George L. Craik

A Compendious History of English Literature and of the English Language from the Norman

George L. Craik

A Compendious History of English Literature and of the English Language from the Norman

ISBN/EAN: 9783741179150

Manufactured in Europe, USA, Canada, Australia, Japa

Cover: Foto ©ninafisch / pixelio.de

Manufactured and distributed by brebook publishing software (www.brebook.com)

George L. Craik

A Compendious History of English Literature and of the English Language from the Norman

HISTORY OF ENGLISH LITERATURE,

AND OF

THE ENGLISH LANGUAGE.

VOL. I.

A

COMPENDIOUS HISTORY

OF

ENGLISH LITERATURE,

AND OF

THE ENGLISH LANGUAGE,

FROM

The Norman Conquest.

WITH NUMEROUS SPECIMENS.

BY

GEORGE L. CRAIK, LL.D.,

PROFESSOR OF HISTORY AND OF ENGLISH LITERATURE IN QUEEN'S COLLEGE, BELFAST.

IN TWO VOLUMES.

VOL. I.

LONDON:

GRIFFIN, BOHN, AND COMPANY,

STATIONERS' HALL COURT.

1861.

PREFACE.

In the largest or loosest sense of the expression a History of English Literature might be taken to mean an account of everything that has been written in the language. But neither is the literature of a language everything that has been written in it, nor would all that has been written in the language necessarily comprehend all its literature, for much true literature may exist, and has existed, without having been written. Literature is composed of words, of thought reduced to the form of words; but the words need not be written; it is enough that they be spoken or sung, or even only conceived. All that writing does is to record and preserve them. It no more endows them with any new character than money acquires a new character by being locked up in a desk or paid into a bank.

But, besides this, if the history of a national literature is to have any proper unity, it can rarely embrace the language in its entire extent. If it should attempt to do so, it would be really the history not of one but of several literatures. In some cases it might even be made a question when it was that the language properly began, at what point of the unbroken thread which undoubtedly connects every form of human speech with a succession of preceding forms out of which it has sprung we are to say that an old language has died and a new one come into existence; but, at any rate, even when the language is admitted to be the same, it not unfrequently differs almost

as much in two of its stages as if it were two languages. We
have a conspicuous example of this in our own English. We
may be said to have the language before us in complete continuity from the seventh century; but the English of the earliest
portion of this long space of time, or what is commonly called
Anglo-Saxon, is no more intelligible to an Englishman of the
present day who has not made it a special study than is German
or Dutch.

The case is even a great deal worse than that. Dutch and
German and other foreign tongues are living; our earliest
English has been dead and buried for centuries. Nay, for a
long time even the fact that it had once existed was all but
universally forgotten. And even since it has come to be once
more studied we know it only as a fossil—as the dust and dry
bones of a language. Of the literature written in it we may
indeed acquire such a conception as we might of a living human
being from a skeleton; but nothing more.

Of that nocturnal portion of our literature, as it may be called,
no critical survey is attempted in the present work. Only the
principal compositions of which it consists, and the names of
their authors, are rapidly enumerated by way of Introduction,
along with the leading particulars of the same kind belonging to
the histories of the Latin, the Welsh, and the Irish literatures
of the same early period.

The history of any national literature, in fact, naturally
divides itself into three portions, all very distinct from one
another, and demanding each a treatment of its own. First,
there is the portion which, as has just been said, may be named
after the night, not perhaps altogether as being the product
of a period of darkness, but as lying now, from distance and
change of circumstances, in the dark to us; secondly, there is
so much of that produced after what seems to us to have been
the rising of the sun as we can look back upon; thirdly, there
is what belongs to our own day, and lies not behind us but

rather before us or around us. Of the three subjects thus presented, the first offers a field chiefly for philological and antiquarian erudition; even the third, not being yet past, does not come properly within the domain of history; the only one that perfectly admits of being treated historically is the daylight or middle division. But that is always both by far the most extensive and also in every other respect the most important.

The survey which is taken in the present work of so much of our English literature as is thus properly historical is no doubt far from complete. Still it will be found to include not only, of course, all our writers of the first class, but also, I believe, all those, without exception, who can be regarded as of any considerable distinction. If that be so, it will, whatever its defects of execution, present a view of the whole subject of which it professes to treat; for it is only great names and great works that make a literature. An account of the writings of Chaucer, of Spenser, of Shakespeare, of Bacon, of Milton, of Dryden, of Pope, of Swift, of Burke, of Burns, of Cowper, would sufficiently unfold the course and revolutions of our English literature from its commencement down to the beginning of the present century. Many names, however, have also been noticed in these volumes which have no pretensions to be considered as even of second-rate importance, but yet some information in regard to which, if it were no more than the date to which each of them belongs, might, it was thought, add to the serviceableness of the work as a book of reference.

Such brief notices are rather for being turned to by means of the Index than for straightforward perusal. The history of our literature, in so far as it is of universal interest, is all contained in the longer and fuller accounts;—the space allotted to which, however, it will be obvious, is not in all cases proportioned to the eminence of the writers. On the contrary, several writers of the first class whose works are in the hands of everybody, as, for example, Shakespeare and Milton, are disposed of without the critical remarks on them being illustrated by any specimens; of others, again, who are less read in the present day, such as Chaucer and Spenser of earlier, Swift and Burke of later, date, the poetry and eloquence are amply exemplified from what they have left us that is most characteristic and remarkable. Any one who will take the trouble to ascertain the fact will find how completely even our great poets and other writers of the last generation have already faded from the view of the present with the most numerous class of the educated and reading public. Scarcely anything is generally read except the publications of the day. Yet nothing is more certain than that no true cultivation can be so acquired. This is the extreme case of that entire ignorance of history, or of what had been done in the world before we ourselves came into it, which has been affirmed, not with more point than truth, to leave a person always a child.

Having already gone over the greater part of the present subject in a work entitled Sketches of the History of Literature and Learning in England, which was published in 1844-5, I have only revised and retouched here, and not sought to rewrite, whatever as it there stood still sufficiently expressed what I had to say. The present work, therefore, it will be understood, comprehends and incorporates all of the former one (now out of print) which it has been considered desirable to preserve. It is, in truth, in the main a republication of that, though with many alterations and some curtailments, as well as considerable additions and enlargements. I have even retained, though hardly coming under the new title, the summaries of the progress of Scientific Discovery in successive periods, as not taking up very much room, and supplying a good many dates and other facts which even in following the history of Literature it is sometimes convenient to have at hand.

The present work, on the other hand, professes to combine the history of the Literature with the history of the Language. The

scheme of the course and revolutions of the Language which is
followed here, and also in the later editions of my Sketches of
the History of the English Language, was first announced by
me in an article published in the Dublin University Magazine
for July, 1857. It is extremely simple, and, resting not upon
arbitrary but upon natural or real distinctions, gives us the only
view of the subject that can claim to be regarded as of a scientific character. In the earliest state in which it is known to us
the English is both a *homogeneous* and a *synthetic* language—homogeneous in its vocabulary, synthetic in its grammatical structure. It has since, though, of course, always operated upon, like
everything human, by the law of gradual change, undergone
only two decided revolutions; the first of which destroyed its
synthetic, the second its homogeneous, character. Thus, in its
second form it is still a homogeneous, but no longer a synthetic
language; in its third it is neither synthetic nor homogeneous,
but has become both analytic in its grammar and composite
in its vocabulary. The three forms may be conveniently
designated :—the First, that of Pure or Simple English; the
Second, that of Broken or Semi-English; the Third, that of Mixed,
or Compound, or Composite English. The first of the three
stages through which the language has thus passed may be considered to have come to an end in the eleventh century; the
second, in the thirteenth century; the third is that in which it
still is.

In another paper, published in the Dublin University Magazine for October, 1857, I applied this view to the explanation of
the action upon the language of the Norman Conquest; the
immediate effect of which was to produce the first of the two
revolutions, its ultimate effect to produce the second. I there,
also, gave an account of the examination of the vocabulary of
our existing English instituted by Dr. J. P. Thommerel, in his
Recherches sur la Fusion du Franco-Normand et de l'Anglo-
Saxon, published at Paris in 1841, in which he showed, in oppo-

sition to all previous estimates, that, of the words collected in
our common dictionaries, instead of two-thirds being of native
origin, as usually assumed, and only one-third of Latin or French
extraction, the fact is just the other way;—two-thirds are foreign
and only one-third native.   I proceeded to remark, however,
that, of the words in common use both in speaking and in
writing, which may be taken as about 10,000 in number, probably full a half are pure English; and that of those in common
colloquial use, which may be about 5,000 in all, probably four-
fifths are of native stock.   "And the 4,000 or 5,000 non-Roman
words," I added, "that are in general use (4,000 in our common
speech, 5,000 in literary composition) compose all the fundamental framework of the language, all that may be called its
skeleton or bony structure, and also perhaps the better part of
its muscular tissue."

The portion of our literature to which the present work is
properly speaking devoted is that of the Third Form of the Language, and may be regarded as commencing with the poetry of
Chaucer in the middle of the fourteenth century.

G. L. C.

P.S. Upon more careful consideration, I find that the simile in
the 9th Iliad is not fairly represented in the translation given
vol. ii. p. 520.   Nothing turns upon it; but I ought not to have
supposed it possible that Homer could have been in anything
inconsistent with truth and nature.

Queen's College, Belfast,
        September, 1861.

CONTENTS.

SPECIMENS.

VOL. I.

CORRECTIONS.

VOL. I.

Page 4, line 26; *after* "and the French" *add:* "The Romaic, or Modern Greek, may be included under the same head."

„ 8, line 6 from foot; *add as foot-note:* "Britannia after the Romans, being an Attempt to Illustrate the Religious and Political Revolutions of that Province in the Fifth and succeeding Centuries [By the late Hon. Algernon Herbert]; vol. i. 4to. 1836, pp. 21, 22."

„ 15, line 22; *for* "various" *read* "oldest."

„ 15, line 3 from foot; *for* "British" *read* "Irish."

„ 28, line 25; *for* "Biscopt" *read* "Biscop."

„ 33, line 25; *dele comma after* "so far."

„ 53, line 8 from foot; *after* "founded" *add* "in England."

„ 57, line 13; *for* "their" *read* "our."

„ 82, line 16 from foot; *after* "annotations" *insert comma.*

„ 92, line 19; *read* "Normannorum fortia facta, deduxit."

„ 106, line 13 from foot; *for* "Saxons" *read* "English."

„ 165, line 2; *for* "be" *read* "is."

„ 168, line 12 from foot; *for* "seemed" *read* "seem."

„ 170, line 12; *for* "tenth" *read* "eleventh."

„ 189, lines 17, 18; *read* "accept such rhymes as might."

„ 245, line 3 from foot; *read* "in the present form of the language."

„ 246, line 5; *after* "what" *insert* "has."

„ 376, line 8; *for* "Lyttelton" *read* "Fortescue."

„ 384, line 4 from foot of text; *for* "slain at Flodden in 1513" *read* "b. 1511, d. 1542."

„ 408, line 18; *for* "eldest" *read* "elder."

„ 500, line 5 from foot; *for* "R. H. Ellis" *read* "R. L. Ellis."

HISTORY

OF

ENGLISH LITERATURE.

LITERATURE AND LANGUAGE.

In tracing, as it is our purpose to do in the present work, the history of English Literature and of the English Language together, we shall be obliged to look at the language principally, or almost exclusively, as we find it employed in the service of the literature. But in its proper nature language is independent of writing. Writing is only a visible representation of language, which in itself consists, not of strokes drawn by the pen, or marks made in any other way, but of sounds uttered by the voice and the organs of articulation. It addresses itself not to the eye but to the ear. There are many languages that have never been written, or visibly represented in any form. Every language that has come to be written has also existed in an unwritten state. No language has been born a written language, any more than it was ever heard tell of that a boy had been born with breeches on. It has been common to talk of language, which is really thought itself, as the dress of thought; with much more truth might writing be called the dress of language. It is an artificial or non-natural addition which language assumes as it grows up and gets civilized,—something that perhaps would not have been needed or thought of in a state of innocence. As matters stand, this contrivance may be necessary for the perfect training of language, for turning it to its full use and developing all its capabilities; but still it is in some sort what his trappings are to the war-horse—a sign and seal of its conquest and bondage.

Letters are the fetters of language, even if they are its golden fetters.

It would be convenient if we had distinctive names for language spoken and language written. In the want of such, perhaps the best thing that could be done in a precisely scientific treatment of the subject would be to understand the common terms *language* and *speech* when used absolutely, or without qualification, as meaning always only language proper or spoken language,—which is what these words, and the only corresponding ones probably in all languages, do mean etymologically— and to distinguish written language as language representative. But for ordinary purposes this is not necessary; as in other cases, the context makes the sense clear, notwithstanding the insufficiency of the expression.

What is never to be forgotten, however, is, that, while writing is unquestionably and by universal admission artificial, language proper is essentially a natural product. It is simply to man what neighing is to the horse or lowing to the bullock. A race or community of human beings without a language would be as extraordinary a phenomenon as a race without hands or without heads. Human beings formed as they ordinarily are, there is every reason to believe, could no more grow up, at least in a state of association, without speech than they could without eating or without breathing. It is the natural, the spontaneous, the inevitable result of their organization. Language, that is, not merely the utterance of articulate sounds, but the employment of words for the expression of thought, or what we may call the conversion of thought into words, is probably as much a necessity of the organization, physical and mental, of the human being as it is an impossibility for that of any of the inferior animals.

As for literature, it is not the synonyme even of written language. It is not either coextensive with that, or limited to that. For want of a better term, we call artistic composition in words, or thought artistically so expressed, literature; but, on the one hand, there is abundance of writing, and of printing too, which is not literature in this proper sense, and, on the other, it is not a necessity of artistic composition that it should be in a written form. Literature, therefore, whatever the etymology of the term may seem to indicate, has no essential connexion with letters.

And its connexion even with language, which is essential, is still no more than such a connexion as is created by the fact that literature consists necessarily of words. It is of thought and emotion transformed into or manifested in language that the fabric of literature is woven. But literature is not, like language, a necessary product of our humanity. Man has been nowhere found without a language: there have been and are many nations and races without a literature. A language is to a people a necessary of existence; a literature is only a luxury. Hence it sometimes happens that the origin of a nation's literature, and the influences which have inspired and moulded it, have been more or less distinct from the sources whence the language has taken its beginning and the inner operating spirit or external circumstances which have modified its shape and character. The literature will generally be acted upon by the language, and the language by the literature; but each may have also had fountains of its own at which the other has not drunk. Thus, for example, it may be affirmed that even those nations of modern Europe which owe their language mostly to the Romans have derived their literature and fine art of every other form, as well as their spirit of philosophical speculation, to a much greater extent from the Greeks. Here too the modern world has inherited from Rome the useful and necessary, from Greece the refined and ornamental;—from the one, language, along with law and government, the art of war offensive and defensive, and the common arts of life; from the other, that which, although not the feeding fruit of the tree or plant, but only its crowning flower, yet alone constitutes true civilization.

THE LANGUAGES OF MODERN EUROPE.

There have in every age been some populations which, for one reason or another, have deemed it necessary or expedient to have each more than one language. Both in ancient and in modern times this has been usual with the inhabitants of border districts. Herodotus mentions some northern races of his day who were all familiar with Greek as well as with their own barbaric speech. In some countries, in addition to the common tongue, there has been another known only to the priesthood: in some the men have had a language of their own, which the women were not permitted to speak or to learn. It is perhaps to be regretted that the use of two languages has not been universal in civilized countries; it might probably be almost as easily acquired as the ordinary power of speaking one language. Possibly this may be one of the educational, or rather social, reforms of another era.

Some of the existing European nations or races are distributed under several governments : there are still several political communities, for instance, both of Germans and of Italians, and that although Germany and Italy form each geographically only one region. But in other cases a community occupying only one country, and living under one and the same government, consists of several races each having a language of its own. In this way it happens that, without including what are called dialects, the number of distinct languages in Europe, though it falls short of the number of political communities, exceeds the number of what we can properly call nations. Some languages, again, such as the Welsh, the Irish, and the Basque, are no longer national forms of speech.

The existing European languages may be nearly all comprehended under five divisions. First, there are the Celtic tongues of Ireland and Wales, and their subordinate varieties. Secondly, there are the tongues founded upon the Latin spoken by the old Romans, and thence called the Romance or the Neo-Latin, that is, the New Latin, tongues; of these the principal are the Italian, the Spanish, and the French. Thirdly, there are what have been variously designated the Germanic, Teutonic, or Gothic tongues, being those which were originally spoken by the various barbarian races by whom the Roman empire of the West was overthrown and overwhelmed (or at the least subjugated, revolutionized, and broken up) in the fifth and sixth centuries. Fourthly, there are the Slavonic tongues, of which the Russian and the Polish are the most distinguished. Fifthly, there are the Tchudic tongues, as they have been denominated, or those spoken by the Finnic and Laponnic races. Almost the only language which this enumeration leaves out is that still preserved by the French and Spanish Biscayans, and known as the Basque, or among those who speak it as the Euskarian, which seems to stand alone among the tongues not only of Europe but of the world. It is supposed to be a remnant of the ancient Iberian or original language of Spain.

The order in which the five sets or classes of languages have been named may be regarded as that of their probable introduction into Europe from Asia or the East, or at any rate of their establishment in the localities of which they are now severally in possession. First, apparently, came the Celtic, now driven on to the farthest west;—after which followed in succession the Latin, the Gothic, the Slavonic, and the Tschudic, pressing upon and urging forward one another like so many waves.

Their present geographical position may also be set forth in few words. Those of the Celtic type are found, as just mentioned, in the West, the Latin generally in the South, the Slavonic in the East, the Tschudic in the North, and the Gothic over the whole of the central region. The chief exception is, that one Tschudic language, the Madgyar, is spoken in Hungary, at the south-eastern extremity of Europe.

The English is essentially or fundamentally a Gothic tongue. That is to say, it is to be classed among those which were spoken by the main division of the barbaric invaders and conquerors of the Roman empire, and which are now spread over the whole of the central portion of the European continent, or what we may call the body of Europe as distinguished from its head and limbs. These Gothic tongues have been subdivided into the High-Germanic, the Low-Germanic, and the Scandinavian; and each of these subordinate groups or clusters has a certain character of its own in addition to the common character by which they are all allied and discriminated from those belonging to quite other stocks. They may be said to present different shades of the same colour. And even in their geographical distribution they lie as it were in so many successive ridges:—the High-Germanic languages farthest south; next to them, the Low-Germanic, in the middle; and then, farthest north, the Scandinavian. The High-Germanic may be considered to be principally represented by the modern classic German; the Low-Germanic by the language of the people of Holland, or what we call the Low Dutch, or simply the Dutch; the Scandinavian, by the Swedish, Danish, or Icelandic.

It may be remarked, too, that the gradation of character among the three sets of languages corresponds to their geographical position. That is to say, their resemblance is in proportion to their proximity. Thus, the High-Germanic and the Scandinavian groups are both nearer in character, as well as in

position, to the Low-Germanic than they are to each other; and
the Low-Germanic tongues, lying in the middle, form as it were
a sort of link, or bridge, between the other two extreme groups.
Climate, and the relative elevation of the three regions, may
have something to do with this. The rough and full-mouthed
pronunciation of the High-Germanic tongues, with their broad
vowels and guttural combinations, may be the natural product
of the bracing mountain air of the south; the clearer and neater
articulation of the Low-Germanic ones, that of the milder
influences of the plain; the thinner and sharper sounds of the
Scandinavian group, that of the more chill and pinching hyper-
borean atmosphere in which they have grown up and been
formed.

EARLY LATIN LITERATURE IN BRITAIN.

When the South of Britain became a part of the Roman empire,
the inhabitants, at least of the towns, seem to have adopted generally the Latin language and applied themselves to the study of
the Latin literature. The diffusion among them of this new taste
was one of the first means employed by their politic conquerors,
as soon as they had fairly established themselves in the island,
to rivet their dominion. A more efficacious they could not have
devised; and, happily, it was also the best fitted to turn their
subjugation into a blessing to the conquered people. Agricola,
having spent the first year of his administration in establishing
in the province the order and tranquillity which is the first
necessity of the social condition, and the indispensable basis of
all civilization, did not allow another winter to pass without
beginning the work of thus training up the national mind to a
Roman character. Tacitus informs us that he took measures for
having the sons of the chiefs educated in the liberal arts, exciting them at the same time by professing to prefer the natural
genius of the Britons to the studied acquirements of the Gauls;
the effect of which was, that those who lately had disdained to
use the Roman tongue now became ambitious of excelling in
eloquence. In later times, schools were no doubt established
and maintained in all the principal towns of Roman Britain, as
they were throughout the empire in general. There are still

extant many imperial edicts relating to these public seminaries, in which privileges are conferred upon the teachers, and regulations laid down as to the manner in which they were to be appointed, the salaries they were to receive, and the branches of learning they were to teach. But no account of the British schools in particular has been preserved. It would appear, however, that, for sometime at least, the older schools of Gaul were resorted to by the Britons who pursued the study of the law : Juvenal, who lived in the end of the first and the beginning of the second century, speaks, in one of his Satires, of eloquent Gaul instructing the pleaders of Britain. But even already forensic acquirements must have become very general in the latter country and the surrounding regions, if we may place any reliance on the assertion which he makes in the next line, that in Thule itself people now talked of hiring rhetoricians to manage their causes. Thule, whatever may have been the particular island or country to which that name was given, was the most northern land known to the ancients.

It is somewhat remarkable that, while a good many names of natives of Gaul are recorded in connexion with the last age of Roman literature, scarcely a British name of that period of any literary reputation has been preserved, if we except a few which figure in the history of the Christian Church. The poet Ausonius, who flourished in the fourth century, makes frequent mention of a contemporary British writer whom he calls Sylvius Bonus, and whose native name is supposed to have been Coil the Good ; but of his works, or even of their titles or subjects, we know nothing. Ausonius, who seems to have entertained strong prejudices against the Britons, speaks of Sylvius with the same animosity as of the rest of his countrymen. Of ecclesiastical writers in Latin belonging to the sixth century, the heresiarch Pelagius and his disciple Celestius, St. Patrick, the apostle of Ireland, with his friend Bishop Secundinus, and the poet Sedulius, are generally regarded as having been natives of the British islands.

Gildas, our earliest historian of whom anything remains, also wrote in Latin. St. Gildas the Wise, as he is styled, was a son of Caw, Prince of Strathclyde, in the capital of which kingdom, the town of Alcluyd, now Dunbarton, he is supposed to have been born about the end of the fifth or beginning of the sixth century. Caw was also father of the famous bard Aneurin : one theory, indeed, is that Aneurin and Gildas were the same person. In his youth Gildas is said to have gone over to

Ireland, and to have studied in the schools of the old national learning that still flourished there; and, like his brother Aneurin (if Aneurin was his brother), he also commenced his career as a bard, or composer of poetry in his native tongue. He was eventually, however, converted to Christianity, and became a zealous preacher of his new religion. The greater part of his life appears to have been spent in his native island; but at last he retired to Armorica, or Little Britain, on the Continent, and died there. He is said to lie buried in the Cathedral of Vannes. Gildas is the author of two declamatory effusions, the one commonly known as his History (De Excidio Britanniæ Liber Querulus), the other as his Epistle (De Excidio Britanniæ et Britonum Exulatione), which have been often printed. The latest edition is that contained in the Monumenta Historica Britannica, 1848; and there is also an edition prepared by Mr. Joseph Stevenson for the English Historical Society, 8vo. London: 1834. A translation of the Epistle was published in 1638; and both works are included in Dr. Giles's Six Old English Chronicles, 1848. They consist principally of violent invectives directed against his own countrymen as well as their continental invaders and conquerors; and throw but little light upon the obscure period to which they relate.

Our next historical writer is Nennius, said to have been a monk of Bangor, and to have escaped from the massacre of his brethren in 613. He too, like Gildas, is held to have been of Welsh or Cumbrian origin: his native name is conjectured to have been Ninian. But there is much obscurity and confusion in the accounts we have of Nennius: it appears to be probable that there were at least two early historical writers of that name. The author of a late ingenious work supposes that the true narrative of the ancient Nennius only came down to the invasion of Julius Cæsar, and is now lost, although we probably have an abridgment of it in the British History (Eulogium Britanniæ, sive Historia Britonum), published by Gale in his Scriptores Quindecim, Oxon. 1691, which, however, is expressly stated in the preface by the author himself to have been drawn up in 858. A very valuable edition of 'The Historia Britonum, commonly attributed to Nennius, from a MS. lately discovered in the Library of the Vatican Palace at Rome,' was published in 8vo. at London, in 1819, by the Rev. W. Gunn, B.D., rector of Irstead, Norfolk; and his greatly improved text has been chiefly followed

In the subsequent edition prepared by Mr. Stevenson for the Historical Society (8vo. London, 1838). The most complete text, however, is probably that given in the Monumenta Historica Britannica, from a collation of no fewer than twenty-six manuscripts. An English version, originally published by Mr. Gunn in his edition of the Vatican text, is reprinted by Dr. Giles in his Six Old English Chronicles. But the most curious and important volume connected with Nennius is that published in 1847 by the Irish Archæological Society, containing an Irish version of his History executed in the fourteenth century, with a translation and Notes by Dr. Todd, together with a large mass of Additional Notes, and an Introduction, by the Hon. Algernon Herbert, who has here discussed nearly all the leading questions in the obscure region of early British antiquities with profuse learning, and at the same time, whatever may be thought of some of his conclusions, with an ingenuity and freshness still more rare and valuable.

Of the Latin writers among the Angles and Saxons any of whose works remain, the most ancient is Aldhelm, abbot of Malmesbury, and afterwards the first bishop of Sherborn, who died in 709. Aldhelm was of the stock of the kings of Wessex, and was initiated in Greek and Latin learning at the school in Kent presided over by the Abbot Adrian, who, like his friend Archbishop Theodore, appears to have been a native of Asia Minor, so that Greek was his native tongue. We are assured by one of his biographers that Aldhelm could write and speak Greek like a native of Greece. He also early associated himself with the monastic brotherhood of Malmesbury, or Meildulfesbyrig, that is, burgh or town of Moildulf, Maildulf, or Meldun, an Irish exile, by whom the monastery had been founded about half a century before the birth of Aldhelm. Among the studies of Aldhelm's after-life are mentioned the Roman law, the rules of Latin prosody, arithmetic, astronomy, and astrology. He is said to have written a tract on the great scientific question of the age, the proper method of computing Easter. Aldhelm's favourite subject, however, would seem to have been the virtue of virginity, in praise of which he wrote first a copious treatise in prose and then a long poem. Both of these performances are preserved, and have been printed. Aldhelm long enjoyed the highest reputation for learning; but his writings are chiefly remarkable for their elaborately unnatural and fantastic rhetoric.

His Latin style bears some resemblance to the pedantic English, full of alliteration and all sorts of barbarous quaintness, that was fashionable among our theological writers in the reigns of Elizabeth and James the First.

But the English name of the times before the Norman Conquest that is most distinguished in literature is that of Beda, or Bede, upon whom the epithet of "The Venerable" has been justly bestowed by the respect and gratitude of posterity. All that we have written by Bede is in the Latin language. He was born some time between the years 672 and 677, at Jarrow, a village near the mouth of the Tyne, in the county of Durham, and was educated in the neighbouring monastery of Wearmouth under its successive abbots Benedict and Ceolfrid. He resided here, as he tells us himself, from the age of seven to that of twelve, during which time he applied himself with all diligence, he says, to the meditation of the Scriptures, the observance of regular discipline, and the daily practice of singing in the church. " It was always sweet to me," he adds, " to learn, to teach, and to write." In his nineteenth year he took deacon's orders, and in his thirtieth he was ordained priest. From this date till his death, in 735, he remained in his monastery, giving up his whole time to study and writing. His principal task was the composition of his celebrated Ecclesiastical History of England, which he brought to a close in his fifty-ninth year. It is our chief original authority for the earlier portion even of the civil history of the English nation. But Bede also wrote many other works, among which he has himself enumerated, in the brief account he gives of his life at the end of his Ecclesiastical History, Commentaries on most of the books of the Old and New Testaments and the Apocrypha, two books of Homilies, a Martyrology, a chronological treatise entitled On the Six Ages, a book on orthography, a book on the metrical art, and various other theological and biographical treatises. He likewise composed a book of hymns and another of epigrams. Most of these writings have been preserved, and have been repeatedly printed. The first edition of the Ecclesiastical History is without date, but it probably appeared at Eslingen, in Germany, between 1471 and 1475. Three other continental editions followed before the end of the fifteenth century ; and no fewer than nine more in the course of the sixteenth. The first edition printed in England was that of Abraham Wheloc, folio, Cam-

bridge, 1644, accompanied by the old vernacular translation
attributed to King Alfred, then also for the first time given to
the world through the press; this was followed by the Jesuit
Chifflet's edition, 4to. Paris, 1681; then came Dr. Smith's greatly
improved edition both of the original Latin and of Alfred's
translation, folio, Cambridge, 1722; and this remained the
standard edition till the appearance of that of Mr. Stevenson
(containing also the Minor Historical Works), under the auspices
of the English Historical Society, in 2 vols. 8vo. 1838-41, and of
that of Mr. Petrie, in the Monumenta, folio, 1848. There are
three continental editions of the entire works of Bede, each
in eight volumes folio, the latest of which was published at
Cologne in 1688. Some additional pieces were published at
London in a quarto volume, by Henry Wharton, in 1693; and
an edition of the complete works of Bede in the original Latin,
accompanied with a translation, was produced by Dr. Giles, in
12 vols. 8vo. London, 1843-44. It appears, from an interesting
account of Bede's last hours by his pupil St. Cuthbert, that he
was engaged at the time of his death in translating St. John's
Gospel into his native tongue. Among his last utterances to his
affectionate disciples watching around his bed were some reci-
tations in the English language: " For," says the account, "he
was very learned in our songs; and, putting his thoughts into
English verse, he spoke it with compunction."

Beside King Alfred's version in the earlier form of the language, there are translations of Bede's Ecclesiastical History into
modern English by Thomas Stapleton (1565), by John Stevens
(1723), and by W. Hurst (1814). Stevens's translation, altered
and corrected, was reproduced by Dr. Giles in 1840, and again
in 1842; and it is given also both in his edition of the complete
works of Bede, and, along with his translation of the Chronicle,
in one of the volumes of Bohn's Antiquarian Library, 1840.
Finally, a new translation of all Bede's Historical Works by the
Rev. Joseph Stevenson forms the second part of volume first of
the collection entitled The Church Historians of England,
London, 1853-54.

Another celebrated English churchman of this age was St.
Boniface, originally named Winfrith, who was born in Devon-
shire about the year 680. Boniface is acknowledged as the
Apostle of Germany, in which country he founded various
monasteries, and was greatly instrumental in the diffusion both

of Christianity and of civilization.   He eventually became archbishop of Mentz, and was killed in East Friesland by a band of
heathens in 755.   Many of his letters to the popes, to the English bishops, to the kings of France, and to the kings of the
various states of his native country, still remain, and are printed
in the collections entitled Bibliotheca Patrum.   We may here
also mention another contemporary of Bede's, Eddius, surnamed
Stephanus, the author of a Latin life of Bishop Wilfrid.   Bede
mentions him as the first person who taught singing in the
churches of Northumberland.

———————

THE CELTIC LANGUAGES AND LITERATURES.

No other branch of what is called the Indo-European family of
languages is of higher interest in certain points of view than the
Celtic.   The various known forms of the Celtic are now regarded
as coming under two great divisions, the Gaelic and the Cymric ;
Ireland being the head seat of the Gaelic (which may therefore
also be called Irish), Wales being the head seat of the Cymric
(which accordingly is by the English commonly called Welsh).
Subordinate varieties of the Irish are the Gaelic of Scotland
(often called Erse, or Erish, that is, Irish), and the Manks, or
Isle of Man tongue (now fast dying out) : other Cymric dialects
are the Cornish (now extinct as a spoken language), and the
Armorican, or that still spoken in some parts of Brittagne.

The probability is, that the various races inhabiting the
British islands when they first became known to the civilized
world were mostly, if not all, of Celtic speech.   Even in the
parts of the country that were occupied by the Caledonians, the
Picts, and the Belgian colonists, the oldest topographical names,
the surest evidence that we have in all cases, and in this case
almost our only evidence, are all, so far as can be ascertained,
Celtic, either of the Cymric or of the Gaelic form.   And then there
are the great standing facts of the existence to this day of a large
Cymric population in South Britain, and of a still larger Gaelic-
speaking population in North Britain and in Ireland.   No other
account of these Celtic populations, or at least of the Welsh,
has been attempted to be given, than that, as their own traditions
and records are unanimous in asserting, they are the remnants
of the races by which the two islands were occupied when they

first attracted the attention of the Romans about half a century before the commencement of the Christian era.

And both the Welsh and the Irish possess a large mass of literature in their native tongues, much of which has been printed, in great part no doubt of comparatively modern production, but claiming some of it, in its substance if not exactly in the very form in which it now presents itself, an antiquity transcending any other native literature of which the country can boast.

Neither the Welsh nor the Irish language and literature, however, can with any propriety be included in a history of English literature and of the English language. The relationship of English to any Celtic tongue is more remote than its relationship not only to German or Icelandic or French or Italian or Latin, but even to Russian or Polish, or to Persian or Sanscrit. Irish and Welsh are opposed in their entire genius and structure to English. It has indeed been sometimes asserted that the Welsh is one of the fountains of the English. One school of last-century philologists maintained that full a third of our existing English was Welsh. No doubt, in the course of the fourteen centuries that the two languages have been spoken alongside of each other in the same country, a considerable number of vocables can hardly fail to have been borrowed by each from the other; the same thing would have happened if it had been a dialect of Chinese that had maintained itself all·that time among the Welsh mountains. If, too, as is probable, a portion of the previous Celtic population chose or were suffered to remain even upon that part of the soil which came to be generally occupied after the departure of the Romans by the Angles, Saxons, and other Teutonic or Gothic tribes, the importers of the English language and founders of the English nation, something of Celtic may in that way have intermingled and grown up with the new national speech. But the English language cannot therefore be regarded as of Celtic parentage. The Celtic words, or words of Celtic extraction, that are found in it, be they some hundreds in number, or be they one or two thousands, are still only something foreign. They are products of another seed that have shot up here and there with the proper crop from the imperfectly cleared soil; or they are fragments of another mass which have chanced to come in contact with the body of the language, pressed upon by its weight, or blown upon

it by the wind, and so have adhered to it or become imbedded in
it. It would perhaps be going farther than known facts warrant
us if we were to say that a Gothic tongue and a Celtic tongue are
incapable of a true amalgamation. But undoubtedly it would
require no common pressure to overcome so strong an opposition
of nature and genius. The Gothic tongues, and the Latin or
Romance tongues also, indeed, belong to distinct branches of what
is called the Indo-European family; but the Celtic branch,
though admitted to be of the same tree, has much more of a
character of its own than any of the others. Probably any other
two languages of the entire multitude held to be of this general
stock would unite more readily than two of which only one was
Celtic. It would be nearly the same case with that of the intermixture of an Indo-European with a Semitic language. It has
been suggested that the Celtic branch must in all probability
have diverged from the common stem at a much earlier date
than any of the others. At any rate, in point of fact the
English can at most be said to have been powdered or sprinkled
with a little Celtic. Whatever may be the number of words
which it has adopted, whether from the ancient Britons or from
their descendants the Welsh, they are only single scattered
words. No considerable department of the English dictionary
is Welsh. No stream of words has flowed into the language
from that source. The two languages have in no sense met and
become one. They have not mingled as two rivers do when
they join and fall into the same channel. There has been no
chemical combination between the Gothic and the Celtic elements, but only more or less of a mechanical intermixture.

We shall limit ourselves to the briefest notice of the remains
of the ancient vernacular literature of Ireland and of Wales.
The earliest literature of which any remains still exist in any of
the native languages of the British Islands must be held to be
the Irish. The Irish were probably possessed of the knowledge
of letters from a very remote antiquity. Although the forms
of their present alphabetical characters are Roman, and are
supposed to have been introduced by St. Patrick in the fifth
century, it is very remarkable that the alphabet, in the number
and powers of its elements, exactly corresponds with that which
Cadmus is recorded to have brought to Greece from Phœnicia.
If we may believe the national traditions, and the most ancient
existing chronicles, the Irish also possessed a succession of bards

from their first settlement in the country, and the names of some
of those that are said to have flourished so early as in the first
century of our era are still remembered; but the eldest bardic
compositions that have been preserved claim to be of the fifth
century. Some fragments of metrical productions to which this
date is attributed are found in the old annalists, and more abundant specimens occur in the same records under each of the succeeding centuries. The oldest existing Irish manuscript,
however, is believed to be the Psalter of Cashel, a collection of
bardic legends, compiled about the end of the ninth century, by
Cormac MacCulinan, bishop of Cashel and king of Munster.
But the most valuable remains of ancient Irish literature that
have come down to us are the various historical records in prose,
called the Annals of Tigernach, of the Four Masters, of Ulster,
and others. Portions of these were first published in the original, accompanied with Latin translations, in Dr. O'Conor's
Rerum Hibernicarum Scriptores Veteres, 4 vols. 4to., Buckingham, 1814–1826; a splendid monument of the munificence of
his Grace the late Duke of Buckingham, at whose expense the
work was prepared and printed, and from the treasures of whose
library its contents were principally derived. Tigernach, the
various of these Irish annalists, lived in the latter part of the
eleventh century; but both his and the other annals profess, and
are believed, to have been compiled from authentic records of
much greater antiquity. They form undoubtedly a collection of
materials in the highest degree precious for the information they
supply with regard to the history both of Ireland and of the
various early British kingdoms. These Annals differ wholly in
character from the metrical legends of Irish history found in the
Book of Cashel and in the other later compositions of the bards.
They consist of accounts of events related for the most part both
with sobriety and precision, and with the careful notation of
dates that might be expected from a contemporary and official
recorder. They are in all probability, indeed, copies of, or compilations from, public records. A much more satisfactory edition
in all respects of the Annals of the Four Masters, which were
compiled in the seventeenth century, and of which only the
portion ending with the year 1171 is in Dr. O'Conor's work,
has since been produced under the auspices of the British
Archæological Society, by Dr. O'Donovan, Professor of the
Celtic Languages in Queen's College, Belfast. This edition

(which was originally brought out in 5 vols. 4to. in 1848-51, and reprinted in 7 vols. 4to. in 1856) contains the Annals from their commencement at the Creation down to their termination in A.D. 1616, and, besides a translation of the whole in English, presents a mass of learned annotation, making it almost a cyclopædia both of Irish history and of Irish topography.* To the Archæological Society, founded in 1840, and now united with the Celtic Society, we owe also many other important publications. And on one which will be perhaps the most important of all that have yet appeared in illustration of the ancient civilization of the country, and to a considerable extent too of the earlier forms of the language, that of the remains of what are called the Brehon Laws, Dr. O'Donovan is understood to have been for some years engaged.

Not of such historic importance, but perhaps still more curious and interesting in other points of view, are the remains we still possess of the early Welsh literature. The Welsh have no national annals to be compared in value with those of the Irish; but some of their Chronicles, fabulous as they evidently are in great part, are undoubtedly of considerable antiquity. It is now almost universally admitted that the famous Latin Chronicle of the Britons, published by Geoffrey of Monmonth in the twelfth century, is really what it professes to be, at least in the main, a translation from a much older Welsh original. The Laws of Howel Dha, who reigned in South Wales in the early part of the tenth century, have been printed with a Latin translation, by Wotton, in his Leges Wallicæ, fol. 1730; and again in the late Record Commission edition of the Ancient Laws and Institutes of Wales, by Aneurin Owen, Esq., fol. 1841. They develop a state of society in which many primitive features are strangely mixed up with a general aspect of considerable civilization, and all the order of a well-established political system. Then there are the singular compositions called the Triads, which are enumerations of events or other particulars, bound together in knots of three, by means of some title or general observation—sometimes, it must be confessed, forced and far-fetched enough—under which it is conceived that they may all be included. Of the Triads, some are moral, and others historical. The historical are certainly not all ancient; for they contain allusions to events

* There is also an English translation of the Annals of the Four Masters, by Owen Connellan, Esq., in one volume, 4to. 1846.

that took place in the reign of our Edward I.; but it appears
most probable that the form of composition which they exemplify
was long in use; and, if so, the comparatively modern character
of some of them does not disprove the antiquity of others. A
late writer, who considers them to be a compilation of the
thirteenth century, admits that they " reflect, in a small and
moderately faithful mirror, various passages of Bardic com
position which are lost."* Then there is the collection of
romantic prose tales known as the Mabinogion, preserved in
a MS. of the fourteenth century, which has now been published,
with an English translation and notes, by Lady Charlotte Guest,
in three sumptuous volumes, 8vo. London, 1838-1850,—one of the
most remarkable feats of the female authorship of our day. The
most voluminous of the ancient Welsh remains, however, are the
poems of the Bards. The authenticity of these compositions
had till recently been regarded as having been established,
beyond dispute, by various investigators, and especially by
Mr. Sharon Turner's elaborate Vindication.† But now again
the judgment of the most advanced Celtic scholarship seems to
be tending the other way.‡ The poems professing to be the
most ancient are those ascribed to the four bards, Aneurin,
Taliesin, Llywarch Hen, and Merdhin, or Merlin, the Cale-
donian, who all appear to have belonged to the sixth century.
A few additional pieces have also been preserved of the seventh,
eighth, ninth, tenth, and eleventh centuries, which are printed
along with these in the first volume of the Myvyrian Archaiology
of Wales, 3 vols. 8vo. Lond. 1801. Much of this early Welsh
poetry is in a strangely mystical style, its general spirit being,
according to one theory, much more Druidical than Christian.
The author of Britannia after the Romans has endeavoured
to show that a partial revival of Druidism was effected in
Wales in the sixth century, principally through the efforts of

* The Hon. Algernon Herbert, in Britannia after the Romans, p. xlv.
† First published separately in 1803, and since, much enlarged, at the
end of the third and subsequent editions of his History of the Anglo-Saxons.
See also the Rev. E. Davies's Celtic Researches, Mr. Probert's Preface
to his edition of Aneurin, and Mr. Herbert's Britannia after the Romans,
pp. l.-vi.
‡ See an important work entitled Taliesin; or, the Bards and Druids of
Britain. A translation of the Remains of the earliest Welsh Bards, and an
Examination of the Bardic Mysteries. By D. W. Nash, Member of the Royal
Society of Literature. 8vo. London, 1858.

the Bards, whose order had formerly composed so distinguished
a part of the Druidical system; and much in the character
of this ancient poetry would seem to favour that supposition,
which does not, however, rest upon this evidence alone.   No
existing manuscript of these poems, we may observe, nor any
other Welsh manuscript, appears to be much older than the
twelfth century.

As the forms of the original English alphabetical characters
are the same with those of the Irish, it is probable that it was
from Ireland the English derived their first knowledge of
letters.   There was certainly, however, very little literature in
the country before the arrival of Augustine, in the end of the
sixth century.   Augustine is supposed to have established
schools at Canterbury; and, about a quarter of a century afterwards, Sigebert, king of the East Angles, who had spent part of
his early life in France, is stated by Bede to have, upon his
coming to the throne, founded an institution for the instruction
of the youth of his dominions similar to those he had seen abroad.
The schools planted by Augustine at Canterbury were afterwards
greatly extended and improved by his successor, Archbishop
Theodore, who obtained the see in 668.   Theodore and his
learned friend Adrian, Bede informs us, delivered instructions to
crowds of pupils, not only in divinity, but also in astronomy,
medicine, arithmetic, and the Greek and Latin languages.
Bede states that some of the scholars of these accomplished
foreigners were alive in his time, to whom the Greek and Latin
were as familiar as their mother-tongue.   Schools now began to
multiply in other parts, and were generally to be found in all
the monasteries and at the bishops' seats.   Of these episcopal
and monastic schools, that founded by Bishop Benedict in his
abbey at Wearmouth, where Bede was educated, and that which
Archbishop Egbert established at York, were among the most
famous.   But others of great reputation at a somewhat later date
were superintended by learned teachers from Ireland.   One was
that of Maildulf at Malmesbury.   At Glastonbury, also, it is
related in one of the ancient lives of St. Dunstan, some Irish
ecclesiastics had settled, the books belonging to whom Dunstan
is recorded to have diligently studied.   The northern parts of the
kingdom, moreover, were indebted for the first light of learning
as well as of religion to the missionaries from Iona, which was
an Irish foundation.

For some ages Ireland was the chief seat of learning in Christian Europe; and the most distinguished scholars who appeared in other countries were mostly either Irish by birth or had received their education in Irish schools. We are informed by Bede that in his day, the earlier part of the eighth century, it was customary for his English fellow-countrymen of all ranks, from the highest to the lowest, to retire for study and devotion to Ireland, where, he adds, they were all hospitably received, and supplied gratuitously with food, with books, and with instruction.* The glory of this age of Irish scholarship and genius is the celebrated Joannes Scotus, or Erigena, as he is as frequently designated,—either appellative equally proclaiming his true birthplace. He is supposed to have first made his appearance in France about the year 845, and to have remained in that country till his death, which appears to have taken place before 875. Erigena is the author of a translation from the Greek of certain mystical works ascribed to Dionysius the Areopagite, which he executed at the command of his patron, the French king, Charles the Bald, and also of several original treatises on metaphysics and theology. His productions may be taken as furnishing clear and conclusive evidence that the Greek language was taught at this time in the Irish schools. Mr. Turner has given a short account of his principal work, his Dialogue De Divisione Naturæ (On the Division of Nature), which he characterises as "distinguished for its Aristotelian acuteness and extensive information." In one place "he takes occasion," it is observed, "to give concise and able definitions of the seven liberal arts, and to express his opinion on the composition of things. In another part he inserts a very elaborate discussion on arithmetic, which he says he had learnt from his infancy. He also details a curious conversation on the elements of things, on the motions of the heavenly bodies, and other topics of astronomy and physiology. Among these he even gives the means of calculating the diameters of the lunar and solar circles. Besides the fathers Austin, the two Gregories, Chrysostom, Basil, Epiphanius, Origen, Jerome, and Ambrosius, of whose works, with the Platonising Dionysius and Maximus, he gives large extracts, he also quotes Virgil, Cicero, Aristotle, Pliny, Plato, and Boethius; he details the opinions of Eratosthenes and of

* Hist. Eccles. iii. 28.

c 2

Pythagoras on some astronomical topics ; he also cites Martianus
Capella. His knowledge of Greek appears almost in every
page." *   The subtle speculations of Erigena have strongly
attracted the notice of the most eminent among the modern
inquirers into the history of opinion and of civilization ; and the
German Tenneman agrees with the French Cousin and Guizot in
attributing to them a very extraordinary influence on the philosophy of his own and of succeeding times. To his writings
and translations it is thought may be traced the introduction into
the theology and metaphysics of Europe of the later Platonism
of the Alexandrian school. It is remarkable, as Mr. Moore has
observed, that the learned Mosheim had previously shown the
study of the scholastic or Aristotelian philosophy to have been
also of Irish origin. "That the Hibernians," says that writer,
"who were called Scots in this [the eighth] century, were
lovers of learning, and distinguished themselves in those times
of ignorance by the culture of the sciences beyond all the other
European nations, travelling through the most distant lands,
both with a view to improve and to communicate their knowledge, is a fact with which I have been long acquainted ; as we
see them in the most authentic records of antiquity discharging,
with the highest reputation and applause, the function of doctor
in France, Germany, and Italy, both during this and the following century. But that those Hibernians were the first teachers
of the scholastic theology in Europe, and so early as the eighth
century illustrated the doctrines of religion by the principles of
philosophy, I learned but lately." †   And then he adduces the
proofs that establish his position.

Among the earlier productions of Irish scholarship may especially be mentioned the two Latin lives of Columba, the founder
of the monastery of Iona, and its abbot from 563 till his death
in 597 ; the first by Cuminius, who succeeded as abbot of Iona in
657 ; the second, which is of much greater length, by Adamnan,
who succeeded to the same office in 679. Both these productions,
the second of which in particular is highly curious, have been
repeatedly printed. ‡

    * Turner, Anglo-Sax. iii. 508.
    † Translated in Moore's Ireland, I. 302
    ‡ The late edition of Adamnan's Life of St. Columba (in which nearly the
whole of the other by Cuminius is incorporated), prepared for the Irish
Archæological and Celtic Society by Dr. Reeves, 4to. Dublin, 1857, while its

DECAY OF THE EARLIEST ENGLISH SCHOLARSHIP.

It should seem not to be altogether correct to attribute the decline and extinction of the earliest literary civilization of the Angles and Saxons wholly to the Danish invasions. The Northmen did not make their appearance till towards the close of the eighth century, nor did their ravages occasion any considerable public alarm till long after the commencement of the ninth; but for a whole century preceding this date, learning in England appears to have been falling into decay. Bede, who died in 735, exactly ninety-seven years before that landing of the Danes in the Isle of Sheppey, in the reign of Egbert, which was followed by incessant attacks of a similar kind, until the fierce marauders at last won for themselves a settlement in the country, is the last name eminent for scholarship that occurs in this portion of the English annals. The historian William of Malmesbury, indeed, affirms that the death of Bede was fatal to learning in England, and especially to history; "insomuch that it may be said," he adds, writing in the early part of the twelfth century, "that almost all knowledge of past events was buried in the same grave with him, and hath continued in that condition even to our times." "There was not so much as one Englishman," Malmesbury declares, "left behind Bede, who emulated the glory which he had acquired by his studies, imitated his example, or pursued the path to knowledge which he had pointed out. A few, indeed, of his successors were good men, and not unlearned, but they generally spent their lives in an inglorious silence; while the far greater number sunk into sloth and ignorance, until by degrees the love of learning was quite extinguished in this island for a long time."

The devastations of the Danes completed what had probably been begun by the dissensions and confusion that attended the

typography, and the maps and other plans by which it is adorned make it one of the handsomest productions of the modern press, is illustrated, in an abundant apparatus of notes and explanatory matter of all kinds, with an extent of research and copiousness of learning which place it on a level with whatever has been recently done best among us in this department of scholarship, if, indeed, any other work has appeared for many years on the subject of the early ecclesiastical history of these islands that deserves to be compared with this admirable edition of a most curious account of the great Scottish missionary of the sixth century, compiled by a writer of the seventh, and preserved to our day in a manuscript of the eighth.

breaking up of the original political system established by the
Angles and Saxons, and perhaps also by the natural decay of the
national spirit among a race long habituated to a stirring and
adventurous life, and now left in undisturbed ease and quiet
before the spirit of a new and more intellectual activity had been
sufficiently diffused among them.   Nearly all the monasteries
and the schools connected with them throughout the land were
either actually laid in ashes by the northern invaders, or were
deserted in the general terror and distraction occasioned by their
attacks.   When Alfred was a young man, about the middle of the
ninth century, he could find no masters to instruct him in any of
the higher branches of learning: there were at that time, according to his biographer Asser, * few or none among the West Saxons

* The Life of King Alfred, professing to have been written by his contemporary and friend Asser, bishop of Sherborn, afterwards Salisbury, one of the
two sees (Winchester being the other) into which the original bishopric of
Wessex was divided in the beginning of the eighth century, is in Latin, and
was first printed, in folio, at London in 1574, along with Alfred's Preface to
his translation of Pope Gregory's Pastorale, at the end of Archbishop Parker's
edition of the English and Norman Historics of Thomas Walsingham. This
first edition of Asser is remarkable as exhibiting the Latin text in what
are called Saxon characters.   The second edition is in Camden's collection (Anglica, Normannica, &c.), fol. Frankfort, 1602; the third in Gale's
Scriptores Quindecim, fol. Oxford, 1691.   It was first published separately
by Francis Wise, in 8vo. at Oxford, in 1722.   And a fifth edition, being the
latest, is given in the Monumenta Historica Britannica, 1848.   Meanwhile
Mr. Thomas Wright, having previously intimated his suspicions in a communication to the Society of Antiquaries, published in their Transactions,
had, in 1842, in the first volume of his Biographia Britannica Literaria, pp.
408-412, stated in full certain reasons which led him to believe that this Life
of King Alfred could not have been written before the end of the tenth century, and that " it was probably the work of a monk who, with no great knowledge of history, collected some of the numerous traditions relating to King
Alfred which were then current, and joined them with the legends in the life
of St. Neot and the historical entries in the Saxon Chronicle; and, to give
authenticity to his work, published it under the name of Asser." Mr. Wright,
however, does not put forward his objections as depriving the biography of all
historical value: " It contains," he admits, " interesting traditions relating to
Alfred's life and character, many of which were without doubt true in substance."   And, since Mr. Wright's work appeared, the authenticity of the
biography has been maintained by the late Dr. Lingard, in an elaborate investigation inserted in the second edition of his History and Antiquities of the
Anglo-Saxon Church, 1845, vol. II. pp. 424-428.   The reader may further be
referred to what is said on this subject by Mr. Hardy in his Preface to the
Monumenta Historica Britannica, pp. 77-81; and by Dr. Pauli in the
Introduction to his Life of Alfred the Great (English translation by Thorpe,
1853, pp. 3-11.   Mr. Hardy holds that the inconsistencies which are to be

who had any scholarship, or could so much as read with propriety and ease. The reading of the Latin language is probably what is here alluded to. Alfred has himself stated, in the preface to his translation of Gregory's Pastorale, that, though many of the English at his accession could read their native language well enough, the knowledge of the Latin tongue was so much decayed, that there were very few to the south of the Humber who understood the common prayers of the church, or were capable of translating a single sentence of Latin into English ; and to the south of the Thames he could not recollect that there was one possessed of this very moderate amount of learning. Contrasting this lamentable state of things with the better days that had gone before, he exclaims, " I wish thee to know that it comes very often into my mind, what wise men there were in England, both laymen and ecclesiastics, and how happy those times were to England ! The sacred profession was diligent both to teach and to learn. Men from abroad sought wisdom and learning in this country, though we must now go out of it to obtain knowledge if we should wish to have it."

---

found in Asser's narrative as we now have it are explained by the fact " that many passages of the printed text formed no part of Asser's work, but were the insertions of Archbishop Parker " from a spurious work which he found bound up with the MS., still in the library of Corpus Christi College, Cambridge, from which he printed his edition. Dr. Pauli, after referring to the continued confidence of the best English and German writers, such as Lappenberg, Pertz, and Kemble, in the general authenticity of the work, adds that he cannot himself altogether avoid considering it in the same light; and, having pointed out various passages which may be suspected, he concludes by stating that he will, nevertheless, frequently refer to it in the course of his own narrative; and, in fact, it is one of his leading authorities. " Lingard," he observes, " brings forward good reasons for differing with Wright." Dr. Giles has given an English translation of Asser in his Six Old English Chronicles, 1848.

Along with Asser's work may be noticed the chronicle of Ethelwerd, which in a few pages of affected, and, in some places, nearly or altogether unintelligible Latin, gives a summary of the course of human affairs from the creation to the year 975. Ethelwerd,—or, as he styles himself, Patricius Consul Fabius Quæstor Ethelwerdus—appears from his Prologue, or dedication, to have been a member of the royal family, a descendant of King Alfred. His work is little more than a dry abstract from the national Chronicle. It is contained in Savile's Collection, 1596, and also in the Monumenta Historica Britannica. There is an English translation of it in Dr. Giles's Six Old English Chronicles, Bohn, 1848, and another by Mr. Stevenson in vol. II. part 2nd. of the Church Historians of England, 1854.

It was not till he was nearly forty years of age that Alfred
himself commenced his study of the Latin language. Before
this, however, and as soon as he had rescued his dominions from
the hands of the Danes, and reduced these foreign disturbers to
subjection, he had exerted himself with his characteristic activity
in bringing about the restoration of letters as well as of peace
and order. He had invited to his court all the most learned men
he could discover anywhere in his native land, and had even
brought over instructors for himself and his people from other
countries. Werfrith, the bishop of Worcester; Ethelstan and
Werwulf, two Mercian priests; and Plegmund, also a Mercian,
who afterwards became archbishop of Canterbury, were some of
the English of whose superior acquirements he thus took advantage. Asser he brought from the western extremity of Wales.
Grimbald he obtained from France, having sent an embassy of
bishops, presbyters, deacons, and religious laymen, bearing
valuable presents to his ecclesiastical superior Fulco, the archbishop of Rheims, to ask permission for the great scholar to be
allowed to come to reside in England. And so in other instances,
like the bee, looking everywhere for honey, to quote the simili-
tude of his biographer, this admirable prince sought abroad in
all directions for the treasure which his own kingdom did not
afford.

His labours in translating the various works that have been
mentioned above from the Latin, after he had acquired that
language, he seems himself to have been half inclined to regard
as to be justified only by the low state into which all learning
had fallen among his countrymen in his time, and as likely perhaps to be rather of disservice than otherwise to the cause of real
scholarship. Reflecting on the erudition which had existed in
the country at a former period, and which had made these
volumes in the learned languages useful that now lay unopened,
" I wondered greatly," he says in the Preface to his translation
of the Pastorale, " that of those good wise men who were formerly
in our nation, and who had all learned fully these books,
none would translate any part into their own language; but I
soon answered myself, and said, they never thought that men
could be so reckless, and that learning would be so fallen. They
intentionally omitted it, and wished that there should be more
wisdom in the land, by many languages being known." He then
called to recollection, however, what benefit had been derived

by all nations from the translation of the Greek and Hebrew
Scriptures, first into Latin, and then into the various modern
tongues; and, "therefore," he concludes, "I think it better, if
you think so (he is addressing Wulfsig, the bishop of London),
that we also translate some books, the most necessary for all men
to know, that we all may know them; and we may do this, with
God's help, very easily, if we have peace; so that all the youth
that are now in England, who are freemen, and possess sufficient wealth, may for a time apply to no other task till they
first well know how to read English. Let those learn Latin
afterwards, who will know more, and advance to a higher condition." In this wise and benevolent spirit he acted. The old
writers seem to state that, besides the translations that have
come down to us, he executed many others that are now lost.

It is probable, though there is no sufficient authority for the
statement, that Alfred re-established many of the old monastic
and episcopal schools in the various parts of the kingdom.
Asser expressly mentions that he founded a seminary for the
sons of the nobility, to the support of which he devoted no less
than an eighth part of his whole revenue. Hither even some
noblemen repaired who had far outgrown their youth, but nevertheless had scarcely or not at all begun their acquaintance with
books. In another place Asser speaks of this school, to which
Alfred is stated to have sent his own son Ethelward, as being
attended not only by the sons of almost all the nobility of the realm,
but also by many of the inferior classes. It was provided with
several masters. A notion that has been eagerly maintained by
some antiquaries is, that this seminary, instituted by Alfred, is
to be considered as the foundation of the University of Oxford.

Up to this time absolute illiteracy seems to have been common even among the highest classes of the English. We have
just seen that, when Alfred established his schools, they were as
much needed for the nobility who had reached an advanced or
mature age as for their children ; and, indeed, the scheme of instruction seems to have been intended from the first to embrace
the former as well as the latter, for, according to Asser's account,
every person of rank or substance who, either from age or want
of capacity, was unable to learn to read himself, was compelled
to send to school either his son or a kinsman, or, if he had
neither, a servant, that he might at least be read to by some one.
The royal charters, instead of the names of the kings, sometimes

exhibit their marks, used, as it is frankly explained, in consequence of their ignorance of letters.

The measures begun by Alfred for effecting the literary
civilization of his subjects were probably pursued under his successors; but the period of the next three quarters of a century,
notwithstanding some short intervals of repose, was on the whole
too troubled to admit of much attention being given to the carrying out of his plans, or even, it may be apprehended, the maintenance of what he had set up. Dunstan, indeed, during his
administration, appears to have exerted himself with zeal in
enforcing a higher standard of learning as well as of morals, or
of asceticism, among the clergy. But the renewal of the Danish
wars, after the accession of Ethelred, and the state of misery and
confusion in which the country was kept from this cause till its
conquest by Canute, nearly forty years after, must have again
laid in ruins the greater part of its literary as well as ecclesiastical establishments. The concluding portion of the tenth
century was thus, probably, a time of as deep intellectual darkness in England as it was throughout most of the rest of Europe.
Under Canute, however, who was a wise as well as a powerful
sovereign, the schools no doubt rose again and flourished. We
have the testimony, so far as it is to be relied upon, of the history
attributed to Ingulphus, which professes to be written immediately after the Norman conquest, and the boyhood of the author
of which is made to coincide with the early part of the reign
of the Confessor, that at that time seminaries of the higher as
well as of elementary learning existed in England. Ingulphus,
according to this account, having been born in the city of
London, was first sent to school at Westminster; and from
Westminster he proceeded to Oxford, where he studied the
Aristotelian philosophy and the rhetorical writings of Cicero.
This is the earliest express mention of the University of Oxford,
if a passage in Asser's work in which the name occurs be, as is
generally supposed, spurious, and if the History passing under
his name was really written by Ingulphus.

The studies that were cultivated in those ages were few in
number and of very limited scope. Alcuin, in a letter to his
patron Charlemagne, has enumerated, in the fantastic rhetoric
of the period, the subjects in which he instructed his pupils in
the school of St. Martin at Paris. "To some," says he, "I
administer the honey of the sacred writings; others I try to

inebriate with the wine of the ancient classics. I begin the
nourishment of some with the apples of grammatical subtlety.
I strive to illuminate many by the arrangement of the stars, as
from the painted roof of a lofty palace." In plain language, his
instructions embraced grammar, the Greek and Latin languages,
astronomy, and theology. In the poem in which he gives an
account of his own education at York, the same writer informs
us that the studies there pursued comprehended, besides grammar,
rhetoric, and poetry, "the harmony of the sky, the labour of the
sun and moon, the five zones, the seven wandering planets; the
laws, risings, and settings of the stars, and the aërial motions
of the sea; earthquakes; the nature of man, cattle, birds, and
wild beasts, with their various kinds and forms; and the sacred
Scriptures."

This poem of Alcuin's is especially interesting for the account
it gives us of the contents of the library collected by Archbishop
Egbert at York, the benefit of which Alcuin had enjoyed in his
early years, and which he seems to speak of in his letter to
Charlemagne, already quoted, as far superior to any collection
then existing in France. He proposes that some of his pupils
should be sent to York to make copies of the manuscripts there
for the imperial library at Tours. Among them, he says, were
the works of Jerome, Hilary, Ambrose, Austin, Athanasius,
Orosius, the Popes Gregory and Leo, Basil, Fulgentius, Cassio-
dorus, John Chrysostom, Athelmus, Bede, Victorinus, Boethius;
the ancient historical writers, as he calls them, Pompeius (most
probable Justin, the epitomizer of the lost Trogus Pompeius),
and Pliny; Aristotle, Cicero; the later poets Sedulius and
Juvencus; Alcuin himself, Clement, Prosper, Paulinus, Arator,
Fortunatus, and Lactantius (writers of various kinds, evidently
thus jumbled together to suit the exigencies of the verse); Virgil,
Statius, Lucan; the author of the Ars Grammatica; the
grammarians and scholiasts, Probus, Phocas, Donatus, Priscian,
and Servius; Eutychius; Pompeius (probably Festus) and Com-
monianus; besides, he adds, many more whom it would be
tedious to enumerate. This was certainly a very extraordinary
amount of literary treasure to be amassed in one place, and by
one man, at a period when books were everywhere so scarce and
necessarily bore so high a price. "Towards the close of the
seventh century," says Warton, in his Dissertation on the Introduction of Learning into England, "even in the Papal library at

Rome, the number of books were so inconsiderable that Pope St. Martin requested Sanctamand, bishop of Maestricht, if possible, to supply this defect from the remotest parts of Germany. In the year 855, Lupus, abbot of Ferrières in France, sent two of his monks to Pope Benedict the Third, to beg a copy of Cicero De Oratore and Quintilian's Institutes, and some other books: 'for,' says the abbot, 'although we have part of these books, yet there is no whole or complete copy of them in all France.' Albert, abbot of Gemblours, who with incredible labour and immense expense had collected a hundred volumes on theological and fifty on profane subjects, imagined he had formed a splendid library. About the year 790 Charlemagne granted an unlimited right of hunting to the abbot and monks of Sithin, for making their gloves and girdles of the skins of the deer they killed, and covers for their books. We may imagine that these religionists were more fond of hunting than of reading. It is certain that they were obliged to hunt before they could read; and, at least, it is probable that under these circumstances, and of such materials, they did not manufacture many volumes. At the beginning of the tenth century books were so scarce in Spain, that one and the same copy of the Bible, St. Jerome's Epistles, and some volumes of ecclesiastical offices and martyrologies often served several different monasteries." [*] To these instances we may add what Bede relates in his History of the Abbots of Wearmouth, in which monastery Benedict Biscopt, the founder, had, about the end of the seventh century, collected a considerable library, at the cost not only of much money, but also of no little personal exertion, having made five journeys to Rome for the purchase of books, relics, and other furniture and decorations for the establishment. Bede records that Benedict sold one of his volumes, a work on cosmography, to his sovereign, Alfred of Northumberland, for eight hides of land.

THE ENGLISH LANGUAGE.

The earliest historically known fact with regard to the English language is, that it was the language generally, if not universally, spoken by the barbaric invaders, apparently for the greater part

[*] History of English Poetry, vol. 1, p. cviii. (edit. of 1824).

of one race or blood, though of different tribes, who, upon the
breaking up of the empire of the West in the fifth century, came
over in successive throngs from the opposite continent, and, after
a protracted struggle, acquired the possession and dominion of the
principal portion of the province of Britain. They are stated to
have consisted chiefly of Angles and Saxons. But, although it is
usual to designate them rather by the general denomination of
the Saxons, or Anglo-Saxons, it is probable that the Saxons
were in reality only a section of the Angles. The *Angles*, of
which term our modern *English* is only another form, appears
to have been always recognized among themselves as the proper
national appellation. They both concurred, Angles and Saxons
alike, after their establishment in Britain, in calling their common country *Angle-land*, or *England*, and their common language
English—that is, the language of the Angles,—as there can be
little doubt it had been called from the time when it first became
known as a distinct form of human speech.

This English language, since become so famous, is ordinarily
regarded as belonging to the Low-Germanic, or middle, group
of the Gothic tongues. That is to say, it is classed with the
Dutch and the Flemish, and the dialects generally of the more
northern and low-lying part of what was anciently called Germany, under which name were included the countries that we
call Holland and the Netherlands, as well as that to which it is
now more especially confined. It appears to have been from
this middle region, lying directly opposite to Britain, that the
Angles and Saxons and other tribes by whom the English language was brought over to that island chiefly came. At any
rate, they certainly did not come from the more elevated region
of Southern Germany. Nor does the language present the distinguishing characteristics of a High-Germanic tongue. What
is now called the German language, therefore, though of the
same Gothic stock, belongs to a different branch from our own.
We are only distantly related to the Germans proper, or the race
among whom the language and literature now known as the
German have originated and grown up. We are, at least in
respect of language, more nearly akin to the Dutch and the
Flemings than we are to the Germans. It may even be doubted
if the English language ought not to be regarded as having more
of a Scandinavian than of a purely Germanic character,—as, in
other words, more nearly resembling the Danish or Swedish

than the modern German. The invading bands by whom it was
originally brought over to Britain in the fifth and sixth centuries were in all ,probability drawn in great part from the
Scandinavian countries. At a later date, too, the population of
England was directly recruited from Denmark, and the other
regions around the Baltic to a large extent. From about the
middle of the ninth century the population of all the eastern and
northern parts of the country was as much Danish as English.
And soon after the beginning of the eleventh century the sovereignty was acquired by the Danes.

The English language, although reckoned among modern languages, is already of respectable antiquity. In one sense, indeed,
all languages may be held to be equally ancient; for we can in
no case get at the beginning of a language, any more than we
can get at the beginning of a lineage. Each is merely the continuation of a preceding one, from which it cannot be separated
in any case except by a purely arbitrary mark of distinction.
Take two portions of the line at some distance from one another,
and they may be very unlike; yet the change which has transformed the one into the other, or produced the one out of the
other, has been, even when most active, so gradual, so perfectly
free always from anything that can be called a convulsion or
catastrophe, so merely a process of growth, however varying in
its rate of rapidity, that there is no precise point at which it can
be said to have begun. This is undoubtedly the way in which
all languages have come into existence: they have all thus grown
out of older forms of speech; none of them have been manufactured or invented. It would seem that human skill could as
soon invent a tree as invent a language. The one as well as the
other is essentially a natural production.

But, taking a particular language to mean what has always
borne the same name, or been spoken by the same nation or
race, which is the common or conventional understanding of the
matter, the English may claim to be older than the great majority
of the tongues now in use throughout Europe. The Basque,
perhaps, and the various Celtic dialects might take precedence
of it; but hardly any others. No one of the still spoken Germanic or Scandinavian languages could make out a distinct proof
of its continuous existence from an equally early date. And the
Romance tongues, the Italian, the Spanish, the French, are all.
recognized as such, confessedly of much later origin.

The English language is recorded to have been known by that name, and to have been the national speech of the same race, at least since the middle of the fifth century. It was then, as we have seen, that the first settlers by whom it was spoken established themselves in the country of which their descendants have ever since retained possession. Call them either Angles (that is, English) or Saxons, it makes no difference; it is clear that, whether or no the several divisions of the invaders were all of one blood, all branches of a common stock, they spoke all substantially the same language, the proper name of which, as has been stated, was the *Anglish*, or *English*, as *England*, or *Angle-land* (the land of the Angles), was the name which the country received from its new occupants. And these names of *England* and *English* the country and the language have each retained ever since.

Nor can it be questioned that the same tongue was spoken by the same race, or races, long before their settlement in Britain. The Angles figure as one of the nations occupying the forest land of Germany in the picture of that country sketched by Tacitus in the first century of our era.

The most distinct and satisfactory record, however, of a language is afforded by what exists of it in a written form. In applying this test or measure of antiquity, the reasonable rule would seem to be, that, wherever we have the clear beginning or end of a distinct body or continuous series of literary remains, there we have the beginning or end of a language. Thus, of what is called the Mœsogothic we have no written remains of later date than the fourth century (or, at any rate, than the sixth, if we reckon from what is probably the true age of the transcripts which we actually possess); and accordingly we hold the Mœsogothic to be a language which has passed away and perished, notwithstanding that there may be some other language or languages still existing of which there is good reason to look upon it as having been the progenitor. But of the English language we have a continuous succession of written remains since the seventh century at least; that is to say, we have an array of specimens of it from that date such as that no two of them standing next to one another in the order of time could possibly be pronounced to belong to different languages, but only at most to two successive stages of the same language. They afford us a record or representation of the language in

which there is no gap.   This cannot be said of any other existing
European tongue for nearly so great a length of time, unless we
may except the two principal Celtic tongues, the Welsh and the
Irish.

The movement of the language, however, during this extended
existence, has been immense. No language ever ceases to move
until it becomes what is called dead, which term, although commonly understood to mean merely that the language has ceased
to be spoken, really signifies, here as elsewhere, that the life is
gone out of it, which is indeed the unfailing accompaniment
of its ceasing to be used as an oral medium of communication.
It cannot grow after that, even if it should still continue to a
certain extent to be used in writing, as has been the case with
the Sanscrit in the East and the Latin in the West,—except
perhaps as the hair and the nails are said sometimes to grow
after the animal body is dead. It is only speaking that keeps
a language alive; writing alone will not do it. That has no
more than a conservative function and effect; the progressive
power, the element of fermentation and change, in a language
is its vocal utterance.

We shall find that the English language, moving now faster,
now slower, throughout the twelve or thirteen centuries over
which our knowledge of it extends, although it has never been
all at once or suddenly converted from one form into another—
which is what the nature of human speech forbids—has yet
within that space undergone at least *two* complete revolutions,
or, in other words, presents itself to us in *three* distinct forms.

Original English :—

commonly called *SAXON*, or *ANGLO-SAXON*.

The English which the Angles and Saxons brought over with
them from the Continent, when they came and took possession
of the greater part of South Britain in the fifth and sixth centuries, differed from the English that we now speak and write
in two important respects. It was an unmixed language; and it
was what is called a synthetic, in contradistinction to an analytic,
language. Its vocables were all of one stock or lineage; and it
expressed the relations of nouns and verbs, not by separate

words, called auxiliaries and particles, but by terminational or other modifications,—that is, by proper conjugation and declension,—as our present English still does when it says, *I loved* instead of *I did love*, or *The King's throne* instead of *The throne of the King*. These two characteristics are what constitute it a distinct form, or stage, of the language:—its synthetic or generally inflected grammatical structure, and its homogeneous vocabulary.

As a subject of philological study the importance of this earliest known form of the English language cannot be over-estimated; and much of what we possess written in it is also of great value for the matter. But the essential element of a literature is not matter, but manner. Here too, as in everything else, the soul of the artistic is form;—beauty of form. Now of that what has come down to us written in this primitive English is, at least for us of the present day, wholly or all but wholly destitute.

There is much writing in forms of human speech now extinct, or no longer in oral use, which is still intelligible to us in a certain sort, but in a certain sort only. It speaks to us as anything that is dead can speak to us, and no otherwise. We can decipher it, rather than read it. We make it out as it were merely by the touch, getting some such notion of it as a blind man might get of a piece of sculpture by passing his hand over it. This, for instance, to take an extreme case, is the position in which we stand in reference to the hieroglyphic inscriptions on the ancient monuments of Egypt. They can be read as the multiplication table can be read. But that is all. There may be nothing more in them than there is in the multiplication table; but if there were, we could not get at it. M. Champollion, indeed, in his enthusiasm, saw a vision of an amatory or bacchanalian song laughing under the venerable veil of one of them; but it is plain that this must have been an illusion. A mummy from one of the neighbouring tombs, embalmed some three or four thousand years ago, might almost as soon be expected to give forth a living voice.

Even the ancient Assyrian inscriptions, which are in alphabetical characters, will certainly never be made to render up to us more than the dead matters of fact that may be wrapt up in them. If there be any grace in the manner in which the facts are related, any beauty of style in the narrative, it has perished irretrievably. But this is what also appears to happen, in a

greater or less degree, in the case even of a language the vocabulary of which we have completely in our possession, and which we
are therefore quite able to interpret so far as regards the substance
of anything written in it, whenever it has for some time—for a
single generation, it may be—ceased both to be spoken and to be
written. Something is thus lost, which seems to be irrecover-
able. The two great classic tongues, it is to be observed, the
old Greek and Latin, although they have both long passed out of
popular use, have always continued to be not only studied and
read by all cultivated minds throughout Europe, but to be also
extensively employed by the learned, at least in writing. And
this has proved enough to maintain the modern world in what
may be called a living acquaintance with them—such an acquaintance as we have with a person we have conversed with,
or a place where we have actually been, as distinguished from
our dimmer conception of persons and places known to us only
by description. The ancient classic literature charms us as well
as informs us. It addresses itself to the imagination, and to our
sense of the beautiful, as well as to the understanding. It has
shape, and colour, and voice for us, as well as mere substance.
Every word, and every collocation of words, carries with it a
peculiar meaning, or effect, which is still appreciated. The
whole, in short, is felt and enjoyed, not simply interpreted.
But a language, which has passed from what we may call its
natural condition of true and full vitality as a national speech
cannot, apparently, be thus far preserved, with something of the
pulse of life still beating in it, merely by such a knowledge of
it being kept up as enables us to read and translate it. Still less
can a language, the very reading of which has been for a time
suspended, and consequently all knowledge whatever of it forgotten, ever be restored to even the appearance of life. It has
become a fossil, and cannot be resuscitated, but only dug up. A
thousand facts warrant us in saying that languages, and even
words, are subject to decay and dissolution as well as the human
beings of whose combined mental and physical organizations they
are the mysterious product; and that, once really dead, nothing
can reanimate their dust or reclothe their dry bones with flesh.

The original form of the English language is in this state. It
is intelligible, but that is all. What is written in it can in a
certain sense, be read, but not so as to bring out from the most
elaborate compositions in it any artistic element, except of the

most dubious and unsatisfactory kind. Either such an element is not present in any considerable degree, or the language is not now intimately enough known for any one to be able to detect it. If it is not literally dumb, its voice has for us of the present day entirely lost its music. Even of the system of measure and arrangement according to which it is ordinarily disposed for the purposes of poetry we have no proper apprehension or feeling. Certain mechanical principles or rules may have been discovered in obedience to which the versification appears to be constructed; but the verse as verse remains not the less for our ears and hearts wholly voiceless. When it can be distinguished from prose at all it is only by certain marks or characteristics which may indeed be perceived by the eye, or counted on the fingers, but which have no expression that excites in us any mental emotion. It is little better than if the composition merely had the words " This is verse " written over it or under it.

In respect of everything else appertaining to the soul of the language, our understanding of it is about equally imperfect. The consequence is, that, although it can be translated, it cannot be written. The late Mr. Conybeare, indeed, has left us a few specimens of verse in it of his own composition; but his attempts are of the slightest character, and, unadventurous as they are, nobody can undertake to say, except as to palpable points of right or wrong in grammar, whether they are well or ill done. The language, though so far, in our hands as to admit of being analyzed in grammars and packed up in dictionaries, is not recoverable in such a degree as to make it possible to pronounce with certainly whether anything written in it is artistically good or bad. As for learning to speak it, that is a thing as little dreamt of as learning to speak the language of Swift's Houyhnhnms.

When the study of this original form of the national speech was revived in England in the middle of the sixteenth century, it had been for well-nigh four hundred years not only what is commonly called a dead language, but a buried and an utterly forgotten one. It may be questioned if at least for three preceding centuries any one had been able to read it. It was first recurred to as a theological weapon. Much in the same manner as the Reformers generally were drawn to the study of the Greek language in maintaining the accordance of their doctrines with those of the New Testament and of the first ages

of Christianity, the English Reformers turned to the oldest
writings in the vernacular tongue for evidence of the comparatively unromanized condition of the early English church.
In the next age history and law began to receive illustration
from the same source. It was not till a considerably later date
that the recovered language came to be studied with much of a
special view to its literary and philological interest. And it is
only within the present century that it has either attracted any
attention in other countries, or been investigated on what are
now held to be sound principles. The specially theological
period of its cultivation may be regarded as extending over the
latter half of the sixteenth century, the legal and historical
period over the whole of the seventeenth, the philological of the
old school over the whole of the eighteenth, and the philological
of the modern school over the nineteenth, so far as it has gone.

If the English language as it was written a thousand years
ago had been left to itself, and no other action from without had
interfered with that of its spontaneous growth or inherent principles of change and development, it might not have remained
so stationary as some more highly-cultivated languages have
done throughout an equal space of time, but its form in the
nineteenth century would in all probability have been only a
comparatively slight modification of what it was in the ninth.
It would have been essentially the same language. As the case
stands, the English of the ninth century is one language, and
the English of the nineteenth century another. They differ at
least as much as the Italian differs from the Latin, or as English
differs from German. The most familiar acquaintance with the
one leaves the other unintelligible. So much is this so that it
has long been customary to distinguish them by different names,
and to call the original form of the national speech Saxon, or
Anglo-Saxon, as if it were not English at all. If the notion be
that the dialect in which most of the ancient English that has
come down to us is written in that which was in use among the
specially Saxon part of the population, that would have been
better indicated by calling it, not Anglo-Saxon, but Saxon
English. But even such a designation would be inapplicable to
those specimens of the language in which there is unquestionably nothing whatever that is specially Saxon, and which recent
investigations have shown to be not inconsiderable in amount, as
well as of high philological importance; and it would also leave

the limitation of the name *English* to the more modern form of the language without any warrant in the facts of the case. Objectionable, however, as may be the common nomenclature, it is still indisputable that we have here, for all practicable purposes, not one language, but two languages. The one may have grown out of the other, and no doubt has done so at least in part or in the main; but in part also the modern language is of quite a distinct stock from the ancient. Of English Literature, therefore, and the English Language, commonly so called, the language and literature of the Angles and Saxons before the twelfth century make no proper part. The history of the latter can only with propriety be glanced at as introductory to that of the former.

The mass of writing that has been preserved in this earlier English is very considerable, but only a small portion of it can be regarded as coming under the head of literature. Even of what has been printed, much, and that not the least interesting and valuable part, has no claim to that title; for example, the numerous mere documents that are given by Hickes in his most learned Thesaurus, and those that compose the six volumes of Mr. Kemble's Codex Diplomaticus. Most of what is of much value or curiosity in the language has now probably been committed to the press — much of it by scholars still living or only recently deceased, both in our own and other countries. The names of Conybeare, Ingram, Sharon Turner, Price, Kemble, Garnett, Miss Gurney, Thorpe, Guest, Bosworth, Fox, Goodwin, Langley, Norman, Offer, Cardale, Vernon, Barnes, Wright, Barrow, Stevenson, Thorkelin, Rask, Jacob Grimm, Leo, Schmidt, Ettmüller, Lappenberg, K. W. Bouterwek, to mention no others, may illustrate the wide diffusion of the interest that in our day has been and still continues to be taken in this field of study.

The epic of Beowulf is the most considerable poetical composition of which this primitive English literature has to boast. It exists only in a single manuscript, of the tenth century, one of those in the Cottonian Collection, from which it was first published, with a Latin translation, at Copenhagen, in 1810, by Dr. G. J. Thorkelin, whose transcript had been made so early as in 1786. A far superior text, however, accompanied by an English translation, notes, and a glossary, was afterwards produced by Mr. Kemble, in two volumes, the first published in 1833 (and again in 1835), the second in 1837. Copious extracts from Beowulf had previously been given by Mr. Sharon Turner in his History of the Anglo-Saxons, 1803; and the English reader will find a complete analysis of the poem, with versions of many passages in blank verse, in Professor Conybeare's Illustrations of Anglo-Saxon Poetry, published in 1826 by his brother, the Rev. W. D. Conybeare. There is likewise an English translation of the whole in rhyme by Professor A. Diedrich Wackerbarth, published in 1849. The only other long work in verse that has been preserved is what is sometimes described as a metrical version of Scripture history by a poet of the name of Cædmon, recorded by Bede as having lived in the seventh century, but which is in fact a collection of separate Scriptural narratives, mostly paraphrased from the book of Genesis, possibly by various writers, and certainly of much later date. It was first published from the only known manuscript, which is of the tenth century, and is now in the Bodleian Library, by the learned Francis Junius, at Amsterdam, in 1655; but a much more commodious and in every way superior edition, with an English translation, was brought out at London in 1832, under the auspices of the Society of Antiquaries, by Mr. Thorpe. Another, by K. W. Bouterwek, in two volumes octavo, was published at Elberfeld in 1847 and 1848. Some remarkable coincidences have often been noticed between Cædmon's treatment of his first subject, that of the Fall, and the manner in which it is treated by Milton, who may very possibly, it has been thought, have looked into his predecessor's performance, unless we should rather suppose that a common ancient source may have supplied some hints to both. There is also another religious poem, on the subject of Judith, preserved in the same Cottonian volume with Beowulf; but it is only a fragment. It was first published by Edward Thwaites in a volume entitled Heptateuchus, containing the Five Books of Moses and other portions of Scripture, Oxford, 1699; and it is reprinted in Thorpe's Analecta Anglo-Saxonica, 1834, and again 1846. Other fragmentary or short pieces are a song attributed to Cædmon (sometimes styled the Elder Cædmon) in King Alfred's translation of Bede, which if genuine must be of the latter part of the seventh century, and would be the oldest specimen of the language that has been preserved; a small portion of a warlike chant, first printed by Hickes (Grammatica Anglo-Saxonica, 192), and styled by Kemble, who has reproduced it in his edition of Beowulf, The Battle of Finnesburh; The

Traveller's Song, first printed by Conybeare; several compositions interspersed in the historical record called the Chronicle, of which the most famous is that on the victory of King Athelstan over the Scots and Danes at a place called Brunanburg in 938; a considerable portion of a poem on the battle of Maldon, fought in 993, originally printed from one of the Cotton manuscripts, in his Johannis Glastoniensis Chronicon, 1726, by Hearne, who, however, mistook it for prose, and since reproduced both by Conybeare and by Thorpe (in the Analecta); and others in the two collections known as the Exeter and the Vercelli Manuscripts, both which have now been edited in full, the former (which is of the eleventh century) by Thorpe in 1842, the latter (having however been previously printed in an appendix to the Record Commission edition of Rymer's Fœdera) by Kemble, for the Ælfric Society, in 1843.

One romance in prose has been discovered, on the mediæval story of Apollonius of Tyre (the same on which the play of Pericles, attributed to Shakespeare, is founded); of this also an edition by Mr. Thorpe, with a literal translation, appeared in 1834. Of the other prose remains the most important are the fragments of the Laws, among which are some of those of Ethelbert, king of Kent, who reigned in the latter part of the sixth and the early part of the seventh century, but evidently reduced to the language of a later age; the Chronicle, the earlier portion of which is chiefly a compilation from the Historia Ecclesiastica of Bede, but which may be regarded as a contemporary register of public events from perhaps about the middle of the tenth century, and which terminates at the close of the reign of Stephen in 1154; the various works of King Alfred, which however, are all in the main only translations from the Latin, though occasionally interspersed with original matter: his Pastorale of Pope Gregory, his Boethius De Consolatione Philosophiæ (with the verse in some of the copies metrically paraphrased and expanded), his English Ecclesiastical History of Bede, and his General History of Orosius; and the various theological, grammatical, and other writings of Alfric, or Ælfric, generally supposed to have been the individual of the same name who was archbishop of Canterbury from 995 to 1006. There are also translations of the Pentateuch, the Psalms, the Gospels, and other parts of Scripture: and numerous lives of saints, besides some treatises on medicine and botany, and a great many

wills, charters, and other legal instruments. Portions of the
laws were given in William Lambarde's Archaionomia, 4to.
1568, and fol. 1643, by Hickes in his Dissertatio Epistolaris
(in the Thesaurus), and in Hearne's Textus Roffensis, Oxford,
1720; and there are complete collections by Wilkins, 1721; by
Dr. Reinhold Schmidt, Leipzig, 1832; and by Thorpe (for the
Record Commission), 1840. Of the Chronicle, of which there
are many manuscripts more or less perfect, a portion was
appended by Wheloc to his Bede's Historia Ecclesiastica, with
Alfred's translation, Cambridge, 1649; the earliest edition of the
whole was that of Bishop Gibson, with a Latin translation,
Oxford, 1692; and there have since appeared that of the Rev.
J. Ingram, London, 1823, and that, by the late Richard
Price, Esq., contained in the Monumenta Historica Britannica,
1848 (coming down, however, only to the Norman Conquest),
both with translations into English. An English MS. translation by the late Richard Gough, Esq., is preserved, with the
rest of his collection, in the Bodleian Library; and another,
printed, but not published, by the late Miss Gurney, of Keswick,
Norfolk, in 1819, has been made the basis of that edited by
Dr. Giles, along with Bede's Ecclesiastical History, in one of
the volumes of Bohn's Antiquarian Library, 1849. The
Chronicle "in part translated," by Mr. Stevenson, is contained
in the First Part of the Second Volume of The Church Historians of England, 1853. Many portions of it are also given in
the original in a volume entitled Ancient History, English and
French, exemplified in a regular dissection of the Saxon
Chronicle, 8vo. Lond. 1830. Of the translations from the Latin
attributed to Alfred the Great, the preface to the Pastorale of
Pope Gregory was first printed, with a Latin translation, by
Archbishop Parker, along with his edition of Asser's (Latin)
Life of Alfred, fol. Lond. 1574; from this it was transferred to
a scarce octavo volume published at Leyden in 1597, with the
title of De Literis et Lingua Getarum, sive Gothorum, by a
writer calling himself Bonaventura Vulcanius Brugensis,
meaning, it has been conjectured, Smidt, or De Smet, of Bruges,
and who has been asserted to have really been Antony Morillon,
secretary to Cardinal Grandvelle; it is also given along with his
reprint of Asser by Camden in his Collection, published at
Francfort in 1603, and in Wise's Asser, 8vo. Oxford, 1722;
and Mr. Wright has inserted it, with an English translation, in

his Biographia Britannica Literaria, 1842, vol. i. pp. 307-400. The version of Boethius De Consolatione Philosophiæ was first edited by Christopher Rawlinson, 8vo. Oxford, 1098; and there are modern editions of the prose, with an English translation and notes, by Mr. J. S. Cardale, 8vo. Lond. 1829, and of the verse (Alfred's claim to which, however, is very doubtful), also with an English translation and notes, by the Rev. Samuel Fox, 8vo. Lond. 1835. Alfred's Orosius was first edited, "with an English translation from the Anglo-Saxon," by the Hon. Daines Barrington, in 1773; and it has been reproduced, with a new translation by Mr. Thorpe, in a very convenient form, along with Dr. R. Pauli's Life of Alfred, in one of the volumes of Bohn's Antiquarian Library, 1853. Alfred's Bede was published, in folio, at Cambridge, first by Wheloc in 1643, and again by Dr. John Smith, with large and learned annotations, in 1722. We may mention that a collection, professing to contain "The Whole Works of King Alfred the Great, with Preliminary Essays Illustrative of the History, Arts, and Manners of the Ninth Century," and calling itself the Jubilee Edition, was produced at London, by "the Alfred Committee," in 2 vols. (commonly bound in 3), in 1852. It consists, however, only of translations into modern English.

The various treatises passing under the name of Alfric, Ælfric, or Elfric, have recently engaged much attention, and the name has been assumed by a society established some years ago for the publication of literary remains in early English. He is known by the titles of the Grammarian and the Abbot; and the writings attributed to him, which are very numerous, are mostly theological and grammatical. The Ælfric Society has published a collection of his Homilies, edited, with a translation, by Mr. Thorpe, in 2 vols. 8vo. 1854; and a Latin grammar, compiled by him in his native language, first published by Somner in his Dictionarium Saxonico-Latino-Anglicum, Oxford, 1659, has been reprinted in part, from a different manuscript, at the expense of Sir Thomas Phillipps. For further information respecting Ælfric and his works the reader is referred to the account of him given by Mr. Wright in the first volume of the Biographia Britannica Literaria, pp. 480-494. His Homilies, Mr. Wright observes, are "written in very easy Anglo-Saxon, and form on that account the best book for the student who is beginning to study the language."

THE NORMAN CONQUEST.

The year 1066 is memorable as that of the Norman Conquest, —the conquest of England by the Normans. The conquests of which we read in the history of nations are of three kinds. Sometimes one population has been overwhelmed by or driven before another as it might have been by an inundation of the sea, or at the most a small number of the old inhabitants of the invaded territory have been permitted to remain on it as the bondsmen of their conquerors. This appears to have been the usual mode of proceeding of the barbarous races, as we call them, by which the greater part of Europe was occupied in early times, in their contests with one another. When the Teuton or Goth from the one side of the Rhine attacked the Celt on the other side, the whole tribe precipitated itself upon what was the object at once of its hostility and of its cupidity. Or even if it was one division of the great Gothic race that made war upon another, as, for instance, the Scandinavian upon any Germanic country, the course that was taken was commonly, or at least frequently, the same. The land was cleared by driving away all who could fly, and the universal massacre of the rest. This primitive kind of invasion and conquest belonged properly to the night of barbarism, but in certain of the extreme parts of the European system something of it survived down to a comparatively late date. Much that we are told of the manner in which Britain was wrested from its previous Celtic occupants by the Angles and Saxons in the fifth and sixth centuries of our era would lead us to think that the enterprise of these invaders was both originally conceived and conducted throughout in this spirit. Nay, for some centuries after this we have the Danes in their descents and inroads upon all parts of the British territories still acting, apparently, in the same style. But, ever from the time of the settlement of the barbarous nations in the more central provinces of the old Roman empire, another kind of conquest had come into use among them. Corrupted and enfeebled as it was, the advanced civilization which they now encountered seems to have touched them as with a spell, or rather could not but communicate to its assailants something of its own spirit. A policy of mere destruction was evidently not the course to be adopted here. The value of the conquest lay mainly in preserving as far as possible both the stupendous material structures and the other works of art by which the soil was everywhere covered and adorned, and the living intelligence and skill of which all these wonders were the product. Hence the second kind of conquest, in which for the first time the conquerors were contented to share the conquered country, usually according to a strictly defined proportional division, with its previous occupants. But this system too was only transitory. It passed away with the particular crisis which gave birth to it; and then arose the third and last kind of conquest, in which there is no general occupation of the soil of the conquered country by the conquerors, but only its dominion is acquired by them.

The first of the three kinds of conquest, then, has for its object and effect the complete displacement of the ancient inhabitants. It is the kind which is proper to the contests of barbarians with barbarians. Under the second form of conquest the conquerors, recognizing a superiority to themselves in many other things even in those whom their superior force or ferocity has subdued, feel that they will gain most by foregoing something of their right to the wholesale seizure and appropriation of the soil, and neither wholly destroying or expelling its ancient possessors, nor even reducing them to a state of slavery, but only treating them as a lower caste. This is the form proper and natural to the exceptional and rare case of the conquest of a civilized by a barbarous people. Finally, there is that kind of subjugation of one people or country by another which results simply in the overthrow of the independence of the former, and the substitution in it or over it of a foreign for a native government. This is generally the only kind of conquest which attends upon the wars of civilized nations with one another.

The conquest of England by the Normans in the year 1006 may be regarded as having been professedly a conquest of this last description. The age of both the first and the second kinds of conquest was over, at least everywhere throughout Europe except it may be only along some few portions of its extreme northern boundary. Both the English and the Normans stood indisputably within the pale of civilization, the former boasting the possession both of Christianity and of a national literature for four or five centuries, the latter, if more recently reclaimed from paganism and barbarism, nevertheless already recognized as one of the most brilliantly gifted of European races, and distinguished for their superior aptitude in the arts both of war and of peace, of polity and of song. And the Norman leader, having with him in his enterprise the approval and sanction of the Church, claimed the English crown as his by right; nor were there probably wanting many Englishmen, although no doubt the general national feeling was different, who held his claim to be fully as good in law and justice as that of his native competitor. In taking the style of the Conqueror with respect to England, as he had been wont to take that of the Bastard with reference to his ancestral Normandy, William, as has been often explained, probably meant nothing more than that he had acquired his English sovereignty for himself, by the nomination or bequest of his relation King Edward, or in whatever other way, and had not succeeded to it under the ordinary rule of descent. Such a right of property is still, in the old feudal language, technically described in the law of Scotland as acquired by conquest, and in that of England by purchase, which is etymologically of the same meaning,—the one word being the Latin *Conquæstus*, or *Conquisitio*, the other *Perquisitio*.

And in point of fact the Normans never transferred themselves in a body, or generally, to England. They did not, like the barbarous populations of a preceding age, abandon for this new country the one in which they had previously dwelt. England was never thus taken possession of by the Normans. It was never colonized by these foreigners, or occupied by them in any other than a military sense. The Norman Duke invaded it with an army, raised partly among his own subjects, partly drawn from other regions of the Continent, and so made himself master of it. It received a foreign government, but not at all a new population.

Two causes, however, meeting from opposite points, and working together, soon produced a result which was to some extent the same that would have been produced by a Norman colonization. The first was the natural demand on the part of William's followers or fellow-soldiers for a share in the profits and advantages of their common enterprise, which would probably in any case have compelled him eventually to surrender his new subjects to spoliation; the second was the equally natural restlessness of the latter under the foreign yoke that had been imposed upon them, by which they only facilitated the process of their general reduction to poverty and ruin.

And to the overthrow thus brought about of the native civilization was added, in the present case, the intrusion of another system of social organization, and of another language possessing also its own literature, to take the place of what was passing away. So that here again were two distinct forces harmoniously, though by movements in opposite directions, co-operating to a common end. At the same time that English culture shrunk and faded, Norman culture flourished and advanced. And the two forces were not balanced or in any way connected, but quite independent the one of the other. English culture went down, not under the disastrous influence of the rival light, but from the failure of its own natural aliment, or because the social structure of which it was the product had been smitten with universal disorganization. It was the withering of life throughout the whole frame that made the eye dim.

The difference, then, between the case of England conquered by the Normans in the eleventh century and that of Italy overrun by the Goths in the fifth, was twofold. First, the Normans did not settle in England, as the barbarous nations of the North did in Italy and other provinces of the subjugated Western empire; but, secondly, on the other hand, the new power which the Norman invasion and conquest of England established in the country was not a barbarism, but another civilization in most respects at least as advanced as the indigenous one;—if younger, only therefore the stronger and more aspiring, and yet, as it proved, not differing so far from that with which it was brought into competition as to be incapable of coalescing with it, if need were, as well as, in other circumstances, with its advantages of position, outshining it or casting it into the shade.

In this way it came to pass that the final result to both the language and the literature of the conquered people was pretty much the same in the two cases. What the barbaric influence, in its action upon the Latin language and literature, wanted of positive vital force it made up for by its mass and weight; the Norman influence, on the contrary, compensated by quality for its deficiency in quantity. There was considerable difference, however, in the process by which the transformation was effected in the two cases, and in the length of time which it occupied. The Gothic barbarism was in the first instance simply destructive; it was not till after some centuries that it came to be visibly or appreciably anything else. But the Norman influence, in virtue of being that, not of a barbarism, but of a civilisation, and especially of a civilization still in all the radiant bloom and buoyant pride of youth, never could have been directly destructive ; from the first moment of their actual contact it must have communicated to the native civilization something of new life.

One thing further may be noted. In both the cases that we have been comparing the result was the combination, both in the language and the literature, of the same two elements ; namely, the Latin (or Classical) and the Gothic (or Germanic, in the largest sense). But the important difference was, that, the basis of the combination remaining in each case what it originally was,—Latin in Italy, in France, in Spain, but Gothic in England—while the language and literature that grew up in each of the former countries came to be in general spirit and character what is called Romance, which must be understood to mean modified Roman, the English language and literature retained their original fundamentally Gothic character, only modified by so much as it has absorbed of a Latin element.

And the remarkable distinction of the English language is, that it is the only one of all the languages of the European world which, thus combining the two elements of the Classic and the Gothic—that is, as we may say, of ancient and of modern civilization—is Gothic, or modern, in its skeleton, or bony system, and in its formative principle, and Classic, or antique, only in what of it is comparatively superficial and non-essential. The other living European languages are either without the Classic element altogether, as are all those of the Scandinavian and Teutonic branches, or have it as their principal and governing element, as is the case with the Italian, the French, and the Spanish, which may all be described as only modernized forms of the Latin. Even in the proportion, too, in which the two elements are combined the English has greatly the advantage over these Romance tongues, as they are called, in none of which is there more than a mere sprinkling of the modern element, whereas in English, although here that constitutes the dominant or more active portion of the compound, the counterpoising ingredient is also present in large quantity, and is influential to a very high degree upon the general character of the language.

It should seem to follow from all this, that, both in its inner spirit and in its voice, both in its constructional and in its musical genius, the English language, and, through that, English literature, English civilization or culture generally, and the whole temper of the English mind, ought to have a capacity of sympathizing at once with the Classical and the Gothic, with the antique and the modern, with the past and the present, to an extent not to be matched by any other speech or nation of Europe.

It so happens, too, that the political fortunes of this English tongue have been in singular accordance with its constitution and natural adaptation, inasmuch as, at the same time that it stands in this remarkable position in the Old World, its position is still more pre-eminent in the New World, whether that designation be confined to the continent of America or understood as including the entire field of modern colonization in every quarter of the globe. The English are the only really colonizing people now extant. As we remember Coleridge once expressing it, it is the natural destiny of their country, as an island, to be the mother of nations. Their geographical position, concurring with their peculiar genius, and with all the other favourable circumstances of the case, gives them the command of the readiest access to the most distant parts of the earth,—a universal highway, almost as free as is the air to the swarming bees. And, accordingly, all the greatest communities of the future, whether they be seated beyond the Atlantic or beyond the Pacific, promise to be communities of English blood and English speech.

ARABIC AND OTHER NEW LEARNING.

The space of about a thousand years, extending from the overthrow of the Western Roman empire, in the middle of the fifth century, to that of the Eastern, in the middle of the fifteenth, may be divided into two nearly equal parts: the first of which may be considered as that of the gradual decline, the second as that of the gradual revival of letters. The former, reaching to the close of the tenth century, nearly corresponds, in its close as well as in its commencement, with the domination in England of the Angles and Saxons. In Europe generally, throughout this long space of time, the intellectual darkness, notwithstanding some brief and partial revivals, deepens more and more on the whole, in the same manner as in the natural day the gray of evening passes into the gloom of midnight. The Latin learning, properly so called, may be regarded as terminating with Boethius, who wrote in the early part of the sixth century. The Latin language, however, continued to be used in literary compositions, as well as in the services of the Church, both in our own country and in the other parts of Europe that had composed the old empire of Rome.

The Danish conquest of England, as completed by the accession of Canute, preceded the Norman by exactly half a century, and throughout this space, the country had, with little interruption, enjoyed a government which, if not always national,—and it was that too for rather more than half of the fifty years—was at any rate acknowledged and submitted to by the whole nation. The public tranquillity was scarcely ever disturbed for more than a moment by any internal commotion, and never at all by attacks from abroad. During this interval, therefore, many of the monastic and other schools that had existed in the days of Alfred, Athelstan, and Edgar, but had been swept away or allowed to fall into decay in the disastrous forty years that succeeded the decease of the last-mentioned monarch, were probably re-established. The more frequent communication with the Continent that began in the reign of the Confessor must also have been favourable to the intellectual advancement of the country. The dawn of the revival of letters in England, therefore, may be properly dated from a point about fifty years antecedent to the Norman Conquest, or from not very long after the commencement of the eleventh century.

Still at the date of the Conquest the country was undoubtedly in regard to everything intellectual in a very backward state. Ordericus Vitalis, almost a contemporary writer, and himself a native of England, though educated abroad, describes his countrymen generally as having been found by the Normans a rustic and almost illiterate people (*agrestes et pene illiteratos*). The last epithet may be understood as chiefly intended to characterize the clergy, for the great body of the laity at this time were everywhere illiterate. A few years after the Conquest, the king took advantage of the general illiteracy of the native clergy to deprive great numbers of them of their benefices, and to supply their places with foreigners. His real or his only motive for making this substitution may possibly not have been that which he avowed; but he would scarcely have alleged what was notoriously not the fact, even as a pretence.

The Norman Conquest introduced a new state of things in this as in most other respects. That event made England, as it were, a part of the Continent, where, not long before, a revival of letters had taken place scarcely less remarkable, if we take into consideration the circumstances of the time, than the next great revolution of the same kind in the beginning of the fifteenth century. In France, indeed, the learning that had flourished in the time of Charlemagne had never undergone so great a decay as had befallen that of England since the days of Alfred. The schools planted by Alcuin and the philosophy taught by Erigena had both been perpetuated by a line of the disciples and followers of these distinguished masters, which had never been altogether interrupted. But in the tenth century this learning of the West had met and been intermixed with a new learning originally from the East, but obtained directly from the Arab conquerors of Spain. The Arabs had first become acquainted with the literature of Greece in the beginning of the eighth century, and it instantly exercised upon their minds an awakening influence of the same powerful kind with that with which it again kindled Europe seven centuries afterwards. One difference, however, between the two cases is very remarkable. The mighty effects that arose out of the second revival of the ancient Greek literature in the modern world were produced almost solely by its eloquence and poetry; but these were precisely the parts of it that were neglected by the Arabs. The Greek books which they sought after with such extraordinary avidity were almost exclusively those that related either to metaphysics and mathematics on the one hand, or to medicine, chemistry, botany, and the other departments of physical knowledge, on the other. All Greek works of those descriptions that they could procure they not only translated into their own language, but in course of time illustrated with voluminous commentaries. The prodigious magnitude to which this Arabic literature eventually grew will stagger the reader who has adopted the common notion with regard to what are called the middle or the dark ages. "The royal library of the Fatimites" (sovereigns of Egypt), says Gibbon, "consisted of 100,000 manuscripts, elegantly transcribed and splendidly bound, which were lent, without jealousy or avarice, to the students of Cairo. . Yet this collection must appear moderate if we can believe that the Ommiades of Spain had formed a library of 600,000 volumes,

44 of which were employed in the mere catalogues. Their capital Cordova, with the adjacent towns of Malaga, Almeria, and Murcia, had given birth to more than 300 writers, and above 70 public libraries were opened in the cities of the Andalusian kingdom."* The difficulty we have in conceiving the existence of a state of things such as that here described arises in great part from the circumstance of the entire disappearance now, and for so long a period, of all this Arabic power and splendour from the scene of European affairs. But, long extinct as it has been, the dominion of the Arabs in Europe was no mere momentary blaze. It lasted, with little diminution, for nearly five hundred years, a period as long as from the age of Chaucer to the present day, and abundantly sufficient for the growth of a body of literature and science even of the wonderful extent that has been described. In the tenth century Arabic Spain was the fountainhead of learning in Europe. Thither students were accustomed to repair from every other country to study in the Arabic schools; and many of the teachers in the chief towns of France and Italy had finished their education in these seminaries, and were now diffusing among their countrymen the new knowledge which they had thence acquired. The writings of several of the Greek authors, also, and especially those of Aristotle, had been made generally known to scholars by Latin versions of them made from the Arabic.

There is no trace of this new literature having found its way to England before the Norman Conquest. But that revolution immediately brought it in its train. " The Conqueror himself," observes a writer who has illustrated this subject with a profusion of curious learning, " patronized and loved letters. He filled the bishoprics and abbacies of England with the most learned of his countrymen, who had been educated at the University of Paris, at that time the most flourishing school in Europe. He placed Lanfranc, abbot of the monastery of St. Stephen at Caen, in the see of Canterbury—an eminent master of logic, the subtleties of which he employed with great dexterity in a famous controversy concerning the real presence. Anselm, an acute metaphysician and theologian, his immediate successor in the same see, was called from the government of the abbey of Bec, in Normandy. Herman, a Norman, bishop of Salisbury, founded a noble library in the ancient cathedral of that

* Decline and Fall of the Rom. Emp. c. lii.

see. Many of the Norman prelates preferred in England by the Conqueror were polite scholars. Godfrey, prior of St. Swithin's at Winchester, a native of Cambray, was an elegant Latin epigrammatist, and wrote with the smartness and ease of Martial; a circumstance which, by the way, shows that the literature of the monks at this period was of a more liberal cast than that which we commonly annex to their character and profession." [*] Geoffrey, also, another learned Norman, came over from the University of Paris, and established a school at Dunstable, where, according to Matthew Paris, he composed a play, called the Play of St. Catharine, which was acted by his scholars, dressed characteristically in copes borrowed from the sacrist of the neighbouring abbey of St. Albans, of which Geoffrey afterwards became abbot. " The king himself," Warton continues, "gave no small countenance to the clergy, in sending his son Henry Beauclere to the abbey of Abingdon, where he was initiated in the sciences under the care of the abbot Grimbald, and Faritius, a physician of Oxford. Robert d'Oilly, constable of Oxford Castle, was ordered to pay for the board of the young prince in the convent, which the king himself frequently visited. Nor was William wanting in giving ample revenues to learning. He founded the magnificent abbeys of Battle and Selby, with other smaller convents. His nobles and their successors co-operated with this liberal spirit in erecting many monasteries. Herbert de Losinga, a monk of Normandy, bishop of Thetford in Norfolk, instituted and endowed with large possessions a Benedictine abbey at Norwich, consisting of sixty monks. To mention no more instances, such great institutions of persons dedicated to religious and literary leisure, while they diffused an air of civility, and softened the manners of the people in their respective circles, must have afforded powerful incentives to studious pursuits, and have consequently added no small degree of stability to the interests of learning." [†]

To this it may be added, that most of the successors of the Conqueror continued to show the same regard for learning of which he had set the example. Nearly all of them had themselves received a learned education. Besides Henry Beauclere,

[*] Warton's Dissertation on Introduction of Learning into England, prefixed to History of English Poetry, p. cxli. (edit. of 1840).
[†] Ibid. Some inaccuracies in Warton's account of Geoffrey and his play are corrected from a note by Mr. Douce.

Henry II., whose father Geoffrey Plantagenet, Earl of Anjou, was famous for his literary acquirements, had been carefully educated under the superintendence of his admirable uncle, the Earl of Gloucester; and he appears to have taken care that his children should not want the advantages he had himself enjoyed; for at least the three eldest, Henry, Geoffrey, and Richard, are all noted for their literary as well as their other accomplishments.

What learning existed, however, was still for the most part confined to the clergy. Even the nobility—although it cannot be supposed that they were left altogether without literary instruction—appear to have been very rarely initiated in any of those branches which were considered as properly constituting the scholarship of the times. The familiar knowledge of the Latin language in particular, which was then the key to all other erudition, seems to have been almost exclusively confined to churchmen, and to those few of the laity who embraced the profession of schoolmasters, as some, at least on the Continent, were now wont to do. The contemporary writer of a Life of Becket relates, that when Henry II., in 1161, sent an embassy to the Pope, in which the Earl of Arundel and three other noblemen were associated with an archbishop, four bishops, and three of the royal chaplains, four of the churchmen, at the audience to which they were admitted, first delivered themselves in as many Latin harangues; and then the Earl of Arundel stood up, and made a speech in English, which he began with the words, " We, who are illiterate laymen, do not understand one word of what the bishops have said to your holiness."

The notion that learning properly belonged exclusively to the clergy, and that it was a possession in which the laity were unworthy to participate, was in some degree the common belief of the age, and by the learned themselves was almost universally held as an article of faith that admitted of no dispute. Nothing can be more strongly marked than the tone of contempt which is expressed for the mass of the community, the unlearned vulgar, by the scholars of this period: in their correspondence with one another especially, they seem to look upon all beyond their own small circle as beings of an inferior species. This pride of theirs, however, worked beneficially upon the whole: in the first place, it was in great part merely a proper estimation of the advantages of knowledge over ignorance; and, secondly, it helped to make the man of the pen a match for him of the sword—the natural

liberator of the human race for its natural oppressor. At the
same time, it intimates very forcibly at once the comparative
rarity of the highly prized distinction, and the depth of the
darkness that still reigned far and wide around the few scattered
points of light.

SCHOOLS AND UNIVERSITIES.

Schools and other seminaries of learning, however, were greatly
multiplied in this age, and were also elevated in their character,
in England as well as elsewhere. Both Archbishop Lanfranc
and his successor Anselm exerted themselves with great zeal in
establishing proper schools in connexion with the cathedrals and
monasteries in all parts of the kingdom; and the object was one
which was also patronized and promoted by the general voice
of the Church. In 1170 it was ordered by the third general
council of Lateran, that in every cathedral there should be
appointed and maintained a head teacher, or scholastic, as was
the title given to him, who, besides keeping a school of his own,
should have authority over all the other schoolmasters of the
diocese, and the sole right of granting licences, without which
no one should be entitled to teach. In former times the bishop
himself had frequently undertaken the office of scholastic of the
diocese; but its duties were rarely efficiently performed under
that arrangement, and at length they seem to have come to be
generally altogether neglected. After the custom was introduced of maintaining it as a distinct office, it was filled in many
cases by the most learned persons of the time. And besides
these cathedral schools there were others established in all the
religious houses, many of which were also of high reputation.
It is reckoned that of religious houses of all kinds there were
founded no fewer than five hundred and fifty-seven between the
Conquest and the death of King John; and, besides those, there
still existed many others that had been founded in earlier times.
All these cathedral and conventual schools, however, appear to
have been intended exclusively for the instruction of persons
proposing to make the Church their profession. But mention is
also made of others established both in many of the principal
cities and even in the villages, which would seem to have been

open to the community at large; for it may be presumed that
the laity, though generally excluded from the benefits of a
learned education, were not left wholly without the means of
obtaining some elementary instruction. Some of these city
schools, however, were eminent as institutes of the highest departments of learning. One in particular is mentioned in the
History ascribed to Matthew Paris as established in the town of
St. Albans, which was presided over by Matthew, a physician,
who had been educated at the famous school of Salorno, in Italy,
and by his nephew Garinus, who was eminent for his knowledge
of the civil and canon laws, and where we may therefore suppose instructions were given both in law and in medicine.
According to the account of London by William Stephanides, or
Fitz-Stephen, written in the reign of Henry II., there were then
three of these schools of a higher order established in London,
besides several others that were occasionally opened by distinguished teachers. The London schools, however, do not seem
to have been academies of science and the higher learning, like
that of St. Albans: Fitz-Stephen's description would rather lead
us to infer that, although they were attended by pupils of different ages and degrees of proficiency, they were merely schools
of grammar, rhetoric, and dialectics. "On holidays," he says,
"it is usual for these schools to hold public assemblies in the
churches, in which the scholars engage in demonstrative or
logical disputations, some using enthymems, and others perfect
syllogisms; some aiming at nothing but to gain the victory, and
make an ostentatious display of their acuteness, while others
have the investigation of truth in view. Artful sophists on
these occasions acquire great applause; some by a prodigious
inundation and flow of words, others by their specious but fallacious arguments. After the disputations other scholars deliver
rhetorical declamations, in which they observe all the rules of
art, and neglect no topic of persuasion. Even the younger boys
in the different schools contend against each other, in verse,
about the principles of grammar, and the preterites and supines
of verbs."

The twelfth century may be considered as properly the age of
the institution of what we now call Universities in Europe,
though many of the establishments that then assumed the
regular form of universities had undoubtedly existed long before
as schools or studia. This was the case with the oldest of the

European universities, with Bologna and Paris, and also, in all probability, with Oxford and Cambridge. But it may be questioned if even Bologna, the mother of all the rest, was entitled by any organization or constitution it had received to take a higher name than a school or *studium* before the latter part of this century. It is admitted that it was not till about the year 1200 that the school out of which the University of Paris arose had come to subsist as an incorporation, divided into nations, and presided over by a rector.* The University of Oxford, properly so called, is probably of nearly the same antiquity. It seems to have been patronized and fostered by Richard I., as that of Paris was by his great rival, Philip Augustus. Both Oxford and Cambridge had undoubtedly been eminent seats of learning long before this time, as London, St. Albans, and other cities had also been; but there is no evidence that either the one or the other had at an earlier date become anything more than a great school, or even that it was distinguished by any assigned rank or privileges above the other great schools of the kingdom. In the reign of Richard I. we find the University of Oxford recognized as an establishment of the same kind with the University of Paris, and as the rival of that seminary.

We have the following account of what is commonly deemed the origin of the University of Cambridge in the continuation of the history of Ingulphus, attributed to Peter of Blois, under the year 1109:—"Joffrid, abbot of Croyland, sent to his manor of Cottenham, near Cambridge, Master Gislebert, his fellow monk, and professor of theology, with three other monks who had followed him into England; who, being very well instructed in philosophical theorems and other primitive sciences, went every day to Cambridge, and, having hired a certain public barn, taught the sciences openly, and in a little time collected a great concourse of scholars; for, in the very second year after their arrival, the number of their scholars from the town and country increased so much that there was no house, barn, nor church capable of containing them. For this reason they separated into different parts of the town, and, imitating the plan of the Studium of Orleans, brother Odo, who was eminent as a grammarian and satirical poet, read grammar, according to the doctrine of Priscian and of his commentator Remigius, to the boys and younger students, that were assigned to him, early in

* See Crevier, Hist. de l'Univ. de Paris, t. 255.

the morning. At one o'clock, brother Terrious, a most acute
sophist, read the Logic of Aristotle, according to the Introductions and Commentaries of Porphyry and Averroes,* to those
who were further advanced. At three, brother William read
lectures on Tully's Rhetoric and Quintilian's Institutions. But
Master Gislebert, being ignorant of the English, but very expert
in the Latin and French languages, preached in the several
churches to the people on Sundays and holidays." † The history
in which this passage occurs is, as will presently be shown, as
apocryphal as that of which it professes to be the continuation ;
but even if we waive the question of its authenticity, there is
here no hint of any sort of incorporation or public establishment
whatever ; the description is merely that of a school set on foot
and conducted by an association of private individuals. And
even this private school would seem to have been first opened
only in the year 1109, although there may possibly have been
other schools taught in the place before. It may be gathered
from what is added, that at the time when the account, if it was
written by Peter of Blois, must have been drawn up (the latter
part of the same century), the school founded by Gislebert and
his companions had attained to great celebrity ; but there is
nothing to lead us to suppose that it had even then become
more than a very distinguished school. "From this little
fountain," he says, "which hath swelled into a great river, we
now behold the city of God made glad, and all England rendered
fruitful, by many teachers and doctors issuing from Cambridge,
after the likeness of the holy Paradise."

Notwithstanding, however, the rising reputation of Oxford
and Cambridge, the most ambitious of the English students continued to resort for part of their education to the more distinguished foreign schools during the whole of the twelfth century.
Thus, it is recorded that several volumes of the Arabian philosophy were brought into England by Daniel Merlac, who,
in the year 1185, had gone to Toledo to study mathematics.
Salerno was still the chief school of medicine, and Bologna of

* The works of Averroes, however, who died in 1198, were certainly not in
existence at the time here referred to. Either Peter of Blois must have been
ignorant of this, or—if he was really the author of the statement—the name
must have been the insertion of some later transcriber of his text.

† Petri Blesensis Continuatio ad Historiam Ingulphi : in Rerum Anglicarum
Script. Vet.: Oxon. 1684, p. 114. The translation is that given by Henry in
his History of Britain.

law, although Oxford was also becoming famous for the latter study. But, as a place of general instruction, the University of Paris stood at the head of all others. Paris was then wont to be styled, by way of pre-eminence, the City of Letters. So many Englishmen, or, to speak more strictly, subjects of the English crown, were constantly found among the students at this great seminary, that they formed one of the four nations into which the members of the university were divided. The English students are described by their countryman, the poet Nigellus Wireker, in the latter part of the twelfth century, in such a manner as to show that they were already noted for that spirit of display and expense which still makes so prominent a part of their continental reputation :—

> Moribus egregii, verbo vultuque venusti,
> Ingenio pollent, consilioque vigent ;
> Ibus pluunt populis, et detestantur avaros,
> Fercula multiplicant, et sine lege bibunt.*

> Of noble manners, gracious look and speech,
> Strong sense, with genius brightened, shines in each.
> Their free hand still rains largess ; when they dine
> Course follows course, in rivers flows the wine.

Among the students at the University of Paris in the twelfth century are to be found nearly all the most distinguished names among the learned of every country. One of the teachers, the celebrated Abelard, is said to have alone had as pupils twenty persons who afterwards became cardinals, and more than fifty who rose to be bishops and archbishops. Thomas à Becket received part of his education here. Several of the most eminent teachers were Englishmen. Among these may be particularly mentioned Robert of Melun (so called from having first taught in that city), and Robert White, or Pullus, as he is called in Latin. Robert of Melun, who afterwards became bishop of Hereford, distinguished himself by the zeal and ability with which he opposed the novel views which the rising sect of the Nominalists were then introducing both into philosophy and theology. He is the author of several theological treatises, none of which, however, have been printed. Robert White, after

* These verses are quoted by A. Wood, Antiq. Oxon., p. 53. The poem in which they occur is entitled Speculum Stultorum, or sometimes Brunellus (from its principal personage). It has been repeatedly printed.

teaching some years at Paris, where he was attended by crowded audiences, was induced to return to his own country, where he is said to have read lectures on theology at Oxford for five years, which greatly contributed to spread the renown of that rising seminary. After having declined a bishopric offered to him by Henry I., he went to reside at Rome in 1143, on the invitation of Celestine II., and was soon after made a cardinal and chancellor of the holy see. One work written by him has been printed, a summary of theology, under the then common title of The Book of Sentences, which has the reputation of being distinguished by the superior correctness of its style and the lucidness of its method.

Another celebrated name among the Englishmen who are recorded to have studied at Paris in those days is that of Nicolas Breakspear, who afterwards became pope by the title of Adrian IV. But, above all others, John of Salisbury deserves to be here mentioned. It is in his writings that we find the most complete account that has reached us not only of the mode of study followed at Paris, but of the entire learning of the age.

RISE OF THE SCHOLASTIC PHILOSOPHY.

At this time those branches of literary and scientific knowledge which were specially denominated the arts were considered as divided into two great classes,—the first or more elementary of which, comprehending Grammar, Rhetoric, and Logic, was called the Trivium; the second, comprehending Music, Arithmetic, Geometry, and Astronomy, the Quadrivium. The seven arts, so classified, used to be thus enumerated in a Latin hexameter:—

> Lingua, Tropus, Ratio, Numerus, Tonus, Angulus, Astra;

or, with definitions subjoined, in two still more singularly constructed verses,—

> *Gram.* loquitur, *Dia.* vera docet, *Rhet.* verba colorat,
> *Mus.* canit, *Ar.* numerat, *Geo.* ponderat, *Ast.* colit astra.

John of Salisbury speaks of this system of the sciences as an ancient one in his day. "The Trivium and Quadrivium," he

says, in his work entitled Metalogicus, "were so much admired by our ancestors in former ages, that they imagined they
comprehended all wisdom and learning, and were sufficient for
the solution of all questions and the removing of all difficulties;
for whoever understood the Trivium could explain all manner of
books without a teacher; but he who was farther advanced, and
was master also of the Quadrivium, could answer all questions
and unfold all the secrets of nature." The present age, however,
had outgrown the simplicity of this arrangement; and various
now studies had been added to the ancient seven, as necessary to
complete the circle of the sciences and the curriculum of a liberal
education.

It was now, in particular, that Theology first came to be
ranked as a science. This was the age of St. Bernard, the last of
the Fathers, and of Peter Lombard, the first of the Schoolmen.
The distinction between these two classes of writers is, that the
latter do, and the former do not, treat their subject in a system-
atizing spirit. The change was the consequence of the cultivation of the Aristotelian logic and metaphysics. When these
studies were first introduced into the schools of the West, they
were wholly unconnected with theology. But, especially at a
time when all the learned were churchmen, it was impossible
that the great instrument of thought and reasoning could long
remain unapplied to the most important of all the subjects
of thought—the subject of religion. It has already been remarked that John Erigena and other Irish divines introduced
philosophy and metaphysics into the discussion of questions
of religion as early as the ninth century; and they are consequently entitled to be regarded as having first set the example
of the method afterwards pursued by the schoolmen. But,
although the influence of their writings may probably be traced
in preparing the way for the introduction of the scholastic
system, and also, afterwards, perhaps, in modifying its spirit,
that system was derived immediately, in the shape in which it
appeared in the eleventh and twelfth centuries, from another
source. Erigena was a Platonist; the spirit of his philosophy
was that of the school of Alexandria. But the first schoolmen,
properly so called, were Aristotelians: they drew their logic and
metaphysics originally from the Latin translations of the works of
Aristotle made from the Arabic. And they may also have been
indebted for some of their views to the commentaries of the

Arabic doctors. But, whether they took their method of philosophy entirely from the ancient heathen sage, or in part from
his modern Mahomedan interpreters and illustrators, it could in
neither case have had at first any necessary or natural alliance
with Christianity. Yet it very soon, as we have said, formed
this alliance. Both Lanfranc and Anselm, although not commonly reckoned among the schoolmen, were imbued with the
spirit of the new learning, and it is infused throughout their
theological writings. Abelard soon after, before he was yet a
churchman, may almost be considered to have wielded it as a
weapon of scepticism. Even so used, however, religion was
still the subject to which it was applied. At last came Peter
Lombard, who, by the publication, about the middle of the twelfth
century, of his celebrated Four Books of Sentences, properly
founded the system of what is called the Scholastic Theology.
The schoolmen, from the Master of the Sentences, as Lombard
was designated, down to Francis Suarez, who died after the
commencement of the seventeenth century, were all theologians.
Although, however, religious speculation was the field of thought
upon which the spirit of the Aristotelian philosophy chiefly
expended itself, there was scarcely any one of the arts or
sciences upon which it did not in some degree seize. The
scholastic logic became the universal instrument of thought and
study : every branch of human learning was attempted to be
pursued by its assistance ; and most branches were more or less
affected by its influence in regard to the forms which they
assumed.

JOHN OF SALISBURY.—PETER OF BLOIS.

John of Salisbury went to complete his education at Paris in
the year 1136. " When I beheld," he writes in a letter to his
friend Becket, " the reverence paid to the clergy, the majesty
and glory of the whole Church, and the various occupations of
those who applied themselves to philosophy in that city, it raised
my admiration as if I had seen the ladder of Jacob, the top of
which reached to Heaven, while the steps were crowded with
angels ascending and descending." The first master whose
lectures he attended was the renowned Abelard, still, after all the
vicissitudes of his life, teaching with undiminished glory, in

the midst of a vast confluence of admiring disciples, on the Mount
of St. Genovieve. " I drank in," says his English pupil, " with
incredible avidity, every word that fell from his lips; but he
soon, to my infinite regret, retired." Abelard lived only a few
years after this date, which he spent in devotion and entire seclusion from the world. John of Salisbury then studied dialectics
for two years under two other masters, one of whom was his
countryman, Robert de Melun, mentioned above. After this he
returned to the study of grammar and rhetoric, which he pursued
for three years under William de Conches, of whose method of
teaching he has left a particular account. It appears to have
embraced a critical exposition both of the style and the matter of
the writers commented upon, and to have been well calculated
to nourish both the understanding and the taste. After this he
spent seven years under other masters, partly in the further pro-
secution of his acquaintance with the writers of antiquity and the
practice of Latin composition, partly in the study of the mathematics and theology. The entire course thus occupied twelve
years; but some, it would appear, devoted the whole of this time
to the study of dialectics, or logic, alone. John of Salisbury's
treatise entitled Metalogicus is intended principally to expose
the absurdity and injurious effects of this exclusive devotion to
the art of wrangling; and, although it must be considered as
written with some degree of satirical licence, the representation
which it gives of the state of things produced by the new spirit
that had gone abroad over the realms of learning is very curious
and interesting. The turn of the writer's own genius was
decidedly to the rhetorical rather than the metaphysical, and he
was not very well qualified, perhaps, to perceive certain of the
uses or recommendations of the study against which he directs
his attack; but the extravagances of its devotees, it may be
admitted, fairly exposed them to his ridicule and castigation.
" I wish," he says in one place, " to behold the light of truth,
which these logicians say is only revealed to them. I approach
them,—I beseech them to instruct me, that, if possible, I may
become as wise as one of them. They consent,—they promise
great things,—and at first they command me to observe a Pytha-
gorean silence, that I may be admitted into all the secrets of
wisdom which they pretend are in their possession. But by-
and-by they permit, and even command me, to prattle and
quibble with them. This they call disputing: this they say is

logic; but I am no wiser." He accuses them of wasting their ingenuity in the discussion of such puerile puzzles as whether a person in buying a whole cloak also bought the cowl; or whether, when a hog was carried to market with a rope tied about its neck, and held at the other end by a man, the hog was really carried to market by the man or by the rope. It must be confessed that, if their logic had been worth much, it ought to have made short work with these questions, supposing them to be worth settling at all. Our author adds, however, that they were declared to be questions which could not be solved, the arguments on both sides exactly balancing each other. But his quarrel with the dialecticians was chiefly on the ground of the disregard and aversion they manifested, in their method of exercising the intellectual powers, to all polite literature, to all that was merely graceful and ornamental. And there can be no question that the ascendancy of the scholastic philosophy was fatal for the time to the cultivation of polite literature in Europe. So long as it reigned supreme in the schools, learning was wholly divorced from taste. The useful utterly rejected all connexion with the beautiful. The head looked down with contempt upon the heart. Poetry and fiction, and whatever else belonged to the imaginative part of our nature, were abandoned altogether to the unlearned, to the makers of songs and lays for the people. It was probably fortunate for poetry, and the kindred forms of literature, in the end, that they were thus left solely to the popular cultivation for a time: they drew nourishment and new life from the new soil into which they were transplanted; and their produce has been the richer and the racier for it ever-since. The revival of polite literature probably came at a better time in the fifteenth than if it had come in the twelfth century. Yet it was not to be expected that, when it was threatened with blight and extinction at the earlier era, its friends should either have been able to foresee its resurrection two or three centuries later, or should have been greatly consoled by that prospect if they had.

John of Salisbury's chief work is his Polycraticon, or, as he further entitles it, A Treatise in eight books, on the Frivolities of Courtiers and the Footsteps of Philosophers (De Nugis Curialium et Vestigiis Philosophorum). " It is," says Warton, " an extremely pleasant miscellany, replete with erudition, and a judgment of men and things which properly belongs to a more sensible and reflecting period. His familiar acquaintance with

the classics appears not only from the happy facility of his language, but from the many citations of the purest Roman authors
with which his works are perpetually interspersed."* He also
wrote Latin verses with extreme elegance. John of Salisbury
died bishop of Chartres in 1182. Peter of Blois (or Petrus
Blesensis), a native of the town in France from which he takes
his name, was another distinguished cultivator of polite literature
in the same age. Among the writings he has left us, his Letters
collected by himself to the number of 134, are especially interesting, abounding as they do in graphic descriptions of the manners
and characters of the time. But neither in elegance of taste and
style, nor in general literary accomplishment, is the Frenchman
to be compared with his English contemporary.

CLASSICAL LEARNING.—MATHEMATICS.—MEDICINE.—LAW.—
BOOKS.

The classical knowledge of this period, however, was almost
confined to the Roman authors, and some of the most eminent of
these were as yet unstudied and unknown. Even John of
Salisbury, though a few Greek words are to be found in his compositions, seems to have had only the slightest possible acquaintance with that language. Both it and the Hebrew, nevertheless,
were known to Abelard and Eloisa; and it is probable that
there were both in England and other European countries a few
students of the oriental tongues, for the acquisition of which
inducements and facilities must have been presented, not only
by the custom of resorting to the Arabic colleges in Spain, and
the constant intercourse with the East kept up by the pilgrimages and the crusades, but also by the numbers of learned
Jews that were everywhere to be found. In England the Jews
had schools in London, York, Lincoln, Lynn, Norwich, Oxford,
Cambridge, and other towns, which appear to have been attended
by Christians as well as by those of their own persuasion. Some
of these seminaries, indeed, were rather colleges than schools.
Besides the Hebrew and Arabic languages, arithmetic and medicine are mentioned among the branches of knowledge that
were taught in them; and the masters were generally the most

* Introd. of Learning into Eng. p. cxx. (ed. 1840).

distinguished of the rabbis.   In the eleventh and twelfth centuries, the age of Sarchi, the Kimchis, Maimonides, and other
distinguished names, rabbinical learning was in an eminently
flourishing state.

There is no certain evidence that the Arabic numerals were yet
known in Europe: they certainly were not in general use.
Although the Elements of Euclid and other geometrical works
had been translated into Latin from the Arabic, the mathematical
sciences appear to have been but little studied.   " The science of
demonstration," says John of Salisbury, in his Metalogicus,
" is of all others the most difficult, and alas! is almost quite
neglected, except by a very few who apply to the study of the
mathematics, and particularly of geometry.   But this last is at
present very little attended to amongst us, and is only studied
by some persons in Spain, Egypt, and Arabia, for the sake of
astronomy.   One reason of this is, that those parts of the works
of Aristotle that relate to the demonstrative sciences are so ill
translated, and so incorrectly transcribed, that we meet with
insurmountable difficulties in every chapter."   The name of the
mathematics at this time, indeed, was chiefly given to the science
of astrology.   " Mathematicians," says Peter of Blois, " are those
who, from the position of the stars, the aspect of the firmament,
and the motions of the planets, discover things that are to come."
Astronomy, however, or the true science of the stars, which was
zealously cultivated by the Arabs in the East and in Spain,
seems also to have had some cultivators among the learned of
Christian Europe.   Latin translations existed of several Greek
and Arabic astronomical works.   In the History attributed to
Ingulphus, is the following curious description of a sort of
scheme or representation of the planetary system called the
Nadir, which is stated to have been destroyed when the abbey of
Croyland was burnt in 1091 : " We then lost a most beautiful and
precious table, fabricated of different kinds of metals, according to
the variety of the stars and heavenly signs.   Saturn was of copper,
Jupiter of gold, Mars of iron, the Sun of latten, Mercury of amber,
Venus of tin, the Moon of silver.   The eyes were charmed, as
well as the mind instructed, by beholding the colure circles, with
the zodiac and all its signs, formed with wonderful art, of metals
and precious stones, according to their several natures, forms,
figures, and colours.   It was the most admired and celebrated
Nadir in all England."   These last words would seem to imply

that such tables were then not uncommon.   This one, it is stated,
had been presented to a former abbot of Croyland by a king of
France.

John of Salisbury, in his account of his studies at Paris, makes
no mention either of medicine or of law.   With regard to the
former, indeed, he elsewhere expressly tells us that the Parisians
themselves used to go to study it at Salerno and Montpellier.
By the beginning of the thirteenth century, however, we find a
school of medicine established at Paris, which soon became very
celebrated.   Of course there were, at an earlier date, persons who
practised the medical art in that city.   The physicians in all the
countries of Europe at this period were generally churchmen.
Many of the Arabic medical works were early translated into
Latin; but the Parisian professors soon began to publish treatises
on the art of their own.   The science of the physicians of this
age, besides comprehending whatever was to be learned respecting the diagnostics and treatment of diseases from Hippocrates,
Galen, and the other ancient writers, embraced a considerable
body of botanical and chemical knowledge.   Chemistry in particular the Arabs had carried far beyond the point at which it
had been left by the ancients.   Of anatomy little could as yet be
accurately known, while the dissection of the human subject was
not practised.   Yet it would appear that physicians and surgeons
were already beginning to be distinguished from each other.
Both the canon and civil laws were also introduced into the
routine of study at the University of Paris soon after the time
when John of Salisbury studied there.   The canon law was
originally considered to be a part of theology, and only took the
form of a separate study after the publication of the systematic
compilation of it called the Decretum of Gratian, in 1151.
Gratian was a monk of Bologna, and his work, not the first
collection of the kind, but the most complete and the best-
arranged that had yet been compiled, was immediately introduced
as a text-book in that university.   It may be regarded as having
laid the foundation of the science of the canon law, in the same
manner as the system of the scholastic philosophy was founded by
Peter Lombard's Book of Sentences.   Regular lecturers upon it
very soon appeared at Orleans, at Paris, at Oxford, and all the
other chief seats of learning in western Christendom; and before
the end of the twelfth century no other study was more eagerly
pursued, or attracted greater crowds of students, than that of the

canon law. One of its first and most celebrated teachers at
Paris was Girard la Pucelle, an Englishman, who afterwards
became bishop of Lichfield and Coventry. Girard taught the
canon law in Paris from 1160 to 1177; and, in consideration of
his distinguished merits and what was deemed the great importance of his instructions, he received from Pope Alexander III.
letters exempting him from the obligation of residing on his
preferments in England while he was so engaged; this being, it
is said, the first known example of such a privilege being
granted to any professor.* The same professors who taught the
canon law taught also, along with it, the civil law, the systematic study of which, likewise, took its rise in this century, and
at the University of Bologna, where the Pandects of Justinian, of
which a more perfect copy than had before been known is said
to have been found in 1137 at Amalfi,† were arranged and first
lectured upon by the German Irnerius,—the Lamp of the Law,
as he was called,—about the year 1150. Both the canon and
the civil law, however, are said to have been taught a few years
before this time at Oxford by Roger, surnamed the Bachelor, a
monk of Bec, in Normandy. The study was, from the first,
vehemently opposed by the practitioners of the common law;
but, sustained by the influence of the Church, and eventually also
favoured by the government, it rose above all attempts to put it
down. John of Salisbury affirms that, by the blessing of God,
the more it was persecuted the more it flourished. Peter of
Blois, in one of his letters, gives us the following curious account
of the ardour with which it was pursued under the superintendence of Archbishop Theobald:—" In the house of my master,
the Archbishop of Canterbury, there are several very learned
men, famous for their knowledge of law and politics, who spend
the time between prayers and dinner in lecturing, disputing,
and debating causes. To us all the knotty questions of the
kingdom are referred, which are produced in the common hall,
and every one in his order, having first prepared himself, declares, with all the eloquence and acuteness of which he is
capable, but without wrangling, what is wisest and safest to be

* Crevier, Hist. de l'Univ. de Paris, I. 241.

† "The discovery of the Pandects at Amalfi," says Gibbon, " is first noticed
(in 1501) by Ludovicus Bologninus, on the faith of a Pisan Chronicle, without
a name or date. The whole story, though unknown to the twelfth century,
embellished by ignorant ages, and suspected by right criticism, is not however
destitute of much internal probability."

done. If God suggests the soundest opinion to the youngest amongst us, we all agree to it without envy or detraction."[*]

Study in every department must have been still greatly impeded by the scarcity and high price of books; but their multiplication now went on much more rapidly than it had formerly done. We have already noticed the immense libraries said to have been accumulated by the Arabs, both in their oriental and European seats of empire. No collections to be compared with these existed anywhere in Christian Europe; but, of the numerous monasteries that were planted in every country, few were without libraries of greater or less extent. A convent without a library, it used to be proverbially said, was like a castle without an armoury. When the monastery of Croyland was burnt in 1091, its library, according to Ingulphus, consisted of 900 volumes, of which 300 were very large. "In every great abbey," says Warton, "there was an apartment called the Scriptorium; where many writers were constantly busied in transcribing not only the service-books for the choir, but books for the library. The Scriptorium of St. Albans abbey was built by Abbot Paulin, a Norman, who ordered many volumes to be written there, about the year 1080. Archbishop Lanfranc furnished the copies. Estates were often granted for the support of the Scriptorium. . . . I find some of the classics written in the English monasteries very early. Henry, a Benedictine monk of Hyde Abbey, near Winchester, transcribed in the year 1178 Terence, Boethius, Suetonius, and Claudian. Of these he formed one book, illuminating the initials, and forming the brazen bosses of the covers with his own hands." Other instances of the same kind are added. The monks were much accustomed both to illuminate and to bind books, as well as to transcribe them. "The scarcity of parchment," it is afterwards observed, "undoubtedly prevented the transcription of many other books in these societies. About the year 1120, one Master Hugh, being appointed by the convent of St. Edmondsbury, in Suffolk, to write and illuminate a grand copy of the Bible for their library, could procure no parchment for this purpose in England."[†] Paper made of cotton, however, was certainly in common use in the twelfth century, though no evidence exists that

---

[*] Ep. vi, as translated in Henry's History of Britain.
[†] Introd. of Learning into England, p. cxvi.

that manufactured from linen rags was known till about the middle of the thirteenth.

THE LATIN LANGUAGE.

During the whole of the Anglo-Norman period, and down to a much later date, in England as in the other countries of Christendom, the common language of literary composition, in all works intended for the perusal of the educated classes, was still the Latin, the language of religion throughout the western world, as it had been from the first ages of the Church. Christianity had not only, through its monastic institutions, saved from destruction, in the breaking up of the Roman empire, whatever we still possess of ancient literature, but had also, by its priesthood and its ritual, preserved the language of Rome in some sort still a living and spoken tongue—corrupted indeed by the introduction of many new and barbarous terms, and illegitimate acceptations, and by much bad taste in style and phraseology, but still wholly unchanged in its grammatical forms, and even in its vocabulary much less altered than it probably would have been if it had continued all the while to be spoken and written by an unmixed Roman population. It would almost seem as if, even in the Teutonic countries, such as England, the services of the church, uninterruptedly repeated in the same words since the first ages, had kept up in the general mind something of a dim traditionary understanding of the old imperial tongue. We read of some foreign ecclesiastics, who could not speak English, being accustomed to preach to the people in Latin. A passage quoted above from the Croyland History seems to imply that Gislebert, or Gilbert, one of the founders of the University of Cambridge, used to employ Latin as well as French on such occasions. So, Giraldus Cambrensis tells us that, in a progress which he made through Wales in 1188, to assist Archbishop Baldwin in preaching a new crusade for the delivery of the Holy Land, he was always most successful when he appealed to the people in a Latin sermon; he asserts, indeed, that they did not understand a word of it, although it never failed to melt them into tears, and to make them come in crowds to take the cross. No doubt they were acted upon chiefly through their ears and their imaginations, and for the most part only supposed that they comprehended what they were listening to; but it is probable that their self-deception was assisted by their catching a word or phrase here and there the meaning of which they really understood. The Latin tongue must in those days have been heard in common life on a thousand occasions from which it has now passed away. It was the language of all the learned professions, of law and physic as well as of divinity, in all their grades. It was in Latin that the teachers at the Universities (many of whom, as well as of the ecclesiastics, were foreigners) delivered their prelections in all the sciences, and that all the disputations and other exercises among the students were carried on. It was the same at all the monastic schools and other seminaries of learning. The number of persons by whom these various institutions were attended was very great: they were of all ages from boyhood to advanced manhood; and poor scholars must have been found in every village, mingling with every class of the people, in some one or other of the avocations which they followed in the intervals of their attendance at the Universities, or after they had finished their education, from parish priests down to wandering beggars.

LATIN POETS—MAPES, ETC.

Much Latin poetry was written in this age by Englishmen, some of it of a popular character. Warton enumerates Joannes Grammaticus,[*] Lawrence, prior of Durham, Robert Dunstable,[†] the historians Henry of Huntingdon, Geoffrey of Monmouth, Eadmer, William of Malmesbury, Giraldus Cambrensis, and Geoffrey de Vinsauf (*Galfridus de Vinosalvo*), John Hanvill,[‡] Alexander Neckam, Walter Mapes, archdeacon of Oxford, and above all Joseph Iscanus, or Joseph of Exeter, whom he characterizes as "a miracle in classical composition;" adding, in regard to one of his works, an epic on the subject of the Trojan war,

---

[*] Mr. Wright (Biog. Brit. Lit., ii. 48) denies the existence of this writer, supposed by Tanner and others to have belonged to the latter part of the eleventh century. The works attributed to him, he says, were certainly written by other persons.

[†] His name appears to have been, not *Robert*, but *Radulph* (or *Ralph*). See Wright's Biog. Brit. Lit., ii. 212.

[‡] Mr. Wright has shown that the name is not *Hanvill* (as given by Warton), but *Hauvill*, or *Hauteville*, in Latin *De Alto Vitro*. See his note on Warton, p. cxxi., and Biog. Brit. Lit., ii. 230, &c.

" The diction of this poem is generally pure, the periods round, and the numbers harmonious; and on the whole the structure of the versification approaches nearly to that of polished Latin poetry." [*] Walter Mapes, or rather Map, who was archdeacon of Oxford, has the credit of having been the author of most of the pieces of Latin poetry belonging to the latter part of the twelfth century which from their form and character may be supposed to have acquired anything like general popularity. In particular the famous drinking song, in rhyming or Leonine verse, beginning—

" Meum est propositum in taberna mori,"

is attributed to this " genial archdeacon." [†]

To Warton's dozen names, or thereby, Mr. Wright, in his account of the writers of the Anglo-Norman Period (Biog. Brit. Lit., vol. ii. 1846), has added about a score of others belonging to Latin poets and versifiers of the first century and a half after the Conquest. Among the most important are those of Guy, or Wido, bishop of Amiens, author of an elegiac poem on the Battle of Hastings, discovered a few years ago at Brussels and since several times printed; Godfrey, prior of Winchester, in the latter part of the eleventh century, whom Mr. Wright designates as " the first and best of the Anglo-Norman writers of Latin verse;" Hilarius, author of three scriptural dramas and a number of shorter pieces, preserved in a single manuscript now in the

* Dissertation on the Introd. of Learning into England, cxvii.-cxxxiv.
† The expression is Warton's (Diss. on Introd. of Learning, p. cxxvi.). The Latin Poems commonly attributed to Walter Mapes have been printed by the Camden Society, as collected and edited by Thomas Wright, Esq., M.A., F.S.A. &c., 4to, Lond. 1841. In an introduction to this volume Mr. Wright remarks:—" The common notion that Walter Mapes was a ' jovial toper' must be placed in the long list of vulgar errors." The drinking song, nevertheless, as commonly given, forms part of one of the pieces which Mr. Wright has printed, one which he admits has been constantly attributed to Mapes, and the authorship of which, he says, he hesitates, without any direct evidence to the contrary, in taking from him; and the only correction which the perusal of the entire poem can make upon the impression produced by the part commonly quoted is to extend the sense in which we must consider the author to have been what he has been designated, the Anacreon of his day. Lord Lyttelton, from whom that epithet is quoted by Warton as a very happy one, has inadvertently written the Anacreon of the eleventh, instead of the twelfth, century. Mapes lived and wrote in the reigns of Henry II. and Richard I.: his death, according to Mr. Wright, " is supposed to have occurred towards the year 1210." (Introd. to Poems, p. vii.)

Bibliothèque Impériale at Paris, from which they were edited in 1838 by M. Champollion-Figeac; John of Salisbury, a work in verse by whom was edited by Professor Christian Petersen, at Hamburgh, in 1843; and Nigellus Wirekor, for whose surname, however, Mr. Wright finds no satisfactory authority, the author, among other pieces, of the Speculum Stultorum referred to in a proceding page.

LATIN CHRONICLERS.

But by far the most valuable portion of our Latin literature of this age consists of the numerous historical works which it has bequeathed to us. As these works have a double interest for the English reader, belonging to the country and the age in which they were written by their subject as well as by their authorship, we will give some account of the most important of them.

The following are the principal collections that have been made in modern times of our old Latin historians or chroniclers:—

1. Rerum Britannicarum, id est, Angliæ, Scotiæ, Vicinarumque Insularum ac Regionum, Scriptores Vetustiores ac Præcipui: (a Hier. Commelino). Fol. Heidelb. & Lugd. 1587.

2. Rerum Anglicarum Scriptores post Bedam Præcipui, ex Vetustissimis MSS. nunc primum in lucem editi: (a Hen. Savile). Fol. Lon. 1596, and Francof. 1601.

3. Anglica, Normannica, Hibernica, Cambrica, a veteribus Scripta, ex Bibl. Gulielmi Camden. Fol. Francof. 1602 and 1603.

4. Historiæ Normannorum Scriptores Antiqui; studio Andreæ Duchesne. Fol. Paris. 1619.

5. Historiæ Anglicanæ Scriptores Decem, ex vetustis MSS. nunc primum in lucem editi: (a Rog. Twysden et Joan. Selden). Fol. Lon. 1652.

6. Rerum Anglicarum Scriptorum Veterum Tomus I^us; Quorum Ingulfus nunc primum integer, cæteri nunc primum, prodeunt: (a Joan. Fell, vel potius Gul. Fulman). Fol. Oxon. 1684. (Sometimes incorrectly cited as the 1st vol. of Gale's Collection.)

7. Historiæ Anglicanæ Scriptores Quinque, ex vetustis Codd. MSS. nunc primum in lucem editi: (a Thom. Gale). Fol. Oxon. 1687. (This is properly the 2nd vol. of Gale's Collection.)

8. Historiæ Britannicæ, Saxonicæ, Anglo-Danicæ, Scriptores Quindecim, ex vetustis Codd. MSS. editi, opera THOMÆ GALE. Fol. Oxon. 1691. (This is properly the 1st vol. of Gale's Collection, though often cited as the 3rd.)

9. Anglia Sacra; sive Collectio Historiarum . . . de Archiepiscopis et Episcopis Angliæ; (a HENRICO WHARTON). 2 Tom. Fol. Lon. 1691.

10. Historiæ Anglicanæ Scriptores Varii, e Codd. MSS. nunc primum editi: (a Jos. SPARKE). Fol. Lon. 1723.

11. Historiæ Anglicanæ circa tempus Conquestus Angliæ a Guilielmo Notho, Normannorum Duce, selecta Monumenta; excerpta ex volumine And. Duchesne; cum Notis, &c.: (a FRANCISCO MASERES). 4to. Lon. 1807.

12. Monumenta Historica Britannica; or, Materials for the History of Britain from the earliest period to the end of the reign of King Henry VII. Published by command of her Majesty. Vol. 1st (extending to the Norman Conquest). Fol. Lon. 1848. (By PETRIE, SHARPE, and HARDY.)

To which may be added :—

13. The series of works printed by the HISTORICAL SOCIETY, from 1838 to 1856, extending to 29 vols. 8vo.; and,

14. The series entitled Rerum Britannicarum Medii Ævi Scriptores, or Chronicles and Memorials of Great Britain and Ireland during the Middle Ages. Published by authority of her Majesty's Treasury, under the direction of the Master of the Rolls. 8vo. Lon. 1857, &c.

INGULPHUS.

The History of the Abbey of Croyland, or, as the place is now called, Crowland, in Lincolnshire, professing to be written by the Abbot Ingulphus, who presided over the establishment from A.D. 1075 till his death, at the age of about eighty, in 1109, was first published from an imperfect copy by Sir Henry Savile in his collection (Lon. 1596, and Francfort 1601); and afterwards in a more complete form by Fulman in his Scriptores Veteres (Oxford 1684). In the interval between these two (the only) editions of the work, the Laws of William the Conqueror, in French, which were wanting in the MS. used by Savile, were published from another MS. by Selden in 1623 in his edition of

Eadmer, and from another by Sir Henry Spelman in 1639 in the first volume of his Concilia. All these four (the only known) MSS. of the work have now disappeared. Of what has become of that used by Savile nothing is known; that from which Selden took his copy of the Laws of the Conqueror seems to have been one which was in the Cotton Library—the same from which Fulman was supplied with a leaf in which his own MS. was defective by his friend Gale*—and that was destroyed by the calamitous fire at Ashburnham House in 1731; that which Spelman transcribed was preserved in the church of Croyland, in a chest locked with three keys, which were kept by the church-wardens, and was believed by him to be what it was reputed, the author's autograph—but, as Selden could not obtain access to it a few years before, so nobody has seen it since, and, when Fulman made inquiry after it in the latter part of the same century, it was no longer to be found;—finally, that employed by Fulman, which belonged to Sir John Marsham, was after-wards given or lent by him to Obadiah Walker, the famous Master of University College, who was turned out at the Revolution in 1688, and all that further appears is that Walker told Bishop Gibson in 1694 that it was then in the library of University College, where however it has not since been found. It seems most likely that it never was deposited there, but was carried off by Walker, who professed to consider it as his own property on the simple principle, which it appears is recognized among antiquarian collectors, that a manuscript belongs to any one who has once, no matter by what means, got it into his pos-session. "The old gentleman," writes Gibson to Dr. Charlett, the then Master of University College, in relating what had just passed between them on the subject, "has too much of the spirit of an antiquary and a great scholar to think stealing a manuscript any sin. He has ordered me not to discover where it is lodged." These particulars are mostly collected from a learned and valuable paper on the sources of Anglo-Saxon history which appeared some years ago in the Quarterly Review,† and to which we shall

* See Rer. Ang. Script. 1684, Præfat., and p. 131.

† Vol. xxxiv. No. 67 (for June, 1826), pp. 248-298. According to Mr. Wright, however (Biog. Brit. Lit., ii. 31), "there is a transcript of the latter part of the sixteenth century among the Arundel MSS. in the British Museum, No. 178, which was evidently the copy from which Savile printed his edition." "The MS. used by Gale [Fulman]," he adds, "is said to exist in the Library at Holkham."

have frequent occasion further to refer. The writer (understood
to be Sir Francis Palgrave) proceeds to show, very ingeniously
and conclusively, that the MS. which Spelman saw at Croyland
could not in all probability have been older than the end of the
thirteenth or the beginning of the fourteenth century, from a
mistranscription of a word in his extract (*Eustra* for *Eusages*),
which was very likely to have taken place in copying a writing
of that date, but could hardly have happened in reading a manuscript of the end of the eleventh century, the age of Ingulphus.
But, if the external evidence for the antiquity and authenticity
of the work be thus defective, the internal evidence may be pronounced to be conclusive against its claim to be accounted either
the composition of Ingulphus or a work of any historical value.
It appears in fact to be, if not altogether what the reviewer calls
it, " an historical novel," at least in the main a monkish forgery
of the thirteenth or fourteenth century, which may possibly contain some things not the produce of the writer's invention, and
found by him in histories or other records now lost, but no statement in which, whatever appearance of probability it may wear,
can be safely received upon its authority. Not only the portion
of the history which relates to the times preceding the pretended
writer's own age, but the account which Ingulphus is made to
give of himself, is full of the most glaring improbabilities, and in
some parts demonstrably false and impossible. For the demonstration, however, we must refer the reader to the article in the
Quarterly Review, the writer of which justly observes that
" anachronisms which merely impeach the *accuracy* of the *historian*
are entirely *fatal to autobiography*." In none of our chroniclers
anterior to the fourteenth century, the reviewer asserts, is there
a single line to be traced that is borrowed from Ingulphus. And
this is a fact of no slight significance :—" If the work," he
remarks, " had existed, it could scarcely have been neglected by
those inveterate compilers." Of course, if the History of Croyland by Ingulphus be rejected, its continuation to A.D. 1118,
attributed to Peter of Blois, which was also contained in the
Cotton and Sir John Marsham's codices, and is published in
Fulman's Collection, must be included in the same sentence, its
pretended author having died long before the date at which,
upon this supposition, the work he professes to continue was
written. There are also three further continuations, bringing
down the narrative, with certain gaps, to the year 1469. An

English translation of the whole, by Mr. H. T. Riley, was published in Bohn's Antiquarian Library, in 1854; and another the same year by Mr. Stevenson in vol. ii. Part 2nd of The Church Historians of England.

WILLIAM OF POITIERS.

Putting Ingulphus and his first continuator aside, our oldest historian of the Conquest will be William of Poitiers (Guillelmus Pictavensis, Piotaviensis, or Pictavinus), whose life of the Conqueror (Gesta Guillelmi Ducis Normannorum et Regis Anglorum) was published by Duchesne in his Historiæ Normannorum Scriptores, Paris, 1619, and has been reprinted by Baron Maseres in his useful selection from that scarce volume, Lon. 1808. A new edition announced as in preparation by the English Historical Society, has never appeared; but a translation into French, originally published at Caen in 1826, is included in M. Guizot's Collection des Mémoires relatifs à l'Histoire de France, jusqu'au 13ᵉ siècle, 31 vols. 8vo. Paris, 1820-35. Unfortunately the only known MS. of the work, which is in the Cotton Library at the British Museum, is imperfect: Ordericus Vitalis (writing in the beginning of the next century) expressly describes the narrative as ending with the death of Earl Edwin in 1070, but what we have of it comes down only to March, or April, 1067. The beginning is also wanting. What remains, however, which includes the English and Norman story from the death of Canute in 1035, when the Norman duke was only eight years old, to his coronation as king of England after the victory of Hastings, and the first acts of his reign, is of the highest value. William of Poitiers was not an Englishman; he was a native of Normandy, and derived his surname of Pictaviensis from having received his education at Poitiers; but he appears to have accompanied his hero and patron on his expedition to England, and, in that as well as in the other parts of his story, to relate for the most part what he had seen with his own eyes. He had been in close attendance upon or connexion with the Conqueror for the greater part of their lives, having first served under him as a soldier, and having afterwards been made his chaplain—if indeed he may not,

like Friar Tuck and Robin Hood in the next age, have officiated
at the same time in both these capacities. No one, therefore,
could have enjoyed better opportunities of observing and appre-
ciating William in all aspects of his character, public and
domestic, as a sovereign and as a man; and Pictaviensis had both
head and heart enough of his own to comprehend the high nature
with which he was thus brought into contact. His biography
of the Conqueror is throughout a cordial and sympathizing
narrative—a full-length picture of a great man drawn at least with
no timid hand. Yet there is no profession or apparent design of
defence or panegyric, and but little direct expression of admiration; that feeling is too natural, too habitual, too much a matter
of course with the worthy chaplain to be very often or very
emphatically expressed; with no misgivings either of his subject
or of his reader, he contents himself for the most part with stating facts, and leaving them to speak for themselves. The work, it
may be added, is written with considerable ambition of eloquence;
Pictaviensis had had a learned education to begin with, which
his campaigning did not knock out of him, so that, when he
returned in his old age to his native country and was made archdeacon of Lisieux, he was esteemed quite a shining light of
scholarship in the Norman Church. In the judgment of Ordericus
Vitalis his Latin is an imitation of that of Sallust; and in the
same subtle and artistic style, we are told, he also wrote much
verse, none of which, however, appears to be now extant.

ORDERICUS VITALIS.

Ordericus Vitalis is the author of a general Ecclesiastical
History, beginning from the Creation and coming down to
A.D. 1141, the whole of which, consisting of thirteen books, and
occupying above 600 folio pages, or more than half of his collection, Duchesne has printed. A greatly improved edition of the
entire work, by M. A. Le Prévost, the publication of which at
Paris was begun in 1838 under the auspices of the Société de
l'Histoire de France, was completed in 5 volumes 8vo. in 1855;
and a reproduction of the old text of Duchesne is stated to form
the 148th volume of the Patrologie of M. l'Abbé Migne, published
the same year. Ordericus, or Ordricus, who assumed the name

of Vitalis on becoming a monk of the monastery of Ouche
(Uticum), otherwise known as that of St. Evroult, in Normandy,
in which he spent the rest of his days, was of English birth: he
was born at a village which he calls Attingosham (Atcham) on
the Severn, in Shropshire, in 1075; and, although he had been
carried to the Continent to be educated for the ecclesiastical profession when he was only in his eleventh year, and spent all the
rest of his life abroad, he continued to take a special interest in
the affairs of his native country, and of its Norman sovereigns,
with whom his father, whom he calls Odelerius, the son of Con-
stantius of Orleans, had probably been nearly connected as principal counsellor (præcipuo consiliario), whatever that may mean,
to Roger Montgomery, Earl of Shrewsbury, who was one of the
followers of the Conqueror. He is accordingly very full in his
account of English transactions from the epoch of the Norman
Conquest; and his history is particularly valuable in the portion
of it from A.D. 1066 to 1070, as in some sort supplying what is
lost of that of Pictaviensis, whose narrative he professes generally
to have followed, although not without both omissions and variations. This portion of the History of Ordericus Vitalis, making
about a thirteenth part of the whole, has been reprinted by
Maseres in his Selecta Monumenta; and there is a French
translation of the entire work by Louis Du Bois, in the collection of ancient French Mémoires, published at Paris under the
superintendence of M. Guizot. (Vols. 25, 26, 27, and 28.) An
English translation, with Notes, by Mr. Thomas Forester, has
appeared in Bohn's Antiquarian Library, in 4 vols., 1853-4.

A remarkable fragment, taken from an ancient book belonging
to the monastery of St. Stephen at Caen, containing an account
of the last hours of the Conqueror, and of his death and funeral,
which Camden has printed in his Collection, and which he conjectures to be probably from the pen of Guillelmus Pictaviensis,
is in fact the concluding portion of the Seventh Book of Ordericus
Vitalis. A translation of it is given by Stow in his Chronicle.
Ordericus has himself told us that Pictaviensis was prevented by
circumstances from bringing down his History, as he had
intended to do, to the death of the Conqueror.

GESTA STEPHANI.—WILLIAM OF JUMIÈGES.

. Another valuable portion of the English history of this period
by a contemporary writer, which Duchesne has published, is the
tract entitled Gesta Stephani, filling about fifty of his pages.
It is by a partisan of Stephen, but is probably the fairest, as it is
the fullest and most distinct, account we have of his turbulent
reign. A new edition of it, prepared by Mr. R. C. Sewell, was
published by the English Historical Society in 1846; and it is
translated, along with the Chronicle of Henry of Huntingdon,
by Mr. Forester, in one of the volumes of Bohn's Antiquarian
Library, 1853.

In Duchesne's Collection is likewise the History, in eight
books, of the Dukes of Normandy, by William, the monk of
Jumièges, surnamed Calculus—Willelmi Calculi Gemmoticensis
Monachi Historia Normannorum—which Camden had printed
before, from a worse manuscript and less correctly, in his
Anglica, Normannica, &c. Of this also there is a French translation in M. Guizot's Collection (vol. 29) : it was originally published at Caen, along with William of Poitiers, in 1826. Gemmoticensis in the earlier part of his work, down to the accession
of Duke Richard II., the great-grandfather of William the Conqueror, in 996, is little more than an abridger of the earlier
Norman historian Dudo (also in Duchesne) ; but there are a few
facts not elsewhere to be found in the sequel, which brings down
the narrative of Norman and English affairs to his own time, and
which is farther continued through the reigns of the Conqueror
and his two sons, apparently by another hand ; for Gemmoticensis dedicates his work to the Conqueror, and Ordericus Vitalis
expressly states that he finished it with the battle of Hastings.

FLORENCE OF WORCESTER.

The earliest of our English chroniclers or annalists, properly
so called, who wrote after the Norman Conquest is commonly
held to be the monk Florence of Worcester, whose work, entitled
Chronicon ex Chronicis, was printed in 4to. at London in 1592,

under the care of Lord William Howard,[*] and reprinted in
folio at Francfort in 1601. Two new editions have recently been
published:—one, by Mr. Petrie, in the Monumenta, 1848; the
other prepared by Mr. Thorpe for the Historical Society, 2 vols.
8vo. 1848-49. It extends from the Creation to the year 1110, in
which the author died; and there is printed along with it a continuation by another writer to the year 1141. It is, for the
greater part, a transcript from the notices of English affairs contained in the General History or Chronology which bears the
name of Marianus Scotus, intermixed with a nearly complete
transcript of Asser's Life of King Alfred, and enlarged in the
times not treated of in that work by ample translations from the
National Chronicle. The Chronicle of Scotus (said to have been
of English birth and descended from a relation of Bede) was a
favourite book in our monasteries in the middle ages; "there
was hardly one in the kingdom," says Bishop Nicolson, "that
wanted a copy of it, and some had several." Besides the
numerous transcripts, which vary greatly, it has been more than
once printed, but never, we believe, in a complete form. Speaking of Florence of Worcester's compilation, the writer of the
article in the Quarterly Review, to which we have more than once
referred, observes: "Some notices are extracted from Bede.
The facts of which the original sources cannot be ascertained are
very few, but important, and occur principally in the early part
of this history. They are generally of that class which we may
suppose to have been derived from the Saxon genealogies.
Though the great mass of information afforded by Florence is
extant in the Saxon Chronicle, still his work is extremely valuable. He understood the ancient Saxon language well—better,
perhaps, than any of his contemporaries; and he has furnished
us with an accurate translation from a text which seems to have
been the best of its kind." The principal value of Florence's
performance in fact consists in its serving as a key to the
Chronicle. One of the volumes of Bohn's Library contains a
translation, by Mr. Forester, of Florence of Worcester, and also

* This was Lord William Howard, Warden of the Western Marches, the
"Belted Will Howard" of Border tradition, whose castle of Naworth, in Cumberland, where his bedroom and library were preserved, with the books and
furniture, in the same state as when he tenanted the apartments more than
two centuries ago, was unhappily consumed a few years ago by an accidental
fire, with all its interesting contents.

of two anonymous continuations of his work, one of which, extending to the year 1141, is accounted of great value. This is not given in the Monumenta, but it is in the other editions. Both Florence and his continuators appear also in the First Part of the Second Volume of The Church Historians of England (1853), " in part translated " by Mr. Stevenson.

MATTHEW OF WESTMINSTER.

The Quarterly Reviewer, however, is inclined to think that Florence was preceded by another writer, the author of the compilation entitled Flores Historiarum, usually ascribed to Matthew of Westminster, who appears to be a fictitious personage. This English History, which has been brought down by other unknown writers to the year 1307 (or to the end of the reign of Edward I.), is based upon another general chronicle similar to that of Marianus Scotus, with the addition of much matter derived apparently from ancient English sources, some of which are now unknown. The writer in the Quarterly Review, who prefers giving the author the name of Florilegus, thinks it probable that his work supplied Florence with certain passages which are not found in the National Chronicle. " Florilegus," he observes, " has retained and quoted a sufficient number of Anglo-Saxonisms, and of Anglo-Saxon phrases, to show that he was in possession of Saxon materials, which he consulted to the best of his ability. He has not used them with the fidelity of Florence of Worcester, for his knowledge of the Anglo-Saxon language was imperfect, but still he is not guilty of any intentional falsification, and, therefore, when he relates probable facts, it is fair to conclude that he is equally veracious, although the Saxon original of his Chronicle be not extant." [*] The work, under the title of Matthæi Westmonasteriensis Flores Historiarum, præcipue de Rebus Britannicis, ab exordio mundi usque ad A.D. 1307, was first published by Archbishop Parker, in folio, at London in 1567, and again in 1570; and was reprinted, in folio, at Francfort in 1601, along with Florence of Worcester. There is an English translation of it, by Mr. C. D. Yonge, making two volumes of Bohn's Library, 1853.

[*] Quarterly Review, No. lxvii. p. 252.

WILLIAM OF MALMESBURY.

The first, in point of merit and eminence, of our Latin
historians of this period is William of Malmesbury, so designated
as having been a monk of that great monastery, although his
proper surname is said to have been Somerset. He was probably born about the time of the Norman Conquest; and,
though of English birth, he intimates that he was of Norman
descent by one parent, putting in a claim on that ground to be
accounted an impartial witness or judge between the two races.
Malmesbury's English History consists of two parts, or rather
distinct works; the first entitled Gesta Regum Anglorum, in
five books, extending from the arrival of the Angles and Saxons
to the year 1120; the second entitled Historia Novella, in three
books, bringing the narrative down to 1142. It has been commonly supposed that the author died in that or the following
year; but there is no evidence that he did not live to a later
date. A portion of the Gesta was printed, as the work of an
unknown author, in Commeline's volume of British writers, in
1587; both the Gesta and the Historia Novella are in Savile's
Collection, 1596 and 1601; and a new and much more correct
edition of the two, by Mr. Thomas Duffus Hardy, in two vols.
8vo. Lon. 1840, forms one of the publications of the Historical
Society. There is a very good English translation of William of
Malmesbury by the Rev. John Sharpe, 4to. Lon. 1815; and
another, professing to be based upon it, by Dr. Giles, makes one
of the volumes of Bohn's Library, 1847. Malmesbury, although
there is an interval of nearly five hundred years between them,
stands next in the order of time after Bede in the series of our
historical writers properly so called, as distinguished from mere
compilers and diarists. His Historics are throughout original
works, and, in their degree, artistic compositions. He has
evidently taken great pains with the manner as well as with the
matter of them. But he also evinces throughout a love of truth
as the first quality of historical writing, and far more of critical
faculty in separating the probable from the improbable than any
other of his monkish brethren of that age who have set up for
historians, notwithstanding his fondness for prodigies and ecclesiastical miracles, in which of course he had the ready and all-
digestive belief which was universal in his time. Of course, too,
he had his partialities in the politics of his own day; and his

account of the contest between Matilda and Stephen may be compared with that of the author of the Gesta Stephani by those who would study both sides of the question. Both his histories are inscribed in very encomiastic dedications to Robert Earl of Gloucester, Matilda's famous champion. Savile's Collection also contains another work of Malmesbury's, his Lives of the Bishops of England (De Gestis Pontificum Anglorum), in four books; and a Life of St. Aldhelm (bishop of Sherborn), assumed to be a fifth book of this work, was afterwards published by Gale in his Scriptores XV. Oxon. 1691, and the same year by Henry Wharton, in the second volume of his Anglia Sacra. Gale's volume contains, besides, a History of the Monastery of Glastonbury by Malmesbury—De Antiquitate Glastoniensis Ecclesiæ; —and Wharton's contains his Life of St. Wulstan. Others of his treatises still remain in manuscript.

EADMER.

The Modern History, or History of His Own Time (Historia Novorum, sive Sui Sæculi), by his contemporary Eadmer, the monk of Canterbury, is noticed by Malmesbury in the Prologue, or Preface, to the First Book of his Gesta, as a lucubration written with a sober festivity of style (sobria sermonis festivitate elucubratum opus). It was first published (folio, Lon. 1623), with learned annotations by Selden, who holds that in style Eadmer equals Malmesbury, and in the value of his matter excels him. It is also added, with the other writings of Eadmer, as a supplement to the Works of Archbishop Anselm, both in Gerberon's edition, folio, Paris, 1675, and in that of the Benedictines, folio, Paris, 1721. Eadmer's History is distributed into six books, and comprehends the reigns of the Conqueror and Rufus, and the first twenty-two years of Henry the First (that is, from A.D. 1066 to 1122). One distinction belonging to Eadmer's narrative is the nearly entire absence of miracles. He probably considered it improper to introduce such high matter into a composition which did not profess to be of a sacred or spiritual nature. Much of his work, however, is occupied with ecclesiastical transactions, which indeed formed almost the entire home politics, and no small part of the foreign politics also, of that age. He has in particular entered largely into the great

controversy between the crown and the pope about investiture;
and one of the most curious parts of his history is a long and
detailed account which he gives of his own appointment to the
bishopric of St. Andrews in Scotland, and his contest about his
consecration with the stout Scottish king, Alexander I.   Mabillon has published a life of St. Wilfrid, by Eadmer, in the
Acta Sanctorum Benedictinorum (Sæc. iii. part. i.); and other
tracts by him are in the Anglia Sacra.

TURGOT, AND SIMEON OF DURHAM: JOHN OF HEXHAM, AND RICHARD
OF HEXHAM.

Eadmer's immediate predecessor in the see of St. Andrews
was Turgot, who had been a monk of Durham before he was
elevated to the primacy of Scotland in 1109.   Perhaps the most
interesting composition that we have from the pen of Turgot is a
life of Malcolm Canmore's queen, Margaret, the sister of Edgar
Atheling, whose confessor he was: it was drawn up at the
request of her daughter Maud, wife of King Henry I., and is
printed in the Acta Sanctorum of the Bollandists.[*]   Selden,
in his learned Preface to the Decem Scriptores, has advanced
strong reasons for believing that the History of the Church of
Durham which passes under the name of Simeon Dunelmensis,
and which that monk appears to have published as his own, was
really written by Turgot; but this view has been disputed in a
disquisition by Thomas Reed, which accompanies an edition of
the History published at London in an octavo volume in 1732 by
the Rev. Thomas Bedford.   It is in four books, and extends over
the time from A.D. 635 to 1095.   This History, along with a
continuation to A.D. 1154, and a History of St. Cuthbert, an
Epistle respecting the Archbishops of York, a tract on the siege
of Durham by the Scots in 969, and a history of English affairs,
entitled De Regibus Anglorum et Dacorum, from A.D. 616 to
1120, which, for anything that is known, are really by Simeon,

* Acta Sanct. Junii, pp. 328-335.   Papebroch, the editor, has printed the
tract, on the authority of one MS. he used, as the work of an unknown monk
of the name of Theodoric: but Lord Hailes has adduced sufficient reasons for
believing it to be by Turgot to whom it is ascribed by Fordun.   See his
Annals of Scotland, i. 30, 37 (edit. of 1819).

are all in Twysden's Collection ; and the English History to A.D
957 is in the Monumenta.   The latter, which is in the form of
compendious annals, is continued to 1154, by John, prior of Hexham (Joannes Hagustaldensis), whose Chronicle is likewise in
Twysden ; as are also two books of Lives of the Bishops of
Hexham, and an historical fragment on the reign of Stephen from
1135 to 1139, including a narrative of the battle of the Standard,
by his successor Prior Richard, together with a short poem in
rhyming Latin verses on that battle by Serlo, a monk of Fountain
Abbey in Yorkshire.

AILRED.

But the best account we have of the battle of the Standard is
that of Ailred, abbot of Rievault, in Yorkshire—Ailredi Abbatis Riovallensis Historia de Bello Standardii—also printed
among the Scriptores X., along with an Epistle on the Genealogy
of the English Kings, a Life of Edward the Confessor, and a
singular relation, entitled De Quodam Miraculo Mirabili, all by
the same writer.   Ailred, Ealred, Elred, Alured, Adilred, Ethelred, or Valred, who is supposed to have died about 1166, and who
is one of the saints of the Roman calendar (his day is the 12th of
January), spent his life in studious retirement, and is the author
of many other treatises, some printed in various collections,
some still remaining in manuscript.*   But those that have been
mentioned are the only ones that relate to English history.   He
often writes with considerable animation, and a decided gift of
popular eloquence may be discerned in his fluent though not
very classical Latin.

GEOFFREY OF MONMOUTH: ALFRED OF BEVERLEY.

The famous British History of Geoffrey of Monmouth was
printed at Paris, in 4to., in 1508, and again in 1509, and it is
also contained in Commeline's Collection, folio, Heidelberg,
1587.   It professes to be, and, as already intimated, in all

-----

* The fullest and most accurate accounts of the writings of Ailred are in
the Biographical Dictionary of the Society for the Diffusion of Useful Knowledge, and in Mr. Wright's Biog. Brit. Lit., ii. 187-190.

probability is in the main, a translation from a Welsh Chronicle,
given to Geoffrey by his friend Walter, archdeacon of Oxford
(a different person from Walter Mapes, the poet, though they
have been usually confounded), who had procured the manuscript in Britany.   It contains in nine books the history of the
Britons, or Welsh, from the era of their leader Brutus, the great-
grandson of the Trojan Æneas, to the death, in 688, of their king
Cadwallo, or Cadwallader, the same personage called by the English historians Cedwall, or Ceadwalla, and represented by them
as King of Wessex.   Geoffrey, archdeacon of Monmouth, and
afterwards bishop of St. Asaph, is a clever and agreeable writer,
and his Latin is much more scholarly than that of the generality
of the monkish chroniclers of his time.   His work, whatever may
be thought of its historical value, has at least the merit of having
preserved the old legends and traditions of the race who were
driven out by the Angles and Saxons in a more complete and
consistent form than we have them elsewhere.   But the outline
of the same story in all its parts, from the Trojan descent to the
wars of Arthur, is found in Nennius, who lived and wrote certainly not later than the middle of the ninth century, or nearly
three centuries before Geoffrey.   The archdeacon of Monmouth,
therefore, was at any rate not the inventor of the fables, if they
be such, to which his name has been generally attached.   At the
most he can only be suspected of having sometimes expanded
and embellished them.   But, if not the creator of Arthur and his
Knights of the Round Table, Geoffrey was their reviver from
almost universal oblivion to sudden and universal notoriety ; his
book, published probably about 1128, and dedicated to the same
Earl of Gloucester whom Malmesbury chose for his patron, obtained immediately the most wonderful currency and acceptance ;
and from the date of its appearance we find a new inspiration,
derived from its pages, pervading the popular literature of
Europe.   Most of the subsequent Latin chroniclers also adopt
more or less of his new version of our early history.   An English translation of Geoffrey of Monmouth by Aaron Thompson,
originally published in an 8vo. volume at London in 1718, was
reprinted in 1842, as " revised by J. A. Giles, LL.D. ;" and it is
included by Dr. Giles in his volume entitled Six Old English
Chronicles (Bohn), 1848.   A detailed analysis of Geoffrey's
work is given by the late George Ellis in his Specimens of
Early English Metrical Romances.

The compendium of Alfred, Alred, or Alured, canon of the collegiate church of St. John at Beverley, in Yorkshire, published by Hearne, in 8vo., at Oxford, in 1716, under the title of Aluredi Beverlacensis Annales, sive Historia de Gestis Regum Britanniæ, Libris IX., comes down to the year 1129, but is in the first five books (making half the work, which consists only of 152 pages altogether) a mere abridgment of Geoffroy of Monmouth. Alured, in fact, though he does not expressly name the archdeacon, sets out with stating that his design simply is to epitomise the new History of the Britons, which everybody was so eager to read, and of which he had himself for some time in vain sought to procure a copy; a fact which is strangely suppressed both by Hearne and by Dr. Campbell in the Biographia Britannica, in their attempts to show that Alured did not copy Geoffroy, but Geoffroy him. Geoffroy's very expressions are sometimes adopted by Alured. What the latter has added in the continuation of the history down to his own time contains scarcely anything not to be found elsewhere. The period from the Norman Conquest, extending over sixty-two years, which may probably have been about that of his own life, is all comprised in the last book, filling twenty-seven pages.

GIRALDUS CAMBRENSIS.

Giraldus Cambrensis, another learned Welshman, who makes a principal figure among our historical writers of the twelfth century, is of somewhat later date than his countryman Geoffroy of Monmouth:—Geoffroy died in 1154; Giraldus, whose proper Welsh name was Gerald Barry, appears to have been born about 1146. His Itinerary and Description of Wales (the first book) — Itinerarium Cambriæ and Descriptio Cambriæ — were published, with learned annotations, by Dr. David Powell, in a 12mo. volume, at London, in 1685; both are included in Camden's Anglica, Normannica, &c., together with his Topography and Conquest of Ireland—Topographia Hiberniæ and Expugnatio Hiberniæ—there published for the first time: and a second book of the Description of Wales, various biographies of English bishops, an account of his own life, entitled De Rebus a Se Gestis, in three books, together with two separate catalogues of his works drawn up by himself, a treatise concerning the Church of St. Asaph (De Jure et Statu Menevensis Ecclesiæ Distinctiones vii.), and two or three other short pieces, are in the second volume of Wharton's Anglia Sacra. An English translation of the Itinerary and of both parts of the Description of Wales, profusely illuminated with engravings as well as with annotations and commentary, was published by Sir Richard Colt Hoare, Bart., in two vols. 4to., Lond. 1806, under the title of The Itinerary of Archbishop Baldwin through Wales, A.D. 1187, by Giraldus de Barri, and forms one of the most magnificent productions of the modern English press.* Many other writings, however, both in prose and verse, are attributed to him, which are either lost (if they ever existed), or remain in manuscript, with the exception of a treatise, called by himself Gemma Ecclesiastica, which is said to have been printed at Mentz without his name in 1549 under the title of Gemma Animæ. Giraldus, though his style abounds in the conceits and false ornaments which constituted the eloquence of his time, is a very lively writer, and he shows a genius both for narrative and description to which nothing is wanting except the influences of a happier age. In literary ardour and industry, at least, he has not often been surpassed. He "deserves particular regard," says Warton, "for the universality of his works, many of which are written with some degree of elegance. He abounds with quotations of the best Latin poets. He was an historian, an antiquary, a topographer, a divine, a philosopher, and a poet. His love of science was so great that he refused two bishoprics; and from the midst of public business, with which his political talents gave him a considerable connexion in the court of Richard the First, he retired to Lincoln for seven years with a design of pursuing theological studies."† The fancy of Giraldus, however, it must be confessed, was more vigorous than either his judgment or his veracity; and much of the matter in his historical works would have suited poetry better than history.

* In his Preface Sir Richard seems to state that he had also reprinted the Itinerary and Description of Wales in the original Latin, but we have never seen the book.

† Dissertation on Introd. of Learning, p. cxxiv.

HENRY OF HUNTINGDON.

Malmesbury's two Histories are followed in Savile's collection by the Eight Books of that of Henry, archdeacon of Huntingdon, extending from the invasion of Julius Cæsar to the accession of Henry II. (A.D. 1154). The work has not been elsewhere printed in full; but a very superior text of the first Six Books, with the exception of the Third, which is only an abridgment of Bede, is given by Mr. Petrie in the Monuments, 1848. Henry of Huntingdon first distinguished himself as a poet, and is said by Leland to have in the earlier part of his life written eight books of Latin epigrams, and eight more of love verses, besides a long didactic poem on herbs, another on spices, and a third on precious stones. His History, which he composed in his more advanced years, is interspersed with a good deal of verse, most of it professing to be quoted, but some of it confessedly his own. Savile describes him as, in respect of historical merit, although separated by a long interval from Malmesbury, yet making as near an approach to him as any other writer of the time, and as deserving to be placed in the first rank of the most diligent explorers and most truthful expounders of the times preceding their own. He is, indeed, more of an antiquary than an historian. His work, in so far as it is a history of his own time, is of little importance. The writer in the Quarterly Review, however, remarks that it is a more ambitious attempt than had been made by such mere annalists as the Saxon chroniclers on the one hand, or such compilers as Florence of Worcester and Simeon of Durham on the other. "Abandoning the simple plan of his predecessors, he divided his History into books, treating distinctly upon each of the kingdoms of the Heptarchy, until their union under Edgar. Huntingdon states that, taking Bede as his basis, he added much from other sources, and borrowed from the chronicles which he found in ancient libraries. His descriptions of battles are often more diffuse than in the Anglo-Saxon chronicles. It has been supposed that, because these scenes and pictures are not warranted by the existing texts, they are mere historical amplifications; but we find no difficulty in believing that the researches of a writer who was considered as a most learned antiquarian should have enabled him to discover a chronicle lost to us, and which contained more fragments of poetry or poetical prose than the chronicles which have been preserved."[*] The second volume of Wharton's Anglia Sacra contains a long Letter from Henry of Huntingdon to his friend Walter, abbot of Ramsay (De Episcopis Sui Temporis), which is full of interesting notices and anecdotes of the kings, prelates, and other distinguished personages of his time. Both the History and this Letter are translated by Mr. Forester in one of the volumes of Bohn's Antiquarian Library, 1853.

ROGER DE HOVEDEN.

The next work printed in Savile's Collection (and his edition is again our only one) is the copious Chronicle of Roger de Hoveden (probably so designated from having been a native of Hoveden, or Howden, in Yorkshire). It fills 430 pages, or not much less than half the volume. Hoveden takes up the narrative at the year 732, where the History of Bede (a north-country man like himself) ends, and brings it down to 1202. His account is particularly full throughout the reigns of Henry II. and Richard I., and the commencement of that of John, making together what may be called his own half-century. The greater portion, indeed, of the 340 pages of which this second or latter part of his annals — Annalium Pars Posterior — consists, is occupied by letters of kings, popes, and prelates, and other public documents; but it contains also an extraordinary number of minute historical details. Hoveden is of all our old chroniclers the most of a matter-of-fact man; he indulges occasionally in an epithet, rarely or never in a reflection; his one notion of writing history seems to be to pack as many particulars as possible into a given space, giving one the notion in perusing his close array of dates and items that he had felt continually pressed by the necessity of economising his paper or parchment. It is true that he has no notion of the higher economy of discrimination and selection; but among the multitude of facts of all kinds that crowd his pages are many that are really curious and illustrative. A translation of Roger de Hoveden by Mr. Henry T. Riley makes two of the volumes of Bohn's Antiquarian Library, 1853.

[*] Quarterly Review, xxxiv. 283.

WILLIAM OF NEWBURGH.

William of Newburgh (in Latin Gulielmus Neubrigensis), so
called from the monastery of Newburgh, in Yorkshire, to which
he belonged,—although his proper name is said to have been
Little, whence he sometimes designates himself Petit, or Parvus,
—has had the luck to have the five books of his English History
from the Conquest to the year 1197 repeatedly printed; first,
in 12mo., at Antwerp in 1567; a second time, with notes by
J. Picard, in 8vo., at Paris in 1610; again, under the care
of the industrious Thomas Hearne, in 3 vols. 8vo., at Oxford in
1719; and still once more, as edited for the Historical Society
by Mr. H. C. Hamilton, in 2 vols., in 1856. It is also in the
collection of Jerome Commelinus. The work of Neubrigensis is
much more what we now understand by a history than those of
either Hoveden or Huntingdon: in the superior purity of its
Latinity it ranks with that of Malmesbury: and it has the same
comparatively artistic character in other respects. But his merit
lies rather in his manner than in his matter; he has disposed the
chief events of the times of which he treats into a regular and
readable narrative, but has not contributed many new facts. He
is famous as having been, so far as is known, the first writer
after Geoffrey of Monmouth who refused to adopt the story of the
Trojan descent of the old Britons, and the other " figments," as
he calls them, of the Welsh historians, which moreover he
accuses Geoffrey of having made still more absurd and monstrous
by his own "impudent and impertinent lies." Whether he
knew enough of the original chronicle which Geoffrey professed
to translate, or of the language in which it was written, to be
entitled to express an opinion upon this latter point, does not
appear. The Welsh maintain that he had a personal spite at
their whole nation: " This William," says Dr. Powell, " put in
for the bishopric of St. Asaph upon the death of the said Geoffrey,
and, being disappointed, fell into a mad humour of decrying the
whole principality of Wales, its history, antiquity, and all that
belongs to it." It must be admitted, too, that, if not guilty of
the same dishonesty and forgery which he imputes to Geoffrey,
William of Newburgh is himself, in credulity at least, a match
for the most fabulous of our old chroniclers.

BENEDICTUS ABBAS.—RALPH DE DICETO.—GERVASE OF CANTERBURY.

One of the most valuable of our chronicles of the twelfth century is that of the Abbot Benedict, embracing the space from A.D. 1170 to 1192, which was published by Hearne, in 2 vols. 8vo., at Oxford in 1735, under the title of Benedictus Abbas Petroburgensis de Vita et Rebus Gestis Henrici II. et Ricardi I. Benedict, though a partisan of Becket, and one of his biographers, was so highly esteemed by Henry II., who had both the eye to discern and the magnanimity to appreciate merit and ability wherever they were to be found, that he was by his direction elected abbot of Peterborough in 1177; and in 1191, after Richard had come to the throne, he was advanced to be Keeper of the Great Seal, in which high office he died in 1193.

Ralph de Diceto, archdeacon of London, who probably died soon after the commencement of the thirteenth century, is the author of two chronicles: the first entitled Abbreviationes Chronicorum, and extending from A.D. 580 to 1148; the second, continuing the narrative, upon a larger scale, to A.D. 1199. Both are published in the Collection of the Scriptores X., where they occupy together not quite 300 columns. They are followed by a brief outline of the controversy between King Henry and Becket—Series Causæ inter Henricum Regem et Thomam Archiepiscopum—which may also perhaps have been drawn up by Diceto. A compendium of the early British History from Brutus to the death of Cadwallader, after Geoffroy of Monmouth, by this writer (Historia Compendiosa de Regibus Britonum), is given in his collection entitled Scriptores XV. by Gale, who says that he had seen a better manuscript of the Abbreviationes Chronicorum than that used by Twysden. He adds a short tract of two or three pages from a manuscript in the Arundel Collection (now in the British Museum) entitled De Partitione Provinciæ in Schiras et Episcopatus et Regna, which he entitles as by Diceto, although in his Preface he describes it as by an unknown writer. There is a short history of the Archbishops of Canterbury to the year 1200 by this Diceto in the second volume of Wharton's Anglia Sacra. Bishop Nicolson complains of it as not only of little value, from its brevity, but as " stuffed with matters foreign to the purpose."

The Chronicle of Gervase of Canterbury—Gervasii Monachi Dorobernensis, sive Cantuarensis, Chronica—from the accession of Henry I. in A.D. 1100 (or 1122, as he reckons, "secundum Evangelium") to the end of the reign of Richard I. and of the century, is published in the collection of the Scriptores X. (col. 1338-1628); together with three shorter pieces by the same writer:—the first, an account of the burning, A.D. 1174, and subsequent restoration of Canterbury Cathedral (Tractatus de Combustione et Reparatione Doroberneusis Ecclesiæ); the second, on the contest between the monks of Canterbury and Archbishop Baldwin (Imaginationes de Discordiis inter Monachos Cantuarienses et Archiepiscopum Baldwinum); the third, a history of the Archbishops of Canterbury (Actus Pontificum Cantuariensis Ecclesiæ) from Augustine to Hubert Walter, who died in 1205, and whom Gervase probably did not long survive. Leland, who gives this writer a high character for his diligent study and accurate and extensive knowledge of the national antiquities, speaks of his History as commencing with the earliest British times, and including the whole of the Saxon period ("tum Britannorum ab origine historiam, tum Saxonum et Normannorum, fortia facta deduxit"). He takes great pains in the portion we have of it to present a correct and distinct chronology; but it is principally occupied with ecclesiastical affairs.

VINSAUF.—RICHARD OF DEVISES.—JOSCELIN DE BRAKELONDA.

An account of the expedition of Richard Cœur de Lion to the Holy Land, in six books, by Geoffroy Vinsauf, has been published, under the title of Itinerarium Regis Anglorum Richardi, et aliorum, in terram Hierosolymorum, by Gale in his Scriptores Quinque (pp. 245—429). A portion of the same work had been previously printed by Bongarsius in his Gesta Dei per Francos, 1611, as a fragment of the History of Jerusalem (Hierosolimitanæ Historiæ Fragmentum) from A.D. 1171 to 1100, by an unknown writer, probably an Englishman. There is a translation of the whole in the volume of Bohn's Antiquarian Library entitled Chronicles of the Crusaders. Geoffrey, or Walter, Vinsauf, or Vinisauf, or Vincent (in Latin de Vino Salvo), was an Englishman by birth, although of Norman parentage, and accompanied Richard on his crusade. His prose is spirited and eloquent, and he was also one of the best Latin

pools of his day. His principal poetical work, entitled De
Nova Poetria (On the New Poetry), has been several times
printed: it "is dedicated," Warton observes, "to Pope Innocent
the Third, and its intention was to recommend and illustrate
the new and legitimate mode of versification which had lately
begun to flourish in Europe, in opposition to the Leonine or
barbarous species." This work, published soon after the death
of King Richard, contains an elaborate lamentation over that
event, which is quoted in what is called Bromton's Chronicle [*]
(written in the reign of Edward III.), and, as both Camden [†]
and Selden [‡] have noted, is referred to by Chaucer in his
Canterbury Tales,[§] although only the latter seems to have
understood the delicate ridicule of the allusion. The "craft
of Galfride" (so he names Vinsauf) is also celebrated by the
great English poet, apparently with much less irreverence, in
his Court of Love,[‖] no doubt composed at a much less advanced
period of his life.

Another valuable contemporary history of the early part of the
reign of Richard the First (from A.D. 1189 to 1192), comprehending the transactions in England as well as abroad, the
Chronicle of Richard of Devises, has been printed for the first
time by the Historical Society:—Chronicon Ricardi Divisiensis
de Rebus Gestis Ricardi Primi, Regis Angliæ; nunc primum
typis mandatum, curante Josepho Stevenson ;—8vo. Lon. 1838.
Divisiensis appears to have written before either Diceto or
Hoveden, and his work forms therefore an authority additional
to and quite independent of theirs.

Finally, we ought not to omit to mention the singularly curious
Chronicle of Jocelin de Brakelonda, printed a few years ago by
the Camden Society — Chronica Jocolini de Brakelonda, de
Rebus Gestis Samsonis Abbatis Monasterii Sancti Edmundi;
nunc primum typis mandata, curante Johanne Gage Rokewode;
4to. Lon. 1840 — which, although professing to record only the
acts of Abbot Samson and the history of the monastery of St.
Edmondsbury, includes also several notices of the public affairs
of the kingdom, as well as lets us see farther into the system of

* In the Scriptores X. col. 1280. The author's name is misprinted Gal-
fridus de Nico Salvo.
† Remains, 7th edit., p. 414.
‡ Præfat. ad Scriptores X. p. xli.
§ Nonne's Preestis Tale, v. 15,353, &c.
‖ v. 11.

English life and society in that remote time than perhaps any
other record that has come down to us. It embraces the space
from 1173 to 1202, comprehending the last sixteen years of the
reign of Henry II., the whole of that of Richard I., and the first
three years of that of John; and it contains repeated personal
notices of all these three kings. Brakelonda's Chronicle has been
translated by Mr. T. E. Tomlins (8vo. Lon. 1840); and Mr. Car-
lyle's brilliant resuscitation of the old Abbot and his century in his
Past and Present, 1843, lives in the memory of most readers of
modern English books.

MONASTIC REGISTERS.

Among the contemporary historical monuments of this age are
also to be reckoned parts at least of several of the monastic
registers, compiled by a succession of writers, which have been
published;—such as that of Melrose, extending from A.D. 735 to
1270 (in Fulman, 1684, and much more carefully edited by Mr.
Stevenson for the Bannatyne Club, 4to. 1835); that of Margan,
from 1066 to 1232 (in Gale, 1687); that of Waverley,* from
1066 to 1291 (in the same collection); those of Ramsay and
Ely, both, as far as printed, coming down to the Conquest (the
former in Gale, 1691, the latter in the same collection, and also,
in part, in the second Seculum of Mabillon's Acta Sanctorum
Benedictinorum); that of Ely by the Priors Thomas and Richard,
from A.D. 156 to 1169 (in Wharton's Anglia Sacra); those of
Holyrood, from A.D. 596 to 1163, and of Abingdon, from 870 to
1131, and the History of the Bishops and Church of Durham
from A.D. 633 to 1214 (all in the same collection). A new and
much improved edition of that of Holyrood was brought out in
1828 for the Bannatyne Club by the late Mr. R. Pitcairn. To these
may be added some of the tracts relating to the great monastery
of Peterborough in Sparke's collection; and several lives of prelates by Malmesbury, Goscelin of Canterbury, Osbern, John of
Salisbury, Eadmer, &c., in Wharton. The Annals of the Monastery of Burton, in Staffordshire, from A.D. 1004 to 1263, and the
continuation of the History of England from 1149 to 1470 (both

---

* The passage, however, from the earlier portion of the Waverley Annals,
which Gale quotes in proof of the writer having lived at the time of the Conquest, is merely a translation from the vernacular Chronicle.

in Fulman), appear to be throughout compilations of a later date. The venerable collection of ancient monuments relating to the church of Rochester and the kingdom of Kent, entitled the Textus Roffensis, which was published by Hearne, in 8vo., at Oxford in 1720, was drawn up by Bishop Ernulphus, who presided over the see of Rochester from A.D. 1115 till his death in 1124; and Heming's Chartulary of the Church of Worcester—Hemingi Chartularium Ecclesiæ Wigorniensis—published by Hearne in two vols. 8vo. in 1723, is of still earlier date, having been compiled in the reign of the Conqueror.

LAW TREATISES.— DOMESDAY BOOK.—PUBLIC ROLLS AND REGISTERS.

We may close the account of the numerous historical writings of the first century and a half after the Conquest by merely noticing, that to the same period belong the earliest work on the common law of England, the Tractatus de Legibus et Consuetudinibus Angliæ, commonly ascribed to the chief justiciary Ranulf de Glanvil, which was first printed, in 4to., at London in 1673, and of which there is an English translation, with notes, by Mr. John Beames, 8vo. Lon. 1812; the Liber Niger, or Black Book of the Exchequer, supposed to have been compiled by Gervase of Tilbury (Gervasius Tilburiensis), who according to some authorities was a nephew of King Henry II., of which there is an edition by Hearne, 2 vols. 8vo. Oxford, 1728, reprinted at London in 1771; and the Dialogus de Scaccario, or Dialogue respecting the Exchequer, probably written by Richard Fitz-Nigel, or Fitz-Neale, bishop of London from A.D. 1189 to 1198, which is printed at the end of Madox's History of the Exchequer, 4to. Lon. 1711, and again 2 vols. 4to. 1769; and of which there is an English translation, 4to. Lon. 1750. Along with these text-books of English law may be noticed the book of the laws and legal usages of the duchy of Normandy, called the Contumes de Normandie, of which there are editions of 1681, 1684, 1694, and 1700, all printed at Rouen, and each, in 2 volumes folio. It hardly belongs to our subject to mention the most venerable of all national registers, the Domesday Book of the Conqueror, printed at London in 1783, in 2 volumes, folio, under the title of Domesday Book, seu Liber Censualis Willelmi Primi Regis Angliæ inter Archivos Regni in Domo Capitulari West-

monasterii conservatus; the Indices printed in 1811, and the
additional volume printed in 1816 containing the Exon Domesday, the Inquisitio Eliensis, the Book of Winchester, and the
Boldon Book; the public documents appertaining to the present
period in the Statutes of the Realm, the Fœdera, the Calendar
of Patent Rolls in the Tower, the Calendar of Rolls, Charters,
and Inquisitions Ad Quod Damnum, the Placitorum Abbreviatio,
the Rotuli Literarum Patentium, the Rotuli Literarum Clausarum,
the Great Rolls of the Pipe of the 31st of Henry I. and of the
3rd of John, the Rotuli Normanniæ, the Rotuli de Oblatis et
Finibus, the Fines in Curia Domini Regis, the Rotuli Curiæ
Regis, the Charter Rolls of John, the Ancient Laws and Institutes
of England from Æthelbert to Henry I., and perhaps one or two
other publications of the late Record Commission; the Concilia
of Spelman, and of Wilkins, &c.

THE FRENCH LANGUAGE IN ENGLAND.

It is commonly asserted that for some reigns after the Norman
Conquest the exclusive language of government and legislation
in England was the French,—that all pleadings, at least in the
supreme courts, were carried on in that language,—and that in
it all deeds were drawn up and all laws promulgated. " This
popular notion," observes a learned living writer, "cannot be
easily supported. . . . Before the reign of Henry III. we cannot
discover a deed or law drawn or composed in French. Instead
of prohibiting the English language, it was employed by the
Conqueror and his successors in their charters until the reign
of Henry II., when it was superseded, not by the French but
by the Latin language, which had been gradually gaining, or
rather regaining, ground; for the charters anterior to Alfred are
invariably in Latin."[*] So far was the Conqueror from showing
any aversion to the English language, or making any such
attempt as is ascribed to him to effect its abolition, that, according to Ordericus Vitalis, when he first came over he strenuously
applied himself to learn it for the special purpose of understanding, without the aid of an interpreter, the causes that were

* Sir Francis Palgrave, Rise and Progress of the English Commonwealth,
vol. I. p. 56.

pleaded before him, and persevered in that endeavour till the
tumult of many other occupations, and what the historian calls
" durior aetas "—a more iron time *—of necessity compelled him
to give it up.† The common statement rests on the more than
suspicious authority of the History attributed to Ingulphus, the
fabricator of which, in his loose and ignorant account of the
matter, has set down this falsehood along with some other things
that are true or probable. Even before the Conquest, the Confessor himself, according to this writer, though a native of
England, yet, from his education and long residence in Normandy, had become almost a Frenchman; and when he succeeded to the English throne he brought over with him great
numbers of Normans, whom he advanced to the highest dignities
in the church and the state. " Wherefore," it is added, " the
whole land began, under the influence of the king and the other
Normans introduced by him, to lay aside the English customs,
and to imitate the manners of the French in many things; for
example, all the nobility in their courts began to speak French
as a great piece of gentility, to draw up their charters and other
writings after the French fashion, and to grow ashamed of their
old national habits in these and many other particulars."‡
Further on we are told, " They [the Normans] held the language
[of the natives] in such abhorrence that the laws of the land and
the statutes of the English kings were drawn out in the Gallic
[or French] tongue; and to boys in the schools the elements of
grammar were taught in French and not in English; even the
English manner of writing was dropped, and the French manner
introduced in all charters and books."§ The facts are more
correctly given by other old writers, who, although not contemporary with the Conquest, are probably of as early a date as
the compiler of the Croyland History. The Dominican friar
Robert Holcot, writing in the earlier part of the fourteenth century, informs us that there was then no institution of children in
the old English—that the first language they learned was the
French, and that through that tongue they were afterwards
taught Latin; and he adds that this was a practice which had

* Quid nos dura refugimus aetas?—Hor. Od. i. 35.
† Excerpta ex Libro iv. Orderici Vitalis, p. 217; edit. Maseres.
‡ Ingulphi Historia, in Savile, 895: or in Fulman, 62. The translation,
which is sufficiently faithful, is Henry's.
§ Id. Savile. 901; Fulman, 71.

been introduced at the Conquest, and which had continued ever since.[*] About the middle of the same century Ranulf Higden, in his Polychronicon, says, as the passage is translated by Trevisa, "This apayringe (impairing) of the birthe tonge is by cause of twoye thinges; oon is for children in scole, aghenes (against) the usage and manor of alle other nacionns, both (be) compelled for to love her (their) owne langage, and for to con-strewe her lessouns and her thingis a Frensche, and havoth sithithe (have since) that the Normans come first into England. Also gentil mennes children both ytaught (be taught) for to speke Frensche from the time that thei both rokked in her cradel, and cunneth (can) speke and playe with a childes brooche; and uplondish (rustic) man wol likne hem self (will liken them-selves) to gentilmen, and fondeth (are fond) with grete bisy-nesse for to speke Frensche, for to be the more ytold of."[†] The teachers in the schools, in fact, were generally, if not uni-versally, ecclesiastics; and the Conquest had Normanized the church quite as much as the state. Immediately after that revolution great numbers of foreigners were brought over, both to serve in the parochial cures and to fill the monasteries that now began to multiply so rapidly. These churchmen must have been in constant intercourse with the people of all classes in various capacities, not only as teachers of youth, but as the instructors of their parishioners from the altar, and as holding daily and hourly intercourse with them in all the relations that subsist between pastor and flock. They probably in this way diffused their own tongue throughout the land of their adoption to a greater extent than is commonly suspected. We shall have occasion, as we proceed, to mention some facts which would seem to imply that in the twelfth century the French language was very generally familiar to the middle classes in England, at least in the great towns. It was at any rate the only language spoken for some ages after the Conquest by our kings, and not only by nearly all the nobility, but by a large proportion even of the inferior landed proprietors, most of whom also were of Norman birth or descent. Ritson, in his rambling, incoherent Dissertation on Romance and Minstrelsy, prefixed to his

---

[*] Lect. in Libr. Sophent. Lect. ii., 4to. Paris, 1518; as referred to by Warton, Hist. Eng. Poetry, i. 5.

[†] Quoted from MS. Harl. 1900, by Tyrwhitt, in Essay on the Language and Versification of Chaucer, prefixed to his edition of the Canterbury Tales.

Ancient English Metrical Romances, has collected, but not in
the most satisfactory manner, some of the evidence we have
as to the speech of the first Norman kings. He does not
notice what Ordericus Vitalis tells us of the Conqueror's meritorious attempt, which does not seem, however, to have been
more successful than such experiments on the part of grown-up
gentlemen usually are; so that he may be allowed to be correct
enough in the assertion with which he sets out, that we have no
information " that William the Bastard, his son Rufus, his
daughter Maud, or his nephew Stephen, did or could speak the
Anglo-Saxon or English language." Reference is then made to
a story told in what is called Bromton's Chronicle respecting
Henry II., which, however, is not very intelligible in all its
parts, though Ritson has slurred over the difficulties. As
Henry was passing through Wales, the old chronicler relates,
on his return from Ireland in the spring of 1172, he found himself on a Sunday at the castle of Cardiff, and stopped there to
hear mass; after which, as he was proceeding to mount his
horse to be off again, there presented itself before him a somewhat singular apparition, a man with red hair and a round
tonsure,[*] lean and tall, attired in a white tunic and barefoot,
who, addressing him in the Teutonic tongue, began, " Gode
Olde Kinge,"[†] and proceeded to deliver a command from Christ,
as he said, and his mother, from John the Baptist and Peter,
that he should suffer no traffic or servile works to be done
throughout his dominions on the sabbath-day, except only such
as pertained to the use of food; " which command, if thou
observest," concluded the speaker, " whatever thou mayest
undertake thou shalt happily accomplish." The king immediately, speaking in French, desired the soldier who held the
bridle of his horse to ask the rustic if he had dreamed all this.
The soldier made the inquiry, as desired, in English; and then,
it is added, the man replied in the same language as before, and
addressing the king said, " Whether I have dreamed it or no,
mark this day; for, unless thou shalt do what I have told thee,

[*] Tonsura rotunda. Scriptores Decem, 1079. The epithet would seem to
imply that there were still in Wales some priests of the ancient British
Church who retained the old national crescent-shaped tonsure, now deemed
heretical.

[†] Henry and his son of the same name were commonly distinguished as the
Old and the Young King from the date of the coronation of the latter (whom
his father survived) in 1170.

and amend thy life, thou shalt within a year's time hear such
news as thou shalt mourn to the day of thy death." And, having
so spoken, the man vanished out of sight. With the calamities
which of course ensued to the doomed king we have here nothing
to do. Although the chronicler reports only the three commencing words of the prophet's first address in what he calls the
Teutonic tongue, there can be no doubt, we conceive, that the
rest, though here translated into Latin, was also delivered in the
same Teutonic (by which, apparently, can only have been meant
the vernacular English, or what is commonly called Saxon). The
man would not begin his speech in one language, and then suddenly break away into another. But, if this was the case,
Henry, from his reply, would appear to have understood English,
though he might not be able to speak it. The two languages,
thus subsisting together, were probably both understood by
many of those who could only speak one of them. We have
another evidence of this in the fact of the soldier, as we have
seen, speaking English and also understanding the king's French.
It is, we suppose, merely so much affectation or bad rhetoric in
the chronicler that makes him vary his phrase for the same
thing from " the Teutonic tongue" (*Teutonica lingua*) in one place
to " English" (*Anglicè*) in another, and immediately after to
" the former language" (*lingua priori*); for the words which he
gives as Teutonic are English words, and, when Henry desired
the soldier to address the priest in English and the soldier did
so, it must have been because that was the language in which he
had addressed the king.*

" King Richard," Ritson proceeds, " is never known to have
uttered a single English word, unless one may rely on the
evidence of Robert Mannyng for the express words, when, of
Isaac King of Cyprus, 'O dele,' said the king, 'this is a folc
Breton.' The latter expression seems proverbial, whether it
alludes to the Welsh or to the Armoricans, because Isaac was
neither by birth, though he might be both by folly. Many great
nobles of England, in this century, were utterly ignorant of the

---

* A somewhat different view of this story is taken by Mr. Luders in his
tract On the Use of the French Language in our ancient Laws and Acts of
State. (Tracts on Various Subjects, p. 100.) He remarks: " The author does
not tell why the ghost spoke German to the king in Wales, or how this
German became all at once good English; nor how it happened that the
groom addressed the German ghost in English." Mr. Luders, therefore, understands "the Teutonic tongue" to mean, not English, but German.

English language." As an instance, he mentions the case, before
noticed by Tyrwhitt, of William Longchamp, bishop of Ely,
chancellor and prime minister to Richard I., who, according to a
remarkable account in a letter of his contemporary Hugh bishop
of Coventry, preserved by Hoveden, did not know a word of
English.[*] The only fact relating to this subject in connexion
with John or his reign that Ritson brings forward, is the speech
which that king's ambassador, as related by Matthew Paris, made
to the King of Morocco :—" Our nation is learned in three idioms,
that is to say, Latin, French, and English." [†] This would go to
support the conclusion that both the French and the Latin
languages were at this time not unusually spoken by persons of
education in England.

THE LANGUE D'OC AND THE LANGUE D'OYL.

French as well as Latin was at least extensively employed
among us in literary composition. The Gauls, the original
inhabitants of the country now called France, were a Celtic
people, and their speech was a dialect of the same great
primitive tongue which probably at one time prevailed over
the whole of Western Europe, and is still vernacular in
Ireland, in Wales, and among the Highlanders of Scotland.
After the country became a Roman province this ancient
language gradually gave place to the Latin; which, however, here as elsewhere, soon became corrupted in the mouths
of a population mixing it with their own barbarous vocables
and forms, or at least divesting it of many of its proper characteristics in their rude appropriation of it. But, as different

---

[*] Linguam Anglicanam prorsus ignorabat.—Hoveden, 704. Ritson, omitting
all mention either of Hoveden or Tyrwhitt, chooses to make a general reference to the chronicle called Bromton's, a later compilation, the author of
which (vide col. 1227) has quietly appropriated Bishop Hugh's Letter, and
made it part of his narrative.

[†] This was a secret mission despatched by John, the historian tells us, in
1213, "ad Admirallium Marmellium, regem magnum Aphricæ, Marrochiæ, et
Hispaniæ, quem vulgus Miramumellinum vocat." The words used by Thomas
Hardington, the one of the three commissioners selected, on account of his
superior gift of eloquence, to be spokesman, were "Gens nostra speciosæ et
ingenuosa tribus pollet idiomatibus erudita, scilicet Latino, Gallico, et Anglico."—Matt. Paris, 243.

depraving or obliterating influences operated in different circumstances, and a variety of kinds of bad Latin were thus produced in the several countries which had been provinces of the empire, so even within the limits of Gaul there grew up two such distinct dialects, one in the south, another in the north. All these forms of bastard Latin, wherever they arose, whether in Italy, in Spain, or in Gaul, were known by the common name of Roman, or Romance, languages, or the Rustic Roman (Romana Rustica), and were by that generic term distinguished from the barbarian tongues, or those that had been spoken by the Celtic, German, and other uncivilized nations before they came into communication with the Romans. From them have sprung what are called the Latin languages of modern Europe—the Italian, the Spanish, and the Portuguese, as well as what we now denominate the French. The Romance spoken in the south of Gaul appears to have been originally nearly, if not altogether, identical with that spoken in the north-east of Spain; and it always preserved a close resemblance and affinity to that and the other Romance dialects of Spain and Italy. It is in fact to be accounted a nearer relation of the Spanish and Italian than of the modern French. The latter is exclusively the offspring of the Romance of northern Gaul, which, both during its first growth and subsequently, was acted upon by different influences from those which modified the formation of the southern tongue. It is probable that whatever it retained of the Celtic ingredient to begin with was, if not stronger or of larger quantity than what entered into the Romance dialect of the south, at any rate of a somewhat different character; but the peculiar form it eventually assumed may be regarded as having been mainly owing to the foreign pressure to which it was twice afterwards exposed, first by the settlement of the Franks in the north and north-east of Gaul in the fifth century (while the Visigoths and Burgundians had spread themselves over the south), and again by that of the Normans in the north-west in the tenth. What may have been the precise nature or amount of the effect produced upon the Romance tongue of Northern Gaul by either or both of these Teutonic occupations of the country, it is not necessary for our present purpose to inquire; it is sufficient to observe that that dialect could not fail to be thereby peculiarly affected, and its natural divergence from the southern Romance materially aided and promoted. The result, in fact, was that

the two dialects became two distinct languages, differing from
one another more than any two other of the Latin languages did
—the Italian, for example, from the Spanish, or the Spanish
from the Portuguese, and even more than the Romance of the
south of Gaul differed from that either of Italy or of Spain.
This southern Romance, it only remains further to be observed,
came in course of time to be called the Provençal tongue; but
it does not appear to have received this name till, in the beginning of the twelfth century, the county of Provence had fallen
to be inherited by Raymond Berenger, Count of Catalonia, who
thereupon transferred his court to Arles, and made that town the
centre and chief seat of the literary cultivation which had
previously flourished at Barcelona.   There had been poetry
written in the Romance of Southern Gaul before this; but it
was not till now that the Troubadours, as the authors of that
poetry called themselves, rose into much celebrity; and hence it
has been maintained, with great appearance of reason, that what
is best or most characteristic about the Provençal poetry is really
not of French but of Spanish origin.   In that case the first
inspiration may probably have been caught from the Arabs.
The greater part of Provence soon after passed into the possession
of the Counts of Toulouse, and the Troubadours flocked to that
city.   But the glory of the Provençal tongue did not last altogether for much more than a century; and then, when it had
ceased to be employed in poetry and literature, and had declined
into a more provincial patois, it and the northern French
were wont to be severally distinguished by the names of
the Langue d'Oc (sometimes called by modern writers the
Occitanian) and the Langue d'Oyl, from the words for *yes*, which
were *oc* in the one, and *oyl*, afterwards *oy* or *oui*, in the other.
Dante mentions them by these appellations, and with this
explanation, in his treatise De Vulgari Eloquio, written in the end
of the thirteenth or beginning of the fourteenth century; and one
of them still gives its name to the great province of Languedoc,
where the dialect formerly so called yet subsists as the popular
speech, though, of course, much changed and debased from what
it was in the days of its old renown, when it lived on the lips of
rank and genius and beauty, and was the favourite vehicle of love
and song.

The Langue d'Oyl, on the other hand, formerly spoken only to
the north of the Loire, has grown up into what we now call the

French language, and has become, at least for literary purposes, and for all the educated classes, the established language of the whole country. Some fond students of the remains of the other dialect have deplored this result as a misfortune to France, which they contend would have had a better modern language and literature if the Langue d'Oc, in the contest between the two, had prevailed over the Langue d'Oyl. It is probable, indeed, that accident and political circumstances have had more to do in determining the matter as it has gone than the merits of the case; but in every country as well as in France—in Spain, in Italy, in Germany, in England—some other of the old popular dialects than the one that has actually acquired the ascendancy has in like manner had its enthusiastic reclaimers against the unjust fortune which has condemned it to degradation or oblivion; and we may suspect that the partiality which the mind is apt to acquire for whatever it has made the subject of long investigation and study, especially if it be something which has been generally neglected, and perhaps in some instances a morbid sympathy with depression and defeat, which certain historical and philosophical speculators have in common with the readers and writers of sentimental novels, are at the bottom of much of this unavailing and purposeless lamentation. The question is one which we have hardly the means of solving, even if any solution of it which might now be attainable could have any practical effect. The Langue d'Oyl is now unalterably established as the French language; the Langue d'Oc is, except as a local patois, irrecoverably dead. Nor are there wanting French archæologists, quite equal in knowledge of the subject to their opponents, who maintain that in this there is nothing to regret, but the contrary—that the northern Romance tongue was as superior to the southern intrinsically as it has proved in fortune, and that its early literature was of far higher value and promise than the Provençal.*

* What has come to be called the French tongue, it may be proper to notice, has no relationship whatever to that of the proper French, or Franks, who were a Teutonic people, speaking a purely Teutonic language, resembling the German, or more nearly the Flemish. This old Teutonic French, which the Franks continued to speak for several centuries after their conquest of Gaul, is denominated by philologists the Frankish, or Francic. The modern French, which is a Latin tongue, has come to be so called, from the accident of the country in which it was spoken having been conquered by the French or Franks—the conquerors, as in other cases, in course of time adopting the language of the conquered, and bestowing upon it their own name.

NORMAN TROUVEURS:—DUKE RICHARD I.—THIBAUT DE VERNON—
TUROLD, OR THEROULDE.—CHANSON DE ROLAND.

It is, at any rate, this early literature of the Langue d'Oyl
which is for us in England of most interest. It is, in fact, in
a manner a part of our own. Not only did it spring up, and
for a long time flourish exclusively, among those same wonderful Normans whose greatest and most enduring dominion has
been established in this island; the greater part of it appears to
have been produced not in France, but in England. This was
first shown by the late Abbé de la Rue in a series of dissertations
published in 1796 and 1797 in the twelfth and thirteenth
volumes of the Archæologia, or Transactions of the Society of
Antiquaries, and subsequently, at more length and with more
elaborate research, in his work entitled Essais Historiques sur
les Bardes, les Jongleurs, et les Trouvères Normands et Anglo-
Normands; 3 vols. 8vo. Caen, 1834.

The earliest recorded writer of French verse appears to be
Richard I., Duke of Normandy, the natural but only son of
William I., son and successor of Rollo, the great founder of the
duchy. Richard, who afterwards acquired for himself the
surname of Sans-peur (the Fearless), was born in 933, was
recognized as duke on the death of his father, ten years after,
and died, after a glorious reign of more than half a century, in
996. Of his poetry, however, nothing remains except the fame,
preserved in the writings of another Trouvère of the next age.
Richard, it may be observed, had been sent by his father to be
educated at Bayeux, where the Danish language was still spoken,
instead of at Rouen, the capital of the duchy, where even
already, only a generation after the arrival of the Normans,
they or their children, as well as the native population, spoke
only French; and his taste for poetry is said to have been first
awakened by the songs of the land of his ancestors. Much of
the peculiar character, indeed, of the early northern French
poetry betokens a Scandinavian inspiration. With this influence
was probably combined that of the old Celtic poetry of Britany,
or Armorica, of which the country now called Normandy had been
originally a part, and with which it still continued to be intimately connected. In this way may be reconciled the various
theories that have been proposed on the subject of the origin of

romantic poetry and fiction in Europe; one deducing it from a Scandinavian, another from a Celtic, a third from an Oriental source; and each, separately looked at, appearing to support itself by facts and considerations of great force. When these several theories were advanced in opposition to one another by ingenious and more or less well-informed speculators of the last century, the distinction between the early language and poetry of the south and those of the north of France had been little attended to, and was very imperfectly understood. Had the love-songs of the Provençal Troubadours, and the lays and tales of the Norman Trouvères, not been confounded together, it might have been perceived that both the internal and the external evidence concurred in assigning, in great part at least, a Saracenic origin to the former, and a mixed Scandinavian and Armorican parentage to the latter.

Another early Norman Trouvère, whose name only has been preserved, is Thibaut de Vernon, who was a canon of Rouen in the early part of the eleventh century, or in the age intermediate between that of Duke Richard Sans-peur and that of the Conqueror. A collection of fifty-nine old French Lives of Saints, of which three are in verse and the rest in prose, has been attributed to De Vernon; but erroneously, as is shown by M. de la Rue. What he really wrote was a verse Life of St. Vandrille (the Abbot Wandregisilus), which appears to be lost.

The renowned minstrel Taillefer, who struck the first blow at the battle of Hastings, is described by his countryman Wace, in the next century, as having dashed on horseback among the ranks of the Saxons, to meet his glorious death, singing of Charlemagne and Roland and Oliver, and the other peers who died at Roncesvaux:—

> De Karlemaigne et de Rollant,
> E d'Oliver, et des vassals,
> Qy morurent en Roncesvala.

Various pieces of ancient verse have been from time to time produced, claiming to be this Song of Roland (as it is styled by several later chroniclers); and it has been generally assumed that it was a short lyrical strain, and a composition of Taillefer's own. Lately, however, much attention has been attracted to a long poem, of nearly three hundred stanzas, or some three thousand lines, which was first published by M. Francisque

Michel from the manuscript in the Bodleian Library, under the title of La Chanson de Roland, ou de Roncevaux (8vo. Paris, 1837), and which is maintained to be the true old epic of which a portion was recited by Taillefer on this occasion. The existence of this poem was, we believe, first pointed out in a note to his edition of Chaucer's Canterbury Tales (v. 13,741), by Tyrwhitt, so many of whose hints and conjectures on such subjects have anticipated or been confirmed by more recent inquiry, and who observes that the "romance, which in the MS. has no title, may possibly be an older copy of one which is frequently quoted by Du Cange, under the title of Le Roman de Roncevaux." "The author's name," he adds, "is Turold, as appears from the last line :—

Ci fait le geste que Turold declinet.*

He is not mentioned by any of the writers of French literary history that I have seen." There are in fact other manuscripts of the work, but of a later age, and exhibiting a modernized text. It appears, however, to have been generally forgotten until it was again mentioned by the late Rev. J. F. Conybeare, in announcing, in the Gentleman's Magazine for August, 1817, his Illustrations of the Early History of English and French Poetry—a work which, unfortunately, he did not live to publish. That same year an analysis of the poem was given in the first volume of the Mémoires et Dissertations de la Société Royale des Antiquaires de France, by M. de Musset, who at the same time announced an edition of it as in preparation by M. Guyot des Herbiers. This, however, never appeared, any more than an edition which was announced in 1832 as then preparing by M. Bourdillon. Nor, although it was subsequently made the subject of much discussion by M. H. Monin, who published a Dissertation upon it in an 8vo. volume, at Paris, in 1832, by M. Paulin Paris, by M. Le Roux de Lincy, in his Analyse du Roman de Garin le Loherain (12mo. Paris, 1835), and other French poetical antiquaries, was the poem made accessible to the public, till M. Michel was enabled to bring out his edition of it (of which the impression, however, was very limited) by the liberality of the French government. But a more sumptuous edition was subsequently produced by the late M. F. Génin—

* Turold is the common contraction for Turoldus.

La Chanson de Roland, Texte Critique; 8vo. Par. 1850—
founded on a further examination, conducted with extraordinary
care, of the original manuscript (which the enthusiastic editor is
inclined to believe to be the very copy that had belonged to
Taillefer)—and illustrated with everything in the way of
explanation and disquisition that any student could desire, or
that rare ingenuity as well as erudition could supply.[*]

Anglo-Norman Poets.—King Henry I.—His Queens, Matilda and Alice.

To our King Henry I., surnamed Beauclerc, or the Scholar,
who was carefully educated under the superintendence of the
learned Lanfranc, afterwards archbishop and saint, M. de la Rue
attributes both an English translation of a collection of Latin
Æsopian fables, mentioned in the next age by Marie de France,
and rendered by her into French verse, and a short poem in
Romance entitled Urbanus, or Le Dictié d'Urbain, being a
sort of code of the rules of politeness as understood and observed
in his day. The evidence, however, is not very conclusive as to
either production; and the English fables, in particular, now
only known from Marie's translation, have been claimed, with
perhaps more probability, for King Alfred, whose name appears
instead of that of Henry in some manuscripts of Marie's work.[†]
Both Henry's queens, it may be noticed, are recorded to have
been, as well as himself, fond of literature and poetry. M. de la
Rue refers to the works of Hildebert, bishop of le Mans, as containing several pieces of Latin poetry addressed to the first of
them, Matildis, or Matilda, the daughter of the Scottish king
Malcolm Canmore and the English Margaret, herself a learned as
well as pious princess. But the liveliest picture of this part of
Queen Matilda's character is that drawn by William of Malmes-

---

[*] See also Lettre sur les Variantes de la Chanson de Roland (édition de
M. F. (Génin), à M. Léon de Bastard, par F. Guessard; Lettre à M. Paulin
Paris, par F. Génin; and Lettre à un Ami sur l'Article de M. Paulin Paris,
inséré dans la Bibliothèque de l'Ecole des Chartes, par F. Génin; all published at Paris in 1851.

[†] See a note upon this subject (which, however, appears not to have con-
vinced De la Rue) by the late Mr. Price, in his edition of Warton's History of
English Poetry. I. lvii.-lxvi.

bury, who, it will be perceived however, is no great admirer of some of the tastes which he describes:—" She had a singular pleasure in hearing the service of God; and on this account was thoughtlessly prodigal towards clerks of melodious voice; addressed them kindly, gave to them liberally, and promised still more abundantly. Her generosity becoming universally known, crowds of scholars, equally famed for verse and for singing, came over; and happy did he account himself who could soothe the ears of the queen by the novelty of his song. Nor on those only did she lavish money, but on all sorts of men, especially foreigners, that, through her presents, they might proclaim her liberality abroad: for the desire of fame is so rooted in the human mind that scarcely is any one-contented with the precious fruits of a good conscience, but is fondly anxious, if he does anything laudable, to have it generally known. Hence, it was generally observed, the disposition crept upon the queen to reward all the foreigners she could, while the others were kept in suspense, sometimes with effectual, but often with empty promises. Hence, too, it arose that she fell into the error of prodigal givers: bringing many claims on her tenantry, exposing them to injuries, and taking away their property; by which, obtaining the credit of a liberal benefactress, she little regarded their earnestness."[*] With all this vanity, however, and love of admiration and applause, if such it is to be called, Matilda is admitted by the historian to have constantly practised the humblest and most self-denying offices of religion: she did not shrink, we are told, either from washing the feet of diseased persons, or even from touching and dressing their sores and pressing their hands for a long time with devout affection to her lips; and her chief pleasure was in the worship of God. It is a trait of the times to find the same person the chief patroness of piety and of poetry. Henry's second queen, also, Adelais, or Alice, of Louvain, is addressed by several of the Norman and Anglo-Norman trouvères as the special protectress of them and their art.

---

[*] Willelmi Malmesbiriensis Gesta Regum Anglorum, lib. v. ad an. 1107; as translated by the Rev. John Sharpe. 4to. London, 1815, p. 516.

PHILIP DE THAN.—GEOFFREY, ABBOT OF ST. ALBANS.

One of those by whom Queen Adelais is thus distinguished is
Philip de Than (anciently Thaon or Thaun), who, if the age of
Throld and his Roman de Roncevaux be disputed, may be regarded
as the earliest of the trouvères any of whose works have certainly
come down to us. He is the author of two French poems of
considerable length; one a treatise on chronological computation,
entitled Li Livre des Creatures; the other, known as The
Bestiary, being a sort of natural history, comprising an account
of both animal and mineral productions. The latter is dedicated
to the English queen, and was probably written between 1120
and 1130. Both poems are mainly compiled from various Latin
originals.[*]

We have already mentioned Geffroy, or Geoffrey, also a native
of Normandy, who died abbot of the monastery of St. Albans in
1146, and his miracle-play of St. Catharine, which is stated by
Matthew Paris to have been acted by the boys attending his
school at Dunstable about the year 1110, and is generally referred to as the earliest drama upon record in any modern
tongue.[†] But in truth we have no information in what language
this lost production of Geoffrey was composed; it may have
been in French, in English, or in Latin, though it is most probable that it was in the first-mentioned tongue. If so, it is by
much the most ancient French play of which the name has been
preserved. Its claim to stand at the head of modern dramatic
literature, however, has been disputed. " Perhaps," observes a
late learned writer, " the plays of Roswitha, a nun of Gandor-
sheim in Lower Saxony, who lived towards the close of the
tenth century, afford the earliest specimens of dramatic composition since the decline of the Roman empire."[‡] These plays
of Roswitha's appear to have been intended only for reading, and
are not known ever to have been acted; but they have been twice
published;—first by Conrad Celtes in 1501, and again by Leonard
Schurtzfleisch in 1707.

* They are both given, with translations, in Mr. Wright's Popular
Treatises on Science written during the Middle Ages. In Anglo-Saxon,
Anglo-Norman, and English. 8vo. London, 1841.
   † See ante, p. 51.
   ‡ Note by Price to Warton's Hist. of Eng. Poet, ii. 6d.

Another of the poetical protégés or celebrators of Queen Adelais
is the unknown author of a poem of between 800 and 900 verses
on the Pilgrimage of St. Brandan.   There were, it appears, in
the sixth century two Irish ecclesiastics of the name of Brandan
or Brendan, both of whom have since been canonized, the day
assigned in the Calendar to the one being the 29th of November,
to the other the 16th of May. It is the latter with whom we
have here to do. He has the credit of having been the founder
of the abbey of Clonfert in Galway; but the most memorable
passage of his history is his voyage, along with some of his
monks, in quest of a more profound seclusion from the world,
which was believed in an after age to have conducted him to one
of the Fortunate Islands, or one of the Canaries according to a
still later interpretation. He did not find the scheme of so
distant a retirement to answer, and he soon returned to Ireland:
but M. de la Rue thinks it probable that he drew up a narrative
of his adventures for the information of the European public of
that day, out of which there grew in course of time the legend
which bears the name of his Voyage to the Terrestrial Paradise,
and which is as full of marvels and miracles as that of Ulysses,
or any of those of Sinbad the Sailor. Indeed, one of Sinbad's
principal wonders, his landing on the whale, is actually found in
the Voyage of St. Brandan.   De la Rue has given copious
extracts from the poem on this subject which he notices, and
which professes to have been composed at the command of
Queen Adelais, and immediately after her marriage in 1121.
But the fullest account of St. Brandan and his Pilgrimage will
be found in the Preface to a more recent publication by M. Achille
Jubinal, entitled La Légende Latine de S. Brandaines, avec
une traduction inédite en prose et en poésie Romane, publiée
d'après les manuscrits de la Bibliothèque du Roi, remontant aux
xi°, xii°, et xiii° siècles; 8vo., Paris, 1830.   Of the French
metrical legend here printed, which is different from the Anglo-
Norman romance analyzed by De la Rue, M. Jubinal states that
there are many manuscripts. It is found as part of a poem of the
thirteenth century written by Gauthier de Metz, entitled Image
du Monde. Several copies of the story in Latin prose also
exist; of the French prose version there is only one known text,
which is in the Bibliothèque Impériale at Paris. It is found,

however, both in verse and prose in most of the other European
tongues—in Irish, in Welsh, in Spanish, in German of various
dialects, in Flemish, in English ; and there are printed editions
of it, both recent and in the earlier ages of typography, in several
of these languages.   M. Jubinal mentions an edition of it in
English prose, printed by Wynken do Worde, in folio, in 1516:
it appears to be a translation from a Latin version contained
in a volume of Lives of the Saints, compiled under the title of
Legenda Aurea, by John Capgrave, who was an English monk
of the fourteenth century, and the author also of a quantity of
verse, some of which still exists, in his native tongue.*   It is
remarkable that St. Brandan, or Brandain, has given his name to
an imaginary island long popularly believed to form one of the
Canary group, although become invisible since his day, or at
least not to be discovered by modern navigators, to whom it was
a frequent object of search from the beginning of the sixteenth
down to so late a date as the beginning of the eighteenth century :
the last expedition in quest of it was fitted out from Spain in
1721.   The Spaniards, who call the lost island San Borendon,
believe it to be the retreat of their King Rodrigo; the Portuguese
assign it to their Don Sebastian.†   The acquaintance of the
modern nations of Europe with the Canary Islands dates only
from about the year 1330, when a French ship was driven upon
one of them in a storm.

Along with this romance on the pilgrimage of St. Brandan may
be noticed another old French poem on a fabulous journey of
Charlemagne to Constantinople and Jerusalem, which is perhaps
of still earlier date, and which has also from the language been
supposed to have been written in England.   An account of it is
given by De la Rue (Essais, ii. 23-32) ; and the poem has been
since published by M. Francisque Michel, from the Royal MS.
10 E. viii., at the British Museum, under the title of Charlemagne, an Anglo-Norman poem of the Twelfth Century, with an
Introduction and a Glossarial Index ; 12mo. Lon. 1836.   It consists of only 870 lines.

* See Warton's Hist. of Eng. Poet., ii. 355 ; and additional note by Park,
p. 514 (edit. of 1821).

† Both the Abbé de la Rue and M. Jubinal refer the reader for information
upon the subject of the Isle of St. Brandan to the Noticias de la Historia de
las islas de Canaria of Dom Joseph de Viera y Clavigo (Madrid, 1672 or
1771).

ANGLO-NORMAN CHRONICLERS:—GAIMAR;—DAVID.

But the farther we pursue the history of this early Norman poetry, the closer becomes its connexion with our own country. Not only does it seek its chief audience in England, but the subjects with which it occupies itself come to be principally or almost exclusively English. The earliest of the old French versifiers of our English history appears to be Geffroy Gaimar, the author of a metrical chronicle, entitled Estorie des Engles (History of the English). It was probably completed about the middle of the twelfth century. Attention was first called to Gaimar and his work by the Abbé de la Rue, who appears, however, to have in part mistaken the sense of the account the old chronicler gives of himself. In the complete work the History of the English was preceded by a Brut d'Angleterre, or History of the Britons, which he had compiled principally, he tells us, from a Latin work, itself a translation from a Welsh original, the good book of Oxford belonging to Walter the archdeacon. Comparing this with what is stated by Geoffrey of Monmouth in the Preface or Dedication to his History, we cannot doubt that that was the Latin original upon which Gaimar worked. He seems to say that he also made some use of another book which he calls the History of Winchester, and of an English book of Washingburgh (in Lincolnshire), where he found accounts of the Roman emperors who possessed the sovereignty of England and of the kings who had held of them. This portion of Gaimar's performance, however, is no longer known to exist. His English History extends from the coming of the Angles and Saxons to the death of William Rufus, and is for the most part based on the vernacular National Chronicle, but owes its chief interest and value to certain legendary matter gathered either from other written sources, or, in some cases perhaps, from mere popular tradition. The first portion of it which was printed was that containing the story of Havelok the Dane, which was given by Sir Frederic Madden in his edition of that romance prepared for the Roxburghe Club, London, 1828. The latter portion of the work, commencing from the Norman Conquest, was published by M. Francisque Michel, at Rouen, in 1835, in the first volume of his collection entitled Chroniques Anglo-Normandes. The portion relating to the period before

the Norman Conquest, again, extending to above 5300 lines in
all, is contained in the Monumenta Historica Britannica, 1848.
Finally, the whole has been edited by Mr. Thomas Wright, for
the Caxton Society, under the title of Gaimar's Anglo-Norman
Metrical Chronicle, with Illustrative Notes and Appendix, containing the Lay of Havelok, the Legend of Ernulf, and the Life
of Horward; 8vo. London, 1850. A translation of Gaimar by
Mr. Stevenson is given in the Second Part of the Third Volume
of The Church Historians of England, 1854.

At the end of his History, Gaimar, who here describes himself
as of Troyes, intimates his intention of writing a separate Life
of King Henry I., of whom he says that he could tell a thousand
things omitted by David, who did not go sufficiently into details
to do justice to the nobleness, the liberality, the magnificence,
and the other brilliant qualities of that great king, although his
chronicle was highly esteemed, and in particular was a favourite
book with the Queen Adelais. Of this David, who is nowhere
else made mention of, nothing is known. His performance was
in verse; Gaimar calls it a *Chanson*. Nor have we any evidence
that Gaimar's own promised Life of King Henry was ever written.

WACE.

The most famous of these writers of early English history in
romance verse is Master Wace—*Maître Wace, clerc lisant* (that is,
writing clerk), as he calls himself—in Latin *Magister Wacius*.
The name is also otherwise written in his own day *Waice*, *Gace*,
Gasse, and *Gasce*; but *Guace*, *Huace*, *Huistace*, *Wistace*, *Extasse*,
Eustace, *Eustache*, are the corruptions of a subsequent age or
modern variations, and *Vate*, which is the form adopted by
some modern writers, is a mere mistranscription.[*] His Christian
name appears to have been Richard. He was a native of the
island of Jersey, where he was probably born in the last decade
of the eleventh century, and of a good family: his father was
one of the Norman barons who accompanied the Conqueror to
England and fought at Hastings; he himself was educated for
the ecclesiastical profession at Caen, and, after passing some

---

[*] *Wace*, however, according to Mr. Wright, is really " merely the vernacular
form of the Latin *Eustacius*."—(Biog. Brit. Lit., II. 208.)

years in other parts of France, and also, it appears, visiting England, he returned and settled in that city, where he spent the rest of his life in writing his several poetical works. In his latter years he was made by Henry II. a canon of Bayeux. The Waces, probably descendants of the poet's father, obtained large possessions in Nottinghamshire and Yorkshire; and another branch continued to flourish for some ages in Normandy. The first of Wace's chronicles is entitled the Brut d'Angleterre,[*] and is in the main a translation into romance verse of eight syllables of the British History of Geoffrey of Monmouth, although it contains also a good many things which are not in Geoffrey. It extends to upwards of 15,000 lines. After finishing his work Wace is said to have presented it to Henry II.'s queen, Eleanor of Aquitaine. Many manuscripts of it exist both in England and in France; and it has now been printed, under the title of Le Roman de Brut, par Wace; avec un Commentaire et des Notes, par Le Roux de Lincy; 2 vols. 8vo. Rouen, 1836, 1838. Wace's other great work is his Roman de Rou, that is, Romance of Rollo. It is a chronicle of the Dukes of Normandy, in two parts: the first, in Alexandrine verses, extending only to the beginning of the reign of the third duke, Richard Sans-peur; the second, in eight-syllable rhymes, coming down to the year 1170, the sixteenth of Henry II. There are nearly 17,000 lines in all. The composition of the first part is stated to have been commenced in 1160, and it appears to have been published by itself; but some years after, on learning that the charge of writing the history of the Dukes of Normandy in verse had been confided by King Henry to another poet named Benoît, Wace, as M. de la Rue supposes, resumed his pen, and, adopting for expedition the easier octosyllabic verse, hastened to complete his task before his rival.[†] The entire work was printed for the

---

[*] The British Chronicles are generally supposed to have been called Bruts from Brutus, the great-grandson of Æneas, who is represented in them as the first king of the Britons; but the author of Britannia after the Romans puts forward a new interpretation. "Brut," he says (p. xlii), "in construction Brut, is reputation, or rumour, and in the secondary sense, a chronicle, or history. It retains that original sense in the French and English word bruit; and, though it is curious that all the Welsh Chronicles begin with the reign of Brutus, we must not be seduced by that accident into etymological trifling."

[†] M. Le Roux de Lincy, however, denies that this latter part of the Roman des Ducs de Normandie is by Wace, or that he ever really attempted in his old age to compete with Benoît.

first time in 1827 at Rouen, in 2 vols. 8vo., under the title of
Le Roman de Rou et des Ducs de Normandie, par Robert
Wace; avec des Notes par Frédéric Pluquet; but, although
M. Pluquet, who had in 1824 published a short notice about
Wace (Notice sur la Vie et les Ecrits de Robert Wace), mostly
copied from the Abbé de la Rue's paper in the Archæologia, was
assisted in the preparation of his edition by M. Auguste le
Prévost, whose notes are often learned and curious, it is evident
that very little knowledge or critical judgment has been em-
ployed in settling the text, which is often manifestly corrupt
either from mistranscription or reliance on a faulty original.
Some of its errors have been pointed out, with sufficient gentleness, by M. Raynouard in a small tract entitled Observations
Philosophiques et Grammaticales sur le Roman de Rou, 8vo.
Rouen, 1829; which ought always to accompany M. Pluquet's
edition.   Mr. Edgar Taylor (author of the volume entitled
Lays of the Minnesingers or German Troubadours, and other
works) has translated so much of the Roman de Rou as relates to
the Conquest of England into English prose, with notes and
illustrations, 8vo. Lond. 1837.   The interest that has been
lately excited by this old Norman poet is further evinced by
the publication of two others of his supposed works; his Shorter
Chronicle of the Dukes of Normandy, in Alexandrine verse, from
Henry II. back to Rollo, which is printed in the first volume
(Part ii. pp. 444-447) of the Mémoires de la Société des Antiquaires de Normandie, 8vo. 1824;[*] and his poem, in verse of
eight syllables, on the establishment by William the Conqueror
of the Festival of the Conception of the Virgin, which was printed
in 8vo. at Caen, in 1842, under the title of L'Etablissement de
la Fête de la Conception Notre Dame, dite la Fête aux Normands; publié pour la première fois d'après les MSS. de la Bibliothèque du Roi, par MM. Mancel et Trebution.   A very limited
impression, also, of another of his romances, entitled La Vie de
St. Nicholas, in about 1500 lines, of which there are several
manuscripts in existence, and some extracts from which are
given by Hickes in his Thesaurus Linguarum Septentrionalium,
is stated by M. Le Roux de Lincy to have been produced by

[*] Both M. Le Roux de Lincy, however, and M. Francisque Michel, a much
higher authority (in the Preface to his Chronique des Ducs de Normandie
par Benoît, 1836, p. xv.), agree in holding this to be the production of a later
writer than Wace.

M. Monmerqué for the Société des Bibliophiles Français, and to
be contained in the seventh volume of their privately printed
Mélanges, 8vo. Paris, 1820-1834. Wace is besides commonly
held to be the author of a Romance about the Virgin, extending
to 1800 verses, and comprising a full account of her life and
death, which is still in manuscript.

BENOIT.

Wace's contemporary and rival, Benoit, also wrote a Chronicle
of the Norman Dukes, though not till some years after Wace had
finished his. Benoit's performance consists of above 30,000 octosyllabic verses, and begins at the first irruption of the Normans
under their leaders Hastings and Bier Ironside, but comes down
no farther than to the end of the reign of Henry I. It was
supposed to have been preserved only in one MS. which is in
the Harleian collection in the British Museum, and from which
it has been printed at Paris, under the care of M. Francisque
Michel, with the title of Chronique des Ducs de Normandie,
par Benoit, Trouvère Anglo-Normand du 12ᵐᵉ siècle, 3 vols.
4to. 1836-44.* But another MS. has since been found in the
Library of the city of Tours. It is, from its fulness and minuteness, one of the most curious monuments we possess of early
Norman history, and contains many details nowhere else to be
found. This Benoit also appears to be the same with the Benoit
de St. More, or St. Maure, by whom we have another long romance of nearly 30,000 verses, entitled the Roman de Troye,
being a legendary history of the Trojan war, founded on the
favourite authorities of the middle ages, the fictitious Dares
Phrygius and Dictys of Crete: their identity had been doubted
by M. Michel in his edition of the Norman Chronicle; but he
was subsequently induced, Mr. Wright informs us (Biog. Brit.
Lit., ii. 262), to change his opinion.

EVERARD.—FRENCH LANGUAGE IN SCOTLAND.

Among those early romance poets, the Abbé de la Rue reckons
a Scotsman, one Everard, who, after having been a monk of

* In the Collection de Documents Inédits sur l'Histoire de France.

Kirkham in Yorkshire, was in 1150 appointed by David I. of
Scotland—that "sore saint to the crown," as he was called
by his successor, the first James—the first abbot of his newly-
founded abbey of Ulme or Holmo-Cultraino in Cumberland.   To
him M. de la Rue attributes a French metrical translation of
what are called the Distichs of Cato, which is said to afford the
earliest-known example in the language of mixed rhymes, that
is, of the alternation of masculine and feminine rhymes, now an
established rule of French poetry.   A romance history of the
Passion of Christ, in 126 strophes, and in the same style with
the Distichs, which is found along with the Latin work in one of
the Arundel MSS., formerly belonging to the Royal Society, now
in the British Museum, the Abbé conceives to be also in all probability by Everard.   But the evidence for identifying the translator of the Distichs with the monk of Kirkham appears, it must
be confessed, to be extremely slight.*   A knowledge of the
French language, nevertheless, seems to have been as general
at this date in Scotland as in England.   Pinkerton, in his Essay
on the Origin of Scotish Poetry, prefixed to his Ancient Scotish
Poems, 2 vols. 8vo. Lond. 1786, after observing that the chief
English poets wrote solely in French for three centuries after
the Conquest—that French was the only language used at court
or by the nobility, nay even by the middle ranks of people—
that Saxon was left merely to the mob—that the apophthegms,
expressions, &c., preserved by historians of the time, are all in
old French—and that probably upwards of a hundred names of
English writers who wrote in French during that interval might
yet be recovered—proceeds to mention some facts which illustrate
the prevalence of the same language in the northern kingdom.
" Upon the murder of Duncan by Macbeth," he remarks, " in
1039, Malcolm, the heir of the crown, fled into England, where
he remained for seventeen years before he was enabled to resume
his kingdom.   Edward the Confessor was king of England from
1041 till 1065, and in his reign we know that French was the
court language in England.   Malcolm surely used this speech,
and his court also.   Many Saxons came to Scotland with him in
1056, and also at the Conquest (1066); but in 1093 they were
all very prudently ordered to leave the kingdom by Dovenald
Ban, his successor.   They were chiefly men of rank ; and, had
they introduced any language, it would have been the French.

* See Wright's Biog. Brit. Lit., ii. 121

. . . . But yet another point requires our attention. In 945,
Edmund king of England gave Cumberland to Malcolm I., king
of Scotland, on condition of homage for it. From this period the
heir of the Scotish crown was always Prince of Cumberland,
and resided as a king in that country. . . . . Now the prince,
it may be supposed, did not use the Gaelic in a country where
it was never spoken; but, remaining there from early youth,
adopted French, the court tongue of England, in which country
his principality was, and to the king of which he was bound to
do homage."* He then mentions that under William of Scotland, in 1165, the coin of that country bears a French inscription; and that Alexander III., in 1249, is stated to have taken
the coronation oath *Latine et Gallice*, in Latin and in French: it
was read in Latin (probably after the ancient formula), and then
expounded in French.† And he concludes:—" French being
the language of the polite, and Latin of the learned, who could
use the vulgar tongue in writing? . . . . I suspect that no Scotish
poet, before Thomas of Ersildon, ventured beyond a ballad when
using his native tongue. Perhaps one or two may have written
a romance in French rhyme, though now lost or unknown. . . . .
The poor bards who entertained the mob might recite ballads and
short romances in the vulgar tongue; but the minstrels who appeared in the king's or in the baron's hall would use French only,
as in England; for had they tried the common language they
would have been sent into the kitchen."‡ By the common
language, Pinkarton means the Pictish, which he conceives to
have been a Gothic dialect nearly allied to the English. In this
notion he is probably wrong: there is every reason to believe
that the Picts spoke a Celtic dialect; but it is true, nevertheless, that the popular speech of the south-eastern half of Scotland
at this period was, as he assumes, a Gothic dialect, though derived not from the Picts, but from the Anglian and Danish settlers, who had occupied the whole of that region partially, and a
great part of it exclusively, ever since the seventh century.

LUC DE LA BARRE.—GUICHARD DE BEAULIEU.

Another early trouvère whose history connects him with England is Luc de la Barre, famous for the satirical rhymes which he

* Essay, p. lxlv.   † Halles, Annals, i. 195.   ‡ Essay, p. lxvi.

composed against Henry I., and for the terrible punishment (the
extinction of his sight) which he drew down upon himself from
the exasperated king.   It appears, however, that it was not till
after repeated and extreme provocation, and the abuse of much
clemency, that Henry took this savage revenge.   De la Barre,
who was a distinguished Norman baron and warrior as well as a
poet, had espoused the cause of Duke Robert in the quarrel between the two brothers; but, although, in the course of the contest of arms for the possession of the duchy, he had been several
times taken prisoner, he had always been dismissed without
ransom by the English king, perhaps out of respect to his
poetical talents or reputation, till he at last, in a fatal hour for
himself, turned against his benefactor with his pen as well as
with his sword.   Henry was perhaps stung more by the in-
gratitude of the poet than by the sharpness of his sarcasms; or,
at any rate, as De la Rue insinuates, if it was an acute feeling of
the wit and the poetry which actuated him, there was still something generous and high-minded even in an excess of such sensibility.   There is nothing, however, of De la Barre's remaining.

Guichard (or Guiscard) de Beaulieu describes himself as a
monk, and is supposed by M. de la Rue to have belonged to
the priory of that name, which was a dependency of the abbey of
St. Albans.   Mr. Wright, however, doubts this, and thinks that
Beaulieu was probably his family name.* His only known work
is a sort of sermon, in French verse, on the vices of the age, consisting of nearly 2000 Alexandrine lines.   It has been edited by
M. Achille Jubinal, 8vo. Paris, 1834.   It appears to have been
intended for a popular audience.   The poetical preacher begins
by telling his hearers that he is not going to speak to them in
Latin, but in Romance, in order that all may understand him.
" The mention of sermons in verse," observes De la Rue, "may
perhaps surprise the reader; but it is certain that at this epoch,
at least among the Normans and the Anglo-Normans, it was customary to read to the people the lives of the Saints in French
verse, on Sundays and holidays."† Guichard's poetry is described as often naïve and graceful in expression, and sweet in
its flow; and he is the first writer who is known to have introduced into the romance poetry the practice of preserving the
same rhyme throughout each stanza or paragraph, extending

* Biog. Brit. Lit., ii. 132.   † Essais, ii. 138.

sometimes to thirty, sixty, or even eighty lines or more*—a fashion followed by many succeeding writers in ten and twelve syllabled verse, and which De la Rue conceives Guichard must have borrowed from the Welsh, or their kindred the Armoricans.

ARTHURIAN ROMANCE:—THE SAINT GREAL.—LUC DU GAST.—BORON.—MAPES.

We cannot here attempt to take up the intricate and obscure question of the origin of the Arthurian body of Romance, including the romances of the Round Table and those of the quest of the Saint Greal, about which so much has been written, in great part to little purpose except to be refuted by the next inquirer. In addition to the earlier speculations of Warburton, Tyrwhitt, Warton, Percy, and Ritson, and to what has been more recently advanced by Ellis, Southey, Scott, Dunlop, and other writers among ourselves, the Preface of the late Mr. Price to his edition of Warton's History of English Poetry (pp. 68, &c.), and the Introduction to Britannia after the Romans (pp. vi. &c.), may be pointed out to the reader's attention. The theory of the author of the last-mentioned treatise is in some respects new and curious. "The great Work," he observes, "and, as I may say, the Alcoran, of Arthurian romance was the Book of the Saint Greal. In truth, it is no romance, but a blasphemous imposture, more extravagant and daring than any other on record, in which it is endeavoured to pass off the mysteries of bardism for direct inspirations of the Holy Ghost." The original work, this writer holds, was actually composed in Welsh, as it professes to have been, in the year 717. "Greal," he says, "is a Welsh word, signifying an aggregate of principles, a magazine; and the elementary world, or world of spirits, was called the *Country of the Greal*. From thence the word Greal, and in Latin Gradalis, came to signify a vessel in which various messes might be mixed up." The Saint Greal, according to the common account in the British romances, which appears to be derived from the

* The commencing stanza of Parise la Duchesse (considered as one of the parts of the Roman des Douze Pairs de France), which has been published under the care of M. G. F. de Martonne, 12mo. Paris, 1836, consists of 119 lines, all ending with the same rhyme.

apocryphal gospel of Nicodemus, is the plate from which Christ
ate his last supper, and which is said to have been appropriated
by Joseph of Arimathea, and to have been afterwards used by
him to collect the blood that flowed from the wounds of the
Redeemer.   It makes a great figure in the romantic history of
Arthur and his Knights of the Round Table, as may be seen in
'he eleventh and subsequent books of the popular compilation
entitled Morte Darthus.   The author of Britannia after the
Romans maintains that the original Welsh Book of the Saint
Greal was unquestionably the work of the bard Tysilio.   De la
Rue holds that the original romances on the quest of the Saint
Greal, or Saint Graal, are to be considered as forming quite a
distinct body of fiction from those relating to the Round Table,
and that much misapprehension has arisen from confounding the
two.   The account given by him is in substance as follows :—
The oldest verse romance on the subject of the Saint Greal appears
to have been composed by Chrétien de Troyes about the year
1170; but of his work only some fragments remain, and the
earliest entire romance now existing which treats of this subject
is the prose Roman de Tristan, written by Luc du Gast, who
was a person of family and property; he calls himself Chevalier and Sire du Chastel du Gast—that is, according to M.
de la Rue, Gast in Normandy, now situated in the canton of
St. Sever, and the department of Calvados.   Although of
Norman descent, however, he was a native and inhabitant of
England: he resided, he tells us, near Salisbury; and, if his
French should not always be correct, he begs his readers to
excuse him on the score of his English birth and breeding.   It
was from this prose romance, the Abbé proceeds to state, and
from a continuation of it by Walter Map, or Mapes, already
mentioned, whose work is entitled Roman des Diverses Quêtes
du Saint Graal, and is dedicated to Henry II., that Chrétien de
Troyes soon after drew the materials of his verse romance, which
is called the Roman du Saint Graal, or sometimes the Roman
de Perceval.   But both Luc du Gast and Walter Map, and also
Robert de Borron, who likewise wrote in this age a prose Roman
du Saint Graal (which, however, is merely a life of Joseph of
Arimathea), all declare that they translated from a Latin
original, which they say had been drawn up by order of King
Arthur himself, and deposited by him in the library of the
cathedral of Salisbury.   Another romance on the subject of the

Saint Greal, which is now lost, is attributed to a writer named
Gace le Blount, who is said to have been a relation of Henry II.
Map, in addition to his Roman des Diverses Quêtes, which is
in two parts, continued the history of the knights who had
engaged in the search for the Saint Greal in a third romance,
also in prose, which he entitled La Mort d'Artur; and he is
also the author of another prose romance on the adventures
of Lancelot du Lac. Upon one of the incidents in this last,
Chrétien de Troyes founded his verse romance, also still extant,
entitled Lancelot de la Charette. From another prose romance
by Robert de Borron, on the subject of the enchanter Merlin, an
Anglo-Norman trouvère of the latter part of the thirteenth
century composed a verse romance, which is still preserved,
entitled Merlyn Ambroise. Finally, in association with his
relation Elie de Borron, and with another writer called Rusticien
de Pise, Robert de Borron produced a prose translation of the
Historia Britonum of Geoffroy of Monmouth, and also the two
romances of Moliadus de Leonois and Giron le Courtois; and
Elie de Borron wrote by himself the Roman de Palamedes. *
    Thus far the Abbé de la Rue. Since his work appeared,
however, some parts of his statement have been corrected or
controverted by M. Michel and other recent writers. In the
elaborate Introduction to his edition of Tristan, to be presently
mentioned (Paris, 1835), M. Michel, accepting his own account
of himself, maintains Luc, or Luces, to whom he attributes either
the invention, or at least the first translation from the Latin, of
that romance, to have been an Englishman, and lord of a château
in the neighbourhood of Salisbury, the name of which is variously
given in the manuscripts as Gat, Gast, Gad, Gant, and Gail.
Henry II., M. Michel further states, delighted with this prose
work of Luce, engaged Walter Map to follow it up in the same
style with the Romance of Lancelot; and Robert de Buron,
Borron, or Bowron, to add that of the Saint Greal: finally,
Hoyle de Buron, a brother, or at least a relation, of Robert,
revised the whole, and gave a unity and completeness to the
cycle by finishing the story of Tristram.
    In the Notice prefixed to his publication, from the MS. in
the Bibliothèque du Roi, now the Bibliothèque Impériale, of the
Roman du Saint Greal, in old French verse (12mo. Bordeaux,
1841), M. Michel states that Map, by order of Henry II., drew

* De la Rue, Essais Historiques, ii. 206—248.

up the Romance of the Saint Graal in Latin from the songs and
lays of the bards of Britany; and that his work was afterwards
translated into French by Robert de Borron. The Roman de
Perceval of Chrestien de Troyes is not, he says, a romance of
the Saint Graal at all; it only contains the last adventures of the
Saint Graal. The poem which he publishes, and which is
incomplete, extends to 4018 octosyllabic lines.*

ROMAN DU ROI HORN.

It will be most convenient to notice here the French metrical
Romance of King Horn (Roman du Roi Horn). This is the
work of a poet who calls himself "Mestre Thomas," and is
regarded by Ritson and M. de la Rue as a composition of the
latter part of the twelfth century, and as the original of the
English Horne Childe, or Geste of Kyng Horn; but by other
eminent authorities, such as Bishop Percy and the late learned
editor of Warton, the English poem has been held to be the

* "Walter Mapes," says Mr. Wright, "was distinguished as a writer in the
Anglo-Norman language, as well as in Latin. It is to him we owe a large
portion of the cycle of the romances of the Round Table in the earliest form
in which they are known. This first series of three romances consists of the
Roman de St. Graal, or the history of the Graal before its pretended arrival in
Britain, brought by Joseph of Arimathea; of the Roman de Merlin; of the
Roman de Lancelot du Lac; of the Quête du Saint Graal, which is a sequel to
the adventures of Lancelot; and of the death of King Arthur, forming the
Roman de la Mort Arthus. The three latter were the work of Mapes, as we
learn from the concluding paragraph of the Mort Arthus, and from a later
writer of another branch of the series, Helie de Borron, who completed the
Roman de Tristan in the reign of Henry III. These authorities appear to
intimate that Mapes translated his romances from a Latin original, which is
distinctly stated in some of the manuscripts; but we have no other evidence
of the existence of such an original, and it is probable that a great part of the
incidents of the story was the work of the writer's own imagination, the whole
being founded on popular legends then floating about."—Biog. Brit. Lit., II.
304.

Mr. Wright adds that the manuscripts containing this series of pure romances, though rather numerous, are mostly no older than the latter half of
the thirteenth century and the beginning of the fourteenth, no one being
known which can be assigned to the age in which the authors lived; and that
from this circumstance, and the fact that most of them were written in France,
they cannot be regarded as representing accurately the language in which
they were originally written.

earlier of the two; and in this latter opinion both Mr. Wright
and Sir F. Madden concur. A few extracts from this French
romance were given by Ritson in the notes to his edition of
the English Geste (Ancient English Metrical Romances, iii.
264–281); others were printed by M. de la Rue (Essais Hist.
ii. 251–260); and a complete edition by M. Francisque Michel has
long been announced, to include also the English romance from a
text prepared by Mr. Wright. Bishop Percy ascribed the English
Kyng Horn to so early a date as "within a century after the
Conquest;" and, although in its present form it is probably not
older than the latter part of the thirteenth century, Mr. Price has
no hesitation in expressing his belief that it owes its origin to a
period even long anterior to the date assigned by Percy.[*]

TRISTAN, OR TRISTREM.

To the author of the Roi Horn or to another Thomas the French
metrical Roman de Tristan is also ascribed. All that remains of
this romance is a fragment of 1811 verses.[†] There can hardly
be a doubt that it is an earlier composition than the English Sir
Tristrem, published by Sir Walter Scott, from the Auchinleck
MS., and attributed by him to Thomas of Ercildown, styled the
Rhymer, who is admitted to have belonged to the latter part of
the thirteenth century; but whether the author of the French
romance be the Thomas of Britany referred to as his chief
authority by Gotfried von Strasburgh, a German minstrel of the
thirteenth century, by whom there remains a long metrical
romance, in his own language, on the subject of Sir Tristrem—
whether he be the same Thomas to whom we owe the Roman
du Roi Horn (which Scott was also inclined to claim as a translation from another English romance of his Thomas of Ercildown),
—and what may be the real connexion between either the French

---

[*] Warton (edit. of 1840), i. 41.

[†] There is another fragment, of 996 verses, of a romance of Tristan, which
has been assumed to belong to the same work; but it appears now to be
agreed that the two fragments are parts of two different poems written by
different authors. Abstracts, in English, by the late Mr. George Ellis are
given of both in the Appendix to Sir Walter Scott's edition of the English
Romance of Sir Tristrem. Both were among the MSS. of the late Mr.
Douce, and are now in the Bodleian Library.

or the German Tristrem and the English—as well as whether
the latter work be the Sir Tristrem of Thomas of Erceildown
mentioned by Robert de Brunne (in the early part of the fourteenth century)—or to what age, country, and author it is to
be assigned—are questions upon which we cannot enter. They
will be found profusely discussed in Scott's Introduction and
Notes to his edition of Sir Tristrem (8vo. Edinb. 1803); in a
long Note, in reply to his views, by Mr. Price, inserted at the
end of the first volume of his edition of Warton's History
(pp. 181-198, and, with additional notes by Mr. Wright, Sir F.
Madden, and the late Rev. Richard Garnett, in the edition of
1840, i. 95-112); in an Advertisement by Mr. Lockhart, prefixed
to his republication of Scott's volume (12mo. Edinb. 1833); in
M. de la Rue's Essais Historiques (ii. 251-269); in a valuable
paper, known to be by Sir Frederick Madden, in the Gentleman's Magazine for October, 1833 (vol. civ., pp. 307-312); and
in M. Michel's elaborate Introduction to his publication of The
Poetical Romances of Tristan in French, in Anglo-Norman, and
in Greek (2 vols. 12mo. London and Paris, 1835).

GUERNES DE PONT SAINTE MAXENCE.

M. de la Rue mentions, in one of his papers in the Archæologia,
a Life of Becket in French verse by a contemporary of the name
of Guernes, an ecclesiastic of Pont Sainte Maxence, in Picardy,
which is curious from the statement of the author that he had
several times read his composition publicly at the tomb of the
archbishop. This, the Abbé observes, would seem to show that,
in the time of Henry II., the Romance or old French was understood in England even by many of the common people.[*]
Guernes appears to have begun his poem in France; but he
came over to England in 1172, and finished it here in 1177. It
consists of above 6000 lines, in stanzas in each of which all the
verses terminate in the same rhyme. The only manuscript of it
known to De la Rue was one in the Harleian collection (No.
270); but another has since been discovered in the ducal library
at Wolfenbüttel, from which the poem has been published by
Immanuel Bekker, under the title of Leben des h. Thomas von

* Archæologia, xII. 394.

Canterbury, Altfranzœisch (8vo. Berlin, 1838). The Wolfenbüttel manuscript, however, wants the beginning, and contains
only about 5220 lines.*

HERMAN.

A writer named Herman, who calls himself a priest, and was
no doubt of English birth, is the author of several religious
romance poems:—a Life of Tobias, in about 1400 verses, written
at the request of William prior of Kenilworth, in Warwickshire
(Kenoilleworth en Ardenne); another of 1152 verses on the
birth of the Redeemer, entitled Les Joies de Notre Dame; a
third of 844 verses on a curious theme,—Smoke, Rain, and
Woman considered as the three disturbers of a man's domestic
comforts,—which was given him, it seems, by Alexander, bishop
of Lincoln; a fourth, in 712 verses, on the Miracles of Magdalen
of Marseilles; a fifth, on the life, death, and burial of the Virgin
Mary; a sixth, a sort of mystery, or scriptural drama, on the
divine scheme of redemption, also written at the request of the
prior of Kenilworth; and a seventh, a History of the ten ancient
Sibyls, extending to 2496 verses, which professes to be a translation from the Latin, and which he composed at the desire of
the Empress Matilda. The era of this poet is ascertained from
that of his patron, Alexander, bishop of Lincoln, who died in
1147, and that of Matilda, who died in 1167, while he was employed on his last-mentioned work.

* An account of Gnermes, nearly the same as in the Archæologia, is given
by De la Rue in his Essais (vol. ii. pp. 809—815), under the name of Gervais de Pont Ste. Maxence. In the Harleian MS. the poem is entitled, in
Latin, Vita Thome Cantuar. per Guernes de Ponte Sti Maxontii. This title
is in a more recent hand than the poem; and under "Guernes" is written
"Garnerius." He is called "Gervais," or "Gervois," by the transcriber of
another work. "This poem," says Mr. Wright, "is especially valuable in a
philological point of view, because we know the exact date at which it was
written. It is historically important as the earliest of the Lives of Becket.
Guernes tells us ... that he had collected his materials from Becket's friends
and acquaintance, that he had repeatedly and carefully corrected it, and that
he had read it many times at the martyr's tomb. His narrative is very clear
and vigorous, and furnishes valuable information not found in the same detail
in the other biographers."—Biog. Brit. Lit. ii. 329.

HUGH OF RUTLAND.—BOSON.—SIMON DU FRESNE.

Other English trouvours of the same age were Hughes de
Rotolande, or Hugh of Rutland, who lived, it seems, according
to his own account, at Credenhill in Cornwall,* and who is the
author of two romances, each containing between 10,000 and
11,000 verses,·the Roman d'Ypomodon and its continuation the
Roman de Protesilaus, which are remarkable as having their
scene in Magna Græcia, or the south of Italy, and as not
drawing their subject from the·Welsh or Armorican legends of
Arthur and his Knights of the Round Table, which were now
become the common source of the chivalrous romance:† a
religious poet of the name of Boson, from whom we have a
volume of lives of nine of the Saints, and who the Abbé de la
Rue thinks may have been the same person with a learned
theologian of that name who was nephew and secretary to Pope
Adrian IV.;‡ and Simon du Fresne, canon of the Cathedral of
Hereford (sometimes called by later authorities Simon Ash), the
friend and correspondent of Giraldus Cambrensis, and well
known among the Latin versifiers of his time, who has left us a
French poem of considerable merit entitled in one manuscript
Dictié du Clerc et de la Philosophie, in another Romance Dame
Fortune, founded on the favourite classic work of the middle
ages, Boethius De Consolatione Philosophiæ.§

CARDINAL LANGTON.

De la Rue has introduced among his Anglo-Norman poets of
the twelfth or the early part of the thirteenth century the great
Stephen Langton, who was archbishop of Canterbury from
1207 to 1228, and also a cardinal. The only undoubted specimen
of Cardinal Langton's French poetry occurs, strangely enough, in
the course of one of his Latin Sermons (preserved in one of the
Arundel MSS., now in the British Museum), where, deserting his
prose and the more learned language, he suddenly breaks out

---

* There is a place of this name in Hereford.
† See an account of these two poems in De la Rue, Essais, II. 285-290.
‡ Id. pp. 297-300.
§ Id. pp. 829-834. See also Wright, Biog. Brit. Lit., II. 349, 850.

into song in the idiom of the trouveurs, and, after having pronounced eight graceful and lively lines relating how "belle Alice" rose betimes, and, having bedecked herself, went out into a garden and there gathered five flowers which she wove into a chaplet, proceeds throughout the remainder of the discourse to make a mystical application of the several points of this little anecdote to the Holy Virgin—exclaiming at the close of each enthusiastic paragraph,

> Ceste est la bele Aliz,
> Ceste est la flur, ceste est le lis.
> (She is the fair Alice,
> She is the flower, she is the lily.)*

"It will be admitted," remarks the Abbé de la Rue, "that the taste for French poetry must have been very general in England when we find the chief prelate of the kingdom taking this way of conciliating the attention of his audience." The Abbé thinks it highly probable that Cardinal Langton is also the author of two poetical pieces which occur in the same manuscript with his sermon; the first a little theological drama on the subject of the Fall and Restoration of Man, the other a canticle or song, of 126 strophes, on the Passion of Christ. Both are stated to be of considerable merit.

— ·

KING RICHARD CŒUR-DE-LION.

Finally, we have to enrol in this list of the early English writers of French poetry the renowned King Richard I., if we may put faith in old tradition. Among the poetical performances attributed to Richard are several Sirventes or *Serventois*,† and his share in the song formerly composed between them, which, according to the well-known story, discovered him in his prison to his faithful minstrel Blondel, the strain begun by the latter having been taken up and finished by the king. But all this, it

---

* Mr. Wright has printed the entire sermon, in his Biog. Brit. Lit., ii. 416, 417.

† M. de la Rue shows that, originally and properly, a *Serventois*, or *Sirvente* (the former the northern, the latter the southern term), was a poem relating to military affairs, from *serventagium* or *sirventagium*, the low Latin for *servitium*, service; according to the definition in Ducange, "Poemata in quibus *servientium* seu militum facta et *arcilla* referuntur."

must be confessed, is not so clear or certain as were to be desired.
The song said to have been sung by Richard and Blondel was
printed by Mademoiselle l'Héritier in her volume entitled La
Tour Ténébreuse et les Jours Lumineux, 12mo. Paris, 1705; it
is in mixed Norman and Provençal; but, unfortunately, the
manuscript from which it professes to have been extracted is now
unknown.   Mlle. l'Héritier also prints as a composition of
Richard a love-song in Norman French.   But the most celebrated composition attributed to Richard is a poem addressed by
him from his prison to his barons of England, Normandy, Poitou,
and Gascony, remonstrating with them for suffering him to
remain so long a captive.   A Provençal version of this poem,
one of the stanzas of which only had been previously quoted by
Crescimbini in his Istoria della Volgar Poesia, was first printed
from a manuscript in the library of San Lorenzo at Florence by
Horace Walpole, in his Catalogue of Royal and Noble Authors,
1758.   It consists of six stanzas of six lines each, with an Envoy
of five lines.   Two English verse translations of it have been
produced; one by Dr. Burney, in his History of Music, the other
by the late Mr. George Ellis, which is given in Park's edition of
the Royal and Noble Authors.   More recently, the appearance
of a version of the same poem in Norman French in Sismondi's
Littérature du Midi de l'Europe (vol. i. p. 149) has raised the
question in which of the two dialects it was originally written.[*]
Meanwhile the Provençal version has been more correctly republished by Raynouard in the fourth volume of his Choix des
Poésies Originales des Troubadours.   And the poetical reputation of Richard has been also enlarged by the appearance of
another Provençal song claiming to be of his inditing in the
Parnasse Occitanien (by the Comte de Rochegude), 2 vols. 8vo.,
Toulouse, 1819.   It cannot be said, however, that any or all of
those effusions, supposing their authenticity to be admitted, tend
to give us a high idea of the genius of the lion-hearted king in this
line,—even if we should not go the length of Walpole, who
declares the particular poem he has printed to be so poor a composition that the internal evidence weighs with him more than
anything else to believe it of his majesty's own fabric.[†]

    [*] See it also in M. Le Roux de Lincy's Recueil de Chants Historiques
(1812), I. 59.
    [†] See, for notices of other compositions attributed to Richard, Wright's
Biog. Brit. Lit., II. 324 –327.

From the Norman Conquest to the termination of the reign of the seventh Norman sovereign, King John, is almost exactly a century and a half, even to a day. The victory of Hastings was gained on the 14th of October, 1066, and John died on the 19th of October, 1216. His death, happening at the time it did, was probably an event of the greatest importance. The political constitution, or system of government, established by the Conquest, —a system of pure monarchy or absolutism—had been formally brought to an end the year before by the grant of the Great Charter wrung from the crown by the baronage, which at any rate tempered the monarchical despotism by the introduction of the aristocratic element into the theory of the constitution ; but this might have proved little more than a theoretical or nominal innovation if John had lived. His death, and the non-age of his son and heir, left the actual management of affairs in the hands of those by whom the constitutional reform had been brought about ; and that reform became a practical reality. At the least, its legal character and authority never were disputed ; no attempt ever was made to repeal it ; on the contrary it was ratified no less than six times in the single reign of Henry III., John's successor ; and it has retained its proper place at the head of the Statute Book down to our own day. Its proper place ; for it is indeed our first organic law, the true commencement or foundation-stone, of the constitution. Before it there was no mechanism in our political system, no balance of forces or play of counteracting elements and tendencies ; nothing but the sort of life and movement that may belong to a stone or a cannon-ball or any other mere mass. The royal power was all in all. With the Charter, and the death of the last despotic king, from whom it was extorted, begins another order of things both political and social. It may be likened to the passing away of the night and the dawning of a new day. In particular, the Charter may be said to have consummated by a solemn legislative fiat the blending and incorporation of the two races, the conquerors and the conquered, which had been actively going on without any such sanction, and under the natural influence of circumstances only, throughout the preceding half-century,—having commenced, we may reckon, perhaps, half a century earlier, or about the middle of the reign of Henry I. There is, at least, not a word in this law making the least reference to any distinction between the two races. Both are spoken of throughout only as English; the nation is again recognized as one, as fully as it had been before either William the Norman or Canute the Dane.

We have thus four successive periods of about half a century each:—The first, from the Danish to the Norman Conquest,—half English, half Danish; the Second, from the Norman Conquest to the middle of the reign of Henry I., in which the subjugated English and their French or Norman rulers were completely divided; the Third and Fourth extending to the date of Magna Charta, and presenting, the former the comparatively slow, the latter the accelerated, process of the intermixture and fusion of the two races. Some of our old chroniclers would make the third half-century also, as well as the first and second, to have been inaugurated by a great constitutional or political event: as the year 1016 is memorable for the Danish and the year 1066 for the Norman Conquest, so in 1116, we are told by Stow, "On the 19th day of April, King Henry called a council of all the States of his realm, both of the Prelates, Nobles, and Commons, to Salisbury, there to consult for the good government of the Commonwealth, and the weighty affairs of the same, which council, taking the name and fame of the French, is called a Parliament;" "and this," he adds, "do the historiographers note to be the first Parliament in England, and that the kings before that time were never went to call any of their Commons or people to council or lawmaking." This theory of the origin of our parliamentary government must, indeed, be rejected;[*] but the year 1116 will still remain notable as that in which Henry, reversing what had been done fifty years before, crossed the sea with an army of English to reduce his ancestral Normandy, or prevent it from falling into the hands of the son of his unfortunate older brother. Even the next stage, half a century further on, when we have supposed the amalgamation of the two races to have assumed its accelerated movement, may be held to be less precisely indicated by such events as the appointment of Becket, said to be the first Englishman since the Conquest promoted to high office either in the Church or the State, to the archbishopric of Canterbury in 1161,—the enactment in 1164 of the Constitu-

[*] See Sir H. Spelman, Concilia; ad an. 1116.

tions of Clarendon, by which the clergy, a body essentially foreign in feeling and to a great extent even of foreign birth, were brought somewhat more under subjection to the law of the land—and the Conquest of Ireland in 1172, to the vast exaltation of the English name and power.

What was the history of the vernacular language for this first century and a half after the Norman Conquest, throughout which everything native would thus seem to have been in a course of gradual re-emergence from the general foreign inundation that had overwhelmed the country? We have no historical record or statement as to this matter: the question can only be answered, in so far as it can be answered at all, from an examination of such compositions of the time in the vernacular tongue as may have come down to us.

The principal literature of this period, it will have been seen from the above notices, was in the Latin and French languages. In the former were written most works on subjects of theology, philosophy, and history; in the latter most of those intended rather to amuse than to inform, and addressed, not to students and professional readers, but to the idlers of the court and the upper classes, by whom they were seldom actually read, or much expected to be read, but only listened to as they were recited or chanted (for most of them were in verse) by others. How far over society such a knowledge of the imported tongue came to extend as was requisite for the understanding and enjoyment of what was thus written in it has been matter of dispute. The Abbé de la Rue conceives that a large proportion even of the middle classes, and of the town population generally, must have been so far frenchified; but later authorities look upon this as an extravagant supposition.

It is, at all events, this French literature only that is to be considered as having come into competition with, or to have taken the place of, the old vernacular literature. The employment of the Latin language in writing by monks, secular churchmen, and other persons who had had a learned education, was what had always gone on in England as in every other country of Western Christendom; there was nothing now in that; we continue to have it after the Conquest just as we had it before the Conquest. But it is quite otherwise with the writing of French; that was altogether a new thing in England, and indeed very much of a new thing everywhere, in the eleventh century:

no specimen of composition in the Langue d'Oyl, in fact, either in verse or in prose, has come down to us from beyond that century, nor is there reason to believe that it had been much earlier turned to account for literary purposes even in France itself. The great mass of the oldest French literature that has been preserved was produced in England, or, at any rate, in the dominions of the King of England, in the twelfth century.

To whatever portion of society in England an acquaintance with this French literature was confined, it is evident that it was for some time after the Conquest the only literature of the day that, without addressing itself exclusively to the learned classes, still demanded some measure of cultivation in its readers or auditors as well as in its authors. It was the only popular literature that was not adapted to the mere populace. We might infer this even from the fact that, if any other ever existed, it has mostly perished. The various metrical chronicles, romances, and other compositions in the French tongue, of the principal of which an account has been given, are very nearly the only literary works which have come down to us from this age. And, while the mass of this produce that has been preserved is, as we have seen, very considerable, we have distinct notices of much more which is now lost. How the French language should have acquired the position which it thus appears to have held in England for some time after the Conquest is easily explained. The advantage which it derived from being the language of the court, of the entire body of the nobility, and of the opulent and influential classes generally, is obvious. This not only gave it the prestige and attraction of what we now call fashion, but, in the circumstances to which the country was reduced, would very speedily make it the only language in which any kind of regular or grammatical training could be obtained. With the native population almost everywhere deprived of its natural leaders, the old landed proprietary of its own blood, it cannot be supposed that schools in which the reading and writing of the vernacular tongue was taught could continue to subsist. This has been often pointed out. But what we may call the social cause, or that arising out of the relative conditions of the two races, was probably assisted by another which has not been so much attended to. The languages themselves did not compete upon fair terms. The French would have in the general esti-

mation a decided advantage for the purposes of literature over
the English. The latter was held universally to be merely a
barbarous form of speech, claiming kindred with nothing except
the other half-articulate dialects of the woods, hardly one of
which had ever known what it was to have any acquaintance
with letters, or was conceived even by those who spoke it to be
fit to be used in writing except on the most vulgar occasions, or
where anything like either dignity or precision of expression
was of no importance; the former, although somewhat soiled
and disfigured by ill usage received at the hands of the uneducated multitude, and also only recently much employed in
formal or artistic eloquence, could still boast the most honourable of all pedigrees as a daughter of the Latin, and was thus
besides allied to the popular speech of every more civilized
province of Western Christendom. The very name by which it
had been known when it first attracted attention with reference
to its literary capabilities was, as we have seen, the Rustic
Latin, or Roman (*Lingua Romana Rustica*). Even without being
favoured by circumstances, as it was in the present case, a
tongue having those intrinsic recommendations would not have
been easily worsted, in a contest for the preference as the organ
of fashionable literature, by such a competitor as the unknown
and unconnected English.

There was only one great advantage possessed by the national
tongue with which it was impossible for the other in the long run
to cope. This was the fact of its being the national tongue, the
speech, actual and ancestral, of the great body of the people.
Even that, indeed, might not have enabled it to maintain its
ground if it had been a mere unwritten form of speech. But it
had been cultivated and trained for centuries both by the
practice of composition, in prose as well as in verse, and by the
application to it of the art of the grammarian. It already possessed a literature considerable in volume, and embracing a
variety of departments. It was not merely something floating
upon men's breath, but had a substantial existence in poems and
histories, in libraries and parchments. In that state it might
cease, in the storm of national calamity, to be generally either
written or read, but even its more literary inflexions and constructions would be less likely to fall into complete and universal
oblivion. The memory, at least, of its old renown would not
altogether die away; and that alone would be found to be much

when, after a time, it began to be again, although in a somewhat
altered form, employed in writing.

The nature of the altered form which distinguishes the written
vernacular tongue when it reappears after the Norman Conquest
from the aspect it presents before that date (or the earliest
modern English from what is commonly designated Saxon or
Anglo-Saxon) is not matter of dispute. "The substance of the
change,", to adopt the words of Mr. Price, the late learned editor
of Warton, "is admitted on all hands to consist in the suppression of those grammatical intricacies occasioned by the inflection
of nouns, the seemingly arbitrary distinctions of gender, the
government of prepositions, &c."[*] It was, in fact, the conversion of an inflectional into a non-inflectional, of a synthetic
into an analytic, language. The syntactical connexion of words,
and the modification of the mental conceptions which they
represent, was indicated, no longer, in general, by those variations which constitute what are called declension and conjugation,
but by separate particles, or simply by juxtaposition; and whatever seemed to admit of being neglected without injury to the
prime object of expressing the meaning of the speaker, or writer,
—no matter what other purposes it might serve of a merely
ornamental or artistic nature—was ruthlessly dispensed with.

A change such as this is unquestionably the breaking up of a
language. In the first instance, at least, it amounts to the
destruction of much that is most characteristic of the language,
—of all that constitutes its beauty to the educated mind, imbued
with a feeling for the literature into which it has been wrought,
—of something, probably, even of its precision as well as of its
expressiveness in a higher sense. It has become, in a manner,
but the skeleton of what it was, or the skeleton with only the
skin hanging loose upon it:—all the covering and rounding flesh
gone. Or we may say it is the language no longer with its old
natural bearing and suitable attire, but reduced to the rags and
squalor of a beggar. Or it may be compared to a material
edifice, once bright with many of the attractions of decorative
architecture, now stripped of all its splendours and left only a
collection of bare and dilapidated walls. It may be, too, that, as
is commonly assumed, a synthetic tongue is essentially a nobler
and more effective instrument of expression than an analytic
one,—that, often comprising a whole sentence, or at least a whole

[*] Preface to Warton's Hist. of Eng. Poetry, p. 81.

clause, in a word, it presents thoughts and emotions in flashes and pictures where the other can only employ comparatively dead conventional signs. But perhaps the comparison has been too commonly made between the synthetic tongue in its perfection and the analytic one while only in its rudimentary state. The language may be considered to have changed its constitution, somewhat like a country which should have ceased to be a monarchy and become a republic. The new political system could only be fairly compared with the old one, and the balance struck between the advantages of the one and those of the other, after the former should have had time fully to develop itself under the operation of its own peculiar principles. Even if it be inferior upon the whole, and for the highest purposes, an analytic language may perhaps have some recommendations which a synthetic one does not possess. It may not be either more natural or, properly speaking, more simple, for the original constitution of most, if not of all, languages seems to have been synthetic, and a synthetic language is as easy both to acquire and to wield as an analytic one to those to whom it is native; nor can the latter be said to be more rational or philosophical than the former, for, as being in the main natural products, and not artificial contrivances, languages must be held to stand all on an equality in respect of the reasonableness at least of the principle on which they are constituted; but yet, if comparatively defective in poetical expressiveness, analytic languages will probably be found, whenever they have been sufficiently cultivated, to be capable, in pure exposition, of rendering thought with superior minuteness and distinctness of detail. With their small tenacity or cohesion, they penetrate into every chink and fold, like water or fine dust.

But the great question in every case of the apparent conversion of a synthetic into an analytic language is, how, or under the operation of what cause or causes, the change was brought about. In the particular case before us, for instance, what was it that converted the form of our vernacular tongue which we find alone employed in writing before the Norman Conquest into the comparatively uninflected form in which it appears in the generality of the compositions which have come down to us from the first ages after that great political and social catastrophe?

First, however, we may remark that there is no proof of the latter form having been really new, or of recent origin, about the

time of the Conquest. All that we can assert is, that soon after
that date it first appears in writing. If it was ever so employed
before, no earlier specimens of it have been preserved. It was
undoubtedly the form of the language popularly in use at the
time when it thus first presents itself in our national literature.
But did it not exist as an oral dialect long before? May it not
have so existed from the remotest antiquity alongside of the
more artificial form which was exclusively, or at least usually,
employed in writing? It has been supposed that even the
classical Greek and Latin, such as we find in books, may have
always been accompanied each by another form of speech, of looser
texture, and probably more of an analytical character, which
served for the ordinary oral intercourse of the less educated
population, and of which it has even been conjectured we may
have some much disguised vestige or resemblance in the modern
Romaic and Italian. The rise, at any rate, of what was long a
merely oral dialect into a language capable of being employed in
literature, and of thereby being gradually so trained and improved as to supplant and take the place of the ancient more
highly inflected and otherwise more artificial literary language of
the country, is illustrated by what is known to have happened in
France and other continental provinces of the old Empire of the
West, where the *Romana Rustica*, as it was called, which was a
corrupted or broken-down form of the proper Latin, after having
been for some centuries only orally used, came to be written
as well as spoken, and, having been first taken into the service
of the more popular kinds of literature, ended by becoming the
language of all literature and the only national speech. So in
this country there may possibly have been in use for colloquial
purposes a dialect of a similar character to our modern analytic
English even from the earliest days of the old synthetic English;
and the two forms of the language, the regular and the irregular, the learned and the vulgar, the mother and the daughter, or
rather, if you will, the elder and the younger sister, may have
subsisted together for many centuries, till there came a crisis
which for a time laid the entire fabric of the old national
civilization in the dust, when the rude and hardy character of
the one carried it through the storm which the more delicate
structure of the other could not stand.

Or was the written English of the twelfth and thirteenth
centuries the same English (or Anglo-Saxon) that was written in

the ninth and tenth, only modified by that process of gradual
change the principle of which was inherent in the constitution of
the language? Was the former neither the sister nor the daughter of the latter, but the latter merely at a different stage of its
natural growth? This is the view that has been maintained by
some eminent authorities. The late Mr. Price, acknowledging it
to be a matter beyond dispute "that some change had taken
place in the style of composition and general structure of the
language" from the end of the ninth to the end of the twelfth
century, adds :—" But that those mutations were a consequence
of the Norman invasion, or were even accelerated by that event,
is wholly incapable of proof; and nothing is supported upon a
firmer principle of rational induction, than that the same effects
would have ensued if William and his followers had remained in
their native soil."[*] The change, as we have seen, may be said to
have amounted to the transformation of the language from one
of a synthetic to one of an analytic constitution or structure;
but Mr. Price contends that, whether it is to be considered as the
result of an innate law of the language, or of some general law
in the organization of those who spoke it, its having been in no
way dependent upon external circumstances,—upon foreign
influence or political disturbance,—is established by the undeni-
able fact that every other language of the Low-German stock
displays the same simplification of its grammar. "In all these
languages," he observes, "there has been a constant tendency to
relieve themselves of that precision which chooses a fresh symbol
for every shade of meaning, to lessen the amount of nice distinctions, and detect as it were a royal road to the interchange of
opinion. Yet, in thus diminishing their grammatical forms and
simplifying their rules, in this common effort to evince a striking contrast to the usual effects of civilization, all confusion has
been prevented by the very manner in which the operation has
been conducted; for the revolution produced has been so gradual
in its progress, that it is only to be discovered on a comparison
of the respective languages at periods of a considerable interval."[†]

The interval that Mr. Price has taken in the present case is
certainly wide enough. What has to be explained is the difference
that we find between the written English of the middle of the
twelfth century and that, not of the age of Alfred, or the end of

the ninth century, but rather of the end of the eleventh. The question is, how we are to account for a great change which would appear to have taken place in the language, as employed for literary purposes, not in three centuries, but in one century, or even in half a century. The English of Alfred continues to be in all respects the English of Alfric, who lived and wrote more than a century later. The National Chronicle, still written substantially in the old language, comes down even to the year 1154. It is probable that we have here the continued employment, for the sake of uniformity, of an idiom which had now become antique, or what is called dead; but there is certainly no evidence or trace of any other form of the national speech having ever been used in writing before the year 1100 at the earliest. The overthrow of the native government and civilization by the Conquest in the latter part of the eleventh century would not, of course, extinguish the knowledge of the old literary language of the country till after the lapse of about a generation. We may fairly, then, regard the change in question as having taken place, in all probability, not in three centuries, as Mr. Price puts the case, but within at most the third part of that space. This correction, while it brings the breaking up of the language into close connexion in point of time with the social revolution, gives it also much more of a sudden and convulsionary character than it has in Mr. Price's representation. The gradual and gentle flow, assumed to have extended over three centuries, turns out to have been really a rapid precipitous descent—something almost of the nature of a cataract—effected possibly within the sixth or eighth part of that space of time.

It may be that there is a tendency in certain languages, or in all languages, to undergo a similar simplification of their grammar to that which the English underwent at this crisis. And it is conceivable that such a tendency constantly operating unchecked may at last produce such a change as we have in the present case, the conversion of the language from one of a synthetic to one of an analytic structure. That may have happened with those other languages of the Low-Germanic stock to which Mr. Price refers. But such was certainly not the case with the English. We have that language distinctly before us for three or four centuries, during which it is not pretended that there is to be detected a trace of the operation of any such tendency. The tendency, therefore, either did not exist, or must have been rendered inoperative by some counteracting influence. If, on the other hand, we are to suppose that, in our own or in any other language, the tendency suddenly developed itself or became active at a particular moment, that would necessarily imply the very operation of a now external cause which Mr. Price's theory denies. It is no matter whether we may or may not be able to point out the cause; that a cause there must have been is unquestionable.

In the case before us, the cause is sufficiently obvious. The integrity of the constitution or grammatical system of the language was preserved so long as its literature flourished; when that ceased to be read and studied and produced, the grammatical cultivation and knowledge of the language also ceased. The two things, indeed, were really one and the same. The literature and the literary form of the language could not but live and die together. Whatever killed the one was sure also to blight the other. And what was it that did or could bring the native literature of England suddenly to an end in the eleventh or twelfth century except the new political and social circumstances in which the country was then placed? What other than such a cause ever extinguished in any country the light of its ancient literature?

Of at least two similar cases we have a perfect knowledge. How long did the classical Latin continue to be a living language? Just so long as the fabric of Latin civilization in the Western Empire continued to exist; so long, and no longer. When that was overthrown, the literature which was its product and exponent, its expression and in a manner its very soul, and the highly artificial form of language which was the material in which that literature was wrought, were both at once struck with a mortal disease under which they perished almost with the generation that had witnessed the consummation of the barbaric invasion. Exactly similar is the history of the classic Greek, only that it continued to exist as a living language for a thousand years after the Latin, the social system with which it was bound up, of which it was part and parcel, lasting so much longer. When that fell, with the fall of the Eastern Empire in the fifteenth century, the language also became extinct. The ancient Greek gave place to the modern Greek, or what is called the Romaic. The conquest of Constantinople by the Turks was to the Greek language the same thing that the Norman Conquest was to the English.

THE THIRTEENTH AND FOURTEENTH CENTURIES.—ASCENDANCY OF THE SCHOLASTIC PHILOSOPHY.

Ever since the appearance of Peter Lombard's Four Books of Sentences, about the middle of the twelfth century, a struggle for ascendancy had been going on throughout Europe between the Scholastic Theology, or new philosophy, and the grammatical and rhetorical studies with which men had previously been chiefly occupied. At first the natural advantages of its position told in favour of the established learning; nay an impulse and a new inspiration were probably given to poetry and the belles-lettres for a time by the competition of logic and philosophy, and the general intellectual excitement thus produced: it was in the latter part of the twelfth century that the writing of Latin verse was cultivated with the greatest success; it was at the very end of that century, indeed, that Geoffrey de Vinsauf, as we have seen, composed and published his poem on the restoration of the legitimate mode of versification, under the title of Nova Poetria, or the New Poetry. But from about this date the tide began to turn; and the first half of the thirteenth century may be described as the era of the decline and fall of elegant litera-ture, and the complete reduction of studious minds under the dominion of the scholastic logic and metaphysics.

In the University of Paris, and it was doubtless the same else-where, from about the middle of the thirteenth century, the ancient classics seem nearly to have ceased to be read; and all that was taught of rhetoric, or even of grammar, consisted of a few lessons from Priscian. The habit of speaking Latin correctly and elegantly, which had been so common an accomplishment of the scholars of the last age, was now generally lost: even at the universities, the classic tongue was corrupted into a base jargon, in which frequently all grammar and syntax were disregarded. This universal revolt from the study of words and of æsthetics to that of thoughts and of things is the most remarkable event in the intellectual history of the species. Undoubtedly all its results were not evil. On the whole, it was most probably the salvation even of that learning and elegant literature which it seemed for a time to have overwhelmed. The excitement of its very novelty awakened the minds of men. Never was there such a ferment of intellectual activity as now sprung up in

Europe. The enthusiasm of the Crusades seemed to have been succeeded by an enthusiasm of study, which equally impelled its successive inundations of devotees. In the beginning of the fourteenth century there were thirty thousand students at the University of Oxford; and that of Paris could probably boast of the attendance of a still vaster multitude. This was something almost like a universal diffusion of education and knowledge. The brief revival of elegant literature in the twelfth century was a premature spring, which could not last. The preliminary processes of vegetation were not sufficiently advanced to sustain any general or enduring efflorescence; nor was the state of the world such as to call for or admit of any extensive spread of the kind of scholarship then cultivated. The probability is, that, even if nothing else had taken its place, it would have gradually become feebler in character, as well as confined within a narrower circle of cultivators, till it had altogether evaporated and disappeared. The excitement of the new learning, turbulent and in some respects debasing as it was, saved Western Europe from the complete extinction of the light of scholarship and philosophy which would in that case have ensued, and kept alive the spirit of intellectual culture, though in the mean while imprisoned and limited in its vision, for a happier future time when it should have ampler scope and full freedom of range.

Almost the only studies now cultivated by the common herd of students were the Aristotelian logic and metaphysics. Yet it was not till after a struggle of some length that the supremacy of Aristotle was established in the schools. The most ancient statutes of the University of Paris that have been preserved, those issued by the pope's legate, Robert de Courçon, in 1215, prohibited the reading either of the metaphysical or the physical works of that philosopher, or of any abridgment of them. This, however, it has been remarked, was a mitigation of the treatment these books had met with a few years before, when all the copies of them that could be found were ordered to be thrown into the fire.[*] Still more lenient was a decree of Pope Gregory IX. in 1231, which only ordered the reading of them to be suspended until they should have undergone correction. Certain heretical notions in religion, promulgated or suspected to have been entertained by some of the most zealous of the early Aristotelians, had awakened the apprehensions of the Church; but the general

* Crevier, Histoire de l'Univ. de Paris, t. 313.

orthodoxy of their successors quieted these fears; and in course of time the authority of the Stagirite was universally recognized both in theology and in the profane sciences.

Some of the most distinguished of the scholastic doctors of this period were natives of Britain. Such, in particular, were Alexander de Hales, styled the Irrefragable, an English Franciscan, who died at Paris in 1245, and who is famous as the master of St. Bonaventura, and the first of the long list of commentators on the Four Books of the Sentences; the Subtile Doctor, John Duns Scotus, also a Franciscan and the chief glory of that order, who, after teaching with unprecedented popularity and applause at Oxford and Paris, died at Cologne in 1308, at the early age of forty-three, leaving a mass of writings, the very quantity of which would be sufficiently wonderful, even if they were not marked by a vigour and penetration of thought which, down to our own day, has excited the admiration of all who have examined them; and William Occam, the Invincible, another Franciscan, the pupil of Scotus, but afterwards his opponent on the great philosophical question of the origin and nature of Universals or General Terms, which so long divided, and still divides, logicians. Occam, who died at Munich in 1347, was the restorer, and perhaps the most able defender that the middle ages produced, of the doctrine of Nominalism, or the opinion that general notions are merely names, and not real existences, as was contended by the Realists. The side taken by Occam was that of the minority in his own day, and for many ages after, and his views accordingly were generally regarded as heterodox in the schools; but his high merits have been recognized in modern times, when perhaps the greater number of speculators have come over to his way of thinking.

MATHEMATICAL AND OTHER STUDIES.

In the mathematical and physical sciences, Roger Bacon is the great name of the thirteenth century, and indeed the greatest that either his country or Europe can produce for some centuries after this time. He was born at Ilchester about the year 1214, and died in 1292. His writings that are still preserved, of which the principal is that entitled his Opus Majus (or Greater Work), show that the range of his investigations included theology, grammar, the ancient languages, geometry, astronomy, chronology, geography, music, optics, mechanics, chemistry, and most of the other branches of experimental philosophy. In all those sciences he had mastered whatever was then known; and his knowledge, though necessarily mixed with much error, extended in various directions considerably farther than, but for the evidence of his writings, we should have been warranted in believing that scientific researches had been carried in that age. In optics, for instance, he not only understood the general laws of reflected and refracted light, and had at least conceived such an instrument as a telescope, but he makes some advances towards an explanation of the phenomena of the rainbow. It may be doubted whether what have been sometimes called his inventions and discoveries in mechanics and in chemistry were for the greater part more than notions he had formed of the possibility of accomplishing certain results; but, even regarded as mere speculations or conjectures, many of his statements of what might be done show that he was familiar with mechanical principles, and possessed considerable acquaintance with the powers of natural agents. He appears to have been acquainted with the effects and composition of gunpowder, which indeed there is other evidence for believing to have been then known in Europe. Bacon's notions on the right method of philosophizing are remarkably enlightened for the times in which he lived; and his general views upon most subjects evince a penetration and liberality much beyond the spirit of his age. With all his sagacity and freedom from prejudice, indeed, he was a believer both in astrology and alchemy; but, as it has been observed, these delusions did not then stand in the same predicament as now: they were "irrational only because unproved, and neither impossible nor unworthy of the investigation of a philosopher, in the absence of preceding experiments." *

Another eminent English cultivator of mathematical science

* Penny Cyclopædia, III. 213. Bacon's principal work, the Opus Majus, was published by Dr. Jebb, in a folio volume, at London in 1733; and several of his other treatises had been previously printed at Frankfort, Paris, and elsewhere. His Opus Minus has also now been edited by Professor Brewer, of King's College, London, and forms one of the volumes of the series entitled Rerum Britannicarum Medii Ævi Scriptores, or Chronicles and Memorials of Great Britain and Ireland during the Middle Ages: published by the authority of Her Majesty's Treasury, under the direction of the Master of the Rolls. 8vo. London, 1857, &c.

in that age was the celebrated Robert Grosseteste, or Grostête, or Grosthead, bishop of Lincoln, the friend and patron of Bacon. Grostête, who died in 1253, and of whom we shall have more to say presently, is the author of a treatise on the sphere, which has been printed. A third name that deserves to be mentioned along with these is that of Sir Michael Scott, famous in popular tradition as a practitioner of the occult sciences, but whom his writings, of which several are extant, and have been printed, prove to have been possessed of acquirements, both in science and literature, of which few in those times could boast. He is commonly assumed to have been proprietor of the estate of Balwearie, in Fife, and to have survived till near the close of the thirteenth century; but all that is certain is that he was a native of Scotland, and one of the most distinguished of the learned persons who flourished at the court of the Emperor Frederick II., who died in 1250.* Like Roger Bacon, Scott was addicted to the study of alchemy and astrology; but those were in his eyes also parts of natural philosophy. Among other works, a History of Animals is ascribed to him; and he is said to have translated several of the works of Aristotle from the Greek into Latin, at the command of the Emperor Frederick. He is reputed to have been eminently skilled both in astronomy and medicine; and a contemporary, John Bacon, himself known by the title of Prince of the Averroists, or followers of the Arabian doctor Averroes, celebrates him as a great theologian.†

These instances, however, were rare exceptions to the general rule. Metaphysics and logic, together with divinity—which was converted into little else than a subject of metaphysical and logical contention—so occupied the crowd of intellectual inquirers, that, except the professional branches of law and medicine, scarcely any other studies were generally attended to. Roger Bacon himself tells us that he knew of only two good mathematicians among his contemporaries—one John of Leyden, who had been a pupil of his own, and another whom he does not name, but who is supposed to have been John Peckham, a Franciscan friar, who afterwards became archbishop of Canterbury. Few students of the science, he says, proceeded farther than the fifth proposition of the first book of Euclid—the well-known asses' bridge. The study of geometry was still confounded in the popular under-

* See article in Penny Cyclopædia, xxI. 101.
† See an article in Michael Scott in Hoyle.

standing with the study of magic—a proof that it was a very rare pursuit. In arithmetic, although the Arabic numerals had found their way to Christian Europe before the middle of the fourteenth century, they do not appear to have come into general use till a considerably later date. Astronomy, however, was sufficiently cultivated at the University of Paris to enable some of the members to predict an eclipse of the sun which happened on the 31st of January, 1310.* This science was indebted for part of the attention it received to the belief that was universally entertained in the influence of the stars over human affairs. And, as astrology led to the cultivation and improvement of astronomy, so the other imaginary science of alchemy undoubtedly aided the progress of chemistry and medicine. Besides Roger Bacon and Michael Scott in the thirteenth century, England contributes the names of John Daustein, of Richard, and of Cremer abbot of Westminster, the disciple and friend of the famous Raymond Lully, to the list of the writers on alchemy in the fourteenth. Lully himself visited England in the reign of Edward I., on the invitation of the king; and he affirms in one of his works, that, in the secret chamber of St. Katharine in the Tower of London, he performed in the royal presence the experiment of transmuting some crystal into a mass of diamond, or adamant as he calls it, of which Edward, he says, caused some little pillars to be made for the tabernacle of God. It was popularly believed, indeed, at the time, that the English king had been furnished by Lully with a great quantity of gold for defraying the expense of an expedition he intended to make to the Holy Land. Edward III. was not less credulous on the subject than his grandfather, as appears by an order which he issued in 1320, in the following terms:—"Know all men, that we have been assured that John of Rous and Master William of Dalby know how to make silver by the art of alchemy; that they have made it in former times, and still continue to make it; and, considering that these men, by their art, and by making the precious metal, may be profitable to us and to our kingdom, we have commanded our well-beloved Thomas Cary to apprehend the aforesaid John and William, wherever they can be found, within liberties or without, and bring them to us, together with all the instruments of their art, under safe and sure custody." The earliest English writer on medicine, whose works have been

* Crevier, ii. 224.

J. 2

printed, is Gilbert English (or Anglicus), who flourished in the thirteenth century; and he was followed in the next century by John de Gaddesdon. The practice of medicine had now been taken in a great measure out of the hands of the clergy; but the art was still in the greater part a mixture of superstition and quackery, although the knowledge of some useful remedies, and perhaps also of a few principles, had been obtained from the writings of the Arabic physicians (many of which had been translated into Latin) and from the instructions delivered in the schools of Spain and Italy. The distinction between the physician and the apothecary was already well understood. Surgery also began to be followed as a separate branch: some works are still extant, partly printed, partly in manuscript, by John Ardern, or Arden, an eminent English surgeon, who practised at Newark in the fourteenth century. A lively picture of the state of the surgical art at this period is given by a French writer, Guy de Cauliac, in a system of surgery which he published in 1363: "The practitioners in surgery," he says, "are divided into five sects. The first follow Roger and Roland, and the four masters, and apply poultices to all wounds and abscesses; the second follow Brunus and Theodoric, and in the same cases use wine only; the third follow Salicoto and Lanfranc, and treat wounds with ointments and soft plasters; the fourth are chiefly Germans, who attend the armies, and promiscuously use charms, potions, oil, and wool; the fifth are old women and ignorant people, who have recourse to the saints in all cases."

Yet the true method of philosophising, by experiment and the collection of facts, was almost as distinctly and emphatically laid down in this age by Roger Bacon, as it was more than three centuries afterwards by his illustrious namesake. Much knowledge, too, must necessarily have been accumulated in various departments by the actual application of this method. Some of the greatest of the modern chemists have bestowed the highest praise on the manner in which the experiments of the alchemists, or hermetic philosophers, as they called themselves, on metals and other natural substances appear to have been conducted. In another field—namely, in that of geography, and the institutions, customs, and general state of distant countries— a great deal of new information must have been acquired from the accounts that were now published by various travellers, especially by Marco Polo, who penetrated as far as to Tartary and China, in

the latter part of the thirteenth century, and by our countryman, Sir John Mandevil, who also traversed a great part of the
East about a hundred years later. Roger Bacon has inserted a
very curious epitome of the geographical knowledge of his time
in his Opus Majus.

UNIVERSITIES AND COLLEGES.

About the middle of the thirteenth century, both in England
and elsewhere, the universities began to assume a new form, by
the erection of colleges for the residence of their members as
separate communities. The zeal for learning that was displayed
in those endowments is the most honourable characteristic of the
age. Before the end of the fourteenth century the following
colleges were founded at Oxford :—University Hall, by William,
archdeacon of Durham, who died in 1249; Baliol College, by
John Baliol, father of King John of Scotland, about 1263; Morton College, by Walter Merton, bishop of Rochester, in 1268;
Exeter College, by Walter Stapleton, bishop of Exeter, about
1315; Oriel College, originally called the Hall of the Blessed
Virgin of Oxford, by Edward II. and his almoner, Adam de
Brom, about 1324; Queen's College, by Robert Eglesfield, chaplain to Queen Philippa, in 1340; and New College, in 1379, by
the celebrated William of Wykeham, bishop of Winchester, the
munificent founder also of Winchester School or College. In
the University of Cambridge the foundations were, Peter House,
by Hugh Dalsham, sub-prior and afterwards bishop of Ely, about
1256; Michael College (afterwards incorporated with Trinity
College), by Horby de Stanton, Chancellor of the Exchequer to
Edward II., about 1324; University Hall (soon afterwards
burnt down), by Richard Badow, Chancellor of the University,
in 1320; King's Hall (afterwards united to Trinity College), by
Edward III.; Clare Hall, a restoration of University Hall, by
Elizabeth de Clare, Countess of Ulster, about 1347; Pembroke
Hall, or the Hall of Valence and Mary, in the same year, by
Mary de St. Paul, widow of Aymer de Valence, Earl of Pem-
broke; Trinity Hall, in 1350, by William Bateman, bishop of
Norwich; Gonvil Hall, about the same time, by Edmond Gonvil,
parson of Terrington and Rushworth, in Norfolk; and Corpus

Christi, or Ben'et (that is, Benedict) College, about 1351, by the United Guilds of Corpus Christi and St. Mary, in the town of Cambridge. The erection of these colleges, besides the accommodations which they afforded in various ways both to teachers and students, gave a permanent establishment to the universities, which they scarcely before possessed. The original condition of these celebrated seats of learning, in regard to all the conveniences of teaching, appears to have been humble in the extreme. Great disorders and scandals are also said to have arisen, before the several societies were thus assembled each within its own walls, from the intermixture of the students with the townspeople, and their exemption from all discipline. But, when the members of the University were counted by tens of thousands, discipline, even in the most favourable circumstances, must have been nearly out of the question. The difficulty would not be lessened by the general character of the persons composing the learned mob, if we may take it from the quaint historian of the University of Oxford. Many of them, Anthony à Wood affirms, were mere "varlets who pretended to be scholars;" he does not scruple to charge them with being habitually guilty of thieving and other enormities; and he adds, "They lived under no discipline, neither had any tutors, but only for fashion sake would sometimes thrust themselves into the schools at ordinary lectures, and, when they went to perform any mischiefs, then would they be accounted scholars, that so they might free themselves from the jurisdiction of the burghers." To repress the evils of this state of things, the old statutes of the University of Paris, in 1215, had ordained that no one should be reputed a scholar who had not a certain master. Another of these ancient regulations may be quoted in illustration of the simplicity of the times, and of the small measure of pomp and circumstance that the heads of the commonwealth of learning could then affect. It is ordered that every master reading lectures in the faculty of arts should have his cloak or gown round, black, and falling as low as the heels—"at least," adds the statute, with amusing naïveté, "while it is new." But this famous seminary long continued to take pride in its poverty as one of its most honourable distinctions. There is something very noble and affecting in the terms in which the rector and masters of the faculty of arts are found petitioning, in 1362, for a postponement of the hearing of a cause in which they were parties. "We have difficulty," they say, "in finding the money to pay the procurators and advocates, whom it is necessary for us to employ—*we whose profession it is to possess no wealth.*" [*] Yet, when funds were wanted for important purposes in connexion with learning or science, they were supplied in this age with no stinted liberality. We have seen with what alacrity opulent persons came forward to build and endow colleges, as soon as the expediency of such foundations came to be perceived. In almost all these establishments more or less provision was made for the permanent maintenance of a body of poor scholars, in other words, for the admission of even the humblest classes to a share in the benefits of that learned education whose temples and priesthood were thus planted in the land. It is probable, also, that the same kind of liberality was often shown in other ways. Roger Bacon tells us himself that, in the twenty years in which he had been engaged in his experiments, he had spent in books and instruments no less a sum than two thousand French livres, an amount of silver equal to about six thousand pounds of our present money, and in effective value certainly to many times that sum. He must have been indebted for these large supplies to the generosity of rich friends and patrons.

LATIN HISTORICAL WORKS OF THE THIRTEENTH AND FOURTEENTH CENTURIES.

Notwithstanding the general neglect of its elegancies, and of the habit of speaking it correctly or grammatically, the Latin tongue still continued to be in England, as elsewhere, the common language of the learned, and that in which books were generally written that were intended for their perusal. Among this class of works may be included the contemporary chronicles, most of which were compiled in the monasteries, and the authors of almost all of which were churchmen.

The Chronicle of Roger de Wendover, hitherto existing only in MS., and in a single copy, has now been published, in the greater part, by the Rev. Henry O. Coxe, for the English Historical Society, under the title of Rogeri de Wendover Chronica, sive Flores Historiarum, 5 vols. 8vo. Lon. 1841-44. The portion omitted is

[*] Crevier, ii. 404.

merely the First Book, which contains the space from the creation
to the commencement of the Christian era, and is abridged in
the Flores Historiarum bearing the name of Matthew of Westminster, together with the first 446 years of Book Second, in
which there is equally little that is peculiar or important. The
remainder of the narrative comes down to the year 1235 (the 19th
of Henry III.), and is very valuable. An English translation
by Dr. Giles of so much of Roger de Wendover's Chronicle as
has been published by Mr. Coxe makes two of the volumes of
Bohn's Antiquarian Library, Lon. 1849. Wendover, who was
probably a native of the place of that name in Buckinghamshire,
became a monk and precentor in the Benedictine monastery
of St. Albans, and died prior of Belvoir, in a cell of that
house, on the 6th of May, 1237. He has compiled the earlier
portion of his work from Bede, Marianus Scotus, some of the
Byzantine writers, Malmesbury, Florence of Worcester, Henry
of Huntingdon, and the other best and most reputable of preceding chroniclers, and in a very workmanlike manner. Mr.
Coxe holds him to be quite as good a writer as Matthew Paris,
whose more celebrated History is, down to the point where that
of Wendover ends, copied from him with few alterations, and
those, Mr. Coxe declares, mostly for the worse even in point of
expression. Mr. Coxe vindicates the claim of Wendover to the
authorship of the portion of the Chronicle bearing his name
which has been thus transcribed by Paris, in answer to some remarks by Mr. Halliwell in the introduction to his late edition of
Rishanger's Chronicle of the Barons' Wars.

The most celebrated English historian of the thirteenth century, however, is Matthew Paris, who was another monk of the
same great monastery of St. Albans, and was also much employed
in affairs of state during the reign of Henry III. He died in
1259 ; and his principal work, entitled Historia Major (the
Greater History), begins at the Norman Conquest, and comes
down to that year. Matthew Paris is one of the most spirited
and rhetorical of our old Latin historians ; and the extraordinary
freedom with which he expresses himself, in regard especially to
the usurpations of the court of Rome, forms a striking contrast
to the almost uniform tone of his monkish brethren. Nor does
he show less boldness in animadverting upon the vices and
delinquencies of kings and of the great in general. These
qualities have in modern times gained him much admiration

among writers of one party, and much obloquy from those of
another. His work has always been bitterly decried by the
Roman Catholics, who at one time, indeed, were accustomed to
maintain that much of what appeared in the printed copies of it
was the interpolation of its Protestant editors. This charge has
now been abandoned; but an eminent Catholic historian of the
present day has not hesitated to denounce the narrative of
the monk of St. Albans as " a romance rather than a history,"
on the ground of the great discrepancy which he asserts he has
found between it and authentic records or contemporary writers,
in most instances when he could confront the one with the other.[*]
The Historia Major of Matthew Paris was first printed at
London in 1571, under the care of Archbishop Parker; and it
has been republished at Zurich in 1606; at London, under the
care of Dr. William Wats, in 1640; at Paris, in 1644; and at
London in 1684. All these editions are in folio. An excellent
French translation, by M. A. Huillard-Bréholles, has lately been
published under the superintendence, or at the cost, of the Duc
de Luynes, in 9 vols. 8vo. Paris, 1840–41, with a few notes by
the translator, but without the Introduction by the Duke, promised on the title-page—at least in the only copy of the work
that has fallen in our way. An English translation, by Dr. Giles,
makes three of the volumes of Bohn's Antiquarian Library. To
the edition published by Dr. Wats, and those that have followed
it, are appended some other historical pieces of the author; and
there also exists, in MS., an abridgment of the Historia Major,
drawn up by himself, and generally referred to as the Historia
Minor.

The History of Matthew Paris was continued by William
Rishanger, another monk of the same abbey, whose narrative
appears to have come down to the year 1322 (the 15th of Edward
II.), although no complete copy is now known to be in existence,
and only the earlier part, extending to the death of Henry III.
(A.D. 1272), has been printed. It is at the end of Wats's edition
of Matthew Paris. Rishanger is also the author of several other
historical tracts, one of the most curious of which, his Chronicle
of the Barons' Wars (preserved in a single MS., with the title of
De Bellis Lewes et Evesham) has been printed for the Camden
Society, under the care of Mr. James Orchard Halliwell, 4to.
Lond. 1840. To Rishanger's narrative Mr. Halliwell has appended

* Dr. Lingard, Hist. of Eng. iii. 100, edit. of 1837.

a collection of miracles attributed to Simon de Montfort, from another MS. in the Cotton Library.

What is commonly called the Chronicle of John Bromton, and is printed among the Decem Scriptores (pp. 721-1284) under the titles of Chronicon Johannis Bromton, and Joralanensis Historia, a Johanne Brompton, Abbate Jurvalensi, Conscripta, has been shown by Selden, in his most learned and curious preface to that collection, not to be either the composition of Bromton, or in any sense a Chronicle of Jorevale or Jorevaux, of which monastery in Yorkshire Bromton, Brompton, or Bramton, was abbot. The book was merely procured for the library of that house while he presided over it, and probably through his means. It does not appear from Selden's account when Bromton lived; but he has proved (p. xli) that the Chronicle must have been written in or after the year 1328, or the second of Edward III. At the commencement the author intimates that it is his design to bring it down to the time of Edward I., but it terminates with the death of Richard I. (A.D. 1199), having set out from the conversion of the Saxons by St. Augustine. It is not therefore, in any part of it, a contemporary history; but the writer has gleaned from some authorities which we do not now possess, and he gives many details which have not elsewhere been preserved.

Among the other Latin chroniclers of this period, whose works have been printed, the following are the principal:—Thomas Wikes, or Wycko, in Latin Wicius, canon regular of Osney, near Oxford, whose chronicle, otherwise called the Chronicle of the Church of Salisbury, fills from p. 21 to p. 120 of Gale's Scriptores Quinque, and, as there printed, extends from the Conquest to the year 1304, although it is afterwards intimated (p. 503) that the last ten pages of it are by another hand; Walter Hemingford, or, as Leland calls him, Hemingoburgus, a monk of Gisborough in Yorkshire, the portion of whose work extending from the Conquest to the year 1273 (being the first three Books) was printed by Gale in the same collection (pp. 453-595), and the remainder, comprehending the reigns of Edward I., Edward II., and the first twenty years of that of Edward III., by Hearne, in 2 vols. 8vo., at Oxford, in 1731, and the whole of which has been edited by Mr. H. C. Hamilton for the Historical Society, in 2 vols. 8vo. Lon. 1848; Robert de Avesbury, register of the court of the Archbishop of Canterbury, whose history of the reign of Edward III., Historia de Mirabilibus Gestis Edwardi III., which is esteemed for its accuracy, but comes down only to A.D. 1356, was published by Hoarne, in 8vo., at Oxford, in 1720; Nicolas Trivet, whose clear and exact history of the reigns of Stephen, Henry II., Richard I., John, Henry III., and Edward I. (or from A.D. 1135 to 1307), is printed in both editions of Father d'Achery's Spicilegium (1671 and 1723), and has also been published separately by Anthony Hall, in 8vo., at Oxford, in 1719, and, as edited by Mr. T. Hog for the Historical Society, 8vo., Lon. 1845; Adam Murimuth, whose short chronicle, extending from A.D. 1303 to 1337, along with a continuation by an anonymous writer to 1380, was printed by Hall as a second volume to his Trivet, in 1721, and has also been edited for the Historical Society by Mr. Hog, 1846; Henry de Knyghton (or Cnitton, as he himself spells the name), a canon of Leicester, the author of a History of English affairs from the time of King Edgar to the death of Richard II., which is printed among the Decem Scriptores (pp. 2297-2742); and the two ecclesiastical historians, Thomas Stubbs and William Thorne, the Chronicle of the acts of the Archbishops of York to A.D. 1373 by the former of whom, and that of the Abbots of St. Augustine's monastery at Canterbury to 1397 by the latter, are in the same collection (pp. 1685-1734, and 1753-2202). The original Latin Polychronicon of Ranulph, or Ralph, Higden, monk of St. Werburgh's in Chester, which ends in 1357, still remains, for the greater part, in MS., only the portion of it relating to the period of English history before the Norman Conquest having been published by Gale among his Scriptores Quindecim (pp. 177-289); but an English translation of the whole by John de Trevisa, who was vicar of Berkeley in Gloucestershire towards the close of the fourteenth century, was printed, in folio, at Westminster, by Caxton in 1482, at the same place by Wynken de Worde in 1485, and at Southwark in 1517, and again in 1527. Besides many insertions, Caxton has added a continuation of the History down to 1460; but it appears that he has also omitted several passages which are found in Trevisa's MS. now in the Harleian collection.

John Fordun, the earliest of the regular Scottish chroniclers, also belongs to the fourteenth century. His History, entitled Scotichronicon, beginning with the creation, comes down only to the end of the reign of David I. (A.D. 1153), but is continued

by Walter Bower, abbot of Inchcolm, to the death of James I.
(A.D. 1437), the materials for the space from 1153 to 1385 having
been collected by Fordun. The portion of the Scotichronicon
actually written by Fordun, being the first five of the sixteen
books, was printed by Gale among his Scriptores Quindecim
(pp. 563-701); and the whole was published by Hearne, at
Oxford, in 5 vols. 8vo. in 1722, and again by Walter Goodall, at
Edinburgh, in 2 vols. folio, in 1759.

The most important of the monastic chronicles belonging to
this period which has been preserved is that called (it does not
appear for what reason) the Chronicle of Lanercost. It has now
been printed for the Bannatyne and Maitland Clubs, under the
superintendence of Mr. Joseph Stevenson, 4to., Edinburgh, 1839.
Before this it existed only in one or two very incorrect modern
transcripts, and in a single original codex (the Cotton MS. D. vii.),
where it is appended, without any break, to an imperfect copy
of what is printed by Savile as Hovedon's History. Hovedon
ends on the reverse of what is numbered as folio 172 of the MS.,
having filled from folio 66 inclusive: the continuation, or Lanercost Chronicle, goes on in one handwriting to the end of the
volume on the reverse of fol. 242. The time which it comprehends is from A.D. 1201 to 1346; and Mr. Stevenson thinks that
it was transcribed about the latter date from the contemporary
register kept, most probably, in the Minorite monastery of
Carlisle. As printed it fills 352 4to. pages; and it abounds in
curious and valuable information relating to the course of events
both in England and in Scotland during the period over which
it extends.

USE AND STUDY OF THE LATIN AND GREEK, THE HEBREW AND OTHER ORIENTAL TONGUES.

Latin was also, for a great part of the thirteenth and fourteenth
centuries, the usual language of the law, at least in writing.
There may, indeed, be some doubt perhaps as to the Charter of
John. It is usually given in Latin; but there is also a French
text first published in the first edition of D'Achery's Spicilegium
(1653-57), xii. 573, &c., which there is some reason for believing
to be the original. " An attentive critical examination of the
French and Latin together," says Mr. Ludors, " will induce

any person capable of making it to think several chapters of the
latter translated from the former, and not originally composed in
Latin."* Yet the Capitula, or articles on which the Great
Charter is founded, are known to us only in Latin. And all the
other charters of liberties are in that language. So is every
statute down to the year 1275. The first that is in French is the
Statute of Westminster the First, passed in that year, the 3rd of
Edward I. Throughout the remainder of the reign of Edward
they are sometimes in Latin, sometimes in French, but more
frequently in the former language. The French becomes more
frequent in the time of Edward II., and is almost exclusively
used in that of Edward III. and Richard II. Still there are
statutes in Latin in the sixth and eighth years of the last-mentioned king. It is not improbable that, from the accession of
Edward I., the practice may have been to draw up every statute
in both languages. Of the law treatises, Bracton (about 1265)
and Fleta (about 1285) are in Latin; Britton (about 1280) and
the Miroir des Justices (about 1320), in French.

Latin was not only the language in which all the scholastic
divines and philosophers wrote, but was also employed by all
writers on geometry, astronomy, chemistry, medicine, and the
other branches of mathematical and natural science. All the
works of Roger Bacon, for example, are in Latin; and it is
worth noting that, although by no means a writer of classical
purity, this distinguished cultivator of science is still one of the
most correct writers of his time. He was indeed not a less
zealous student of literature than of science, nor less anxious for
the improvement of the one than of the other: accustomed himself to read the works of Aristotle in the original Greek, he
denounces as mischievous impositions the wretched Latin translations by which alone they were known to the generality of his
contemporaries: he warmly recommends the study of grammar
and the ancient languages generally; and deplores the little
attention paid to the Oriental tongues in particular, of which he
says there were not in his time more than three or four persons
in Western Europe who knew anything. It is remarkable that
the most strenuous effort made within the present period to
revive the study of this last-mentioned learning proceeded from

* Tracts on the Law and History of England (1810), p. 308. D'Achery's
French text may also be read in a more common book, Johnson's History of
Magna Charta, 2nd edit. (1772), pp. 182—234.

another eminent cultivator of natural science, the famous Raymond Lully, half philosopher, half quack, as it has been the fashion to regard him. It was at his instigation that Clement V., in 1311, with the approbation of the Council of Vienne, published a constitution, ordering that professors of Greek, Hebrew, Arabic, and Chaldaic should be established in the universities of Paris, Oxford, Bologna, and Salamanca. He had, more than twenty years before, urged the same measure upon Honorius IV., and its adoption thus was only prevented by the death of that pope. After all, it is doubtful if the papal ordinance was ever carried into effect. There were, however, professors of strange, or foreign, languages at Paris a few years after this time, as appears from an epistle of Pope John XXII. to his legate there in 1325, in which the latter is enjoined to keep watch over the said professors, lest they should introduce any dogmas as strange as the languages they taught.*

Many additional details are collected by Warton in his Dissertation on the Introduction of Learning into England. He is inclined to think that many Greek manuscripts found their way into Europe from Constantinople in the time of the Crusades. " Robert Grosthead, bishop of Lincoln," he proceeds, " an universal scholar, and no less conversant in polite letters than the most abstruse sciences, cultivated and patronized the study of the Greek language. This illustrious prelate, who is said to have composed almost two hundred books, read lectures in the school of the Franciscan friars at Oxford about the year 1230. He translated Dionysius the Areopagite and Damascenus into Latin. He greatly facilitated the knowledge of Greek by a translation of Suidas's Lexicon, a book in high repute among the lower Greeks, and at that time almost a recent compilation. He promoted John of Basingstoke to the archdeaconry of Leicester, chiefly because he was a Greek scholar, and possessed many Greek manuscripts, which he is said to have brought from Athens into England. He entertained, as a domestic in his palace, Nicholas, chaplain of the abbot of St. Albans, surnamed Graecus, from his uncommon proficiency in Greek ; and by his assistance he translated from Greek into Latin the testaments of the twelve patriarchs. Grosthead had almost incurred the censure of excommunication for preferring a complaint to the pope that most of the opulent benefices in England were occu-

* Crevier, Hist. de l'Univ. de Paris, ii. 112. 227.

pied by Italians. But the practice, although notoriously founded on the monopolizing and arbitrary spirit of papal imposition, and a manifest act of injustice to the English clergy, probably contributed to introduce many learned foreigners into England, and to propagate philological literature."* "Bishop Grosthead," Warton adds, " is also said to have been profoundly skilled in the Hebrew language. William the Conqueror permitted great numbers of Jews to come over from Rouen, and to settle in England, about the year 1087. Their multitude soon increased, and they spread themselves in vast bodies throughout most of the cities and capital towns in England, where they built synagogues. There were fifteen hundred at York about the year 1189. At Bury in Suffolk is a very complete remain of a Jewish synagogue of stone, in the Norman style, large and magnificent. Hence it was that many of the learned English ecclesiastics of those times became acquainted with their books and language. In the reign of William Rufus, at Oxford the Jews were remarkably numerous, and had acquired a considerable property; and some of their rabbis were permitted to open a school in the university, where they instructed not only their own people, but many Christian students, in the Hebrew literature, about the year 1054. Within two hundred years after their admission or establishment by the Conqueror, they were banished the kingdom. This circumstance was highly favourable to the circulation of their learning in England. The suddenness of their dismission obliged them, for present subsistence, and other reasons, to sell their moveable goods of all kinds, among which were large quantities of Rabbinical books. The monks in various parts availed themselves of the distribution of these treasures. At Huntingdon and Stamford there was a prodigious sale of their effects, containing immense stores of Hebrew manuscripts, which were immediately purchased by Gregory of Huntingdon, prior of the abbey of Ramsey. Gregory speedily became an adept in the Hebrew, by means of these valuable acquisitions, which he bequeathed to his monastery about the year 1250. Other members of the same convent, in consequence of these advantages, are said to have been equal proficients in the same language, soon after the death of Prior Gregory; among whom were Robert Dodford, librarian of Ramsay, and Laurence Holbeck, who compiled a Hebrew Lexicon. At Oxford, great multitudes

* Hist. of Eng. Poet, i. cxxxv.

of their books fell into the hands of Roger Bacon, or were bought
by his brethren, the Franciscan friars of that university."* The
general expulsion of the Jews from England did not take place
till the year 1290, in the reign of Edward I.; but they had been
repeatedly subjected to sudden violence, both from the populace
and from the government, before that grand catastrophe.

LAST AGE OF THE FRENCH LANGUAGE IN ENGLAND.

The French language, however, was still in common use
among us down to the latter part of the reign of Edward III.
It is well remarked by Pinkerton that we are to date the ces-
sation of the general use of French in this country from the
breaking out of "the inveterate enmity" between the two
nations in the reign of that king.† Higden, as we have seen,
writing before this change had taken place, tells us that French
was still in his day the language which the children of gentlemen were taught to speak from their cradle, and the only
language that was allowed to be used by boys at school; the
effect of which was, that even the country people generally
understood it and affected its use. The tone, however, in which
this is stated by Higden indicates that the public feeling had
already begun to set in against these customs, and that, if they
still kept their ground from use and wont, they had lost their
hold upon any firmer or surer stay. Accordingly about a quarter
of a century or thirty years later his translator Trevisa finds it
necessary to subjoin the following explanation or correction : —
" This .maner was myche yused tofore the first moreyn [before
the first murrain or plague, which happened in 1349], and is
siththe som dele [somewhat] ychaungide. For John Cornwaile,
a maister of gramar, chaungide the lore [learning] in gramar scole
and construction of [from] Frensch into Englisch, and Richard
Pencriche lerned that maner teching of him, and other men of
Pencriche. So that now, the yere of owre Lord a thousand thre

* Hist. of Eng. Poet., I. cxxxvi.
† Essay on the Origin of Scotish Poetry, prefixed to Ancient Scotish
Poems, 1786, vol. i. p. lxiii. Some curious remarks upon the peculiar political
position in which England was held to stand in relation to France in the first
reigns after the Conquest may be read in Tink's Preface to his Scripturvs
Quinqueviæ.

hundred foure score and fyve, of the secunde King Rychard after the Conquest nyne, in alle the gramer scoles of England children leveth Frensch, and construeth and lerneth an [in] Englisch, and haveth thereby avauntage in oon [one] side and desavauntage in another. Her [their] avauntage is, that thei lerneth hor [their] g'amer in lasse tyme than children were wont to do: desavauntage is, that now children of gramer scole kunneth [know] no more Frensch than can hor lifte [knows their left] heole; and that is harm for hem [them], and [if] thei schul passe the see and travaile in strange londes, and in many other places also. Also gentilmen haveth now mych ylefte for to teche her [their] children Frensch."*

A few years before this, in 1362 (the 36th of Edward III.), was passed the statute ordaining that all pleas pleaded in the king's courts should be pleaded in the English language, and entered and enrolled in Latin; the pleadings, or oral arguments, till now having been in French, and the enrolments of the judgments sometimes in French, sometimes in Latin. The reasons assigned for this change in the preamble of the act are, " because it is often showed to the king by the prelates, dukes, earls, barons, and all the commonalty, of the great mischiefs which have happened to divers of the realm, because the laws, customs, and statutes of this realm be not commonly holden and kept in the same realm, for that they be pleaded, shewed, and judged in the French tongue, which is much unknown in the said realm, so that the people which do implead, or be impleaded, in the king's court, and in the courts of other, have no knowledge nor understanding of that which is said for them or against them by their sergeants and other pleaders; and that reasonably the said laws and customs the rather shall be perceived and known, and better understood, in the tongue used in the said realm, and by so much every man of the said realm may the better govern himself without offending of the law, and the better keep, save, and defend his heritage and possessions; and in divers regions and countries, where the king, the nobles, and other of the said realm have been, good governance and full right is done to every person, because that their laws and customs be learned and used in the tongue of the country."

Yet, oddly enough, this very statute (of which we have here

* As quoted by Tyrwhitt, from Harl. MS. 1900, in Essay on the Language, &c., of Chaucer.

quoted the old translation) is in French, which, whatever might
be the case with the great body of the people, continued down
to a considerably later date than this to be the mother-tongue of
our Norman royal family, and probably also that generally
spoken at court and at least in the upper house of parliament.
Ritson asserts that there is no instance in which Henry III. is
known to have expressed himself in English. "King Edward I.
generally," he continues, "or, according to Andrew of Wyntoun,
constantly, spoke the French language, both in the council and
in the field, many of his sayings in that idiom being recorded by
our old historians. When, in the council at Norham, in 1291-2,
Anthony Beck had, as it is said, proved to the king, by reason
and eloquence, that Bruce was too dangerous a neighbour to be
king of Scotland, his Majesty replied, *Par le sang de dieu, vous avez
bien enchanté*, and accordingly adjudged the crown to Baliol; of
whom, refusing to obey his summons, he afterwards said, *A ce fol
felon tel folie fais? S'il ne voult venir à nous, nous viendrons à lui.*[*]
There is but one instance of his speaking English; which was
when the great sultan sent ambassadors, after his assassination,
to protest that he had no knowledge of it. These, standing at a
distance, adored the king, prone on the ground; and Edward said
in English (*in Anglico*), *You, indeed, adore, but you little love, me.*
Nor understood they his words, because they spoke to him by an
interpreter.[†] King Edward II., likewise, who married a French
princess, used himself the French tongue. Sir Henry Spelman
had a manuscript, in which was a piece of poetry entitled *De le
roi Edward le fiz roi Edward, le chanson qu'il fist meismes*, which Lord
Orford was unacquainted with. His son Edward III. always
wrote his letters or despatches in French, as we find them preserved by Robert of Avesbury; and in the early part of his reign
even the Oxford scholars were confined in conversation to Latin
or French.[‡] . . . . There is a single instance preserved of this
monarch's use of the English language. He appeared in 1349 in
a tournament at Canterbury with a white swan for his impress,
and the following motto embroidered on his shield :—

---

* For these two speeches, the latter of which, by-the-by, he points as if he
did not understand it, Ritson quotes the Scotichronicon (Fordun), ii. 147, 156.
  † For this anecdote Ritson quotes Hemingford (in Gale), p. 591.
  ‡ The authority for this last statement is a note in Warton's Hist. of Eng.
Poet. i. 6 (edit. of 1824).

> Hay, hay, the wythe swan !
> By Godes soul I am thy man !*

Lewis Beaumont, bishop of Durham, 1317, understood not a word of either Latin or English. In reading the bull of his appointment, which he had been taught to spell for several days before, he stumbled upon the word *metropolitice*, which he in vain endeavoured to pronounce; and, having hammered over it a considerable time, at last cried out, in his mother tongue, *Seit pour dite ! Par Seynt Lowys il ne fu pas curteis qui ceste parole ici escrit.*† The first instance of the English language which Mr. Tyrwhitt had discovered in the parliamentary proceedings was the confession of Thomas, Duke of Gloucester, in 1308. He might, however, have met with a petition of the mercers of London ten years earlier (*Rot. Parl.* iii. 225). The oldest English instrument produced by Rymer is dated 1366 (vii. 526); but an indenture in the same idiom betwixt the abbot and convent of Whitby, and Robert the son of John Bustard, dated at York in 1343,‡ is the earliest known."§

ANGLO-NORMAN POETS.

French metrical romances and other poetry, accordingly, continued to be written in England, and in many instances by Englishmen, throughout the thirteenth and fourteenth centuries. Of the Anglo-Norman poets of this period one of the most famous is a lady, Marie, who describes herself as of France, but who appears to have resided in England in the time of Henry III. Her poems—consisting principally of Lais,‖ or lays, the subjects of which she professes to have found in the Bas Breton, or

---

* " See Warton's Hist. of Eng. Poet. ii. 231 (l. 36, in edit. of 1824). He had another, ' It is as it is ;' and may have had a third, ' Ha St. Edward ! Ha St. George.' "

† " Robert de Graystanes, Anglia Sacra, i. 761—' Take it as said ! By St. Lewis, he was not very civil who wrote this word here.' "

‡ " Charlton's History of Whitby, 247."

§ Dissertation on Romance and Minstrelsy, pp. lxxv.-lxxxvi. We have not thought it necessary to preserve Ritson's peculiar spelling, adopted, apparently, on no principle except that of deviating from the established usage.

‖ The derivation of this word remains, we believe, an unsolved puzzle, or at least a subject of dispute, among etymologists. One conjecture would make it to be the same word with *lia*.

Celtic tongue of Britany, and of Fables in the manner of Æsop,
translated, she says, from an English version made by a king of
England, by which she probably means a collection attributed
to Alfred the Great, although another theory is that she refers
to a work by Henry I.—were first brought into notice by
Tyrwhitt (Introductory Discourse to the Canterbury Tales of
Chaucer, notes 24 and 20): they were afterwards made the
subject of a paper by the Abbé de la Rue, in the Archæologia
(vol. xiii. pp. 35-67, published in 1797); and they have since
been published by M. B. de Roquefort under the title of Poésies
de Marie de France, ou Recueil de Lais, Fables, et autres productions de cette femme célèbre, 2 vols. 8vo. Paris, 1820. An
account, including nearly a complete translation, of the Lais,
which are twelve in number (besides two which M. de Roquefort
has printed, apparently without any authority for assigning them
to Marie), is given by Ellis in his Early English Metrical
Romances (Appendix ii. to Introduction, pp. 143-200);* and
the reader may also consult what has been written about Marie
by Ritson, in a note to the romance of Emare (Ancient English
Metrical Romances, iii. 330), by Mr. Price, in a long and elaborate note upon Warton (Hist. of Eng. Poet., i. lxxiv.-lxxxvi.),
and by the Abbé de la Rue (in his Essais Historiques, iii. 47-100).
Le Grand d'Aussy has given prose versions or paraphrases of
forty-three of Marie's Fables in his work entitled Fabliaux ou
Contes du xiime et du xiiime Siècles, &c.

Marie is mentioned as his contemporary by Denis Pyram, or
Pyramus, who was also probably a native of France, but lived at
the court of Henry III., and was in his earlier years the author
of many serventois, anacreontic songs, and other gay pieces, but
whose only remaining compositions are two religious poems
written in the sobriety and penitence of his old age: the first, on
the life and martyrdom of St. Edmond, in 3280 verses; the
second, in 714 verses, on the miracles of the same royal saint.†

Another trouvéur of this date was no less a person than the
famous Grostête, bishop of Lincoln, already mentioned. Grostête,
who was an Englishman, a native of Suffolk, is the author of a

---

* He has also printed, in vol. iii. pp. 291-307, an account, communicated by
Sir Walter Scott, of an early English translation of one of them, the Lai le
Freine, contained in the Auchinleck MS. in the Advocates' Library, Edin-
burgh.

† See De la Rue, Essais Historiques, iii. 101-106.

religious romance of 1746 lines on the favourite subject of the Fall and Restoration of Man, which he sometimes called the Chastel, d'Amour (by which expression the Virgin Mary is meant), sometimes the Roman des Romans; and there is also attributed to him another French poem of much greater length, which M. de la Rue thinks is the same that is preserved in one of the royal manuscripts at the British Museum (MS. Reg. 16 x. ix.), and is in that copy entitled Traité des Péchés et des Vertus, although spoken of by other copyists as the Manuel. It consists of more than 7000 verses.

The title by which Grostête's second work is commonly referred to is the Manuel des Péchés; but the only known French poem bearing this title appears to be the work of a later writer, William of Wadington, who lived in the end of the thirteenth or beginning of the fourteenth century. It is a translation, but with much additional matter, from a Latin poem entitled Floretus, which was printed both in folio at London, and in 4to. at Caen, in the same year, 1512.* Wadington's Manuel, which contains nearly 10,000 verses,† exists in several manuscripts; of which two in the Harleian collection have at the end a farewell address to the reader, explaining his object in undertaking the translation. It was, he says, with a view of making the beauties of the Floretus be felt by a people who ran eagerly after everything written in French verse, and that the work might be understood by great and small; which proves, observes the Abbé de la Rue, that the knowledge of the French language was then generally diffused in England. Wadington also asks his readers to pardon the faults he may have committed, whether in expression or in regard to the laws of rhyme, on the ground that, being an Englishman by birth, it was impossible that he should write French verse with perfect purity and correctness.

A peculiar subject which engaged many of the French poets of the thirteenth century was the history of Alexander the Great; about a dozen trouveurs of France and England are enumerated who devoted themselves to this singular chapter of the romance of chivalry, and several of their performances still survive, although they can scarcely in any case be assigned with certainty

* De la Rue, Essais, iii. 226. In a paper in the Archæologia, vol. xii. pp. 240, &c. (read in 1798, published in 1800), this date is given 1520.
† De la Rue, Essais, iii. 241. In the Archæologia (vol. xiii.) he says nearly 6000.

to their proper authors. One Roman d'Alexandre is attributed,
at least in some copies, to a Thomas of Kent, who is placed by
some authorities in the twelfth century ;[*] by others, about the
beginning of the fourteenth ;[†] and who, it has been suggested,
may possibly be the author of the French romance of Le Roi
Horn, and also the Thomas referred to by Robert de Brunne
as the original narrator of the story of Sir Tristrem, which upon
this supposition must have first appeared in Norman French.[‡]
Another celebrated early French romance is that of Havelok le
Danois—founded on a well-known story of the Saxon era, relating to the town of Grimsby in Lincolnshire—which has been
very ably edited for the Roxburgh Club by Sir Frederick Madden,
along with the somewhat shorter relation of the same adventures
which is found in Gaimar's continuation of Wace's Brut, and a
much longer English poem on the same subject.[§] M. de la Rue,
however, seems to have shown that the learned editor is mistaken
in attributing to the separate Roman (which extends to 1106
lines) the priority in point of time over the version given by
Gaimar (containing 818 lines); and to have proved that it
belongs not to the earlier part of the twelfth, but to the
thirteenth century.[‖]

Other trouveurs of this period, connected with England either
by birth, residence, or the subjects of their poetry, are :—Chardry,
supposed to have been born in Gloucestershire in the thirteenth
century, the author of several religious romances,—one (of 2924
verses) on the lives of Saint Barlaam and St. Josaphat, another
(of 1750 verses) on the legend of the Seven Sleepers, a third (of

---

[*] See M. Vanpraet, Catalogue de la Vallière, ii. 160.

[†] De la Rue, Essais, ii. 358.

[‡] See Remarks on Sir W. Scott's Sir Tristrem (known to be by Sir Frederick Madden) in Gent. Mag. for October, 1833 (vol. ciii., part ii., p. 308);
and also the Introduction to Havelok by the same gentleman, p. xlvii.

[§] The Ancient English Romance of Havelok the Dane, accompanied by
the French text; with an introduction, notes, and a glossary. 4to, London,
1828. See also Examination of the Remarks on the Glossary to the ancient
Metrical Romance of Havelok the Dane, in a Letter to Francis Douce, Esq.,
F.A.S., by S. W. Singer, addressed to Henry Petrie, Esq., Keeper of his
Majesty's Records in the Tower of London, by the Editor of Havelok. 4to,
Lond. 1829. The French Romance, with a translation of part of Sir Frederick
Madden's Introduction, was republished, in crown 8vo., at Paris, in 1833, by
M. Francisque Michel, with the title of Lai d'Havelok le Danois; treizième
Siècle. The publication is dedicated to the Abbé de la Rue, by "son admi-
rateur et son ami."

[‖] Essais Historiques, iii. 114-120.

about 2000 verses) entitled Le Petit Plet, being a dispute
between an old and a young man on the happiness and misery
of human life; * Adam de Ros, an English monk of the same age.
from whom we have a poem on the legend of the descent of St.
Paul to the infernal regions; † Hélio of Winchester, the translator of the Distichs of Cato, for the use, as he says, of those of
the English who, not understanding Latin, spoke only the
Romance (or French); ‡ the anonymous author of a continuation of Wace's Brut, in the common octosyllabic verse, in which
he brings down the history, in a fierce anti-Norman spirit, from
the death of Cadwallader at the close of the seventh century to
the twenty-fourth year of the reign of Henry III. (A.D. 1240),
telling, among other things not elsewhere to be found, a remarkable story of a prophetic revelation made to the Conqueror
touching the fates of his three sons; § Pierre du Ries, a Norman,
described as a writer of true poetical genius, who is the author
of the romance of Anseis de Carthage, one of the Paladins of
Charlemagne, in 10,850 verses, of the Roman de Beuves de
Hamton et de s'amie Josiane, fille du Roi d'Armenie (our
English Bevis of Hampton), in 18,525 verses, and of a continuation of a romance on the subject of Judas Machabeus begun by
Gautier de Belleperche; || Godfrey of Waterford, an Irish
Dominican monk, the author of a verse translation of the pretended Trojan History of Dares Phrygius, and also of several
other versions of Latin works into French prose; ¶ Robert Bikez,
the writer, in the latter part of the thirteenth century, of the
Lai du Corn, founded on a very popular Arthurian fiction; **
two anonymous writers of the same age, to each of whom we
owe a short poem on the Purgatory of St. Patrick (one of about
1800, and the other of about 700 verses); †† Walter of Exeter, a
Franciscan monk of Cornwall, to whom is attributed the romance

* New De la Rue, Essais, iii. 127–138.
† Id. 139–145.
‡ Id. 150, 151; see also Tyrwhitt, Essay, note 65.
§ Id. 157–160; also in Archaeologia, xiii. 242–246.
|| Id. 170–170.
¶ Id. p. 211.
** See Tyrwhitt, Discourse, note 24; Warton, Hist. ii. 432; and De la Rue,
Essais, iii. 216.
†† De la Rue, Essais, iii. 215. Upon this subject see St. Patrick's Pur-
gatory, an Essay on the Legends of Purgatory, Hell, and Paradise, current
during the Middle Ages; by Thomas Wright, Esq. 8vo. Lond. 1844.

of Guy de Warwick, et de Felice fille du Comte de Bukingham
(extending to nearly 11,500 verses); and Peter de Langtoft, a
canon of the priory of St. Augustine at Bridlington, in Yorkshire, who has left us a translation of the British History of
Geoffrey of Monmouth, a continuation of the English story in
the same style from the arrival of the Saxons to the reign of
Edward I., a Life of that King, a translation of Herbert de
Bosham's Latin Life of Becket, and one or two shorter pieces,
all in French verse.*

FRENCH PROSE ROMANCES.—FROISSART.

Down to the end of the twelfth century verse was probably
the only form in which romances, meaning originally any compositions in the Romance or French language, then any narrative
compositions whatever, were written; in the thirteenth, a few
may have appeared in prose; but before the close of the
fourteenth prose had become the usual form in which such
works were produced, and many of the old metrical romances
had been recast in this new shape. The early French prose
romances, however, do not, like their metrical predecessors,
belong in any sense to the literature of this country: many of
them were no doubt generally read for a time in England as well
as in France; but we have no reason for believing that any of
them were primarily addressed to the English public, or were
written in England or by English subjects, and even during the
brief space that they continued popular they seemed to have
been regarded as foreign importations. Their history, therefore,
is no part of our present subject. But there is one remarkable
product of the French literature of the fourteenth century which
must be made an exception, the Chronicle of the inimitable Sire
Jean Froissart. This work, indeed, has, in everything except
the language in which it is written, nearly as much of an
English as of a French interest. Froissart was a native of
Valenciennes, where he appears to have been born about 1337;
but the four Books of his Chronicle,—which relates principally to
English affairs, though the narrative embraces also the course of
events in France, Flanders, Scotland, and other countries,—com

* De la Rue, Essais, iii. 231-239.

prehend the space from 1320 to 1400, or the whole of the reigns
of our Edward III. and Richard II. For the first thirty years of
this space he intimates that his authority was a previous writer,
Jean le Bel, canon of Liège, whom he greatly praises for his
diligence and accuracy; and some years ago the Chronicle of
Le Bel, which was supposed to have perished, was discovered in
the library of the old Dukes of Burgundy at Brussels, when it
turned out that Froissart's first eighty chapters are almost a
literal transcript from his predecessor. Froissart, however, is
rather of authority as a painter of manners than as an historian
of events; for his passion for the marvellous and the decorative
was so strong, that the simple fact, we fear, would have had little
chance of acceptance with him in any case when it came into
competition with a good story. In his own, and in the next age,
accordingly, his history was generally reckoned and designated
a romance. Caxton, in his Boke of the Ordre of Chevalrye or
Knighthood, classes it with the romances of Lancelot and
Percival; and indeed the Roman au Chroniques seems to have
been the title by which it was at first commonly known. On
the other hand, however, it is fair to remember that a romance
was not in those days held to be necessarily a fiction. Froissart's
Chronicle is certainly the truest and most lively picture that
any writer has bequeathed to us of the spirit of a particular era;
it shows "the very age and body of the time his form and
pressure." In a higher than the literal sense, the most apocryphal incidents of this most splendid and imaginative of gossips
are full of truth; they cast more light upon the actual men and
manners that are described, and bring back to life more of the
long-buried past, than the most careful details of any other
historian. The popularity of Froissart's Chronicle has thrown
into the shade his other productions; but his highest fame in his
own day was as a writer of poetry. His greatest poetical work
appears to have been a romance entitled Meliador, or the
Knight of the Sun of Gold; and he also wrote many shorter
pieces, chants royaux, ballads, rondeaux, and pastorals, in what
was then called the New Poetry, which, indeed, he cultivated
with so much success that he has by some been regarded as its
inventor.* On his introduction to Richard II., when he paid his

* See Warton, Hist. of Eng. Poetry, ii. 173, 300.—" It is a proof of the decay
of invention among the French in the beginning of the fourteenth century,
that about that period they began to translate into prose their old metrical

last visit to England in 1396, he presented that monarch, as he tells us, with a book beautifully illuminated, engrossed with his own hand, bound in crimson velvet, and embellished with silver bosses, clasps and golden roses, comprehending all the pieces of Amours and Moralities which he had composed in the twenty-four preceding years. Richard, he adds, seemed much pleased, and examined the book in many places; for he was fond of reading as well as speaking French.

RESURRECTION OF THE ENGLISH LANGUAGE.

But for the last fifty years of the fourteenth century the French language had been rapidly losing the position it had held among us from the middle of the tenth, and becoming among all classes in England a foreign tongue. We have already produced the testimonies of Higden writing immediately before the commencement of this change, and of Trevisa after it had been going on for about a quarter of a century; to these may now be added what Chaucer writes, probably within ten years after the date (1385) which Trevisa expressly notes as that of his statement. In the Prologue to his Testament of Love, a prose work, which seems to have been far advanced, if not finished, in 1392,* the great father of our English poetry, speaking of those of his countrymen who still persisted in writing French verse, expresses himself thus:—" Certes there ben some that spoke thyr poyay maior in Frenche, of whyche speche the Frenche men have as good a fantasye as we have in hearing of French mennes Englyshe." And afterwards he adds, " Let, then, clerkes endyten in Latyn, for they have the propertye in science and the knowinge in that facultye, and lotte Frenchmen in theyr Frenche also endyte theyr queynt termes, for it is kyndly [natural] to theyr mouthes; and let us shewe our fantasyes in

---

romances, ... At length, about the year 1380, in the place of the Provencial a new species of poetry succeeded in France, consisting of Chants Royaux, Balades, Roundeaux, and Pastorales. This was distinguished by the appellation of the New Poetry."

* See Tyrwhitt's Account of the Works of Chaucer, prefixed to his Glossary.

suche wordes as we learneden of our dames tonge." French, it
is evident from this, although it might still be a common acquire-
ment among the higher classes, had ceased to be the mother-
tongue of any class of Englishmen, and was only known to those
to whom it was taught by a master. So, the Prioress in the
Canterbury Tales, although she could speak French " ful fayre
and fetialy," or neatly, spoke it only

> " After the scole of Stratford atte Bowe,
> For Frenche of Paris was to hire [her] unknowe."*

From this, as from many other passages in old writers, we learn
that the French taught and spoken in England had, as was indeed
inevitable, become a corrupt dialect of the language, or at least
very different from the French at Paris. But, as the foreign
tongue lost its hold and declined in purity, the old Teutonic
speech of the native population, favoured by the same circumstances and course of events which checked and depressed its
rival, and having at last, after going through a process almost
of dissolution and putrefaction, began to assume a new organization, gradually recovered its ascendancy.

We have already examined the first revolution which the
language underwent, and endeavoured to explain the manner in
which it was brought about. It consisted in the disintegration
of the grammatical system of the language, and the conversion of
it from an inflectional and synthetic into a comparatively non-
inflected and analytic language. The vocabulary, or what we
may call the substance of the language, was not changed; that
remained still purely Gothic, as it always had been; only the
old form or structure was broken up or obliterated. There was
no mixture or infusion of any foreign element; the language

* It is impossible to believe with Sir Harris Nicolas, in his otherwise very
clear and judicious Life of Chaucer (8vo. Lond. 1643; additional note, p. 142),
that Chaucer perhaps here meant to intimate that the prioress could not
speak French at all, on the ground that the expression " French of Stratford-
at-Bow" is used in a tract published in 1586 (Ferne's Blazon of Gentrie), to
describe the language of English heraldry. In the first place the phrase is not
there "a colloquial paraphrase for English," but for the mixed French and
English, or, as it might be regarded, Anglicized or corrupted French, of our
heralds. But, at any rate, can it be supposed for a moment that Chaucer
would take so roundabout and fantastic a way as this of telling his readers
so simple a fact, as that his prioress could speak her native tongue? He
would never have spent three words upon such a matter, much less three
lines.

was as it were decomposed, but was not adulterated, and the process of decomposition may be regarded as having been the work of the eleventh century, and as having been begun by the Danish Conquest and consummated by the Norman.

This first revolution which the language underwent is to be carefully distinguished from the second, which was brought about by the combination of the native with a foreign element, and consisted essentially in the change made in the vocabulary of the language by the introduction of numerous terms borrowed from the French. Of this latter innovation we find little trace till long after the completion of the former. For nearly two centuries after the Conquest the English seems to have been spoken and written (to the small extent to which it was written) with scarcely any intermixture of Norman. It only, in fact, began to receive such intermixture after it came to be adopted as the speech of that part of the nation which had previously spoken French. And this adoption was plainly the cause of the intermixture. So long as it remained the language only of those who had been accustomed to speak it from their infancy, and who had never known any other, it might have gradually become changed in its internal organization, but it could scarcely acquire any additions from a foreign source. What should have tempted the Saxon peasant to substitute a Norman term, upon any occasion, for the word of the same meaning with which the language of his ancestors supplied him? As for things and occasions for which now names were necessary, they must have come comparatively little in his way; and, when they did, the capabilities of his native tongue were sufficient to furnish him with appropriate forms of expression from its own resources. The corruption of the English by the intermixture of French vocables must have proceeded from those whose original language was French, and who were in habits of constant intercourse with French customs, French literature, and everything else that was French, at the same time that they, occasionally at least, spoke English. And this supposition is in perfect accordance with the historical fact. So long as the English was the language of only a part of the nation, and the French, as it were, struggled with it for mastery, it remained unadulterated;—when it became the speech of the whole people, of the higher classes as well as of the lower, then it lost its old Teutonic purity, and received a larger alien admixture from the alien lips through which it passed. Whether this was a fortunate circumstance, or the reverse, is another question. It may just be remarked, however, that the English, if it had been left to its own spontaneous and unassisted development, would probably have assumed a character resembling rather that of the Dutch or the Flemish than that of the German of the present day.

The commencement of this second revolution, which changed the very substance of the language, may most probably be dated from about the middle of the thirteenth century, or about a century and a half after the completion of the first, which affected, not the substance or vocabulary of the language, but only its form or grammatical system.

SECOND ENGLISH:—
COMMONLY CALLED *SEMI-SAXON.*

The chief remains that we have of English verse for the first two centuries after the Conquest have been enumerated by Sir Frederic Madden in a comprehensive paragraph of his valuable Introduction to the romance of Havelock, which we will take leave to transcribe:—" The notices by which we are enabled to trace the rise of our Saxon poetry from the Saxon period to the end of the twelfth century are few and scanty. We may, indeed, comprise them all in the Song of Canute recorded by the monk of Ely [Hist. Elyens. p. 505 apud Gale), who wrote about 1166; the words put into the mouth of Aldred archbishop of York, who died in 1069 [W. Malmesb. de Gest. Pontif. l. i. p. 271); the verses ascribed to St. Godric, the hermit of Finchale, who died in 1170 [Rits. Bibliogr. Poet.]; the few lines preserved by Lambarde and Camden attributed to the same period [Rits. Anc. Songs, Diss. p. xxviii.]; and the prophecy said to have been set up at Hera in the year 1189, as recorded by Benedict Abbas, Roger Hoveden, and the Chronicle of Lanercost [Rits. Metr. Rom. Diss. p. lxxiii.]. To the same reign of Henry II. are to be assigned the metrical compositions of Layamon [MS. Coll. Cal. A. ix, and Otho C. xiii.] and Orm [MS. Jun. 1], and also the legends of St. Katherine, St. Margaret, and St. Julian [MS. Bodl. 34], with some few others, from which we may learn with tolerable accuracy the state of the language at that time, and its gradual formation from the Saxon to the shape it subsequently assumed.

From this period to the middle of the next century nothing
occurs to which we can affix any certain date; but we shall probably not err in ascribing to that interval the poems ascribed to
John de Guldevorde [MSS. Cott. Cal A. ix., Jes. Coll. Oxon. 29],
the Biblical History [MS. Bennet Cant. R. 11] and Poetical
Paraphrase of the Psalms [MSS. Cott. Vesp. D. vii., Coll. Benn.
Cant. O. 6, Bodl. 921] quoted by Warton, and the Moral Ode
published by Hickes [MSS. Digby 4, Jes. Coll. Oxon. 29].
Between the years 1244 and 1258, we know, was written the
versification of part of a meditation of St. Augustine, as proved
by the age of the prior who gave the MS. to the Durham Library
[MS. Eccl. Dun. A. iii. 12, and Bodl. 42]. Soon after this time
also were composed the earlier Songs in Ritson and Percy (1264),
with a few more pieces which it is unnecessary to particularize.
This will bring us to the close of Henry III.'s reign and beginning of his successor's, the period assigned by our poetical
antiquaries to the romances of Sir Tristrem, Kyng Horn, and
Kyng Alesaunder." *

The verse that has been preserved of the song composed by
Canute as he was one day rowing on the Nen, while the holy
music came floating on the air and along the water from the choir
of the neighbouring minster of Ely—a song which we are told
by the historian continued to his day, after the lapse of a
century and a half, to be a universal popular favourite †—is very
nearly such English as was written in the fourteenth century.
This interesting fragment properly falls to be given as the first
of our specimens :—

> Merie sungen the muneches binnen Ely
> Tha Cnut Ching rew there by :
> Roweth, cnihtes, noer the lant,
> And here we thes muneches seng.

That is, literally,—

> Merry (sweetly) sung the monks within Ely
> That (when) Cnute King rowed thereby :
> Row, knights, near the land,
> And hear we these monks' song.

---

* The Ancient English Romance of Havelok the Dane; Introduction,
p. xlii. We have transferred the references, inclosed in brackets, from the
bottom of the page to the text.

† Quæ usque hodie in choris publice cantantur, et in proverbiis memo-
rantur.

Being in verse and in rhyme, it is probable that the words are
reported in their original form; they cannot, at any rate, be much
altered.

The not very clerical address of Archbishop Aldred to Ursus
Earl of Worcester, who refused to take down one of his castles
the ditch of which encroached upon a monastic churchyard, consists, as reported by William of Malmesbury (who by-the-by
praises its elegance) of only two short lines:—

> Hatest thou* Urse?
> Have thou God's curse.

The hymn of St. Godric has more of an antique character. It
is thus given by Ritson, who professes to have collated the Royal
MS. 5 F. vii., and the Harleian MS. 322, and refers also to Matt.
Parisiensis Historia, pp. 119, 120, edit. 1640, and to (MS. Cott.)
Nero D. v:—

> Sainte Marie [clane] virgine,
> Moder Jhesu Cristes Nazarene,
> On fo [or fong] schild, help thin Godric,
> On fang bring hegilich with tho in Godes riche.
> Sainte Marie, Christe's bur,
> Maidens clenhad, moderes flur,
> Dilie min sinne [or seunen], rix in min mod,
> Bring me to winne with the selfd God.

"By the assistance of the Latin versions," adds Ritson, "one
is enabled to give it literally in English, as follows:—Saint
Mary [chaste] virgin, mother of Jesus Christ of Nazareth, take,
shield, help thy Godric; take, bring him quickly with thee
into God's kingdom. Saint Mary, Christ's chamber, purity of a
maiden, flower of a mother, destroy my sin, reign in my mind,
bring me to dwell with the only God."

Two other short compositions of the same poetical eremite are
much in the same style. One is a couplet said to have been sung
to him by the spirit or ghost of his sister, who appeared to him
after her death and thus assured him of her happiness:—

> Crist and Sainte Marie swa on scamel me ledde
> That ic on this erde ne silde with mine bare fote Itredde.

Which Ritson translates:—"Christ and Mary, thus supported,
have me brought, that I on earth should not with my bare foot
tread."

* That is, Hightest thou (art thou called)? Malmesbury's Latin translation
is, "Vocaris Ursus: habeas Dei maledictionem." But the first line seems to
be interrogative.

The other is a hymn to St. Nicholas:—

> Sainte Nicholaes, Godes druth,
> Tymbre us faire scone hus.
> At thi burth, at thi bare,
> Sainte Nicholaes, bring us wel there.

"That is," says Ritson, "Saint Nicholas, God's lover, build us a fair beautiful house. At thy birth, at thy bier, Saint Nicholas, bring us safely thither."

As for the rhymes given by Lambarde and Camden as of the twelfth century, they can hardly in the shape in which we have them be of anything like that antiquity: they are, in fact, in the common English of the sixteenth century. Lambarde (in his Dictionary of England, p. 36) tells us that a rabble of Flemings and Normans brought over in 1173 by Robert Earl of Leicester, when they were assembled on a heath near St. Edmonds Bury, "fell to dance and sing,

> Hoppe Wylikin, hoppe Wyllykin,
> Ingland is thyne and myne, &c."

Camden's story is that Hugh Bigott, Earl of Norfolk, in the reign of Stephen used to boast of the impregnable strength of his castle of Bungey after this fashion:—

> " Were I in my castle of Bungey,
> Upon the river of Waveney,
> I would ne care for the king of Cockeney."

THE HERE PROPHECY.

What Sir Frederick Madden describes as "the prophecy said to have been set up at Here in the year 1180" is given by Ritson as follows:—

> Whan thu sees in Here hert yrerel,
> Than sulen Engles in three be ydelet:
> That an into Yrland al to late waie,
> That other into Puille mid prude hleve,
> The thridde into Airhahen herd all wreken drechegen.

These lines, which he calls a "specimen of English poetry. apparently of the same age" (the latter part of the 12th century),

Ritson says are preserved by Benedictus Abbas, by Hoveden, and
by the Chronicle of Lanercost; and he professes to give them,
and the account by which they are introduced, from "the
former," by which he means the first of the three. But in truth
the verses do not occur as he has printed them in any of the
places to which he refers. Benedictus Abbas (p. 622) has two
versions of them, the second of which he introduces by the word
"roetims" (more correctly); there is a third in the printed
Hoveden; what Ritson has mistaken for the Lanercost Chronicle
is an imperfect manuscript of Hoveden (Cotton MS. Claud. D.
vii. fol. 101), in which they occur very nearly as printed in his
Hoveden by Savile—the only difference of any importance being,
that the MS. has in the fourth line "bi lone," whereas Savile
(both in the London edition 1596, fol. 386 r°, and in the Francfort edition 1601, p. 678) has "bi scuo." Ritson's transcript is
evidently taken either from the manuscript or the printed
Hoveden: it is quite unlike either of the versions given by
Benedictus. But it is a very inaccurate transcript: to pass over
minor variations, all the four originals, for instance, have "sul"
or "sale" before "into Yrland" in the third line; and the last
line stands nowhere as Ritson has given it:—in the first copy of
Benedictus it is, "The thirde in hayre haugben hort alle
ydregho;" in the second it is, "The thride in hiro athen hert
alle wreke y-droghe;" in the MS. Hoveden it is "The thriddo
into airhahen herd alle Wrek y drehogon" (or perhaps
"drehogra"); in the printed Hoveden it is, "The thridde into
Airhahen herd all wreke y drechegen." The line in any of the
four forms in which we have it, appears to be entirely unintelligible; and indeed the verses are manifestly corrupt throughout,
although a sort of sense may be made out of most of the others.
"Puillo" is "Apulia;" and the "wreko" in the last line may
have something to do with a law about wrecks which both
Benedict and Hoveden immediately go on to state that Richard
proclaimed at this time, A.D. 1190, after his successful military
operations against King Tancred in Sicily and Calabria (or
Apulia); but what is "Airhahen?" or where, can any one tell,
is the town of "Here," of which Ritson and others who quote or
refer to verses speak so familiarly? Over this name the second
version in Benedict has the word "Host" printed, with a point
of interrogation, as if intended for a gloss. But the most remarkable circumstance of all is, that there is no ground at all for

supposing, as is done by Ritson and Sir Frederic Madden, that
the verses were ever inscribed or set up upon any house at
"Here" or elsewhere. What is said both by Benedict and
Hoveden (who employ nearly the same words) is simply that
the figure of a hart was set upon the pinnacle of the house, in
order, as was believed, that the prophecy contained in the verses
might be accomplished—which prophecy, we are told immediately before, had been found engraven in ancient characters upon stone tables in the neighbourhood of the place. It is
clearly intended to be stated that the prophecy was much older
than the building of the house, and the erection of the figure of
a stag, in the year 1190. This is sufficiently conveyed in
Ritson's own translation. What he means, therefore, by saying,
" As the inscription was set up when the house was built, before
the death of Henry the Second, in 1189," is not obvious. Benedict says that the house was built by Ranulfus, or Ralph (not
" Randal," as Ritson translates it) Fitzstephen (Ranulfo, filio
Stephani); Hoveden, by William; which latter Ritson, we do
not know upon what authority, intimates is the correct name.
Both chroniclers state that the place, which was a royal town
(*villam regis Angliæ*), had been given to Fitzstephen by King
Henry, that is, probably, Henry II., as Ritson assumes; but
this, we repeat, determines nothing as to the age of the verses,
which were, or were supposed to be, of much earlier date than
either the erection of the house or the grant of the property.

———

THE BRUT OF LAYAMON.

Layamon, or, as he is also called, Laweman—for the old character represented in this instance by our modern *y* is really
only a guttural (and by no means either a *j* or a *z*, by which it
is sometimes rendered)—tells us himself that he was a priest,
and that he resided at Ernley, near Radstone, or Redstone,
which appears to have been what is now called Arley Regis, or
Lower Arley, on the western bank of the Severn, in Worcestershire. He seems to say that he was employed in the services of
the church at that place:—" ther he book made" (there he
book read). And the only additional information that he gives
us respecting himself is, that his father's name was Leovenath
(or Louca, as it is given in the later of the two texts).

His Brut, or Chronicle of Britain (from the arrival of Brutus
to the death of King Cadwalader in A.D. 689), is in the main,
though with many additions, a translation of the French Brut
d'Angleterre of Wace, which is itself, as has been stated above,
a translation, also with considerable additions from other
sources, of Geoffrey of Monmouth's Latin Historia Britonum,
which again professes, and probably with truth, to be translated from a Welsh or Breton original. So that the genealogy
of the four versions or forms of the narrative is :—first, a Celtic
original, believed to be now lost; secondly, the Latin of
Geoffrey of Monmouth; thirdly, the French of Wace; fourthly,
the English of Layamon. The Celtic or British version is of
unknown date; the Latin is of the earlier, the French of the
latter, half of the twelfth century; and that of Layamon would
appear to have been completed in the first years of the thirteenth.
We shall encounter a second English translation from Wace's
French before the middle of the fourteenth.

The existence of Layamon's Chronicle had long been known,
but it had attracted very little attention till comparatively recent
times. It is merely mentioned even by Warton and Tyrwhitt—
the latter only remarking (in his Essay on the Language and
Versification of Chaucer), that, "though the greatest part of
this work of Layamon resembles the old Saxon poetry, without
rhyme or metre, yet he often intermixes a number of short
verses of unequal lengths, but rhyming together pretty exactly,
and in some places he has imitated not unsuccessfully the regular
octosyllabic measure of his French original." George Ellis, in
his Specimens of the Early English Poets, originally published in 1790, was, we believe, the first to introduce Layamon
to the general reader, by giving an extract of considerable
length, with explanatory annotations, from what he described
as his " very curious work," which, he added, never had been,
and probably never would be, printed. Subsequently another
considerable specimen, in every way much more carefully and
learnedly edited, and accompanied with a literal translation
throughout into the modern idiom, was presented by Mr. Guest
in his History of English Rhythms, 1838 (ii. 113-120). But
now the whole work has been edited by Sir Frederic Madden,
for the Society of Antiquaries of London, in three volumes 8vo.
1847. This splendid publication, besides a Literal Translation,
Notes, and a Grammatical Glossary, contains the Brut in two

texts, separated from each other by an interval apparently of
about half a century, and, whether regarded in reference to
the philological, to say nothing of the historical, value and
importance of Layamon's work, or to the admirable and altogether satisfactory manner in which the old chronicle is exhibited and illustrated, may fairly be characterized as by far
the most acceptable present that has been made to the students
of early English literature in our day.

His editor conceives that we may safely assume Layamon's
English to be that of North Worcestershire, the district in which
he lived and wrote.   But this western dialect, he contends, was
also that of the southern part of the island, having in fact
originated to the south of the Thames, whence, he says, it
gradually extended itself " as far as the courses of the Severn,
the Wye, the Tame, and the Avon, and more or less pervaded
the counties of Gloucestershire, Worcestershire, Herefordshire,
Warwickshire, and Oxfordshire,"—besides prevailing "throughout the channel counties from east to west,"—notwithstanding
that several of the counties that have been named, and that of
Worcester especially, had belonged especially to the non-Saxon
kingdom of Mercia.   "The language of Layamon," he farther
holds, "belongs to that transition period in which the groundwork of Anglo-Saxon phraseology and grammar still existed,
although gradually yielding to the influence of the popular
forms of speech.   We find in it, as in the later portion of the
Saxon Chronicle, marked indications of a tendency to adopt
those terminations and sounds which characterise a language
in a state of change, and which are apparent also in some other
branches of the Teutonic tongue."   As showing "the progress
made in the course of two centuries in departing from the
ancient and purer grammatical forms, as found in Anglo-Saxon
manuscripts," he mentions "the use of *a* as an article;—the
change of the Anglo-Saxon terminations *a* and *an* into *e* and *en*,
as well as the disregard of inflexions and genders;—the masculine forms given to neuter nouns in the plural;—the neglect
of the feminine terminations of adjectives and pronouns, and
confusion between the definite and indefinite declensions; the
introduction of the preposition *to* before infinitives, and occasional use of weak preterites of verbs and participles instead of
strong;—the constant occurrence of *en* for *on* in the plurals of
verbs, and frequent elision of the final *e*;—together with the

uncertainty in the rule for the government of prepositions."
In the earlier text one of the most striking peculiarities is
what has been termed the *nunnation*, defined by Sir Frederic
as "consisting of the addition of a final *n* to certain cases of
nouns and adjectives, to some tenses of verbs, and to several
other parts of speech." The western dialect, of which both
texts, and especially the earlier, exhibit strong marks, is further
described as perceptible in the " termination of the present tense
plural in *th*, and infinitives in *i, ie,* or *y ;* the forms of the plural
personal pronouns, *heo, heore, heom ;* the frequent occurrence of
the prefix *i* before past participles ; the use of *v* for *f ;* and prevalence of the vowel *u* for *i* or *y,* in such words as *dude, hudde,*
hulle, putte, hure, &c." " But," it is added, " on comparing the
two texts carefully together, some remarkable variations are
apparent in the later, which seem to arise, not from its having
been composed at a more recent period, but from the infusion
of an Anglian or Northern element into the dialect." From
these indications the learned editor is disposed to think that
the later text "may have been composed or transcribed in one
of the counties conterminous to the Anglian border, and he
suggests that "perhaps we might fix on the eastern side of
Leicestershire as the locality."

One thing in the English of Layamon that is eminently deserving of notice with reference to the history of the language
is the very small amount of the French or Latin element that is
found in it. "The fact itself," Sir F. Madden observes, "of a
translation of Wace's poem by a priest of one of the midland
counties is sufficient evidence how widely the knowledge of the
writings of the *trouvères* was dispersed, and it would appear a
natural consequence, that not only the outward form of the
Anglo-Norman versification, but also that many of the terms
used in the original would be borrowed. This, however, is
but true in a very trifling degree, compared with the extent of
the work ; for, if we number the words derived from the French
(even including some that may have come directly from the
Latin), we do not find in the earlier text of Layamon's poem so
many as fifty, several of which were in usage, as appears by the
Saxon Chronicle, previous to the middle of the twelfth century.
Of this number the later text retains about thirty, and adds to
them rather more than forty which are not found in the earlier
version ; so that, if we reckon ninety words of French origin in

both texts, containing together more than 50,800 lines, we shall be able to form a tolerably correct estimate how little the English language was really affected by foreign converse, even as late as the middle of the thirteenth century."*

Layamon's poem extends to nearly 32,250 lines, or more than double the length of Wace's Brut. This may indicate the amount of the additions which the English chronicler has made to his French original. That, however, is only one, though the chief, of several preceding works to which he professes himself to have been indebted. His own account is :—

> He nom the Englisch boc
> Tha makede Seint Beda ;
> An other he nom on Latin,
> Tha makede Seinte Albin,
> And the feire Austin,
> The fulluht broute hider in.
> Boc he nom the thridde,
> Leide ther amidden,
> Tha makede a Frenchis clerc,
> Wace was ihoten,
> The wel couthe writen,
> And he hoo yef thare aethelen
> Aelienor, tha wes Henries quene,
> Thes heyes kinges.
> Layamon leide theos boc,
> And tha leaf wende.
> He heom leofliche bi-hoold ;
> Lithe him beo Drihten.
> Fetheren he nom mid fingren,
> And fiede on boc-felle,
> And tha sothe word
> Sette to-gathere,
> And tha thre boc
> Thrumde to ane.

That is, literally :—

> He took the English book
> That Saint Bede made ;
> Another he took in Latin,
> That Saint Albin made,
> And the fair Austin,
> That baptism brought hither in.

---

* Preface xxiii.

The third book he took,
[And] laid there in midst,
That made a French clerk,
Wace was [he] called,
That well could write,
And he it gave to the noble
Eleanor, that was Henry's queen,
The high king's.
Layamon laid [before him] these books,
And the leaves turned.
He them lovingly beheld;
Merciful to him be [the] Lord.
Feather (pen) he took with fingers,
And wrote on book-skin,
And the true words
Set together,
And the three books
Compressed into one.

His English book was no doubt the translation into the vernacular tongue, commonly attributed to King Alfred, of Bede's
Ecclesiastical History, which Layamon does not seem to have
known to have been originally written in Latin. What he says
about his Latin book is unintelligible. St. Austin died in
A.D. 604; and the only Albin of whom anything is known was
Albin abbot of St. Austin's at Canterbury, who is mentioned by
Bede as one of the persons to whom he was indebted for assistance in the compilation of his History; but he lived more than
a century after St. Austin (or Augustine). Some Latin chronicle,
however, Layamon evidently had; and his scholarship, therefore, extended to an acquaintance with two other tongues in
addition to the now obsolete classic form of his own.

The principal, and indeed almost the only, passage in Layamon's poem from which any inference can be drawn as to the
precise time when it was written, is one near the end (p. 31,
070-80) in which, speaking of the tax called Rome-foch, Rome-
scot, or Peter-penco, he seems to express a doubt whether it will
much longer continue to be paid—

Drihte wat hu longe
Theo lagen scullen ilaeste
(The Lord knows how long
The law shall last).

This his learned editor conceives to allude to a resistance which
it appears was made to the collection of the tax by King John

and the nobility in the year 1205; and that supposition, he
further suggests, may be held to be fortified by the manner in
which Queen Eleanor, who had retired to Aquitaine on the
accession of John, and died abroad at an advanced age in 1204,
is spoken of in the passage quoted above from what we may call
the Preface, written, no doubt, after the work was finished—
" Aelienor, the wes Henries quone."

" The structure of Layamon's poem," Sir Frederic observes,
" consists partly of lines in which the alliterative system of the
Anglo-Saxons is preserved, and partly of couplets of unequal
length rhiming together. Many couplets, indeed, occur which
have both of these forms, whilst others are often met with which
possess neither.   The latter, therefore, must have depended
wholly on accentuation, or have been corrupted in transcription.
The relative proportion of each of these forms is not to be ascertained without extreme difficulty, since the author uses them
everywhere intermixed, and slides from alliteration to rhime, or
from rhime to alliteration, in a manner perfectly arbitrary. The
alliterative portion, however, predominates on the whole greatly
over the lines rhiming together, even including the imperfect or
assonant terminations, which are very frequent." Mr. Guest,
Sir Frederic notes, has shown by the specimen which he has
given with the accents marked in his English Rhythms (ii. 114-
124), " that the rhiming couplets of Layamon are founded on the
models of accentuated Anglo-Saxon rhythms of four, five, six, or
seven accents."

Layamon's poetical merit, and also his value as an original
authority, are rated rather high by his editor. His additions to
and amplifications of Wace, we are told, consist in the earlier
part of the work " principally of the speeches placed in the
mouths of different personages, which are often given with quite
a dramatic effect." " The text of Wace," it is added, " is enlarged
throughout, and in many passages to such an extent, particularly
after the birth of Arthur, that one line is dilated into twenty ;
names of persons and localities are constantly supplied, and not
unfrequently interpolations occur of entirely new matter, to the
extent of more than an hundred lines. Layamon often embel-
lishes and improves on his copy; and the meagre narrative of
the French poet is heightened by graphic touches and details,
which give him a just claim to be considered, not as a mere
translator, but as an original writer."

"It is a remarkable circumstance," Sir Frederic afterwards
remarks, "that we find preserved in many passages of Layamon's
poem the spirit and style of the earlier Anglo-Saxon writers.
No one can read his descriptions of battles and scenes of strife
without being reminded of the Ode on Athelstan's victory at
Brunanburh. The ancient mythological genders of the sun and
moon are still unchanged; the memory of the *Witena-gemot* has
not yet become extinct; and the neigh of the *Aengest* still seems
to resound in our ears. Very many phrases are purely Anglo-
Saxon, and, with slight change, might have been used in
Cædmon or Ælfric. A foreign scholar and poet, versed both in
Anglo-Saxon and Scandinavian literature, has declared, that,
tolerably well read as he is in the rhiming chronicles of his own
country, and of others, he has found Layamon's beyond comparison the most lofty and animated in its style, at every
moment reminding the reader of the splendid phraseology of
Anglo-Saxon verse." This is the Rev. N. F. S. Grundtvig, of
Copenhagen, in a prospectus which he put forth in 1830, containing proposals for publishing Layamon and other ancient
English works.

We cannot do better than give as our specimen of Layamon's
poetry King Arthur's account of his dream, to which both
Sir Frederic Maiden and Sharon Turner have called attention. "The dream of Arthur as related by himself to his companions in arms," Sir Frederic observes, " is the creation of a
mind of a higher order than is apparent in the creeping rhimes
of more recent chroniclers." It runs thus :—

> To niht a mine slepe,
> [To night in my sleep]
> Ther ich lai on bure,
> [Where I lay in bower (chamber)]
> Me imette a swevon;
> [I dreamt* a dream]
> Ther wure ich ful sari sem.
> [Therefore I full sorry am]
> Me imette that mon me hof
> [I dreamt† that men raised me]
> Uppen are halle.
> [Upon a hall]
> Tha halle ich gon bestriden,
> [The hall I gan bestride]

---

* Rather, There met me, there occurred to me ?
† It occurred to me ?

Swulc ich wolde riden
  [So as I would ride]
Alle tha lond tha ich ah
  [All the land that I owned]
Alle ich ther oner sah.
  [All I there over-saw]
And Walwain sat binoren me ;
  [And Walwain sat before me]
Mi swerd he bar an honde
  [My sword he bare in hand].
Tha com Moddred faren ther
  [Thre came Modred to fare (go) there]
Mid unimete uolke,
  [With unmeasured (unnumbered) folk]
He bar an his honde
  [He bare in his hand]
Ane wlax stronge.
  [An axe strong]
He bigon to hewene
  [He began to hew]
Hardliche switbe,
  [Hardily exceedingly]
And tha postes for-heon alle
  [And the posts thoroughly-hewed all]
Tha beolden up tho halle.
  [That held up the hall]
Ther ich isay Weaheuer eke,
  [There I saw Weahever (Guinever, the Queen) eke]
Wimmonen leofnest me :
  [Of women loveliest to me]
Al there muche halle rof
  [All the great (mickle) hall roof]
Mid hire honden heo to-droh,
  [With her hands she drew (down)]
Tha halle gon to haeklen,
  [The hall gan to tumble]
And ich hackl to grunden,
  [And I tumbled to ground]
That mi riht aerm to-brac.
  [That my right arm broke]
Tha sehde Modred, Hauo that I
  [Then said Modred, Have that]
Adun neol tha halle
  [Adown fell the hall]
And Walwain gon to nalle,
  [And Walwain gan to fall]
And feol a there eortho ;
  [And fell on the earth]

His armes brekeen beine.
  [His arms brake both]
And ich igrap mi swcord leofe
  [And I grasped my dear sword]
Mid mire luoft honde,
  [With my left hand]
And smaet of Modred is haft,
  [And smote off Modred his head]
That hit wond a theue neld;
  [That it rolled (wended) on the field]
And tha quene ich al to-snaðhde,
  [And the queen I all cut to pieces (snedded)]
Mid deore mine sweorde,
  [With my dear sword]
And avodthen ich heo adun sette
  [And then I her adown set]
In ane swarto putte,
  [In a black pit]
And al mi uole riche
  [And all my rich (great) people]
Bette to fleme,
  [Set to flight]
That nuste ich under Cristo
  [That I wist not under Christ]
Whar heo bicomen weoren.
  [Where they were become (gone)]
Buten mi seolf ich gond atstonden
  [But myself I gan stand]
Uppen ane woldan
  [Upon a wold (or weald)]
And ich ther wondrien agon
  [And I there gan to wander]
Wide ycond than moren.
  [Wide over the moors]
Ther ich imh gripes
  [There I saw gripes (griffons)]
And grisliche fughelas.
  [And grisly fowls (birds)]
Tha com an guldene leo
  [Then came a golden lion]
Lithen ouer dune.
  [To glide over the down]
Deoren swithe hende,
  [A beast (deer) very handsome]
Tha ure Drihten make.
  [That our Lord made]
Tha leo me orn forth to,
  [The lion ran forward to me]

And lueng me bi than middle,
  [And took me by the middle]
And forth hire gun yeongen
  [And forth herself gan move]
And to there me wende.
  [And to the sea went]
And ich iseeh thae vthen
  [And I saw the waves]
I there me driuen ;
  [In the sea drive]
And the leo i than ulode
  [And the lion in the flood]
I wende with me seultis.
  [Went with myself]
Tha wit I sae comen,
  [When we in sea came]
Tha vthen me hire binomen.
  [The waves *from* me her took]
Com ther an fisc lithe,
  [Came there a fish to glide]*
And seruden me to lotale.
  [And brought me to land]
Tha wes ich al wet,
  [Then was I all wet]
And weri of soryen, and sexe.
  [And weary from sorrow, and sick]
Tha gon ich iwakien
  [When I gan to awake]
Swithe ich gon to quakien ;
  [Greatly I gan to quake]
Tha gon ich to binien
  [Then gan I to tremble]
Swule ich al fur barne.
  [As *if* I all with fire burned]
And swa ich habbe al niht
  [And so I have all night]
Of mine swenene swithe ithoht ;
  [Of my dream much thought]
For ich what to iwisse
  [For I wot to certainty]
Agan is al mi blisse ;
  [Agan is all my bliss]
For a to mine liue
  [For aye to (throughout) my life]

---

* That is, A fish approached. Unless we should understand *lithe* to be an
epithet of the fish. But the later text, " Com ther a fisc swemme " is against
that.

Soryen Ich mot driye.
[Sorrow I must endure]
Wale that Ich nabbe here
[Welaway (alas) that I have not here]
Weuhauer mine quene!
[Wenhaver, my queen].

28014—28003.

Here is evidently a considerable amount of true poetic life in
the conception, and also, as far as the apparent rudeness of the
language will admit—if we ought not perhaps rather to say as far
as the imperfect knowledge of its laws now attainable enables us
to form a judgment—considerable care and aptness of expression.
The conclusion of the address, in particular, is worked up to
no contemptible height of artistic elegance, as well as pathos.
Let the strange antiquated spelling only be regulated according
to the system with which we are all at present familiar, and, if
we will accept what are called assonant rhymes, as well as the
ordinary consonant ones—such as *night* and *thought*, *here* and
quern—and also sometimes, perhaps, consent to be satisfied without
rhyme at all in consideration of certain alliterative artifices, the
beauty of which, it must be confessed, has now become of somewhat difficult appreciation—we shall not find it deficient in
harmony, any more than in a graceful and expressive simplicity
of diction :—

And away I hab all night
Of min-e sweeven swythe ythought ;
For I wot to ywiss
Agone is all my bliss ;
For aye to min-e liv-e
Sorien I mote dri-e.
Wall-e! that I nab here
Wenhavere min-e queen !

This will represent pretty nearly the manner in which the
lines would probably be read by Layamon and his contemporaries.

The philological interest and importance of this work of
Layamon's are greatly enhanced by the fortunate circumstance
of its having come down to us in two texts, the one evidently
somewhat more recent than the other. Both have been most
judiciously given by Sir Frederic Madden—to whom, indeed,

we may be said to be chiefly indebted for the preservation of the
latter one, the manuscript containing which was so greatly
injured by the deplorable fire that was allowed to seize upon
the Cottonian Collection in the early part of last century as to be
regarded as having been rendered almost entirely illegible and
useless till he took the reparation of its fragments in hand, and
had them bound and inlaid, after they had been collected and
partially restored, about the year 1827, under the superintendence of the Rov. J. Forshall, his predecessor as keeper of the
MSS. in the British Museum. Of about 27,000 lines of which
this second edition, as it may be called, is calculated to have
consisted (for it is slightly condensed from the first), not quite
2,400 are supposed to be wholly lost, and only about 1,000 more
are in a partially injured state. So that, of the 32,250 lines, of
which the poem in its more extended form consists, we have
still between 23,000 and 24,000 perfect in both editions,—an
amount of material for comparison which leaves us hardly anything to regret in the loss of the 3,000 or 4,000 that have
perished. Fortunately the earlier edition appears to be complete.
It is contained in the Cott. MS. Caligula A. ix., the handwriting
of which is of the early part of the thirteenth century: the
other in the MS. Otho C. xiii., the handwriting of which is
supposed to be of the latter part of the same century. The
first text may be regarded as giving us probably the west
country English of about the year 1200, the second that of
1250.

The later text for the most part follows the earlier line for
line, though with occasional omissions; the differences which it
exhibits are confined to the substitution of more modern forms
for such vocables, constructions, and modes of expression as had
gone out of use or of fashion since the poem first appeared.
Unfortunately the manuscript has suffered considerably in the
part containing Arthur's dream; but many lines are still entire.
The first six, for instance, stand thus:—

> To niht in mine bedde
> Thar ich lay in loure,
> Me imette a sweuen;
> Thar fore ich sori bam.
> Me mette that men me selte
> Vppon one balke.

And here are the concluding six lines :--

> For ich wot al mid iwisse
> Agon his al min blisse ;
> For nuero to mine lifue
> Sorewe ich mot dribe.
> Wele that ich nadde her
> Mine cwenne Gwennyfer !

It ought to be observed that, although we have given throughout the u and v exactly as they stand in the printed edition, these are really only two ways of writing what was regarded as the same letter, and that in both texts sometimes the u is to be sounded like our modern v, sometimes the v like our modern u. Thus, *suenen* was pronounced *sweven*, *uore uore*, *ouer-n uppen*, *auerr avere*, &c.

THE ORMULUM.

Another metrical work of considerable extent, that known as the Ormulum, from Orm, or Ormin, which appears to have been the name of the writer, has been usually assigned to the same, or nearly the same age with the Brut of Layamon. It exists only in a single manuscript, which there is some reason for believing to be the author's autograph, now preserved in the Bodleian Library among the books bequeathed by the great scholar Francis Junius, who appears to have purchased it at the Hague in 1650 at the sale of the books of his deceased friend Janus Ulitius, or Vlitius (van Vliet), also an eminent philologist and book-collector. It is a folio volume, consisting of 90 parchment leaves, besides 29 others inserted, upon which the poetry is written in double columns, in a stiff but distinct hand, and without division into verses, so that the work had always been assumed to be in prose till its metrical character was pointed out by Tyrwhitt in his edition of Chaucer's Canterbury Tales, 1775. Accordingly no mention is made of it by Warton, the first volume of whose History was published in 1774. But it had previously been referred to by Hickes and others; and it has attracted a large share of the attention of all recent investigators of the history of the language. It has now been printed in full, under the title of The Ormulum; Now first edited from the

Original Manuscript in the Bodleian, with Notes and a glossary, by Robert Meadows White, D.D., late Fellow of St. Mary Magdalene College, and formerly Professor of Anglo-Saxon in the University of Oxford; 2 vols. 8vo. Oxford, at the University Press, 1852.

The Ormulum is described by Dr. White as being "a series of Homilies, in an imperfect state, composed in metre without alliteration, and, except in very few cases, also without rhyme; the subject of the Homilies being supplied by those portions of the New Testament which were read in the daily service of the Church." The plan of the writer is, we are further told, "first to give a paraphrastic version of the Gospel of the day, adapting the matter to the rules of his verse, with such verbal additions as were required for that purpose. He then adds an exposition of the subject in its doctrinal and practical bearings, in the treatment of which he borrows copiously from the writings of St. Augustine and Ælfric, and occasionally from those of Beda." "Some idea," it is added, "may be formed of the extent of Ormin's labours when we consider that, out of the entire series of Homilies, provided for nearly the whole of the yearly service, nothing is left beyond the text of the thirty-second." We have still nearly ten thousand long lines of the work, or nearly twenty thousand as Dr. White prints them, with the fifteen syllables divided into two sections, the one of eight the other of seven syllables,—the latter, which terminates in an unaccented syllable, being prosodically equivalent to one of six, so that the whole is simply our still common alternation of the eight-syllabled and the six-syllabled line, only without either rhyme or even alliteration, which makes it as pure a species of blank verse, though a different species, as that which is now in use.

The list of the texts, or subjects of the Homilies, as preserved in the manuscript, extends to 242, and it appears to be imperfect. Ormin plainly claims to have completed his long self-imposed task. Here is the beginning of the Dedication to his brother Walter, which stands at the head of the work:—

   Nu, brotherr Wallterr, brotherr min
    [Now, brother Walter, brother mine]
   Afflerr the flæshes kinde;
    [After the flesh's kind (or nature)]
   Annd brotherr min i Crisstenndom
    [And brother mine in Christendom (or Christ's kingdom)]

Thurrh fulluhht and thurrh trowwthe;
  [Through baptism and through truth]
Annd brotherr min I Godess hus,
  [And brother mine in God's house]
Yet o the thride wise,
  [Yet on (in) the third wise]
Thurrh thatt witt hafenn takenn ba
  [Though that we two have taken both]
An reghellboc to folghenn,
  [One rule-book to follow]
Unnderr kanunnkess had and lif,
  [Under canonic's (canon's) rank and life]
Swa summ Sannt Awwstin settde;
  [So as St. Austin set (or ruled)]
Icc hafe don swa summ thu badd
  [I have done so as thou bade]
Annd forthedd te thin wille;
  [And performed thee thine will (wish)]
Icc hafe wennd innntill Ennglissh
  [I have wended (turned) into English]
Goddspelless hallghe lare,
  [Gospel's holy lore]
Affterr thatt little witt tatt me
  [After that little wit that me]
Min Drihhtin hafethth lenedd.
  [My Lord hath lent]
Thu thohhtesst tatt itt mihhte well
  [Thou thoughtest that it might well]
Till mickell frame turrnenn
  [To mickle (much) profit turn]
Yiff Ennglissh follk, forr lufe off Crist,
  [If English folk for love of Christ]
Itt wollde yerne lernenn,
  [It would earnestly learn]
Annd follghenn itt, and fillenn itt
  [And follow it, and fulfil it]
Withth thohht, withth word, withth dede.
  [With thought, with word, with deed]
Annd forrthi gerrndesst tu thatt icc
  [And because thou desiredst that I]
Thiss werrc the shollde wirrkenn;
  [This work thee should work]
Annd icc itt hafe forthedd te,
  [And I it have performed thee]
Acc all thurrh Cristess hellpe;
  [But all through Christ's help]
Annd unnc birrth bathe thannkenn Crist
  [And us two it behoves both (to) thank Christ]

Thatt itt ias brohht till ende.
  [That it is brought to end]
Icc hafe sammned o thiss boc
  [I have collected on (or in) this book]
Tha Goddspelless nehh alle
  [The Gospels nigh all]
Thatt sinndenn o the mess-boc
  [That are on (or in) the mass-book]
Inn all the yer att messe.
  [In all the year at mass]
Annd ayy afterr the Goddspell stannt
  [And aye after the Gospel stands]
Thatt tatt the Goddspell menethth
  [That that the Gospel meaneth]
Thatt mann birrth spellenn to the follc
  [That one ought (to) declare to the folk]
Off theyyre saule nede ;
  [Of (or for) their soul (or soul's) need]
Annd yet taer tekenn mare inoh
  [And yet there in addition more enough]
Thu shallt tacronno findenn
  [Thou shalt thereon (or therein) find]
Off thatt tatt Cristess hallghe thed
  [Of that that Christ's holy people]
Birrth trowwenn wel and folghenn.
  [Behove (to) believe well and follow]
Icc hafe sett her o thiss boc
  [I have set here on (or in) this book]
Amang Goddspelless wordess,
  [Among (the) Gospel's words]
All thurrh me sellfenn, manig word
  [All through myself many (a) word]
The rime swa to fillen ;
  [The rhyme so to fill]
Acc thu shallt findenn thatt min word
  [But thou shalt find that my word]
Eyywhaer thaer itt iss ekedd
  [Everywhere there (or where) it is eked (or added)]
Mayy hellpenn tha thatt redenn itt
  [May help them that read it]
To unn and tunnderrstanndenn
  [To see and to understand]
All thiss te bettre bu theyym birrth
  [All this the better how them it behoveth]
The Goddspel unnderrstanndenn.
  [The Gospel (to) understand]   .

Ono remarkable feature in this English is evidently something very peculiar in the spelling. And the same system

is observed throughout the work. It is found on a slight examination to consist in the duplication of the consonant whenever it follows a vowel having any other than the sound which is now for the most part indicated by the annexation of a silent *e* to the single consonant, or what may be called the *name* sound, being that by which the vowel is commonly named or spoken of in our modern English. Thus *pane* would by Ormin be written *pan*, but *pan pann*; *mean men*, but *men menn*; *pine pin*, but *pin pinn*; *own on*, but *on onn*; *tune tun*, but *tun tunn*. This, as Mr. Guest has pointed out, is, after all, only a rigorous carrying out of a principle which has always been applied to a certain extent in English orthography,—as in *tally*, or *tall*, *berry*, *witty*, *folly*, *dull*, as compared with *tale*, *beer*, *white*, *lone*, *mule*. The effect, however, in Ormin's work is on a hasty inspection to make his English seem much more rude and antique than it really is. The entry of the MS. in the catalogue of Vliet's library, as quoted by Dr. White, describes it as an old Swedish or Gothic book. Other early notices speak of it as semi-Saxon, or half Danish, or possibly old Scottish. Even Hickes appears to have regarded it as belonging to the first age after the Conquest.

Ormin attaches the highest importance to his peculiar system of orthography. Nevertheless, in quoting what he says upon the subject in the subsequent passage of his Dedication we will take the liberty, for the sake of giving a clear and just idea of his language to a reader of the present day, to strip it of a disguise which so greatly exaggerates its apparent antiquity :—

And whase willen shall this book
[And whoso shall wish this book]
Eft other sithe writen,
[After (wards) (an) other time (to) write]
Him bidde icc that he't write right,
[Him bid I that he it write right]
Swa sum this book him teacheth,
[So as this book him teacheth]
All thwert out after that it is
[All athwart (or through) out after that (or what) it is]
Upo this firste biane.
[Upon this first example]
With all swilk rime als here is set
[With all such rhyme as here is set]
With all se fele wordes
[With all so many words]
And tat he looke well that he
[And that he look well that he]

An bookstaff write twien
   [A letter write twice]
Eywhere there it uppo this book
   [Wherever there (or where) it upon this book]
Is written o that wise,
   [Is written on (or in) that wise]
Looke he well that he't write away
   [Look he well that he it write on]
For lie ne may nought elles
   [For he may not else]
On English writen right te word,
   [On (or in) English write right the word]
That wite he well te soothe,
   [That wot (or know) he well to (or for) sooth (or truth)]

Thus presented, Ormin's English certainly seems to differ much less from that of the present day than Layamon's. His vocabulary may have as little in it of any foreign admixture; but it appears to contain many fewer words that have now become obsolete; and both his grammar and his construction have much more of a modern character and air. Dr. White has not thought it necessary to subjoin any such translation to his author as Sir Frederic Madden rightly judged was indispensable in the case of Layamon. He confesses, also, that, while the handwriting, the ink, and the material of the manuscript would seem to assign it to the earlier part of the thirteenth century, "the grammatical forms and structure of the language rather indicate a later period." "We meet," he says, "with neglect of gender and number, a frequent use of prepositions substituted for the casal endings of nouns, and the rejection of the prefix *ge* in all those parts of speech which receive it in pure Anglo-Saxon.... There is also for the most part a simplicity in grammatical forms and in the construction of sentences." Of the amount of any French or Latin element that there may be in the vocabulary we do not find that he says anything. But it is evidently very small, probably not greater than we have found it to be in Layamon's work.

The Brut of Layamon was undoubtedly written in the south-west of England: the dialect of the Ormulum is thought to betray a Scandinavian character, and to point to a north-eastern, or at least an eastern, county as the part of the kingdom in which and for which it was written. Dr. Latham assigns it to Northumbria. Mr. Guest is "inclined to fix on some county north of Thames, and south of Lincoln." And the late Mr. Garnett,

Dr. White tells us, expressed his opinion in a letter to him that " the Ormulum was written a hundred miles or upwards to the south of Durham, and considered Peterborough not an unlikely locality."

On the whole, it may be assumed that, while we have a dialect founded on that of the Saxons specially so called in Layamon, we have a specially Anglian form of the national language in the Ormulum; and perhaps that distinction will be enough, without supposing any considerable difference of date, to explain the linguistic differences between the two. There is good reason for believing that the Anglian part of the country shook off the shackles of the old inflectional system sooner than the Saxon, and that our modern comparatively uninflected and analytic English was at least in its earliest stage more the product of Anglian than of purely Saxon influences, and is to be held as having grown up rather in the northern and north-eastern parts of the country than in the southern or south-western.[*]

* Ormin's orthography, if minutely examined, might probably be made to throw considerable light upon the pronunciation of our ancestors. From the short extract given above, for example, the following inferences, among others, might be deduced:—The name *Christ* and the commencing syllable of *Christendom* would appear to have been when the Ormulum was composed distinguished in pronunciation in the same manner as they still are, the former taking the long or name sound of the vowel, the latter the short or shut sound. The case is different, however, so far as the evidence of this passage goes, with the name *God* and the commencing syllable of the word *Gospel*, which also then took a *d*; while the *o* of *Gospel* (or *Godspel*) was undoubtedly pronounced, as it still is, with the short sound, the *o* of *God* would appear, at least according to one mode of speaking, to have taken the name sound, so that the word would be pronounced exactly as we now pronounce the word *good*. So in the present day many people distinguish the proper name *Job* by giving the *o* the name sound as in *robe*. This pronunciation is the more deserving of notice, as being in accordance with other evidence opposed to the common notion of there being any connexion between *God* and the adjective *good* (which is the *God* of *Gospel*, or *Godspel*, = the good tidings, or εὐαγγέλιον). In the English of the period before the Conquest the two words were always distinguished by the adjective being written with an accent, *gód*; but, the vowel being the same in both, this can hardly be taken to indicate the same distinction which we now make between *God* and *good*. In other passages of the Ormulum, however, we have the sacred name also written with the double *d*, which would seem to show that the present pronunciation was already beginning to drive out the other older one. But this instance must be held to make it somewhat questionable whether, in what is called the Anglo-Saxon form of the language, the accent, at least universally, is to be taken to indicate that the vowel over which it is placed had the name sound. The testimony of the Ormulum, at any rate, is apparently decisive to

THE ANCREN RIWLE.

There is also to be mentioned, along with the Brut of Layamon and the Ormulum, a work of considerable extent in prose which has been assigned to the same interesting period in the history of the language, the Ancren Riwle, that is, the Anchorites', or rather Anchoresses' Rule, being a treatise on the duties of the monastic life, written evidently by an ecclesiastic, and probably one in a position of eminence and authority, for the direction of three ladies to whom it is addressed, and who, with their domestic servants or lay sisters, appear to have formed the entire community of a religious house situated at Taronte (otherwise called Tarrant-Kaines, Kainoston, or Kingston) in Dorsetshire. This

the fact that, of the two words at present under consideration, the one which used to be written without the accent was pronounced with the same sound, and the other, formerly taking the accent, with the shut sound. *God* was sounded *good*, and *gód* was sounded *gud* or *gudd*. This was undoubtedly the case if Ormin's distinctive spelling here indicates the same thing that it usually does.

Again, *pear* and *here* and *read* appear, from the manner in which Ormin writes them, to have all been pronounced in his day as they are at present; and so, no doubt, they then said *to sern* (with the old termination of the infinitive) for our *to see*, not *to see* (which Ormin would have given as *sren*). But, on the other hand, *yet* and *well* were apparently then pronounced *yeet* and *weel*, and *here* with the long *a* as in *care* (the following consonant, besides, being an *f* instead of a *r*). There may be some doubt, perhaps, in regard to the *o* in *brother* and *word* and *look* and *love*, and the *dom* of *Christendom*. All we can say is, that it seems not to have been the ordinary shut sound; it might be going too far to assume that people formerly said *brouther* and *wourd* and *Christendoum* and *brouk* and *loof* (or *leuf*). Probably both the *w* and the *k* were recognised as having a softening effect upon the vowel, so that they might pronounce it rather as we still do in *Worcester* and *Wolverhampton* and *Wolsey* and *worsted* and *wolf* and *woman* and *Bolingbroke* and *Pembroke* and other similar words (some of which have exchanged the *ou* for *oo* in our modern spelling).

Ormin has evidently taken the greatest pains with his orthography, and it is for the most part very uniform. It may be doubted if any other language possesses a record of its ancient pronunciation at all approaching in distinctness and completeness to what we thus have for the English in the single manuscript in which his work has been preserved, thanks to his singular scrupulosity in this particular. It is probably a unique instance of any considerable knowledge having been transmitted upon positive evidence of a part of human speech which has usually for the greater part perished with those upon whose lips it once lived, and is only at best to be imperfectly recovered, after some generations have passed away, by conjectural speculation, mostly of a very dubious and unsatisfactory character.

work too has now been printed, having been edited for the
Camden Society in 1853 by the Rev. James Morton, B.D. It is
preserved in four manuscripts, three of them in the Cottonian
Collection, the other belonging to Corpus Christi College, Cambridge; and there is also in the Library of Magdalen College,
Oxford, a Latin text of the greater part of it. The entire work
extends to eight Parts, or Books, which in the printed edition
cover 215 quarto pages. Mr. Morton, who has appended to
an apparently careful representation of the ancient text both a
glossary and a version in the language of the present day, has
clearly shown, in opposition to the commonly received opinion,
that the work was originally written in English, and that the
Latin in so far as it goes is only a translation. This, indeed,
might have been inferred as most probable in such a case, on the
mere ground that we have here a clergyman, however learned,
drawing up a manual of practical religious instruction for
readers of the other sex, even without the special proofs which
Mr. Morton has brought forward. The conclusion to which he
states himself to have come, after carefully examining and comparing the text which he prints with the Oxford MS., is, that
the Latin is " a translation, in many parts abridged and in some
enlarged, made at a comparatively recent period, when the language in which the whole had been originally written was
becoming obsolete." In many instances, in fact, the Latin translator has misunderstood his original. Mr. Morton has also thrown
great doubts upon the common belief that the authorship of the
work is to be ascribed to a certain Simon de Gandavo, or Simon
de Ghent, who died Bishop of Salisbury in 1315. This belief
rests solely on the authority of an anonymous note prefixed to
the Latin version of the work preserved in Magdalen College,
Oxford; and Mr. Morton conceives that Simon is of much too
late a date. It might have been thought that the fact of the
work having been written in English would of itself be conclusive against his claim; but the Bishop of Salisbury, it seems,
was born in London or Westminster; it was only his father who
was a native of Flanders. On the whole, Mr. Morton is inclined
to substitute in place of Bishop Simon a Richard Poor, who
was successively Bishop of Chichester, of Salisbury, and of
Durham, and who was a native of Tarente, where also, it seems,
he died in 1237. Of this prelate Matthew Paris speaks in very
high terms of commendation.

Two other mistakes in the old accounts are also disposed of:—that the three recluses to whom the work is addressed belonged to the monastic order of St. James, and that they were the sisters of the writer. He merely directs them, if any ignorant person should ask them of what order they were, to say that they were of the order of St. James, who in his canonical epistle has declared that pure religion consists in visiting and relieving the widow and the orphan, and in keeping ourselves unspotted from the world; and in addressing them as his dear sisters, "he only," as Mr. Morton explains, "uses the form of speech commonly adopted in convents, where nuns are usually spoken of as sisters or mothers, and monks as brothers or fathers."

Upon what is the most important question relating to the work, regarded as a documentary monument belonging to the history of the language, the learned editor has scarcely succeeded in throwing so much light. Of the age of the manuscripts, or the character of the handwriting, not a word is said. It does not even appear whether any one of the copies can be supposed to be of the antiquity assumed for the work upon either the new or the old theory of its authorship. The question is left to rest entirely upon the language, which, it is remarked, is evidently that of the first quarter of the thirteenth century, not greatly differing from that of Layamon, which has been clearly shown by Sir F. Madden to have been written not later than 1205.

The English of the Ancren Rule is, indeed, rude enough for the highest antiquity that can be demanded for it. "The spelling," Mr. Morton observes, "whether from carelessness or want of system, is of an uncommon and unsettled character, and may be pronounced barbarous and uncouth." The language he considers to be what is commonly called Semi-Saxon, or "Anglo-Saxon somewhat changed; and in the first of the various stages through which it had to pass before it arrived at the copiousness and elegance of the present English." This statement is perhaps not quite consistent with the doctrine which afterwards seems to be laid down, that no particular effect was produced upon the language of England by the Norman Conquest, that it only after that revolution continued to go on in the same course of gradual disintegration, or simplification, which it had been running for some centuries, suffering nothing more of change than it would have done if the Normans had never invaded the country. If that were so, how can the stage in which it is supposed to have been found some short time after the Conquest to with propriety spoken of as the *first* of a series? But is it possible to believe that so complete a social revolution as the Conquest, affecting everything else in the country, should have left the language, which is always to so great an extent the expression or reflection of everything else, untouched? The gradual change that may have been proceeding for some time before is not inconsistent with or any disproof of the more sudden and violent change which may have taken place at this crisis, precipitating the ruin of the already decaying original system of the language, just as the shaking of a tree, by a blast of wind or in any other way, would bring down at once a shower of leaves or blossoms, which, although beginning to wither or lose their hold, might still have hung on for a considerable time longer if the tree had not been thus rudely assailed.

In this work, according to Mr. Morton, the inflections which originally marked the oblique cases of substantive nouns, and also the distinctions of gender, are for the most part discarded. " Yet," he adds, " as these changes are partial and incomplete, enough of the more ancient characteristics of the language is left to justify the inference that the innovations are recent. Not only is *es* of the genitive case retained, but we very often meet with the dative and the accusative in *e* and the accusative in *en*, as *then, the.* We also meet occasionally with the genitive plural in *re*, from the Saxon *ra*, and *ne* and *ene*, from *ena.** . . . The cases and genders of adjectives are generally disused, but not always. . . The moods and tenses of verbs are little altered from the older forms, and in many words they are not changed at all. The infinitive, which in pure Saxon ends invariably in *an*, is changed into *en.*" In only three infinitives, *warnie* (to warn), *i-wurthe* (to be), and *windwe* (to winnow), has the final *n* dropped off; nor does the language exhibit any of the other Scandinavian peculiarities which mark what Hickes calls the Dano-Saxon, or what is known to modern philology as the Anglian dialect. From this, and from its general resemblance to the older text of Layamon, which appears to have been produced on the banks of the Severn, Mr. Morton thinks it most probable that the English we have in the Rule is that of the West of England in the thirteenth century.

* Does not the very title of the book afford us also an instance of a genitive plural in *en*; *ancren* = of anchoresses? This, however, appears to be rare.

In ono particular, however, it differs remarkably from Layamon's English. In that, as we have seen, Sir F. Maddon found
in above 32,000 verses of the older text only about 50 words of
French derivation, and only about 90 in all in the 57,000 of both
texts; whereas in the present work the infusion of Norman
words is described as large. But this, as Mr. Morton suggests, is
" owing probably to the peculiar subjects treated of in it, which
are theological and moral, in speaking of which terms derived
from the Latin would readily occur to the mind of a learned
ecclesiastic much conversant with that language, and with the
works on similar subjects written in it."

A few sentences from the Eighth or last Part, which treats of
domestic matters, will afford a sufficient specimen of this curious
work :—

Ye ne schulen eten vleschs ne seim buten ine muchele secnesse ; other
hwoso is ener feble eteth potage blitheliche; and wunketh ou to lutel
drunch. Notheless, leone austren, ower mete and ower drunch haueth ·
ithuht me lease then ich wolde. Ne neste ye nenne dei to bread and to
watere, bute ye habben leaue. Sum ancre maketh hire lord mid hire
gistes withuten. Thet is to mucho ureondschipe, aor, of alle ordres
theonne is hit unkaindelukest and mest ayean ancre ordre, thet is al deod
to the worlde. Me haneth i-herd ofte siggen thet deode men speken mid
cwike men ; auh thet beo eten mid cwike men ne woud ich neuer yete.
Ne makie ye none gistninges ; ne ne tulle ye to the yete uon mukutho
harlos ; thauh ther nere non other vœl of (hit ?) bute hore methlease
muth, hit wolde other hwule letten heauenliche thouhtes.

[That is, literally :—Ye not shall eat flesh nor lard but in
much sickness; or whoso is ever feeble may eat potage blithely;
and accustom yourselves to little drink. Nevertheless, dear
sisters, your meat and your drink have seemed to me less than I
would (have it). Fast ye not no day to bread and to water but
ye have leave. Some anchoresses make their board (or meals)
with their friends without. That is too much friendship, for, of
all orders, then is it most unnatural and most against anchoress
order, that is all dead to the world. One has heard oft say that
dead men speak with quick (living) men ; but that they eat with
quick men not found I never yet. Make not ye no banquetings,
nor allure ye not to the gate no strange vagabonds ; though
there were not none other evil of it but their measureless mouth
(or talk), it would (or might) other while (sometimes) hinder
heavenly thoughts.]

And again :—

Ye, mine leoue sustren, ne schulen habben no best, bute kat one. Ancre thet haueth eihte thuncheth bet husewif, aso Marthe was, then ancre; ne none wha mei beo beon Marie, mid grithfulnesse of heorte. Vor theonne mot heo theocben of the kues foddre, and of heorde-monne huire, oluhnen thene heiward, warien hwon me punt hire, and yelden, thauh, the hermes. Wat Crist, this is lodlich thing hwon me maketh in tune of ancre eihta. Thauh, yif eul mot nede habben ku, loke thet heo none monne ne ellie ne ne hermie; ne thet hire thouht ne beo nout theron i-meaned. Ancre ne ouh nout to habben no thing thet drawe utward hire heorte. None cheffare ne driue ye. Ancre thet is cheapild, heo cheapeth hire soule the chepmon of helle. Ne wite ye nout in oure huse of other monnes thinges, ne eihte, ne clothes; ne nout ne underuo ye the chirche uestiment, ne thene caliz, bute yif strencthe hit makie, other muchel nie; vor of swuche witunge is i-kumen muchel vuel oftesithen. Withinnen ower wonnes ne lete ye nenne mon slepen. Yif muchel neode mid alle maketh breken ower hus, the hwule thet it ener is i-broken, loke thet ye habben therinne mid ou one wummon of clene line deies and nihtes.

Uorthi thet no mon ne i-sihth ou, ne ye i-seoth nenne mon, wel mei dou of ower clothes, leon heo hwite, leon heo blake; but thet heo beon unorne and warme, and wel i-wrouhte, uelles wel i-tawed; and habbeth aso monie ase ou to-neodeth, to bedde and eke to rugge.

Next flesshe ne schal mon werien no linene cloth, bute yif bit beo of herde and of greate hoordun. Stamin habbe hwoso wule; and hwoso wille mei beon buten. Ye schulen liggen in on heater, and i-gurd. Ne bere ye non iren, ne here, ne irspiles felles; ne ne beate on ther mide, no mid schurge i-letheret ne i-leaded; ne mid holle ne mid breres ne ne biblodge hire sulf withuten schriftes leaue; ne ne nime, et enes, to veole disciplines. Ower schone beon greate and warme. Ine sumer ye habbeth leaue uorto gon and sitten baruot; and hosen withuten unumpes; and ligge inne ham hwoso liketh. . . . Hing ne broche nabbe ye; ne gurdel i-menbrel, ne gloven, ne no swuch thing thet ou ne deih forto habben . . . .

Ye ne schulen senden lettres, ne underuon lettres, ne writen, buten leaue. Ye schulen beon i-dodded four sithen ithe yere, uorto lihten ower heaued; and ase ofte i-leten blod; and oftere yif neod is; and hwoso mei beon ther withuten, Ich hit mei wel i-tholien.

[Literally :—Ye, my dear sisters, shall not have no beast but (a) cat only. (An) anchoress that hath cattle seems (a) better housewife, as Martha was, than anchoress, nor no wise may she be Mary with peacefulness of heart. For then must she think of the cow's fodder, and of the herdsman's hire, flatter the heyward (cattle-keeper), defend (herself) when they pound her (put her cattle in the pound), and pay, moreover, the harms (damages). Knoweth Christ, this is (an) ugly thing when they make moan (complaint) in town of anchoress's cattle. Though

if any must needs have (a) cow, look that she no man not annoy
nor not harm, nor that her thought not be not thereon fastened.
(An) anchoress not ought not to have nothing that draweth
outward her heart. No chaffering not drive ye (no buying and
selling carry ye on). (An) anchoress that is a chafferer, she
chaffereth her soul with the chapman of hell. Nor take ye not
charge in your house of other men's things, nor cattle, nor
clothes; nor not receive ye not (under your care) the church
vestments, nor the chalice, but if (unless) strength it make
(force compel it), or much fear; for of such charge-taking is
come much evil oftentimes. Within your walls let ye not no
man sleep. If much need (strong necessity), withal (however),
make (cause) to use your house, the while that (so long as) it
over is used look that ye have therein with you a woman of clean
life days and nights.

Because that no man neither seeth you, nor ye see no man,
well may (ye) do of (with) your clothes, be they white, be they
black; but (see) that they be plain and warm and well made,
skins well tawed; and have as many as it needeth you, to bed
and eke to back.

Next the flesh shall not one wear no linen cloth, but if it be
of harda and of great (coarse) canvas. A stamin (shirt of
woollen and linen) may have whoso will, and whoso will may be
without. Ye shall lie in a garment, and girt. Nor bear (carry)
ye not iron, nor hair (haircloth), nor hedgehog skins; nor beat
not yourselves therewith, nor with scourge leathered nor
leaded; nor with holly nor with briars not blood not herself
(yourselves) without shrift's (shriver's) leave; nor take not, at
once, too many disciplines (flagellations). (Let) your shoes be
large and warm. In summer ye have leave for to go and sit
barefoot; and (to wear) hose without vamps; and whoso liketh
may lie in them. . . . Ring nor brooch do not ye have, nor
girdle ornamented, nor gloves, nor no such thing that it not
behoveth you for to have. . . .

Ye shall not send letters, nor receive letters, nor write without
leave. Ye shall be cropped four times in the year, for to lighten
your head; and as often let blood, and oftener if need is; and
whoso may be there-without (may dispense with this) I it may
well endure.]

METRICAL LEGENDS.—LAND OF COKAYNE—GULDEVORD.—WILLE
GRIS.—EARLY ENGLISH SONGS.

With regard to the metrical Legends of Saints and other
pieces, which have been assigned by Hickes and Warton to the
twelfth century, it is in the highest degree probable, as already
remarked, that none of them belong to an earlier period than
the latter part of the thirteenth, and that some are not even of
that antiquity. It is impossible, for instance, to believe that
the celebrated satirical poem on the Land of Cokayne, which
Warton holds to have been "evidently written soon after the
Conquest, at least before the reign of Henry the Second," can,
in the form in which we have it, be older than the year
1300, if it be even quite so old.* Price has noted † that "a
French fabliau bearing a near resemblance to this poem, and
possibly the production upon which the English minstrel
founded his song, has been published in the new edition of
Barbazan's Fabliaux et Contes, Paris 1808, vol. iv. p. 175;" and
Sir Frederic Madden has no doubt that the French composition
is the original.‡ It is undoubtedly of the thirteenth century.
The English poem, which he also assumes to be a translation,
is given in full by Ellis (Specimens of Early English Poets, 4th
edit., i. 83—95); and abundant samples of the other fugitive and
anonymous poetry which has been attributed to the same age,
but the alleged antiquity of which is in many cases equally disputable, may be found in Hickes and in Warton.

As we have had occasion to show that there is no authority in
the Lanercost Chronicle for one specimen of early verse cited
thence by Ritson, we may here insert a couplet therein given
under the year 1244, which has generally escaped attention.
A Norfolk peasant boy, named William, had left his father's
house and set out to seek his fortune, with no companion or
other possession but a little pig (porcellus), whence the people
used to call him *Willy Grice*;§ but having in his wanderings

* In a note to the 1810 edition of Warton's History, I. 8, Mr. Wright says:—
"The identical MS. from which Hickes transcribed this poem is in the Harleian Collection, No. 913. I have traced its history satisfactorily. It was
written early in the fourteenth century, and this poem is a composition of at
the most five or six years earlier."

† Note on Warton (1824), I. 12.   ‡ Ibid. (1840), I. 8.

§ *Grice*, which is of frequent occurrence in Piers Plowman, and continued
in use in England at least down to the middle of the sixteenth century, is
still the common word for a pig in Scotland.

in France met with a rich widow, whom he wooed and wed,
he became in the end a great man in that country: still he
piously remembered his early life of poverty and vagrancy, and,
among the other ornaments of one of the apartments of his fine
house, to which he used to retire every day for an hour's meditation and self-communion, he had himself pictured, leading the
pig as he used to do with a string, with this superscription in
his native tongue :—

> Wille Gris, Wille Gris!
> Thinche twat thou was, and qwat thou es.

Some of our earliest songs that have been preserved undoubtedly belong to about the middle of the thirteenth century.
The well-known lines beginning "Sumer is i-cumen in," first
printed by Warton in the Additions to his History, from the
Harleian MS. 978, being the oldest English song that has been
found with the musical notes annexed, appear to be of this
antiquity;[*] and so likewise may be some of the other pieces
which Warton has quoted from another of the Harleian MSS.
(2253). But the compositions of this kind of most certain date
are some referring to the public events of the day, and evidently
written at the time; such as the ballad about the battle of Lewes
(fought in 1264), and others in Percy's Reliques, in Ritson's
Ancient Songs, and in Mr. Wright's collection printed for the
Camden Society, and entitled The Political Songs of England,
from the Reign of John to that of Edward II., 4to. Lond. 1839.

EARLY ENGLISH METRICAL ROMANCES.

From the thirteenth century also we are probably to date the
origin or earliest composition of English metrical romances; at
least, none have descended to the present day which seem to
have a claim to any higher antiquity. There is no absolutely
conclusive evidence that all our old metrical romances are translations from the French; the French original cannot in every
case be produced; but it is at least extremely doubtful if any
such work was ever composed in English except upon the
foundation of a similar French work. It is no objection that
the subjects of most of these poems are not French or continental,

---

[*] In a note to the 1840 edition of Warton, Sir F. Madden states that the
Harleian MS. 978 is certainly of the middle of the thirteenth century.

but British—that the stories of some of them are purely English or
Saxon: this, as has been shown, was the case with the early
northern French poetry generally, from whatever cause, whether
simply in consequence of the connection of Normandy with this
country from the time of the Conquest, or partly from the
earlier intercourse of the Normans with their neighbours the
people of Armorica, or Bretagne, whose legends and traditions,
which were common to them with their kindred the Welsh, have
unquestionably served as the fountain-head to the most copious
of all the streams of romantic fiction. French seems to have
been the only language of popular literature (apart from more
songs and ballads) in England for some ages after the Conquest;
if even a native legend, therefore, was to be turned into a
romance, it was in French that the poem would at that period
be written. It is possible, indeed, that some legends might
have escaped the French trouvours, to be discovered and taken
up at a later date by the English minstrels; but this is not
likely to have happened with any that were at all popular or
generally known; and of this description, it is believed, are all
those, without any exception, upon which our existing early
English metrical romances are founded. The subjects of these
compositions—Tristrem, King Horn, Havelok, &c.—could hardly
have been missed by the French poets in the long period during
which they had the whole field to themselves: we have the most
conclusive evidence with regard to some of the legends in
question that they were well known at an early date to the
writers in that language;—the story of Havelok, for instance, is
in Gaimar's Chronicle;—upon this general consideration alone,
therefore, which is at least not contradicted by either the internal
or historical evidence in any particular case, it seems reasonable
to infer that, where we have both an English and a French
metrical romance upon the same subject, the French is the
earlier of the two, and the original of the other. From this it is,
in the circumstances, scarcely a step to the conclusion come to by
Tyrwhitt, who has intimated his belief " that we have no English
romance prior to the age of Chaucer which is not a translation or
imitation of some earlier French romance." * Certainly, if this
judgment has not been absolutely demonstrated, it has not been
refuted, by the more extended investigation the question has
since received.

* Essay on the Language of Chaucer, note 55.

PUBLICATIONS OF PERCY—WARTON—TYRWHITT—PINKERTON—HER-
BERT—RITSON—ELLIS—SCOTT—WEBER—UTTERSON—LAING—
HARTSHORNE—THE ROXBURGHE CLUB—THE BANNATYNE—THE
MAITLAND—THE ABBOTSFORD—THE CAMDEN SOCIETY.

The first account, in any detail, of our early English metrical
romances was given by Percy, in the third volume of his
Reliques of Ancient English Poetry, first published in 1765.
In this Essay, of twenty-four pages (extended to thirty-eight in
the fourth edition of the work, 1794), he gave a list of thirty
of these poems, to which, in subsequent editions, he added
nine more. Then came the first volume of Warton's History of
English Poetry, in 1774, with a much more discursive examination at least of parts of the subject, and ample specimens of
several romances. Tyrwhitt's edition of the Canterbury Tales
of Chaucer followed the next year, with many valuable notices
on this as well as other matters belonging to our early literature
in the interesting preliminary Essay on the Language and Versification of his author, which is in fact a history of the language
down to the end of the fourteenth century. In 1792 Pinkerton
inserted the Scotch metrical romance of Gawan and Galogras,
from an Edinburgh edition of 1508, in his collection of Scotish
Poems, reprinted from scarce editions, 3 vols. 8vo., Lond.; and
he also gave in his last volume, as one of " three pieces before
unpublished," that of Sir Gawan and Sir Galaron of Galloway; which was copied into Sibbald's Chronicle of Scottish
Poetry (i., pp. xv. &c.), 4 vols. 8vo., Edinb. 1802. In 1796
appeared Roberts the Douyll, a metrical Romance, from an
ancient illuminated MS. (8vo., Lond.), printed for I. Herbert;
whose name is also at the end of a short prefatory advertisement, in which it is stated that the MS. agreed, word for
word, with a remaining fragment of an edition of the poem
which appears to have been printed early in the sixteenth century by Wynken de Worde, or Pynson. The volume has a
number of engravings, which are very curious, and seem to be
fac-similes of the illuminations in the MS.[*] In 1802 Ritson
published at London his 3 vols. 8vo. of Ancient English
Metrical Romances, containing, besides his Dissertation on
Romance and Minstrelsy, which fills 220 pages of the first
volume, the romances, in their entire length, of Ywaine and

[*] See a note on the legend of Robert the Devil, by Sir F. Madden, in the
1840 edition of Warton, L 187, and another by Mr. R. Taylor, pp. 207, 208.

Gawin (4032 lines); of Launfal, or Launfal Miles, a translation from the French of Marie by Thomas Chestre in the reign of Henry VI. (1044 lines); of Lybeaus Disconus, that is, Le Beau Desconnu, or The Fair Unknown, sometimes called Lybius Disconius (2130 lines); of The Geste of Kyng Horn (1546 lines); of The Kyng of Tars and the Soudan of Dammas (1148 lines); of Emare (1035 lines); of Sir Orpheo (510 lines); of The Chronicle of Engleland (1030 lines); of Le Bone Florence of Rome (2189 lines); of The Erle of Tolous (1216 lines); of The Squyr of Lowe Degre (1132 lines); and of The Knight of Curtesy and the Fair Lady of Fagnell (500 lines): together with 133 pages of Notes, including the imperfect romance of Horn Childe and Maiden Rimnild (about 1150 lines) from the Auchinleck MS. in the Advocates' Library at Edinburgh: the whole being followed by a Glossary, filling about 60 pages; in commendation of which, however, very little can be said. With the exception of The Squyr of Lowe Degre, and The Knight of Curtesy, which are from rare black-letter copies of the sixteenth century, all the pieces in this collection of Ritson's are transcribed from manuscripts, most of them unique. A more successful attempt to diffuse a knowledge of this portion of our ancient poetical literature was made by Mr. George Ellis, in his Specimens of Early English Metrical Romances, 3 vols. 8vo., first published in 1805. Besides an Historical Introduction on the Rise and Progress of Romantic Composition in France and England—followed by an Analysis (by Mr. Douce) of the MS. work of Petrus Alphonsus entitled De Clericali Disciplina, and an account, amounting almost to a complete translation, of the twelve Lays of Marie of France— this work, of which a second edition appeared in 1811, contained extended analytical reviews of the romances of Merlin, Morte Arthur, Guy of Warwick, Sir Bevis of Hamptoun, Richard Cœur de Lion, Roland and Ferragus, Sir Otuel, Sir Ferumbras, The History of the Seven Wise Masters, Florence and Blaucheflour, Robert of Cysille, Sir Isumbras, Sir Triamour, The Life of Ipomydon, Sir Eglamour of Artois, Lai le Fraine, Sir Eger, Sir Grahame, and Sir Graysteel, Sir Degore, Roswal and Lillian, and Amys and Amylion. Most of these romances may be considered of later date than those published by Ritson: Mr. Ellis, indeed, on his title-page describes them as "chiefly written during the early part of the fourteenth century." Meanwhile, in 1804, Walter Scott had published at Edinburgh, in royal 8vo., the romance of Tristrem, from the Auchinleck MS., describing it on his title-page as a work of the thirteenth century, written in Scotland, by Thomas of Ercildoune, popularly called The Rhymer, and maintaining that theory in an elaborate and ingenious Introduction and a large body of curious illustrative annotation. One of the Appendices to this volume, which has been several times reprinted, contained an account of the contents of the Auchinleck MS., consisting of forty-four pieces in all of ancient poetry, complete or imperfect. Scott, it may be remarked, here acknowledges that there can be little doubt of the volume, which consists of 334 leaves of parchment, the writing being in double columns, in a nearly uniform hand of the earlier part of the fourteenth century, having been compiled in England; and many circumstances, he says, lead him to conclude that the MS. has been written in an Anglo-Norman convent. In 1810, Scott's friend, Mr. Henry Weber, brought out at Edinburgh, in 3 vols. 8vo., his collection entitled Metrical Romances of the Thirteenth, Fourteenth, and Fifteenth Centuries, published from Ancient MSS.; with an introduction, Notes, and a Glossary. This work contains the romances of King Alisaunder (8034 lines), Sir Cleges (540 lines), Lay le Freine (402 lines), Richard Coer de Lion (7136 lines), The Lyfe of Ipomydon (2346 lines), Amis and Amiloun (2495 lines), The Proces of the Seuyn Sages (4002 lines), Octouian Imperator (1962 lines), Sir Amadas (778 lines), and the Huntyng of the Hare (270 lines). The next collection that appeared was that of Mr. Edward Vernon Utterson, entitled Select Pieces of Early Popular Poetry; republished principally from early printed copies in the Black Letter; 2 vols. 8vo., Lond. 1817. It contained the metrical romances or tales of Syr Tryamoure (1593 lines), Syr Isenbras (855 lines), Syr Degore (803 lines), Syr Gowghter (685 lines); besides a number of other pieces (occupying the second volume) which cannot be included under that denomination. Next followed Mr. David Laing's three collections:—the first entitled Select Remains of the Ancient Popular Poetry of Scotland, 4to., Edinb. 1822; containing twenty-five pieces in all, among which are The Awntyrs of Arthure at the Terne Watholyn, being another copy, from a MS. of the fifteenth century in the library of Lincoln cathedral, of Pinkerton's Sir Gawan and Sir Galaron of Galloway; and the tale of Orfeo and Heurodis (that is, Orpheus and Eurydice), from the Auchinleck MS., being another and very different version of Ritson's Sir Orpheo: the second, entitled Early Metrical Tales, 8vo., Edinb. 1826; containing the History of Sir Eger, Sir Grahame, and Sir Graysteel (2860 lines), The History of Roswall and Lillian, which Mr. Laing had already printed separately in 1822 (876 lines), together with other poems and shorter pieces, all from earlier printed copies: the third, entitled The Knightly Tale of Golagras and Gawane, and other Ancient Poems, black letter, 4to., 1837; being a reprint of a unique volume in the Advocates' Library, printed by W. Chapman and A. Myllar, in 1508, and containing eleven pieces in all, among which, besides Golagras and Gawane, are The Tale of Orpheus and Eurydice (another version, attributed to Robert Henryson), and Sir Eglamour of Artoys, which is analyzed in Ellis. This last-mentioned volume is extremely scarce, only seventy-four copies, most of them more or less damaged, having been saved from a fire at the printer's. The unique volume of which it is a reprint, and which is in a very decayed state, was presented to the Advocates' Library by a medical gentleman of Edinburgh, about 1788, and is understood to have been picked up somewhere in Ayrshire. One of the pieces, The Portous of Noblenes, the last in the collection, is in prose. Then came the Rev. Charles Henry Hartshorne's Ancient Metrical Tales, printed chiefly from Original Sources, 8vo., Lond. 1829, containing, besides several pieces in other kinds of poetry, The Romance of King Athelstone, Florice and Blanchefour (apparently from the Auchinleck MS.), and a portion of the alliterative romance of Willyam and the Werwolf. There have also been printed, by the Roxburghe Club, Le Morte Arthure; the Adventures of Sir Launcelot du Lake, 4to., Lond. 1819, from the Harleian MS. 2252, being one of those analyzed by Ellis; Chevelere Assigne— that is, the Chevalier au Cygne, or Knight of the Swan—from the Cotton MS. Cal. A. 2, being a translation of a portion of a French romance, which is also preserved (with a short Introduction and Glossary by Mr. Utterson), 4to., Lond. 1820; The Ancient English Romance of Havelok the Dane, accompanied by the French text, with an Introduction, Notes, and a Glossary, by Frederic Madden, Esq. (now Sir F. Madden), 4to., Lond. 1828; and The Ancient English Romance of William and the Werwolf, edited, with an Introduction and Glossary, by Sir Frederic Madden, 4to., Lond. 1832: by the Bannatyne Club,

The Buik of Alexander the Great, reprinted from the Metrical
Romance printed at Edinburgh, by Arbuthnot, about the year
1580, 4to., Edinb. 1834 ; The Seven Sages, in Scotch metre, by
John Rolland of Dalkeith, reprinted from the edition of 1578,
4to., Edinb. 1837 ; The Scottish Metrical Romance of Lancelot
du Lak, from a MS. of the Fifteenth century (edited by Joseph
Stevenson, Esq.), 4to., Edinb. 1839 ; and Syr Gawayne, a Col-
lection of Ancient Romance Poems, by Scottish and English
Authors, relating to that celebrated Knight of the Round Table,
with an Introduction, Notes, and a Glossary, by Sir Frederic
Madden (including Syr Gawayn and the Grene Knygbt, The
Awntyrs of Arthure at the Terne Walbolyne, The Knightly
Tale of Golagros and Gawane, and an Appendix of shorter
pieces), 4to., Lond. 1839 : by the Maitland Club, Sir Bevis of
Hamtoun, a Metrical Romance, now first edited from the Auchinleck MS. (by W. B. D. D. Turnbull, Esq.), 4to., Edinb. 1838 :
by the Bannatyne and Maitland Clubs in conjunction, Clariodus,
a Metrical Romance, from a MS. of the Sixteenth Century (edited
by Edward Piper, Esq.), 4to., Edinb. 1830 : by the Abbotsford
Club, the Romances of Rowland and Vernagu, and Otuel, from
the Auchinleck MS. (edited by A. Nicholson, Esq.), 4to., 1836 ;
and Arthour and Merlin, a Metrical Romance, from the Auchinleck MS. (edited by Mr. Turnbull), 4to., 1838 : and by the
Camden Society, Three Early English Metrical Romances, with
an Introduction and Glossary, edited by John Robson, Esq., 4to.,
Lond. 1842; the three Romances (which are edited from a MS.
of the fifteenth century, called the Ireland MS. from its former
possessor of that name) being The Anturs of Arthor at the
Tarnewathelan (other versions of which, as already noticed,
have been printed by Pinkerton, Laing, and Madden *) ; Sir

* Mr. Robson (who is rather sparing of distinct references) says (Introduction, p. xii.) that this romance was first printed by Pinkerton in his Scottish
Ballads ; remarking again (p. xvi.) that " Pinkerton published it as a Scottish
ballad." The collection, in fact, in which Pinkerton published it, as mentioned above, was entitled Scottish Poems, 1792. The curious notice of this
proceeding by Ritson, to which Mr. Robson refers, occurs in his Ancient
English Metrical Romances, vol. iii. p. 230. In a note on Ywaine and Gawin,
where he says, " Two other romances on the same subject, but in a dialect and
metre peculiar to Scotland, are printed in Pinkerton's Scotish Poems; the one
from an edition at Edinburgh in 1508, the other from a MS., the property of
the present editor, which the said Pinkerton came by very dishonestly." It
appears from a letter of Ritson's, dated December 26, 1792, published in the
Gentleman's Magazine for January, 1793 (vol. xliii. p. 32', that he was then

Amadace (a different version of which is in Weber's Collection);
and The Avowynge of King Arther, Sir Gawan, Sir Kaye, and
Sir Bawdewyn of Bretau, which is here printed for the first
time.

History of the English Metrical Romance.

Although, however, it thus appears that a very considerable
body of our early romantic poetry has now been made generally
accessible, it is to be observed that only a small proportion of
what has been printed is derived from manuscripts of even so
early a date as the fourteenth century, and that many of the
volumes which have just been enumerated are merely re-impres-
sions of compositions which cannot be traced, at least in the
form in which we have them, beyond the sixteenth. Of the
undoubted produce of the thirteenth century in this kind of
writing we have very little, if we except the romances of Kyng
Horn, Sir Tristrem, Haveloc, and Sir Gawaine, with perhaps
two or three others in Ritson and Weber. It is probable, indeed,
that many of the manuscripts of later date are substantially transcripts from earlier ones; but in such cases, even when we have
the general form of the poems as first written tolerably well preserved, the language is almost always more or less modernized.
The history of the English metrical romance appears shortly to
be, that at least the first examples of it were translations from the

in possession of the MS., which had belonged to his friend Mr. Baynes, of
Gray's Inn, and that his complaint against Pinkerton was, that the latter had
printed the poem from a transcript made by a third party many years before,
which transcript the gentleman who made it declared he had never considered fit for the press; assuring Ritson, moreover, on his refusal to allow a
collation of the original, for which Pinkerton had applied, that the piece
should not be printed by the latter at all. Pinkerton, in his Preface, or Pre-
liminaries (vol. i. p. xxx.), merely says that the poem "was copied many years
ago by a learned friend, from a MS. belonging to Mr. Baynes, of Gray's Inn,
who was a noted collector of romances of chivalry." The MS. afterwards got
into the possession of the late Mr. Douce, and is now, with the rest of his collection, in the Bodleian Library. In another place (p. xviii.) Mr. Robson
observes, "Sir Walter Scott, where he alludes to this poem in his Minstrelsy,
asserts that it is not prior to the reign of James the Fifth of Scotland; but in
his Introduction to Sir Tristrem he is satisfied that it was written long
before the conclusion of the thirteenth century." The passages in which
Scott advances these contradictory opinions are in the Minstrelsy, iv. 147,
and Sir Tristrem, p. 57 (Poetical Works, edition of 1833).

French;—that there is no evidence of any such having been produced before the close of the twelfth century;—that in the thirteenth century were composed the earliest of those we now possess
in their original form;—that in the fourteenth the English took the
place of the French metrical romance with all classes, and that
this was the era alike of its highest ascendancy and of its most
abundant and felicitous production;—that in the fifteenth it was
supplanted by another species of poetry among the more educated classes, and had also to contend with another rival in the
prose romance, but that, nevertheless, it still continued to be
produced, although in less quantity and of an inferior fabric,—
mostly, indeed, if not exclusively, by the mere modernization
of older compositions—for the use of the common people;—and
that it did not altogether cease to be read and written till after
the commencement of the sixteenth. From that time the taste
for this earliest form of our poetical literature (at least counting
from the Norman Conquest) lay asleep in the national heart till
it was re-awakened in our own day by Scott, after the lapse
of three hundred years. But the metrical romance was then
become quite another sort of thing than it had been in its proper
era, throughout the whole extent of which, while the story was
generally laid in a past age, the manners and state of society
described were, notwithstanding, in most respects those of the
poet's and of his readers' or hearers' own time. This was
strictly the case with the poems of this description which were
produced in the thirteenth, fourteenth, and fifteenth centuries;
and even in those which were accommodated to the popular taste
of a later day much more than the language had to be partially
modernized to preserve them in favour. When this could no
longer be done without too much violence to the composition, or
an entire destruction of its original character, the metrical romance
lost its hold of the public mind, and was allowed to drop into
oblivion. There had been very little of mere antiquarianism in
the interest it had inspired for three centuries. It had pleased
principally as a picture or reflection of manners, usages, and a
general spirit of society still existing, or supposed to exist. And
this is perhaps the condition upon which any poetry must ever
expect to be extensively and permanently popular. We need not
say that the temporary success of the metrical romance, as revived
by Scott, was in great part owing to his appeal to quite a different, almost an opposite, state of feeling.

We give no specimens of our early English metrical romances, because no extracts such as we could afford room for from one or two of them could do much, or almost anything, to convey a notion of the general character of those compositions. Although written in verse, they are essentially not so much poems as histories, or narrative works. At least, what poetry is in them lies almost always in the story rather than in anything else. The form of verse is manifestly adopted chiefly as an aid to the memory in their recitation. Even the musical character which the romance poetry is supposed originally to have had, if it ever was attempted to be maintained in long compositions of this description (which it is difficult to believe), appears very early to have been abandoned. Hence, when reading became a more common accomplishment, and recitation fell into comparative disuse, the verse came to be regarded as merely an impediment to the free and easy flow of the story, and was, by general consent, laid aside. Such being the case, it is easy to understand that an old metrical romance is hardly to be better represented by extracts than an architectural structure would be by a bit of one of the walls. Even the more ornamented or animated passages derive most of their effect from the place they occupy, or the connexion in which they stand with the rest. The only way, therefore, of exhibiting any of these compositions intelligibly or fairly is to print the whole, or at the least, if only portions of the story are produced in the words of the original, to give the rest of it—somewhat abridged, it may be—in modern language. This latter method has been very successfully followed by Ellis in his Specimens, which work will be found to take a general survey of nearly the whole field of fiction with which our early English metrical romances are conversant.

Another thing to be observed of these compositions is, that they are in very few cases ascribed to any particular writer. Nor have they, in general, any such peculiarity of style as might mark and distinguish their authorship. A few only may be accounted exceptions—among them the romance of Tristrem,—and, if so, we may understand what Robert de Brunne means when he appears to speak of its English as strange and quaint; but usually their style is merely that of the age in which they were written. They differ from one another, in short, rather in the merit of the story itself than by anything in the manner of telling it. The expression and the rhyme are both, for the most

part, whatever comes first to hand. The verse, irregular and
rugged enough withal, is kept in such shape and order as it has
by a crowd of tautologies, expletives, and other blank phrases
serviceable only for filling up a gap, and is altogether such
verse as might apparently be almost improvised or chanted ex-
tempore. These productions, therefore, are scarcely to be considered as forming any part of our literature, properly so called,
interesting as they are on many accounts,—for the warm and
vigorous imagination that often revels in them, for their vivid
expression of the feelings and modes of thought of a remote age,
for the light they throw upon the history of the national manners
and mind, and even of the language in its first rude but bold
essays to mimic the solemnities of literary composition.

METRICAL CHRONICLE OF ROBERT OF GLOUCESTER.

Nearly what Biography is to History are the metrical romances
to the versified Chronicle of Robert of Gloucester, a narrative of
British and English affairs from the time of Brutus to the end of
the reign of Henry III., which, from events to which it alludes,
must have been written after 1297.[*] All that is known of the
author is that he was a monk of the abbey of Gloucester. His
Chronicle was printed—"faithfully, I dare say," says Tyrwhitt,
"but from incorrect manuscripts"—by Hearne, in 2 vols. 8vo.,
at Oxford, in 1724; and a re-impression of this edition was
produced at London in 1810. The work in the earlier part of it
may be considered a free translation of Geoffrey of Monmouth's
Latin History; but it is altogether a very rude and lifeless composition. "This rhyming chronicle," says Warton, "is totally
destitute of art or imagination. The author has clothed the
fables of Geoffrey of Monmouth in rhyme, which have often a
more poetical air in Geoffrey's prose." Tyrwhitt refers to
Robert of Gloucester in proof of the fact that the English
language had already acquired a strong tincture of French;
Warton observes that the language of this writer is full of
Saxonisms, and not more easy or intelligible than that of what he

* This has been shown by Sir F. Madden in his Introduction to Havelock the
Dane, p. lii.

calls " the Norman Saxon poems" of Kyng Horn and others
which he believes to belong to the preceding century.

Robert of Gloucester's Chronicle, as printed, is in long lines
of fourteen syllables, which, however, are generally divisible
into two of eight and six, and were perhaps intended to be
so written and read. The language appears to be marked by
the peculiarities of West Country English. Ample specimens
are given by Warton and Ellis; we shall not encumber our
limited space with extracts which are recommended by no
attraction either in the matter or manner. We will only
transcribe, as a sample of the language at the commencement of
the reign of Edward I., and for the sake of the curious evidence
it supplies in confirmation of a fact to which we have more than
once had occasion to draw attention, the short passage about the
prevalence of the French tongue in England down even to this
date, more than two centuries after the conquest :—

" Thus come lo! Engelonde into Normannes honde,
  And the Normans ne couthe speke tho bote her owe speche,
  And speke French as dude atom, and here chyldren dude al so teche,
  So that heymen of thys lond, that of her blod come,
  Holdeth alle thulke speche that hii of hem nome.
  Vor bote a man couthe French, me tolth of hym well lute :
  Ac lowe men holdeth to Englysm and to her kunde speche yute.
  Ich wene ther be no man in world contreyes none
  That ne holdeth to her knnde speche, but Engelond one.
  Ac wel me wot vor to conne bothe wel yt ya,
  Vor the more that a man con the more worth be ya."

That is, literally :—Thus lo ! England came into the hand of
the Normans : and the Normans could not speak then but their
own speech, and spoke French as they did at home, and their
children did all so teach ; so that high men of this land, that
of their blood come, retain all the same speech that they of them
took. For, unless a man know French, one talketh of him
little. But low men hold to English, and to their natural speech
yet. I imagine there be no people in any country of the world
that do not hold to their natural speech, but in England alone.
But well I wot it is well for to know both ; for the more that a
man knows, the more worth he is.

A short composition of Robert of Gloucester's on the Martyrdom
of Thomas à Boket was printed by the Percy Society in 1845.

ROBERT MANNYNG, OR DE BRUNNE.

Along with this chronicle may be mentioned the similar performance of Robert Mannyng, otherwise called Robert de Brunne
(from his birthplace,* Brunne, or Bourne, near Deping, or
Market Deeping, in Lincolnshire), belonging as it does to a date
not quite half a century later. The work of Robert de Brunne is
in two parts, both translated from the French : the first, coming
down to the death of Cadwalader, from Wace's Brut; the
second, extending to the death of Edward I., from the French or
Romance chronicle written by Piers, or Peter, de Langtoft, a
canon regular of St. Austin, at Bridlington, in Yorkshire, who
has been mentioned in a former page,† and who appears to have
lived at the same time with De Brunne. Langtoft, whose
chronicle, though it has not been printed, is preserved in more
than one manuscript, begins with Brutus; but De Brunne, for
sufficient reasons it is probable, preferred Wace for the earlier
portion of the story, and only took to his own countryman and
contemporary when deserted by his older Norman guide. It is
the latter part of his work, however, which, owing to the subject,
has been thought most valuable or interesting in modern times;
it has been printed by Hearne, under the title of Peter Langtoft's
Chronicle (as illustrated and improved by Robert of Brunne),
from the death of Cadwalader to the end of K. Edward the First's
reign ; transcribed, and now first published, from a MS. in the
Inner Temple Library, 2 vols. 8vo. Oxford, 1725; [reprinted
London, 1810.] This part, like the original French of Langtoft, is
in Alexandrine verse of twelve syllables ; the earlier part, which
remains in manuscript, is in the same octosyllabic verse in which
its original, Wace's chronicle, is written. The work is stated in
a Latin note at the end of the MS. to have been finished in
1338. Ritson (Bibliographia Poetica, p. 33) is very wroth with
Warton for describing De Brunne as having "scarcely more
poetry than Robert of Gloucester;"—"which only proves,"
Ritson says, "his want of taste or judgment." It may be
admitted that De Brunne's chronicle exhibits the language in a
considerably more advanced state than that of Gloucester, and
also that he appears to have more natural fluency than his pro-

---

* See a valuable note on De Brunne in Sir Frederic Madden's *Havelok*,
Introduction, p. xiii.
† *See ante*, p. 168.

decessor; his work also possesses greater interest from his occasionally speaking in his own person, and from his more frequent expansion and improvement of his French original by new matter; but for poetry, it would probably require a "taste or judgment" equal to Ritson's own to detect much of it. It is in the Prologue prefixed to the first part of his Chronicle that the famous passage occurs about the romance of Sir Tristrem, its strange or quaint English, and its authors, Thomas and Ercildonne (assumed to be the same person), and Kendale, which has given rise to so much speculation and controversy. De Brunne is also the author of two other rhyming translations : one, of the Latin prose treatise of his contemporary, the Cardinal Bonaventura, De Cœna et Passione Domini, et Pœnis S. Mariæ Virginis, which title he converts into Medytacium of the Soper of our Lorde Jhesu, and also of his Passyun, and eke of the Peynes of hys swete Modyr mayden Marye; the other a very free paraphrase of what has commonly been described as the Manuel de Péché (or Manual of Sin) of Bishop Grostête, but is, in fact, the work with the same title written by William de Wadington.[*] Copious extracts from these, and also from other translations of which it is thought that De Brunne may possibly be the author, are given by Warton, who, if he has not sufficiently appreciated the poetical merits of this writer, has at any rate awarded him a space which ought to satisfy his most ardent admirers.[†]

ROLLE, OR HAMPOLE.—DAVIE.

Other obscure writers in verse of the earlier part of the fourteenth century were Richard Rolle, often called Richard Hampole, or of Hampole, a hermit of the order of St. Augustine, who lived in or near the nunnery of Hampole, four miles from Doncaster, and after his death, in 1349, was honoured as a saint, and who is the author, or reputed author, of various metrical paraphrases of parts of Scripture, and other prolix theological effusions, all of which that are preserved (Ritson has enumerated seventeen of them) slumber in manuscript, and are not likely to be disturbed; and Adam Davie, who rather pre-

---

[*] See ante, p. 163; and notes by Price and Madden to Warton, i. 54.
[†] Hist. of Eng. Poet., i. pp. 55–70.

cocled Rolle, being reckoned the only poet belonging to the reign of Edward II., and to whom are also attributed a number of religious pieces, preserved only in one manuscript, much damaged, in the Bodleian, besides the metrical romance of the Life of Alexander, of which two copies exist, one in the Bodleian, the other in the library of Lincoln's Inn; but there is every reason for believing that this last-mentioned work, which is printed in Weber's collection under the title of Kyng Alisaunder, and is one of the most spirited of our early romances, is by another author. There is no ground for assigning it to Davie except the circumstance of the Bodleian copy being bound up with his Visions, Legends, Scripture Histories, and other much more pious than poetical lucubrations; and its style is as little in his way as its subject.

LAWRENCE MINOT.

Putting aside the authors of some of the best of the early metrical romances, whose names are generally or universally unknown, perhaps the earliest writer of English verse who deserves the name of a poet is Lawrence Minot, who lived and wrote about the middle of the fourteenth century, and of the reign of Edward III. His ten poems in celebration of the battles and victories of that king, preserved in the Cotton MS. Galba E. ix., which the old catalogue had described as a manuscript of Chaucer, the compiler having been misled by the name of some former proprietor, Richard Chawser, inscribed on the volume, were discovered by Tyrwhitt while collecting materials for his edition of the Canterbury Tales, in a note to the Essay on the Language and Versification of Chaucer prefixed to which work their existence was first mentioned. This was in 1775. In 1781 some specimens of them were given (out of their chronological place) by Warton in the third volume of his History of Poetry. Finally, in 1790, the whole were published by Ritson under the title of Poems written anno MCCCLII., by Lawrence Minot; with Introductory Dissertations on the Scottish Wars of Edward III., on his claim to the throne of France, and Notes and Glossary, 8vo. London; and a reprint of this volume appeared in 1825. Of the 250 pages, or thereby, of which it consists, only about 50 are occupied by the poems, which are ten in number, their

subjects being the Battle of Halidon Hill (fought 1333); the
Battle of Bannockburn (1314), or rather the manner in which
that defeat, sustained by his father, had been avenged by
Edward III.; Edward's first Invasion of France (1339); the
Sea-fight in the Swine, or Zwin * (1340); the siege of Tournay
(the same year); the Landing of the English King at La
Hogue, on his Expedition in 1346; the Siege of Calais (the
same year); the Battle of Neville's Cross (the same year);
the Sea-fight with the Spaniards off Winchelsea (1350); and
the Taking of the Guisnes (1352). It is from this last
date that Ritson, somewhat unwarrantably, assumes that all
the poems were written in that year. As they are very various
in their form and manner, it is more probable that they were
produced as the occasions of them arose, and therefore that they
ought rather to be assigned to the interval between 1333 and
1352. They are remarkable, if not for any poetical qualities of a
high order, yet for a precision and selectness, as well as a force,
of expression, previously, so far as is known, unexampled in
English verse. There is a true martial tone and spirit too in
them, which reminds us of the best of our old heroic ballads,
while it is better sustained, and accompanied with more refinement of style, than it usually is in these popular and anonymous compositions. As a sample we will transcribe the one on
Edward's first expedition to France, omitting a prologue, which
is in a different measure, and modernizing the spelling where it
does not affect the rhyme or rhythm :—

> Edward, owre comely king,
> In Braband has his woning[1]
>   With many comely knight;
> And in that land, truely to tell,
> Ordains he still for to dwell
>   To time[2] he think to fight.

> Now God, that is of mightes mast,[3]
> Grant him grace of the Holy Ghast
>   His heritage to win;
> And Mary Moder, of mercy free,
> Save our king and his meny[4]
>   Fro sorrow, shame, and sin.

----

* To the south of the Isle of Cadsand, at the mouth of the West Scheldt.

[1] Dwelling.   [2] Till the time.   [3] Most of might.

[4] Followers.

Thus in Brabant has he been,
Where he before was seldom seen
　For to prove their japes;[1]
Now no langer will he spare,
But unto France fast will he fare
　To comfort him with grapes.

Furth he fared into France;
God save him fro mischance,
　And all his company!
The noble Duke of Brabant
With him went into that land,
　Ready to live or die.

Then the rich flower de lice[2]
Was there full little price;
　Fast he fled for feared:
The right heir of that countrèe
Is comen,[3] with all his knightes free,
　To shake him by the beard.

Sir Philip the Valays[4]
Wit his men in tho days
　To battle had he thought:[5]
He bade his men them purvey
Withouten langer delay;
　But he ne held it nought.

He brought folk full great won,[6]
Aye seven against[7] one,
　That full well weaponed were,
But soon when he heard secry[8]
That king Edward was near thereby,
　Then durst he nought come near.

In that morning fell a mist,
And when our Englishmen it wist,
　It changed all their cheer;
Our king unto God made his boon,[9]
And God sent him good comfort soon;
　The weather wex full clear.

---

[1] Jeers.　　　[2] Fleur de lis.　[3] Come.
[4] Philip VI. de Valois, king of France.
[5] The meaning seems to be, "Informed his men in those days that he had
a design to fight." Unless, indeed, wit be a mistranscription of with.
[6] Number.　　　　[7] Against.　　　　[8] Report.
[9] Prayer, request.—Ritson. Perhaps, rather, vow or bond.

Our king and his men held the field
Stalworthly with spear and shield,
　And thought to win his right ;
With lordes and with knightes keen,
And other doughty men hydeen[1]
　That war full frek[2] to fight.

When Sir Philip of France heard tell
That king Edward in field wald[3] dwell,
　Then gained him no glee :[4]
He traisted of no better boot,[5]
Bot both on horse and on foot
　He basted him to flee.

It seemed he was feared for strokes
When he did fell his greate oaks
　Obout[6] his pavilionn ;
Abated was then all his pride,
For langer there durst he nought bide ;
　His boast was brought all down.

The king of Beme[7] bad cares cold,
That was full hardy and bold
　A steed to umstride :[8]
He and the king als[9] of Naverne[10]
War fair feared[11] in the fern
　Their hevids[12] for to hide.

And leves[13] well it is no lie,
And field hat[14] Flemangry[15]
　That king Edward was in,
With princes that were stiff and bald,
And dukes that were doughty tald[16]
　In battle to begin.

The princes, that were rich on raw,[17]
Gert[18] nakers[19] strike, and trumpes blaw,
　And made mirth at their might,

---

[1] Perhaps "besides." The word is of common occurrence, but of doubtful
or various meaning.　[2] Were full eager.　[3] Would (was dwelling).
[4] The meaning seems to be, "then no glee, or joy, was given him"
(acerroit ei).　[5] He trusted in no better expedient, or alternative.
[6] About. .　[7] Bohemia.　[8] Bestride.　[9] Also.
[10] Navarro.　[11] Were fairly frightened.　[12] Heads.
[13] Believe.　[14] Was called.　[15] The village of La Flamengrie.
[16] Reckoned.　[17] Apparently, "arranged richly clad in a row."
[18] Caused.　[19] Tymbals.

Both alblast[1] and many a bow
War ready railed[2] upon a row,
    And full frek for to fight.

Gladly they gave meat and drink,
So that they suld the letter swink,[3]
    The wight[4] men that there were.
Sir Philip of France fled for doubt,
And bied him bame with all his rout:
    Coward! God Give him care!

For there then had the lily flower
Lorn all halely[5] his honour,
    That so gat fled[6] for feard;
Bot our king Edward come full still?
When that he trowed no harm him till,[7]
    And keeped him in the beard.[8]

ALLITERATIVE VERSE.—PIERS PLOUGHMAN.

It may be observed that Minot's verses are thickly sprinkled
with what is called *alliteration*, or the repetition of words having
the same commencing letter, either immediately after one another,
or with the intervention only of one or two other words generally
unemphatic or of subordinate importance. Alliteration, which
we find here combined with rhyme, was in an earlier stage of
our poetry employed, more systematically, as the substitute for
that decoration—the recurrence, at certain regular intervals, of
like beginnings, serving the same purpose which is now accomplished by what Milton has contemptuously called "the jingling
sound of like endings." To the English of the period before the
Conquest, until its very latest stage, rhyme was unknown, and
down to the tenth century our verse appears to have been constructed wholly upon the principle of alliteration. Hence,
naturally, even after we had borrowed the practice of rhyme
from the French or Romance writers, our poetry retained for a
time more or less of its original habit. In Layamon, as we have
seen, alliterative and rhyming couplets are intermixed; in other
cases, as in Minot, we have the rhyme only pretty liberally be-

[1] Arblast, or crossbow.
[2] Should the better labour.
[3] Got put to flight?
[4] Stout.
[5] Lost wholly.
[6] Came back quietly at his ease.
[7] When he perceived there was no harm intended him.
[8] Perhaps, "kept his beard untouched."

spangled with alliteration. At this date, in fact, the difficulty probably would have been to avoid alliteration in writing verse; all the old customary phraseologies of poetry had been moulded upon that principle; and indeed alliterative expression has in every age, and in many other languages as well as our own, had a charm for the popular ear, so that it has always largely prevailed in proverbs and other such traditional forms of words, nor is it yet by any means altogether discarded as an occasional embellishment of composition, whether in verse or in prose. But there is one poetical work of the fourteenth century, of considerable extent, and in some respects of remarkable merit, in which the verse is without rhyme, and the system of alliteration is almost as regular as what we have in the poetry of the times before the Conquest. This is the famous Vision of Piers Ploughman, or, as the subject is expressed at full length in the Latin title, Visio Willielmi de Petro Ploughman, that is, The Vision of William concerning Piers or Peter Ploughman. The manuscripts of this poem, which long continued to enjoy a high popularity, are very numerous, and it has also been repeatedly printed: first in 1550, at London, by Robert Crowley, "dwelling in Elye rentes in Holburne," who appears to have produced three successive impressions of it in the same year; again in 1561, by Owen Rogers, "dwellyng neare unto great Saint Bartelmewes gate, at the sygne of the Spred Egle;" next in 1813, under the superintendence of the late Thomas Dunham Whitaker, LL.D.; lastly, in 1842, under the care of Thomas Wright, Esq., M.A., F.R.S., &c. The early editions, and also Dr. Whitaker's, are in quarto and in black letter. Mr. Wright's is in the common type, and in the much more commodious form of two volumes duodecimo; and, furnished as it is with an introduction, notes, and a glossary, all very carefully and learnedly compiled, is as superior in all other respects as it is in cheapness and convenience for perusal to Dr. Whitaker's costly and cumbrous publication. Whitaker, moreover, whose acquirements in this department of study were very slender, has selected a text widely differing from the common one, and which has evidently no claim to the preference with which he has honoured it; that given by Mr. Wright (who has added in the notes the most important of the variations exhibited by Dr. Whitaker's edition) differs very little, except in greater accuracy, from that first printed by Crowley, while it is derived from what appears to be " the best and oldest manuscript now in existence." Dr. Whitaker's notes and glossary are contemptible; and his running paraphrase, which accompanies the text, will be found much more frequently to slur over, when it does not mistake, the obscure passages of the original, than to explain, or attempt to explain, them.

Of the author of Piers Ploughman scarcely anything is known. He has commonly been called Robert Langland: but there are grounds for believing that his Christian name was William, and it is probable that it is himself of whom he speaks under that name throughout his work. He is supposed to have been a monk, and he seems to have resided in the West of England, near the Malvern Hills, where he introduces himself at the commencement of his poem as falling asleep "on a May morwenynge," and entering upon his dreams or visions. The date may be pretty nearly fixed. In one place there is an allusion to the treaty of Bretigny made with France in 1360, and to the military disasters of the previous year which led to it; in another passage mention is made of a remarkable tempest which occurred on the 15th of January, 1362, as of a recent event. " It is probable," to quote Mr. Wright, " that the poem of Piers Ploughman was composed in the latter part of this year, when the effects of the great wind were fresh in people's memory, and when the treaty of Bretigny had become a subject of popular discontent."[*] We may assume, at least, that it was in hand at this time.

We cannot attempt an analysis of the work. It consists, in Mr. Wright's edition, where the long line of the other editions is divided into two, of 14,696 verses, distributed into twenty sections, or Passus as they are called. Each passus forms, or professes to form, a separate vision; and so inartificial or confused is the connection of the several parts of the composition (notwithstanding Dr. Whitaker's notion that it had in his edition " for the first time been shown that it was written after a regular and consistent plan "), that it may be regarded as being in reality not so much one poem as a succession of poems. The general subject may be said to be the same with that of Bunyan's Pilgrim's Progress, the exposition of the impediments and temptations which beset the crusade of this our mortal life; and the method, too, like Bunyan's, is the allegorical; but the spirit of the poetry is not so much picturesque, or even descriptive, as satirical.

* Introduction, p. xii.

Vices and abuses of all sorts come in for their share of the exposure and invective; but the main attack throughout is directed against the corruptions of the church, and the hypocrisy and worldliness, the ignorance, indolence, and sensuality, of the ecclesiastical order. To this favourite theme the author constantly returns with new affection and sharper zest from any less high matter which he may occasionally take up. Hence it has been commonly assumed that he must have himself belonged to the ecclesiastical profession, that he was probably a priest or monk. And his Vision has been regarded not only as mainly a religious poem, but as almost a puritanical and Protestant work, although produced nearly two centuries before either Protestanism or Puritanism was ever heard of. In this notion, as we have seen, it was brought into such repute at the time of the Reformation that three editions of it were printed in one year. There is nothing, however, of anti-Romanism, properly so called, in Langland, either doctrinal or constitutional; and even the anti-clerical spirit of his poetry is not more decided than what is found in the writings of Chaucer, and the other popular literature of the time. In all ages, indeed, it is the tendency of popular literature to erect itself into a power adverse to that of the priesthood, as has been evinced more especially by the poetical literature of modern Europe from the days of the Provençal troubadours. In the Canterbury Tales, however, and in most other works where this spirit appears, the puritanism (if so it is to be called) is merely one of the forms of the poetry; in Piers Ploughman the poetry is principally a form or expression of the puritanism.

The rhythm or measure of the verse in this poem must be considered as accentual rather than syllabical—that is to say, it depends rather upon the number of the accents than of the syllables. This is, perhaps, the original principle of all verse; and it still remains the leading principle in various kinds of verse, both in our own and in other languages. At first, probably, only the accented syllables were counted, or reckoned of any rhythmical value; other syllables upon which there was no emphasis went for nothing, and might be introduced in any part of the verse, one, two, or three at a time, as the poet chose. Of course it would at all times be felt that there were limits beyond which this licence could not be carried without destroying or injuring the metrical character of the composition; but

these limits would not at first be fixed as they now for the most
part are. The elementary form of the verse in Piers Ploughman
demands a succession of four accented syllables—two in the first
hemistich or short line, and two in the second; but, while each
of those in the first line is usually preceded by either one or two
unaccented syllables, commonly only one of those in the second
line is so preceded. The second line, therefore, is for the most
part shorter than the first. And they also differ in regard to the
alliteration: it being required that in the first both the accented
or emphatic syllables, which are generally initial syllables, should
begin with the same letter, but that in the second only the first
accented syllable should begin with that letter. This is the
general rule; but, either from the text being corrupt or from the
irregularity of the composition, the exceptions are very numerous.[*] We may merely add, that, although in our extracts
we shall for the convenience of printing, and for the greater
intelligibility, follow Mr. Wright's edition, as in other respects,
so in the bisection of the long line of the manuscripts and the
other editions into two short ones, only marking the structural
distinction between the first and second, which he does not, we
suspect that the true prosody requires these short lines to be regarded rather as hemistichs than as entire verses, and sometimes
only as false hemistichs—that is to say, that the correct prosodical division would be, not in all cases where he has placed it, but
occasionally in the middle of the word with which he closes his
first line. But this is a matter of little moment. We shall adopt
the plan of modernizing the spelling in all cases in which there
can be no doubt that the pronunciation is not thereby affected.

The poem begins as follows :—

> In a summer season,
> When soft was the sun,
> I shoop me into shrowds[1]
> As I a sheep[2] were;

---

[*] Mr. Wright observes that, when alliterative poetry was written in the
fifteenth century, the writers, instead of three, "not unfrequently inserted four
or five alliterative words in the same [long] line, which would certainly have
been considered a defect in the earlier writers." But this defect, if it be one,
is very frequent in Piers Ploughman. It occurs, for instance, in the two commencing lines of the poem, at least as printed in Mr. Wright's edition.

[1] I put myself into clothes.

[2] A shepherd.

In habit as an hermit
  Unholy of werkes,[1]
Went wide in this world
  Wonders to hear;
Ac[2] on a May morwening
  On Malvern hills
Me befel a ferly,[3]
  Of fairy me thought.
I was weary for-wandered,[4]
  And went me to rest
Under a broad[5] bank,
  By a burn's[6] side;
And as I lay and leaned,
  And looked on the waters,
I slumbered into a sleeping,
  It swayed so mury.[7]
Then gan I meten[8]
  A marvellous swoven,[9]
That I was in a wilderness,
  Wist I never where;
And, as I beheld into the east
  On high to the sun,
I seigh[10] a tower on a toft[11]
  Frielicho ymaked,[12]
A deep dale beneath,
  A donjon therein,
With deep ditches and darke,
  And dreadful of sight.
A fair field full of folk
  Found I there between,
Of all manner of men,
  The mean and the rich,
Working[13] and wandering
  As the world asketh.
Some putten hem[14] to the plough,
  Playden full seld,[15]
In setting and sowing
  Swonken[16] full hard.

---

[1] Whitaker's interpretation is, "in habit, not like an anchorite who keeps his cell, but like one of those unholy hermits who wander about the world to see and hear wonders." He reads, "That went forth in the werl," &c.

[2] And.	[5] Wonder.	[4] Worn out with wandering.
[3] Broad.	[6] Stream's.	[7] It sounded so pleasant
[8] Meet.	[9] Dream.	[10] Saw.
[11] An elevated ground.	[12] Handsomely built.	[13] Working.
[14] Put them.	[15] Played full seldom.	[16] Laboured.

And women that wasters
  With gluttony destroyeth.[1]
And some putten hem to pride,
  Apparelled hem thereafter,
In countenance of clothing
  Comen disguised,[2]
In prayers and penances
  Putten hem many,[3]
All for the love of our Lord
  Liveden full strait,[4]
In hope to have after
  Heaven-riche bliss;[5]
As anchors and heremites[6]
  That holden hem in hir' cells,
And coveten nought in country
  To carryen about,
For no likerous lisade
  Hir liksme to please.[8]
And some chosen chaffer;[9]
  They choveden[10] the better,
As it seemeth to our sight
  That swich me thriveth.[11]
And some murths to make
  As minstrelics con,[12]
And geten gold with hir glee,[13]
  Guiltless, I lieve.[14]
Ac japers and jangellers[15]
  Judas' children,
Feignen hem fantasies
  And fools hem maketh,
And han hir[16] wit at will
  To werken if they wold.
That Poul preacheth of hem
  I wol nat prove[17] it here:
But qui loquitur turpiloquium[18]
  Is Jupiter's hine.[19]

---

[1] Wan that which wasters with gluttony destroy.
[2] Came disguised. Whitaker reads, "In countenance and in clothing."
[3] Many put them, applied themselves to, engaged in.
[4] Lived full strictly. [5] The bliss of the kingdom of heaven.
[6] Anchorites and eremites or hermits. [7] Hold them in their.
[8] By no likerous living their body to please. [9] Merchandise.
[10] Achieved their end. [11] That such men thrive.
[12] And some are skilled to make mirths, or amusements, as minstrels.
[13] And got gold with their minstrelsy. [14] Believe.
[15] But jesters and jugglers. [16] Have their. [17] Will not prove.
[18] Whoso speaketh ribaldry. [19] Our modern hind, or servant.

Bidders[1] and beggars
  Fast about yede,[2]
With hir bellies and hir bags
  Of bread full y-crammed,
Faiteden[3] for hir food,
  Foughten at the ale:
In gluttony, God wot,
  Go they to bed,
And risen with ribaudry,[4]
  Tho Roberd's knaves;[5]
Sleep and sorry slewth[6]
  Sueth[7] hem ever.
Pilgrims and palmers
  Plighten hem togider[8]
For to seeken Saint Jame
  And saintes at Rome:
They wenten forth in hir way[9]
  With many wise tales,
And hadden leave to lien[10]
  All hir life after.
I saigh some that saiden[11]
  They had y-sought saintes:
To each a tale that they told
  Hir tongue was tempered to lie[12]
More than to say sooth,
  It seemed by hir speech.
Hermits on an heap,[13]
  With hooked staves,
Wenten to Walsingham,
  And hir wenches after;
Great lobies and long,
  That loath were to swink,[14]
Clothed hem in copes
  To be knowen from other,
And shopen hem[15] hermits
  Hir ease to have.
I found there freres,
  All the four orders,

---

[1] Petitioners. [2] Went. [3] Flattered. [4] Rise with ribaldry.

[5] These Robertsmen—a class of malefactors mentioned in several statutes of the fourteenth century. The name may have meant originally Robin Hood's men, as Whitaker conjectures.

[6] Sloth. [7] Pursue.

[8] Gather them together. [9] They went forth on their way.

[10] To lie. [11] I saw some that said.

[12] In every tale that they told their tongue was trained to lie.

[13] In a crowd. [14] Labour. [15] Made themselves.

Preaching the people
  For profit of hem selve :
Glosed the gospel
  As hem good liked ;[1]
For covetise of copes[3]
  Construed it as they would.
Many of these master freres
  Now clothen hem at liking,[2]
For hir money and hir merchandize
  Marchen togeders.
For sith charity hath been chapman,
  And chief to shrive lords,
Many ferlies han fallen[4]
  In a few years :
But holy church and hi[5]
  Hold better togeders,
The most mischief on moold[6]
  Is mounting well fast.
There preached a pardoner,
  As he a priest were ;
Brought forth a bull
  With many bishops' seals,
And said that himself might
  Assoilen hem all,
Of falsehede of fasting,[7]
  Of avowes y-broken.
Lewed[8] men leved[9] it well,
  And liked his words ;
Comen up kneeling
  To kissen his bulls :
He bonched[10] hem with his brevet,[11]
  And bleared hir eyen,[12]
And raught with his ragman[13]
  Ringes and brooches.

Here it will be admitted, we have both a well-filled canvas and a picture with a good deal of life and stir in it. The satiric touches are also natural and effective ; and the expression clear, easy, and not deficient in vigour. We will now present a portion of the Fifth Passus, which commences thus :—

---

[1] As it seemed to them good.   [3] Covetousness of copes or rich clothing.
[2] Clothe themselves to their liking.   [4] Many wonders have happened.
[5] Unless holy church and they.   [6] The greatest mischief on earth.
[7] Of breaking fast-days.   [8] Ignorant.   [9] Loved.
[10] Stopped their mouths.   [11] Little brief.   [12] Dadimmed their eyes.
[13] Reached, drew in, with his catalogue or roll of names ?

The king and his knights
  To the kirk went,
To hear matins of the day,
  And the mass after.
Then waked I of my winking,
  And wo was withal
That I ne had slept sadder[1]
  And y-seighen[2] more.
Ac ere I had faren[3] a furlong
  Faintise me hent,[4]
That I ne might ferther a foot
  For de-faut of sleeping,
And sat softly adown,
  And said my believe,
And so I babbled on my beads,
  They brought me asleep.
And then saw I much more
  Than I before of told;
For I seigh the field full of folk
  That I before of said,
And how Reason gan arrayen him
  All the reaum to preach,[5]
And with a cross afore the king
  Comsed[6] thus to teachen :—
He preved that these pestilences[7]
  Were for pure sin,
And the south-western wind
  On Saturday at even[8]
Was pertlich[9] for pure pride,
  And for no point else.
Pyries[10] and plum-trees
  Were puffed to the earth,
In ensample that the segges[11]
  Sholden do the better;
Beeches and broad oaks
  Were blowen to the ground,
Turned upward hir tails,
  In tokening of dread
That deadly sin ere doomsday
  Shall for-done[12] hem all.

---

[1] Sounder.   [2] Seen.   [3] But ere I had walked.
[4] Faintness seized me.   [5] To preach to all the realm.   [6] Commenced.
[7] The three great pestilences which desolated England and the rest of Europe in the reign of Edward III. occurred in 1348-1349, 1361-1362, and 1369.
[8] The great tempest of Saturday, Jan. 15, 1362.   [9] Manifestly.
[10] Pear-trees.   [11] Men, people.   [12] Undo, ruin.

The account of Reason's sermon is continued at great length;
after which the repentance of his auditors is narrated as follows :—

> Pernel Proudheart
>   Flat her[1] to the earth,
> And lay long ere she loked,
>   And "Lord, Mercy," cried,
> And bi-highte[2] to him
>   That us all made
> She should unsowen her serk[3]
>   And set there an hair,
> To affaiten[4] her flesh,
>   That fierce was to sin.
>
>   .   .   .   .   .
>
> Envy with heavy heart
>   Asked after shrift,
> And carefully mea culpa
>   He comsed[5] to shew.
> He was as pale as a pellet,[6]
>   In the palsy he seemed ;
> And clothed in a kaury maury[7]
>   I couth it nought descrive,
> In kirtle and courtepy,[8]
>   And a knife by his side ;
> Of a frere's frock
>   Were the fore-sleeves ;
> And as a leek that had y-lay
>   Long in the sun,
> So looked he with lean cheeks
>   Lowering foul.
> His body was to-bollen[9] for wrath
>   That he boot[10] his lips ;
> And wringing he yede[11] with the fist ;[12]
>   To wreaken himself he thought
> With werks or with words
>   When he seigh his time.
> Each a word that he warp[13]
>   Was of a nedder's[14] tongue ;

---

[1] Threw herself down. [2] Promised. [3] Shirt.
[4] Tame. [5] Commenced. [6] Snowball.
[7] In Cole's Dictionary this is given as a Dutch word, and interpreted
"mock-garments." Wright, in his Dictionary of Obsolete and Provincial
English has caury, worm-eaten. But see post, p. 212.
[8] A short coat. [9] Was swollen. [10] Bit.
[11] Went. [12] Fist. [13] Each word that he uttered.
[14] An adder's.

Of chiding and of chalenging
  Was his chief lifiode ;[1]
With backbiting and blamear[2]
  And bearing of false witness.
" I wold been y-shrive," quod this shrew,
  " And[3] I for shame durst ;
I wold be gladder, by God,
  That Gib had mischance
Than though I had this week[4] y-won
  A wey[5] of Essex cheese.
I have a neighbour by me ;
  I have annoyed him oft,
And lowen[6] on him to lords
  To doon him lese his silver,[7]
And made his friends be his foon[8]
  Thorough my false tongue :
His grace and his good haps
  Grieven me full sore.
Between many and many
  I make debate oft,
That both life and limb
  Is lost thorough my speech.
And when I meet him in market
  That I most hate,
I hailse him hendly[9]
  As I his friend were ;
For[10] he is doughtier than I
  I dare do none other ;
Ac[11] had I mastery and might
  God wot my will !
And when I come to the kirk,
  And should kneel to the rood,
And pray for the people
  As the priest teacheth,
For pilgrims and for palmers,
  For all the people after,
Then I cry on my knees
  That Christ give hem sorrow
That beareo away my bowl
  And my broke sheta.[12]
Away fro the auter[13] then
  Turn I mine eyen,

---

[1] Livelihood (way of living).   [2] Reproach, besmearing.   [3] If, an.
[4] Week.   [5] 256 pounds.   [6] Lied?
[7] To make him lose his money.   [8] Foes.
[9] I salute him politely.   [10] Because.   [11] But.
[12] That bore away my bowl and shut my breast.   [13] Altar.

And behold Ellen
   Hath a new coat :
I wish then it were mine,
   And all the web after.
And of men's losing[1] I laugh ;
   That liketh mine heart :
And for his winning I weep,
   And wail the time,
And deem that they doen ill
   There I do well werse.[2]
Whoso under-nymeth[3] me hereof,
   I hate him deadly after.
I wold that such a wight
   Were my knave ;[4]
For whoso hath more than I,
   That angereth me sore.
And thus I live loveless,
   Like a luther[5] dog,
That all my body boineth[6]
   For bitter of my gall.
I might nought eat many years
   As a man ought,
For envy and evil will
   Is evil to defy.[7]
May no sugar nor sweet thing
   Assuage my swelling ?
Ne no diapenidion[8]
   Drive it fro mine heart ?
Ne neither shrift ne shame,
   But whoso shrape[9] my maw ?"
" Yes, readily," quod Repentance,
   And rad him to the best ;[10]
" Sorrow of sins
   Is salvation of souls."
" I am sorry," quod that segge ;[11]
   I am but seld other ;[12]
And that maketh me thus meagre
   For[13] I ne may me venge.

---

[1] Losing.
[2] Where I do still worse (bien plus pis).
[3] Mr. Wright translates undertake, takes possession of. Here, perhaps, the meaning is, takes me up in speech, chucks me for that.
[4] Servant.
[5] Vicious.
[6] Swelleth.
[7] Ill to digest.
[8] Electuary.
[9] Unless one should scrape. It may perhaps be doubted if these last three couplets are intended to be taken interrogatively.
[10] Counselled him for the best.
[11] Man.
[12] I am seldom otherwise.
[13] Because.

Amonges burgeses have I be
  Dwelling in London,
And gart[1] backbiting be a broker
  To blame men's ware:
When he sold and I bought,
  Then was I ready
To lie and to lower on my neighbour,
  And to lack his chaffer.[2]
I woll amend this if I may,
  Thorough might of God Almighty."

The cases of Wrath, Covetousness, Gluttony, and Sloth follow
at equal or greater length; and then comes the passage in which
Piers Ploughman is first mentioned. The people having been
persuaded by the exhortations of Repentance and Hope to set
out in quest of Truth,—

A thousand of men tho[3]
  Throngen togeders,
Cried upward to Christ,
  And to his clean moder,
To have grace to go with them
  Truthe to seek.
Ac[4] there was wight none so wise
  The way thider couth,[5]
But blustreden[6] forth as beasts
  Over bankes and hills;
Till late was an long
  That they a leod[7] met,
Apparelled as a paynim
  In pilgrimes' wise.
He bar a borden y-bound
  With a broad list,
In a with-wind wise[8]
  Y-wounden about;
A bowl and a bag
  He bar by his side,
And hundred of ampuls[9]
  On his hat setten,
Signs of Sinai,
  And shells of Galice,

---

[1] Caused.
[2] To disparage his merchandise.
[3] Then.
[4] But.
[5] Knew.
[6] Wandered along aimlessly.
[7] Person.
[8] Withy-wand-wise.
[9] Ampulla, small vessels of holy water or oil?

And many a crouch[1] on his cloak,
   And keyes of Rome,
And the Vernicle[2] before,
   For[3] men shold know
And see by his signs
   Whom he sought had.
The folk frayned[4] him first
   Fro whennes he come.
" From Sinai," he said,
   " And from our Lord's sepulchre :
In Bethlem and in Babiloyn,
   I have been in both ;
In Armony[5] and Alisandre,
   In many other places.
Ye may see by my signs,
   That sitten on mine hat,
That I have walked full wide
   In weet and in dry,
And sought good saints
   For my soul's health."
" Knowestow aught a corseint[6]
   That men call Truth ?
Coudestow aught wissen us the way[7]
   Where that wye[8] dwelleth ?"
" Nay, so me God help,"
   Said the gome[9] then,
" I saigh never palmer
   With pike ne with scrip
Asken after him ere
   Till now in this place."

Then the narrative goes on, as printed and pointed by Mr.
Wright, who has no note upon the passage—

" Peter," quod a ploughman,
   And put forth his head,
" I know him as kindly
   As clerk doth his bookes :
Conscience and kind[10] wit
   Kenned[11] me to his place,

---

[1] Cross.	[2] The Veronica, or miraculous picture of Christ.
[3] In order that.	[4] Questioned.
[5] Armenia.	[6] Knowest thou of any relic.
[7] Couldest thou tell us aught of the way.	[8] Man.
[9] Man.	[10] Natural.
	[11] Showed.

And diden me suren him sikerly[1]
　To serven him for ever,
Both to sow and to set
　The while I swink[2] might.
I have been his follower
　All this fifty winter,
Both y-sowen[3] his seed
　And sued[4] his beasts,
Within and withouten
　Waited his profit.
I dig and I delve,
　I do that Truth hoteth:[5]
Some time I sow
　And sometime I thresh;
In tailors' craft and tinkers' craft
　What Truth can devise;
I weave and I wind
　And do what Truth hoteth," &c.

It is difficult to understand what meaning we are to give to the word "Peter," understood as part of the Ploughman's speech. Whitaker's interpretation is "One Peter, a ploughman, now put forth his head;" and in a note upon the passage, which in his edition occurs in the eighth *passus*, and stands "Peter quoth a Ploughman," he says, "As Piers Ploughman, who now first appears, is evidently the speaker, we must, notwithstanding the arrangement of the words, understand them to mean, ' Quoth Peter a ploughman.'" But it is evident that this sense cannot be got out of the words as they stand.[*] The line is pos-

---

[1] And did assure (determine or fix) me to him securely (firmly).
[2] Labour.　　　[3] Sowed.　　　[4] Tended.　　　[5] Ordereth.

[*] From its position the word *Peter* would almost seem to be nothing more than an exclamation. It does not appear to have been noticed that we have the same form of expression in two passages of Chaucer's House of Fame; in book II, l. 526, where, to the question of the eagle,

　　　　"And what sown is it like? quod he,"

the author answers,

　　　　"Peter! like the beating of the sea,
　　　　Quod I, against the rocks below:"—

and again in book III., l. 910, where it is used by the eagle in addressing the author (elsewhere called Geffrey, see II. 221)—

　　　　"Peter! that is now mine intent,
　　　　Quod he to me."　　　　　　　　　　[Perhaps

sibly corrupt; and indeed the whole passage, though one on
which so much of the structure of the poem hinges, exhibits
other traces of having suffered from the carelessness or ignorance
of the transcribers. It differs widely throughout in the two
editions. But everything relating to the personage from whom
the work takes its name would almost seem to be designedly
involved in confusion and obscurity. The Ploughman ends his
speech, of which we have quoted the commencement, by telling
his auditors that, if they wish to know where Truth dwells, he
is ready to show them the way to his residence; upon which,
proceeds the story,—

> " Yea, leve¹ Piers," quod these pilgrims,
>   And proffered him hire,
> For to wend with hem
>   To Truth's dwelling-place.
> " Nay, by my soul's help,"² quod Piers,
>   And gan for to swear,
> I nold fang a ferthing,
>   For Saint Thomas' shrine ;³
> Truth wold love me the lass⁴
>   A long time thereafter.
> Ac if you wilneth to wend well⁵
>   This is the way thider :—
> Ye moten⁶ go thorough Meekness,
>   Both men and wives,
> Till ye come into Conscience," &c.

The personage who thus speaks is afterwards constantly designated Piers, or sometimes Perkin, the Ploughman, and he makes
a considerable figure throughout the sixth and seventh *Passus*;

Perhaps " Peter! quod a Ploughman" means no more than what we find a few
pages after :—

> " Quod Perkin the Ploughman,
>   By Saint Peter of Rome !"—l. 3799.

Besides, the Ploughman, we believe, is never afterwards called *Peter*; but
always either *Piers* or *Perkin*.

¹ Dear.
² Should not this be *helth*, or *health*? The Saxon character for *th* is very
apt to be mistaken for a *p*.
³ I would not take a farthing, if you were to offer me all the wealth of
St. Thomas's shrine.   ⁴ Less.
⁵ But if you wish to go well.   ⁶ Must.

after which we hear little more of him till we come to the sixteenth. In the eighteenth *Passus* "the character of Piers the Ploughman," according to Mr. Wright's view (Introduction, p. xxiv.), "is identified with that of the Saviour." Whitaker, who generally calls him "the mysterious personage," conceives (Introductory Discourse, p. xxviii.) that Piers in the latter part of the poem is intended to be the representative of the Church. Taking the church as meaning, not the clergy or the ecclesiastical system, but the body of the faithful, it would not perhaps be impossible to understand Piers as sustaining that character throughout the work.

PIERS PLOUGHMAN'S CREED.

The popularity of Langland's poem appears to have brought alliterative verse into fashion again even for poems of considerable length; several romances were written in it, such as that of William and the Werwolf, that of Alexander, that of Jerusalem, and others; and the use of it was continued throughout the greater part of the fifteenth century. But the most remarkable imitation of the Vision is the poem entitled Piers the Ploughman's Creed, which appears to have been written about the end of the fourteenth century: it was first printed separately at London, in 4to. by Reynold Wolfe, in 1553; then by Rogers, along with the Vision, in 1561. In modern times it has also been printed separately, in 1814, as a companion to Whitaker's edition of the Vision; and, along with the Vision, in Mr. Wright's edition of 1842. The Creed is the composition of a follower of Wyclif, and an avowed opponent of Romanism. Here, Mr. Wright observes, "Piers Ploughman is no longer an allegorical personage: he is the simple representative of the peasant rising up to judge and act for himself—the English *sans-culotte* of the fourteenth century, if we may be allowed the comparison." The satire, or invective, in this effusion (which consists only of 1697 short lines), is directed altogether against the clergy, and especially the monks or friars; and Piers or Peter is represented as a poor ploughman from whom the writer receives that instruction in Christian truth which he had sought for in vain from every order of these licensed teachers. The language is quite as antique as that of the Vision, as may appear from the following passage, in which Piers is introduced:—

Then turned I me forth,
    And talked to myself
Of the falsehede of this folk,
    How faithless they weren.
And as I went by the way
    Weeping for sorrow,
I see a seely[1] man me by
    Upon the plough honged.[2]
His coat was of a clout[3]
    That cary[4] was y-called;
His hood was full of holes,
    And his hair out;
With his knopped shoon[5]
    Clouted full thick,
His ton[6] toteden[7] out
    As he the lond tredded;
His hosen overhongen his hoc-shynes[8]
    On everich a side,
All beslomered[9] in fen[10]
    As he the plough followed.
Twey[11] mittens as meter[12]
    Made all of clouts,
The fingers weren for-weard[13]
    And full of fen honged.
This whit[14] waaled[15] in the feen[16]
    Almost to the ancle;
Four rotheren[17] him beforn,
    That feeble were worthy;[18]
Men might reckon each a rib[19]
    So rentful[20] they weren.
His wife walked him with,
    With a long goad,
In a cutted coat
    Cutted full high,

---

[1] Simple.   [2] Hang, bent, over.   [3] Cloth.
[4] Is not this the same word that we have in cary maary (vid. sup. p. 234)? It would seem to be the same of a kind of cloth.
[5] Knobbed shoen.   [6] Toes.   [7] Peeped.
[8] Neither of Mr. Wright's explanations seems quite satisfactory: "crooked shins;" or "the shin towards the hock or ankle?"
[9] Beslubbed.   [10] Mud.   [11] Two.
[12] Mr. Wright suggests fitter; which does not seem to make sense.
[13] Were worn out.   [14] Wight.   [15] Dirtied himself.
[16] Fen, mud.   [17] Oxen (the Four Evangelists).
[18] Became? Perhaps the true reading is forthy, that is, for that.
[19] Each rib.   [20] Meagre?

Wrapped in a winnow[1] sheet
To weären her fro weders,[2]
Barefoot on the bare ice,
That the blood followed.
And at the lond's end[3] lath[4]
A little croun-bolle,[5]
And thereon lay a little child
Lapped in clouts,
And tweyn of twey years old[6]
Upon another side.
And all they songen[7] o[8] song,
That sorrow was to hearen;
They crieden all o cry,
A careful note.
The seely man sighed sore,
And said, "Children, beth[9] still."
This man looked upon me,
And leet the plough stonden;[10]
And said, "Seely man,
Why sighest thou so hard?
Gif thee lack lifelode,[11]
Lene thee ich will[12]
Swich[13] good as God hath sent:
Go we, leve brother."[14]

Alliterative verse, the most ancient form of our poetry, would seem to have been revived, and brought into fashion or favour again for a time, after having been long disused, by its successful employment in the Visions of Piers Ploughman, and the popularity of that work. Both Warton in his History, and Percy in an Essay published in the second volume of his Reliques, have noticed several other alliterative poems, in addition to the Creed, which, although not all strictly speaking to be regarded as imitations of Langland's performance, probably owed their existence mainly to the example he had set. In some of them the alliteration is carried much further than in the Visions, the jingle, or juggle, of like *beginnings*, as Milton might have called

[1] Winnowing.
[2] The meaning seems to be, "to protect her from the weather."
[3] The end of the field.   [4] Lieth?
[5] Mr. Wright explains by "crum-bowl."
[6] Two of two years old.   [7] Sang.   [8] One.
[9] Be.   [10] Let the plough stand.
[11] If livelihood lack, or be wanting to, thee.
[12] Give or lend thee I will.   [13] Such.
[14] Let us go, dear brother.

it, being introduced, not according to a rule only in certain
places of the verse, but apparently to the utmost extent that the
writer found possible by availing himself of all the resources of
his vocabulary.   Here, for instance, is the commencing stanza of
a Hymn to the Virgin, given by Warton :—

> Hail hro yow, Marie, moodur and may,[1]
>   Mylde, and meke, and merciable ;[2]
> Heyl, follicbe[3] fruit of sothfast fay,[4]
>   Agayn uche stryf[5] studefast and stable !
> Huil, sothfast soul in uche a may,[6]
>   Undur the son[7] is non so able.
> Heil, logge[8] that ur lord in lay,
>   The formast that never was founden in fable ![9]
> Heil, trewe, trouthfull, and tretable ![10]
>   Heil, cheef ! chosen of chastite ![11]
> Heil, homely, hende,[12] and amyable
>   To preye for us to thi sone so fre !

---

[1] Mother and maid.	[2] Merciful.
[3] Baptismal ?	[4] Truth-fast faith.
[5] Against each strife stedfast.	[6] In each assay, or trial.
[7] The sun.	[8] Lodge.
[9] The formost that ever was found in story ?	
[10] Tractable.	[11] Chosen (ychosen) chief of chastity.
[12] Gentle, courteous.	

THIRD ENGLISH.

(MIXED OR COMPOUND ENGLISH.)

GEOFFREY CHAUCER.

The Vision of Piers Ploughman is our earliest poetical work of any considerable extent that may still be read with pleasure; but not much of its attraction lies in its poetry. It interests us chiefly as rather a lively picture (which, however, would have been nearly as effective in prose) of much in the manners and general social condition of the time, and of the new spirit of opposition to old things which was then astir; partly, too, by the language and style, and as a monument of a peculiar species of versification. Langland, or whoever was the author, probably contributed by this great work to the advancement of his native tongue to a larger extent than he has had credit for. The grammatical forms of his English will be found to be very nearly, if not exactly the same with those of Chaucer's; his vocabulary, if more sparingly admitting the non-Teutonic element, still does not abjure the principle of the same composite constitution; nor is his style much inferior in mere regularity and clearness. So long a work was not likely to have been undertaken except by one who felt himself to be in full possession of the language as it existed: the writer was no doubt prompted to engage in such a task in great part by his gift of ready expression; and he could not fail to gain additional fluency and skill in the course of the composition, especially with a construction of verse demanding so incessant an attention to words and syllables. The popularity of the poem, too, would diffuse and establish whatever improvements in the language it may have introduced or exemplified. In addition to the ability displayed in it, and the popular spirit of the day with which it was animated, its position in the national literature naturally and deservedly gave to the Vision of Piers Ploughman an extraordinary influence: for it has the distinction (so far as is either known or probable) of being the earliest original work, of any magnitude, in the language. Robert of Gloucester and Robert de Brunne, Langland's predecessors, were both, it may be remembered, only translators or paraphrasts.

If Langland, however, is our earliest original writer, Chaucer
is still our first great poet, and the true father of our literature,
properly so called.   Compared with his productions, all that
precedes is barbarism.   But what is much more remarkable is,
that very little of what followed in the space of nearly five
centuries that has elapsed since he lived and wrote is worthy of
being compared with what he has left us.   He is in our English
poetry almost what Homer is in that of Greece, and Dante in
that of Italy—at least in his own sphere still the greatest light.

Although, therefore, according to the scheme of the history of
the language which has been propounded, the third form of it, or
that which still subsists, may be regarded as having taken its
commencement perhaps a full century before the date at which
we are now arrived, and so as taking in the works, not only of
Langland, but of his predecessors from Robert of Gloucester
inclusive, our living English Literature may be most fitly held
to begin with the poetry of Chaucer.   It will thus count an
existence already of above five centuries.   Chaucer is supposed
to have been born about the beginning of the reign of Edward
III.—in the year 1328, if we may trust what is said to have
been the ancient inscription on his tombstone ; so that he had
no doubt begun to write, and was probably well known as
a poet, at least as early as Langland.   They may indeed
have been contemporaries in the strictest sense of the word,
for anything that is ascertained.   If Langland wrote the
Creed of Piers Ploughman, as well as the Vision, which
(although it has not, we believe, been suggested) is neither
impossible nor very unlikely, he must have lived to as late, or
very nearly as late, a date as Chaucer, who is held to have died
in 1400.   At the same time, as Langland's greatest, if not only,
work appears to have been produced not long after the middle of
the reign of Edward III., and the composition of Chaucer's
Canterbury Tales not to have been begun till about the middle of
that of Richard II., the probability certainly is, regard being
had to the species and character of these poems, each seemingly
impressed with a long experience of life, that Langland, if not
the earlier writer, was the elder man.

The writings of Chaucer are very voluminous ; comprising, in
so far as they have come down to us, in verse, The Canterbury
Tales; the Romaunt of the Rose, in 7701 lines, a translation
from the French Roman de la Rose of Guillaume de Lorris and

Jean de Meun; Troilus and Cresside, in Five Books, on the same subject as the Filostrato of Boccaccio; The House of Fame, in Three Books; Chaucer's Dream, in 2235 lines; the Book of the Duchess (sometimes called the Dream of Chaucer), 1334 lines; the Assembly of Fowls, 694 lines; the Flower and the Loaf, 595 lines; the Court of Love, 1442 lines; together with many ballads and other minor pieces: and in prose (besides portions of the Canterbury Tales), a translation of Boethius' De Consolatione Philosophiæ; the Testament of Love, an imitation of the same treatise; and a Treatise on the Astrolabe, addressed to his son Lewis in 1391, of which, however, we have only two out of five parts of which it was intended to consist. All these works have been printed, most of them more than once; and a good many other pieces have also been attributed to Chaucer which are either known to be the compositions of other poets, or of which at least there is no evidence or probability that he is the author. Only the Canterbury Tales, however, have as yet enjoyed the advantage of anything like careful editing. Tyrwhitt's elaborate edition was first published, in 4 vols. 8vo., in 1775, his Glossary to all the genuine works of Chaucer having followed in 1778; and another edition, presenting a new text, and also accompanied with notes and a Glossary, was brought out by Mr. T. Wright for the Percy Society in 1847.

In his introductory Essay on the Language and Versification of Chaucer, Tyrwhitt observes, that at the time when this great writer made his first essays the use of rhyme was established in English poetry, not exclusively (as we have seen by the example of the Vision of Piers Ploughman), but very generally, " so that in this respect he had little to do but to imitate his predecessors." But the metrical part of our poetry, the learned editor conceives, " was capable of more improvement, by the polishing 'of the measures already in use, as well as by the introduction of new modes of versification." " With respect," he continues, " to the regular measures then in use, they may be reduced, I think, to four. First, the long Iambic metre, consisting of not more than fifteen nor less than fourteen syllables, and broken by a cæsura at the eighth syllable. Secondly, the Alexandrine metre, consisting of not more than thirteen syllables nor less than twelve, with a cæsura at the sixth. Thirdly, the Octosyllable metre, which was in reality the ancient dimeter Iambic. Fourthly, the stanza of six verses, of which the first, second, fourth, and fifth were in the complete octosyllable metre, and the third and last catalectic—that is, wanting a syllable, or even two." The first of these metres Tyrwhitt considers to be exemplified in the Ormulum, and probably also in the Chronicle of Robert of Gloucester, if the genuine text could be recovered; the second, apparently, by Robert de Brunne, in imitation of his French original, although his verse in Hearne's edition is frequently defective: the third and fourth were very common, being then generally used in lighter compositions, as they still are. "In the first of those metres," he proceeds, "it does not appear that Chaucer ever composed at all (for I presume no one can imagine that he was the author of Gamelyn), or in the second; and in the fourth we have nothing of his but the Rhyme of Sire Thopas, which, being intended to ridicule the vulgar romancers, seems to have been purposely written in their favourite metre. In the third, or octosyllable metre, he has left several compositions, particularly an imperfect translation of the Roman de la Rose, which was probably one of his earliest performances, The House of Fame, The Dethe of the Duchesse Blanche, and a poem called his Dreme: upon all which it will be sufficient here to observe in general, that, if he had given no other proofs of his poetical faculty, these alone must have secured to him the pre-eminence above all his predecessors and contemporaries in point of versification. But by far the most considerable part of Chaucer's works is written in that kind of metre which we now call the Heroic, either in distichs or stanzas; and, as I have not been able to discover any instance of this metre being used by any English poet before him, I am much inclined to suppose that he was the first introducer of it into our language." It had been long practised by the writers both in the northern and southern French; and within the half century before Chaucer wrote it had been successfully cultivated, in preference to every other metre, by the great poets of Italy—Dante, Petrarch, and Boccaccio. Tyrwhitt argues, therefore, that Chaucer may have borrowed his new English verse either from the French or from the Italian.

That the particular species of verse in which Chaucer has written his Canterbury Tales and some of his other poems had not been used by any other English poet before him, has not, we believe, been disputed, and does not appear to be disputable, at least from such remains of our early poetical literature as we now possess. Here, then, is one important fact. It is certain, also, that the French, if not likewise the Italian, poets who employed the decasyllabic (or more properly hendecasyllabic *) metre were well known to Chaucer. The presumption, therefore, that his new metre is, as Tyrwhitt asserts, this same Italian or French metre of ten or eleven syllables (our present heroic verse) becomes very strong.

Moreover, if Chaucer's verse be not constructed upon the principle of syllabical as well as accentual regularity, when was this principle, which is now the law and universal practice of our poetry, introduced? It will not be denied to have been completely established ever since the language acquired in all material respects its present form and pronunciation—that is to say, at least since the middle of the sixteenth century : if it was not by Chaucer at the end of the fourteenth, by whom among his followers in the course of the next hundred and fifty years was it first exemplified?

At present it is sufficient to say that no one of his successors throughout this space has hinted that any improvement, any change, had been made in the construction of English verse since Chaucer wrote. On the contrary, he is generally recognized by them as the great reformer of our language and our poetry, and as their master and instructor in their common art.

* In the Italian language, at least, the original and proper form of the verse appears to have consisted of eleven syllables; whence the generical name of the metre is endecasyllabo, and a verse of ten syllables is called endecasyllabo tronco, and one of twelve, endecasyllabo sdrucciolo. But these variations do not affect the prosodical character of the verse, which requires only that the tenth should be in all cases the last accented syllable. The modern English heroic, or, as we commonly call it, ten-syllabled verse, still admits of being extended by an eleventh or even a twelfth unaccented syllable: although, from the constitution of our present language as to syllabic emphasis, such extension is with us the exception, not the rule, as it is (at least to the length of eleven syllables) in Italian. It may be doubted whether Chaucer's type or model line is to be considered as decasyllabic or hendecasyllabic: Tyrwhitt was of opinion that the greater number of his verses, when properly written and pronounced, would be found to consist of eleven syllables; and this will seem probable, if we look to what is assumed, on the theory of his versification which we are considering, to have been the pronunciation of the language in his day. At the same time many of his lines evidently consist (even on this theory) of ten syllables only; and such a construction of verse for ordinary purposes is become so much more agreeable to modern usage and taste that his poetry had better be so read whenever it can be done, even at the cost of thereby somewhat violating the exactness of the ancient pronunciation.

By his friend and disciple Occleve he is called " the first finder
of our fair langage." So Lydgate, in the next generation,
celebrates him as his master—as "chief poet of Britain"—as

> — " he that was of making soverain,
> Whom all this lande of right ought prefer,
> Sith of our langage he was the lode-ster "—

and as—

> " The noble rhethor poet of Britain,
> That worthy was the laurer to have
> Of poetrye, and the palm attain ;
> That made first to distil and rain
> The gold dew-drops of speech and eloquence
> Into our tongue through his excellence,
> And found the flowres first of rhetorio
> Our rode speech only to enlumine," &c.

A later writer, Gawin Douglas, sounds his praise as—

> " Venerable Chaucer, principal poet but[1] peer,
> Heavenly trumpet, orlege,[2] and regulere ;[3]
> In eloquence balm, condict,[4] and dial,
> Milky fountain, clear strand, and rose rial,"[5]

in a strain, it must be confessed, more remarkable for enthusiastic
vehemence than for poetical inspiration. The learned, and at
the same time elegant, Leland, in the next age describes him as
the writer to whom his country's tongue owes all its beauties :—

> " Anglia Chaucerum veneratur nostra poetam,
>   Cui veneres debet patria lingua suas ;"

and again, in another tribute, as having first reduced the language
into regular form :—

> " Linguam qui patriam redegit illam
>   In formam."

And such seems to have been the unbroken tradition down to
Spenser, who, looking back through two centuries, hails his
great predecessor as still the " well of English undefiled."

If now we proceed to examine Chaucer's verse, do we find it
actually characterized by this regularity, which indisputably
has at least from within a century and a half of his time been the
law of our poetry? Not, if we assume that the English of
Chaucer's time was read in all respects precisely like that of our
own day. But are we warranted in assuming this ? We know
that some changes have taken place in the national pronun-

---

[1] Without.   [2] Horologe, clock or watch.
[3] Regulator.   [4] Condiment.   [5] Royal.

ciation within a much shorter space. The accentuation of
many words is different even in Shakespeare and his contemporaries from what it now is: even since the language has been
what we may call settled, and the process of growth in it nearly
stopped, there has still been observable a disposition in the accent
or syllabic emphasis to project itself with more precipitation than
formerly, to seize upon a more early enunciated part in dissyllables and other polysyllabic words than that to which it was
wont to be attached. For example, we now always pronounce
the word *aspect* with the accent on the first syllable; in the time
of Shakespeare it was always accented on the last. We now call
a certain short composition an *éssay*; but only a century ago it
was called an *esśáy*: "And write next winter," says Pope,
"more essays on man." Probably at an earlier period, when
this change was going on more actively, it was part of that
general process by which the Teutonic, or native, element in our
language eventually, after a long struggle, acquired the ascendancy over the French element; and, if so, for a time the
accentuation of many words would be unfixed, or would oscillate
between the two systems—the French habit of reserving itself
for the final syllable, and the native tendency to cling to a prior
portion of the word. This appears to have been the case in
Chaucer's day: many words are manifestly in his poetry accented
differently from what they are now (as is proved, upon either
theory of his prosody, when they occur at the end of a verse),
and in many also he seems to vary the accent—pronouncing, for
instance, *lángage* in one line, *langáge* in another—as suits his convenience. But again, under the tendency to elision and abbreviation, which is common to all languages in a state of growth,
there can be no doubt that, in the progress of the English
tongue, from its first subjection to literary cultivation in the
middle of the thirteenth century to its final settlement in the
middle of the seventeenth, it dropt and lost altogether many
short or unaccented syllables. Some of these, indeed, our
poets still assert their right to revive in pressing circumstances:
thus, though we now almost universally elide or suppress the *e*
before the terminating *d* of the preterites and past participles of
our verbs, it is still sometimes called into life again to make a
distinct syllable in verse. Two centuries ago, when perhaps it
was generally heard in the common speech of the people (as it
still is in some of our provincial dialects), and when its sup-

pression in reading prose would probably have been accounted
an irregularity, it was as often sounded in verse as not, and the
licence was probably considered to be taken when it was elided.
The elision, when it took place, was generally marked by the
omission of the vowel in the spelling. If we go back another
century, we find the pronunciation of the termination as a
distinct syllable to be clearly the rule and the prevailing
practice, and the suppression of the vowel to be the rare exception. But even at so late a date as the end of the sixteenth
and the beginning of the seventeenth century, other short vowels
as well as this were still occasionally pronounced, as they were
almost always written. Both the genitive or possessive singular
and the nominative plural of nouns were, down to this time,
made by the addition not of *s* only, as now, but of *es* to the
nominative singular; and the *es* makes a distinct syllable sometimes in Shakespeare, and often in Spenser. In Chaucer, therefore, it is only what we should expect that it should generally be
so pronounced : it is evident that originally, or when it first
appeared in the language, it always was, and that the practice of
running it and the preceding syllable together, as we now do,
has only been gradually introduced and established.

. Up to this point Tyrwhitt's theory of Chaucer's versification
may be said to be admitted on all hands. It is allowed that in
reading Chaucer's verses we should generally sound as distinct
syllables the *ed* at the end of verbs and the *es* when it is the
plural or possessive termination of a noun; and also that we
must give many words a different accentuation from what they
now possess. But this is not enough to make the verse in all
cases syllabically regular.

The deficiencies of Chaucer's metres, Tyrwhitt contends, are to
be chiefly supplied by the pronunciation of what he calls "the
e feminine ;" by which he means the *e* which still terminates so
many of our words, but is now either totally silent and ineffective
in the pronunciation, or only lengthens or otherwise alters the
sound of the preceding vowel—in either case is entirely inoperative upon the syllabication. Thus, such words as *large*,
strange, *time*, &c., he conceives to be often dissyllables, and such
words as *Romains*, *sentence*, often trisyllables, in Chaucer. Some
words also he holds to be lengthened a syllable by the intervention of such an *e*, now omitted both in speaking and writing,
in the middle—as in *jug-e-ment*, *command-e-ment*, *vouch-e-safe*, &c.

Wallis, the distinguished mathematician, in his Grammar of the English Language (written in Latin, and published about the middle of the seventeenth century) had suggested that the origin of this silent *e* probably was, that it had originally been pronounced, though somewhat obscurely, as a distinct syllable, like the French *e* feminine, which still counts for such in the prosody of that language. Wallis adds, that the surest proof of this is to be found in our old poets, with whom the said *e* sometimes makes a syllable, sometimes not, as the verse requires. "With respect to words imported directly from France," observes Tyrwhitt, "it is certainly quite natural to suppose that for some time they retained their native pronunciation." "We have not indeed," he continues, "so clear a proof of the original pronunciation of the Saxon part of our language; but we know, from general observation, that all changes of pronunciation are generally made by small degrees; and, therefore, when we find that a great number of those words which in Chaucer's time ended in *e* originally ended in *a*, we may reasonably presume that our ancestors first passed from the broader sound of *a* to the thinner sound of *e* feminine, and not at once from *a* to *e* mute. Besides, if the final *e* in such words was not pronounced, why was it added? From the time that it has confessedly ceased to be pronounced it has been gradually omitted in them, except where it may be supposed of use to lengthen or soften the preceding syllable, as in *hope*, *name*, &c. But according to the ancient orthography it terminates many words of Saxon original where it cannot have been added for any such purpose, as *herts*, *childe*, *olde*, *wilde*, &c. In these, therefore, we must suppose that it was pronounced as *e* feminine, and made part of a second syllable, and so, by a parity of reason, in all others in which, as in these, it appears to have been substituted for the Saxon *a*." From all this Tyrwhitt concludes that "the pronunciation of the *e* feminine is founded on the very nature of both the French and Saxon parts of our language," and therefore that "what is generally considered as an *e* mute, either at the end or in the middle of words, was anciently pronounced, but obscurely, like the *e* feminine of the French." In a note, referring to an opinion expressed by Wallis, who, observing that the French very often suppressed this short *e* in their common speech, was led to think that the pronunciation of it would perhaps shortly be in all cases disused among them, as among ourselves, he adds: " The prediction has certainly failed; but, notwithstanding, I will venture to say that when it was made it was not unworthy of Wallis's sagacity. Unluckily for its success, a number of eminent writers happened at that very time to be growing up in France, whose works, having since been received as standards of style, must probably fix for many centuries the ancient usage of the e feminine in poetry, and of course give a considerable check to the natural progress of the language. If the age of Edward III. had been as favourable to letters as that of Louis XIV.; if Chaucer and his contemporary poets had acquired the same authority here that Corneille, Molière, Racine, and Boileau have obtained in France; if their works had been published by themselves, and perpetuated in a genuine state by printing; I think it probable that the e feminine would still have preserved its place, in our poetical language at least, and certainly without any prejudice to the smoothness of our versification."

In supporting his views by these reasons, Tyrwhitt avoids having recourse to any arguments that might be drawn from the practice of Chaucer himself—that being in fact the matter in dispute; but his main proposition, to the extent at least of the alleged capacity of the now silent final e to make a distinct syllable in Chaucer's day, appears to be demonstrated by some instances in the poet's works. Thus, for example, in the following couplet from the Prologue to the Canterbury Tales, unless the word Rome which ends the first line be pronounced as a dissyllable, there will be no rhyme:—

> " That straight was comen from the court of Rome;
> Full loud he sang—Come hither, love, to me."

So again, in the Canon Yeoman's Tale, we have the following lines:—

> " And when this alchymister saw his time,
> His'th up, Sir Priest, quod he, and stondeth by me,"

in the first of which time must evidently in like manner be read as a word of two syllables. The same rhyme occurs in a quatrain in the Second Book of the Troilus and Cresside:—

> " All easily now, for the love of Marte,
> Quod Pandarus, for every thing hath time,
> So long abide, till that the night departe
> For all so sicker as thou liest here by me."

Finding *Rome* and *time* to be clearly dissyllables in these passages, it would seem that we ought, as Tyrwhitt remarks (Note on Prol. to Cant. Tales, 674), to have no scruple so to pronounce them and other similar words wherever the metre requires it.

Such is the outline of Tyrwhitt's theory, which, it must be admitted, is at least extremely plausible, and which was long universally assented to. Of late, however, it has been attacked from several quarters, and on various grounds. The question is one which is of fundamental and central importance in the history of our language and literature, and which therefore may not unprofitably detain us for a few pages more.

The first person, we believe, who intimated a distinct dissent from Tyrwhitt's conclusions was the late Dr. Nott, in an elaborate Dissertation on the State of English Poetry before the Sixteenth Century, prefixed to his edition of The Works of the Earl of Surrey, 4to. Lon. 1815. Dr. Nott's object is to prove that the present system of our versification, the principle of which is syllabical as well as accentual regularity, was the invention of Surrey in the middle of the sixteenth century, and that down to that date our verses of every kind were all what he is pleased to call "rhythmical and not metrical;"—that is, as he explains the expression, "they did not consist, as our verses do at present, of a certain number of feet, each foot of two syllables, but they were constructed so as to be recited with a certain rhythmical cadence; for which reason they seem to have been called Verses of cadence." (Diss. p. cli.)

This nomenclature, at least, is unfortunate. The phrase, "verse of cadence" is Lydgate's; but, whatever may be its import, it certainly was not the only kind of verse known in Chaucer's time; for in his House of Fame (ii. 115) Chaucer himself is described in an address to him by the Eagle as having long been given to apply his wit

> "To make bokes, songis, and ditis,
> *In rhyme or ellis in cadence.*"

It is remarkable that this passage, so clearly implying, as it would seem, that, besides verse of cadence, Chaucer was acquainted with a different sort of verse, which he distinguishes by the name of rhyme, should have escaped the attention of Dr. Nott, or should not be anywhere noticed by him. Further, it appears from a passage in the Troilus and Cresside (v. 1796),

which the learned editor does quote (Diss. clxiii.), that Chaucer
himself considered his verse in that work to be metrical: it is
where, after having thus gracefully dismissed his finished work,—

> "Go, little book! go, little tragedy!
> There God my Maker yet ere that I die
> So send me might to make some comedy:
> But, little book, make thou thee none envie,
> But subject ben unto all poesie,
> And kiss the steps whereas thou seest pace
> Of Virgil, Ovid, Homer, Lucan, Stace,"—

he proceeds in the next stanza to express his earnest hope that
transcribers and reciters may be withheld from violating his
metre:—

> "And, for there is so great diversity
> In English and in writing of our tongue,
> So pray I to God that none miswrite thee
> Ne thee mismetre for defaut of tongue."

These passages may not be absolutely irreconcilable with the
position that Chaucer's verse was not constructed upon the
principle of syllabical regularity; but they show that Dr. Nott
has not been happy in the selection of his epithets when he
affirms that the only kinds of verse known in Chaucer's time
were all "verses of cadence" and all "not metrical." To
speak, as he does, of the feet of our present verses as all consisting each of *two* syllables is another obvious error of expression.

Dr. Nott maintains that Chaucer's supposed employment of
the final and now silent *e* as a distinct syllable could not have
been derived from the similar use of the *e* feminine in French
poetry; but he satisfies himself with a mere expression of his
conviction on this point. "It remains," he says, "yet to be
proved that the use of the *e* feminine, such as is here contended
for, was then established in French poetry. It seems clear to
me that it was not; nor do I doubt but that every one will
arrive at the same conclusion who will give himself the trouble
to examine dispassionately the early French poets, and particularly the manuscript copies of their works." It is probable
that French verse was anciently written with less regularity
than it afterwards acquired; and in the earlier poets of that
language, therefore, the prosodical use of what is called the
e feminine may both seem and be somewhat capricious; but it is

a startling assumption that such use is altogether a modern invention. Upon this supposition it behoved Dr. Nott to point out when and by whom so extraordinary an innovation was introduced. It is strange he should not have perceived that his notion attributes to some comparatively recent French poet the very same thing which he properly objects to as unlikely to have happened in the case of Chaucer—that, in his own words, " if Chaucer really did employ the *e* feminine in his versification in the manner supposed, it must have been a contrivance purely of his own invention "—" a supposition this," he adds, " which, I apprehend, few will be disposed to maintain." (Diss. p. cxliii.)

But the supposition in question is one which nobody has ever advanced with regard to Chaucer. " It appears to me incredible," says Dr. Nott, a few sentences before, " that Chaucer, who was remarkable for his common sense and practical view of things, meaning to form a standard style in language, should begin by introducing a novel mode of pronunciation, which, being contrary to common usage, could not be generally adopted." This is an absurdity of the learned editor's own making. Tyrwhitt does not imagine that Chaucer introduced any novel mode of pronunciation; he conceives that the pronunciation of the language found, according to his view, in Chaucer's poetry was the common pronunciation of the time. If the poetry of Chaucer is to be so read, so undoubtedly is that also of Langland, and Minot, and De Brunne, and Robert of Gloucester, and all our other early English poetry. What Chaucer introduced, and borrowed from the poetry of France or Italy, if he introduced or thence borrowed anything, was not the occasional pronunciation of the final *e* as a distinct syllable, but the general principle of metrical regularity, to which he adapted this and all the other points of the ancient and established national mode of speech. What particular advantage could he have gained by merely multiplying in this or in any other way the number of syllables in the language? It is an odd notion for Dr. Nott to take up that Chaucer's only object in his supposed reformation of our verse was to contrive some ready way of always spinning out his line into ten or eleven syllables. A method of reducing it within those dimensions would have been found equally convenient, if he had ever thought of resorting to any such unheard of and absurd devices. But it is not necessary for the refutation of the claim set up by Dr. Nott in favour of the Earl of

Surrey, that we should suppose Chaucer to have made any change whatever in the principles of English versification. If it be only admitted that his verses are constructed upon the principle of syllabical regularity, it does not matter, for this question, whether those of his predecessors are so or not. His versification may surpass theirs only by this common principle being applied by him with more care, skill, and success than it was by them. He may have made no innovation in the structure of our verse whatever, and borrowed nothing from the poets of France or Italy except only their superior correctness and elegance.

The only one of Dr. Nott's arguments which has much or indeed any apparent force is that which he draws from the manner in which all our early poetry, that of Chaucer included, is stated to be written in the ancient manuscripts. "In all those MSS.," he says, "the cæsura in the middle, and the pause at the end of the line, are pointed out with a precision that leaves no room for conjecture. The points or marks made use of have no reference whatever to punctuation: they never occur but at the place of cæsura in the middle of the line, or at the pause at the end of it; and are often made with red paint, the better to catch the eye. When the mark of cæsura is omitted, an interval is generally left in the middle of the line, between the two hemistichs. The second hemistich frequently begins with a capital, though the introduction of a capital there, instead of assisting, often confuses the sense." (Diss. p. clii.) "An impartial consideration of the subject," he afterwards observes, "and a reference to good MSS., must, I think, lead us to conclude that Chaucer had not a metrical system of numbers in contemplation; but that, on the contrary, he designed his verses to be read, like those of all his contemporaries, with a cæsura and rhythmical cadence." (Id., p. clix.) Again, speaking particularly of the manuscripts of Chaucer's poems, he says, "In those MSS. either the cæsura, or the pause at the end of the line, and sometimes both the pause and the cæsura, are almost always noted, and that in so careful a manner as makes it questionable whether there be any MS. of good date and authority in which one or both of them is not noted, either by a point or a virgule; though the virgule or point may in some instances have been obliterated. Why this particularity, which must have been designed to answer some practical purpose, should not have been noticed by the several editors of Chaucer's works, I am at a loss to say. The omission is the more remarkable, as it could not have escaped observation that all the MSS. agree in fixing the cæsura in every line, with hardly any variation, at the same place. This is another evident mark of design, amounting to little less than proof that Chaucer not only meant his verses to be rhythmical, but did all he could to settle what their rhythm should be." (Id., p. clxiii.) Finally, he remarks on the subject of the cæsura:—" Its use, and the object proposed by it, is confirmed by the appearance of the early printed editions of Chaucer's works. In the editions subsequent to 1532 the cæsura is almost entirely disused ; if it was retained, it seems to have been retained by accident. The reason is obvious. Our English versification had then become metrical. The cæsura was, therefore, no longer wanted for general purposes; it was consequently omitted, though, strictly speaking, in some works it ought to have been retained. But in the editions previous to 1532 the case was different. The rhythmical cadence was then still in use, and therefore the division of the hemistich was still to be continued." (Id., p. clxix.) Surrey's Poems were first printed in .1557; but there were editions of Chaucer in 1542, 1546, and 1555, which must be understood according to this statement to be all without the cæsura. Would it not appear, then, that metrical verse, upon Dr. Nott's own showing, had been introduced from fifteen to twenty-five years before Surrey's poems were given to the world? It is true they were written some years before, for Surrey was put to death in January 1547; but they can hardly have been supposed to have been already so widely diffused in manuscript as to have revolutionized the national versification. When the Chaucer of 1542, the first edition without the cæsura, was published, Surrey, according to the common account, was not more than twenty-three or twenty-four years old. Even Dr. Nott does not pretend that he was more than twenty-six.[*]

What Dr. Nott calls the pause at the *end* of the line seems to have nothing to do with the question he raises in regard to the nature of Chaucer's versification. Of course, it is admitted upon either, and must be admitted upon any, system that a line is such an integral section as may be properly separated by a

[*] See Memoir, prefixed to Works, p. x.

point or other divisional mark if it be thought necessary. As
poetry is now written, nothing of the kind is required; the
limits of the line or verse cannot be more distinctly indicated
than they are by each being kept standing by itself; and it is
not easy to see what practical purpose could be contemplated by
retaining the points at the end of the line after this method was
introduced. Probably it was merely a retention from habit of a
usage to which transcribers and readers had become accustomed,
and which was no doubt very serviceable while verse was
written continuously like prose, as it generally or always was in
the earliest era of our language. We may, therefore, put aside
altogether so much of the above statement as refers to this *final*
point or pause. Let us see, then, how the fact stands as to the
other and only important mark, that of the cæsura, as Dr. Nott
calls it, in the middle of each verse. He sets out by telling us
that both the cæsura in the middle *and* the pause at the end of
the line are always pointed out with perfect precision ; but this
broad assertion is very far from being adhered to when he comes
to specify particulars. The next form in which we have the
statement is, that, "when the mark of cæsura is omitted, an
interval is *generally* left in the middle of the line." Then, in
still more qualified phrase, we are informed that in the manuscripts of Chaucer's poetry "*either* the cæsura *or* the pause at the
end of the line, and *sometimes* both, are *almost* always noted." He
persists, however, in maintaining the careful manner in which
this notation of the pause or pauses has been attended to in all
good manuscripts, although he admits that the virgule or point
may in some instances have been obliterated; and he affirms,
as we have seen, (though not very consistently with his previous
admission of its being only in *some* manuscripts that the cæsura
is noted at all,) "that *all* the manuscripts [of Chaucer] agree in ·
fixing the cæsura, in every line, with hardly any variation, at
the same place."

Let us now turn to his examples. One will suffice to show
how far his statements are borne out, even in their most limited
form. The first seven lines of the Canterbury Tales are professed to be given from three different manuscripts. Of one of
those, the Lansdowne MS. 907, the account given is, that in
this passage the cæsura or middle pause is not marked at
all, either by point or virgule; but that elsewhere we have
the lines cut, not uniformly into two portions by a single

virgule, but sometimes into two, sometimes into three, sometimes into four portions by a succession of such strokes. This
is a phenomenon of which Dr. Nott's theory seems to take no
account. All he has to say in regard to it is, that the frequent
recurrence of the virgule may be suspected to be intended " to
mark some rules in recitation, with which we now are unacquainted." The two other manuscripts, Harl. MSS. 1758 and
7333, as here quoted, differ as to the place of the middle pause
in the very first line ; and in three of the remaining six
lines where the one has only a point the other has both a
point and a virgule, in a fourth verse only a virgule, and in
a fifth a point followed by a capital letter. But it is hard to
say what dependence can be safely placed even upon this
apparent amount of agreement. It so happens that the same
passage has been printed from the same two manuscripts by
Mr. Guest in his History of English Rhythms (2 vols. 8vo.
London, 1838, vol. i., p. 215), and the variations between his
transcripts and those of Dr. Nott are not a little startling.
Dr. Nott evidently did not intend to preserve the old spelling,
although for the object he had here in view that would have
been almost necessary ; but some of the liberties he appears to
have taken go far beyond the reformation of the antique verse in
that particular. In his extract from the MS. 1758, which
extends to eight verses, in the first line he might perhaps defend
his change of *wit* into *with*, and of *swote* (for sweet) into *sote* ; in
the third line, *vain* instead of *vyne* (or vein) is probably a typographical erratum ; in the fourth, the substitution of *vertu* for
virtue, though not very intelligible, and indeed the very reverse
of what might have been expected, is still not a very wide
deviation ; but the printing of *had* for *hath* in the second line is
an instance of unpardonable inattention ; and to transform the
eighth line from

> " Into the ram his half cours ronne."

as it stands in Mr. Guest's transcript, into

> " Hath in the Ram . his half course y-run."

is proceeding to so great a length as to destroy all reliance upon
such a mode of pretending to exhibit the testimony of ancient
manuscripts, or upon any conclusions so supported. But the
discrepancies between the two transcripts of the other MS.

bear more upon the question of the middle pause or cæsura;
for, according to Mr. Guest's exhibition of this text, there is
in three of the seven lines, the first, second, and sixth, actually
no mark of any such pause at all.   Mr. Guest states that in
this manuscript " the pause, when inserted, is often nothing
more than a mere scratch of the pen;" and, so far from regarding either manuscript as a good one, or as carefully written in
regard to the divisional point, he describes " the occasional
omission or misplacing of the dot as perfectly in keeping
with the general inaccuracy" of both.   His extract extends
to eighteen lines; and in regard to eight of the ten not already
examined we are enabled to compare the two Harleian MSS.
with another then belonging to the Marquess of Stafford,
of which a transcript to that extent is given by Dr. Nott.
Passing over other differences, we find that in the Harl. MS.
7333, the middle pause is wanting altogether in the second,
fourth, and eighth; that it is also wanting in the third of the
Stafford MS.; and that in the fifth it is placed differently in all
the three MSS.   It is also wanting in the ninth line in the
Harl. MS. 1758.

It seems plain that of such confusion and uncertainty as this
little or nothing can be made, and that any attempt to exhibit,
in printing Chaucer's poetry, the cæsura or middle pause in each
verse as noted in the manuscripts would be impracticable, even
if it were ever so important. But is this cæsural mark, in fact,
of any importance in determining the nature of Chaucer's versification?   Mr. Guest holds, as well as Dr. Nott, that each line
in Chaucer consists properly of two parts, which the cæsural
mark was designed to indicate: "Still, as it seems to me," he
observes, after describing the irregularity with which this mark
is introduced in the manuscripts, " we can only come to one
conclusion in examining these manuscripts; namely, that each
verse was looked upon as made up of two sections, precisely in
the same way as the alliterative couplet of the Anglo-Saxons." *
Yet Mr. Guest finds no difficulty in reconciling with the principles of syllabical rhythm this fact of the division of each verse
by the cæsural mark, which Dr. Nott regards as demonstrative
of the rhythm being not syllabical but only accentual.

Nor is there, in truth, anything in the cæsura to decide the

* History of English Rhythms, i. 216.

matter either one way or the other. The middle pause, as found
in the manuscripts of Chaucer, appears to be as consistent with
the syllabical as with the merely accentual scanning of the
verse, if the right text be followed. For example, in printing
the first eighteen lines of the Canterbury Tales with accentual
marks, to show in what manner the verse was, as he apprehends,
recited, Dr. Nott gives the first line thus:—

"When that April | with his shoures soote ;"

marking the three syllables, *when*, *with*, and *shour* as long, the
last syllable of *April* and the word *soote* with a grave accent, and
the syllables *that*, *his*, and *es* (of *shoures*) as short; the first
syllable of *April* being left without any mark. It is not very clear
what all the parts of this apparatus of notation are intended to
mean; but certainly, however the words so set down may be
meant to be read or sung, they are not reducible to the regular
metre of our modern heroic verse. It is by no means either
certain or probable, however, that *when* is Chaucer's word; the
reading adopted by Tyrwhitt is *whanne*, which he regards as a
dissyllable, and he has as good a right to select that form, which
occurs in some of the manuscripts, as Dr. Nott has to select the
monosyllabic form, *when*, or *whan*, from other manuscripts, for the
purposes of *his* theory. The next five lines are every one of
them, even as printed by Dr. Nott, of perfect metrical regularity;
the caesura is also where it should be upon either system; the
only thing that interferes with their being read like any modern
English heroic verse is Dr. Nott's own notation of their supposed
temporal and accentual character. All that is wanting to make
the seventh line a correct modern verse, is to be read *younge* (in
two syllables) with Tyrwhitt, instead of *young* with Nott, there
being manuscript authority for both forms. The eighth line
Dr. Nott prints—

"Hath in the Ram | half his course y-run."

We doubt whether there be any authority for this form of the
verse; but, at any rate, Tyrwhitt's form,

"Hath in the Ram his halfe cours y-ronne"

(where *halfe* is a dissyllable), is supported by the Harleian MS.
7333. In the ninth line Nott obtains his text by changing the
dissyllabic *smale* of both the Harleian MSS. into the modern

monosyllable *small*. The next three lines are equally regular
upon either system. The thirteenth line will scan metrically,
even as given by Nott, provided we reckon *strange* a dissyllable;
but we do not know where he has got his text: it does not
agree with either of the Harleian MSS., and as little with the
Stafford MS. as exhibited by himself in another page. The last
five lines, again, are regular upon both systems.

Upon the whole it does not appear that the cæsural mark of the
manuscripts can be regarded as indicating or proving, at the
most, anything more than that, by the rule of the verse, the
place where it fell should always be at the termination and
never in the middle of a word—a rule which is also generally,
though not always, observed in our modern prosody. As far
as can be ascertained, the two parts into which, when it is
employed, it divides each of Chaucer's lines, are as much the
hemistichs of what Dr. Nott calls a metrical, as of what he calls
a merely rhythmical, verse.

We do not understand what notion of the harmony of English
verse can have led Dr. Nott to quote the following line from the
Canterbury Tales—

"In her is high beauty withouten pride"—

as one which, unless read rhythmically (as he calls it) has no
principle of harmony at all, even if we read *beauty* with the
accent on the last syllable. It is in fact a perfectly correct
heroic verse according to the strictest laws of our modern prosody. Yet he asserts that, if Chaucer had followed that prosody,
he would unquestionably have written the verse—

"In her high beauty is withouten pride"—

thus making it a perfect Iambic decasyllabic line, "by the
transposition of a single word." Let the reader who has any
feeling of Chaucer's direct, natural, manly diction, or even of the
most common proprieties of speech, decide. Yet upon this single
instance Dr. Nott lays it down that a large proportion of
Chaucer's verses cannot be read metrically "without doing the
utmost violence to our language; all which verses are harmonious as verses of cadence, if read with the cæsura rhythmically;"
and further, that *all* those verses might easily, by a slight transposition, have been reduced to the pure Iambic decasyllabic
measure, "if Chaucer had either known that mode of versifica-

tion, or intended to have adopted it." Such an assertion, by-the-by, would be a somewhat bold one, even if a hundred instances were quoted instead of one, and those really instances in point.

While insisting that Chaucer's verses are constructed upon what he describes as the rhythmical principle, which he has begun by defining as independent of the number of feet or syllables, Dr. Nott, strangely enough, admits that the chief improvement which Chaucer made in our versification was the introduction of the line of ten syllables (Diss. p. clviii.); and he afterwards repeatedly calls his verses "Decasyllabic" (or, as he more usually chooses to express himself, "Decasyllables"). But he cannot possibly mean that Chaucer's versification is, upon his theory, really syllabically, any more than that it is accentually, correct, according to our modern notions. In fact, of the eighteen lines which he has printed from the commencement of the Canterbury Tales, "to show in what manner rhythmical Decasyllabic verses were recited," no fewer than seven are, according to his own notation, not decasyllabic at all: they are verses of nine syllables (sometimes with an unaccented syllable at the end, which counts for nothing in prosody), not of ten.[*]

Finally, before dismissing Dr. Nott and his theory, we may remark that no attempt is made by him or it to meet the apparently conclusive proof of the now silent final *e* having been enunciable as a distinct syllable in Chaucer's age derived from the occurrence of such rhymes as *Ro-me* and *to me*, *ti-me* and *by me*. Indeed he expressly states (Diss. p. clxxxiii. note), that with the exception of a passage in Occleve, of which he shows that the received reading is most probably incorrect (and which, by-the-by, would scarcely have been in point at any rate), he had

---

[*] Either from a misprint or from something in his system of notation which is not explained, it is difficult with regard to certain of these lines to say in what manner Dr. Nott intends that they should be read. For instance, in the couplet (as he prints it),

"And palmeres to seeken strange strandes,
    To serve halwes couth in sundry londes,"

the appearance of ten syllables is given to each of the two lines by throwing a double accent upon the terminating words *strandes*, *londes*—as if the rhyme lay in the *des*. But it is plain that, if *strandes* and *londes* are to be accounted disyllables, we have here what is called a double rhyme—which can only count as one syllable in the measure—just as in the immediately preceding couplet, which Dr. Nott himself prints—

"So pricketh them nature in their courages ;
    Then longen folk to go on pilgrimages."

nowhere met with a single rhyme " to justify the notion that
the final *e*, which we properly call the *e* mute, was ever pronounced."

More recently, however, Tyrwhitt's main principle for the
scanning of Chaucer's verse, the occasional pronunciation of this
now mute final *e*, has been attacked, or at least denounced, on other
grounds and by a higher authority. The late Mr. Richard Price,
in his edition of Warton's History of English Poetry (4 vols. 8vo.
Lon. 1824), assigns an origin to this termination which he considers to be altogether irreconcilable with Tyrwhitt's view of it.
The change of orthography from the Anglo-Saxon forms which
has taken place in a numerous class of our English words,
Mr. Price maintains, " has arisen solely from the abolition of the
accentual marks which distinguish the long and short syllables."
" As a substitute for the former," he says, " the Norman scribes,
or at least the disciples of the Norman school of writing, had
recourse to the analogy which governed the French language:
and, to avoid the confusion which would have sprung from
observing the same form in writing a certain number of letters
differently enounced and bearing a different meaning, they elongated the word, or attached as it were an accent instead of super-
scribing it. From hence has emanated an extensive list of terms
having final e's and duplicate consonants; which were no more
the representatives of additional syllables than the acute or grave
accent in the Greek language is a mark of metrical quantity."
And he adds in a note:—" The converse of this can only be
maintained under an assumption that the Anglo-Saxon words
of one syllable multiplied their numbers after the Conquest, and
in some succeeding century subsided into their primitive simplicity." * Again, he observes in another place, " The Anglo-
Saxon á was pronounced like the Danish aa, the Swedish å, or
our modern o in more, fore, &c. The strong intonation given to
the words in which it occurred would strike a Norman ear as
indicating the same orthography that marked the long syllables
of his native tongue, and he would accordingly write them with
an o final. It is from this cause that we find hár, sár, hát, bát,
wá, án, bén, stán, &c., written hore (hore), sore, hote (hot),
bote (boat), woe, one, bone, stone, some of which have been
retained. The same principle of elongation was extended to all
the Anglo-Saxon vowels that were accentuated; such as réc,

* Preface to Warton, p. (114).

reke (rook), lif, life, góde, gode (good), sour, shure (shower);
and hence the majority of those e's mute upon which Mr. Tyrwhitt has expended so much unfounded speculation."[*] And the
complete development of these doctrines is promised in a sup-
plementary volume, which was announced under the title of
Illustrations of Warton's History of English Poetry, containing
[among other things] an examination of Mr. Tyrwhitt's Essay
on the Language and Versification of Chaucer; but which has
never appeared.

Upon this view of the matter let us hear a living writer who
must be regarded as the highest authority on the earlier forms
of the language. "The most frequent vowel endings of Anglo-
Saxon substantives," says Mr. Guest (Hist. of Eng. Rhythms,
i. 26), "were a, e, u. All the three were in the fourteenth century represented by the e final." And afterwards, in explaining
the origin of our present mode of indicating the long quantity
of a vowel preceding a single consonant by the annexation of an
e, he observes (Id. p. 108):—"In the Anglo-Saxon there was a
great number of words which had, as it were, two forms; one
ending in a consonant, the other in a vowel. In the time of
Chaucer all the different vowel endings were represented by the
e final; and so great is the number of words which this writer
uses, sometimes as monosyllables, and sometimes as dissyllables,
with the addition of the e, that he has been accused of adding to
the number of his syllables whenever it suited the convenience
of his rhythm. In his works we find hert and herte, bed and bedde,
erth and erthe, &c. In the Anglo-Saxon we find corresponding
duplicates, the additional syllable giving to the noun, in almost
every case, a new declension, and in most a new gender. In
some few cases the final e had become mute even before the time
of Chaucer, and was wholly lost in the period which elapsed
between his death and the accession of the Tudors. Still, however, it has its ground in our manuscripts, and are our, rose a
rose, &c., though pronounced as monosyllables, were still written
according to the old spelling. Hence it came gradually to be
considered as a rule, that when a syllable ended in a single consonant and mute e the vowel was long." "Such," concludes
Mr. Guest, "is clearly the origin of this very peculiar mode of
indicating the long vowel; and it seems to me so obvious, that
I always felt surprise at the many and various opinions that

[*] Note to Warton, Vol. I. p. c. ii.

have been hazarded upon the subject. We could not expect
much information from men who, like Tyrwhitt, were avowedly
ignorant of the early state of our language; but even Hickes
had his doubts whether the final *e* of the Anglo-Saxon words
were mute or vocal; and Rask, notwithstanding his triumph
over that far superior scholar, has fallen into this his greatest
blunder. Price, whose good sense does not often fail him, supposes this mode of spelling to be the work of the Norman, and
the same as the 'orthography that marked the long syllables of
his native tongue.' As if the *e* final were mute in Norman
French!" Throughout his work, Mr. Guest assumes the syllabic
quality of the final *e* in Chaucer's verse, exactly as is done by
Tyrwhitt. "After the death of Chaucer," he asserts (vol. i.
p. 80), "the final *e*, so commonly used by that poet and his contemporaries, fell into disuse. Hence many dissyllables became
words of one syllable, *mone* became moon, and *sunne* sun; and
the compounds into which they entered were curtailed of a syllable." If it be meant that the change spoken of took place
immediately or very soon after the death of Chaucer, the assertion is one which it would probably be somewhat difficult to make
good. We should doubt if the new pronunciation was generally
introduced before the commencement of the sixteenth century.*

* An important view of the final *e* in the English of the period from the
Norman Conquest down at least to the end of the fourteenth century has been
for the first time propounded by Mr. Guest. He believes that it has, at least
in many cases, a grammatical, as well as a prosodical, value; that it is the
remnant of or substitute for the vowel of inflection belonging to the original
form of the language. Thus, in the expression *shoures sote* (showers sweet),
he holds the *e* of *sote* to be the sign of the plural; and that of *rote* in the expression *to the rote* (to the root) to be the distinctive termination of the dative
singular. In other cases, again, he conceives that the *e* distinguishes what is
called (as in modern German) the definite from the indefinite form of the adjective; in others, the adverb from the adjective (*brighte*, for example, being
the former, equivalent to our modern brightly, bright the latter). See his
English Rhythms, I. 29–34. It is, there can be little doubt, this short *e*, we may
here remark, commuted into a short *i*, which we have in such modern forms
as *handicraft* and *handiwork*. They are other forms of *handcraft* and *handwork*
(both recently, if not still, belonging to the language), not of *handy craft* and
handy work, which would be expressions having a different meaning altogether.
A misunderstanding of this matter is probably what has led to the absurd
neologism which has been current on title-pages for the last few years, first
employed by a distinguished noble author (of much higher authority in
legal than in linguistic learning), and forthwith adopted, of course, by the
numerous class to whom any thing and every thing new recommends itself as
certain to be right—the same who some years before at once and unanimously

A fact elsewhere noticed by Mr. Guest, we may just remark, although not adduced by him for that purpose, meets Mr. Price's objection about the unlikelihood or impossibility of many Anglo-Saxon monosyllables having after the Conquest been elongated into dissyllables, and having then in some succeeding century reverted to their original monosyllabic condition. If it were necessary to make such an assumption as this in order to vindicate Tyrwhitt's theory of Chaucer's versification, the thing supposed is no more than what has actually happened. As Mr. Guest has observed (vol. i. p. 40), "The dissyllables containing y and w seem to have been once so numerous in our language, that many words, both English and foreign, were adapted to their pronunciation, and thus gained a syllable: *scur* A. S. became shower, and *fleur* Fr. became flower. Change of pronunciation has again reduced them to their original dimensions."

On the whole, then, we may say that substantially Tyrwhitt's theory remains unshaken; and we shall, in our extracts, assume that the mode proposed by him of reading the verse of Chaucer and his contemporaries is the true one. The reader, to whom it may be new, will find, after a very little practice, that the ear soon gets accustomed to the peculiarities of pronunciation required; and the slight air of archaism which they impart rather adds to the effect of the poetry, so that we come to prefer the retention of these obsolete forms to any substitution, however delicately made, that would aim at modernizing it or making it more intelligible. We shall not, however, in our transcripts, attempt to indicate the pronunciation by any accentual or other marks; being of opinion with Tyrwhitt that "a reader who cannot perform such operations for himself had better not trouble his head about the versification of Chaucer."

" The notion, probably, which most people have of Chaucer," to borrow a few sentences of what we have written elsewhere, " is merely that he was a remarkably good poet for his day;

took to writing *Dover* instead of *Dovor* on no better ground than that the former spelling had appeared painted on some stage-coach—the neologism which turns our perfectly correct old *Handbook* (the *Handbuch* of the Germans) into *Handy Book!* Are we to have also handy ball, and handy barrow, and handy basket, and handy breadth, and handy maidro? It is the same as if we were to call a rainbow a rainy bow, or a fire-shovel a fiery shovel, or a hairbrush a hairy brush, or a hand-draw a handy draw.

but that, both from his language having become obsolete, and from the advancement which we have since made in poetical taste and skill, he may now be considered as fairly dead and buried in a literary, as well as in a literal, sense. This, we suspect, is the common belief even of educated persons and of scholars who have not actually made acquaintance with Chaucer, but know him only by name or by sight;—by that antique-sounding dissyllable that seems to belong to another nation and tongue, as well as to another age; and by that strange costume of diction, grammar, and spelling, in which his thoughts are clothed, fluttering about them, as it appears to do, like the rags upon a scarecrow.

"Now, instead of this, the poetry of Chaucer is really, in all essential respects, about the greenest and freshest in our language. We have some higher poetry than Chaucer's—poetry that has more of the character of a revelation, or a voice from another world: we have none in which there is either a more abounding or a more bounding spirit of life, a truer or fuller natural inspiration. He may be said to verify, in another sense, the remark of Bacon, that what we commonly call antiquity was really the youth of the world: his poetry seems to breathe of a time when humanity was younger and more joyous-hearted than it now is. Undoubtedly he had an advantage as to this matter, in having been the first great poet of his country. Occupying this position, he stands in some degree between each of his successors and nature. The sire of a nation's minstrelsy is of necessity, though it may be unconsciously, regarded by all who come after him as almost a portion of nature—as one whose utterances are not so much the echo of hers as in very deed her own living voice—carrying in them a spirit as original and divine as the music of her running brooks, or of her breezes among the leaves. And there is not wanting something of reason in this idolatry. It is he alone who has conversed with nature directly, and without an interpreter—who has looked upon the glory of her countenance unveiled, and received upon his heart the perfect image of what she is. Succeeding poets, by reason of his intervention, and that imitation of him into which, in a greater or less degree, they are of necessity drawn, see her only, as it were, wrapt in hazy and metamorphosing adornments, which human hands have woven for her, and are prevented from perfectly discerning the outline and the movements of her form by that encumbering investiture. They are the fallen race, who have been banished from the immediate presence of the divinity, and have been left only to conjecture from afar off the brightness of that majesty which sits throned to them behind impenetrable clouds : he is the First Man, who has seen God walking in the garden, and communed with him face to face.

"But Chaucer is the Homer of his country, not only as having been the earliest of her poets (deserving to be so called), but also as being still one of her greatest. The names of Spenser, of Shakspeare, and of Milton are the only other names that can be placed on the same line with his.

"His poetry exhibits, in as remarkable a degree perhaps as any other in any language, an intermixture and combination of what are usually deemed the most opposite excellences. Great poet as he is, we might almost say of him that his genius has as much about it of the spirit of prose as of poetry, and that, if he had not sung so admirably as he has done of flowery meadows, and summer skies, and gorgeous ceremonials, and high or tender passions, and the other themes over which the imagination loves best to pour her vivifying light, he would have won to himself the renown of a Montaigne or a Swift by the originality and penetrating sagacity of his observations on ordinary life, his insight into motives and character, the richness and peculiarity of his humour, the sharp edge of his satire, and the propriety, flexibility, and exquisite expressiveness of his refined yet natural diction. Even like the varied visible creation around us, his poetry too has its earth, its sea, and its sky, and all the "sweet vicissitudes" of each. Here you have the clear-eyed observer of man as he is, catching 'the manners living as they rise,' and fixing them in pictures where not their minutest lineament is or ever can be lost : here he is the inspired dreamer, by whom earth and all its realities are forgotten, as his spirit soars and sings in the finer air and amid the diviner beauty of some far-off world of its own. Now the riotous verse rings loud with the turbulence of human merriment and laughter, casting from it, as it dashes on its way, flash after flash of all the forms of wit and comedy : now it is the tranquillizing companionship of the sights and sounds of inanimate nature of which the poet's heart is full—the springing herbage, and the dew-drops on the leaf, and the rivulets glad beneath the morning ray and dancing to their own simple music. From mere narrative and playful

humour up to the heights of imaginative and impassioned song,
his genius has exercised itself in all styles of poetry, and won
imperishable laurels in all."[*]

It has been commonly believed that one of the chief sources
from which Chaucer drew both the form and the spirit of his
poetry was the recent and contemporary poetry of Italy—that
eldest portion of what is properly called the literature of modern
Europe, the produce of the genius of Petrarch and Boccaccio and
their predecessor and master, Dante. But, although this may
have been the case, it is by no means certain that it was so; and
some circumstances seem to make it rather improbable that
Chaucer was a reader or student of Italian. Of those of his
poems which have been supposed to be translations from the
Italian, it must be considered very doubtful if any one was
really derived by him from that language. The story of his
Palamon and Arcite, which, as the Knight's Tale, begins the
Canterbury Tales, but which either in its present or another
form appears to have been originally composed as a separate
work, is substantially the same with that of Boccaccio's heroic
poem in twelve books entitled Le Teseide—a fact which, we
believe, was first pointed out by Warton. But an examination
of the two poems leads rather to the conclusion that they are
both founded upon a common original than that the one was
taken from the other. Boccaccio's poem extends to about 12,000
octosyllabic, Chaucer's to not many more than 2000 decasyllabic,
verses; and not only is the story in the one much less detailed
than in the other, but the two versions differ in some of the
main circumstances.[†] Chaucer, moreover, nowhere mentions
Boccaccio as his original; on the contrary, as Warton has himself noticed, he professes to draw his materials, not from the
works of any contemporary, but from "olde Stories," and "olde
bookes that all this story telleth more plain."[‡] Tyrwhitt, too,
while holding, as well as Warton, that Chaucer's original was
Boccaccio, admits that the latter was in all probability not the
inventor of the story.[§] Boccaccio himself, in a letter relating to

* Printing Machine. No. 37 (1835).

† See this pointed out by Dr. Nott (who nevertheless assumes the one
poem to be a translation from the other), in a note to his Dissertation on the
State of English Poetry before the Sixteenth Century, p. cclxxiv.

‡ Warton's Hist. Eng. Poetry, ii. 179.

§ Introductory Discourse to Canterbury Tales, Note (13).

his poem, describes the story as very ancient, and as existing in
what he calls *Latino volgare*, by which he may mean rather the
Provençal than the Italian.* In fact, as both Warton and
Tyrwhitt have shown, there is reason to believe that it had previously been one of the themes of romantic poetry in various
languages. The passages pointed out by Tyrwhitt in his notes
to Chaucer's poem, as translated or imitated from that of Boccaccio, are few and insignificant, and the resemblances they
present would be sufficiently accounted for on the supposition of
both writers having drawn from a common source. Nearly the
same observations apply to the supposed obligations of Chaucer
in his Troilus and Creseide to another poetical work of Boccaccio's, his Filostrato. The discovery of these was first announced by Tyrwhitt in his Essay prefixed to the Canterbury
Tales. But Chaucer himself tells us (ii. 14) that he translates his poem "out of Latin;" and in other passages (i. 394,
and v. 1653), he expressly declares his "auctor" or author,
to be named *Lollius*. In a note to the Parson's Tale, in the
Canterbury Tales, Tyrwhitt assumes that Lollius is another
name for Boccaccio, but how this should be he confesses himself
unable to explain. In his Glossary (a later publication), he
merely describes Lollius as "a writer from whom Chaucer professes to have translated his poem of Troilus and Creseide,"
adding, "I have not been able to find any further account of
him." It is remarkable that he should omit to notice that Lollius
is mentioned by Chaucer in another poem, his House of Fame
(iii. 378), as one of the writers of the Trojan story, along with
Homer, Dares Phrygius, Livy (whom he calls Titus), Guido of

---

* The letter is addressed to his mistress (la Fiametta), Mary of Aragon, a
natural daughter of Robert king of Naples. "Trovate," he says, "una anti-
chissima storia, ed al più delle genti non manifesta, in Latino volgare," &c.
The expression here has a curious resemblance to the words used by Chaucer
in enumerating his own works in the Legende of Good Women, v. 420,—

> "He made the boke that hight the House of Fame, &c.
> And all the love of Palamon and Arcite
> Of Thebes, *though the story is knowen lite.*"

Tyrwhitt's interpretation of these last words is, that they seem to imply that
the poem to which they allude, the Palamon and Arcite (as first composed),
had not made itself very popular. Both he and Warton understand the
Latino volgare, as meaning the Italian language in this passage of the letter
to La Fiametta, as well as in a stanza which he quotes from the Teseide in
Discourse, Note (9).

Colonna, and "English Galfrid," that is, Geoffrey of Monmouth.
The only writer of the name of Lollius of whom anything is
now known appears to be Lollius Urbicus, who is stated to
have lived in the third century, and to have composed a history
of his own time, which, however, no longer exists.[*] But our
ignorance of who Chaucer's Lollius was does not entitle us to
assume that it is Boccaccio whom he designates by that name.
Besides, the two poems have only that general resemblance
which would result from their subject being the same, and their
having been founded upon a common original. Tyrwhitt (note
to Parson's Tale), while he insists that the fact of the one being
borrowed from the other "is evident, not only from the fable
and characters, which are the same in both poems, but also from
a number of passages in the English which are literally translated from the Italian," admits that "at the same time there are
several long passages, and even episodes, in the Troilus of which
there are no traces in the Filostrato;" and Warton makes the
same statement almost in the same words.[†] Tyrwhitt acknowledges elsewhere, too, that the form of Chaucer's stanza in the
Troilus does not appear ever to have been used by Boccaccio,
nor does he profess to have been able to find such a stanza in any
early Italian poetry.[‡] The only other composition of Chaucer's
for which he can be imagined to have had an Italian original is
his Clerk's Tale in the Canterbury Tales, the matchless story of
Griselda. This is one of the stories of the Decameron; but it
was not from Boccaccio's Italian that Chaucer took it, but from
Petrarch's Latin, as he must be understood to intimate in the
Prologue, where he says, or makes the narrator say—

> " I woll you tell a tale which that I
> Learned at Padowe of a worthy clerk,
> As preved by his works and his werk :
> He is now dead and nailed in his chest ;
> I pray to God so yeve his soule rest.
> Francis Petrarch, the laureat poet,
> Highte this clerk, whose rhethorike sweet
> Enlumined all Itaille of poetrie." ·

Petrarch's Latin translation of Boccaccio's tale , as Tyrwhitt
states, printed in all the editions of his works, under the title of

---

* See Warton, Hist. Eng. Poetry, ii. 220; and Vossius, de Historicis La-
tinis, ed. 1651, p. 176.

† Hist. Eng. Poetry, ii. p. 221, note.

‡ Essay, § 9.

De Obedientia et Fide Uxoria Mythologia (a Myth on Wifely Obedience and Faithfulness).[*] But, indeed, Chaucer may not have even had Petrarch's translation before him; for Petrarch, in his letter to Boccaccio, in which he states that he had translated it from the Decameron, only recently come into his hands, informs his friend also that the story had been known to him many years before. He may therefore have communicated it orally to Chaucer, through the medium of what was probably their common medium of communication, the Latin tongue, if they ever met, at Padua or elsewhere, as it is asserted they did. All that we are concerned with at present, is the fact that it does not appear to have been taken by Chaucer from the Decameron: he makes no reference to Boccaccio as his authority, and, while it is the only one of the Canterbury Tales which could otherwise have been suspected with any probability to have been derived from that work, it is at the same time one an acquaintance with which we know he had at least the means of acquiring through another language than the Italian. To these considerations may be added a remark made by Sir Harris Nicolas:—" That Chaucer was not acquainted with Italian," says that writer, " may be inferred from his not having introduced any Italian quotation into his works, redundant as they are with Latin and French words and phrases." To which he subjoins in a note: "Though Chaucer's writings have not been examined for the purpose, the remark in the text is not made altogether from recollection; for at the end of Speght's edition of Chaucer's works translations are given of the Latin and French words in the poems, but not a single Italian word is mentioned.[†]

---

* It is strange that Warton, Hist. Eng. Poetry, ii. 250, should say that this translation was never printed.

† Life of Chaucer, p. 23. Sir Harris had said before :—" Though Chaucer undoubtedly knew Latin and French, it is by no means certain, notwithstanding his supposed obligations to the Decameron, that he was as well acquainted with Italian. There may have been a common Latin original of the main incidents of many if not of all the Tales for which Chaucer is supposed to have been wholly indebted to Boccaccio, and from which original Boccaccio himself may ┐ ╮ have ╮ taken." Beside the Clerk's Tale, which has been noticed above, ╮ only stories in the Canterbury Tales which are found in the Decameron are the Reeve's Tale, the Shipman's Tale, and the Franklin's Tale ; but both Tyrwhitt and Warton, while maintaining Chaucer's obligations in other respects to the Italian writers, admit that the two former are much more probably derived from French Fabliaux (the particular fabliau, indeed, on which the Reeve's Tale appears to be founded has been published

T 2

It may be questioned, then, if much more than the fame of
Italian song had reached the ear of Chaucer; but, at all events,
the foreign poetry with which he was most familiar was certainly that of France. This, indeed, was probably still accounted everywhere the classic poetical literature of the modern
world; the younger poetry of Italy, which was itself a derivation from that common fountain-head, had not yet, with all its
real superiority, either supplanted the old lays and romances of
the trouvères and troubadours, or even taken its place by their
side. The earliest English, as well as the earliest Italian, poetry
was for the most part a translation or imitation of that of France.
Of the poetry written in the French language, indeed, in the
eleventh, twelfth, and thirteenth centuries, the larger portion, as
we have seen, was produced in England, for English readers,
and to a considerable extent by natives of this country. French
poetry was not, therefore, during this era, regarded among us as
a foreign literature at all; and even at a later date it must have
been looked back upon by every educated Englishman as rather
a part of that of his own land. For a century, or perhaps more,
before Chaucer arose, the greater number of our common versifiers had been busy in translating the French romances and
other poetry into English, which was now fast becoming the
ordinary or only speech even of the educated classes; but this
work had for the most part been done with little pains or skill,
and with no higher ambition than to convey the mere sense of
the French original to the English reader. By the time when
Chaucer began to write, in the latter half of the fourteenth century, the French language appears to have almost gone out of
use as a common medium of communication; the English on the
other hand, as we may see by the poetry of Langland and Minot
as compared with that of Robert of Gloucester, had, in the course
of the preceding hundred years, thrown off much of its primitive
rudeness, and acquired a considerable degree of regularity and
flexibility, and general fitness for literary composition. In these
circumstances, writing in French in England was over for any

by Le Grand); and the Franklin's Tale is expressly stated by Chaucer himself
to be a Breton lay. He nowhere mentions Boccaccio or his Decameron, or
any other Italian authority. Of the Pardoner's Tale, "the mere outline," as
Tyrwhitt states, is to be found in the Cento Novelle Antiche; but the greater
part of that collection is borrowed from the Contes and Fabliaux of the French.

good purpose: Chaucer himself observes in the prologue to his
prose treatise entitled the Testament of Love:—"Certes there
ben some that speak their poesy matter in French, of which
speech the Frenchmen have as good a fantasy as we have in hearing of Frenchmen's English." And again:—"Let, then, clerks
enditen in Latin, for they have the property of science and the
knowinge in that faculty; and let Frenchmen in their French
also endite their quaint terms, for it is kindly [natural] to their
mouths; and let us show our fantasies in such words as we
learneden of our dames' tongue." The two languages, in short,
like the two nations, were now become completely separated, and
in some sort hostile: as the Kings of England were no longer
either Dukes of Normandy or Earls of Poitou, and recently a
fierce war had sprung up still more effectually to divide the one
country from the other, and to break up all intercourse between
them, so the French tongue was fast growing to be almost as
strange and distinctly foreign among us as the English had
always been in France. Chaucer's original purpose and aim
may be supposed to have been that of the generality of his immediate predecessors, to put his countrymen in possession of some
of the best productions of the French poets, so far as that could
be done by translation; and with his genius and accomplishments, and the greater pains he was willing to take with it, we
may conjecture that he hoped to execute his task in a manner
very superior to that in which such work had hitherto been performed. With these views he undertook what was probably his
earliest composition of any length, his translation of the *Roman
de la Rose*, begun by Guillaume de Lorris, who died about 1260,
and continued and finished by Joan de Meun, whose date is
about half a century later. "This poem," says Warton, "is
esteemed by the French the most valuable piece of their old
poetry. It is far beyond the rude efforts of all their preceding
romancers; and they have nothing equal to it before the reign
of Francis the First, who died in the year 1547. But there is a
considerable difference in the merit of the two authors. William
of Lorris, who wrote not one quarter of the poem, is remarkable
for his elegance and luxuriance of description, and is a beautiful
painter of allegorical personages. John of Meun is a writer of
another cast. He possesses but little of his predecessor's inventive and poetical vein; and in that respect, he was not properly
qualified to finish a poem begun by William of Lorris. But he

has strong satire and great liveliness. He was one of the wits of
the court of Charles le Bel. The difficulties and dangers of a
lover in pursuing and obtaining the object of his desires are the
literal argument of this poem. This design is couched under the
argument of a rose, which our lover after frequent obstacles
gathers in a delicious garden. He traverses vast ditches, scales
lofty walls, and forces the gates of adamantine and almost impregnable castles. These enchanted fortresses are all inhabited
by various divinities; some of which assist, and some oppose,
the lover's progress."* The entire poem consists of no fewer
than 22,734 verses, of which only 4,149 are the composition of
William of Lorris. All this portion has been translated by
Chaucer, and also about half of the 18,586 lines written by
De Meun: his version comprehends 13,105 lines of the French-
poem. These, however, he has managed to comprehend in 7701
(Warton says 7699) English verses: this is effected by a great
compression and curtailment of De Meun's part; for, while the
4149 French verses of De Lorris are fully and faithfully rendered in 4432 English verses, the 8956 that follow by De Meun
are reduced in the translation to 3269. Warton, who exhibits
ample specimens both of the translation and of the original, considers that Chaucer has throughout at least equalled De Lorris,
and decidedly surpassed and improved De Meun. We can afford
space for only one short extract: the poet represents himself as
having seen all that he relates in a dream, the account of which
he thus begins:—

> That it was May me thoughten tho,[1]
> It is five year or more ago,
> That it was May thus dreamed me
> In time of love and jollity,
> That all thing ginneth waxen gay;
> For there is neither busk nor hay[2]
> In May that it n'ill shrowded been,[3]
> And it with newe leaves wrene:[4]
> These woodes eke recoveren green
> That dry in winter been to seen,
> And the earth waxeth proud withal
> For sote[5] dews that on it fall,   •

---

* Hist. Eng. Poetry. ii. 209.

[1] Then.   [2] Bush nor hedgerow.   [3] Will not be shrouded or covered.
[4] Itself hide, or cover.   [5] Sweet.

And the pover[1] estats forget
In which that winter had it set;
And then becometh the ground so proud
That it will have a newe shrowd,
And make so quaint his robe and fair
That it had hews an hundred pair,
Of grass and floures Ind and Pers,[2]
And many hewes full diverse;
That is the robe I mean, ywis,
Through which the ground to praisen is.[3]
The birdes, that han left their song
While they had suffered cold full strong
In weathers gril,[4] and derk to sight,
Been in May for the sunne bright
So glad, that they shew in singing
That in their heart is such liking,
That they mote singen and been light:
Then doth the nightingale her might
To maken noise and singen blithe;
Then is blissful many a sithe[5]
The chalaundre[6] and the popinjay;
Then younge folk intenden[7] aye
For to been gay and amorous,
The time is then so savourous.
Hard is his heart that loveth nought
In May, when all this mirth is wrought,
When he may on these branches hear
The smale birdes singen clear,
Their blissful swete song pitous.
And in this season delitous,
When love affirmeth[8] alle thing,
Methought one night, in my sleeping,
Right in my bed full readily,
That it was by the morrow early;
And up I rose and gan me clothe;
Anon I wish[9] mine hondes both;
A silver needle forth I drew
Out of a guiler[10] quaint enow,
And gan this needle thread anon;
For out of town me list to gone,

---

1 Poor.

2 Indian and Persian.

3 Is to be praised? if this be the true reading. The French is, "l'arquoy la terre mieulx se prise."

4 Grim, dreary.

5 Time.

6 Goldfinch.

7 Address themselves.

8 Strengtheneth.

9 Washed.

10 Needle-case.

The soun of briddes[1] for to hear
That on the buskes[2] singen clear.
In the sweet season that leif is.[3]
With a thread basting[4] my sleeves,
Alone I went in my playing,
The smale fowles' song hearkening.
That plained them full many a pair
To sing on boughes blossomed fair ;
Jollif[5] and gay, full of gladness,
Toward a river gan me dress[6]
Which that I heard ren[7] faste by;
For fairer playen none saw I
Than playen me by that rivere ;
For from an hill that stude[8] there near
Came down the stream full stiff and bold ;
Clear was the water, and as cold
As any well is, soth to sain,[9]
And some deal lass[10] it was than Seine ;
But it was straighter, wele away ;[11]
And never saw I ere that day
The water that so wele liked[12] me ;
And wonder glad was I to see
That lusty[13] place and that rivere.
With that water that ran so clear
My face I wish ; tho saw I wele
The bottom ypaved every deal[14]
With gravel, full of stones shern ;
The meadows, softe, sote, and green,
Beet[15] right upon the water side ;
Full clear was then the morrow tide,[16]
And full attempre[17] out of drede :[18]
Tho gan I walken through the mead,
Downward ever in my playing
Nigh to the river's side coasting.

No verse so flowing and harmonious as this, no diction at once
so clear, correct, and expressive, had, it is probable, adorned and
brought out the capabilities of his native tongue when Chaucer
began to write. Several of his subsequent poems are also in

---

[1] Birds.	[2] Bushes.	[3] Pleasing.
[4] Stitching.	[5] Jolly.	[6] Direct.
[7] Run.	[8] Stood.	[9] Sooth to say.
[10] Somewhat less.		[11] Well-away, well-a-day, alas.
[12] So well pleased.	[13] Pleasant.	[14] Everywhere.
[15] Perhaps a misprint for been.		[16] The morning.
[17] Temperate.		[18] Without doubt.

whole or in part translations; the Troilus and Cresside, the Legend of Good Women (much of which is borrowed from Ovid's Epistles), and others. But we must pass over these, and will take our next extract from his House of Fame, no foreign original of which has been discovered, although Warton is inclined to think that it may have been translated or paraphrased from the Provençal. Chaucer, however, seems to appear in it in his own person; at least the poet or dreamer is in the course of it more than once addressed by the name of Geoffrey. And in the following passage he seems to describe his own occupation and habits of life. It is addressed to him by the golden but living Eagle, who has carried him up into the air in his talons, and by whom the marvellous sights he relates are shown and explained to him :—

> First, I, that in my feet have thee,
> Of whom thou hast great fear and wonder,
> Am dwelling with the God of Thunder,
> Which men ycallen Jupiter,
> That doth me flyen full oft fer [1]
> To do all his commandement ;
> And for this cause he hath me sent
> To thee ; harken now by thy trouth ;
> Certain be bath of thee great routh,[2] .
> For that thou hast so truëly
> So long served ententifly [3]
> His blinde nephew Cupido,
> And the fair queen Venus also,
> Withouten guerdon ever yet ;
> And natheless [4] hast set thy wit
> Although in thy head full lit is
> To make bokes, songs, and dittes,
> In rhime or elles in cadence,
> As thou best canst, in reverence
> Of Love and of his servants eke,
> That have his service sought and seek ;
> And painest thee to praise his art,
> Although thou haddest never part ;
> Wherefore, so wisely God me bless,
> Jovis yhalt [5] it great humbless,

And virtue eke, that thou wilt make
Anight¹ full oft thine head to ache
In thy study, so thou ywritest,
And ever more of Love enditest,
In honour of him and praisings,
And in his folkes furtherings,
And in their matter all devisest,
And not him ne his folk despisest,
Although thou may'st go in the dance
Of them that him list not avance:
Wherefore, as I now said, ywis,
Jupiter considreth well this,
And als, beau sire,² of other things,
That is, that thou hast no tidings
Of Loves folk if they be glade,
Ne of nothing else that God made,
And not only fro³ fer countree
That no tidinges comen to thee,
Not of thy very neighebores,
That dwellen almost at thy dores,
Thou hearest neither that ne this;
For, when thy labour all done is,
And hast made all thy reckonings,
Instead of rest and of new things,
Thou goest home to thine house anon,
And, all so dumb as any stone,
Thou sittest at another book,
Till fully dased is thy look,
And livest thus as an hermit,
Although thine abstinence is lit;
And therefore Jovis, through his grace,
Will that I hear thee to a place
Which that yhight the House of Fame, &c.

From the mention of his *reckonings* in this passage, Tyrwhitt conjectures that Chaucer probably wrote the House of Fame while he held the office of Comptroller of the Customs of Wools, to which he was appointed in 1374. It may be regarded, therefore, as one of the productions of the second or middle stage of his poetical life, as the Romaunt of the Rose is supposed to have been of the first. The House of Fame is in three books, comprising in all 2190 lines, and is an exceedingly interesting poem on other accounts, as well as for the reference which Chaucer seems to make in it to himself, and the circumstances of his own

----

¹ O'nights, at night.   ² Fair sir.   ³ From.

life. Another evidence which it carries of the somewhat advanced years of the writer, is the various learning and knowledge with which it is interspersed. Here, for instance, is the
doctrine of gravitation as explained by the all-accomplished
Eagle:—

> Geffrey, thou knowest full well this,
> That every kindly[1] thing that is
> Thath a kindly stead, there[3] he
> May best in it conserved be;
> Unto which place every thing,
> Thorough his kindly inclining,
> Ymeveth[3] for to comen to
> When that it is away therefro;
> As thus, lo, thou may'st all day see,
> Take any thing that heavy be,
> As stone, or lead, or thing of weight,
> And bear it ne'er so high on height,
> Let go thine hand it falleth down;
> Right so, say I, by fire, or soun,
> Or smoke, or other thinges light,
> Alway they seek upward on height;
> Light things up and heavy down charge
> While everich of them be at large;
> And for this cause thou may'st well see
> That every river to the sea
> Inclined is to go by kind;
> And, by these skilles as I find,
> Have fishes dwelling in flood and sea,
> And trees eke on the earthe be:
> Thus every thing by his reason
> Hath his own proper mansion,
> To which he seeketh to repair
> There as it shoulden nat appair.[4]
> Lo this sentence is knowen couth
> Of every philosopher's mouth,
> As Aristotle and Dan Platon
> And other clerkes many one.
> And, to confirmen my reasoun,
> Thou wottest well that speech is soun,
> Or elles no man might it hear;
> Now hearken what I woll thee lear.

---

[1] Natural.　　　　[3] Where.　　　　[3] Moveth.
[4] Where it should not impair, or suffer declension.

And then the learned bird proceeds in the like strain to deliver
a lecture on the production and propagation of sound :—

> Soun is nought but air ybroken,
> And every speeche that is spoken,
> Whe'r[1] loud or privy, foul or fair,
> In his substance ne is but air,
> For, as flame is but lighted smoke,
> Right so is soun but air ybroke.
> But this may be in many wise,
> Of the which I will thee devise,[2]
> As soun cometh of pipe or harp;
> For when a pipe is blowen sharp
> The air is twist with violence
> And rent : lo, this is my sentence.
> Eke, when that men harp-stringes smite,
> Wheder that it be moch or lite,[3]
> Lo, with the stroke the air it breaketh,
> And right so breaketh it when men speaketh.
> Thus wost[4] thou well what thing is speech :
> Now henceforth I will thee teach
> How everich speeche, voice, or soun,
> Through his multiplicatioun,
> Though it were piped of a mouse,
> Mote[5] nedes come to Fame's House.
> I prove it thus, taketh heed now,
> By experience; for, if that thou
> Threw[6] in a water now a stone,
> Well wost thou it will make anon
> A little roundle as a circle,
> Peraventure as broad as a covircle ;[7]
> And right anon thou shalt see wele
> That circle cause another wheel,
> And that the third, and so forth, brother,
> Every circle causing other
> Much broader than himselfen was ;
> And thus, from roundle to compass,
> Each abouten other going
> Ycauseth of others stirring,
> And multiplying evermo,
> Till that it be so far ygo
> That it at bothe brinkes be ;
> Although thou mayest it not see

---

[1] Whether. [2] Instruct. [3] Much or little.
[4] Knowest. [5] Must.
[6] Probably a misprint, or mistranscription, for *throw*. [7] Pothid.

> Above, yet goeth it alway under,
> Although thou think it a great wonder;
> And whoso saith of truth I vary,
> Bidde him preven[1] the contrary;
> And right thus every word, ywis,
> That loud or privy yspoken is
> Ymoveth first an air about,
> And of his moving, out of doubt,
> Another air anon is moved.
> As I have of the water proved
> That every circle causeth other,
> Right so of air, my leive brother,
> Everich air another stirroth
> More and more, and speech up beareth,
> Or voice, or noise, or word, or soun,
> Aye through multiplicatioun,
> Till it be at the House of Fame, &c.

He then applies this fact of sound tending up into the air, till it find its stead or home, the House of Fame, to the confirmation of what he had before delivered on the general law of gravitation or attraction. In another place, we have an illustration drawn from a novelty which we might have thought had hardly yet become familiar enough for the purposes of poetry. The passage, too, is a sample of the wild, almost grotesque imagination, and force of expression, for which the poem is remarkable:—

> What did this Æolus? but he
> Took out his blacke trompe of brass,
> That fouler than the devil was,
> And gan this trompe for to blow
> As all the world should overthrow.
> Throughout every region
> Ywent this foule trompes soon,
> *As swift as pellet out of gun*
> *When fire is in the powder run:*
> And such a smoke gan out wend
> Out of the foule trompes end,
> Black, blue, and greenish, swartish, red,
> As dooth where that men melt lead,
> Lo all on high from the tewel:[2]
> And thereto one thing saw I well,
> That aye the ferther that it ran
> The greater wexen it began,
> As doth the river from a well;
> And it stank as the pit of hell.

---

[1] Prove.   [2] Funnel.

The old mechanical artillery, however, is alluded to in another passage as if also still in use :—

> And the noise which that I heard,
> For all the world right so it fered[1]
> As doth the routing[2] of the stone
> That fro the engine is letten gone.

All through the poem runs the spirit of the strange barbarous classical scholarship of the middle ages.   The Æneid is not altogether unknown to the author ; but it may be questioned if his actual acquaintance with the work extended much beyond the two opening lines, which are pretty literally rendered in six octosyllabic verses near the beginning of the first book.   An abridgment, indeed, of the entire story of Æneas, as told by Virgil, follows ; but that might have been got at second-hand. The same mixture of the classic and the Gothic occurs throughout that is found in all the poetry, French and Italian as well as English, of this era.   For instance :—

> There heard I playing on an harp,
> That ysounded both well and sharp,
> Him Orpheus full craftily ;
> And on this other side fast by
> Ysat the harper Orion,
> And Eacides Chirion,
> And other harpers many one,
> And the Briton Glaskirion, &c.

Orion here is probably a mistake (not, we fear, a typographical one) for Arion.   Why Chirion (by whom Chiron seems to be intended) is called Eacides we do not know—unless the epithet be a misprint for Eacides, or Æacides, applied to the Centaur (by a somewhat violent licence) as the instructor of Achilles. In a subsequent passage the confusion is more perplexing :—

> There saw I then Dan Citherus,
> And of Athens Dan Proserus,
> And Marcia, that lost her skin,
> Both in the face, body, and chin,
> For that she would envyer, lo !
> To pipen bett[3] than Apollo.

---

[1] Fared, proceeded.   [2] Roaring.   [3] Better.

> There saw I famous old and young
> Pipers of all the Dutche tongue,
> To learnen love dances, springs,
> Reyes,[1] and the strange things.

Here, we apprehend, Dan Citherus is none other than Mount Cithaeron. Dan Proserus is possibly the unfortunate Procris, who was daughter of the Athenian king Erectheus. Mercia, "that lost her skin," is undoubtedly the famous piper Marsyas, turned into a woman, by a metamorphosis of which there is no record in Ovid.

As a specimen of the strong painting that characterizes this poem, its crowded and variegated canvas, and the dramatic life that moves and hurries on the action, we will give a portion of the poet's account of his last adventure, his visit to what we may call, with Warton, the House or Labyrinth of Rumour, which went round and round continually, as swift as thought, making such a noise as might have been heard from the north of France to Rome. It was made of twigs, and was all over holes and chinks—or, as the poem says,

> And eke this house hath of entries
> As many as leaves been on trees
> In summer when that they been green;
> And on the roof yet may men seen
> A thousand holes and well mo,
> To letten the sound out ygo;
> And by day in every tide
> Been all the doors open wide,
> And by night each one is unshet;
> No porter is there none to let[2]
> No manner tidings in to pace;
> No never rest is in that place,
> That it is filled full of tidings
> Either loud or of whisperings.
> And ever all the House's angles
> Is full of rownings[3] and of jangles,[4]
> Of werres,[5] of peace, of marriages,
> Of rests, of labour, of viages, &c.

The House, which was shaped like a cage, and sixty miles long, stood in a valley; and, after he has gazed upon it with astonishment for a short time, the poet eagerly begs his guide,

---

[1] A kind of Dutch dance.   [2] Hinder.   [3] Whisperings.
[4] Babblou,   [5] Wars.

the Eagle, to convey him to it, and show him what it contains.
The answer of the Eagle seems to refer to some actual circumstance or passage of Chaucer's history : —

> But certain one thing I thee tell,
> That, but[1] I bringen thee therein,
> Ne shall thou never con the gin[2]
> To come into it, out of doubt,
> So fast it whirleth, lo, about.
> But, sith that Jovis of his grace,
> As I have said, will thee solace
> Finally with these like[3] things,
> These uncouth[4] sightes and tidings,
> To pass away thine heaviness,
> Such routh hath he of thy distress
> That thou suffredest debonairly
> And woste[5] thy selven utterly,
> Wholly desperate of all bliss,
> Sith that fortune hath made amiss[6]
> The sote[7] of all thine hearte's rest
> Languish, and eke in point to brest ;[8]
> But he, through his mighty melite,[9]
> Will do thee ease, all be it lite.[10]

The imperial bird, accordingly, took up the poet again in its
"tone," or claws (toes), and, conveying him into the whirling
house by a window, set him down on the floor.   Then, he
proceeds,

> ————Such great congregation
> Of folk as I saw roam about,
> Some it within and some without,
> N'as never seen, ne shall be eft[11] . . . .
> And every wight that I saw there
> Rowned everich[12] in other's ear
> A news tiding privily,
> Or else he told it openly,
> Right thus, and said, Ne wost nat thou
> That is betidden,[13] lo! right now ?
> No, certes, quod he ; tell me what ;
> And then he told him this and that,

---

[1] Unless.   [2] Know the contrivance (engine).
[3] Same.   [4] Strange (unknown).   [5] Wastest.
[6] Unluckily.   [7] Swift.   [8] On the point of bursting.
[9] Not understood.   [10] Little.   [11] Again.
[12] Whispered every one.   [13] Knowest thou not that which is befallen.

And swore thereto that it was soth;
Thus hath he said, and thus he doth,
And this shall be, and this heard I say,
That shall be found, that dare I lay;
That all the folk that is on live
Ne have the cunning to descrive
Tho thinges that I hearden there,
What aloud and what in the ear.
But all the wonder most was this,
When one had heard a thing, ywis,
He came straight to another wight,
And gan him tellen anon right
Tho same tale that to him was told
Or it a furlong way was old,
And began somewhat for to ech [1]
Unto this tiding in his speech
More than ever it spoken was,
And nat so soon departed n'as
Tho fro him that he ne ymet [2]
With the third man, and, ere he let [3]
Any stound, [4] he ytold him also; [5]
Weren the tidings sooth or false,
Yet wold he tell it natheless,
And evermore with mo increase
Than it was erst: thus north and south
Went every tiding from mouth to mouth,
And that increasing ever mo,
As fire is wont to quicken and go
From a sparkle sprongen [6] amiss,
Till all a city brent up is,
And when that that was full up-sprong,
And waxen more on every tongue
Than [7] er it was, and went anon
Up to a window out to goon,
Or but [8] it might out there ypass,
It gan out creep at some crevass,
And flew forth faste for the nones. [9]
And sometime I saw there at ones
A leasing [10] and a sad soothsaw, [11]
That gonnen of aventure draw, [12]

---

1 Add (eke).   2 And no sooner was departed then from him that he met.
3 Stopped, delayed.   4 Moment.   5 Also.
6 Sprang.   7 Before.   8 Ere ever.
9 For the occasion (the nonce).   10 Lie, falsehood.
11 Grave truth.   12 Began by chance to draw.

Out at a window for to pace,
And when they metten in that place
They were achecked[1] bothe two,
And neither of them might out go,
For each other they gan so crowd,
Till each of them gan cryen loud,
Let me gon first; Nay, but let me,
And here I wol ensuren thee
With vows, that[2] thou wolt do so,
That I shall never fro thee go,
But be alway thine own sworn brother;
We wol meddle[3] us each in other,
That no man, be he ne'er so wroth,
Shall have one of us two, but both
At ones, as bruide his leve,[4]
Come we a morrow or on eve,
Be we yeried or still yrowned.
Thus saw I falas and sooth compowned
Togeder fly for o[5] tiding.
Thus out at holes gan to wring[6]
Every tiding straight to Fame;
And she gan yeven[7] each his name
After her disposition,
And yeve them eke duration,
Some to wexen and wanen soon,
As doth the fair and white moon,
And let him goon: there might I seen
Winged wonders full fast flyen,
Twenty thousand all in a rout
As Æolus them blew about.
And, Lord! this house in alle times
Was full of shipmen and pilgrimes
With scrippes bretful[8] of leasings,
Intermeddeled with tidings;
And eke, alone by them selve,
A many thousand times twelve
Saw I eke of these pardoners,
Currours,[9] and eke of messangers,
With boxes crommed full of lies
As ever vessel was with lees.
And, as I altherfastest[10] went
About, and did all mine intent[11]

---

1 Checked, stopped.	3 Apparently a misprint for "and," that is, *if*.
2 Intermix.	4 Without his leave?	5 One.
6 To squeeze out?	7 Give.	8 Topful.
9 Couriers.	10 Fastest of all.	11 Endeavour.

Me for to playen,[1] and for to hear,[2]
And eke a tiding for to hear
That I had heard of some countree,
That shall not now be told for me,
For it no need is (readily
Folk can ysing it bet than I,
For all mote[3] out, or late or rathe,[4]
Alle the sheaves in the lathe)[5]
I hearden a great noise withal
Within a corner of the hall,
There[6] men of love tidings told;
And I gan thiderward behold,
For I saw renning every wight
As fast as that they hadden might;
And everich cried, What thing is that?
And some said, I n'ot[7] never what:
And when they were all on an heap,
Tho they behind gonnen up leap,
And clamben up on other fast,
And up the noise on highen cast,
And treaden fast on other's heels,
And stamp as men done after eels;
But at the last I saw a man,
Which that I nought describe ne can,
But he ysemed for to be
A man of great auctority.

At the apparition of this unnamed personage the poet awakens
from his dream, and the poem ends.

Through such deeper thinking and bolder writing as this
Chaucer appears to have advanced from the descriptive luxuriance of the Romaunt of the Rose to his most matured style in
the Canterbury Tales. This is not only his greatest work,
but it towers above all else that he has written, like some palace
or cathedral ascending with its broad and lofty dimensions from
among the common buildings of a city. His genius is another
thing here altogether from what it is in his other writings.
Elsewhere he seems at work only for the day that is passing
over him; here, for all time. All his poetical faculties put forth
a strength in the Canterbury Tales they have nowhere else shown;
not only is his knowledge of life and character greater, his style

---

[1] To play or amuse myself?   [2] Learn.   [3] Must.   [4] Late or soon.
[5] Barn. Urry misprints the word "lathe." His punctuation also shows
that he did not understand the passage.
[6] Where.   [7] Know not (ne wot).

firmer, clearer, more flexible, and more expressive, his humour
more subtle and various, but his fancy is more nimble-winged,
his imagination far richer and more gorgeous, his sensibility
infinitely more delicate and more profound. And this great
work of Chaucer's is nearly as remarkably distinguished by its
peculiar character from the great works of other poets as it is
from the rest of his own compositions. Among ourselves at
least, if we except Shakespeare, no other poet has yet arisen to
rival the author of the Canterbury Tales in the entire assemblage
of his various powers. Spenser's is a more aerial, Milton's
a loftier song; but neither possesses the wonderful combination
of contrasted and almost opposite characteristics which we have in
Chaucer :—the sportive fancy, painting and gilding everything,
with the keen, observant, matter-of-fact spirit that looks through
whatever it glances at; the soaring and creative imagination,
with the homely sagacity, and healthy relish for all the realities
of things; the unrivalled tenderness and pathos, with the
quaintest humour and the most exuberant merriment; the
wisdom at once and the wit; the all that is best, in short, both
in poetry and in prose, at the same time.

The Canterbury Tales is an unfinished, or at least, as we have
it, an imperfect work; but it contains above 17,000 verses,
besides more than a fourth of that quantity of matter in prose.
The Tales (including the two in prose*) are twenty-four in
number; and they are interspersed with introductions to each,
generally short, called prologues, besides the Prologue to the
whole work, in which the pilgrims or narrators of the tales are
severally described, and which consists of between 800 and 900
lines. The Prologue to the Wife of Bath's Tale is fully as long.
All the twenty-four tales are complete, except only the Cook's
Tale, of which we have only a few lines, the Squire's Tale,

* Mr. Guest conceives that one of these prose tales, the Tale of Melibœus,
(that told by the poet himself), is a specimen of the kind of poetry called
cadence, of which mention is made in a passage that has been quoted in a preceding page from the House of Fame (Hist. Eng. Rhythms, ii. 253—258).
"As the tale proceeds," he says, "the rhythmical structure gradually disap-
pears." Tyrwhitt, after informing us that Mr. William Thomas, in one of his
MS. notes upon the copy of Urry's edition presented by him to the British
Museum, had observed that this tale seems to have been written in blank
verse, adds : "It is certain that in the former part of it we find a number of
blank verses intermixed in a much greater proportion than in any of our
author's other prose writings; but this poetical style is not, I think, remarkable beyond the first four or five pages."

which remains "half-told," and the burlesque Tale of Sir
Thopas, which is designedly broken off in the middle. Of the
nineteen complete tales in verse, the longest are the Knight's
Tale of 2250 verses, the Clerk's Tale of 1156, and the Merchant's
Tale of 1172.* The entire work, with the exception of the
prose tales and the Rime of Sir Thopas (205 lines), is in decasyllabic (or hendecasyllabic) verse, arranged either in couplets
or in stanzas.

The few extracts we can give cannot, of course, convey any
notion of this vast and various poem to those who are not acquainted with it; but those who are may have their recollection
of it refreshed, and the curiosity of other readers may be excited,
though not satisfied, by the two or three passages we shall now
subjoin.

The general Prologue is a gallery of pictures almost un-
matched for their air of life and truthfulness. Here is one of
them :—

> There was also a nun, a Prioress
> That of her smiling was full simple and coy,
> Her greatest oathe n'as but by Saint Loy ;¹
> And she was cleped² Madame Eglantine.
> Full well she sange the service divine,
> Entuned in her nose full sweetely ;
> And French she spake full fair and fetisly ³
> After the school of Stratford atte Bow,
> For French of Paris was to her unknow.⁴
> At meate was she well ytaught withal ;
> She let no morsel from her lippes fall,
> Ne wet her fingers in her sauce deep ;
> Well could she carry a morsel and well keep
> Thatte no droppe ne fell upon her breast :
> In curtesy was set full much her lest.⁵
> Her over-lippe wiped she so clean
> That in her cuppe was no ferthing⁶ seen

---

* Some of the old editions add the following spurious tales :—The Cook's
Tale of Gamelyn, in 1787 short verses; the Ploughman's Tale, with a short
prologue, in 1363 alternately rhyming verses; and the Merchant's Second
Tale, or the History of Beryn, in 3289 lines, preceded by the prologue of the
Pardoner and Tapster, in 729 lines. These are all rejected by Tyrwhitt.

¹ That is Saint Eloy or Eligius. Oaths here, according to Mr. Guest, is the
old genitive plural (originally athe), meaning of oaths.
² Called.   ⁵ Neatly.   ⁴ Unknown.
³ Pleasure.   ⁶ Smallest spot.

Of grease when she dronken had her draught.
Full semely after her meat she raught.[1]
And sikerly[2] she was of great disport,
And full pleasant and amiable of port,
And pained[3] her to counterfeiten cheer
Of court, and been estatelich of manere,
And to been holden digne[4] of reverence.

But for to speaken of her conscience,
She was so charitable and so pitous
She wolde weep if that she saw a mouse
Caught in a trap, if it were dead or bled.
Of smale houndes had she that she fed
With roasted flesh, and milk, and wastel bread ;
But sore wept she if one of them were dead,
Or if men smote it with a yerde[5] smart :
And all was conscience and tender heart.

Full semely her wimple ypinched was ;
Her nose tretis,[6] her eyen grey as glass ;
Her mouth full small, and thereto[7] soft and red,
But sikerly she had a fair forehead ;
It was almost a spanne broad, I trow ;
For hardily[8] she was not undergrow.[9]
Full fetise[10] was her cloak, as I was ware.
Of smale coral about her arm she bare
A pair of beades gauded all with green ;[11]
And thereon heng[12] a brooch of gold full sheen,
On which was first ywritten a crowned A,
And after, *Amor vincit omnia.*

As a companion to this perfect full length, we will add that of
the Mendicant Friar :—

A Frere there was, a wanton and a merry,
A limitour,[13] a full solemne man ;
In all the orders four is none that can
So much of dalliance and fair langage.
He had ymade full many a marriage
Of younge women at his owen cost ;
Until[14] his order he was a noble post
Full well beloved and familier was he
With franklins[15] over all in his countree,

---

[1] Reached.	[2] Surely.	[3] Took pains.	[4] Worthy.
[5] Yard, rod.	[6] Long and well proportioned.		
[7] In addition to that.	[8] Certainly.	[9] Undergrown, of a low stature.	
[10] Neat.	[11] Having the gauds or beads coloured green.		
[12] Hung.	[13] A friar licensed to beg within a certain district.		
[14] Unto.	[15] Freeholders of the superior class.		

And eke with worthy women of the town ;
For he had power of confession,
As said him selfe, more than a curat,
For of his order he was a licenciat.
Full swoetly hearde he confession,
And pleasant was his absolution.
He was an easy man to give penance
There as he wist to han a good pitance ;[1]
For unto a poor order for to give
Is signe that a man is well yshrive ;[2]
For, if he gave, he durste make avant,[3]
He wiste that a man was repentant ;
For many a man so hard is of his heart
He may not weep although him sore smart ;
Therefore, instead of weeping and prayeres,
Men mote give silver to the poore freres.

His tippet was aye farsed[4] full of knives
And pinnes for to given faire wives :
And certainly he had a merry note ;
Well could he sing and playen on a rote.[5]
Of yeddings[6] he bare utterly the pris.[7]
His neck was white as is the flower de lis;[8]
Thereto he strong was as a champioun,
And knew well the taverns in every town,
And every hosteler and gay tapstere,
Better than a lazar or a beggere ;
For unto swich[9] a worthy man as he
Accordeth nought[10] as,[11] by his facultee,[12]
To haven with sick lazars acquaintance ;
It is not honest, it may not avance,[13]
As[14] for to dealen with no swich poorail[15]
But all with rich and sellers of vitail.[16]
And, over[17] all, there as[18] profit should arise,
Curteis[19] he was, and lowly of service ;
There n'as no man no where so virtuous ;
He was the best begger in all his house ;

---

[1] Where he knew he should have a good pittance or fee.
[2] Shriven.　　[3] Boast.　　[4] Stuffed.
[5] A musical instrument so called.　　[6] Stories, romances.　　[7] Prize.
[8] Fleur de lis, lily.　　[9] Such.　　[10] It suits not, is not fitting.
[11] As in this and in other forms seems to have the effect of merely generating or giving indefiniteness to the expression.
[12] Having regard to his quality or functions?　　[13] Profit.
[14] As in the fourth line preceding.　　[15] Poor people.
[16] Victual.　　[17] In addition to.　　[18] Wherever.
[19] Courteous.

And gave a certain ferme[1] for the grant
None of his brethren came in his haunt ;
For, though a widow hadde but a shoe,
So pleasant was his *In principio*,
Yet would he have a ferthing or he went ;
His purchase[2] was well better than his rent.
And rage he could as it had been a whelp :
In lovedays[3] there could be mochel[4] help ;
For there was he nat[5] like a cloisterere
With threadbare cope, as is a poor scholere ;
But he was like a maister or a pope :
Of double worsted was his semi-cope,
That round was as a bell out of the press.[6]
Somewhat he lisped for his wantonness,
To make his English sweet upon his tongue ;
And in his harping, when that he had sung,
His eyen twinkled in his head aright,
As don the sterres[7] in a frosty night.
This worthy limitour, was clep'd Huberd.

It may be observed in all these extracts how fond Chaucer is
of as it were welding one couplet and one paragraph to another,
by allowing the sense to flow on from the last line of the one
through the first of the other, thus producing an alternating
movement of the sense and the sound, instead of making the one
accompany the other, as is the general practice of our modern
poetry. This has been noticed, and a less obvious part of the
effect pointed out, by a poet of our own day, who has shown how
well he felt Chaucer by something more and much better than
criticism. " Chaucer," observes Leigh Hunt, " took the custom
from the French poets, who have retained it to this day. It
surely has a fine air, both of conclusion and resumption ; as
though it would leave off when it thought proper, knowing how
well it could recommence." [*] It is so favourite a usage with
Chaucer, that it may be sometimes made available to settle the
reading, or at least the pointing and sense of a doubtful passage.
And it is also common with his contemporary Gower.

[1] Farm. [2] What he got by tagging and the exercise of his profession.
[3] Days formerly appointed for the amicable settlement of differences.
[4] Much.   [5] Not.
[6] Not understood. It is the bell or the semicope that is described as out of
the press!   [7] As do the stars.
[*] Preface to Poetical Works, 8vo. Lon. 1832. See also Mr. Hunt's fine
imitation and continuation of the Squire's Tale in the Fourth Number of the
Liberal. Lon. 1823.

The following is the first introduction to the reader of Emily, the heroine of the Knight's Tale of Palamon and Arcite :—

Thus passeth year by year, and day by day,
Till it fell once in a morrow of May
That Emily, that fairer was to seen
Than is the lily upon his stalke green,
And fresher than the May with floures new
(For with the rose colour strof[1] her hue ;
I n'ot[2] which was the finer of them two)
Ere it was day, as she was wont to do,
She was arisen and all ready dight,
For May wol have no slogardy[3] a night ;
The season pricketh every gentle heart,
And maketh him out of his sleep to start,
And saith, Arise, and do thine observance.
    This maketh Emily han[4] remembrance
To don honour to May, and for to rise.
Yclothed was she fresh for to devise ;
Her yellow hair was broided[5] in a tress
Behind her back, a yarde long I guess ;
And in the garden as the sun uprist[6]
She walketh up and down where as her list :[7]
She gathereth floures partie[8] white and red
To make a sotel[9] gerlond[10] for her head :
And as an angel heavenlich she sung.

Of the many other noble passages in this Tale we can only present a portion of the description of the Temple of Mars :—

Why should I not as well eke tell you all
The portraiture that was upon the wall
Within the Temple of mighty Mars the Red ?
All painted was the wall in length and bred[11]
Like to the estres[12] of the grisley place
That hight[13] the great Temple of Mars in Trace,[14]
In thilke[15] cold and frosty region
There as Mars hath his sovereign mansion.
    First on the wall was painted a forest,
In which there wonneth[16] neither man ne beast ;

---

1 Strove.
4 Have.
7 Uprise.
10 Subtle, artfully contrived.
13 The interior.
16 That same.

3 Wot not, know not.
6 With enactnem (point devise).
8 Where it pleaseth her.
11 Garland.
14 Is called.
15 Dwelleth.

2 Sloth.
5 Braided.
9 Mixed of.
12 Breadth.
13 Thrace.

With knotty knarry barren trees old,
Of stubbes sharp and hidous to behold;
In which there ran a rumble and a swough,[1]
As though a storm should bresten[2] every bough ;
And downward from an hill under a bent[3]
There stood the Temple of Mars Armipotent,
Wrought all of burned[4] steel, of which the entree
Was long, and strait, and ghastly for to see ;
And thereout came a rage and swich a vise[5]
That it made all the gates for to rise.
The northern light in at the dore shone ;
For window on the wall ne was there none
Through which men mighten any light dissern.
The door was all of adamant[6] etern,
Yclenched overthwart and endelong[7]
With iron tough, and, for to make it strong,
Every pillar the temple to sustene
Was tonne-great,[8] of iron bright and shene.
There saw I first the dark imagining
Of Felony, and all the compassing ;
The cruel Ire, red as any gled ;[9]
The Picke-purse, and eke the pale Dread ;
The Smiler with the knife under the cloak ;
The shepen[10] brenning[11] with the blake smoke ;
The treason of the murdering in the bed ;
The open wer,[12] with woundes all bebled ;
Contek[13] with bloody knife and sharp menace ;
All full of chirking[14] was that sorry place.
The sleer[15] of himself yet saw I there ;
His hearte-blood hath bathed all his hair ;
The nail ydriven in the shod[16] on hight ;
The colde death, with mouth gaping upright.
Amiddes of the Temple sat Mischance,
With discomfort and sorry countenance :
Yet saw I Woodness[17] laughing in his rage,
Armed Complaint, Outhees,[18] and fierce Outrage ;
The carrain[19] in the bush, with throat ycorven ;[20]
A thousand slain, and not of qualm ystorven ;[21]

---

[1] A long sighing noise, such as in Scotland is called a sugh.
[2] Was going to break.   [3] A declivity.   [4] Burnished.
[5] A violent blast ?   [6] Adamant.   [7] Across and lengthways.
[8] Of the circumference of a tun.   [9] Burning coal.   [10] Stable.
[11] Burning.   [12] War.   [13] Contention.   [14] Disagreeable sound.
[15] Slayer.   [16] Hair of the head.   [17] Madness.   [18] Outcry.
[19] Carrion.   [20] Cut.   [21] Died (starved).

The tyrant, with the prey by force yraft ;[1]
The town destroyed ;—there was nothing laft.[2]

. . . .

The statue of Mars upon a carte[3] stood
Armed, and looked grim as he were wood ;[4]
And over his head there shinen two figures
Of sterres, that been cleped in scriptures[5]
That one Puella, that other Rubeus.
This God of Armes was arrayed thus:
A wolf there stood beforn him at his feet
With eyen red, and of a man he eat.

Chaucer's merriment, at once hearty and sly, has of course
the freedom and unscrupulousness of his time ; and much of the
best of it cannot be produced in our day without offence to our
greater sensitiveness, at least in the matter of expression.
Besides, humour in poetry, or any other kind of writing, can
least of all qualities be effectively exemplified in extract: its
subtle life, dependent upon the thousand minutiæ of place and
connection, perishes under the process of excision ; it is to
attempt to exhibit, not the building by the brick, but the living
man by a " pound of his fair flesh." We will venture, however,
to give one or two short passages. Nothing is more admirable
in the Canterbury Tales than the manner in which the character
of the Host is sustained throughout. He is the moving spirit of
the poem from first to last. Here is his first introduction to us
presiding over the company at supper in his own

gentle hostelry, *
That hights the Tabard faste by the Bell,

in Southwark, on the evening before they set out on their pilgrimage :—

Great cheere made our Host us everich one,
And to the supper set he us anon,
And served us with vitail of the best ;
Strong was the wine, and well to drink us lest.[6]
A seemly man our Hoste was with all
For to han been a marshal in an hall ;
A large man he was, with eyen steep ;
A fairer burgess is there none in Cheap ;
Bold of his speech, and wise, and well ytaught,
And of manhood ylaked[7] right him naught :

---

[1] Reft.   [2] Left.   [3] Car, chariot.   [4] Mad.
[5] Stars that are called in books.   [6] It pleased us.   [7] Lacked.

> Eke thereto[1] was he right a merry man;
> And after supper playen he began,
> And spake of mirth amonges other things,
> When that we hadden made our reckoniugs,
> And said thus: Now, Lordings, truely
> Ye been to me welcome right heartily;
> For, by my troth, if that I shall not lie,
> I saw nat this yer swich[2] a company
> At ones in this herberwe[3] as is now;
> Fain would I do you mirth an I wist how;
> And of a mirth I am right now bethought
> To don you ease, and it shall cost you nought.
> Ye gon to Canterbury; God you speed,
> The blisful martyr quite you your meed:
> And well I wot as ye gon by the way
> Ye shapen[4] you to talken and to play;
> For truely comfort ne mirth is none
> To riden by the way dumb as the stone;
> And therefore would I maken you disport,
> As I said erst, and don you some comfort.
> And if you liketh all by one assent
> Now for to stonden[5] at my judgement,
> And for to werchen[6] as I shall you say
> To morrow, when ye riden on the way,
> Now, by my fader's soule that is dead,
> But ye be merry[7] smiteth[8] off my head:
> Hold up your hondes withouten more speech.

They all gladly assent; upon which mine Host proposes further that each of them (they were twenty-nine in all, besides himself) should tell two stories in going, and two more in returning, and that, when they got back to the Tabard, the one who had told the "tales of best sentence and most solace" should have a supper at the charge of the rest. And, adds the eloquent, sagacious, and large-hearted projector of the scheme,

> —for to make you the more merry
> I woll my selven gladly with you ride
> Right at mine owen cost, and be your guide.
> And who that woll my judgement withsay[9]
> Shall pay for all we spenden by the way.

---

[1] In addition, besides, also.   [7] Such.   [2] Inn.
[4] Prepare yourselves, intend. [5] Stand. [6] Work, do.
[7] If ye shall not be merry.
[8] Smite. The imperative has generally this termination.
[9] Resist, oppose, withstand.

Great as the extent of the poem is, therefore, what has been executed, or been preserved, is only a small part of the design; for this liberal plan would have afforded us no fewer than a hundred and twenty tales. Nothing can be better than the triumphant way in which mine Host of the Tabard is made to go through the duties of his self-assumed post;—his promptitude, his decision upon all emergencies, and at the same time his good feeling never at fault any more than his good sense, his inexhaustible and unflagging fun and spirit, and the all-accommodating humour and perfect sympathy with which, without for a moment stooping from his own frank and manly character, he bears himself to every individual of the varied cavalcade. He proposes that they should draw cuts to decide who was to begin; and with how genuine a courtesy, at once encouraging and reverential, he first addresses himself to the modest Clerk, and the gentle Lady Prioress, and the Knight, who also was "of his port as meek as is a maid:"—

> Sir Knight, quod he, my maister and my lord,
> Now draweth cut, for that is mine accord.
> Cometh near, quod he, my Lady Prioress;
> And ye, Sir Clerk, let be your shamefastness,
> Ne studieth nought; lay hand to, every man.

But for personages of another order, again, he is another man, giving and taking jibe and jeer with the hardest and boldest in their own style and humour, only more nimbly and happily than any of them, and without ever compromising his dignity. And all the while his kindness of heart, simple and quick, and yet considerate, is as conspicuous as the cordial appreciation and delight with which he enters into the spirit of what is going forward, and enjoys the success of his scheme. For example,—

> When that the Knight had thus his tale told,
> In all the company n'as there young ne old
> That he ne said it was a noble storie,[1]
> And worthy to be drawen to memorie,[1]
> And namely[2] the gentles everich one.
> Our Hoste lough[3] and swore, So mote I gone,[4]
> This goth aright; unbokeled is the male;[5]
> Let see now who shall tell another tale,

---

[1] Probably pronounced *sto-ri-e* and *me-mo-ri-e*.   [2] Especially.
[3] Laughed.   [4] So may I fare well.   [5] Unbokeled is the budget.

For trisely this game is well begonne :
Now telleth ye, Sir Monk, if that ye conne,[1]
Somewhat to quiten with[2] the Knighte's tale.
    The Miller, that for-drunken[3] was all pale,
So that uneouthe[4] upon his horse he sat,
He n'old avalen[5] neither hood ne hat,
Ne abiden[6] no man for his courtesy,
But in Pilate's voice[7] he gan to cry,
And swore, By armes, and by blood and bones,
I can[8] a noble tale for the nones,[9]
With which I wol now quite the Knightes tale.
    Our Hoste saw that he was drunken of ale,
And said, Abide, Robin, my leve[10] brother ;
Some better man shall tell us first another ;
Abide and let us werken[11] thriftily.
    By Cockles soul, quod he, that woll not I,
For I woll speak, or elles go my way.
    Our Host answered, Tell on a devil way ;
Thou art a fool ; thy wit is overcome.
Now, hearkeneth, quod the Miller, all and some ;
But first I make a protestatioun
That I am drunk, I know it by my soun,
And therefore, if that I misspeak or say,
Wite it[12] the ale of Southwark, I you pray.

The Miller is at last allowed to tell his tale—which is more
accordant with his character, and the condition he was in, than
with either good morals or good manners ;—as the poet observes :—

What should I more say, but this Millere
He n'old his wordes for no man forbere,
But told his cherle's[13] tale in his manere :
Methinketh that I shall rehearse it here :
And therefore every gentle wight I pray
For Cockles love, as deem not that I say,
Of evil intent, but that I mote rehearse
Their tales all, al be they better or werse,
Or elles falsen some of my matere :
And, therefore, whoso list it not to hear,

---

[1] Can.   [2] To requite.   [3] Very drunk.
[4] With difficulty.   [5] Would not doff or lower.   [6] Stop for.
[7] "In such a voice as Pilate was used to speak with in the Mysteries.
Pilate, being an odious character, was probably represented as speaking with a
harsh disagreeable voice."—*Tyrwhitt.*
[8] Know.   [9] For the nonce, for the occasion.   [10] Dear.
[11] Go to work.   [12] Lay the blame of it on.   [13] Churl's.

Turn over the leaf, and chese[1] another tale;
For he shall find enow, both great and smale,
Of storial thing that toucheth gentiless,
And eke morality and holiness.

The Miller's Tale is capped by another in the same style from his fellow "churl" the Reve (or Bailiff)—who before he begins, however, avails himself of the privilege of his advanced years to prelude away for some time in a preaching strain, till his eloquence is suddenly cut short by the voice of authority:—

When that our Host had heard this sermoning,
He gan to speak as lordly as a king,
And saide, What amounteth all this wit?
What, shall we speak all day of holy writ?
The devil made a Reve for to preach,
Or of a souter[2] a shipman or a leech.[3]
Say forth thy tale, and tarry not the time;
Lo Deptford,[4] and it is half way prime;[5]
Lo Greenwich, there many a shrew is in:[6]
It were all time thy Tale to begin.

The last specimen we shall give of " our Host " shall be from the Clerk's Prologue :—

Sir Clerk of Oxenford, our Hoste said,
Ye ride as still and coy as doth a maid
Were newe spoused, sitting at the board;
This day ne heard I of your tongue a word.
I trow ye study abouten some sophime,[7]
But Salomon saith that every thing hath time.
For Godde's sake as beth[8] of better cheer;
It is no time for to studien here.
Tell us some merry tale by your fay;[9]
For what man that is entered in a play
He needes must unto the play assent.
But preacheth not, as freres don in Lent,
To make us for our olde sinnes weep,
Ne that thy tale make us not to sleep.
Tell us some merry thing of aventures;
Your terms, your coloures, and your figures,

---

[1] Choose.　　[2] Cobbler.　　[3] Physician.　　[4] Deptford.
[5] Tyrwhitt supposes this means half-past seven in the morning.
[6] In which (wherein) is many a shrew.
[7] Sophism, perhaps generally for a logical argument.
[8] Be.　　[9] Faith.

Keep them in store till so be ye indite
High style, as when that men to kinges write.
Speaketh so plain at this time, I you pray,
That we may understonden what ye say.

 This worthy Clerk benignely answerd;
Hoste, quod he, I am under your yerde;
Ye have of us as now the governance,
And therefore would I do you obeisance,
As far as reason asketh hardily.[1]
I wol you tell a tale which that I
Learned at Padow of a worthy clerk,
As proved[2] by his wordes and his werk:
He is now dead and nailed in his chest;
I pray to God so yeve his soule rest.
Francis Petrarch, the laureat poete
Highte this clerk, whose rhethoricke sweet
Enlumined all Itaille of poetry,
As Linian[3] did of philosophy,
Or law, or other art particulere;
But death, that wol not suffre us dwellen here
But as it were a twinkling of an eye,
Them both hath slain, and alle we shall die.

And our last specimen of the Canterbury Tales, and also of
Chaucer, being a passage exhibiting that power of pathos in the
delicacy as well as in the depth of which he is unrivalled, shall
be taken from this tale told by the Clerk, the exquisite tale of
Griselda. Her husband has carried his trial of her submission
and endurance to the last point by informing her that she must
return to her father, and that his now wife is " coming by the
way :"—

 And she again answerd in patience :
My lord, quod she, I wot, and wist alway,
How that betwixen your magnificence
And my povert no wight ne can ne may
Maken comparison : it is no nay :
I ne held me never digne[4] to be your manere
To be your wife, ne yet your chamberere.[5]

 And in this house there[6] ye me lady made
(The highe God take I for my witness,
And all so wisly[7] be my soule glade)
I never held me lady no maistresse,

But humble servant to your worthiness,
And ever shall, while that my life may dure,
Aboven every worldly creature.

That ye so long, of your benignity,
Han' holden me in honour and nobley,¹
Whereas² I was not worthy for to be,
That thank I God and you, to whom I pray
Foryeld⁴ it you : there is no more to say.
Unto my fader gladly wol I wend,
And with him dwell unto my lives end.

God shieldë swich a lordes wife to take
Another man to husband or to make.⁵

And of your newe wife God of his grace
So grant you weale and prosperity ;
For I wol gladly yielden her my place,
In which that I was blissful wont to be :
For, sith it liketh you, my lord, quod she,
That whilome weren all my hertes rest,
That I shall gon, I wol go where you list.

But, thereas⁶ ye me profer swich dowair⁷
As I first brought, it is well in my mind
It were my wretched clothes, nothing fair,
The which to me were hard now for to find.
O goode God! how gentle and how kind
Ye semed by your speech and your visage
The day that maked was our marriage!

But sooth is said, algate⁸ I find it true,
For in effect it preved⁹ is on me,
Love is not old as when that it is new.
But certes, Lord, for non adversity¹⁰
To dien in this case, it shall not be
That ever in word or werk I shall repent
That I you yave mine heart in whole intent.

My lord, ye wot that in my fader's place
Ye did me strip out of my poore weed,
And richely ye clad me of your grace :
To you brought I nought elles, out of drede,¹¹
But faith, and nakedness, and maidenheds :

---

¹ Have.　　² Nobility.　　³ Where.　　⁴ Repay.　　⁵ Mate.
⁶ Whereas.　　⁷ Such dower.　　⁸ In every way.　　⁹ Proved.
¹⁰ For no unhappiness that may be my lot, were it even to die?
¹¹ Doubt.

And here again your clothing I restore,
And eke your wedding ring, for evermore.

The remnant of your jewels ready be
Within your chamber, I dare it safely sayn.
Naked out of my fader's house, quod she,
I came, and naked I mote turn again.
All your pleasance wold I follow fain :
But yet I hope it be not your intent
That I smockless out of your palace went.

   .   .   .   .   .

Let me not like a worm go by the way :   .
Remember you, mine owen lord so dear,
I was your wife, though I unworthy were.

   .   .   .   .   .

The smock, quod he, that thou hast on thy bake
Let it be still, and bear it forth with thee.
But well unneathes[1] thilke[2] word he spake,
But went his way for ruth and for pitee.
Before the folk herselven strippeth she,
And in her smock, with foot and head all bare,
Toward her father's house forth is she fare.[3]

The folk her followen weeping in her way,
And Fortune aye they cursen as they goon :
But she fro weeping kept her eyen drey,[4]
Ne in this time word ne spake she none.
Her fader, that this tiding heard anon,
Curseth the day and time that nature
Shope him[5] to been a lives[6] creature.

There is scarcely perhaps to be found anywhere in poetry a
finer burst of natural feeling than in the lines we have printed
in italics.

JOHN GOWER.

Contemporary with Chaucer, and probably born a few years
earlier, though of the two—he survived to the latest date, for his
death did not take place till the year 1408, was John Gower.
It is affirmed by Leland in his Commentarii de Scriptoribus
Britannicis that he was of the ancient family, said to have been
seated at Stitenham, or Sittenham, in Yorkshire, before the

---

[1] With great difficulty.   [2] This same.   [5] Gone.
[4] Dry.   [3] Formed.   [6] Living.

Conquest, of which the Duke of Sutherland is now the head;
and Mr. Todd, in his valuable Illustrations of the Lives and
Writings of Gower and Chaucer (8vo. Lon. 1810), has pub-
blished a deed from the charter-chest of the Duke (then Marquis
of Stafford), dated at Stitenham in 1348, to which the first of the
subscribing witnesses is *Johannes Gower*, and an endorsement
upon which, but in a hand which is admitted to be at least a
century later, states this person to have been " Sir John Gower
the poet." This would make Gower to have been born before
1326 at the latest, and to have been some years beyond eighty
when he died; which is consistent enough with the manner in
which his name is generally mentioned by old writers along with
but before that of Chaucer, and with the express statement in
some of the earlier accounts that he was the senior of the two.
But it has since been conclusively shown by Sir Harris Nicolas
that no reliance can be placed upon these assertions and inferences, and that Gower was really not a North of England, but a
South of England man, and resided in the county of Kent.*
It is proved, however, by his will, published by Mr. Todd (and
previously by Gough, in his Sepulchral Monuments, 2 vols. fol.
1786), that he was a person of condition, and possessed of considerable property. He and Chaucer were friends, as well as
contemporaries and brother-poets; and there appears to be no
sufficient reason for the notion that has been taken up by most of
the modern biographers of the latter that they were alienated
from one another in their old age.† It may be safely assumed, at
least, that their friendship remained unbroken down to 1393,
the year in which Gower, as he tells us himself, finished his
Confessio Amantis, where near the end he puts the following
compliment to Chaucer into the mouth of Venus:—

> And greet well Chaucer when ye meet,
> As my disciple and my poete;
> For in the floures of his youth,
> In sundry wise, as he well couth,
> Of ditties and of songes glade,
> The which he for my sake made,
> The land fulfilled is over all;
> Whereof to him in special,

* Retrospective Reviews, Second Series, ii., 111; and Dr. Pauli's Introductory Essay to the Confessio Amantis.
† See the remarks of Sir Harris Nicolas, in his Life of Chaucer, p. 39.

> Above all other, I am most bold :[1]
> Forthy[2] now in his dayes old
> Thou shalt him tell this message,
> That he upon his latter age,
> To set an end of all his werk,
> As he which is mine owne clerk,
> Do make his Testament of Love,
> As thou hast done thy shrift above,
> So that my court it may record.

This was certainly liberal repayment for Chaucer's dedication to his friend, probably many years before, of his Troilus and Cresside, or rather of half that work, in the following sober lines :—

> O moral Gower! this boke I direct
> To thee, and to the philosophical Strood,
> To vouchesauf there need is to correct
> Of your benignities and zeales good.

The epithet here bestowed upon Gower is not perhaps exactly the one which a poet would most covet; but it has stuck, and *Moral Gower* is the name by which he has generally passed over since. "O *Moral Gower*, and Lydgate laureat," exclaims the Scottish poet Dunbar, in his Golden Targe. "*Moral Gower*, whose sententious dew adown reflareth with fair golden beams," says Hawes in his Pastime of Pleasure. "And near them sat old *Moral Gower*, with pleasant pen in hand," writes the author of A Dialogue both pleasant and pitiful, Lon. 1573.[*] But his publisher, Bertholet the printer, is the most severe of all: in the dedication prefixed to his edition of the Confessio Amantis, 1532, he naively remarks: "It was not much greater pain to that excellent clerk, the *Moral John Gower*, to compile the same noble work than it was to me to print it." "No man," he adds, alluding to the former edition by Caxton, in 1483, "will believe it without conferring both the prints, the old and mine, together."

Gower is the author of three great poetical works (sometimes spoken of as one, though they do not seem to have had any connection of plan or subject) ; the Speculum Meditantis, which is, or was, in French ; the Vox Clamantis, which is in Latin ; and the Confessio Amantis, which is in English. But the first,

---

[1] Beholden.   [2] Therefore.
[*] Quoted by Mr. Todd in Illustrations, Introduction, p. xxix.

although an account of it, founded on a mistake, has been given
by Warton, has certainly not been seen in modern times, and has
in all probability perished. We have other specimens, however,
of Gower's talents as a French and also as a Latin poet in certain
short pieces in both these languages preserved in a volume in the
Duke of Sutherland's library at Trentham (Staffordshire), of which
an account has been given by Warton (Hist. Eng. Poetry, II. 314
—341), and another, more full, particular, and exact, by Mr. Todd
(Illustrations, pp. 93—108). Speaking of Gower's Latin poetry,
Warton says that he "copied Ovid's elegiacs with some degree
of purity, and with fewer false quantities and corrupt phrases
than any of our countrymen had yet exhibited since the twelfth
century." [*] Of the French pieces in the Trentham volume,
which consist of fifty *Balades*, or sonnets, he observes, "They
have much real and intrinsic merit. They are tender, pathetic,
and poetical; and place our old poet Gower in a more advan-
tageous point of view than that in which he has hitherto been
usually seen. I know not if any even among the French poets
themselves, of this period, have left a set of more finished
sonnets; for they were probably written when Gower was a
young man, about the year 1350. Nor had yet any English
poet treated the passion of love with equal delicacy of sentiment,
and elegance of composition." [†] Four of these French sonnets are
given by Warton, and more correctly, with the addition of a
fifth, by Todd; and the entire contents of the volume were
edited for the Roxburghe Club in 1818 by the present Duke of
Sutherland (then Earl Gower) under the title of *Balades* and
other Poems, by John Gower, printed from the original MS.,
Latin and French; Black Letter, 4to. London. Gower was
probably one of the last Englishmen who attempted the composition of poetry in French; and at the end of one of the pieces
in this volume he asks forgiveness of his reader for any inaccuracies he may have committed in the foreign idiom, on the
ground of his English birth and his therefore not being master
of the French eloquence:—

> Et si jeo mai de François la faconde,
> Pardonetz moi qe jeo de ceo forvoie.
> Jeo sui Engloia.

The Vox Clamantis was edited for the Roxburghe Club in 1850 by the Rev. H. G. Coxe. It consists of seven Books in Latin elegiacs. "The greater bulk of the work," says Dr. Pauli, "the date of which its editor is inclined to fix between 1382 and 1384, is rather a moral than an historical essay; but the First Book describes the insurrection of Wat Tyler in an allegorical disguise; the poet having a dream on the 11th of June 1381, in which men assumed the shape of animals. The Second Book contains a long sermon on fatalism, in which the poet shows himself no friend to Wiclif's tenets, but a zealous advocate for the reformation of the clergy. The Third Book points out how all orders of society must suffer for their own vices and demerits; in illustration of which he cites the example of the secular clergy. The Fourth Book is dedicated to the cloistered clergy and the friars, the Fifth to the military; the Sixth contains a violent attack on the lawyers; and the Seventh subjoins the moral of the whole, represented in Nebuchadnezzar's dream, as interpreted by Daniel."[*] The allusion in the title seems to be to St. John the Baptist, and to the general clamour then abroad in the country.

The Confessio Amantis has been several times printed;—by Caxton in 1483, by Bertholet in 1532 and again in 1554; and by Alexander Chalmers in the second volume of his English poets, 1810; but all these previous editions have been superseded by the very commodious and beautiful one of Dr. Reinhold Pauli, in 3 vols. 8vo., London, 1857.

We will avail ourselves of Dr. Pauli's account of the course in which the work proceeds:—"The poem opens by introducing the author himself, in the character of an unhappy lover in despair. Venus appears to him, and, after having heard his prayer, appoints her priest called Genius, like the mystagogue in the picture of Cobes, to hear the lover's confession. This is the frame of the whole work, which is a singular mixture of classical notions, principally borrowed from Ovid's Ars Amandi, and of the purely medieval idea, that as a good Catholic the unfortunate lover must state his distress to a father confessor. This is done with great regularity and even pedantry: all the passions of the human heart, which generally stand in the way of love, being systematically arranged in the various books and

---

[*] Introd. Essay to Confessio Amantis.

subdivisions of the work. After Genius has fully explained the
evil affection, passion, or vice under consideration, the lover
confesses on that particular point; and frequently urges his
boundless love for an unknown beauty, who treats him cruelly,
in a tone of affectation which would appear highly ridiculous in a
man of more than sixty years of age, were it not a common
characteristic of the poetry of the period. After this profession
the confessor opposes him, and exemplifies the fatal effects of
each passion by a variety of opposite stories, gathered from
many sources, examples being then, as now, a favourite mode of
inculcating instruction and reformation. At length, after a
frequent and tedious recurrence of the same process, the confession is terminated by some final injunctions of the priest—
the lover's petition in a strophic poem addressed to Venus—the
bitter judgment of the goddess, that he should remember his old
age and leave off such fooleries .... his cure from the wound
caused by the dart of love, and his absolution, received as if by
a pious Roman Catholic." *

Such a scheme as this, pursued through more than thirty thousand verses, promises perhaps more edification than entertainment; but the amount of either that is to be got out of the Confessio Amantis is not considerable. Ellis, after charitably
declaring that so long as Moral Gower keeps to his morality he
is "wise, impressive, and sometimes almost sublime," is compelled to add, "But his narrative is often quite petrifying; and,
when we read in his work the tales with which we had been
familiarised in the poems of Ovid, we feel a mixture of surprise
and despair at the perverse industry employed in removing every
detail on which the imagination had been accustomed to fasten.
The author of the Metamorphoses was a poet, and at least sufficiently fond of ornament; Gower considers him as a mere
annalist; scrupulously preserves his facts; relates them with
great perspicuity; and is fully satisfied when he has extracted
from them as much morality as they can be reasonably expected
to furnish."† In many cases this must be little enough.

We shall confine our specimens of Gower's poetry to two
short passages from the Confessio Amantis. The first is the tale
of the coffers or caskets, in the Fifth Book, which has been given
by Todd after a collation of the printed editions with the best

* Introductory Essay, p. xxxiv.
† Specimens of the Early English Poets, i. 179.

manuscripts :* this is the story, whether found by him in Gower
or elsewhere, from which Shakspeare is supposed to have taken
the hint of the incident of the caskets in his Merchant of
Venice :—

<blockquote>
In a cronique thus I read :
About a kinge, as must need,
There was of knightes and squiers
Great rout and eke of officers :
Some of long time him hadden served,
And thoughten that they have deserved
Avancement, and gone without ;
And some also bren of the rout
That comen but a while agon,
And they avanced were anon.

There olde men upon this thing,
So as they durst, again¹ the king
Among themself² complainen oft :
But there is nothing said so soft
That it ne cometh out at last :
The king it wist, and als³ so fast
As he which was of high prudence :
He shope⁴ therefore an evidence
Of them that plainen in the cas,⁵
To know in whose default it was ;
And all within his own intent,
That none may wiste what it meant.
Anon he let two coffers make
Of one semblance, and of one make,
So lich,⁶ that no life thilke throw⁷
That one may fro that other know :
They were into his chamber brought,
But no man wot why they be wrought ;
And natheless⁸ the king hath bede⁹
That they be set in privy stede,¹⁰
As he that was of wisdom sly ;
When¹¹ he thereto his time sy,¹²
</blockquote>

---

* Illustrations, pp. 145—150 ; Notes, pp. 151—158.
¹ Against.
² Gower, like Chaucer and Langland, writes hem for what we now call them ;
but we have taken the liberty throughout of discarding that peculiarity.
³ Also.   ⁴ Contrived.   ⁵ Case.
⁶ Like.   ⁷ No person at any particular time ?
⁸ Nevertheless.   ⁹ Bidden.   ¹⁰ Place.
¹¹ Gower, also, like the other writers of his time, has whan and than, where
we now say when and then.
¹² Saw. The old spelling is sich and sik.

All privily, that none it wist,
His owne handes[1] that one chest
Of fine gold, and of fine perle,[2]
The which out of his treasury
Was take, anon he filled full;
That other coffer of straw and mull,[3]
With stones meynd,[4] he filld also :
Thus be they full both two.

So that erlich[5] upon a day
He had within, where he lay,
There should be to form his bed
A board upset and faire spread :
And then he let the coffers set
Upon the board, and did them set.
He knew the names well of tho
The which again him grutchod so,[6]
Both of his chamber and of his hall ;
Anon and sente for them all,
And saido to them in this wise :—

There shall no man his hap[7] despise :
I wot well ye have longe served,
And God wot what ye have deserved ;
But if it is along on[8] me
Of that ye unavanced be,
Or elles if it belong on yow,
The soothe shall be proved now :
To stoppe with your evil word,
Lo ! here two coffers on the board ;
Chese[9] which you list of bothe two,
And witteth[10] well that one of tho
Is with tresor so full begon[11]
That, if ye happe therupon,
Ye shall be riche men for ever :
Now chese and take which you is levor ;[12]
But be ye well ware that ye take,
For of that one[13] I undertake[14]
There is no manner good therein
Whereof ye mighten profit win.

---

[1] Hands.   [2] Jewellery.   [3] Rubbish.
[4] Mingled.   [5] Early.   [6] Fetch.
[7] Those who against him grudged (or grumbled) so.
[8] Fortune.   [9] Owing to.
[10] Choose.   [11] Know, understand ye.
[12] Begun, used in a general sense, nearly with the effect of made.
[13] Is more agreeable to you.   [14] The one.
[15] Promise, engage, assure you.

Now goth[1] together of one assent,
And taketh your avisement;
For, but I you this day avance,
It stant upon your owne chance,
All only in default of grace;
No shall be showed in this place
Upon you alle well afin[2]
That no defaulte shall be min.

They kneelen all, and with one voice
The king they thonken of this choice;
And after that they up arise,
And gon aside and them avise;
And at laste they accord
(Whereof their tale to record
To what issue they be fall)
A knight shall speake for them all.
He kneeleth down unto the king,
And saith that they upon this thing,
Or for to win, or for to lose,[3]
Been all avised for to chose.

Tho[4] took this knight a yerd on hond,[5]
And goth there as the coffers stond,
And with assent of everich one
He layeth his yerde upon one,
And saith[6] the king how thilke[7] same
They chese in reguerdon[8] by name,
And prayeth him that they might it have.

The king, which wold his honour save,
When he had heard the common voice,
Hath granted them their owne choice,
And took them thereupon the key,
And, for he wold it were seo[9]
What good they have as they suppose,
He bade anon the coffer unclose—
Which was fulfilled with straw and stones!
Thus be they served all at ones.[10]

Tho king then, in the same stede,[11]
Anon that other coffer unlede,[12]
Whereas they sighen[13] great richess,
Well more than they couthen guess.

---

[1] Go.
[4] Then.
[7] This.
[10] Once.
[12] Undid.

[2] In the end.
[5] A yard, or rod, in hand.
[8] In guerdon, or reward.
[11] Place.
[13] Where they saw.

[3] Lose.
[6] Saith to, telleth.
[9] It were seen?

Lo! saith the king, now may ye see
That there is no default in me ;
Forthy[1] myself I wol acquite,
And beareth ye your owne wite[2]
Of that fortune hath you refused.
    Thus was this wise king excused :
And they left off their evil speech,
And mercy of their king beseech.

Our other extract we give in the old spelling, as it was
contributed to the Pictorial History of England by Sir Henry
Ellis from a very early MS. of the poem in the Harleian Collection, No. 3490 :—

In a Croniq I fynde thus,
How that Caius Fabricius
Wich whilome was consul of Rome,
By whome the lawes yede and come,[3]
Whan the Sampnitees to him brouht
A somme of golde, and hym by saubt
To done hem fanoure in the lawe,
Towarde the golde he gan hym drawe :
Whereof, in alle mennes loke,
A parte in to his honde he tooke,
Wich to his mouthe in alle haste
He put hit for to smelle and taste,
And to his ibe and to his ere,
Bot he ne fonde no comfort there :
And thanne he be gan it to despise,
And tolde vnto hem in this wise :
" I not what is with golde to thryve,
Whan none of alle my wittes fyve
Fynt savour ne delite ther inne ;
So is it bot a nyce sinne
Of golde so ben to coveitous.
Bot ho is riche an glorious
Wich hath in his subieccion
The men wich in possession
Ben riche of gold, and by this skille,[4]
For he may alday whan he wille,
Or be him leef or be him loth,
Justice don vppon hem bothe."
Lo thus he seide, and with that worde
He threwe to fore hem on the borde

[1] Therefore.
[2] Went and came.
[3] Blame.
[4] For this reason.

The golde oute of his honde anon,
And selde hem that he wolde none,
So that he kepte his liberte,
To do justice and equite,
Without lucre of such richesse.
There be nowe fewe of such I gesse,
For it was thilke tyme used
That every juge was refused,
Wich was nut frende to commoun riht ;
Bot thei that wolden stonde vpriht
For trouth only to do justice
Preferred were in thilke office,
To deme and juge common lawe,
Wich nowe men seyn is alle withdrawe.
To set a lawe and keep it naught
There is no common profit sonbt,
But, above alle, natheles,
The lawe wich is made for pees
Is good to kepe for the beste,
For that art alle men in reste.

The manuscripts of the Confessio Amantis are very numerous.
There are no fewer than ten in the Bodleian Library ; and
several others are in the British Museum, at Cambridge, at
Trinity College, Dublin, and in private collections.   Dr. Pauli's
text, in which he has regulated the spelling in conformity to the
demands of the verse, which he apparently assumes to have
been as regular as that of Chaucer is held to be by Tyrwhitt,
is founded on the printed edition of 1532, collated chiefly with
the Stafford MS., and with those in the Harleian Collection numbered 7184, 3869, and 3490.   The poem extends to eight Books,
and is expressly stated by the author to have been finished in
the sixteenth year of Richard II., that is, in the year 1393.   It
had been begun some years before, at the command of that king,
at a time when, as it seems to be intimated, Gower was labouring
under ill health—

Though I sikenesse have upon honde,
And long have had—

though it is not quite clear that these words are not intended to
describe his condition at the conclusion of his task.   He particularly gives it as his reason for choosing the vernacular
tongue—

—— for that fewe men endite
In our Englishe.

BARBOUR.

This latter part of the fourteenth century is also the age of the birth of Scottish poetry; and Chaucer had in that dialect a far more worthy contemporary and rival than his friend and fellow Englishman Gower, in John Barbour. Of Barbour's personal history but little is known. He was a churchman, and had attained to the dignity of Archdeacon of Aberdeen by the year 1357; so that his birth cannot well be supposed to have been later than 1320. He is styled Archdeacon of Aberdeen in a passport granted to him in that year by Edward III. at the request of David de Bruce (that is, King David II. of Scotland), to come into England with three scholars in his company, for the purpose, as it is expressed, of studying in the University of Oxford; and the protection is extended to him and his companions while performing their scholastic exercises, and generally while remaining there, and also while returning to their own country. It may seem strange that an Archdeacon should go to college; but Oxford appears to have been not the only seat of learning to which Barbour resorted late in life with the same object. Three other passports, or safe-conducts, are extant which were granted to him by Edward at later dates:—the first, in 1364, permitting him to come, with four horsemen, from Scotland, by land or sea, into England, to study at Oxford, or elsewhere, as he might think proper; the second, in 1365, by which he is authorized to come into England, and travel throughout that kingdom, with six horsemen as his companions, as far as to St. Denis in France; and the third, in 1368, securing him protection in coming, with two valets and two horses, into England, and travelling through the same to the king's other dominions, on his way to France (*versus Franciam*) for the purpose of studying there, and in returning thence. Yet he had also been long before this employed, and in a high capacity, in civil affairs. In 1357 he was appointed by the Bishop of Aberdeen one of his two Commissioners deputed to attend a meeting at Edinburgh about the ransom of the king. Nothing more is heard of him till 1373, in which year he appears as one of the auditors of Exchequer, being styled Archdeacon of Aberdeen, and clerk of probation (*clerico probacionis*) of the royal household. In his later days he appears to have been in the receipt of two royal pensions, both probably bestowed upon him by Robert II.,

who succeeded David II. in 1370; the first one of 10l. Scots
from the customs of Aberdeen, the other one of 20s. from the
borough mails, or city rents, of the same town. An entry in the
records of Aberdeen for 1471 states on the authority of the
original roll, now lost, that the latter was expressly granted to
him " for the compilation of the book of the Acts of King Robert
the First." In a passage occurring in the latter part of this work,
he himself tells us that he was then compiling it in the year 1375.
All that is further known of him is, that his death took place
towards the close of 1395. Besides his poem commonly called
The Bruce, another metrical work of his entitled The Broite or
The Brute, being a deduction of the history of the Scottish kings
from Brutus, is frequently referred to by the chronicler Wynton
in the next age; but no copy of it is now believed to exist. Of
the Bruce only one MS. was till lately supposed to be extant, a
transcript made in 1489 preserved in the Advocates' Library,
and it was from this that the last and best edition of the poem
was printed by Dr. Jamieson, in 4to. at Edinburgh, in 1820; but
another MS. dated 1488, has since been discovered in the Library
of St. John's College, Cambridge. It appears to have been
printed before the close of the sixteenth century. A " Patrick
Gordon, gentleman," as he designates himself, the author of a
metrical work, entitled The Famous History of the Renowned
and Valiant Prince, Robert, surnamed the Bruce, King of Scotland, which first appeared at Dort in 1615, alludes to Barbour's
previous performance on the same subject as " the old printed
book;" and Mr. David Laing, in a note to his edition of Dunbar
(Edinburgh, 1834), p. 40, states that he is possessed of an edition
of Barbour's poem, in small 4to. and black letter, which, although it has lost the title-page, appears to have been printed at
Edinburgh about the year 1570. The oldest edition known to
Dr. Jamieson was an Edinburgh one of 1616. It was reprinted
at the same place in 1620 and 1670; at Glasgow in 1672; and
again at Edinburgh in 1714 (the title-page, however, being
usually dated 1758). The first critical edition was that by
Pinkerton, published in 3 vols. 8vo. at London in 1790; the last
and best, is that by the Rev. Dr. John Jamieson, forming the first
volume of The Bruce and Wallace, 2 vols. 4to. Edinburgh, 1820.
We may notice by the way that Gordon, who speaks with great
contempt of Barbour's " outworn barbarous speech," and ill-
composed and immethodical work, tells a story in the Preface to

his Famous History about a still older poem on the exploits of
Bruce, written by "a monk of the Abbey of Melrose, called
Peter Fenton" in the year 1369, a manuscript copy of which,
"old and torn, almost illegible, in many places wanting leaves,"
yet having the beginning, had been put into his hands by his
"loving friend, Donald Farquharson." "It was," he says, "in old
rhime like to Chaucer, but wanting in many parts; and especially
from the field of Bannockburn forth it wanted all the rest
almost, so that it could not be gotten to the press; yet such as I
could read thereof had many remarkable tales, worthy to be
noted, and also probable, agreeing with the truth of the history,
as I have followed it, as well as the other." "One cannot help
regretting," Dr. Jamieson sensibly remarks, "that Gordon,
instead of bestowing his labour on a new poem, had not favoured
the public with even the fragments of that written by Fenton."
It would have been something if he had even informed us what
he had done with the manuscript (if he did not put it into the
fire upon finding that he could not read it). He writes the date,
1369, in words at full length; but he is evidently not a person
upon whose testimony much reliance can be placed, as to such a
matter. It is a suspicious circumstance, as is hinted by Macpherson, the editor of Wynton's Chronicle, that that writer, though
he often quotes Barbour, has never once mentioned Fenton.*

The Scotch in which Barbour's poem is written was undoubtedly the language then commonly in use among his countrymen,
for whom he wrote and with whom his poem has been a popular
favourite ever since its first appearance. By his countrymen, of
course, we mean the inhabitants of southern and eastern, or
Lowland Scotland, not the Celts or Highlanders, who have always
been and still are as entirely distinct a race as the native Irish
are, and always have been, from the English in Ireland, and to
confound whom either in language or in any other respect with
the Scottish Lowlanders is the same sort of mistake that it would
be to speak of the English as being either in language or lineage
identical with the Welsh. Indeed, there is a remarkable simi-
larity as to this matter in the circumstances of the three countries: in each a primitive Celtic population, which appears to
have formerly occupied the whole soil, has been partially expelled by another race, but still exists, inhabiting its separate
locality (in all the three cases the maritime and mountainous

* Wyntown's Chronicle, by Macpherson (1795), Pref. p. xxix.

wilds of the west), and retaining its own ancient and perfectly distinct language. The expulsion has been the most sweeping in England, where it took place first, and where the Welsh form now only about a sixteenth of the general population; it has been carried to a less extent in Scotland, where it was not effected till a later age, and where the numbers of the Highlanders are still to those of the Lowlanders in the proportion of one to five or six; in Ireland, where it happened last of all, the new settlers have scarcely yet ceased to be regarded as foreigners and intruders, and the ancient Celtic inhabitants, still covering, although not possessing, by far the greater part of the soil, the larger proportion of them, however, having relinquished their ancestral speech, continue to be perhaps six or eight times as numerous as the Saxons or English. For in all the three cases it is the same Saxon, or at least Teutonic, race before which the Celts have retired or given way: the Welsh, the Scottish Highlanders, and the native Irish, indeed, all to this day alike designate the stranger who has set himself down beside them by the common epithet of the Saxon. We know that other Teutonic or northern races were mixed with the Angles and Saxons in all the three cases: not only were the English, who settled in Scotland in great numbers, and conquered Ireland, in the eleventh and twelfth centuries, in part French Normans, but the original Normans or Danes had in the eighth and ninth centuries effected extensive settlements in each of the three countries. Besides, the original English were themselves a mixed people; and those of them who were distinctively Saxons were even the old hereditary enemies of the Danes. Still, as the Saxons, Angles, and Jutes were as one people against the Scandinavian Danes, or their descendants the French Normans, so even Saxons and Danes, or Normans, were united everywhere against the Celts. As for the language spoken by the Lowland Scots in the time of Barbour, it must have sprung out of the same sources, and been affected by nearly the same influences, with the English of the same age. Nobody now holds that any part of it can have been derived from the Picts, who indeed originally occupied part of the Lowlands of Scotland, but who were certainly not a Teutonic but a Celtic people. Lothian, or all the eastern part of Scotland to the south of the Forth, was English from the seventh century, as much as was Northumberland or Yorkshire: from this date the only difference that could

have distinguished the language there used from that spoken in
the south of England was probably a larger infusion of the
Danish forms; but this characteristic must have been shared in
nearly the same degree by all the English then spoken to the
north of the Thames. Again, whatever effect may have been
produced by the Norman Conquest, and the events consequent
upon that revolution, would probably be pretty equally diffused
over the two countries. In the twelfth and thirteenth centuries
both the Normans themselves and their literature appear to have
acquired almost the same establishment and ascendancy in Scotland as in England. We have seen that French was the language of the court in the one country as well as in the other, and
that Scottish as well as English writers figure among the imitators of the Norman trouveurs and romance poets. Afterwards
the connexion of Scotland with France became much more intimate and uninterrupted than that of England; and this appears
to have affected the Scottish dialect in a way which will be
presently noticed. But in Barbour's day, the language of
Teutonic Scotland was distinguished from that of the south of
England (which had now acquired the ascendancy over that of
the northern counties as the literary dialect), by little more than
the retention, perhaps, of a good many vocables which had become obsolete among the English, and a generally broader enun-
ciation of the vowel sounds. Hence Barbour never supposes
that he is writing in any other language than English any more
than Chaucer; that is the name by which not only he, but his
successors Dunbar and even Lyndsay, always designate their
native tongue: down to the latter part of the sixteenth century,
by the term *Scotch* was generally understood what is now called
the *Gælic*, or the *Erse* or *Ersh* (that is, Irish), the speech of the
Celts or Highlanders. Divested of the grotesque and cumbrous
spelling of the old manuscripts, the language of Barbour is quite
as intelligible at the present day to an English reader as that of
Chaucer; the obsolete words and forms are not more numerous
in the one writer than in the other, though some that are used
by Barbour may not be found in Chaucer, as many of Chaucer's
are not in Barbour; the chief general distinction, as we have
said, is the greater breadth given to the vowel sounds in the
dialect of the Scottish poet. The old termination of the present
participle in *and* is also more frequently used than in Chaucer,
to whom however it is not unknown, any more than its modern

substitute *ing* is to Barbour. The most remarkable peculiarity of the more recent form of the Scottish dialect that is not found in Barbour is the abstraction of the final *l* from syllables ending in that consonant preceded by a vowel or diphthong: thus he never has *a'*, *fu'*, *fa'* or *fou'*, *pou*, *kow*, for *all*, *fall*, *full*, *poll*, *kole*, &c. The subsequent introduction of this habit into the speech of the Scotch is perhaps to be attributed to their imitation of the liquefaction of the *l* in similar circumstances by the French, from whom they have also borrowed a considerable number of their modern vocables, never used in England, and to whose accentuation, both of individual words and of sentences, theirs has much general resemblance, throwing the emphasis, contrary, as already noticed, to the tendency of the English language, upon one of the latter syllables, and also running into the rising in many cases where the English use the falling intonation.

The Bruce is a very long poem, comprising between twelve and thirteen thousand lines, in octosyllabic metre, which the two last editors have distributed, Pinkerton into twenty, Jamieson into fourteen, Books. It relates the history of Scotland, and especially the fortunes of the great Bruce, from the death of Alexander III. in 1286, or rather, from the competition for the crown, and the announcement of the claims of Edward I. as lord paramount, on that of his daughter, Margaret the Maiden of Norway, in 1290—the events of the first fifteen or sixteen years, however, before Bruce comes upon the stage, being very succinctly given—to the death of Bruce (Robert I.) in 1329, and that of his constant associate and brother of chivalry, Lord James Douglas, the bearer of the king's heart to the Holy Land, in the year following. The 12,500 verses, or thereby, may be said therefore to comprehend the events of about twenty-five years; and Barbour, though he calls his work a "romaunt," as being a narrative poem, professes to relate nothing but what he believed to be the truth, so that he is to be regarded not only as the earliest poet but also as the earliest historian of his country. Fordun, indeed, was his contemporary, but the Latin chronicle of that writer was probably not published till many years after his death. And to a great extent Barbour's work is and has always been regarded as being an authentic historical monument; it has no doubt some incidents or embellishments which may be set down as fabulous; but these are in general very easily distinguished from the main texture of the narrative,

which agrees substantially with the most trustworthy accounts
drawn from other sources, and has been received and quoted as
good evidence by all subsequent writers and investigators of
Scottish history, from Andrew of Wynton to Lord Hailes inclusive. This is Barbour's own introduction of himself to his
readers; and the passage, besides explaining the design of his
work, affords a fair example of the worthy archdeacon's manly
bearing, and forcible and cordial style :—

> Stories to read are delitable,
> Suppose that they be nought but fable;
> Then[1] suld[2] stories that suthfast[3] were,
> An they war[4] said on gud[5] manere,
> Have double pleasance in hearing.
> The first pleasance is the carping;[6]
> And the tother the suthfastness,
> That shaws[7] the thing right as it wes;[8]
> And such thinges that are likand[9]
> Till mannes hearing are pleasand.
> Therefore I wald[10] fain set my will,
> Gif[11] my wit might suffice theretill,
> To put in writ a suthfast story,
> That it lest[12] aye furth in memory,
> Swa[13] that na[14] time of length it let,[15]
> Ne ger[16] it haily[17] be foryet.[18]
> For auld[19] stories, that men reads,
> Represents to them the deeds
> Of stalwart folk, that livit are,[20]
> Right as they then in presence ware.[21]
> And certes they suld weil have prize
> That in their time were wight[22] and wise;
> And led their life in great travail,
> And oft, in hard stour[23] of battail,

---

1 Barbour's word, like Chaucer's, is than.　　　3 Should.
2 True.　　　4 If they were.
5 Good. It may perhaps be doubted if the a here, and in other cases, was
yet pronounced like the French a
6 The narrative, the story.　　　7 Shows.　　　8 Was.
9 Agreeable.　　　10 Would.　　　11 If.
12 Last　　　13 So (probably pronounced sway).
14 No.　　　15 Hinder, stop.　　　16 Nor cause.
17 Wholly.　　　18 Forgotten.　　　19 Old.
20 Lived early, formerly.　　　21 Were.　　　22 Valiant.
23 Peril. Was the ou yet pronounced as in French ?

> Wan right great price of chivalry
> And war voidit of cowardy;[1]
> As wes King Robert of Scotland,
> That hardy wes of heart and hand ;
> And gud Schir James of Douglas,
> That in his time sa worthy was,
> That of his price and his bounty
> In ser landes renownit was he.
> Of them I think this book to may :[2]
> Now God give grace that I may swa
> Treat it, and bring it till ending.
> That I say nought but suthfast thing.

Some of the grammatical forms here, it may be observed, are
even more modern than those we find in the English poetry of
the same age; in particular, Barbour uses our present *they*, *them*,
and *their* (or in the old spelling, *thai*, *thaim*, and *thar*), where
Chaucer and his countrymen still adhere to the Saxon *hey*, or *hi*,
hem, and *hir* or *her*. This may serve, with other considerations,
to refute the notion taken up by some modern writers, that
Barbour is an imitator of Chaucer: the Bruce, in fact, is an
earlier poem than the Canterbury Tales, and, as it was written
by Barbour in his old age, the probability is, that the Scottish
poet was absolutely the predecessor of the English; but at any
rate there is no more reason to believe that he imitated Chaucer
than that Chaucer imitated him. The one is never mentioned or
alluded to by the other, and there is no ground for supposing
that they were even acquainted with each other's works. From
his habits of locomotion, and frequent journeys to England, a
suspicion might arise that Barbour intended to write in the language of that country; but such a supposition is negatived by
the dialectic peculiarities which, notwithstanding a general resemblance in other respects, still distinguish his style from that
of his English contemporaries. That his language, we may add,
has not been modernized by the transcriber upon whom we are
dependent for the present text is, to a great extent, proved by
several considerable passages of the poem which are quoted by
Wynton being found with scarcely any variation in the work of
that chronicler, of which we have one manuscript believed to be
of as early a date as the year 1430 at the latest, or within little
more than a quarter of a century from the time when Barbour
lived. Besides, his language, as we have it, does not differ from

---

[1] Voided, or told, of cowardice.   [2] Make.

that of Wynton, who was his contemporary, although he was born perhaps thirty years later, and although he appears not to have composed his chronicle till after the commencement of the fifteenth century.

Barbour is far from being a poet equal to Chaucer; but there is no other English poet down to a century and a half after their day who can be placed by the side of the one any more than of the other. He has neither Chaucer's delicate feeling of the beautiful, nor his grand inventive imagination, nor his wit or humour; but in mere narrative and description he is, with his clear, strong, direct diction, in a high degree both animated and picturesque, and his poem is pervaded by a glow of generous sentiment, well befitting its subject, and lending grace as well as additional force to the ardent, bounding spirit of life with which it is instinct from beginning to end. The following passage, which occurs near the commencement, has been often quoted (at least in part); but it is too remarkable to be omitted in any exemplification of the characteristics of Barbour's poetry. He is describing the oppressions endured by the Scots during the occupation of their country by the English king, Edward I., after his deposition of his puppet Baliol:—

> And gif that ony man them by
> Had ony thing that was worthy,
> As horse, or hund, or other thing,
> That was pleasand to their liking!
> With right or wrang it wald have they.
> And gif ony wald them withsay,
> They suld swa do, that they suld tine[1]
> Other[2] land or life, or live in pine.
> For they dempt[3] them efter their will,
> Takand na kepe[4] to right na skill.[5]
> Ah! what they dempt them felonly![6]
> For gud knightis that war worthy,
> For little enchesoun[7] or them[8] nane
> They hangit be the neckbane.
> Alas[9] that folk, that ever was free,
> And in freedom wont for to be,

<hr>

[1] Lose.   [2] Either.   [3] Doomed, judged.
[4] Taking no heed, paying no regard.   [5] Reason.
[6] Ah! how cruelly they judged them!   [7] Cause.
[8] Both the sense and the metre seem to require that this *them* (in orig. *thame*) should be transferred to the next line; "they hangit them."
[9] Also, thus.

Through their great mischance and folly,
War treated then so wickedly,
That their faes' their judges ware :
What wretchedness may man have mais?[1]
  Ah! Freedom is a noble thing!
Freedom mays[2] man to have liking;[3]
Freedom all solace to man gives :
He lives at ease that freely lives!
A noble heart may have nane ease,
Na ellis nought that may him please
Giff freedom fail ye : for free liking
Is yarnit[5] ower[6] all other thing.
Na he that aye has livit free
May nought knaw well the property,[7]
The anger, na the wretched doom,
That is couplit[9] to foul thirldoom.[8]
But gif he had assay't it,
Then all perquer[10] he suld it wit ;
And suld think freedom mair to prise
Than all the gold in warld that is.

It is, he goes on to observe, by its contrary, or opposite, that
the true nature of everything is best discovered :—the value and
blessing of freedom, for example, are only to be fully felt in
slavery ; and then the worthy archdeacon, who, although the
humorous is not his strongest ground, does not want slyness or a
sense of the comic, winds up with a very singular illustration,
which, however, is more suited to his own age than to ours, and
may be suppressed here without injury to the argument.

But Barbour's design, no doubt, was to effect by means of this
light and sportive conclusion an easy and harmonious descent
from the height of declamation and passion to which he had been
carried in the preceding lines. Throughout his long work he
shows, for his time, a very remarkable feeling of the *art* of
poetry, both by the variety which he studies in the disposition
and treatment of his subject, and by the rare temperance and
self-restraint which prevents him from ever overdoing what he is
about either by prosing or raving. Even his patriotism, warm
and steady as it is, is wholly without any vulgar narrowness or
ferocity : he paints the injuries of his country with distinctness

---

¹ Faes.   ³ More.   ² Makes.
⁴ Pleasure.   ⁵ Yearned for, desired.   ⁶ Over, above.
⁷ The quality, the peculiar state or condition?
⁹ Coupled, attached.   ⁸ Thraldom.   ¹⁰ Exactly.

and force, and celebrates the heroism of her champions and
deliverers with all admiration and sympathy; but he never runs
into either the gasconading exaggerations or the furious depre-
ciatory invectives which would, it might be thought, have better
pleased the generality of those for whom he wrote. His understanding was too enlightened, and his heart too large, for that.
His poem stands in this respect in striking contrast to that of
Harry, the blind minstrel, on the exploits of Wallace, to be
afterwards noticed; but each poet suited his hero—Barbour, the
magnanimous, considerate, and far-seeing king; Blind Harry,
the indomitable popular champion, with his one passion and
principle, hatred of the domination of England, occupying his
whole soul and being.

We will now give one of Barbour's portraits—that of Sir James
of Douglas, the second figure in his canvas :—

> All men lovit him for his bounty !¹
> For he was of full fair effer,²
> Wise, courtais, and deboner ;
> Large and lovand als wes he,
> And ower all thing lovit lawty.³
> Lawty to love is greatumly :⁴
> Through lawty lives men righteously :
> With a' virtue and lawty
> A man may yet sufficiand be :
> And but⁵ lawty may nane have price,
> Whether he be wight, or be he wise ;
> For where it fallis na virtue
> May be of price, na of value,
> To mak a man so gud that he
> May simply callit gud man be.
> He was in all his deedes leal ;⁶
> For him dedeigned⁷ nought to deal
> With treachery ; na with falset :⁸
> His heart on high honour was set ;
> And him conteinit⁹ on sic manere
> That all him lovit that were him near.
> But he was sought so fair that we
> Suld speak greatly of his beauty :

¹ Goodness of nature and disposition.
² Appearance, or rather, perhaps, demeanour, bearing.
³ Loyalty.   ⁴ Great, magnanimous ?
⁵ One. The reading seems doubtful.   ⁶ Without.
⁷ Loyal, true, faithful.   ⁸ He deigned (it deigned him).
⁹ Falsehood.   ¹⁰ Conteined, held him in ?

In visage was he some deal grey,
And had black hair, as ic¹ heard say ;
But of limmes he was well made,
With banes great, and shuldres braid.
His body was well made and lennie,²
As they that saw him said to me.
When he was blythe³ he was lovely,
And meek and sweet in company ;
But wha in battle might him see
All other countenance had he.
And in speech⁴ lispit he some deal ;
But that set him right wonder well,
Till gud Ector of Troy might he
In mony thinges likent be.
Ector had black hair, as he had ;
And stark limmes, and right weil made ;
And lispit alsua⁵ as did he ;
And was fulfillit of beauty ;
And was curtais, and wise, and wight.
But of manheid and mickle might
Till Ector dar I nane compare
Of all that ever in warldes ware.
The whether,⁶ in his time as wrought he
That he suld greatly lovit be.

The only other passage for which we can make room is a short
extract from the narrative of the great day of Bannockburn,
which occupies altogether about 2000 lines of the poem, or
the whole of the eighth and ninth Books of Dr. Jamieson's
edition :—

There might men see men felly fight ;
And men that worthy war and wight
Do mony worthy vassalage.⁷
They faught as they war in a rage ;
For, when the Scottis archery
Saw their fayes⁸ so sturdily
Stand in to battle them again,⁹
With all their might and all their main
They laid on as men out of wit ;
And where they with full strak¹⁰ might hit

---

¹ I.
² These three words seem not to be in the MS., and the last of them at
least may be doubted.   ³ Cheerful, in good spirits.
⁴ Speech.   ⁵ Also.   ⁶ However.
⁷ Acts of valiant service.   ⁸ Foes.
⁹ Against.   ¹⁰ Stroke.

There might na armour stint their strak.
They to-fruhit[1] that they might ower-tak ;[2]
And with axes sic duntes[3] gave,
That they holmes and heades clave.
And their fayes right hardily
Met them, and dang on them doughtily
With wapins[4] that were styth[5] of steel :
There was the battle strekit[6] weil.
Sa great din there was of dints,
As wapins upon armour stints ;[7]
And of speares sa great bresting ;[8]
And sic thrang, and sic thristing ;[9]
Sic girning[10] graning,[11] and sa great
A noise as they gan other beat ;
And enemies[12] on every side ;
Givand and takand woundes wide ;
That it was hideous for to hear.
All their four battles with that were
Fechtand[13] in a front hailly.[14]
Ah ! mighty God, how doughtily
Schir Edward the Bruce and his men
Amang their fais conteinit them[15] then !
Fechtand in sa gud covine,[16]
Sa hardy, worthy, and sa fine,
That their vaward rushit was,
And maugre theirs, left the place ;[17]
And, till their great rout,[18] to warrand[19]
They went, that tane had upon hand[20]
Sa great annoy that they war effrayit
For Scottis, that them hard arrayit,
That than war in a schiltrum[21] all.
Wha happent into that fight to fall,
I trow again he suld nought rise.
There men might see on mony wise

---

[1] Quite broke in pieces. [2] Whatever they might overtake.
[3] Such blows. [4] Weapons. [5] Strong.
[6] Struck, foughten. [7] Rest, strike. [8] Breaking.
[9] Thrusting. [10] Grinning. [11] Groaning.
[12] War-cries. [13] Fighting.
[14] Wholly. Fighting all at once front to front?
[15] Maintained themselves? [16] Combination (covenant).
[17] The meaning evidently is, that the van of the English was broken, and left its ground, in spite of the efforts of its own side to support it.
[18] To their great confusion. [19] A place of shelter or refuge.
[20] Who had received?
[21] Supposed to mean a body of troops drawn up in a round form.

Hardiments[1] eschevit[3] doughtily;
And mony, that wight war and hardy,
Soon lyand under feet all dead,
Where all the field of blud was red.
Armee and whites[5] that they bare
With blud war so defoulit there,
That they might not descryit be.[4]
Ah, mighty God! wha then might see
That Stewart, Walter, and his rout,
And the gud Douglas, that was so stout,
Fechtand into that stalwart stour,[5]
He suld say[6] that till all honour
They war worthy, that in that fight
So fast pressit their fayes might,
That them rushit whar they yede.[7]
There men might see mony a steed
Fleand on stray,[8] that lord had nane.
Ah Lord! wha then gud tent had tane[9]
Till the gud Earl of Murrave[10]
And his, that so great routes gave,
And faught so fast in that betail,
Tholand[11] sic paines and travail,
That they and theirs made sic delat
That where they come they made them gat,[12]
Then might men hear ensignies[13] cry,
And Scottis men cry hardily,
On them! On them! On them! They fail;
With that so hard they gan assail,
And slew all that they might ower ta;[14]
And the Scottis archers alsua[15]
Shot amang them so doliverly,[16]
Engrievand them so greatomly,[17]

---

[1] Hardy deeds. [2] Achieved.
[3] Coats of white woollen. [4] Described.
[5] Fighting in that strong tumult of battle. [6] He would say.
[7] That drove them back wherever they went.
[8] Flying astray, at large. [9] Good heed had taken.
[10] Murray. [11] Sustaining.
[12] Out? But the word is perhaps wrong. Dr. Jamieson, whose pointing frequently shows that he did not understand the text, affords us no light or assistance in any of its difficulties by the miserable glossary which he has appended to his edition.
[13] Dr. Jamieson's only interpretation of the term is word of war. Here at least it seems rather to mean ensigns or standard-bearers, who raised the way-cry.
[14] Overtake. [15] Also.
[16] Nimbly, dexterously (our modern cleverly). [17] Distressing them so greatly.

That, what for them that with them faught,
That awa great routes to them raught,[1]
And preasit them full eagerly;
And what for arrows that felly
Mony great woundes gan them ma,[1]
And slew fast of their horse alsua,
That they wandyst[1] a little wey;
They dread sa greatly then to dey[1]
That their covine was wer and wer;[1]
For they that fechtand with them wer
Set hardiment, and strength, and will,
And heart, and courage als, thereuntil
And all their main, and all their might,
To put them fully to the flight.

This, it must be allowed, if not quite a Homeric strain, is strenuous and valiant writing for a Scottish archdeacon, advanced in years, of the fourteenth century.

COMPOUND ENGLISH PROSE.—MANDEVIL.—TREVISA.—WICLIF.— CHAUCER.

To the fourteenth century belong the earliest specimens of prose composition in our present mixed English that have been preserved. Among Sir Henry Ellis's contributions to the Pictorial History of England are two very curious extracts from the Arundel MS., No. 57, in the British Museum, entitled Ayenbyte of Inwyt, exemplifying the dialect of Kent in 1340. At the beginning of the MS. is this inscription:—" This boc is dan Michelis of Northgate, ywrite an Englis of his ozene hand; and is of the bochouse of Saynt Austine's of Cantorbori under the letters CC." The first of the passages (which occurs on folio 48), is as follows:—

The yonge gribound that is yet al novis that yernth efter eche heste that yernth bevore him, and ne maketh bote him weri and his time lyese. Ther of zet Yaopes the fable of the little hounde and of the lesse. The hond at eche time that he yherth his lhord cometh hom, he yernth to yeus hym, and lharth about his swere, and the lhord him maketh uayre chiere and him froteth, and maker him greate feste. The asse him be thozte thous wolde ich do, and ano wolde mi lhord me loule, beterre he wolde me make joye

---

[1] It should probably be wrought (wrought).
[2] Recoil for fear.
[3] That their combination was worse and worse.
[4] Maka.
[5] Die.

thet ieh serui eche daye thanne thise hounde thet him serueth of nazt. Hit nes nas longe afterward thet the asse ne yzez his lhord come hom, he biginth to lheap and yernth to yene him, and him pranth the net abuute his zuere and biginth zinge grauntliche. The sergeos thet hit y seze noine sieoes and byste than asse rint to the uolle, and ther of thet he wende habbe worthesipe and guod he hedde samne and harm.

The other passage (which occurs on folio 82, and which gives the date of the manuscript) comprises the Kentish version of the Lord's Prayer, Ave Maria, and Creed, after an introductory paragraph, which, it will be observed, although written as prose, is really in rhyme :—

Nou iche wille that ye ywryte hou hit is y'went : thet this boc is ywrite mid Englisc of Kent. This boc is ymad nor lewede men, vor uader and nor musler and uor other ken ham uor to lerze uram alle manyere zen that ine hare in wytte ne blete ne uoul wou. Huo ase God is his name yred thet this boc made God him yeue thet bread of angles of heuene and ther to his red and ondernonge his zaulo huanne thet he is dyad. Amen.

Ymende thet this boc is uolueld ine the eue of the holy apostles Symon and Judas of ane brother of the cloystre of Sanynt Austin of Caunterberi ine the years of our lhordes beringe, 1340.

Pater Noster.—Vader oure thet art ine heuene y halzed by thi name, cominde thi riche, y worthe thi wil ase in heuene ine erthe, bread oure eche dayes yef ous to day, and nor let ous oure yeldinges ase and we norieteth oure yelderes, and ne ous led nazt in to nondinge, ac vri ous uram queade. zo by hit.

Ave Maria.—Hayl Marie of thonke uol. ... dby mid the, yblissed thou ine wymmen, and yblissed thet onet of thine wombe. zuo by hit.

Credo.—Ich leue ine God uader almizti, makere of heuene and of erthe, and ine Jesu Crist his zone onlepi our lhord, that ykend is of the holy Gost, ybore of Marie mayde, ypyned under Pontis Pilate, ynayled a rode, dyade and be bered, yede down to helle, thane thridde day arus uram the dyade, stenz to heuenes, sit athe rizt half of God the uader almizti, thannes to comene he is to deme the quike and the dyade. Ich yleue ine the holy Gost, holy cherche generalliche, meneue of halzen, leaneue of zennes, of uleswe arisinge, and lyf eurelestinde. zuo by hit.

The sound here represented by z in certain words, such as *almizti*, it should be noticed, is really a guttural, the same which at a later date came to be usually indicated by gh. In fact the character is a g, or something between a g and a y, and not at all our modern z.

Sir Henry adds that the Harleian MS. No. 1022, contains several tracts in Northern English, of nearly the same age; among which is a poem on the Decalogue, translated from the Latin in 1357, at the request of Archbishop Horseley, by John

do Tavstoke, a monk of St. Mary's, York. "The reader," it is
further stated, " who is inquisitive as to dialects will find among
the Harleian manuscripts one, No. 221, which contains a Dictionary in English and Latin, the former language in the dialect
of the East Country, compiled ninety years later by a friar
preacher, a recluse at Lynne in Norfolk."

Our oldest Mixed English prose author is Sir John Mandevil,
whose Voyages and Travels, a singular repertory of the marvellous
legends of the middle ages, have been often printed. The best
editions are that published in 8vo., at London, in 1725, and the
reprint of it in the same form in 1839, " with an introduction,
additional notes, and a glossary, by J. O. Halliwell, Esq., F.S.A.,
F.R.A.S." The author's own account of himself and of his book
is given in an introductory address, or Prologue :—

And, for als moch as it is long time passed that there was no general
passage ne vyage over the sea, and many men desiren for to hear speak of
the Holy Lond, and ben[1] thereof great solace and comfort, I, John Maun-
deville, knight, all be it I be not worthy, that was born in England, in the
town of Saint Albons, passed the sea in the year of our Lord Jesu Christ
1322, in the day of Saint Michel ; and bider-to have ben[2] longtime over
the sea, and have seen and gone thorough many divers londs, and many
provinces, and kingdoms, and isles, and have passed thorough Tartary,
Persie, Ermonie[3] the Little and the Great; thorough Libye, Chaldee, and
a great part of Ethiop; thorough Amazoyn, Ind the Lass and the More, a
great party ; and thorough out many other isles, that ben abouten Ind ;
where dwellen many divers folks, and of divers manners and laws, and of
divers shapps of men. Of which londs and isles I shall speak more plainly
hereafter. And I shall devise you some party of things that there ben,[4]
when time shall ben after it may best come to my mind ; and specially
for hem[2] that will[5] and are in purpose for to visit the Holy City of
Jerusalem, and the holy places that are thereabout. And I shall tell the
way that they should holden thider. For I have often times passed and
ridden the way, with good company of many lords, God be thanked.

And ye shull understond that I have put this book out of Latin into
French, and translated it agen out of French into English, that every
man of my nation may understood it. But lords and knights, and other
noble and worthy men, that con[6] Latin but little, and han ben beyond
the sea, knowen and understonden gif I err in devising, for forgetting or
else; that they mowe[7] redress it and amend it. For things passed out,
of long time, from a man's mind, or from his sight, turnen soon into forgetting ; because that mind of man ne may not ben comprehended ne
withholden for the frcelty of mankind.

---

[1] Have.	[2] Been.	[3] Armenia.	[4] Be.
[5] Them ('em).	[5] Wish.	[6] Know.	[7] May.

Mandevil is said to have returned to England in 1356, or after an absence of thirty-four years; and, as he is recorded to have died at Liege in 1371, his book must have been written early in the latter half of the fourteenth century. Of the many copies of it which exist in manuscript, some are as old as the close of that century; so that the language may be presumed to have been preserved nearly as he wrote it. Divested of the old spelling, it will be seen from the above specimen to be still very readily intelligible; indeed it is remarkable for its clearness and correctness. Our other extracts, however, shall be given with the spelling of the time, as exhibited in the Cottonian MS. Titus c. xvi., which is believed to have been written about the year 1400. The following is the Seventh Chapter, entitled Of the Pilgrimages in Jerusalem, and of the Holy Places thereabouts, as contributed after that MS. to the Pictorial History of England by Sir Henry Ellis.

After for to speke of Jerusalem the holy cytee, see schull undirstondo that it stont full faire betwene hilles, and there be no ryveres ne welles, but watar cometh by condyte from Ebron. And see schulle understondo that Jerusalem of olde tyme, unto the tyme of Melchisedech, was cleped Jebus; and after it was clept Salem, unto the tyme of Kyng David, that put these two names to gider, and cleped it Jebusalem. And after that Kyng Salomon cleped it Jerosolomye. And after that men cleped it Jerusalem, and so it is cleped zit. And aboute Jerusalem is the kyngdom of Surrye.[1] And there besyde, is the lond of Palestyne. And besyde it is Ascalon. And besyde that is the lond of Maritanie. But Jerusalem is in the lond of Judee; and it is clept Jude, for that Judas Machabeus was kyng of that contree. And it marcheth estward to the kyngdom of Arabye; on the south syde to the lond of Egipt; and on the west syde to the grete see. On the north syde toward the kyngdom of Surrye, and to the see of Cypre.

In Jerusalem was wont to be a Patriark and Erchebyshopes, and Bisshoppes abouten in the contree. Abowte Jerusalem be theise cytees; Ebron at seven myle, Jerico at six myle, Bersabee at eyght myle, Ascalon at xvii myle, Jaff at xvi myle, Ramatha at iij myle, and Bethleem at ij myle. And a ij myle from Bethleem toward the southe is the chirche of Beynt Karitot that was abbot there, for whom thei maden moche doel[2] amongs the monks whan he scholde dye, and zit be in-moornynge in the wise that thei maden her[3] lamentacon for him the first tyme, and it is full gret pytee to beholde. This contree and lond of Jerusalem hath ben in many dyverse nacones hondes. And often therfore hath the contree suffred meche tribulacion for the synne of the people that duelle ther: for

---

[1] Syria.　　　[2] Dolour, sorrow (Fr. dule).　　　[3] Their.

that contree hath he in the honds of all nacyones : that is to seyne of Jewes, of Chananees, Assiryenes, Perses, Medoynes, Macedoynes, of Grekes, Romaynes, of Cristenmen, of Sarrazines, Barbaryenes, Turkes, Tartaryenes, and of manye othere dyverse nacyons. For God wole not that it be longe in the honds of traytours ne of synneres, be thei cristene or other. And now have the hethene men holden that lond in her honds al ser and more. But thei schull not holde it longe zif God wold.

And we schull undirstonde that whan men comen to Jerusalem her first pilgrymage is to the chirche of the Holy Sepulcr wher oure Lord was burryed, that is with oute the cytee on the north syde. But it is now enclosed in with the ton wall. And there is a full fair chirche all rownd, and open above, and covered with leed. And on the west syde is a fair tour and an high for belles strongly made. And in the myddes of the chirche is a tabernacle as itwor a lytyll hows, made with a low lityll dore ; and that tabernacle is made in manor of a half a compas right curiously and richely made of gold and azure and othere riche coloures, full nobelyche made. And in the ryght side of that tabernacle is the sepulcre of oure Lord. And the tabernacle is viij fote long and v fote wyde, and xj fote in heghte. And it is not longe sithe the sepulcre was all open, that men myghte kisse it and touche it. But for pilgrymes that comen thider peyned hem to breke the ston in pecees, or in poudr; therefore the Soudan[1] hath do make a wall aboute the sepulcr that noman may towche it. But in the left syde of the wall of the tabernacle is well the heighte of a man, is a gret ston, to the quantytee of a mannes hed, that was of the holy sepulcr, and that ston kissen the pilgrymes that comen thider. In that tabernacle ben no wyndowes, but it is all made light with lampes that hangen befor the sepulcr. And there is a lampe that hongeth before the sepulcr that brenneth light, and on the Gode fryday it goth out be him self, at that hour that oure Lord roos fro deth to lyve. Also within the chirche at the right syde besyde the queer of the churche is the Mount of Calvarye, wher oure Lord was don on the cros. And it is a roche of white colour, and a lytill medled with red. And the cros was set in a morteys in the same roche, and on that roche dropped the woundes of our Lord, whan he was pyned on the cros, and that is cleped Golgatha. And men gon up to that Golgatha be degrees.[2] And in the place of that morteys was Adames bed found after Noes flode, in tokene that the synnes of Adam schokle ben bought in that same place. And upon that roche made Abraham sacrifice to our Lord. And there is an Awter, and before that Awter lyen Godefray de Boloyne, and Bawdewyn, and othere cristene Kyngs of Jerusalem. And ther nygh wher our Lord was crucyfied is this writen in Greew,[3] *Otheos builios yemon psionis ergast, suthius rmeentis gye,*[4] that is to seyne in Latyn, 'Hic Deus noster Rex, ante secula, operatus est salutem in medio terre;' that is to seye 'This God

---

[1] Sultan.   [2] Steps.   [3] Greek.

[4] In the printed editions the Greek is ὁ δὲ βασιλεὺς ἡμῶν πρὸ αἰῶνος εἰργάσατο σωτηρίαν ἐν μέσῳ τῆς γῆς.

oure Kyng, before the worldes, hath wrought hele in mydde of the Erthe.'
And also on that roche where the cros was sett, is writen with in the
roche these wordes, *Cyos myst ys basis toupisteon they thermofy*,' that is to
mayne in Latyn, 'Quod vides est fundamentum totius fidei Mundi hujus;'
that is to seye, 'That thou seest is ground of all the world and of this
feyth.' And see schull vndirstonde that whan oure Lord was don upon
the cros, he was xxxiij zer and lij monethes of olde. And the prophecye
of David sayth that, 'Quadraginta annis proximus fui generacioni huic;'
that is to seye, 'Forty zeer was I neighbore to this kynrede.' And thus
schulde it seme that the prophecyes ne wor not trewe, but thei ben bothe
trewe : for in old tyme men maden o zeer of x monethes, of the whiche
March was the firste and December was the last. But Gayus that was
Emperour of Rome patten thilke ij monethes there to Janyuer and
Feverer, and ordeyned the zeer of xij monethes, that is to seye ccc.lxv
dayes, without leep zerr, after the propre cours of the Sonne. And
therefore after cowntynge of x monethes of the zerr, he dyede in the xl
zeer as the prophete seyde : and after the zeer of xij monethes he was of
age xxxiij zeer and iij monethes. Also within the Mount of Calvarie, on
the right side, is an Awter, wher the piler lyzth that oure lord Jhesu was
bounden to whan he was scourged ; and there besyde iiij sole, ben liij
pilers of ston that allweys droppen water. And somme seyn that thei
wepen for our Lordes deth. And nygh that awtier is a place under erthe
xlij degrees of depnesse, wher the only croys was founden by the wytt of
Seynte Elyne, under a roche wher ther Jewes had hidde it. And that
was the verray croys assayed. For thei founden iij crosses, on of our
Lord, and ij of the ij thefes. And Seynte Elyne preved hem on a ded
body that aros from deth to lyve, whan that it was leyd on it that our
Lord dyed on. And there by in the wall is the place wher the iiij nayles
of our Lord were hidd, for he had ij in his honds, and ij in his feet : and
of on of theise the Emperour of Constantynople made a brydill to his hors,
to ber him in bataylle, and thorgh vertue there of he overcam his enemyes,
add wan all the lond of Asye the lesse, that is to seye Turkye, Ermonye the
lasse and the more, and from Surrye to Jerusalem, from Arabye to Persie,
from Mesopotaymе to the kingdom of Halappa,[2] from Egypte the highe
and the lowe, and all the othere kyngdomes unto the depe of Ethiope, and
in to Ynde the lesse that thanne was cristerne. And there was in that
tyme many gode holy men and holy Heremytes of whom the book of
Fadres lyfes speketh and thei ben now in paynemes and Sarazines
honds. And in mydds of that chirche is a compas, in the whiche Joseph
of Aramathie leyde the body of our Lord whan he had taken him down of
the croys, and wer he wasshed the wounds of our Lord. And that
compas, sey men is the mydds of the world. And in the chirche of the
Sepulchre on the north syde is the place wher oure Lord was put in preson.
For he was in preson in many places. And ther is a partye of the cheyne

---

[1] In the printed editions, ὃ ἐθεὶς, ἐστὶ βάσις τῆς πίστεως ὅλης τοῦ κόσμου
τούτου. [2] Aleppo.

that he was bounden with. And ther he appered first to Marie Magdaleyne, whan he was rysen, and sche wende[1] that he had ben a gardener.
In the chirche of Seynt Sepuker was wont to be chanons of the ordr of
Seynt Augustyn, and hadden a Priour, but the Patriark was her
sovereyn. And with onte the dores of the chirche, on the right syde as
men gone upward xviij greces,[2] seyd our Lord to his moder, ' *Mulier, ecce
filius tuus*,' that is to seye, ' Woman, lo thi sone.' And after that he
seyde to John his disciple, ' *Ecce Mater tua*,' that is to seyne, ' Lo behold
thi moder.' And theise words he seyde on the cros. And on theise greces
went our Lord whan he bar the cros on his schulder. And under this
grees is a chapell and in that chapell syngen prestes, Yndyenes,[3] that is to
seye prests of Ynde, noght after onre law, but after her, and al wey thei
maken her sacrement of the awtier, seyenge *Pater noster* and othere
prayeres ther with. With the whiche preyeres thei seye the words that
the sacrement is made of. For thei ne knowe not the addicions that many
Popes han made, but thei synge with gode devocion. And there ner is
the place where that onre Lord rested him whan he was wery for berynge
of the cros. And see schull understonde that before the chirche of the
Sepulcre is the cytee more feble than in ony other partie, for the grete
playn that is betwene the chirche and the citee. And toward the est syde,
with onte the walles of the cytee, is the Vale of Josaphath, that toucheth
to the walles as though it wer a large dych. And above that Vale of
Josaphath out of the cytee is the chirche of Seynt Stevene wher he was
stoned to deth. And there beside is the gildene[4] zate that may not be
opened, be the which zate onr Lord entred on Palmesonday upon an asse,
and the zate opened azenst him whan he wolde go unto the Temple.
And zit apperen the steppes of the asses feet in iiij places of the degrees
that ben of full harde ston. And before the chirche of Seynt Sepuler
toward the south, a ca pass is the gret Hospitall of Seynt John, of the
whiche the Hospitleres hadd here foundacion. And with Inne the Palays
of the seke men of that Hospitall be sixe score and iiij pileres of ston.
And in the walles of the hows, with onte the nombre abovesayd, there be
lillj pileres that beren up the hows. And fro that Hospitall to go toward
the est is a full fayr chirche that is clept Notre Dame la graund. And
than is there another chirche right nygh that is clept Notre Dame de
Latyne. And there were Marie Cleophes and Marie Magdaleyne and teren
here heer,[5] whan our Lord was peyned in the cros.

The following is the account of Mahomet in the fourteenth
chapter.

And see schull vnderstonde that Machometo was born in Arabye, that
was first a pore knave that kept cameles that wenten with marchantes for
marchandise, and so befell that he wente with the marchandes in to Egipt, ·
and thei were thanne cristene in tho[6] partyes. And at the desartes of

---

| [1] Weened, thought. | [2] Steps. | [3] Indians. |
| [4] Gilded. | [5] Tore their hair. | [6] Those. |

Arabye he wente in to a chapell wher a Eremyte duelte.   And whan he
entred in to the chapell, that was but a lytill and a low thing, and had
but a lityl dor' and a low, than the entree began to wexe so gret and so
large, and so high, as though it had be of a gret mynstr, or the zate of a
paleys.   And this was the first myracle the Sarazins seyn that Machomete
dide in his zouthe.   After began ho for to wexe wyse and riche; and he
was a gret Astronomer; and, after, he was gouernour and prince of the
lond of Corrodane, and he gouerned it full wisely, in such manere, that
whan the Prince was ded, he toke the lady to wyfe that highte Gadrige.
And Machomete fell often in the grete sikenesse that men calle the fallynge
euyll.   Wherfore the lady was full sory that euere scho toke him to
husbonde.   But Machomete made hire to beleeve that all tymes when he
fell so, Gabriel the angel cam for to speke with him, and for the grete light
and brightnesse of the angell, he myghte not susteyne him fro fallynge.
And therefore the Sarazins seyn that Gabriel cam often to speke with him.
This Machomete regned in Arabye, the zeer of our Lord Jhesu Crist sixe
hundred and ten, and was of the generacion of Ysmael, that was Abra-
hames sone that he gat upon Agar his chambrere; [2] and therefore ther be
Sarazins that be clept Ismaelytenes; and summe Agarzenes, of Agar, and
the othere propurly be clept Sarrazines of Sarra; and summe be clept
Moabytes, and summe Amonytes, for the two sones of Loth, Moab and
Amon, that he begatt on his daughtres, that were aftirward grete erthely
princes.   And also Machomete loued wel a gode heremyte that duelled in
the desertes, a myle from Mount Synay in the weye that men gon fro
Arabye toward Caldee, and toward Ynde, o [3] day Iorney fro the See wher
the Marchaunts of Venyse comen often for merchandise.   And so often
wente Machomete to this heremyte that all his men were wrothe, for he
wolde gladly bere this heremyte preche, and make his men wake all
nyght; and therefore his men thoughten to putte the heremyte to deth;
and so befell vpon a nyght that Machomete was dronken of god wyn
and he fell on slepe, and his men toke Machomete's swerd out of his
schethe, while he slepte, and there with thei slowgh this heremyte and
putte his swerd al blody in his schethe azen.   And at morwe whan
he found the heremyte ded, he was fully sory and wroth, and wolde haue
don his men to deth, but thei all with on accord (said) that he him self had
slayn him whan he was dronken and schewed him his swerd all blody,
and he trowed that thei hadden seyd soth. [4]   And than he cursed the
wyn, and all tho that drynken it.   And therefore Sarrazines that be
deuout drynken neuer no wyn, but sum drynken it priuyly, for zif thei
dronken it openly thei scholde ben reproued.   But thei drynken gode
beuerage, and swete and noryshynge, that is made of Galamell, and that
is that men maken sugr' of that is of right gode sauor, and it is gode for
the brest.   Also it befalleth sumtyme that cristene men become Sarazines outher for pouertee or for symplenesse, or elles for her owne wykked-

---

ness. And therefore the Archidamyn or the Flamyn, as¹ our Echebisshopp or Bisshopp, whan he receyueth hem seyth thus: *Ia illec alla syla Machomet ruers alla*, that is to seye, " There is no God but on and Machomete his messager."

We have already had occasion to quote a short passage from John de Trevisa's translation of Higden's Polychronicon, in speaking of the new mode of teaching Latin in schools, through the medium of English instead of French, which Trevisa tells us had been introduced shortly before the time at which he was then writing, which was the year 1385. His translation of Higden, which was undertaken at the request of Thomas Lord Berkeley, to whom he was chaplain, is stated at the end to have been finished in 1387. It was printed by Caxton in 1482, with a continuation bringing down the narrative from 1357, at which Higden had stopped, to 1460; but, besides that Trevisa's text is extensively altered in this edition both by insertions and omissions, his language is modernized throughout. " I, William Caxton, a simple person," says the worthy printer, in his Preface, " have endeavoured me to writ first over all the said book of Polychronicon, and somewhat have changed the rude and old English, that is to wit, certain words which in these days be neither used ne understood." Yet not more than the ordinary span of a single human life had elapsed since the translation had been executed by Trevisa, no doubt in the current English of his day; such was the rapid growth of the language in the earlier half of the fifteenth century. Besides the Polychronicon, Trevisa rendered several other works from the Latin into his mother tongue; and some of his other translations are still preserved in manuscript. Of a version of the whole of both the Old and New Testaments, however, which he is said to have executed, nothing is now known.

The oldest English translation we have of the Bible is that of Wiclif. John de Wiclif, or Wycliffe, died at about the age of sixty in 1384, and his translation of the Scriptures from the Vulgate appears to have been finished two or three years before. The New Testament has been several times printed: first in folio in 1731 under the care of the Rev. John Lewis; next in 4to. in 1810 under that of the Rev. H. H. Baber; lastly in 4to. in 1841, and again in 1846, in Bagster's English Hexapla. And now the

Old Testament has also been given to the world from the
Clarendon press, at the expense of the University of Oxford,
admirably edited by the Rev. J. Forshall and Sir Frederick
Madden, in four magnificent quartos, Oxford, 1850. The following extracts from Wiclif's Bible were communicated to the
Pictorial History of England by Sir Henry Ellis from one of the
best manuscripts of the entire translation, the Royal MS. 1 C. viii.
in the British Museum. The first from the Old Testament, consists of part of the fifteenth chapter of Exodus, containing the
Song of Moses :—

Thanne Moises song, and the sones of Israel, this song to the Lord;
and thei seiden, Synge we to the Lord for he is magnified gloriousli; he
castide down the hors and the stiere into the see. My strengthe and my
preisyng is the Lord, and he is maad to me into heelthe; this is my God:
y schal glorifie hym the God of my fadir: and y schal enhaunce hym:
the Lord is as a man fiʒter: his name is almiʒti. He castide doun into
the see the charis of Farao and his oost, his chosun princes weren drenchid
in the reed see, the deepe watris hiliden them; thei ʒeden doun into the
depthe as a stoon. Lord thi riʒt hond is magnyfied in strengthe: Lord
thi riʒt hond smoot the enemye: and in the mychilnesse of thi glorie thou
hast put doun all thyn adversaryes; thou sentist thine ire that devouride
hem as stobil: and watris weren gaderid in the spirit of thi woodnesse;
flowinge watir stood: deep watris weren gaderid in the middis of the see:
the enemy seide, Y schal pursue and y schal take, y schal departe spuylis:
my soule schal be fillid: I schal drawe out my swerde: myn hond schal
sle hem. Thi spirit blew; and the see hilide hem, thei weren drenchid as
leed, in grete watris. Lord, who is lyk thee in stronge men: who is lyk
thee: thou art greet doere in boolynesse; ferdful and p'isable, and doyng
miracles; thou heldist forth thine hond, and the erthe devouride hem:
Thou were ledere, in thi merci, to thi puple, which thou aʒen bouʒtest,
and thou hast bore hym, in thi strengthe, to thin holi dwellyng place:
puplis stieden and weren wroothe: sorewis heldyn the dwelleris of Flistiym;
thanne the pryncis of Edom weren disturblid; trembling heelde the stronge
men of Moab: all the dwelleris of Canaan weren starke. Inward drede
falle on hem: and outward drede in the greetnesse of thin arm. Be thei
maad unmoovable as a stoon, til thi puple passe, lord, til this thi puple
passe. Whom thou weldidist, thou schalt brynge hem in and thou schalt
plaunte in the hil of thin eritage: in the moost stidefast dwellyng place
which thou hast wrouʒt, Lord, Lord, thi seyntuarie which thin hondis
made stidefast. The Lord schal regne in to the world and forth'e.
Forsothe Farao a ridere entride with his charis and knyʒtis in to the see:
and the Lord brouʒte the watris of the see on him; sotheli the sones of
Israel ʒeden bi the drie place, in the myddis of the see.

Therfore Marie profetesse, the sister of Aaron, tooke a tympan in hir
hond, and all the wymmen ʒeden out aftir hyr with tympans companyes:

to which sche song before and mekle, Synge we to the Lord: for he is
magnyfied gloriously, he castkle doun into the see the hors and the stiere
of hym.

The specimen selected from the New Testament is the last
chapter of St. Luke :—

But in o day of the woke ful cerli thei camen to the grave, and broughten
swete smelling spicrs that thei hadden arayed. And thei founden the
stoon turnyd awey fro the graue. And thei geiten in and foundun not the
bodi of the Lord Jhesus. And it was don, the while thei weren astonyed
in thought of this thing, lo twey men stodun bisidis hem in schynyng
cloth. And whanne thei dredden and bowiden her semblaunt into erthe,
thei seiden to hem, what seeken ye him that lyueth with deede men?
He is not here: but he is risun: bane ye minde how he spak to you
whanne he was yit in Golilee, and seide, for it behoueth mannes sone to be
bitaken into the hondis of synful men: and to be crucifyed: and the
thridde day to rise agen? And thei bithoughten on blse wordis, and thei
geiten agen fro the graue: and teeklen alle these thingis to the elleuene
and to alle othere. And there was Marye Maudeleyn and Jone and Marye
of James, and othere wymmen that weren with hem, that seiden to
Apostlis these thingis. And these wordis were myn bifore hem as
madnesse and thei bileueden not to hem; but Petre roos up and ran to
the graue, and he bowide doun, and sigh the lynen clothis liynge aloone,
and he wente by himsilf, woudrynge on that that was don.

And lo tweyne of him wenten in that day into a castel, that was fro
Jerusalem the space of sixty furlongis, by name Emaus. And thei
speken togidre of alle these thingis that hadden bifalle. And it was don
the while thei talkiden, and soughten by himsilf: Jesus himsilf neighede
and wente with hem. But her yghen weren holdun, that thei knewen him
not. And he seide to hem, What ben these wordis that ye speken togidere
wondringe: and ye ben sorewful? And oon, whos name was Cleofas,
answerde and seyde, Thou thi silf art a pilgrim in Jerusalem, and hast
thou not knowun what thingis ben don in it those dayes? To whom he
seyde, What thingis? and thei seiden to him, Of Jhesus of Nazareth, that
was a man profete myghti in werk and word bifore God and al the puple.
And how the higheste preestis of our Princis bitoken him into dampnacioun
of deeth: and crucifieden him. But we hopiden that he schulde haue
agen boughte Israel: and now on alle these thingis, the thridde day is to
day that these thingis weren don. But also summe wymmen of ouris
maden us aferd whiche bifore day weren at the graue. And when his
bodi was not foundun, thei camen and seiden that they sighen also a sight
of aungels, which seiden that he lyueth. And summe of ouren wenten to
the graue, and thei foundun so as the wymmen seiden; but they foundun
not him. And he seide to him, A foolis and slowe of herte to bileue in
alle thingis that the profetis han spoken; Wher it bihofte not Crist to
suffre these thingis, and so to entre into his glorye? And he began at
Moyses and at alle the profetis and declaride to hem in alle scripturis that
weren of him. And thei camen nygh the castel whidir thei wenten: and

he made countenaunce that he wolde go ferthir. And thei constreyneden him and seiden, Dwelle with us, for it draweth to nyght, and the day is now bowed doun; and he entride with them. And it was don the while he sat at the mete with hem, he took breed and blisside and brak, and took to hem. And the yghen of hem weren opened, and thei knewen hem; and he vanyschide fro her yghen. And thei seiden togidere, Wher oure herte was not brennynge in us, while he spak to us in the weye, and opened to us Scripturis? And thei risen up in the same our and wenten agen into Jerusalem, and foundun the ellevene gaderid togidre, and hem that weren with him, seiynge, that the Lord is risun verili: and apperid to Symount. And thei tolden what thingis weren don in the weye, and how thei knewen him in the brakinge of bred. And the while thei spaken these thingis Jhesus stood in the myddil of hem and seide to hem; Pees to you, I am, nyl ye drede: but thei weren affrayed and agast and gessiden him to be a spirit. And he seide to hem, what ben ye troubled; and thoughtis camen up into youre hertis? Se ye my hondis and my feet; for I my silf am, feele ye and se ye, for a spirit hath not flesch and boonus as ye seen that I have. And whenne he hadde seid this thing; he schewide houdis and feet to hem. And yet while thei bileueden not and wondriden for Joye; he seide, Han ye here ony thing that schal be etun? and thei profriden to him a part of a fisch roostyd, and a honycomb. And whanne he hadde etun bifore hem, he toke that that lefte and gaf to hem, and seyde to hem, These ben the wordis that I spak to you, whanne I was yit with you, for it is nede that alle thingis ben fulfillid that ben writun in the Lawe of Moyses and in the profetis and in Salmes of me. Thanne he openide to hem with that thei schulden undirstonde Scripturis. And he seide to hem, For thus it is writun, and thus it bihofte Crist to suffre; and rise agen fro death in the thridde day; and penaunce and remissioun of synnes to be prechid in his name into alle folkis bigynnynge at Jerusalem. And ye ben witnessis of these thingis. And I schal send the biheest of my fadir into you, but sitte ye in the citee till that ye ben clothid with vertu fro an high. And he leidde hem forth into Bethanye; and whan hise hondis weren lift up, he blesside hem. And it was don the while he blessid hem he departide fro hem, and was borun into hevene. And thei worschipiden and wenten agen into Jerusalem, with gret ioye; and weren euer more in the temple heriynge and blessinge God.

It would appear from these two specimens that the English of this early version of the Bible is considerably less antique in the New Testament than in the Old. Wiclif is also the author of many original writings in his native language, in defence of his reforming views in theology and church government, some of which have been printed, but most of which that are preserved still remain in manuscript. His style is everywhere coarse and slovenly, though sometimes animated by a popular force or boldness of expression.

Chaucer is the author of three separate works in prose; a

translation of Boethius de Consolatione Philosophiæ, printed by Caxton, in folio, without date, under the title of The Boke of Consolacion of Philosophie, wich that Boecius made for his Comforte and Consolacion ; a Treatise on the Astrolabe, addressed to his son Lewis, in 1391, and printed (at least in part) in the earlier editions of his works ; and The Testament of Love, an apparent imitation of the treatise of Boethius, written towards the end of his life, and also printed in the old editions of his collected works. But, perhaps, the most highly finished, and in other respects also the most interesting, of the great poet's prose compositions are the Tale of Meliboeus and the Parson's Tale, in the Canterbury Tales. The former, which he tells himself as one of the company of pilgrims, and which is a very close translation from a French treatise, entitled Le Livre de Melibee et de Dame Prudence (existing both in prose and verso), has been supposed, as mentioned in a preceding page, to be written in a sort of blank measure or rhythm, perhaps, Mr. Guest thinks, the same that is called *cadence* in the House of Fame : the following extract is from the earlier portion of the Tale, where the rhythmical style is conceived to be most marked :—

This Melibee answerd unto his wife Prudence ; I purpose not, quod he, to werken by thy counsel for many causes and reasons, for certes every wight wold hold me than [1] a fool ; this is to says, if I for thy counselling wold change things that been ordained and affirmed by so many wise men. Secondly, I say that all women ben wick, and none good of hem [2] all ; for of a thousand men, saith Salomon, I found o [3] good man ; but certes of all women good woman found I never. And also, certes, if I governed me by thy counsel it should seem that I had yeve [4] thee over me the maistry ; and God forbid that it so were ; for Jesus Sirach saith, that if the wif have the maistry she is contrarious to her husband ; and Salomon sayeth, Never in thy life, to thy wife, ne to thy child, ne to thy friend, ne yeve no power over thyself ; for better it were that thy children ax [5] of thee thinges that hem needeth, than thou ax thyself in the hands of thy children. And also, if I wol werch by they counselling, certes it must be some time secree [6] till it were time that it be knowen ; and this ne may not be if I should be counselled by thee. For it is written, the janglery of women ne can nothing hide, save that which they wot not. After, the philosopher sayeth, In wicked counsel women venquishen men. And for these reasons I ne owe not [7] to be counselled by thee. [8]

---

[1] Then.   [2] Them.   [3] One.   [4] Given.
[5] Ask.   [6] Secret.   [7] Ought not.
[8] These three last sentences are not in the MSS., but are an insertion of Tyrwhitt's, translated from the French *Melibee*.

When Dame Prudence, full debonairly and with great patience, had
heard all that her husband liked for to say, then asked she of him licence
for to speak, and said in this wise: My lord, quod she, as to your first
reason it may lightly been answered, for I say that it is no folly to change
counsel when the thing is changed, or else when the thing seemeth otherwise than it seemed before.   And moreover I say, though that ye have
sworn and behight[1] to perform your emprise, and nevertheless ye waive to
perform thilk same emprise by just cause, men should not say therefore ye
were a liar ne forsworn, for the book saith that the wise man maketh no
leasing when he turneth his courage[2] for the better.   And, all be it that
your emprise be established and ordained by great multitude of folk, yet
thar[3] you not accomplish thilk ordinance, but you liketh,[4] for the truth of
things and the profit ben rather founden in few folk that ben wise and full
of reason, than by great multitude of folk there[5] every man cryeth and
clattereth what him liketh; soothly swich[6] multitude is not honest.   As
to the second reason, whereas ye say that all women ben wick; save your
grace, certes ye despise all women in this wise, and he that all despiseth, as
saith the book, all displeaseth.   And Senek saith, that who so wol have
sapience shall no man dispraise, but he shall gladly teach the science that
he can[7] without presumption or pride, and swich things as he nought can
he shall not be ashamed to lear hem,[8] and to inquere of less folk than
himself.   And, sir, that there hath ben full many a good woman may
lightly be preved; for certes, sir, our lord Jesu Christ wold never han
descended to be born of a woman if all women had be wicked; and after
that, for the great bounty that is in women, our lord Jesu Christ, when he
was risen from death to life, appeared rather to a woman than to his apostles.
And, though that Salomon said he found never no good woman, it followeth
not therefore that all women be wicked; for, though that he ne found no
good woman, certes many another man hath found many a woman full good
and true; or else, peradventure, the intent[9] of Salomon was this, that in
sovereign bounty[10] he found no woman; this is to say, that there is no
wight that hath sovereign bounty save God above, as he himself recordeth
in his Evangelies; for there is no creature so good that him ne wanteth
somewhat of the perfection of God that is his maker.   Your third reason
is this: ye say that if that ye govern you by my counsel it should seem
that ye had yeve me the maistry and the lordship of your person. Sir,
save your grace, it is not so; for, if so were that no man should be counselled, but only of hem that han lordship and maistry of his person, men
nold not be counselled so often; for, soothly, thilk man that asketh
counsel of a purpose, yet hath he free choice whether he wol work after
that counsel or none.   And as to your fourth reason, there as yesain,[11]
that the janglery of women can hide things that they wol not, as whoso

---

[1] Engaged, pledged yourself.   [5] Heart, inclination.
[2] It behoveth.   [4] Unless it liketh you.   [5] Where.
[6] Such.   [7] Knows, understands.   [8] Learn them.
[9] Meaning.   [10] Goodness.   [11] Whereas you say.

saith that a woman cannot hide that she wot; sir, these words ben understood of women that ben janglereeses and wicked, of which women men
sain that three things driven a man out of his house, that is to say, smoke,
dropping of rain, and wicked wives; and of swich women Salomon saith,
that a man were better dwell in desert than with a woman that is riotous;
and, sir, by your leave, that am not I; for ye have full often assayed my
great silence and my great patience, and eke how well that I can hide and
hele¹ things that men oughten secretly to hiden. And, soothly, as to your
fifth reason, whereas ye say that in wicked counsel women venquishen men,
God wot that thilk reason stant here in no stead; for understondeth now
ye axen counsel for to do wickedness, and if ye wol werken wickedness,
and your wife restraineth thilk wicked purpose, and overcometh you by
reason and by good counsel, certes your wife ought rather to be praised
than to be blamed: thus should ye understond the philosopher that saith,
In wicked counsel women venquishen hir² husbonds. And there as ye
blamen all women and hir reasons, I shall show you by many ensamples
that many women have been full good, and yet ben,³ and hir counsel
wholesome and profitable. Eke some men han said that the counsel of
women is either too dear or else too little of price; but all be it so that
full many a woman be bad, and hir counsel vile and nought worth, yet
han men founden full many a good woman, and discreet and wise in
counselling. Lo Jacob thorough the good counsel of his mother Rebeck,
wan the benison of his father and the lordship over all his brethren.
Judith, by her good counsel, delivered the city of Bethuly, in which she
dwelt, out of the hond of Holofern, that had it besieged and wold it
all destroy. Abigail delivered Nabal, her housbond, fro David the king,
that wold han slain him, and appeased the ire of the king by her wit, and
by her good counselling. Hester, by her counsel, enhanced greatly the
people of God, in the reign of Assuerus the king. And the same bounty
in good counselling of many a good woman moun⁴ men read and tell.
And, further more, whan that our Lord had created Adam, our form⁵
father, he said in this wise; It is not good to be a man alone: make we to
him an help semblable to himself. Here moun ye see that if that women
weren not good, and hir counsel good and profitable, our Lord God of
heaven wold neither had wrought hem ne called hem help of man, but
rather confusion of man. And then said a clerk once in two verses, what
is better than gold? Jasper. What is better than Jasper? Wisdom.
And what is better than wisdom? Woman. And what is better than a
good woman? Nothing. And, sir, by many other reasons moun ye seen
that many women ben good, and hir counsel good and profitable . . .

Whan Melibee had heard the words of his wife Prudence, he said thus:
I see well that the word of Salomon is sooth; for he saith that words that
ben spoken discreetly by ordinance ben honeycombs, for they yeven

¹ Conceal.　　² Their.　　³ Still are.
　　⁴ May.　　⁵ First, original.

sweetness to the soul and wholesomeness to the body; and, wife, because
of thy sweet words, and eke for I have preved and assayed thy great
sapience and thy great truth, I wol govern me by thy counsel in all thing.

This is probably one of the passages that have been conceived
to have most of a rhythmical character; yet its balanced style
does not go beyond what is not uncommon in rhetorical prose.
Part of the measured march of the language may arise from the
French tale, in perhaps its original form, having been in verse.
What is called the Personce (or Parson's) Tale, which winds up
the Canterbury Tales, as we possess the work, is a long moral
discourse, which, for the greater part, is not very entertaining,
but which yet contains some passages curiously illustrative of
the age in which it was written. Here is part of what occurs in
the section headed De Superbia (Of Pride), the first of the seven
mortal sins. Tyrwhitt justly recommends that the whole
"should be read carefully by any antiquary who may mean
to write De re Vestiaria of the English nation in the fourteenth
century."   .

Now ben there two manner of prides: that on of hem[1] is within the
heart of a man, and that other is without; of which soothly there for said
things, and mo[2] than I have said, appertainen to pride that is within
the heart of man. And there be other spices[3] that ben withouten; but,
natheles, that on of these spices of pride is sign of that other, right as the
gay leavesell[4] at the tavern is sign of the wine that is in the cellar. And
this is in many things, as in speech and countenance, and outrageous
array of clothing; for certes if there had ben no sin in clothing Christ wold
not so soon have noted and spoken of the clothing of thilk rich man in the
Gospel: and, as Saint Gregory saith, that precious clothing is culpable,
for the dearth of it, and for his softness, and for his strangeness and
disguising, and for the superfluity or for the inordinate scantiness of it.
Alas! may not a man see as in our days the sinful costlew array of clothing,
and namely[5] in too much superfluity, or else in too disordinate scantiness.

As to the first sin, in superfluity of clothing, which that maketh it so
dear, to the harm of the people, not only the cost of the embrouding,[6]
the disguising, indenting or barring, ownding,[7] palling,[8] winding, or
bending, and semblable waste of cloth in vanity; but there is also the

---

[1] The one of them.   [2] More.   [3] Species, kinds.
[4] The meaning of this word, which at a later date appears to have been
pronounced and written leasel, is unknown. See Tyrwhitt's note to Cant.
Tales, v. 4059, and Glossary, ad verbum; and note by the editor, Mr. Albert
Way, on pp. 300, 301, of the Promptorium Parvulorum, vol. i., printed for
the Camden Society, No. Lxxxi. 1843.   [5] Especially.
[6] Embroidering.   [7] Imitating waves.   [8] Imitating poles.

costlew furring in hir gowns, so moch pounsoning[1] of chisel to maken holes, so moch dagging[2] of sheers, with the superfluity in length of the foresaid gowns, trailing in the dong and in the mire, on horse and eke on foot, as well of man as of woman, that all thilk training is verily (as in effect) wasted, consumed, threadbare, and rotten with dong, rather than it is yoven to the poor, to great damage of the foresaid poor folk, and that in sondry wise; this is to sayn, the more that cloth is wasted, the more must it cost to the poor people, for the scarceness; and, furthermore, if so be that they wolden yeve swich pounsoned and dagged clothing to the poor people, it is not convenient to wear for hir estate, ne suffisant to bote[3] hir necessity, to keep hem fro the distemperance of the firmament....

Also the sin of ornament or of apparel is in things that appertain to riding, as in too many delicate horse that ben holden for delight, that ben so fair, fat, and costlew; and also in many a vicious knave that is sustained because of hem; in curious harness, as in saddles, croppers, peitrels, and bridles, covered with precious cloth and rich, barred and plated of gold and of silver; for which God saith by Zachary the prophet, I wol confound the riders of swich horse. These folk taken little regard of the riding of God's son of heaven, and of his harness, when he rode upon the ass, and had none other harness but the poor clothes of his disciples, ne we read not that ever he rode on any other beast. I speak this for the sin of superfluity, and not for honesty when reason it requireth. And, moreover, certes pride is greatly notified in holding of great meiny,[4] when they ben of little profit, or of right no profit, and namely when that meiny is felonious and damagerous to the people by hardiness of high lordship, or by way of office; for certes swich lords sell than hir lordship to the devil of hell, when they sustain the wickedness of hir meiny; or else when these folk of low degree, as they that holden hostelries, sustainen theft of hir hostellers, and that is in many manner of deceits; thilk manner of folk ben the flies that followen the honey, or else the hounds that followen the carrain; swich foresaid folk stranglen spiritually hir lordships; for which thus saith David the prophet, Wicked death mot come unto thilk lordships, and God yeve that they mot descend into hell all down, for in hir houses is iniquity and shrewedness, and not God of heaven: and certes, but if they done amendment, right as God yave his benison to Laban by the service of Jacob, and to Pharaoh by the service of Joseph, right so wol God yeve his malison to swich lordships as sustain the wickedness of hir servants, but they come to amendment. Pride of the table appeareth eke full oft; for certes rich men be cleped[5] to feasts, and poor folk be put away and rebuked; and also in excess of divers meats and drinks, and namely swich manner bake meats and dish meats brenning[6] of wild fire, and painted and castled with paper, and semblable waste, so that it is abusion to think; and eke in too great preciousness of vessel, and curiosity of minstrelsy, by which a man is stirred more to the delights of luxury.

---

[1] Punching.	[2] Slitting.	[3] Help (boot).
[4] Body of menials.	[5] Called, invited.	[6] Burning.

LITERATURE AND LEARNING IN THE FIFTEENTH CENTURY.— UNIVERSITIES.

A few facts which are important rather as forming epochs in the chronology of our subject, and for the results by which they were followed, than in themselves, constitute the main part of the history of learning and literature in England during the fifteenth century. The actual contributions of this age to our national literature are smaller in amount and value than those of any preceding space of time of the same length since the Norman Conquest. The ferment of studious enthusiasm which had been excited in men's minds in the beginning of the preceding century had, in a great measure, spent itself before the beginning of this. According to an oration delivered before the pope and cardinals by Richard Fitz-Ralph, Archbishop of Armagh, in 1357, the 30,000 students of the University of Oxford had even by that time decreased to about 6000. The popular veneration for learning had also, from various causes, undergone a corresponding decline; and, instead of the honours formerly paid by all classes to talent and scholarship, and the crowding of eager multitudes around every eminent doctor wherever he appeared, we perceive now the aspect of a general indifference, and encounter occasional instances of the votaries of science and letters begging their bread, and of their unappreciated acquirements being turned into matter of ridicule and mockery by the insolence of rank and wealth. Anthony Wood, the quaint historian of the University of Oxford, relates a story of two itinerating students of this age, who, having one day presented themselves at a baronial castle, and sought an introduction by the exhibition of their academical credentials, in which they were each described as gifted, among other accomplishments, with a poetical vein, were ordered by the baron to be suspended in a pair of buckets over a draw-well, and dipped alternately into the water, until each should produce a couplet on his awkward situation; it was not till after a considerable number of duckings that the unfortunate captives finished the rhymes, while their involuntary ascents and descents during the process of concoction were heartily enjoyed by the baron and his company. It would be unfair, indeed, to judge of the general state of things from one or two anecdotes of this kind, although such consequences are only

what might be expected when scholars took to perambulating
the country as mendicants, with recommendations to the charity
of the benevolent by the chancellors of their universities, as we
are assured was now become customary; but the circumstances
of our own country at least, in this age, must have proved in no
small degree depressing to all liberal pursuits.

Although much of the popular effervescence had evaporated,
however, the love of knowledge was still alive and active in
many of the more select order of minds, prompting them to
zealous exertions both in its acquisition and its diffusion. In
the course of the fifteenth century, very nearly forty new universities were founded in the different countries of Europe. In
our own several new colleges were added both to Oxford and
Cambridge. In the former university, Lincoln College was
founded in 1430 by Richard Flemyng, Bishop of Lincoln,
though only completed about 1475 by his successor, Thomas
Rotherham; All Souls was founded in 1437 by Chicheley,
Archbishop of Canterbury, with the design of providing a perpetual service of prayers and masses for the souls of all the
faithful departed, and especially of those who had fallen or
should fall in the French wars; and Magdalen, which soon
became one of the wealthiest academical establishments in
Europe, was founded by William Pattyn, or De Waynflete,
Bishop of Winchester and Lord Chancellor of England, who
began the erection of the fabric in 1458, and lived to witness its
completion in 1479. Cambridge received the additions, of King's
College, founded in 1441, on a scale of great liberality and magnificence, by Henry VI., who established, about the same time,
the celebrated school of Eton, to be a nursery for his college; of
Queen's College, founded in 1446, by Henry's consort, Margaret
of Anjou; and of Catherine Hall, founded in 1475, by Robert
Woodlark, the third provost of King's College. Extensive public
buildings, which came to be known by the name of the New
Schools, were also erected at Oxford in 1439, by Thomas Hoke-
norton, Abbot of Osney, for the delivery of lectures in metaphysics, natural philosophy, moral philosophy, astronomy,
geometry, music, arithmetic, logic, rhetoric, and grammar. The
foundation of a divinity school and of a public library was laid
in the same university about 1427; and, although the building
was often interrupted, it was, at length, through the liberal
donations of Humphrey Duke of Gloucester, Cardinal John

Kemp, Archbishop of York, his nephew Thomas Kemp, Bishop of London, and other benefactors, completed in 1480, when it formed the most magnificent structure of which the university yet had to boast. The building of public schools was also begun at Cambridge, in 1443, at the expense of the university, and finished, by the aid of various contributors, about 1475.

More interesting, however, than these extensions of former establishments, is the founding of a temple to Learning in a part of the island in which no permanent abode had ever before been built for her. The first of the Scottish universities, that of St. Andrews, rose a few years after the commencement of the fifteenth century, out of the scheme of a few men of letters in that city, who, probably on the suggestion of the Bishop, Henry Wardlaw, formed themselves into an association for giving instruction in the sciences then usually taught in universities to all who chose to attend their lectures, and are supposed to have begun teaching about the year 1410. Their names, as recorded by the father of Scottish history, and eminently worthy to be preserved, were Lawrence Lindores, who undertook to explain the Fourth Book of the Master of the Sentences; Richard Cornel, Archdeacon of Lothian, John Litster, canon of St. Andrews, John Shevez, official of St. Andrews, and William Stephen, who lectured on the civil and canon laws; and John Gyll, William Fowler, and William Crosier, who taught logic and philosophy.* The institution, with this apparatus of professors, was already, in everything but in form, a university—and such it is styled in the charter or grant of privileges which Wardlaw hastened to bestow upon it. In that instrument, which is dated the 27th of February, 1411, the bishop speaks of the university as having been already actually instituted and founded by himself, saving the authority of the apostolic see, and laudably begun by those to whom he addresses himself, the venerable doctors, masters, bachelors, and scholars dwelling in his city of St. Andrews. He now proceeded more formally to endow the new seminary, in so far as his jurisdiction extended, with all the rights and liberties of a university. Two years afterwards, bulls of confirmation, &c., in the usual terms, were obtained from Benedict XIII., the one of the three contending popes who was acknowledged by the kingdom of Scotland. Benedict's bulls are six in number, all dated the same day, the 28th of August, 1413, at Paniscola, in

* Fordun, Scotichronicon.

Aragon, where that pope kept his court. They profess to be granted at the request of the Scottish king (though James I. was then a prisoner in England), and of the bishop, prior, and chapter of St. Andrews, whose project of establishing a university, or *studium generale*, in that city, is expressly stated to have been formed with the counsel, consent, and common participation of the three estates of the realm of Scotland.* The bishop and his associates, it is declared, had been stirred up to the undertaking by the consideration of the many dangers and inconveniences to which the clergy of that kingdom who desired to be instructed in theology, the canon and civil laws, medicine, and the liberal arts were exposed, from wars and other impediments in their journeys to foreign *studia generalia*, in consequence of there being no such institution to which they might resort in their own country. The several papal bulls were brought to St. Andrews by Henry de Ogilby, M.A., on the 3rd of February, 1414, when they were received with processions and ringing of bells, and every demonstration of public joy. When King James returned ten years after this from England, he found the new seminary already firmly established, and still flourishing under the protection of its founder, Wardlaw, who had also been the instructor of his own boyhood. James granted it a charter confirming all its privileges and immunities, dated at Perth, the 31st of March, 1432; and, if we may believe the historian Hector Boecius, it flourished so greatly under his patronage, that it soon came to have among its teachers no fewer than thirteen doctors of divinity, and eight doctors of laws, as well as a prodigious multitude of students. The good and enlightened Bishop Wardlaw presided over the see of St. Andrews till the year 1444, when the university found in James Kennedy a worthy successor to his virtues and public spirit, as well as to his place. As yet the institution was little more than an incorporated association, without any permanent endowments, and with scarcely any buildings except a few public lecturing rooms; it was a university, therefore, but as yet without a college. Its first college—that of St. Salvator—was built and endowed by Kennedy, whose original foundation charter was confirmed, in a bull no

* Quod olim de consilio, consensu, et communi tractatu trium statuum personarum regni Scotiæ—are the words of the bull of foundation.—See Evidence taken by the Commissioners for visiting the Universities of Scotland, vol. iii. p. 171.

longer extant, by Pope Nicholas V., who died in 1455. A second charter was granted by Kennedy, at his castle of St. Andrews, on the 4th of April, 1458, and confirmed by Pope Pius II., in a bull dated at Rome, the 13th of September, in the same year. In this the whole scheme of the establishment is minutely detailed, and a complete body of rules laid down for its government. One of the bishop's ordinances is curiously illustrative of the easy morality of the time. Having given some solemn directions as to the hours at which masses were to be said in all time coming by the members of the college, who were all to be clergymen, he proceeds to enjoin that all the members of the said college shall live decently as becomes ecclesiastics, "so as not," it is added, "to keep concubines publicly, nor to be common nightwalkers or robbers, or habitually guilty of other notorious crimes; and if any of them is so (which it is earnestly hoped may not be the case) let him be corrected by his superior; if he prove incorrigible, let him be deprived and another put in his place."[*] By another bull, dated the 25th of February, 1468, Pope Paul II. granted to the Principal and Masters of the college of St. Salvator the right of bestowing degrees in theology and the arts, "in consideration," as it is expressed, "of its high and well-known reputation among the other colleges of the realm of Scotland."[†] The other colleges here spoken of could be nothing more than grammar schools; but the passage proves, what, indeed, is well established by other evidence, that such schools already existed in many of the monasteries and principal towns. It was at these that the Scottish youth were prepared for their attendance upon foreign universities.

Another of the Scottish universities—that of Glasgow—was also founded within this same century. The bull of foundation was granted at the request of James II. in 1450, by Nicholas V., who was "distinguished by his talents and erudition, and particularly by his munificent patronage of Grecian literature."[‡] Other

---

[*] Ordinamus insuper, quod omnes dicti collegii honeste vivant, ut decet ecclesiasticos, ita quod non habeant publicas concubinas, nec sint communes noctivagi seu brigantes, aut aliis notoriis criminibus intenti: et si talis sit (quod absit) per superiorem suum, &c.—See Evidence taken by the Commissioners for visiting the Universities of Scotland, vol. iii. 278.

[†] Quod inter alia collegia regni Scotis collegium ejusdem ecclesie egregium ac notabile reputatur.—Ibid., 273.

[‡] Report of the Scottish University Commissioners, p. 213. See a character

royal and episcopal charters were subsequently granted by King James II. (20th April, 1453); by Bishop Turnbull (1st December, 1453); by Bishop Muirhead (1st July, 1461); and by King James III. (10th December, 1472).* But, "in none of the papal, royal, or episcopal letters of privilege, of a date prior to the Reformation," observes the writer of the able and elaborate account of the University of Glasgow appended to the General Report of the late Commission of Inquiry into the State of the Universities of Scotland, " is there any distinct trace of the constitution of the university; and it can scarcely be said that any of those documents refers to the existence of a *college*, or to the possession of any property. It does not appear that it was the intention of the founder of the university that the members should live *collegialiter*, maintained at a public table, and resident within the walls of a separate building. . . . . Universities might be established (and some still exist on the Continent) without having even class-rooms for the students. The University of Paris subsisted in great efficiency from the age of Charlemagne to the middle of the thirteenth century (a period of nearly five hundred years) without having any schools or places of auditory, except such as were hired in the houses of individuals. During the first twenty years after the foundation of the university of St. Andrews, great inconvenience was suffered, not merely from the want of such rooms, but from the multiplicity of schools in the different religious houses, all of them claiming to be considered as constituent parts of the university; and even after a Pædagogium was founded in 1430, for the schools and halls of the Faculty of Arts, and for chambers to be used by the students in that Faculty, the studies of the Faculties of Theology and Law were conducted in other buildings; and the congregations of the university continued for at least 130 years to be held in the Augustinian Priory."† A piece of ground, however, with the buildings upon it, in the High-street of the city, was granted to the University of Glasgow by James, the first Lord Hamilton, in 1460, being the site on which the college stands at the present day.

---

of Pope Nicholas V. by Gibbon—who observes that his "fame has not been adequate to his merits"—in Decline and Fall of Rom. Emp. ch. 66.

* Evidence of Univ. Com. ii. 230—233.

† Report, p. 214.

REVIVAL OF LETTERS.—INVENTION OF PRINTING.

Dark and unproductive as was the greater part of the fifteenth century in England and France, the revival of letters in the western world dates from this age.[*] For a considerable time before the capture of Constantinople by the Turks, in 1453, the course of political events in the eastern empire had led to a more frequent intercourse than heretofore between its subjects and their fellow Christians of the west, and had not only drawn some of the most distinguished ornaments of the Byzantine court, including three of the emperors themselves, to visit the Latin kingdoms, but had induced several learned Greeks to come over and settle in Italy. "In their lowest servitude and depression," as Gibbon has said in one of his well-poised sentences, "the subjects of the Byzantine throne were still possessed of a golden key that could unlock the treasures of antiquity,—of a musical and prolific language, that gives a soul to the objects of sense, and a body to the abstractions of philosophy." It cannot, perhaps, be said that the knowledge of the Greek tongue was ever entirely lost in western Europe; there were probably in every age a few scholars who had more than a merely elementary acquaintance with it. It is certain, however, that it was not a common study even among the most learned. The most eminent universities—such as Bologna, Paris, and Oxford—were without any regular Professor of Greek. Even the few who did read the language, seem to have read only the writings in it on science and philosophy. Warton has shown that both the Iliad and the Odyssey were apparently wholly unknown, or at least not understood, in Europe from the fourth to the fourteenth century.[*] The renewed intercourse that has been mentioned between the East and the West, beginning in the early part of the latter century, rapidly effected a great revolution in this respect. Petrarch, about the year 1340, began the study of the language of Homer, under the instructions of the learned Barlaam, who had come to Italy as ambassador from Andronicus the Younger; and, although the separation of the two friends soon after stopped the Tuscan at the threshold of the new literature, his friend Boccaccio twenty years later was more fortunate

* Hist. of Eng. Poetry, L 128, and II. 892.

in obtaining the assistance of Leontius Pilatus, a disciple of
Barlaam, and, under his guidance, penetrated to its inner glories.
At a still later date, the destruction of their ancient empire
drove a crowd of illustrious Greek exiles to Italy—the Cardinal
Bessarion, Theodore Gaza, George of Trebizond, John Argy-
ropulus, Demetrius Chalcondyles, Janus Lascaris, and others—
some of whom taught their native language in the universities
and chief towns of that country, while the rest, by their translations, by their writings, and their converse with the public
mind in various ways, assisted in diffusing a taste for it and a
knowledge of it even beyond the Alps. Nor, as Gibbon has
remarked, 'was the ardour of the Latins in receiving and trea-
suring up this new knowledge inferior to that of their Greek
guests in imparting it. The merits of Pope Nicholas V., in the
patronage of Greek literature, have been already noticed. During
the eight years that he wore the tiara (from 1447 to 1455) this
active and liberal head of the Christian church added five thousand volumes to the library of the Vatican. Many of these were
Greek books, or translations of them into Latin. "To his munificence," continues the great historian, "the Latin world was
indebted for the versions of Xenophon, Diodorus, Polybius,
Thucydides, Herodotus, and Appian; of Strabo's Geography, of
the Iliad, of the most valuable works of Plato and Aristotle, of
Ptolemy and Theophrastus, and of the Fathers of the Greek
church. The example of the Roman pontiff was preceded or
imitated by a Florentine merchant, who governed the republic
without arms and without a title. Cosmo of Medicis was the
father of a line of princes whose name and age are almost
synonymous with the restoration of learning; his credit was
ennobled into fame; his riches were dedicated to the service of
mankind: he corresponded at once with Cairo and London; and
a cargo of Indian spices and Greek books was often imported in
the same vessel. In his palace distress was entitled to relief,
and merit to reward: his leisure hours were delightfully spent in
the Platonic academy; he encouraged the emulation of Demetrius Chalcondyles and Angelo Politian; and his active missionary, Janus Lascaris, returned from the East with a treasure
of two hundred manuscripts, fourscore of which were as yet
unknown in the libraries of Europe.*

Gibbon adds, that, "after a short succession of foreign

* Decline and Fall of Rom. Emp. ch. 66.

2 A 2

teachers, the tide of emigration subsided; but the language of Constantinople was spread beyond the Alps; and the natives of France, Germany, and England imparted to their country the sacred fire which they had kindled in the schools of Florence and Rome." Although, however, it has been necessary, for the sake of chronological distinctness, to notice the revival of learning in Europe in this place, the light of that great day-spring scarcely reached our own country within the period with which we are now occupied. The Greek language did not begin to be taught at Oxford till towards the very close of the fifteenth century. The case was different with regard to the other most memorable incident in the history of literature which illustrates the age of which we are now treating. The three towns, of Haerlem in Holland and of Mayence and Strasburg in Germany, contend for the honour of having given birth, shortly before the middle of this century, to the art of printing. The claim of Haerlem rests upon a tradition that one of its citizens, Lawrence (or Laurent) Janszoon Coster, had, without assistance or communication with any other individual, not only invented the art, but brought it to perfection, through the successive stages of wooden types, types of cut metal, and types cast in the modern fashion, before the year 1441; in which year one of his servants named John—whom some suppose to have been John Fust—made his escape to Mayence, carrying with him both the secret and a quantity of Coster's types and implements, with which he began to print in the last-mentioned city in the following year. Among those who reject this story there is little disagreement as to the persons to whom the several parts of the invention are to be attributed; the principal dispute is, whether the art was first practised at Mayence or at Strasburg. The supporters of the pretensions of Coster of Haerlem, we have said, assort his claims to the invention both of the art of printing and of the art of typo-founding. These are properly to be considered as two perfectly distinct inventions; and, though coming the one in aid of the other, the latter was nearly as great an improvement upon the former, as the notion of printing with moveable types was upon the process, long previously practised in China, of producing impressions from blocks of wood and other materials.* The

* We have elsewhere endeavoured to state more distinctly than had previously been done in what it really is that the invention of printing essentially consists.—See Art. *Printing* in Penny Cyclopædia, xix. 14—18.

principle of the one consisted in making the same type available in the production of many different words and pages; the principle of the other consisted in making one cutting serve for the production of many copies of the same type. They proceeded, in fact, in opposite directions; the object of the former was attained by the contrivance of separate types, by the breaking down of the one block into many pieces: the latter was suggested by viewing the different types of each letter as essentially the same, that is to say, by bringing together, as it were, the many into one. The Germans agree in venerating three names as those of the fathers of the whole art of printing—John Gutenberg, or Gutenberger; Peter Schœffer, otherwise called Opilio; and John Fust. The share which Fust had in the matter is involved in some obscurity. According to one account, he merely interested himself warmly in the invention, and, being wealthy, assisted Gutenberg, who was poor, with the means of carrying on his operations. It is admitted that the grand fundamental conception of printing with separate or moveable types is due to Gutenberg alone. And to Schœffer is attributed, with equal unanimity, the invention of casting types of metal by means of a matrix. For this happy improvement — without which, indeed, printing with moveable types would have been checked in its natural development, like an animal or a plant left without adequate nourishment,—Schœffer, who was at the time in the service of Gutenberg and Fust, is said to have received from the latter his only daughter in marriage. The first servants of this high mystery, however, were not of the class of ordinary workmen; the fabrication of books, which even in its most mechanical forms had hitherto always been an employment of an intellectual nature, was not now committed to persons without any literary education; Schœffer had studied in his youth at the University of Paris, and his scholarly acquirements had no doubt in the first instance recommended him to Gutenberg as a fit assistant in his scholarly craft.

PRINTING IN ENGLAND.—CAXTON.

The art of printing had been practised nearly thirty years in Germany before it was introduced either into England or France —with so tardy a pace did knowledge travel to and fro over the earth in those days, or so unfavourable was the state of these countries for the reception of even the greatest improvements in the arts. At length a citizen of London secured a conspicuous place to his name for ever in the annals of our national literature, by being, so far as is known, the first of his countrymen that learned the new art, and certainly the first who either practised it in England, or in printing an English book. William Caxton was born, as he tells us himself, in the Weald of Kent, it is supposed about the year 1412. Thirty years after this date his name is found among the members of the Mercers' Company in London. Later in life he appears to have repeatedly visited the Low Countries, at first probably on business of his own, but afterwards in a sort of public capacity,—having in 1464 been commissioned, along with another person, apparently also a merchant, by Edward IV. to negotiate a commercial treaty with the Duke of Burgundy. He was afterwards taken into the household of Margaret Duchess of Burgundy. It was probably while resident abroad, in the Low Countries or in Germany, that he commenced practising the art of printing. He is commonly supposed to have completed before the end of the year 1471 impressions of Raoul le Fevre's Recueil des Histoires de Troyes, in folio; of the Latin oration of John Russell on Charles Duke of Burgundy being created a Knight of the Garter, in quarto; and of an English translation by himself of Le Fevre's abovementioned history, in folio; "whyche sayd translacion and werke," says the title, "was begonne in Brugis in 1468, and ended in the holy cyte of Colen, 19 Sept. 1471." But these words undoubtedly refer only to the translation; and sufficient reasons have lately been advanced by Mr. Knight for entertaining the strongest doubts of any one of the above-mentioned books having been printed by Caxton.* The earliest work now known, which we have sufficient grounds for believing to have been printed by Caxton, is another English translation by himself, from the French, of a moral treatise entitled The Game and Playe of the Chesse, a folio volume, which is stated to have been "finished the last day of March, 1474." It is generally supposed that this work was printed in England; and the year 1474 accordingly is assumed to have been that of the introduction of

* See William Caxton, a Biography, 12mo, Lond. 1844, pp. 103, &c. This work has since been expanded into The Old Printer and the Modern Press, 8vo, 1854

the art into this country. It is certainly known that Caxton was resident in England in 1477, and had set up his press in the Almonry, near Westminster Abbey, where he printed that year, in folio, The Dictes and Notable Wyse Sayenges of the Phylosophers, translated from the French by Anthony Woodville, Earl Rivers. From this time Caxton continued both to print and translate with indefatigable industry for about a dozen years, his last publication with a date having been produced in 1490, and his death having probably taken place in 1491, or 1492.* Before he died he saw the admirable art which he had introduced into his native country already firmly established there, and the practice of it extensively diffused. Theodore Rood, John Lettow, William Machelina, and Wynkyn de Worde, foreigners, and Thomas Hunt, an Englishman, all printed in London both before and after Caxton's death. It is probable that the foreigners had been his assistants, and were brought into the country by him. A press was also set up at St. Albans by a schoolmaster of that place, whose name has not been preserved; and books began to be printed at Oxford so early as the year 1478. It would even appear that before the end of this period some exportation of the productions of the English press had commenced. At the end of a Latin translation of the Epistles of Phalaris, printed at Oxford in 1485, is a Latin couplet, boasting that the English, who had been wont to be indebted for books to the Venetians, now sold books themselves to other nations.†

An enumeration of the principal works printed by Caxton will present the best view that can be given of the popular literature of the time; for of course he employed his press in the multiplication, and his pen in the translation, of the kind of books most in request among the reading portion of his countrymen. The predominant spirit of the age was still a mixture of devotion and romance; the clergy and the nobility were also at once the best educated and the wealthiest classes; accordingly the religious books and the romances form the two largest divisions in the list. The former comprises the Pilgrimage of

* See article on Caxton in Penny Cyclopædia, vol. vi. p. 593; and with much more fulness of detail and illustration in Mr. Knight's Biography of Caxton.

† Celatos, Veneti, nobis transmittere libros
Cedite; nos aliis venditmus, O Veneti.

Middleton's Origin of Printing in England, p. 10.

the Soul, from the French; Liber Festivalis, or Directions for keeping Feasts all the Year; Quatuor Sermones (or Four Sermons), in English; The Golden Legend (a collection of Lives of the Saints), three editions; The Art and Craft to know well to Die, from the French; Infantia Salvatoris (the Infancy of our Saviour); The Life of St. Catherine of Sens; Speculum Vitæ Christi, or Mirror of the Blessed Life of Jesu Christ; Directorium Sacerdotum (a Directory of Church Worship); A Book of Divers Ghostly Matters; The Life of St. Wynefrid; The Provincial Constitutions of Bishop Lyndwood of St. Asaph, in Latin; the Profitable Book of Man's Soul, called the Chastising of God's Children; and one or two others. Several of these—such as the Lives of the Saints—might come almost equally under the title of books of romance. The works more properly relating to romance and chivalry, however, are the following: The History of Troy, already mentioned (which Caxton at least translated, if he did not print it); The Book of the whole Life of Jason; Godfrey of Boloyn; The Knight of the Tower, from the French; The Book of the Order of Chivalry or Knighthood, from the French; The Book Royal, or the Book for a King; A Book of the Noble Histories of King Arthur and of Certain of his Knights; The History of the Noble, Right Valiant, and Right Worthy Knight Paris and of the Fair Vienne; The Book of Feats of Arms and of Chivalry, from the French of Christine of Pisa; and the History of King Blanchardine and Queen Eglantine his Wife. To these may be added, the History of Renard the Fox, translated by Caxton from the German; and the Subtle Histories and Fables of Æsop, from the French. In English poetry there are the following works of Chaucer, Gower, and Lydgate:—of the first, The Tales of Canterbury, two editions; The Book of Fame; Troylus and Creseide: and some minor poems:—of the second, The Confessio Amantis, that is to say, in English, the Confession of the Lover:—of the third, The Work (or Court) of Sapience; The Life of our Lady; and some minor poems along with those of Chaucer. And here we may take note of the honourable conscientiousness of our first English printer, so worthy of his high vocation as the leader in the great enterprise of giving at once universal diffusion and an imperishable existence to the literature of his country. The manuscript from which he had printed his first edition of the Canterbury Tales happened unluckily, to quote Tyrwhitt's description, "to be one of the very worst, in all respects, that he could possibly have met with." This he himself, as he tells us in the preface to his second edition, discovered some time afterwards, whereupon he did not rest till he had produced this second edition from another much more correct manuscript—"for to satisfy the auctor," as he expresses it, "whereas tofore by ignorance I erred in hurting and defaming his book in divers places, in setting in some things that he never said ne made, and leaving out many things that he made which been requisite to be set in it." None of the ancient Latin classics were printed in England during the fifteenth century; but the list of the productions of Caxton's press contains English translations of Cicero's Treatises on Old Age and on Friendship; of Boëthius's Consolation of Philosophy, by Chaucer; of the Sayings of the Philosophers; of Virgil's Æneid, from the French; and of the works called Cato Magnus and Cato Parvus, also from the French. This was by no means a contemptible beginning of the work of transfusing the wisdom and poetry of antiquity into the mother tongue. Provision was also made for the readers of history, though not so plentifully as for those of romance. The list contains the following historical and topographical works: The Chronicles of England; The Description of Britain; The Polychronicon; The Life of Charles the Great, twice printed; and the Siege of the Noble and invincible City of Rhodes. Caxton also printed the statutes of the first year of Richard III., and those of the first, second, and third parliaments of Henry VII. Among a few other publications of a miscellaneous description, the following may be mentioned as relating to morals and the conduct of life: The Game of Chess, already noticed; The Moral Proverbs of Christine of Pisa; The Book of Good Manners; The Doctrinal of Sapience, from the French; and A Boke for Travellers. On the whole, the first books that were printed in England were, for the most part, we see, books for the general reader: none of them were works of recondite learning or science, or adapted to the tastes and studies only of particular classes; if they were not all equally edifying, they were all as much as possible addressed to the great body of the reading public—the only audience that was then sufficiently numerous to call into profitable exercise the multiplying powers of the press.

BOOKS AND LIBRARIES.

It follows, that it was only books of a certain description the price of which was at first reduced by the new invention. For a considerable time after the art of printing came into use, we find the price of many books still as excessive as ever, and the same anxious precautions taken for their security that had been usual when the only mode of multiplying a volume was by its repeated transcription. In 1471, for example, when Louis XI. of France wished to borrow from the Faculty of Medicine at Paris a copy of the works of the Arabian physician Rhasis, that he might have a transcript made for his own library, the Faculty, in a formal letter, took credit for extraordinary loyalty in assenting to the application, and, after all, would not let the king have the book until he had not only deposited in pledge for it a considerable quantity of valuable plate, but procured a nobleman to join with him as surety in a deed by which he bound himself to return it uninjured under a considerable forfeiture.* On a manuscript of Matthew Paris, now in the British Museum, there is an inscription, in Latin, dated 1st June, 1488, in the handwriting and with the signature of John Russell, then Bishop of Lincoln, in which whosoever shall obliterate or destroy the bishop's memorandum respecting the ownership of the volume is solemnly declared to be accursed.† At this time by far the greater number of books were still unprinted; and every considerable library consisted chiefly of manuscripts, just as it did before the invention of the art of printing. Warton has collected the following facts respecting the libraries of the fifteenth century, and the inconveniences and impediments to study which must have been produced by the scarcity of books. "The famous library established in the University of Oxford by that munificent patron of literature, Humphrey Duke of Gloucester, contained only 600 volumes. [It was opened in the year 1480.] About the commencement of the fourteenth century, there were only four classics in the Royal Library at Paris: these were, one copy of Cicero, Ovid, Lucan, and Boëthius; the rest were chiefly books

* Crevier, Hist. de l'Univ. de Paris, iv. 557.

† Warton, Dissert. on Introd. of Learning into Eng. p. cxi. The volume is one of the Royal MSS., marked 14 C vii. It appears, from an inscription in the author's own hand, to have been a presentation copy from himself, probably to some church or monastery.

of devotion, which included but few of the Fathers; many treatises of astrology, geomancy, chiromancy, and medicine, originally written in Arabic, and translated into Latin or French; pandects, chronicles, and romances. The whole consisted of 900 volumes. They were deposited in three chambers (in the Louvre), which, on this occasion, were wainscoted with Irish oak, and ceiled with cypress, curiously carved. The windows were of painted glass, fenced with iron bars and copper wire. The English became masters of Paris in the year 1425; on which event the Duke of Bedford, Regent of France, sent this whole library—then consisting of only 853 volumes, and valued at 2223 livres—into England; where, perhaps, they became the groundwork of Duke Humphrey's library, just mentioned."[*] In another place the same writer furnishes the following additional information respecting Duke Humphrey, and his munificence as a book collector:—"About the year 1440 he gave to the University of Oxford a library, containing 600 volumes, only 120 of which were valued at 1000*l*. They were the most splendid and costly copies that could be procured, finely written on vellum, and elegantly embellished with miniatures and illuminations: among the rest was a translation into French of Ovid's Metamorphoses. Only a single specimen of these valuable volumes was suffered to remain: it is a beautiful manuscript, in folio, of Valerius Maximus, enriched with the most elegant decorations, and written in Duke Humphrey's age, evidently with a design of being placed in this sumptuous collection. All the rest of the books—which, like this, being highly ornamented, looked like missals, and conveyed ideas of popish superstition—were destroyed or removed by the pious visitors of the University in the reign of Edward VI., whose zeal was equalled only by their ignorance, or perhaps by their avarice."[†] Several of the volumes of Duke Humphrey's library, however, still remain in various collections. In the library of Oriel College, Oxford, is a copy of John Capgrave's Commentary on Genesis, in the author's handwriting, preceded by a Dedication to the Duke, the beautifully illuminated initial letter of which represents Capgrave humbly presenting his book to his patron. The volume contains also an entry, in French, in the

handwriting of the Duke, recording it to have been presented to
him in the year 1438. Warton goes on to state that the patronage of Duke Humphrey was not confined to English scholars.
Many of the most celebrated writers of France and Italy solicited
his favour and shared his bounty. He also employed several
learned foreigners in transcribing and in making translations of
Greek works into Latin. The only literary production which
has been ascribed to this distinguished patron of letters is a
small tract on Astronomy; and it appears to have been only
compiled at his instance, after tables which he had constructed.
In the library of Gresham College, however, there is a scheme
of astronomical calculations which bears his name. "Astronomy," says Warton, " was then a favourite science ; nor is it to
be doubted that he was intimately acquainted with the polite
branches of knowledge, which now began to acquire estimation,
and which his liberal and judicious attention greatly contributed
to restore."*

TIPTOFT, EARL OF WORCESTER.—WOODVILLE, EARL RIVERS.

The most distinguished among the English nobility of this rude
age for learning and intellectual tastes, was John Tiptoft, originally Lord Tiptoft, who was created Earl of Worcester by
Henry VI. He afterwards, however, attached himself to the
Yorkist family, for which he was put to death by Warwick,
during the short restoration of Henry VI., in 1470—his execution being the only vindictive act of bloodshed by which that
revolution was stained. The latest continuation of the history
of the Abbey of Croyland (printed by Fulman, in his Rerum
Anglic. Scriptor., pp. 449—540) asserts that the earl had, by
his cruelty in the office of Constable of the Tower, acquired the
hatred of the people, who called him " the Butcher;" but general
and passionate imputations of this kind cannot be allowed to go
for much in the inflammation and ferocity of such a contest as
then agitated men's minds. The more specific statement of
other writers is, that Worcester was sent to the block under the
pretence of punishing him for cruelty of which he had been
guilty many years before, while exercising the government of

* Hist. of Eng. Poetry, ii. 330.

Ireland, particularly towards two infant sons of the Earl of Desmond. As Walpole has well said, " it was an unwonted strain of tenderness in a man so little scrupulous of blood as Warwick, to put to death so great a peer for some inhumanity to the children of an Irish lord ; nor does one conceive why he sought for so remote a crime : he was not often so delicate. Tiptoft seems to have been punished by Warwick for leaving Henry for Edward, when Warwick had thought fit to quit Edward for Henry."[*] Others of the old chroniclers ascribe the charges brought against him to the malice of his enemies. He was probably singled out for destruction as being the ablest and most dangerous man of his party; for Worcester was distinguished for his political and military talents, as well as for his scholarship. It would be strange, at any rate, if his intellectual acquirements—which raised him so high above the herd of his fellow-nobles, and the great body of his countrymen—should, instead of softening and humanizing him, according to the ancient poet's celebration of the effect of " having faithfully learned the ingenuous arts,"[†] have had an influence of the very opposite kind upon his nature and conduct. The Earl of Worcester was an ardent lover of books, and was, as well as Duke Humphrey, a liberal contributor to the shelves of the rising public library of the University of Oxford. On his return from a pilgrimage to Jerusalem, after residing for some years at Padua and Venice, and making great purchases of manuscripts in both those places, he repaired to Rome to satisfy his longing curiosity with a sight of the library of the Vatican, and drew tears of delight from Pope Pius II. (the learned Æneas Sylvius), by a Latin oration which he pronounced before him. Of his literary performances, the principal one that remains is the translation of Cicero's Treatise on Friendship, which was published by Caxton. He was one of the chief patrons of this earliest English printer, who says of him that he was one " to whom he knew none like among the lords of the temporality for science and moral virtue,"—a far better testimony to his worth than the party-spirit of the Croyland historian, or even the temporary clamour of the populace, if such did make itself heard against him in the triumph of the opposite faction, is of the reverse. He was only in his forty-second year when he was

* Royal and Noble Authors.
† Ovid, Ex Ponto, Lib. II. Ep. 9, v. 47.

put to death; " at which death," says Caxton, " every man that was there might learn to die, and take his death patiently."

Fuller has said that " the axe then did at one blow cut off more learning than was left in the heads of all the surviving nobility." Yet there still survived a noble contemporary of Tiptoft, " by no means," to use the words of Walpole, " inferior to him in learning and politeness, in birth his equal, by alliance his superior, greater in feats of arms, and in pilgrimages more abundant." This was Anthony Widville, or Woodville, Lord Scales and Earl Rivers, the brother of the fair queen of Edward IV. By a fate closely resembling that of the Earl of Worcester, the brave and accomplished Lord Rivers was beheaded at Pomfret Castle, by order of the Protector Gloucester, afterwards Richard III., along with the queen's son Sir Richard Grey, and other victims, on the 23rd of June, 1483. The earl, when he thus perished, had not completed his forty-first year. At a famous combat which took place in Smithfield, between Rivers, then Lord Scales, and Anthony the Bastard of Burgundy, in 1467, the Earl of Worcester presided as Lord High Constable; so that two of the chief figures at this one of the latest real passages of arms held in England, were the two Englishmen the most distinguished of their time for those intellectual tastes and accomplishments in the diffused light of which the empire of chivalry and the sword was ere long to fade away, as the stars disappear before the sun. Walpole has drawn the character of Earl Rivers in his most graphic style:—" The credit of his sister, the countenance and example of his prince, the boisterousness of the times, nothing softened, nothing roughened the mind of this amiable lord, who was as gallant as his luxurious brother-in-law, without his weaknesses—as brave as the heroes of either Rose, without their savageness—studious in the intervals of business—and devout after the manner of those whimsical times, when men challenged others whom they never saw, and went barefoot to visit shrines in countries of which they had scarce a map." He was also one of Caxton's great patrons, and was the author of several of those translations from the French which the latter printed. In a manuscript copy, in the archbishop's library at Lambeth, of one of these translations—that of the Dicts and Sayings of the Philosophers (which Rivers executed for the instruction of his nephew, the young Prince of Wales, to whom he was governor)—there is an interesting

illumination, in which the earl is represented introducing
Caxton to Edward IV., his queen, and the prince. In this
instance, Earl Rivers condescended to translate a translation,
for the original of the Dicts and Sayings is in Latin. He was
also the author of the metrical version of the Proverbs of Christine of Pisa, and of another of Caxton's publications named
Cordial, or Memorare Novissima, both from the French. But
these and the other translations in which the art of printing,
on its first establishment among us, exercised its powers of
multiplying the fountains of knowledge and of mental gratifica-
tion were, as Walpole observes, as much new and real presents
to the age as original works would have been. To Lords Worcester and Rivers this writer conceives their country to have
been in a great measure indebted for the restoration of learning.
"The countenance, the example," he remarks, " of men, in their
situation, must have operated more strongly than the attempts
of an hundred professors, benedictines, and commentators."[*]

SCIENCE IN ENGLAND.—ALCHEMISTS.

Although Chaucer had already set the example of writing on
scientific subjects in the mother tongue by his treatise on the
Astrolabe—the oldest work in English now known to exist on
any branch of science[†]—this department of study was but very
little cultivated in England during the present period. The
short list of English scientific works during the fifteenth century
does not contain a single name remembered, or deserving of
being remembered, in the history of science.[‡] The dreams of
astrology and alchemy still captivated and bewildered almost
all who turned their attention either to mathematical or natural
philosophy. The only difference of opinion with regard to these
mysterious pursuits was whether they were or were not forbidden by the law of God. Nobody doubted the most marvel-

* Royal and Noble Authors, vol. I.
† See Book of Table Talk, i. 199.
‡ See all those whose names have been recovered enumerated, with notices
of their insignificant performances, in a paper on the English Mathematical
and Astronomical Writers between the Norman Conquest and the year 1600,
in the Companion to the Almanac for 1837, pp. 22—26.

lons of their pretensions; but many thought a skill in them was
rather an inspiration from the prince of darkness than light from
heaven. Probably, however, it was not any feeling of this kind
that occasioned an act of parliament passed in the beginning of
the reign of Henry IV., making it felony to practise the transmutation of metals, there designated "the multiplying of gold
or silver, or the craft of multiplication:"* the prohibition has
more the look of having been dictated by political or economical
considerations, as if there had been some apprehension that the
operations of the multipliers might possibly affect the value of
the king's coin. Henry VI., at any rate, with all his piety, was
as great a patron of the alchemists as Edward III. had been
before him. These impostors practised with abundant success
upon his weakness and credulity, repeatedly inducing him to
advance- them money wherewith to prosecute their idle operations, as well as procuring from him protections, which he sometimes prevailed upon the parliament to confirm, from the
penalties of the statute that has just been mentioned. In one
of these protections granted to the three "famous men," John
Fauceby, John Kirkeby, and John Rayny, which was confirmed
by parliament, 31st May, 1456, the object of the researches of
the said philosophers is described to be "a certain most precious
medicine, called by some the mother and queen of medicines;
by some the inestimable glory; by others the quintessence; by
others the philosopher's stone; by others the elixir of life;
which cures all curable diseases with ease, prolongs human life
in perfect health and vigour of faculty to its utmost term, heals
all healable wounds, is a most sovereign antidote against all
poisons, and is capable," the enumeration of virtues concludes,
" of preserving to us, and our kingdom, other great advantages,
such as the transmutation of other metals into real and fine gold
and silver."† The philosopher's stone, and the elixir of life, it
will be observed, are here spoken of as one and the same medicine, contrary, we believe, to the common notion. The power
attributed to the medicine, also, in the prolongation of life
scarcely goes the length of the accounts usually given. Fauceby,
here mentioned, is elsewhere designated the king's physician.
Another of Henry's physicians was Gilbert Kymer, who was a
clergyman, and among other ecclesiastical promotions, held the
offices of dean of Salisbury and chancellor of the University of

* Stat. Henry IV., c. iv.   † Fœdera, xi. 570.

Oxford. From this example we may perceive that the practice
of medicine was still, to some extent, in the hands of the clergy.
The art itself appears to have made little or no progress within
the present period; indeed it may be doubted if the knowledge
that had formerly been derived from the Arabic authors
and schools was not now diminished rather than increased.
Almost the only medical work that appeared in England in the
fifteenth century, even the title of which is now remembered, is
the Dietarium de Sanitatis Custodia (or Dietary for the Preservation of Health) of this Dr. Gilbert Kymer. It is a tract
consisting of twenty-six chapters, and is dedicated, like so many
others of the productions of the learned of this age, both in
England and other countries, to the great patron of literature,
Humphrey Duke of Gloucester. Surgery was also in as rude a
state as ever. It appears, from a record in the Fœdera, that in
Henry V.'s army which won the battle of Agincourt there was
only one surgeon, a certain John Morstede, fifteen assistants, whom
he had pressed under a royal warrant, not having yet landed.
Of these assistants three were also to act as archers, the whole
number having the pay of common archers, and Morstede himself only that of a man-at-arms. The art, indeed, was hardly yet
considered as anything more than a species of mechanical handicraft. It deserves to be noted, however, that the operation of
lithotomy was successfully performed at Paris for the first time,
at least by any modern surgeon, in the year 1474, on a condemned criminal, whose life was granted by the king to the
petition of the physicians and surgeons of the city, that he might
serve, according to the philosophic maxim, as the *corpus vile*, or
worthless subject, of the experiment.

LATIN CHRONICLERS.

Of the literary productions of this age the literary merits are
in general of the humblest description. Among the Latin
historians, or chroniclers, Thomas Walsingham may be accounted
one of the best, if not the chief. He was a Benedictine of the
Abbey of St. Albans, and is the author of two works; one a
History of England, entitled Historia Brevis, which begins at

1273, where Matthew Paris ends, and extends to the beginning
of the reign of Henry VI.; the other a History of Normandy,
under the title of Ypodigma Neustriæ, from the first acquisition
of the duchy by Rollo the Dane. The style of these chronicles
is sufficiently rude and unpolished; but they are very full and
circumstantial, and the English History, even in the earlier
part of it, contains many things not mentioned by any contemporary writer.* The compilation of English History by
Thomas Otterbourne, a Franciscan friar, from the landing of
Brutus to the year 1420, is held in small estimation.† A much
more valuable performance is the Chronicon of John de Whethamstede, Abbot of St. Albans, although it only extends from
the year 1441 to 1461.‡ Whethamstede was a person of judgment as well as of considerable learning. He was an especial
favourite with Duke Humphrey, who was accustomed to visit
him in his monastery, where the monks, however, accused their
abbot of spending too much of his time in study and in writing
books, though he was a most liberal benefactor to their establishment. But probably neither the libraries he built and furnished
both at St. Albans and at Oxford, the organs and pictures with
which he adorned the church and chapels of his monastery, nor
the extensive additions which he made to its buildings, compensated in their estimation for tastes and habits so different
from their own. Another of the Latin historians of this period
whose name is connected with Duke Humphrey is the Italian,
Titus Livius Forojuliensis, as he calls himself, the author of a
Life of Henry V.§ He was invited to England by the duke,
who appointed him to be his poet and orator. His Life of
Henry V., however, is very little else than an abridgment of the
work on the same subject by Thomas de Elmham,‖ Prior of
Lynton, whose barbarous style does not prevent his performance
from being one of great historical value. The Italian affects to
imitate the style of the illustrious ancient whose name he
assumes; but he is, as may be supposed, a very modern Livy.
Another of these annalists is William Botoner, or William of

---

* Published together by Archbishop Parker. fol. Lon. 1571. Also in
Camden's Anglica, &c. fol. Francof. 1603.
† Published by Hearne, in 2 vols. 8vo. Oxon. 1732.
‡ Published by Hearne, along with Otterbourne.
§ Published by Hearne, 8vo. Oxon. 1716.
‖ Published by Hearne, 8vo. Oxon. 1727.

Worcester, the author of a chronicle extending from 1324 to 1491, which is nearly all a compilation, and of very little value.[*] Botoner is also the author of the translation of Cicero's Treatise on Old Age, already mentioned as one of Caxton's publications. The last of this class of writers we shall mention is John Rossus, or Rosse, of Warwick, the author of what he calls a History of the Kings of England,[†] which, nevertheless, commences with the creation of the world. Although it does not contain much that is interesting till the author comes down to his own age, the latter part of the fifteenth century, it furnishes some curious details both of the events and the manners of that time.

FRENCH CHRONICLERS.

Two French writers, Monstrelet and Comines, may be considered as in some sort belonging to this period of English history. Monstrelet, whose narrative extends from 1400 to 1452 (with a supplement coming down to 1467 by another hand), is a very faithful but not a very lively chronicler of the contentions of the houses of Orleans and Burgundy, and of the wars of the English in France, in his own day. Comines, an actor to a considerable extent in the affairs which he relates, is a writer of a superior stamp. His Memoirs extend from 1464 to 1498, a period comprehending nearly the whole reign of Louis XI. of France, whom Comines may be said to make his hero, and whose singular character gives much of a dramatic life to the narrative of the historian. Comines has none of the chivalrous enthusiasm of Froissart, and no other excitement of a very warm or imaginative character to make up for the want of it; but observation, sagacity, and an unaffected, straightforward way of writing, give him a great power of carrying his reader along with him. He is the best authority for the French transactions of the reign of our Edward IV.

[*] Published by Hearne, in the Appendix to the Liber Niger Scaccarii. 2 vols. 8vo. Oxon. 1728.
[†] Published by Hearne, 8vo. Oxon. 1716.

ENGLISH CHRONICLERS.

This age also affords us two or three English chroniclers. The series of our modern English chronicles may perhaps be most properly considered as commencing with John de Trevisa's translation of Higden, with various additions, which, as already mentioned, was finished in 1387, and was printed, with a continuation to 1460, by Caxton, in 1482. After Trevisa comes John Harding, who belongs to the fifteenth century; his metrical Chronicle of England coming down to the reign of Edward IV.* The metre is melancholy enough; but the part of the work relating to the author's own times is not without value. Harding is chiefly notorious as the author, or at least the collector and producer, of a great number of charters and other documents attesting acts of fealty done by the Scottish to the English kings, which are now generally admitted to be forgeries. Caxton himself must be reckoned our next English chronicler, as the author both of the continuation of Trevisa and also of the concluding part of the volume entitled The Chronicles of England, published by him in 1480,—the body of which is translated from a Latin chronicle by Douglas, a monk of Glastonbury, who lived in the preceding century. Neither of these performances, however, is calculated to add to the fame of the celebrated printer. To this period we may also in part assign the better known Concordance of Histories of Robert Fabyan, citizen and draper of London; though the author only died in 1512, nor was his work printed till a few years later. Fabyan's history, which begins with Brutus and comes down to his own time, is in the greater part merely a translation from the preceding chroniclers; its chief value consists in a number of notices it has preserved relating to the city of London.†

BISHOP PECOCK.—FORTESCUE.—MALORY.

Of the English theological writers of the age immediately following that of Wiclif, the most noteworthy is Reynold

---

* First printed by Grafton in 1543. The most recent edition is that by Sir H. Ellis, 4to. Lond. 1812.

† First published in 1516. The last edition is that of Sir H. Ellis, Lond. 4to. 1811.

Pecock, Bishop of Asaph and afterwards of Chichester. As may be inferred from these ecclesiastical dignities, Pecock was no Wiclifite, but a defender of the established system both of doctrine and of church government: he tells us himself, in one of his books, that twenty years of his life had been spent for the greater part in writing against the Lollards. But, whatever effect his arguments may have produced upon those against whom they were directed, they gave little satisfaction to the more zealous spirits on his own side, who probably thought that he was too fond of reasoning with errors demanding punishment by a cautery sharper than that of the pen; and the end was that he was himself, in the year 1457, charged with heresy, and, having been found guilty, was first compelled to read a recantation, and to commit fourteen of his books, with his own hands, to the flames at St. Paul's Cross, and then deprived of his bishopric, and consigned to an imprisonment in which he was allowed the use neither of writing materials nor of books, and in which he is supposed to have died about two years after. One especial heresy alleged to be found in his writings was, that in regard to matters of faith the church was not infallible. Bishop Pecock's Life has been ably and learnedly written by the Rev. John Lewis, to whom we also owe biographies of Wiclif and of Caxton. His numerous treatises are partly in English, partly in Latin. Of those in English the most remarkable is one entitled The Repressor, which he produced in 1449. A short specimen, in which the spelling, but only the spelling, is modernized, will give some notion of his manner of writing, and of the extent to which the language had been adapted to prose eloquence or reasoning of the more formal kind in that age :—

"Say to me, good sir, and answer hereto: when men of the country upland bringen into London in Midsummer eve branches of trees fro Bishop's Wood, and flowers fro the field, and betaken tho[1] to citizens of London for to therewith array her[2] houses, shoulden men of London, receiving and taking the branches and flowers, say and hold that the branches grewen out of the carts which broughten hem[3] to London, and that tho carts or the hands of the bringers weren grounds and fundaments of the branches and flowers? God forbid so little wit be in her heads. Certes, though Christ and his apostles weren now living at London, and would bring, so as is now said, branches from Bishop's Wood, and flowers

---

[1] Take them, or those.   [2] Their.   [3] Them.

from the fields, into London, and woulden hem deliver to men, that they make therewith her houses gay, into remembrance of St. John Baptist, and of this that it was prophesied of him, that many shoulden joy of his birth, yet the men of London, receiving so the branches and flowers, oughten not say and feel that the branches and flowers grewen out of Christ's hands. The branches grewen out of the boughs upon which they in Bishop's Wood stooden, and the boughs grewen out of stocks or truncheons, and the truncheons or shafts grewen out of the root, and the root out of the next earth thereto, upon which and in which the root is buried. So that neither the cart, neither the hands of the bringers, neither the bringers ben the grounds or fundaments of the branches."

The good bishop, we see, has a popular and lively as well as clear and precise way of putting things. It may be doubted, nevertheless, if his ingenious illustrations would be quite as convincing to the earnest and excited innovators to whom they were addressed as they were satisfactory to himself.

Another eminent English prose writer of this date was Sir John Fortescue, who was Lord Chief Justice of the King's Bench under Henry VI., and to whom the king is supposed to have also confided the great seal at some time during his expulsion from the throne. Fortescue is the author of various treatises, some in English, some in Latin, most of which, however, still remain in manuscript. One in Latin, which was first sent to press in the reign of Henry VIII., and has been repeatedly reprinted since, is commonly referred to under the title of De Landibus Legum Angliæ. It has also been several times translated into English. This treatise is drawn up in the form of a dialogue between the author and Henry's unfortunate son, Edward Prince of Wales, so barbarously put to death after the battle of Tewkesbury. Fortescue's only English work that has been printed was probably written at a later date, and would appear to have had for its object to secure for him, now that the Lancastrian cause was beaten to the ground, the favour of the Yorkist king, Edward IV. It was first published, in 1714, by Mr. John Fortescue Aland, of the Middle Temple, with the title of The Difference between an Absolute and Limited Monarchy, as it more particularly regards the English Constitution,—which, of course, is modern, but has been generally adopted to designate the work. The following passage (in which the spelling is again reformed) will enable the reader to compare Fortescue as a writer with his contemporary Pecock, and is also curious both for its matter and its spirit :—

And how so be it that the French king reigneth upon his people *dominio regali*, yet St. Lewis, sometime king there, ne any of his predecessors set never tallies ne other impositions upon the people of that land without the consent of the three estates, which, when they may be assembled, are like to the court of Parliament in England. And this order kept many of his successors till late days, that Englishmen kept such a war in France that the three estates durst not come together. And then, for that cause, and for great necessity which the French king had of goods for the defence of that land, he took upon him to set tallies and other impositions upon the commons without the assent of the three estates; but yet he would not set any such charges, nor hath set, upon the nobles, for fear of rebellion. And, because the commons, though they have grudged, have not rebelled, nor be hardy to rebel, the French kings have yearly sithen[1] set such charges upon them, and so augmented the same charges as the same commons be so impoverished and destroyed that they may uneath[2] live. They drink water, they eat apples, with bread, right brown, made of rye. They eat no flesh, but if it be selden[3] a little lard, or of the entrails or heads of beasts slain for the nobles and merchants of the land. They wear no woollen, but if it be a poor coat under their uttermost gurment, made of great canvas, and passen not their knee; wherefore they be gartered and their thighs bare. Their wives and children gone barefoot. They may in none otherwise live; for some of them that was wont to pay to his landlord for his tenement which he hireth by the year a scute[4] payeth now to the king, over[5] that scute, five scutes. Where-through they be artied[6] by necessity, so to watch, labour, and grub in the ground for their sustenance, that their nature is much wasted, and the kind of them brought to nought. They gone crooked, and are feeble, not able to fight nor to defend the realm; nor have they weapon, nor money to buy them weapon, withal; but verily they live in the most extreme poverty and misery; and yet they dwell in one of the most fertile realms of the world. Where-through the French king hath not men of his own realm able to defend it, except his nobles, which bearen not such impositions, and therefore they are right likely of their bodies; by which cause the king is compelled to make his armies, and retinues for defence of his land, of strangers, as Scots, Spaniards, Aragoners, men of Almayne,[7] and of other nations; else all his enemies might overrun him; for he hath no defence of his own, except his castles and fortresses. Lo! this the fruit of his *jus regale*.

It is in the same spirit that the patriotic chief justice elsewhere boasts, that there were more Englishmen hanged for robbery in one year than Frenchmen in seven, and that "if an

---

[1] Since.   [2] Scarcely, with difficulty (uneasily).
[3] Seldom, on rare occasions.
[4] An *escut*, or *ecu* (*d'or*), about three shillings and fourpence.
[5] In addition to, over and above.   [6] Compelled.
[7] Germany.

Englishman be poor, and see another having riches which may
be taken from him by might, he will not spare to do so."

Fortescue was probably born not much more than thirty years
after Pecock; but the English of the judge, in vocabulary, in
grammatical forms, in the modulation of the sentences, and in its
air altogether, might seem to exhibit quite another stage of the
language.

Although both Pocock and Lyttelton lived to see the great
invention of printing, and the latter at any rate survived the
introduction of the new art into his native country, no production
of either appears to have been given to the world through the
press in the lifetime of the writer. Perhaps this was also the
case with another prose writer of this date, who is remembered,
however, less by his name than by the work of which he is the
author, and which still continues to be read, the famous history
of King Arthur, commonly known under the name of the Morte
Arthur. This work was first printed by Caxton in the year
1485. He tells us in his prologue, or preface, that the copy was
given him by Sir Thomas Malory, Knight, who took it, out of
certain books in French, and reduced it into English. Malory
himself states at the end, that he finished his task in the ninth
year of King Edward IV., which would be in 1469 or 1470.
The Morte Arthur was several times reprinted in the course of
the following century and a half, the latest of the old editions
having appeared in a quarto volume in 1634. From this, two
reprints were brought out by different London booksellers in the
same year, 1816; one in three duodecimos, the other in two.[*]
But the standard modern edition is that which appeared in two
volumes quarto in the following year, 1817, exactly reprinted
from Caxton's original edition, with the title of The Byrth, Lyfe,
and Actes of Kyng Arthur; of his noble Knyghtes of the Rounde
Table, &c., with an Introduction and Notes, by Robert Southey.
Malory, whoever he may have been (Leland says he was Welsh),
and supposing him to have been in the main only a translator,
must be admitted to show considerable mastery of expression ;
his English is always animated and flowing, and, in its earnestness and tenderness, occasionally rises to no common beauty and

---

[*] In Mr. Bohn's new edition of Lowndes's ' Bibliographer's Manual ' it is
stated that the *former* was edited by Haslewood. Should it not be the *latter* ?
It is the more correct of the two, and forms part of the series known as
Walker's Classics.

eloquence. The concluding chapters in particular have been much admired. We extract a few sentences :—

Then Sir Lancelot, ever after, eat but little meat, nor drank, but continually mourned until he was dead ; and then he sickened more and more, and dried and dwindled away. For the bishop, nor none of his fellows, might not make him to eat, and little he drank, that he was soon waxed shorter by a cubit than he was, that the people could not know him. For evermore day and night he prayed [taking no rest], but needfully as nature required ; sometimes he slumbered a broken sleep ; and always he was lying grovelling upon King Arthur's and Queen Guenever's tomb ; and there was no comfort that the bishop, nor Sir Bors, nor none of all his fellows could make him ; it availed nothing.

Oh ! ye mighty and pompous lords, winning in the glorious transitory of this unstable life, as in reigning over great realms and mighty great countries, fortified with strong castles and towers, edified with many a rich city ; yea also, ye fierce and mighty knights, so valiant in adventurous deeds of arms, behold ! behold ! see how this mighty conqueror, King Arthur, whom in his human life all the world doubted,[1] yea also the noble Queen Guenever, which sometime sat in her chair adorned with gold, pearls, and precious stones, now lie full low in obscure fosse, or pit, covered with clods of earth and clay ! Behold also this mighty champion, Sir Lancelot, peerless of all knighthood ; see now how he lieth grovelling upon the cold mould ; now being so feeble and faint, that sometime was so terrible : how, and in what manner, ought ye to be so desirous of worldly honour so dangerous ? Therefore, me thinketh this present book is right necessary often to be read ; for in all[2] ye find the most gracious, knightly, and virtuous war, of the most noble knights of the world, whereby they got praising continually ; also me seemeth, by the oft reading thereof, ye shall greatly desire to accustom yourself in following of those gracious knightly deeds ; that is to say, to dread God and to love righteousness, faithfully and courageously to serve your sovereign prince ; and, the more that God hath given you the triumphal honour, the meeker ought ye to be, ever fearing the unstableness of this deceitful world.

. . . .

And so, within fifteen days, they came to Joyous Guard, and there they laid his corpse in the body of the quire, and sung and read many psalters and prayers over him and about him ; and even his visage was laid open and naked, that all folk might behold him. For such was the custom in those days, that all men of worship should so lie with open visage till that they were buried. And right thus as they were at their service there came Sir Ector de Maris, that had sought seven years all England, Scotland, and Wales, seeking his brother Sir Lancelot. . . .

And then Sir Ector threw his shield, his sword, and his helm from him ; and when he beheld Sir Lancelot's visage, he fell down in a swoon ; and,

---

[1] Dreaded (held as redoubtable).   [2] It ?

when he awoke, it were hard for any tongue to tell the doleful complaints that he made for his brother. "Ah, Sir Lancelot," said he, "thou wert head of all Christian knights."—"And now, I dare say," said Sir Bors, "that Sir Lancelot, there thou liest, thou wert never matched of none earthly knight's hands. And thou wert the courtliest knight that ever bare shield; and thou wert the truest friend to thy lover that ever bestrode horse; and thou wert the truest lover, of a sinful man, that ever loved woman; and thou wert the kindest man that ever stroke with sword; and thou wert the goodliest person that ever came among press of knights; and thou wert the meekest man, and the gentlest, that ever ate in hall among ladies; and thou wert the sternest knight to thy mortal foe that ever put spear in rest."

ENGLISH POETS.—OCCLEVE; LYDGATE.

The most numerous class of writers in the mother tongue belonging to this time, are the poets, by courtesy so called. We must refer to the learned and curious pages of Warton, or to the still more elaborate researches of Ritson,[*] for the names of a crowd of worthless and forgotten versifiers that fill up the annals of our national minstrelsy from Chaucer to Lord Surrey. The last-mentioned antiquary has furnished a list of about seventy English poets who flourished in this interval. The first known writer of any considerable quantity of verse after Chaucer is Thomas Occleve. Warton places him about the year 1420. He is the author of many minor pieces, which mostly remain in manuscript—although "six of peculiar stupidity," says Ritson, "were selected and published" by Dr. Askew in 1796;—and also of a longer poem, entitled De Regimine Principum (On the Government of Princes), chiefly founded on a Latin work, with the same title, written in the thirteenth century by an Italian ecclesiastic Egidius, styled the Doctor Fundatissimus, and on the Latin treatise on the game of chess of Jacobus de Casulis, another Italian writer of the same age—the latter being the original of the Game of the Chess, translated by Caxton from the French, and printed by him in 1474. Occleve's poem has never been published—and is chiefly remembered for a drawing of Chaucer by the hand of Occleve, which is found in one of the manuscripts of it now in the British Museum.[†] Occleve

[*] Bibliographia Poetica.

[†] Harl. MS. 4866. This portrait, which is a half-length, is coloured. There is a full-length portrait in another copy of Occleve's Poems in Royal MS. 17 D. vi.—See Life of Chaucer, by Sir Harris Nicolas, pp. 104. &c

repeatedly speaks of Chaucer as his master and poetic father,
and was no doubt personally acquainted with the great poet.
All that Occleve appears to have gained, however, from his
admirable model is some initiation in that smoothness and regularity of diction of which Chaucer's writings set the first great
example. His own endowment of poetical power and feeling
was very small—the very titles of his pieces, as Warton remarks,
indicating the poverty and frigidity of his genius.

By far the most famous of these versifiers of the fifteenth
century is John Lydgate, the monk of Bury, whom the Historian
of our Poetry considers to have arrived at his highest point of
eminence about the year 1430. Ritson has given a list of about
250 poems attributed to Lydgate. Indeed he seems to have
followed the manufacture of rhymes as a sort of trade, furnishing
any quantity to order whenever he was called upon. On one
occasion, for instance, we find him employed by the historian
Whethamstede, who was abbot of St. Albans, to make a translation into English, for the use of that convent, of the Latin
legend of its patron saint. "The chronicler who records a part
of this anecdote," observes Warton, "seems to consider Lydgate's
translation as a matter of mere manual mechanism; for he adds,
that Whethamstede paid for the translation, the writing, and
illuminations, one hundred shillings."[*] Lydgate, however,
though excessively diffuse, and possessed of very little strength
or originality of imagination, is a considerably livelier and more
expert writer than Occleve. His memory was also abundantly
stored with the learning of his age; he had travelled in France
and Italy, and was intimately acquainted with the literature of
both these countries; and his English makes perhaps a nearer
approach to the modern form of the language than that of any
preceding writer. His best-known poem consists of nine books
of Tragedies, as he entitles them, respecting the falls of princes,
translated from a Latin work of Boccaccio's: it was printed at
London in the reign of Henry VIII. A Selection from the
Minor Poems of Dan John Lydgate, edited by Mr. Halliwell,
has been printed for the Percy Society, 8vo. Lon. 1840.

[*] Hist. Eng. Poetry, vol. ii. p. 363.

SCOTTISH POETS.—WYNTON; JAMES I.; HENRYSON; HOLLAND;
BLIND HENRY.

The most remarkable portion of our poetical literature belonging to the fifteenth century (as also, we shall presently find, of
that belonging to the first half of the sixteenth), was contributed
by Scottish writers. The earliest successor of Barbour was
Andrew of Wyntown, or Wynton, a canon regular of the Priory
of St. Andrews, and Prior of the Monastery of St. Serf's Inch in
Lochleven, one of the establishments subordinate to that great
house, who is supposed to have been born about 1350, and whose
Originale Cronykil of Scotland appears to have been finished in
the first years of the fifteenth century. It is a long poem, of
nine books, written in the same octosyllabic rhyme with the
Bruce of Barbour, to which it was no doubt intended to serve
as a kind of introduction. Wynton, however, has very little of
the old archdeacon's poetic force and fervour; and even his
style, though in general sufficiently simple and clear, is, if anything, rather ruder than that of his predecessor—a difference
which is probably to be accounted for by Barbour's frequent
residences in England and more extended intercourse with the
world. The Chronykil is principally interesting in an historical
point of view, and in that respect it is of considerable value and
authority, for Wynton, besides his merits as a distinct narrator,
had evidently taken great pains to obtain the best information
within his reach with regard to the events both of his own and
of preceding times. The work begins (as was then the fashion),
with the creation of the world, and comes down to the year 1408;
but the first five books are occupied rather with general than
with Scottish history. The last four books, together with such
parts of the preceding ones as contain anything relating to
British affairs, were very carefully edited by the late Mr. David
Macpherson (the author of the well-known Annals of Com-
merce and other works), in two volumes 8vo. Lon. 1795. It
is deserving of notice that a considerable portion of Wynton's
Chronicle is not his own composition, but was the contribution
of another contemporary poet; namely, all from the 10th chapter
of the Eighth to the 10th chapter of the Ninth Book inclusive,
comprising the space from 1324 to 1390, and forming about a
third of the four concluding books. This he conscientiously

acknowledges, in very careful and explicit terms, both at the beginning and end of the insertion. We may give what he says in the latter place, as a short sample of his style:—

> This part last treated beforn,
> Fra Davy the Brus our king was born,
> While[1] his sister son Robert
> The Second, our king, than called Stuert,
> That nest[2] him reigned successive,
> His days had ended of his live,
> Wit ye well, wes nought my dite;[3]
> Thereof I dare nue well acquite.
> Wha that it dited, nevertheless,
> He showed him of mair cunnandnes[4]
> Than me commendis[4] his treatise,
> But[5] favour, wha[6] will it clearly prize.
> This part wes written to me send;
> And I, that thought for to mak end
> Of that purpose I took on hand,
> Saw it was well accordland
> To my matere; I wes right glad;
> For I was in my travail and;
> I eked[7] it here to this dite,
> For to mak me some respite.

This is interesting as making it probable that poetical, or at least metrical, composition in the national dialect was common in Scotland at this early date.

Of all our poets of the early part of the fifteenth century the one of greatest eminence must be considered to be King James I. of Scotland, even if he be only the author of The King's Quair (that is, the King's quire or book), his claim to which has scarcely been disputed. It is a serious poem, of nearly 1400 lines, arranged in seven-line stanzas; the style in great part allegorical; the subject, the love of the royal poet for the lady Joanna Beaufort, whom he eventually married, and whom he is said to have first beheld walking in the garden below from the window of his prison in the Round Tower of Windsor Castle. The poem was in all probability written during his detention in England, and previous to his marriage, which took place in

[1] Till.   [2] Next.   [3] Writing.
[4] He showed himself of more cunning (skill) than I who commend.
[5] Without.   [6] Whosoever.   [7] Added.

February 1424, a few months before his return to his native
country. In the concluding stanza James makes grateful mention
of his—

> maisters dear
> Gower and Chaucer, that on the steppis sate
> Of rhetorick while they were livand here,
> Superlative as poets laureate,
> Of morality and eloquence ornate;

and he is evidently an imitator of the great father of English
poetry. The poem too must be regarded as written in English
rather than in Scotch, although the difference between the two
dialects, as we have seen, was not so great at this early date as
it afterwards became, and although James, who was in his
eleventh year when he was carried away to England in 1405 by
Henry IV., may not have altogether avoided the peculiarities
of his native idiom. The Quair was first published from the
only manuscript (one of the Selden Collection in the Bodleian
Library), by Mr. W. Tytler at Edinburgh, in 1783; there have
been several editions since. The following specimen is transcribed from the text given by Mr. George Chalmers, in his
Poetic Remains of some of the Scottish Kings, now first collected,
8vo. Lon. 1824; though without adhering in all cases either to
his spelling, his pointing, or his explanations :—

> Where as in ward full oft I would bewail
>   My deadly life, full of pain and penance,
> Saying right thus, What have I guilt to fail[1]
>   My freedom in this world and my pleasance?[2]
>   Sen[2] every wight has thereof suffisance
> That I behold, and I a creature
> Put from all this, hard is mine aventure.[3]
>
> The bird, the beast, the fish eke in the sea,
>   They live in freedom everich in his kind,
> And I a man, and lacketh liberty!
>   What shall I sayn, what reason may I find,
>   That fortune should do so? Thus in my mind

---

[1] What guilt have I (what have I been guilty of) so that I should want
(be deprived of).
[2] Since.   [3] Hap. lot. fate.

My folk I would argue;[1] but all for nought;
Was none that might that on my paines wrought.[2]

Then would I say, Gif God me had devised
  To live my life in thraldom thus and pine,
What was the cause that he more me comprised[3]
  Than other folk to live in such ruine?
  I suffer alone among the figures nine;[4]
Ane weeful wretch, that to no wight may speed,[5]
And yet of every lives[6] help has need!

The longe days and the nighter eke
  I would bewail my fortune in this wise;
For which again[7] distress comfort to seek
  My custom was on morrow for to rise,
  Early as day; O happy exercise!
By thee came I to joy out of torment:—
But now to purpose of my first intent.

Bewailing in my chamber thus alone,
  Despaired of all joy and remedy,
Fortirit[8] of my thought and woe-begone,
  And to the window gan I walk in hy[9]
  To see the world and folk that went forby,[10]
As, for the time though I of mirthes food
Might have no more, to look it did me good.

Now was there made, fast by the Toures wall,
  A garden fair, and in the corners set
Ane herber[11] green, with wandes long and small
  Railed about; and so with trees set,
  Was all the place, and hawthorn hedges knet,[12]
That life[13] was none walking there forby
That might within scarce any wight espy.

---

[1] According to Chalmers this means, "I would argue with my attendants—the Earl of Orkney and others of his train." We suspect the word *folk* to be a mistranscription—perhaps for fate.

[2] There was no one that might do what had any effect in relieving my sufferings?—if the line be not corrupt.   [3] Doomed, forced (comprised).

[4] "Of all the nine numbers mine is the most unlucky."—*Chalmers.*

[5] To no man may do service.   [6] Living person.   [7] Against.

[8] Tired. The termination here is Scotch. The MS. appears to have been written in Scotland. Other printed editions have *Fortirid.*   [9] Haste.

[10] Past? "Forby" in modern Scotch means besides.

[11] Ellis says, "probably an arbour:"—Chalmers, "a garden plot set with plants and flowers—a grove with an arbour railed with trellis-work, and close set about with trees."

[12] Knit.   [13] Living person.

So thick the bewes[1] and the leaves green
  Beshaded all the alleys that there were,
And middes[2] every herber might be seen
  The sharpe, greene, sweete juniper,
  Growing so fair with branches here and there,
That, as it seemed to a life without,
The bewes spread the herber all about.

And on the smale greene twistes sate
  The little sweete nightingale, and song
So loud and clear the hymnes consecrate
  Of loves use, now soft now loud among,
  That all the gardens and the walles rung
Right of their song and on the couple next[3]
Of their sweet harmony; and lo the text:—

Worshippe, ye that lovers been, this May,
  For of your bliss the kalends are begun,
And sing with us, Away, winter, away!
  Come summer, come, the sweet season and sun;
  Awake, for shame! that have your heavens won,[4]
And amorously lift up your heades all;
Hark Love, that list you to his mercy call.

The description of the lady whom he afterwards sees " walking
under the Tower,"—at whose sudden apparition, " anon," he
says,—

—" astart[5]
  The blood of all my body to my heart"—

is exceedingly elaborate, but is too long to be quoted. Ellis has
given the greater part of it in his Specimens.[6] Two other
poems of considerable length, in a humorous style, have also
been attributed to James I.—Peebles to the Play, and Christ's
Kirk on the Green, both in the Scottish dialect; but they are
more probably the productions of his equally gifted and equally
unfortunate descendant James V. (slain at Flodden in 1513).
Chalmers, however, assigns the former to James I. As for the
two famous comic ballads of The Gaberlunyie Man, and the Jolly
Beggar, which it has been usual among recent writers to speak

[1] Boughs. [2] Amidst.
[3] Not understood. Tytler thinks "couple" relates to the pairing of the
birds; Ellis and Chalmers, that it is a musical term.
[4] " Ye that have attained your highest bliss "—*Tytler.*
[5] Started up.
[6] Vol. i. pp. 305—309.

of us by one or other of those kings, there seems to be no reasonable ground—not even that of tradition of any antiquity—for assigning them to either.

Chaucer, we have seen, appears to have been unknown to his contemporary Barbour; but after the time of James I. the Scottish poetry for more than a century bears evident traces of the imitation of the great English master. It was a consequence of the relative circumstances of the two countries, that, while the literature of Scotland, the poorer and ruder of the two, could exert no influence upon that of England, the literature of England could not fail powerfully to affect and modify that of its more backward neighbour. No English writer would think of studying or imitating Barbour; but every Scottish poet who arose after the time of Chaucer had passed the border would seek, or, even if he did not seek, would still inevitably catch, some inspiration from that great example. If it could in any circumstances have happened that Chaucer should have remained unknown in Scotland, the singular fortunes of James I. were shaped as if on purpose to transfer the manner and spirit of his poetry into the literature of that country. From that time forward the native voice of the Scottish muse was mixed with this other foreign voice. One of the earliest Scottish poets after James I. is Robert Henryson, or Henderson, the author of the beautiful pastoral of Robin and Makyne, which is popularly known from having been printed by Bishop Percy in his Reliques.[*] He has left us a continuation or supplement to Chaucer's Troilus and Creseide, which is commonly printed along with the works of that poet under the title of The Testament of Fair Creseide. All that is known of the era of Henryson is that he was alive and very old about the close of the fifteenth century. He may therefore probably have been born about the time that James I. returned from England. Henryson is also the author of a translation into English or Scottish verse of Æsop's Fables, of which there is a MS. in the Harleian Collection (No. 3865), and which was printed at Edinburgh in 8vo. in

---

[*] Vol. ii. pp. 73-78. It was first printed in Ramsay's Evergreen, 12mo. Edin. 1724. (Or see second edition, Glasgow, 1824.) It is also in Lord Hailes's Ancient Scottish Poems (from the Bannatyne MS.) 8vo. Edin. 1770. And an edition of this Poem, and of the Testament of Creseide, by the late George Chalmers, was printed for the Bannatyne Club, in 4to. at Edinburgh, in 1824.

1021, under the title of The Moral Fables of Æsop the Phrygian, compyled into eloquent and ornamental meter, by Robert Henrison, schoolmaster of Dumferling. A reimpression of this edition (limited to 68 copies) was executed at Edinburgh, in 4to., in 1832, for the members of the Maitland Club. To Henryson, moreover, as has been already noticed, Mr. Laing attributes the tale of Orpheus and Eurydice contained in the collection of old poetry, entitled The Knightly Tale of Golagrus and Gawane, &c., reprinted by him in 1827.

Contemporary, too, with Henryson, if not perhaps rather before him, was Sir John or Richard Holland, whose poem entitled The Buke of the Howlat (that is, the owl) was printed, under the care of Mr. Laing, in 4to. at Edinburgh in 1823 for the Bannatyne and Abbotsford Clubs. It had been previously printed, with less correctness, by Pinkerton in his Scotish Poems, 3 vols. 8vo. 1792; and also in the first volume of Sibbald's Chronicle of Scottish Poetry, 4 vols. 8vo. 1802. Holland's poem, a wild and rugged effusion in alliterative metre, cannot be charged as an imitation of Chaucer, or of any other English writer of so late a date.

Another Scottish poet of this time the style and spirit as well as the subject of whose poetry must be admitted to be exclusively national is Henry the Minstrel, commonly called Blind Harry, author of the famous poem on the life and acts of Wallace. The testimony of the historian John Major to the time at which Henry wrote is sufficiently express: " The entire book of William Wallace," he says, " Henry, who was blind from his birth, composed in the time of my infancy (*nens infantiæ tempore cudit*), and what things used popularly to be reported wove into popular verse, in which he was skilled." Major is believed to have been born about 1409; so that Henry's poem may be assigned to the end of the third quarter of the fifteenth century. There is reason to believe that it was printed at Edinburgh as early as 1520; but the oldest impression now known is an Edinburgh one in 4to. of the year 1570. There were many reprints of it in the seventeenth and eighteenth centuries, some of them greatly modernized in the language and otherwise altered: the standard edition is that published from a manuscript dated 1488 by Dr. Jamieson along with Barbour's poem, 4to. Edin. 1820. The Wallace, which is a long poem of about 12,000 decasyllabic lines, used to be a still greater favourite than was The Bruce with the author's

countrymen; and Dr. Jamieson does not hesitate to place Harry
as a poet before Barbour. In this judgment, however, probably
few critical readers will concur, although both Warton and Ellis,
without going so far, have also acknowledged in warm terms the
rude force of the Blind Minstrel's genius. It may be remarked,
by the way, that were it not for Major's statement, and the
common epithet that has attached itself to his name, we should
scarcely have supposed that the author of Wallace had been
either blind from his birth or blind at all. He nowhere himself
alludes to any such circumstance. His poem, besides, abounds
in descriptive passages, and in allusions to natural appearances
and other objects of sight: perhaps, indeed, it might be said that
there is an ostentation of that kind of writing, such as we meet
with also in the modern Scotch poet Blacklock's verses, and
which it may be thought is not unnatural to a blind person.
Nor are his apparent literary acquirements to be very easily
reconciled with Major's account, who represents him as going
about reciting his verses among the nobility (*coram principibus*),
and thereby obtaining food and raiment, of which, says the historian, he was worthy (*victum, et vestitum, quo dignus erat, nactus
est*). "He seems," as Dr. Jamieson observes, "to have been
pretty well acquainted with that kind of history which was
commonly read in that period." The Doctor refers to allusions
which he makes in various places to the romance histories of
Hector, of Alexander the Great, of Julius Cæsar, and of Charlemagne; and he conceives that his style of writing is more
richly strewed with the more peculiar phraseology of the writers
of romance than that of Barbour. But what is most remarkable
is that he distinctly declares his poem to be throughout a translation from the Latin. The statement, which occurs toward the
conclusion, seems too express and particular to be a mere imitation of the usage of the romance-writers, many of whom appeal,
but generally in very vague terms, to a Latin original for their
marvels:—

> Of Wallace life wha has a further feel[1]
> May show forth mair with wit and eloquence;
> For I to this have done my diligence,
> Efter the proof given fra the Latin book
> Whilk Maister Blair in his time undertook,

[1] Knowledge.

> In fair Latin compiled it till ane end :
> With thir witness the mair is to commend.[1]
> Bishop Sinclair than lord was of Dunkell ;
> He gat this book, and confirmed it himself
> For very true ; therefore he had no drede ;[2]
> Himself had seen great part of Wallace deed.
> His purpose was till have sent it to Rome,
> Our fader of kirk thereon to give his doom.
> But Maistre Blair and als Shir Thomas Gray
> Efter Wallace they lestit[3] mony day :
> Thir twa[4] knew best of Gud Schir William's deed,
> Fra sixteen year while[5] nine and twenty yeid.[6]

In another place (Book V. v. 538 et seq.) he says :—

> Maistre John Blair was oft in that message,
> A worthy clerk, baith wise and right savage.
> Lewit[7] he was before in Paris town
> Amang maisters in science and renown.
> Wallace and he at hame in schul had been :
> Soon efterwart, as verity is seen,
> He was the man that principal undertook,
> That first compiled in dite[8] the Latin book
> Of Wallace life, right famous in renown ;
> And Thomas Gray, person of Libertown.

Blind Harry's notions of the literary character are well exemplified by his phrase of a "worthy clerk, baith wise and right savage." He himself, let his scholarship have been what it may, is in spirit as thorough a Scot as if he had never heard the sound of any other than his native tongue. His gruff patriotism speaks out in his opening lines :—

> Our antecessors, that we suld of read,
> And hold in mind their noble worthy deed,
> We lat owerslide,[9] through very sleuthfulness,
> And casts us ever till other business.
> Till honour enemies is our hail[10] intent ;
> It has been seen in thir times bywent :

---

[1] We do not profess to understand this line. *Thir* is Scotch for *thir*. *Mair* is *mar* in Jamieson. [2] Doubt.
[3] Survived (lasted). [4] These two.
[5] Till. [6] Went, passed.
[7] Dr. Jamieson's only interpretation is "allowed, left."
[8] Writing. [9] Allow to slip out of memory. [10] Whole.

Our auld enemies comen of Saxons blud,
That never yet to Scotland wald do gud,
Bot ever on force and contrar hail thair will,
How great kindness there has been kythe[1] them till.
It is well knawn on many divers side
How they have wrought into their mighty pride
To hald Scotland at under evermair:
But God above has made thair might to pair.[2]

Of the fighting and slaying, which makes up by far the greater
part of the poem, it is difficult to find a sample that is short
enough for our purpose. The following is a small portion of what
is called the battle of Shortwoodshaw :—

On Wallace set a bicker bauld and keen ;
A bow he bare was big and well beseen,
And arrows als, baith lang and sharp with aw ;[3]
No man was there that Wallace bow might draw.
Right stark he was, and in to sooer gear ;[4]
Bauldly he shot amang they[5] men of wer.[6]
Ane angel heade[7] to the buiks he drow
And at a shot the foremost soon he slew.
Inglis archers, that hardy war and wight,
Amang the Scots bickered with all their might ;
Their aweful shot was felon[8] for to bide ;
Of Wallace men they woundit sore that tide ;
Few of them was sicker[9] of archery ;
Better they were, an they gat even party,
In field to bide either with swerd or spear.
Wallace perceivit his men tuk mickle deir :[10]
He gart[11] them change, and stand nought in to stead ;[12]
He cast all ways to save them fra the dead.[13]
Full great travail upon himself tuk he ;
Of Southron men feil[14] archers he gart dee.[15]
Of Longcashler[16] bowmen was in that place
A mair[17] archer aye waitit on Wallace,

---

[1] Shown.
[2] Dr. Jamieson's only interpretation is *caw*. It would almost seem as if we had here the modern Scottish *witha'* for *withall*.
[3] In sure warlike accoutrements.
[4] War.
[5] Those.
[6] Diminish, impair.
[7] The barbed head of an arrow.
[8] Terrible.
[9] Sure.
[10] Took much hazard, ran much risk.
[11] Caused.
[12] Stand not in their place. Perhaps it should be "o stead," that is, one place.
[13] Death.
[14] Many.
[15] Caused die.
[16] Lancashire.
[17] Skilful.

> At ane opine,[1] whar he usit to repair ;
> At him he drew a sicker shot and sair
> Under the chin, through a collar of steel
> On the left side, and hurt his halse[2] some deal.
> Astonied he was, but nought greatly aghast ;
> Out fra his men on him he followit fast ;
> In the turning with gud will has him ta'en
> Upon the crag,[3] in sunder straik the bain.

It will be seen from this specimen that the Blind Minstrel is a vigorous versifier. His descriptions, however, though both clear and forcible, and even not unfrequently animated by a dramatic abruptness and boldness of expression, want the bounding airy spirit and flashing light of those of Barbour. As a specimen of his graver style we may give his Envoy or concluding lines :—

> Go, noble book, fulfillit of gud sentence,
> Suppose thou be barren of eloquence :
> Go, worthy book, fulfillit of sutheast deed ;
> But in langage of help thou hast great need.
> Whan gud makers[4] rang weil into Scotland,
> Great fault was it that nane of them ye faind.[5]
> Yet there is part that can thee weil avance ;
> Now hide thy time, and be a remembrance.
> I you beseek of your benevolence,
> Wha will nought lou,[6] lak nought[7] my eloquence ;
> (It is weil knawn I am a burel[8] man)
> For here is said as gudly as I can ;
> My sprite feeles ne termes asperans.[9]
> Now beseek God, that giver is of grace,
> Made hell and erd,[10] and set the heaven above,
> That he us grant of his dear lestand[11] love.

---

[1] Open place?   [2] Neck.   [3] Throat
[4] Poets.   [5] Found.   [6] Love?
[7] Neuff not at.   [8] Hurtish, clownish.
[9] Understands no lofty (aspiring) terms. But it seems impossible that asperans can rhyme to grace.
[10] Earth.   [11] Lasting.

In no age, as we have found, even the darkest and most barren
of valuable produce, that has elapsed since learning was first
planted among us, had there failed to be something done in the
establishment of nurseries for its shelter and propagation. The
fifteenth century, though it has left us little enduring literature
of any kind, is distinguished for the number of the colleges that
were founded in the course of it, both in this country and in the
rest of Europe. This, indeed, was the natural and proper direction for the first impulse to take that was given by the revival
of letters: the actual generation upon which the new light
broke was not that in which it was to be expected it should do
much more than awaken the taste for true learning, or at most
the ambition of excellence; the power of accomplishment could
only come in the next era. The men of the latter part of the
fifteenth century, therefore, were most fitly and most usefully
employed in making provision for the preservation and trans-
mission to other times of the long-lost wisdom and eloquence
that had been found again in their day—in building cisterns and
conduits for the precious waters that, after having been hidden
for a thousand years, had burst their founts, and were once more
flowing over the earth. The fashion of founding colleges, and
other seminaries of learning, continued to prevail in this country
both down to the Reformation in religion, and for some time
after that mighty revolution. In the University of Oxford,
Brazennose College was founded in 1511 by William Smith,
Bishop of Lincoln, and Sir Richard Sutton, of Prusbury, in
Cheshire; Corpus Christi in 1517, by Henry VII.'s minister
Richard Fox, successively Bishop of Exeter, of Bath and Wells,
of Durham, and of Winchester; Cardinal College by Wolsey in
1525, which, however, before the buildings had been half
finished, was suppressed by the king on the cardinal's fall in
1529; the college of Henry VIII. by that king in 1532, a continuation, but on a much smaller scale, of Wolsey's design, which
was also dissolved in 1545, when that of Christ Church was
erected in its stead by Henry, to be both a college and at the
same time a cathedral establishment for the new bishopric of
Oxford; Trinity, on the old foundation of Durham College, by
Sir Thomas Pope, in 1554; St. John's, on the site of Bernard
College, by Sir Thomas White, alderman and merchant-tailor of

London, in 1557; and Jesus, by Dr. Hugh Price, Queen Elizabeth contributing part of the expense, in 1571. In Cambridge
there were founded Jesus College, in 1496, by John Alcock,
Bishop of Ely; Christ's College, in 1505, by Margaret, Countess
of Richmond, the mother of Henry VII.; St. John's, by the
same noble lady, in 1508; Magdalen, or Maudlin, begun in 1519
by Edward Stafford, the unfortunate Duke of Buckingham, and,
after his execution for high treason in 1521, completed by the
Lord Chancellor, Thomas Lord Audley; Trinity, in 1546, by
Henry VIII., who at the same time endowed four new professor-
ships in the University, one of theology, one of law, one of Hebrew, and one of Greek; Caius College, properly an extension
of the ancient foundation of Gonville Hall, by Dr. John Caius, or
Key, in 1557; Emanuel, in 1584, by Sir Walter Mildmay,
Chancellor of the Duchy of Lancaster and of the Exchequer;
and Sidney-Sussex College, in 1594, by the widow of Thomas
Radcliffe, Earl of Sussex, originally the Lady Frances Sidney.
In Scotland a new university was erected in Aberdeen, under
the name of King's College, by a bull of Pope Alexander VI.,
granted at the request of King James IV., in 1494, the principal
endower, however, being William Elphinstone, bishop of the
see; a second college, that of St. Leonard's (now forming, with
St. Salvator's, what is called the United College), was founded in
the University of St. Andrews, in 1512, by Alexander Stuart,
archbishop of the see, and John Hepburn, prior of the metro-
politan church; another college, that of St. Mary, now exclusively
appropriated to the theological faculty, was founded in the same
university in 1537, by Archbishop James Beaton; a fourth university, that of Edinburgh, was erected by King James VI. in
1582; and a fifth, that of Marischal College, Aberdeen, by George
Earl Marischal, in 1593. In Ireland, the university of Trinity
College, Dublin, was founded by Queen Elizabeth, in 1591. Along
with these seminaries might be mentioned a great number of
grammar schools; of which the chief were that of St. Paul's, London, founded by Dean Colet, in 1509; that of Ipswich, by Cardinal
Wolsey, at the same time with his college at Oxford, the fate of
which it also shared; Christ Church, London, by Edward VI., in
1553; Westminster School, by Queen Elizabeth, in 1560; and
Merchant Tailors' School by the London civic Company of that
name, in 1568. In Scotland, the High School of Edinburgh was
founded by the magistrates of the city in 1577.

CLASSICAL LEARNING.

Many of these colleges and schools were expressly established
for the cultivation of the newly revived classical learning, the
resurrection of which in the middle of the fifteenth century
revolutionized the ancient studies everywhere as soon as its
influence came to be felt. It scarcely reached England, however, as we have already intimated, till towards the close of that
century. Indeed, Greek is said to have been first publicly
taught in this country in St. Paul's school, by the famous grammarian William Lilly, who had studied the language at Rhodes,
and who was appointed the first master of the new school in
1512. Dean Colet himself, the founder, although accounted one
of the best-educated men of his time, had, during the seven years
he spent at Magdalen College, Oxford, only acquired a knowledge of some of the Greek authors through the medium of Latin
translations. Among the most distinguished of the early patrons
of the new learning after it had been thus introduced were the
two prelates and statesmen Fox and his greater *protégé* and successor Wolsey, both of whom, in the colleges founded by them
that have just been mentioned, made especial provision for the
teaching of the two classic tongues. The professor of Latin—or
of Humanity, as he is designated—in Corpus Christi College,
was expressly enjoined to extirpate *barbariem* from the new
society (*barbariem a nostro alveario extirpet*). The Greek professor
was ordered to explain the best Greek classics ; " and the poets,
historians, and orators in that language," observes Warton,
" which the judicious founder, who seems to have consulted the
most intelligent scholars of the times, recommends by name on this
occasion, are the purest, and such as are most esteemed even in
the present improved state of ancient learning." * Wolsey evinced
the interest he took in the new studies, not only by his great
school at Ipswich and his college at Oxford, but by founding in
that university some years before, along with various other pro-
fessorships, one for Rhetoric and Humanity and another for
Greek. " So attached was Wolsey," says the writer we have just
quoted, " to the new modes of instruction, that he did not think
it inconsistent with his high office and rank to publish a general

* Hist. Eng. Poet. Sect. xxxvi.

address to the schoolmasters of England, in which he orders them to institute their youth in the most elegant literature." And the high eulogium of Erasmus on the great cardinal is, that " he recalled to his country the three learned languages, without which all learning is lame."

A violent struggle, however, was for some time maintained against these innovations by the generality of those who had been educated in the old system, and by the always numerous and powerful host of the enemies and mistrusters of all innovation, whether from self-interest or other motives. Colet, in a letter to Erasmus, relates that one of the prelates of the church, esteemed among the most eminent for his learning and gravity, had, in a great public assembly, censured him in the severest terms for suffering the Latin poets to be taught in his new seminary, which on that account he styled a house of idolatry. This last expression would almost warrant us in suspecting that the prelate, whose name is not mentioned, was one of those inclined to the new opinions in religion: and at this time the new learning was probably rather distasteful than otherwise to that class of persons, zealously patronised as it was by Fox, Wolsey, and others, the heads of the party attached to the ancient faith. A few years afterwards a change took place in this respect: the reformers in religion became also the chief supporters of the reformation in learning, as was fit and natural both from the sameness in the general character and direction of the two movements, and also for an especial reason, which operated with very powerful effect. This was the surpassing importance speedily acquired in the contest between the two religions by the great principle on which the Reformers took their stand, of the omnipotence of the authority of the Scriptures in regard to all the points in debate between them and their opponents. Not custom or tradition, not the decrees of popes or councils, not even the Latin Vulgate translation, but the original text of the Greek New Testament alone, necessarily became, as soon as this principle was proclaimed, the grand ultimate criterion with them for the trial and decision of all doubts and disputes, and the armoury from which they drew their chief weapons both of defence and of assault. At first, it is true, this view does not appear to have been generally taken either by the one party or the other. The first editions of the Greek Testament that were given to the world were that contained in the

Complutensian Polyglot, the magnificent present to literature of Cardinal Ximenes, printed in 1514, but not published till 1522, and that of Erasmus, which appeared in 1516, both of which may be said to have proceeded from the bosom of the ancient church. Even from the first, however, many of the clergy, though principally rather from their extreme ignorance and illiteracy than from any fears they entertained of its unsettling people's faith, raised a considerable outcry against the New Testament of Erasmus: they seem to have seriously believed that the book was an invention of his own, and that he was attempting to establish a new religion. But the opposition to the Greek Scriptures, and to Greek literature generally, assumed a much more decided character when it was seen what use the friends of the new opinions in religion made of both, and how commonly an inclination in favour of the said new opinions went along with the cultivation of the new language. Erasmus for some time attempted to expound the Greek Grammar of Chryso-loras in the public schools at Cambridge; but his lectures were nearly unattended, and a storm of clamour was raised against him on all hands. His New Testament was actually proscribed by the authorities of the University, and a severe fine was denounced against any member who should be detected in having the book in his possession. Both in England and throughout Europe the universities were now generally divided into Greeks and Trojans; the latter class, who were those opposed to the new learning, usually comprehending all the monks and other most bigoted partisans of the old faith.[*]

Although, however, the revolt of Luther and his followers against the authority of Rome and many of the established doctrines in religion thus incidentally aided for a time the study and diffusion of classical scholarship, neither the subsequent progress of the Reformation in England nor its ultimate establishment operated with a favourable effect in the first instance upon the state of the universities or the general interests of learning. Henry VIII. himself, "from his natural liveliness of temper and love of novelty," as Warton puts it, or, as perhaps it might be more correctly expressed, from mere accident or caprice, was favourably disposed to the new studies, and his authority and influence were of considerable use in sup-

[*] The reader will recollect Addison's humorous notices of the modern Greeks and Trojans, in the Spectator, Nos. 239 and 245.

porting them at first against their numerous and powerful opponents. Erasmus relates that, in 1519, when one of the university preachers at Oxford had harangued with great violence
against the study of the Scriptures in their original languages,
Henry, who happened to be resident at the time at the neighbouring royal manor of Woodstock, and had received an account
of the affair from his secretary, the learned Richard Pace, and
Sir Thomas More, issued an order commanding that the said
study of the Greek and Hebrew Scriptures should not only be
permitted for the future, but made an indispensable branch of
the course of academical instruction. Some time after, one of
the royal chaplains, preaching at court, having attacked the new
Greek learning, was, after his sermon, commanded by the king
to maintain his opinions in a solemn disputation with More, by
whose wit and learning of course he was very speedily van-
quished, and forced to make a humiliating admission of his
errors and ignorance: he at last declared that he was now
better reconciled to the Greek tongue, inasmuch as he found that
it was derived from the Hebrew; but, although he fell upon his
knees and begged pardon for any offence he had given, Henry
dismissed him with a command that he should never again
presume to preach before him. One of the first causes, however, although it was only of temporary operation, that interrupted the progress of classical learning at the universities, has
been thought to have been the stir excited throughout Christendom by the question of Henry's divorce from Queen Katharine.
" The legality of this violent measure," observes Warton,
" being agitated with much deliberation and solemnity, wholly
engrossed the attention of many able philologists, whose genius
and acquisitions were destined to a much nobler employment,
and tended to revive for a time the frivolous subtleties of
casuistry and theology." Then, the still more eager and widely
extended doctrinal discussions to which the progress of the
Reformation itself gave rise, came to operate over a much longer
period with a similar effect. In this universal storm of
polemics, " the profound investigations of Aquinas," continues
Warton, " once more triumphed over the graces of the Ciceronian
urbanity; and endless volumes were written on the expediency
of auricular confession, and the existence of purgatory. Thus
the cause of polite literature was for a while abandoned; while
the noblest abilities of Europe were wasted in theological specu-

lation, and absorbed in the abyss of controversy." Another
great temporary check was now also given, Warton conceives, to
the cause of the progress and diffusion of sound learning in
England by the dissolution of the monasteries. " These seminaries," he observes, " though they were in a general view the
nurseries of illiterate indolence, and undoubtedly deserved to be
suppressed under proper restrictions, contained invitations and
opportunities to studious leisure and literary pursuits. On this
event, therefore, a visible revolution and decline in the national
state of learning succeeded. Most of the youth of the kingdom
betook themselves to mechanical or other illiberal employments,
the profession of letters being now supposed to be without
support or reward. By the abolition of the religious houses,
many towns and their adjacent villages were utterly deprived of
their only means of instruction. At the beginning of the reign
of Elizabeth, Williams, Speaker of the House of Commons, complained to her majesty, that more than an hundred flourishing
schools were destroyed in the demolition of the monasteries, and
that ignorance had prevailed ever since. Provincial ignorance,
at least, became universal, in consequence of this hasty measure
of a rapacious and arbitrary prince. What was taught in the
monasteries was not always perhaps of the greatest importance,
but still it served to keep up a certain degree of necessary
knowledge." The many new grammar schools that arose in
different parts of the country after the destruction of the monasteries were partly, no doubt, called into existence by the vacuum
thus created ; which, however, they did very little to fill up in .
so far as the rural population was concerned, although they
may have sufficed for most of the great towns.

Both the old monastic schools and the new foundations, however, being considered, to a certain extent, as charitable institutions, were principally attended by the children of persons in
humble or at least in common life ; among the higher classes it
seems to have been the general custom for boys as well as girls
to be educated at home, or under the superintendence of private
tutors. A notion of the extent and manner of training which
youths of rank underwent in their earliest years may be obtained
from some letters which have been printed, addressed to Henry's
minister, Cromwell, by the tutor of his son Gregory.* This
young man, whose capacity is described as rather solid than

* King Henry the Eighth's Scheme of Bishoprics, &c., 8vo. Lond. 1838.

quick, divided his time under different masters among various studies and exercises, of which English, French, writing, playing at weapons, casting of accounts, and " pastimes of instruments," are particularly enumerated. One master is stated to be in the habit of " daily hearing him to read somewhat in the English tongue, and advertising him of the natural and true kind of pronunciation thereof, expounding also and declaring the etymology and native signification of such words as we have borrowed of the Latins or Frenchmen, not even so commonly used in our quotidian speech." According to a common practice, two other youths, probably of inferior station, appear to have been educated along with young Cromwell; and between him and them, the account continues, " there is a perpetual contention, strife, and conflict, and in manner of an honest envy, who shall do best not only in the French tongue (wherein Mr. Vallance, after a wondrously compendious, facile, prompt, and ready way, not without painful diligence and laborious industry, doth instruct them), but also in writing, playing at weapons, and all other their exercises." In the end a confident hope is expressed that, " whereas the last summer was spent in the service of the wild goddess Diana," the present shall be consecrated to Apollo and the Muses, to the no small profit of the young man, as well as to his father's good contentation and pleasure. This letter is dated in April; another written in September (apparently of the same year), by which time the boy had begun the study of some new branches, especially Latin and instrumental music, enters into some more minute and curious details of how he spent his time. " First," says his tutor, " after he hath heard mass, he taketh a lecture of a dialogue of Erasmus' colloquium called Pietas Puerilis, wherein is described a very picture of one that should be virtuously brought up; and, for cause it is so necessary for him, I do not only cause him to read it over, but also to practise the precepts of the same; and I have also translated it into English, so that he may confer therein both together, whereof, as learned men affirm, cometh no small profect, which translation pleaseth it you to receive by the bringer hereof, that ye may judge how much profitable it is to be learned." From this it may be inferred that the original Latin would have been unintelligible to Cromwell, and that that able man was above being flattered by having a knowledge of the learned tongues ascribed to him which he did not possess.

The letter goes on—" After that he exerciseth his hand in writing one or two hours, and readeth upon Fabian's Chronicles as long; the residue of the day he doth spend upon the lute and virginal." Vocal music at least, it may be observed, if not instrumental, was always one of the branches of education taught at the old monastic, cathedral, and other free schools; a circumstance originating no doubt, in the connection of those schools with the church, in the services of which singing bore so important a part. Lastly, the tutor gives an account of the out-of-door exercises followed by his pupil, intellectual instruction, however, being by no means disregarded even in some of these :— " When he rideth, as he doth very oft, I tell him by the way," he says, " some history of the Romans or the Greeks, which I cause him to rehearse again in a tale. For his recreation he useth to hawk, and hunt, and shoot in his long bow, which frameth and succeedeth so well with him that he seemeth to be thereunto given by nature." This training, so far as it is detailed, appears to have been judiciously contrived for laying the foundation of a good and solid education both of the mental and physical faculties.

The reforming spirit of the early part of the sixteenth century was, as always happens, in the shape it took in the popular mind, much more of a destructive than of a constructive character; and even the wisest of the persons in authority, by whom the mighty movement was guided and controlled, were necessarily, to a certain extent, under the influence of the same presumptuous temper, without a share of which, indeed, they would not have been fitted to restrain the more impetuous multitude to the extent they did. But in its application to the universities, as in other cases, this spirit of mere demolition, and contempt for all that was old and established, displayed itself in some things in a very rampant style. The scorn, in particular, with which it treated the whole mass of the ancient philosophy of the schools, was of the most sweeping description. The famous Duns Scotus, so long the lord of opinion, now underwent, in full measure, the customary fate of deposed sovereigns. A royal visitation of the two universities, by commissioners of Cromwell's appointment, took place in 1535, when injunctions were issued abolishing altogether the reading of the works of the most subtle Doctor. The tone of triumph in which Dr. Layton, one of the Oxford commissioners, announces this reform to Cromwell

is highly characteristic. "We have set Dunce," he writes, "in
Bocardo,* and have utterly banished him Oxford for ever, with
all his blind glosses." The despised tomes, formerly so much
reverenced, Layton goes on to intimate, were now used by any
man for the commonest uses; he had seen them with his own
eyes nailed upon posts in the most degrading situations. "And
the second time we came to New College," he proceeds, "after
we had declared your injunctions, we found all the great
quadrant court full of the leaves of Dunce, the wind blowing
them into every corner. And there we found one Mr. Greenfield,
a gentleman of Buckinghamshire, gathering up part of the same
book leaves, as he said, therewith to make him sewern or
blawnahers to keep the deer within his wood, thereby to have
the better cry with his hounds." † The scholastic philosophy,
however, which was thus banished from the universities, was in
fact the whole philosophy, mental and physical, then taught, and
its abolition consequently amounted to the ejection, for the time,
of philosophical studies from the academical course altogether.
The canon law was another of the old studies, hitherto of chief
importance, that was at the same time put down: degrees in the
canon law were prohibited; and, in place of the canon lecture, a
civil lecture, that is, a lecture on the civil law, was appointed to
be read in every college, hall, and inn. ·

For a short space, the excitement of novelty, and the exertions of a few eminent instructors, made classical learning
popular at Oxford and Cambridge, and enabled it in some degree
to serve as a substitute for those other abandoned studies to
which it ought only to have been introduced as an ally. The
learned Ascham boasts, in one of his letters, that, whereas
almost the only classics hitherto known at Cambridge had been
Plautus, Cicero, Terence, and Livy, all the chief Greek poets,
orators, and historians, Homer, Sophocles, Euripides, Demos-
thenes, Isocrates, Herodotus, Thucydides, and Xenophon, were
now universally and critically studied. This prosperous state
of Greek scholarship was principally owing to the example and
exertions of the two distinguished professors of that language,
Thomas Smith and John Cheke: even the controversy about

* A Figure or form of syllogism of the school logic, which terminated in a
negative conclusion. The expression, therefore, implies that Scotus was, as it
were, annihilated.

† Strype, Eccles. Mem. i. 335.

the proper pronunciation of the language that arose between the latter and Bishop Gardiner, who, as Warton observes, "loved learning, but hated novelties," contributing its share to excite a general interest about Greek literature, as well as to throw new 'light upon the particular subject in dispute. But both Cheke and Smith were soon withdrawn from their academic labours to other fields; and with them the spirit of true learning and taste, which they had awakened at Cambridge, seems also to have taken its departure. At Oxford the case was no better; there, Ascham remarks that a decline of taste in both the classic tongues was decidedly indicated by a preference of Lucian, Plutarch, and Herodian, in Greek, and of Seneca, Gellius, and Apuleius, in Latin, to the writers of the older and purer eras of ancient eloquence. Even divinity itself, as Latimer complains, ceased to be studied. "It would pity a man's heart," he says, "to hear what I hear of the state of Cambridge: what it is in Oxford I cannot tell. There be few that study divinity but so many as of necessity must furnish the colleges." So true is it that no one branch of learning or science can long continue to flourish amid the general neglect and decay of the other branches that compose along with it the system of human knowledge.

The first establishment of the Reformation under Edward VI., instead of effecting the restoration of learning, only contributed to its further discouragement and depression. "The rapacious courtiers of this young prince," as Warton observes, "were perpetually grasping at the rewards of literature . . . . . Avarice and zeal were at once gratified in robbing the clergy of their revenues, and in reducing the church to its primitive apostolical state of purity and poverty. The opulent see of Winchester was lowered to a bare title; its amplest estates were portioned out to the laity; and the bishop, a creature of the Protector Somerset, was contented to receive an inconsiderable annual stipend from the exchequer. The bishopric of Durham, almost equally rich, was entirely dissolved. A favourite nobleman in the court occupied the deanery and treasurership of a cathedral, with some of its best canonries . . . . In every one of these sacrilegious robberies the interest of learning also suffered. Exhibitions and pensions were, in the mean time, subtracted from the students in the universities. Ascham, in a letter to the Marquis of Northampton, dated 1550, laments the ruin of grammar-schools throughout England, and predicts the speedy extinction of the universities from this growing calamity. At Oxford the public schools were neglected by the professors and pupils, and allotted to the lowest purposes. Academical degrees were abrogated as anti-christian. Reformation was soon turned into fanaticism. Absurd refinements, concerning the inutility of human learning, were superadded to the just and rational purgation of Christianity from the papal corruptions. The spiritual reformers of these enlightened days, at a visitation of the last-mentioned university, proceeded so far in their ideas of a superior, rectitude, as totally to strip the public library, established by that munificent patron, Humphrey Duke of Gloucester, of all its books and manuscripts."

A very curious account of the state of the university of Cambridge in this reign is contained in a sermon, preached in 1550, by a Thomas Lever, Fellow of St. John's College, some extracts from which Strype has preserved. Formerly "there were," says Lever, "in houses belonging to the University of Cambridge, two hundred students of divinity, many very well learned, which be now all clean gone home; and many young toward scholars, and old fatherly doctors, not one of them left. One hundred also, of another sort, that, having rich friends, or being beneficed men, did live of themselves in hostels and inns, be either gone away or else fain to creep into colleges and put poor men from bare livings. These both be all gone, and a small number of poor, godly, diligent students, now remaining only in colleges, be not able to tarry and continue their studies for lack of exhibition and help." The description which follows of the studies and mode of living of the poorer and more diligent students is very interesting :—" There be divers there which rise daily about four or five of the clock in the morning, and from five till six of the clock use common prayer, with an exhortation of God's word in a common chapel; and from six until ten of the clock use ever either private study or common lectures. At ten of the clock they go to dinner, whereas they be content with a penny piece of beef among four, having a few pottage made of the broth of the same beef, with salt and oatmeal, and nothing else. After this slender diet, they be either teaching or learning until five of the clock in the evening; whereas they have a supper not much better than their dinner. Immediately after which they go either to reasoning in problems, or to some other study, until it be nine or ten of the clock; and then, being without fires, are fain to walk or run up and down half an hour, to get a heat on their feet when they go to bed."[*] Latimer, in a sermon preached about the same time, expresses his belief that there were then ten thousand fewer students in the kingdom than there had been twenty years before.

In the reign of Mary, who was herself a learned queen, and a considerable benefactress of both universities, classical learning had a distinguished patron in Cardinal Pole, who was as illustrious for his literary acquirements as he was for his birth and station. In his short tenure of power, however, he was not able to accomplish much against the adverse circumstances of the time. It appears that to him Sir Thomas Pope, the founder of Trinity College, Oxford, which was endowed in this reign more especially for the cultivation of classical scholarship, submitted the statutes of his new institution. "My Lord Cardinal's Grace," says Sir Thomas, in a letter of his which has been preserved, "has had the overseeing of my statutes. He much likes well that I have therein ordered the Latin tongue to be read to my scholars. But he advises me to order the Greek to be more taught there than I have provided. This purpose I well like; but I fear the times will not bear it now. I remember when I was a young scholar at Eton, the Greek tongue was growing apace; the study of which is now alate much decayed." The fact here stated is especially honourable to Pole, seeing that by this time the Greek language, as that of the original text of the New Testament, to which the Reformers made all their appeals, had come to be regarded by the generality of Romanists as a peculiarly Protestant and almost heretical study. The return of the old religion, however, with its persecutions and penal fires, did not prove on the whole more favourable to the interests of learning than to any of the other interests of the national happiness and civilization.

Nor did the final establishment of the reformed church, nor all the prosperity of the next reign, for a long time bring back good letters to the universities. A few facts will show their state throughout a great part of that reign. In the first place,

so few persons now received a university education, that for
many years a large proportion of the clergy of the new church
were mere artificers and other illiterate persons, some of whom,
while they preached on Sundays, worked at their trades on
weekdays, and some of whom could hardly write their names.
In the year 1563, we are, informed by Anthony Wood, there
were only three divines in the university of Oxford who were
considered capable of preaching the public sermons.   It has
been sometimes alleged that the growing influence of Puritanism
was one of the chief causes of the continued neglect and depression in which learning was now left; but it is a remarkable fact,
that the three Oxford preachers were all Puritans, as were also
many of the most distinguished ornaments of both universities at
a later date. In 1567, so low was still the state of classical
literature in the country, that when Archbishop Parker in that
year founded three scholarships in Cambridge, the holders of
which were to be "the best and ablest scholars" elected from
the most considerable schools in Kent and Norfolk, all the
amount of qualification he required in them was, that they
should be well instructed in the grammar, "and, if it may be,"
it was added, "such as can make a verse."   As one instance of
the extreme ignorance of the inferior clergy in the latter part
of the sixteenth century, Warton mentions, on the authority of
the episcopal register, that "in the year 1570, Horne, Bishop of
Winchester, enjoined the minor canons of his cathedral to get
by memory, every week, one chapter of St. Paul's Epistles in
Latin; and this formidable task, almost beneath the abilities of
an ordinary schoolboy, was actually repeated by some of them,
before the bishop, dean, and prebendaries, at a public episcopal
visitation of that church." The anecdote, at least, presents the
bishops and minor canons of those times in a strange light. The
accomplished critic we have just quoted is of opinion that the
taste for Latin composition in the reign of Elizabeth had much
degenerated from what it was in that of Henry VIII. The
Latinity of Ascham's prose, he maintains, has no eloquence; and
even Buchanan's Latin poetry, although he admits that its versification and phraseology are splendid and sonorous, he will not
allow to be marked with the chaste graces and simple ornaments
of the Augustan age. "One is surprised," he adds, "to find the
learned Archbishop Grindal, in the statutes of a school which he
founded and amply endowed (in 1583), recommending such

barbarous and degenerate classics as Palingenius, Sedulius, and Prudentius to be taught in his new foundation. These, indeed, were the classics of a reforming bishop; but the well-meaning prelate would have contributed much more to the success of his intended reformation by directing books of better taste and less piety."[*]

The whole of the sixteenth century, however, will deserve the epithet of a learned age, notwithstanding the state of the schools and universities, and of what are called the learned professions, if we look either to the names of eminent scholars by which every portion of it is adorned, or to the extent to which the study of the learned languages then entered into the education of all persons, women as well as men, who were considered to be well educated. In the earlier part of it, besides Cranmer, Ridley, Tunstal, Gardiner, Pole, and other churchmen of distinguished acquirements, we have Richard Pace, Sir John Cheke, and Sir Thomas Smith, Colet the founder and Lilly the first master of St. Paul's School,—all already mentioned; William Grocyn, another of the first and also one of the very greatest of the English Grecians; the equally elegant and industrious John Leland, the father of English antiquities, and the chief preserver in his day of the old knowledge that would otherwise have perished, as well as one of the most successful cultivators of the new; Doctor Thomas Linacer, the first English physician, and as a scholar scarcely second to any, of his country or of his age; and the all-accomplished Sir Thomas More, perhaps the happiest genius of his time, the one of its profound scholars, at all events, unless we are to except his illustrious friend Erasmus, whose natural genius was the least oppressed by his erudition, and whose erudition was the most brightened with wit, and informed by a living spirit better than that of books. Of somewhat later celebrity are the names of Roger Ascham, who is more famous, however, for his English than for his Latin writings; of Dr. Walter Haddon, the most Ciceronian of English Latinists; of Buchanan, perhaps the most of a poet of all the modern writers of Latin verse; not to mention Archbishop Parker, Bishop Andrews, and other eminent churchmen. The number of very great English scholars, however, in the reign of Elizabeth was not so considerable as in that

* Hist. of Eng. Poet. iii. 283.

of her father, when classical studies were not only cultivated
with perhaps a truer appreciation of the highest models, but
afforded, besides, almost the only field for intellectual exercise
and display. Still this kind of learning continued to be fashionable ; and a familiar, if not a profound, acquaintance with both
the Latin and the Greek languages was diffused to an unusual
extent among persons of the highest rank. Henry VIII. was
himself a scholar of considerable pretensions ; he is said to have,
as a younger son, been educated for the church : and to this
accident, which gave the country its first pedant king, it may
perhaps have been also indebted for its succession of learned
princes, which lasted for more than a century, Henry, as it
were, setting the fashion, which it afterwards became a matter of
course to follow. His son, though born to the throne to which
he succeeded, received a schoolmastering fit for a bishop ; and so
also did both his daughters. Erasmus has commended the Latin
letters of Mary, some of which are preserved, as well as others
in French and in Spanish. Elizabeth was not only a Latin,
French, Spanish, and Italian scholar, but also a proficient in
Greek, in which language her tutor Ascham tells us she used,
even after she came to the throne, to read more every day than
some prebendaries of the church read of Latin in a whole
week. But this was especially the age of learned ladies ; and
every reader will remember the names of Lady Jane Grey, of
whose studies in Plato the same writer we have just mentioned
has drawn so interesting a picture, and some of whose Latin
· epistles are still extant, especially one to her sister, written the
night before her death, in a Greek Testament, in which she had
been reading ; of Mary, Countess of Arundel ; her daughter-in-
law, Joanna Lady Lumley ; and the younger sister of the latter,
Mary Duchess of Norfolk, all of whom were the authoresses of
various translations from the Greek into Latin and English ; of
the two Margarets, the female luminaries of the household of Sir
Thomas More, the friend who became the wife of her learned tutor,
Dr. John Clement, and who is said to have so delighted in and
almost worshipped More, that she would sometimes commit a
fault purely that she might be chid by him—such moderation
and humanity were there in his anger ; the other, his affectionate
and favourite daughter who married his biographer Roper, and
was accounted the most learned woman of her time ; and of
the four wonderful daughters of Sir Anthony Cooke—Mildred,

the eldest, married to Lord Burghley, whose name has been embalmed by the muse of Buchanan; Anne, the second, the governess of Edward VI., and afterwards the wife of Sir Nicholas Bacon, and the mother of the illustrious Viscount St. Alban; Elizabeth, the third, the wife, first of Sir Thomas Hobby, then of Lord Russell; and the youngest, Catherine, who married Sir Henry Killigrew, and is celebrated not only for her Latin and Greek, but even for her Hebrew erudition. " It became fashionable in this reign (that of Elizabeth)," says Warton, " to study Greek at court. The maids of honour indulged their ideas of sentimental affection in the sublime contemplation of Plato's Phædo; and the queen, who understood Greek better than the canons of Windsor, and was certainly a much greater pedant than her successor, James I., translated Isocrates. But this passion for the Greek language soon ended where it began; nor do we find that it improved the national taste, or influenced the writings of the age of Elizabeth."

Old Harrison has a curious and characteristic passage on this learned court. " This further," he observes, " is not to be omitted, to the singular commendation of both sorts and sexes of our courtiers here in England, that there are very few of them which have not the use and skill of sundry speeches, besides an excellent vein of writing, before-time not regarded." He does not, however, seem to have a more favourable notion of the moral effect of these novel and showy accomplishments than Warton has expressed respecting their influence on the national literature and taste: " Would to God," he exclaims, " the rest of their lives and conversations were correspondent to these gifts! For, as our common courtiers, for the most part, are the best learned and endued with excellent gifts, so are many of them the worst men, when they come abroad, that any man shall either hear or read of." Harrison's words, which are surprisingly bold to have been published at the time, seem here to be gallantly confined to the men of the court; but other contemporary testimonies do not disguise the fact that many of the women were as dissolute as their male associates. The honest old painter of the living manners of his time may be thought, perhaps, to hint at something of the kind in what follows:—" Truly it is a rare thing with us now to hear of a courtier which hath but his own language. And to say how many gentlewomen and ladies there are that, beside sound knowledge of the Greek and Latin tongues, are thereto no less skilful

in Spanish, Italian, and French, or in some one of them, it
resteth not in me; sith I am persuaded that, as the noblemen
and gentlemen do surmount in this behalf, so these come very
little or nothing at all behind them for their parts; which
industry God continue, *and accomplish that which otherwise is wanting.*"
Yet he winds up his description with a very laudatory flourish.
"Beside these things," he proceeds, "I could in like sort set
down the ways and means, whereby our ancient ladies of the
court do shun and avoid idleness, some of them exercising their
fingers with the needle, others in caul-work, divers in spinning
of silk, some in continual reading either of the Holy Scriptures,
or histories of our own or foreign nations about us, and divers in
writing volumes of their own, or translating of other men's into
our English and Latin tongue, whilst the youngest sort in the
mean time apply their lutes, citterns, pricksong, and all kind of
music, which they use only for recreation sake, when they have
leisure, and are free from attendance upon the queen's majesty,
or such as they belong unto." Many of the eldest sort he goes
on to celebrate as "also skilful in surgery and distillation of
waters, besides sundry other artificial practices pertaining to the
ornature and commendations of their bodies;" and "there are
none of them," he adds, "but when they be at home can help to
supply the ordinary want of the kitchen with a number of delicate
dishes of their own devising." At last, coming directly to the
morals of the court, he declares that, whereas some great princes'
courts beyond the seas have been likened unto hell on account of
the dissipation and debauchery prevailing in them, all such
"enormities are either utterly expelled out of the court of
England, or else so qualified by the diligent endeavour of the
chief officers of her grace's household, that seldom are any of
those things apparently seen there without due reprehension,
and such severe correction as belongeth to those trespasses."
"Finally," he concludes, "to avoid idleness, and prevent sundry
transgressions otherwise likely to be committed and done, such
order is taken that every office hath either a Bible, or the Book
of the Acts and Monuments of the Church of England, or both,
besides some histories and chronicles, lying therein, for the
exercise of such as come into the same; whereby the stranger
that entereth into the court of England upon the sudden shall
rather imagine himself to come into some public school of the
universities, where many give ear to one that readeth, than into

a prince's palace, if you confer the same with those of other nations." *

This flattering description of the English court is very different from that given by Ascham, in his Schoolmaster, who tells us that, although it did indeed contain many fair examples for youth to follow, yet they were, "like fair marks in the field out of a man's reach, too far off to shoot at well;" while the generality of persons to be found there were the worst of characters. Some private letters of the time of Elizabeth, also, which have been printed, describe the court as a place where there was "little godliness and exercise of religion," and where "all enormities reigned in the highest degree." But what it is more important

* Description of England, b. II. c. 15. To this may be added a curious passage which Strype gives in his Life of Archbishop Parker, from an Epistle to Queen Katherine Parr by Nicholas Udall (of whom we shall have more to say some pages onward), found in a translation of The First Tome or Volume of the Paraphrase of Erasmus upon the New Testament, executed partly by himself, partly by others, among them the Princess Mary, who is said to have done part of the Gospel of St. John, which was published in 1549, in the reign of Edward VI. :—" But now in this gracious and blissful time of knowledge, in which it hath pleased God Almighty to reveal and show abroad the light of his most holy gospel, what a number is there of noble women, especially here in this realm of England, yea and how many in the years of tender virginity, not only as well seen and as familiarly traded in the Latin and Greek tongues as in their own mother language, but also both in all kinds of profane literature and liberal arts exacted, studied, and exercised, and in the Holy Scripture and Theology so ripe that they are able aptly, cunningly, and with much grace, either to indite or translate into the vulgar tongue, for the public instruction and edifying of the unlearned multitude. Neither is it now a strange thing to hear gentlewomen, instead of most vain communication about the moon shining in the water [so we still familiarly call a thing of no sense or significance a matter of moonshine], to use grave and substantial talk in Latin and Greek, with their husbands, of godly matters. It is now no news in England for young damsels, in noble houses and in the courts of princes, instead of cards and other instruments of idle trifling, to have continually in their hands, either Psalms, homilies, and other devout meditations, or else Paul's Epistles, or some book of Holy Scripture matters, and as familiarly to read or reason thereof in Greek, Latin, French, or Italian, as in English. It is now a common thing to see young virgins so nursed and trained in the study of letters, that they willingly set all other vain pastimes at nought for learning's sake. It is now no news at all to see queens, and ladies of most high state and progeny, instead of courtly dalliance, to embrace virtuous exercises of reading and writing, and with most earnest study, both early and late, to apply themselves to the acquiring of knowledge, as well in all other liberal arts and disciplines as also most or especially of God and his most holy word."

for our present purpose to observe is, that the learning which
existed in this age, however remarkably it may have shone forth
in particular instances, was by no means generally diffused even
among the higher classes, while the generality of the lower and
many even of the middle classes remained to the end of the
period almost wholly uneducated and illiterate.   It is a question
whether the father of Shakespeare, an alderman of Stratford, could
write his name; and probably, throughout the community, for
one that was scholar enough to subscribe his signature there were
a dozen who could only make their marks.   With all the advancement the country had made in many respects, it may be doubted
if popular education was farther extended at the close of the reign
of Elizabeth than it was at the commencement of that of her
father or her grandfather.   Even the length of time that printing
had now been at work, and the multiplication of books that must
have taken place, had probably but very little, if at all, extended
the knowledge and the habit of reading among the mass of the
people.   The generation that grew up immediately after the
discovery of the art of printing, and that first welcomed the
Reformation and the translated Bible, perhaps read more than
their grandchildren.

PROSE WRITERS:—MORE; ELYOT; TYNDAL; CRANMER; LATIMER.

The fact most deserving of remark in the progress of English
literature, for the first half of the sixteenth century, is the
cultivation that now came to be bestowed upon the language in
the form of prose composition,—a form always in the order of
time subsequent to that of verse in the natural development of a
national language and literature.   Long before this date, indeed,
Chaucer, in addition to what he did in his proper field, had given
proof of how far his genius proceeded his age by several examples
of composition in prose, in which may be discerned the presence
of something of the same high art with which he first elevated
our poetry; but, besides that his genius drew him with greatest
force to poetry, and that the foreign models upon which he seems
chiefly to have formed himself led him in the same direction, the
state of the English language at that day perhaps fitted it better
for verse than for prose, or rather, it had not yet arrived at the

point at which it could be so advantageously employed in prose
as in verse. At all events Chaucer had no worthy successor as a
writer of prose, any more than as a writer of poetry, till more
than a century after his death. Meanwhile, however, the
language, though not receiving much artificial cultivation, was
still undergoing a good deal of what, in a certain sense, might be
called application to literary purposes, by its employment both
in public proceedings and documents, and also in many popular
writings, principally on the subject of the new opinions in
religion, both after and previous to the invention of printing.
In this more extended use and exercise, by persons of some
scholarship at least, if not bringing much artistic feeling and
skill to the task of composition, it must, as a mere language, or
system of vocables and grammatical forms, have not only sustained
many changes and modifications, but, it is probable, acquired on
the whole considerable enlargement of its capacities and powers,
and been generally carried forward towards maturity under the
impulse of a vigorous principle of growth and expansion. But
it is not till some time after the commencement of the sixteenth
century that we can properly date the rise of our classical prose
literature. Perhaps the earliest compositions that are entitled to
be included under that name are some of those of Sir Thomas
More, especially his Life and Reign of King Edward V., which
Rastell, his brother-in-law, by whom it was first printed in 1557,
from, as he informs us, a copy in More's handwriting, states to
have been written by him when he was under-sheriff of London,
in the year 1513.[*] Most of More's other English writings are
of a controversial character, and are occupied about subjects both
of very temporary importance, and that called up so much of
the eagerness and bitterness of the author's party zeal as con-

---

[*] Sir Henry Ellis, however, in the Preface to his edition of Harding's
Chronicle (4to. 1812), has called attention to what had not before been
noticed, namely, that the writer speaks as if he had been present with
Edward IV. in his last sickness, which More could not have been, being
then (in 1483) only a child of three years old; and Sir Henry informs
that the manuscript from which the tract was printed by Rastell, although
in More's handwriting, could have been only a copy made by him of a
narrative drawn up by some one else, very probably Cardinal Morton. But,
although Morton was a person of distinguished eloquence, the style is surely
far too modern to have been proceeded from a writer who was born within ten
years after the close of the fourteenth century, the senior of More by seventy
years.

siderably to disturb and mar both his naturally gentle and benignant temper and the oily eloquence of his style; but this historic piece is characterised throughout by an easy narrative flow which rivals the sweetness of Herodotus. It is certainly the first English historic composition that can be said to aspire to be more than a mere chronicle.

The following is an extract from Sir Thomas More's Dialogue concerning Heresies (chap. 14), written in 1528:—

Some priests, to bring up a pilgrimage in his parishe, may devise some false felowe sayeing himselfe to come seke a saint in hys chyrch, and there solemnly say, that he hath gotten hys syght. Than shall ye have the belles rong for a miracle. And the foode folke of the country soon made foles. Than women commynge thither with their candels. And the Person hyenge of some lame begger iii or iiii payre of theyr olde crutches, with all pennes sprot in men and women of wex, thrust thorowe divers places, some with arrowes, and some wyth rusty knyves, wyll make his offerynges for one vij yere worth twise hys tythes.

Thys is, quoth I, very trouth that suche thynges may be, and sometime so be in dede. As I remember me that I have hard my father tell of a begger, that in Kyng Henry his daies the sixt cam with his wife to Saint Albonis. And there was walking about the towne begging, a fyve or six dayes before the kinges commynge thither, salenge that he was borne blinde, and never sawe in hys lyfe. And was warned in hys dreame, that he shoulde come out of Berwyke, where he said he had ever dwelled, to seke Saynt Albon, and that he had ben at his shryne, and had not bene holpen. And therefore he woulde go seke hym at some other place, for he had hard some say sins he came that Sainct Albonys body shold be at Colon, and in dede such a contencion hath ther ben. But of trouth, as I am surely informed, he lieth here at Saint Albonis, saving some reliques of him, which thei there shew shrined. But to tell you forth, whan the kyng was comen, and the towne full, sudaynlye thys blind man, at Saint Albonis shryne had his sight agayne, and a myracle solemply rongen, and Te Deum songen, so that nothyng was talked of in al the towne, but this myracle. So happened it than that duke Humfry of Gloucester, a great wyse man and very wel lerned, having great joy to se such a myracle, called the pore man unto hym. And first shewing him self joyouse of Goddes glory so shewed in the getting of his sight, and exortinge hym to mekenes, and to none ascribing of any part the worshyp to him self nor to be proude of the peoples prayse, which would call hym a good and a godly man thereby. At last he loked well upon his eyen, and asked whyther he could never se nothing at al, in all his life before. And whan as well his wyfe as himself affermed fastely no, than he loked advisedly upon his eien again, and askd, I beleve you very wel, for me thinketh that ye cannot se well yet. Yes syr, quoth he, I thanke God and his holy marter, I can se nowe as well as any man. Ye can, quoth the Duke; what colour is my gowne? Then anone the begger told him. What colour, quoth he, is this man's gowne? He told him also; and so forthe, without any sticking, he told him the names of al the colours that coulde bee shewed him. And whan my lord saw that, he bad him "walke faytoure," and made him be set opnuly in the stockes. For though he could have sene sundenly by miracle the dyfference betwene divers colours, yet coulde he not by the syght so sudenly tel the names of all these colours but if he had known them before, no more than the names of all the men that he should sodenly se. Lo therfore I say, quad your frende, who may bee sure of such thynges whan such pageantes be played before all the towne?*

The letter which Sir Thomas More wrote to his wife in 1528, after the burning of his house at Chelsea, affords one of the best specimens of the epistolary style of this period:—

Maistres Alyce, in my most harty wise I recommend me to you; and, whereas I am enfourmed by my son Heron of the losse of our barnes and of our neighbours also, with all the corn that was therein, albeit (saving God's pleasure) it is gret pitie of so much good corne lost, yet sith it hath liked hym to sende us such a chaunce, we must and are bounden, not only to be content, but also to be glad of his visitacion. He sente us all that we have loste: and, sith he hath by such a chaunce taken it away againe, his pleasure be fulfilled. Let us never grudge ther at, but take it in good worth, and hartely thank him, as well for adversitie as for prosperite. And peradventure we have more cause to thank him for our losse then for our winning; for his wisdome better seeth what is good for vs then we do our selves. Therfore I pray you be of good chere, and take all the howsold with you to church, and there thanke God, both for that he hath given us, and for that he hath taken from us, and for that he hath left us, which if it please hym he can encrease when he will. And if it please hym to leave us yet lesse, at his pleasure be it.

I pray you to make some good ensearche what my poore neighbours have loste, and bid them take no thought therfore: for and I shold not leave myself a spone, ther shal no pore neighbour of mine here no losse by any chaunce happened in my house. I pray you be with my children and your household merry in God. And devise some what with your freindes, what wayes wer best to take, for provision to be made for corne for our household, and for sede thys yere comming, if ye thinke it good that we kepe the ground stil in our handes. And whether ye think it good that we so shall do or not, yet I think it were not best sodenlye thus to leave it all up, and to put away our folke of our farme till we have somwhat

---

* Sir Thomas More's Works, by Rastell, 4to. 1557, p. 134. This story, it may be remembered, is introduced in the second part of what is called Shakespeare's Henry the Sixth (Act II. Scene I). And it also occurs in the older version of that play, first published, so far as is known, in 1594, under the title of The first part of the Contention between the two famous Houses of York and Lancaster.

advised us thereon. How beit if we have more nowe then ye shall nede, and which can get them other maisters, ye may then dischargo us of them. But I would not that any man were sodenly sent away bo woto nere wether.

At my comming hither I perceived none other but that I shold tary still with the Kinges Grace. But now I shal (I think), because of this chance, get leave this next weke to come home and so you : and then shall we further devyse together uppon all thinges what order shalbe brst to take. And thus as hartely fare you well with all our children as ye can wisho. At Woodestok the thirde daye of Septembre by the hand of

your loving husbande

THOMAS MORE Knight.[*]

Along with More, as one of the earliest writers of classic English prose, may be mentioned his friend Sir Thomas Elyot, the author of the political treatise entitled The Governor, and of various other works, one of which is a Latin and English Dictionary, the foundation of most of the compilations of the same kind that were published for a century afterwards. More was executed in 1535, and Elyot also died some years before the middle of the century. William Tyndal's admirable translations of the New Testament and of some portions of the Old, and also numerous tracts by the same early reformer in his native tongue, which he wrote with remarkable correctness as well as with great vigour and eloquence, appeared between 1526 and his death in 1536. Next in the order of time among our more eminent prose writers may be placed some of the distinguished leaders of the Reformation in the latter part of the reign of Henry VIII. and in that of Edward VI., more especially Archbishop Cranmer, whose compositions in his native tongue are of considerable volume, and are characterized, if not by any remarkable strength of expression or weight of matter, yet by a full and even flow both of words and thought. On the whole, Cranmer was the greatest writer among the founders of the English Reformation. His friends and fellow-labourers, Ridley and Latimer, were also celebrated in their day for their ready popular elocution ; but the few tracts of Ridley's that remain are less eloquent than learned, and Latimer's discourses are rather quaint and curious than either learned or eloquent in any lofty sense of that term. Latimer is stated to have been one of the first English students of the Greek language ; but this could

* Sir Thomas More's Works, by Rastell, 4to. 1557. pp. 1418, 1419.

hardly be guessed from his Sermons, which, except a few scraps
of Latin, show scarcely a trace of scholarship or literature of any
kind. In addressing the people from the pulpit, this honest,
simple-minded bishop, feeling no exaltation either from his
position or his subject, expounded the most sublime doctrines of
religion in the same familiar and homely language in which the
humblest or most rustic of his hearers were accustomed to chaffer
with one another in the market-place about the price of a yard of
cloth or a pair of shoes. Nor, indeed, was he more fastidious
as to matter than as to manner: all the preachers of that age
were accustomed to take a wide range over things in general, but
Latimer went beyond everybody else in the miscellaneous assort-
ment of topics he used to bring together from every region of
heaven and earth,—of the affairs of the world that now is as well
as of that which is to come. Without doubt his sermons must have
been lively and entertaining far beyond the common run of that
kind of compositions; the allusions with which they abounded to
public events, and to life in all its colours and grades, from the
palace to the cottage, from the prince to the peasant,—the
anecdotes of his own experience and the other stories the old
man would occasionally intersperse among his strictures and
exhortations,—the expressiveness of his unscrupulous and often
startling phraseology,—all this, combined with the earnestness,
piety, and real goodness and simplicity of heart that breathed
from every word he uttered, may well be conceived to have had
no little charm for the multitudes that crowded to hear his living
voice; even as to us, after the lapse of three centuries, these
sermons of Latimer's are still in the highest degree interesting
both for the touches they contain in illustration of the manners
and social condition of our forefathers, and as a picture of a very
peculiar individual mind. They are also of some curiosity and
value as a monument of the language of the period; but to what
is properly to be called its literature, as we have said, they can
hardly be considered as belonging at all.

The following extract from Latimer's third sermon preached
before King Edward VI. at Westminster, 22nd March, 1549, was
contributed by Sir Henry Ellis, to the Pictorial History of
England. "We copy the original edition," says Sir Henry,
"with all its spellings and provincialisms; a volume of so great
rarity as not to be found in any of the libraries which have been
brought together at the British Museum:"—

Syr, what forme of preachinge woulde you appoynt me to preache before
a kynge ? Wold you have me for to preache nothynge as concernynge a
kynge in the kynges sermon ? Have you any commission to appoynt me
what I shall preach ? Besydes thys, I asked hym dyvers other questions,
and he wold make no answere to none of them all. He had nothyng to
say. Then I turned me to the kyng, and submitted my selfe to his Grace,
and sayed, I never thoughte my selfe worthy, nor I never sued to be a
preacher before youre Grace, but I was called to it, would be wyllyng (if
you mislyke me) to geve place to my betters. For I graunt ther be a
great many more worthy of the roume than I am. And, if it be your
Grace's pleasure so to allowe them for preachers, I could be content to here
ther boke after theym. But if your Grace allowe me for a preacher I
would desyre your Grace to geve me leave to discharge my conscience.
Geve me leve to frame my doctrine accordyng to my audience. I had byne
a very dolt to have preached so at the borders of your realm as I preach
before your Grace. And I thanke Almyghty God, whych hath alwayes byne
remedy, that my sayinges were well accepted of the kynge, for like a
gracious Lord he turned into a nother communicacyon. It is even as the
Scripture sayeth Cor Regis in manu Domini, the Lorde dyrected the
kynges hart. Certaine of my frendes came to me wyth teares in their
eyes, and told me they loked I should have bene in the Tower the same
nyghte. Thus have I ever more bene burdened wyth the werde of sedition.
I have offended God grevousiye, transgressyng hys law, and but for his
remedy and his mercye I wold not loke to be saved. As for sedicion, for
oughte that I knowe, me thynkes I shoulde not nede Christe, if I might so
saye. But if I be cleare in any thynge, I am clear in thys. So farre as I
knowe myne owne herte, there is no man further from sedicion then I,
whyche I have declared in all my doynges, and yet it hath bene ever layed
to me. An other tyme, when I gave over myne offyce, I should have
receyved a certaine dutye that they call a Pentecostall; it came to the
summe of fyftye and fyve pound, I sent my Commissarye to gather it, but
he coulde not be suffered. For it was sayed a sedicion should ryse upon it.
Thus they burdened me ever wyth sedicion. So thys gentilman commeth
up nowe wyth sedicion. And wott ye what? I chaunched in my last
Sermon to speake a mery worde of the Newe Shilling (to refreshe my
auditory), howe I was lyke to put away my newe shillynge for an olde
grote; I was herein noted to speake sediciously. Yet I comfort my self in
onethyng, that I am not alone, and that I have a fellowe. For it is conso-
latio miserorum, it is the comforte of the wretched, to have companye.
When I was in trouble, it was objected an sayed unto me that I was
syngular, that no man thought as I thought, that I love a syngularyte in
all that I dyd, and that I woke a way contrarye to the kynge and the
whole parliamente, and that I was travayled wyth them that had better
wyttes then I, that I was contrary to them al. Marye, syr, thys was a sore
thunder bolte. I thought it an yrkesome thynge to be a lone, and to have
no fellowe. I thoughte it was possyble it myghte not be true that they
tolde me. In the vii of John the Priestes sente out certayne of the Jewes

to bryng Christ unto them vyolentlye. When they came into the Temple and harde hym preache, they were so moved wyth his preachynge that they returned home agayne, and sayed to them that sente them, *Nunquam sic locutus est homo ut hic homo*, There was never man spake lyke thys man. Then answered the Pharysees, *Num et vos seducti estis?* What ye brayne-syeke foules, ye hastly preken, ye dunklye poulkes, ye huddes, do ye bileve hym? are ye seduced also? *Nunquis ex Principibus credidit in eum?* Did ye see any great man or any great offycer take hys part? don ye so any boldly follow hym but braggerlye fyshers, and suche as have nothynge to take to? *Nunquis ex Pharisæis?* Do ye se any holy man? any perfect man? any learned man take hys parte? *Turba quæ ignorat legem execrabilis est.* Thys laye people is accursed; it is they that knowe not the lawe that takes hys parte, and none.

Lo here the Pharises had nothynge to choke the people wyth al but ignoraunce. They dyd as oure byshoppes of Englande, who upbrayded the people alwayes with ignoraunce, where they were the cause of it them selves. There were, sayeth St. John, *Multi ex principibus qui crediderunt in eum*; manye of the chyefe menne beleved in hym, and that was contrarye to the Pharisyes saying, Oh then by lyke they bilyed him, he was not alone.

So, thoughte I, there be more of myne opinion then I; I thought I was not alone. I have nowe gotten one felowe more, a companyon of axlytyon, and wot ye who is my felowe? Esaye the prophete. I spake but of a lytle preaty shyllynge; but he speaketh to Hierusalem after an other sorte, and was so bold to meddle with theyr coine. Thou proude, thou covetouse, thou hautye cytye of Hierusalem, *Argentum tuum versum est in scoriam*: thy sylver is turned into what? Into testyons? *Scoriam*, into drosse. Ah sedicious wretch, what had he to do wyth the mynte? Why should not he have lefte that matter to some master of pulicy to reprove? Thy silver is drosse, it is not fine, it is counterfaite, thy silver is turned, thou haddest good sylver. What pertayned that to Esay? Mary he espyed a pece of divinity in that pulici, he threateneth them Gods vengeance for it. He went to the rote of the matter, which was covetousnes. He espyed two poyntes in it, that eythere it came of covetousness whych became hym to reprove, or els that it tended to the hurte of the pore people, for the noughtynes of the sylver was the occasion of dearth of all thynges in the realme. He imputeth it to them as a great cryme. He may be called a mayster of sedicion in dede. Was not this a sedyciouse harlot to tell them thys to theyr beardes? to theyr face?

Generally it may be observed, with regard to the English prose of the earlier part of the sixteenth century that it is both more simple in its construction, and of a more purely native character in other respects, than the style which came into fashion in the latter years of the Elizabethan period. When first made use of in prose composition, the mother-tongue was written as it was spoken; even such artifices and embellishments as are always prompted by the nature of verse were here scarcely aspired after or thought of; that which was addressed to and specially intended for the instruction of the people was set down as far as possible in the familiar forms and fashions of the popular speech, in genuine native words, and direct unincumbered sentences; no painful imitation of any learned or foreign model was attempted, nor any species of elaboration whatever, except what was necessary for mere perspicuity, in a kind of writing which was scarcely regarded as partaking of the character of literary composition at all. The delicacy of a scholarly taste no doubt influenced even the English style of such writers as More and his more eminent contemporaries or immediate followers; but whatever eloquence or dignity their compositions thus acquired was not the effect of any professed or conscious endeavour to write in English as they would have written in what were called the learned tongues.

The age, indeed, of the critical cultivation of the language for the purposes of prose composition had already commenced; but at first that object was pursued in the best spirit and after the wisest methods. Erasmus, in one of his Letters, mentions that his friend Dean Colet laboured to improve his English style by the diligent perusal and study of Chaucer and the other old poets, in whose works alone the popular speech was to be found turned with any taste or skill to a literary use; and doubtless others of our earliest classic prose writers took lessons in their art in the same manner from those true fathers of our vernacular literature. And even the first professed critics and reformers of the language that arose among us proceeded in the main in a right direction and upon sound principles in the task they undertook. The appearance of a race of critical and rhetorical writers in any country is, in truth, always rather a symptom or indication than, what it has frequently been denounced as being, a cause of the corruption and decline of the national literature. The writings of Dionysius of Halicarnassus and of Quintilian, for instance, certainly did not hasten, but probably rather contributed to retard, the decay of the literature of ancient Greece and Rome. The first eminent English writer of this class was the celebrated Roger Ascham, the tutor of Queen Elizabeth, whose treatise entitled Toxophilus, the School or Partitions of Shooting, was published in 1545. The design of Ascham, in this performance, was not only to recommend to his countrymen the use of their

old national weapon, the bow, but to set before them an example
and model of a pure and correct English prose style. In his
dedication of the work, To all the Gentlemen and Yeomen of
England, he recommends to him that would write well in any
tongue the counsel of Aristotle,—"To speak as the common
people do, to think as wise men do." From this we may perceive
that Ascham had a true feeling of the regard due to the great
fountain-head and oracle of the national language—the vocabulary
of the common people. He goes on to reprobate the practice of
many English writers, who by introducing into their compositions, in violation of the Aristotelian precept, many words of
foreign origin, Latin, French, and Italian, made all things dark
and hard. "Once," he says, "I communed with a man which
reasoned the English tongue to be enriched and increased thereby,
saying, Who will not praise that feast where a man shall drink at
a dinner both wine, ale, and beer? Truly, quoth I, they be all
good, every one taken by himself alone : but if you put malmsey
and sack, red wine and white, ale and beer and all, in one pot,
you shall make a drink neither easy to be known, nor yet wholesome for the body." The English language, however, it may be
observed, had even already become too thoroughly and essentially
a mixed tongue for this doctrine of purism to be admitted to the
letter; nor, indeed, to take up Ascham's illustration, is it universally true, even in regard to liquids, that a salutary and palatable
beverage can never be made by the interfusion of two or more
different kinds. Our tongue is now, and was many centuries
ago, not, indeed, in its grammatical structure, but in its vocabulary, as substantially and to as great an extent Neo-Latin as
Gothic; it would be as completely torn in pieces and left the
mere tattered rag of a language, useless for all the purposes of
speaking as well as of writing, by having the foreign as by
having the native element taken out of it. Ascham in his own
writings uses many words of French and Latin origin (the latter
mostly derived through the medium of the French); nay, the
common people themselves of necessity did in his day, as they do
still, use many such foreign words, or words not of English
origin, and could scarcely have held communication with one
another on the most ordinary occasions without so doing. It is
another question whether it might not have been more fortunate
if the original form of the national speech had remained in a state
of celibacy and virgin purity; by the course of events the

2 E 2

Gothic part of the language has, in point of fact, been married to the Latin part of it; and what God or nature has thus joined together it is now beyond the competency of man to put asunder. The language, while it subsists, must continue to be the product of that union, and nothing else. As for Ascham's own style, both in his Toxophilus, and in his Schoolmaster, published in 1571, three years after the author's death, it is not only clear and correct, but idiomatic and muscular. That it is not rich or picturesque is the consequence of the character of the writer's mind, which was rather rhetorical than poetical. The publication of Ascham's Toxophilus was soon followed by an elaborate treatise expressly dedicated to the subject of English composition—The Art of Rhetorick, for the use of all such as are studious of Eloquence, set forth in English, by Thomas Wilson. Wilson, whose work appeared in 1553, takes pains to impress the same principles that Ascham had laid down before him with regard to purity of style and the general rule of writing well. But the very solicitude thus shown by the ablest and most distinguished of those who now assumed the guardianship of the vernacular tongue to protect it from having its native character overlaid and debased by an intermixture of terms borrowed from other languages, may be taken as evidence that such debasement was actually at this time going on; that our ancient English was beginning to be oppressed and half suffocated by additions from foreign sources brought in upon it faster than it could absorb and assimilate them. Wilson, indeed, proceeds to complain that this was the case. While some "powdered their talk with over-sea language," others, whom he designates as "the unlearned or foolish fantastical, that smell but of learning," were wont, he says, "so to Latin their tongues," that simple persons could not but wonder at their talk, and think they surely spake by some revelation from heaven. It may be suspected, however, that this affectation of unnecessary terms, formed from the ancient languages, was not confined to mere pretenders to learning. Another well-known critical writer of this period, Webster Puttenham, in his Art of English Poesy, published in 1582, but believed to have been written a good many years earlier, in like manner advises the avoidance in writing of such words and modes of expression as are used "in the marches and frontiers, or in port towns where strangers haunt for traffic sake, or yet in universities, where scholars use much peevish affectation of

words out of the primitive languages;" and he warns his readers
that in some books were already to be found "many inkhorn
terms so ill affected, brought in by men of learning, as preachers
and schoolmasters, and many strange terms of other languages by
secretaries, and merchants, and travellers, and many dark words,
and not usual nor well-sounding, though they be daily spoken at
court." On the whole, however, Puttenham considers the best
standard both for speaking and writing to be "the usual speech
of the court, and that of London and the shires lying about
London within sixty miles, and not much above." This judgment is probably correct, although the writer was a gentleman
pensioner, and perhaps also a cockney by birth.

SCOTTISH PROSE WRITERS.

Before the middle of the sixteenth century a few prose writers
had also appeared in the Scottish dialect. A digest of practical
theology composed for the use of King James IV. in his native
tongue, by a priest called John de Irlandia, in the year 1490,
still exists in MS. (apparently an autograph of the author), in
the Advocates' Library at Edinburgh. "This work," says
Leyden, who has given an account of it, with some extracts, in
the Preliminary Dissertation prefixed to his edition of The
Complaint of Scotland, " exhibits a curious specimen of the
Scottish language at that period; and the style as well as the
orthography are more uniform, and approach nearer the modern
standard, than those of some writers who lived almost a century
later." A moral treatise entitled The Portcous [that is, the
vade mecum or manual] of Noblenes, translated from the French
by Andrew Cadiou was printed at Edinburgh in 1508. The
conclusion of it, the only portion that is known to have been
preserved, is reprinted by Leyden in his Dissertation (pp.
203—208); and also by Mr. David Laing, in his collection
entitled The Knightly Tale of Golagrus and Gawane, &c. Edin.
1827. The Scottish History of Hector Boethius, or Boecius
(Ikeee or Boyce), translated from the Latin by John Bellendon,
was printed at Edinburgh in 1537; and a translation by the
same person of the first Five Books of Livy remained in MS.
till it was published at Edinburgh, in 4to. in 1829; a second

edition of the translation of Boccius having also been brought out there, in two vols. 4to., the same year. But the most remarkable composition in Scottish prose of this era is The Complaynt of Scotland, printed at St. Andrews in 1548, which has been variously assigned to Sir James Inglis, knight, a country gentleman of Fife, who died in 1554; to Wedderburn, the supposed author of the Compendious Book of Godly and Spiritual Songs and Ballats (reprinted from the edition of 1621 by Sir John Grahame Dalzell, 8vo. Edinburgh, 1801); and by its modern editor, the late John Leyden, in the elaborate and ingenious Dissertation prefixed to his reprint of the work, 8vo. Edinburgh, 1801, to the famous poet, Sir David Lyndsay. This is a very extraordinary piece of writing, as a short extract or two will show. For the better comparison of the language in all respects with that spoken and written in England at the same date, we shall, in our first specimen, preserve the original spelling. The following is from a long episode which occurs in the middle of the work, entitled Ane Monolog of the Actor :—*

There eftir i herd the rumour of rammasche¹ fioilis ande of beystis that maid grite beir,² quhilk past besyde burnis³ and boggis on grene bankis to seik ther sustentatione. There brutal sound did redond to the hie skyis, qnhil the depe hou⁴ cauernis of cleuchis, and rotche⁵ craggis ansuert vitht⁶ ane hie son, of that ssmyn sound as thay⁷ beystis hul blauen. It aperit be presumyng and presupusing that blabermul eccho had beene hid in ane hou hole, cryand hyr half ansueir, quhen narcissus rycht sorye socht for his saruandis,⁸ quhen he vas in ane forrest, far fra ony folkis, and there eftir for loue of eccho he drounit in ane drau vel. non to tel treutht of the beystis that maid sic beir, and of the dyn that the foulis did, ther syndry soundis hed nothir temperance nor tune. for fyrst furtht on the fresche feildis, the nolt⁹ maid noyis vitht mony loud lou. baytht horse and meyris did fast nee, and the fulis orcchyr.¹⁰ the bullis began to buller,¹¹ quhen the achelp began to blait, because the calfis began tyl mo,¹² quhen the doggis berkit. than the snyne began to quhryne¹³ quhen thai herd

<hr />

¹ Collected.   ² Noise (birr).   ³ Rivulets.
⁴ Hollow.   ⁵ Rock ; or, perhaps, rocky ?   ⁶ With.
⁷ Those.   ⁸ Servants.   ⁹ Neat.
¹⁰ An imitative word expressing the cry of a foul.   ¹¹ Roar.
¹² Imitative word for cry of a calf.   ¹³ Imitative word for cry of swine.

the nene tair,' quhilk gart[2] the hennis kekkul[3] quhen the cokis crew, the abokyus began to peu[4] quhen the gled[5] quhimsillit. the sun follouit the fei geise, and gart them' cry alaik. the gayslingis[6] cryit quhilk quhilk, and the dukis cryit quaik. the ropern[7] of the rauyben gart the cras crope, the backlit craulis cryit varrok varrok, quhen the suannis murnit, ho came the gray goul[8] mau pronostikat ane storm. the turtil began for to greit, quhen the cuschet[9] roulit.[10] the titlene[11] folkuit the goilk,[12] ande gart byr sing guk guk. the dou[13] croulit[14] byr and sang that soundit lyik sorrou. robenn and the litil vran var hamely in vyntir. the langolyue[15] of the suallou gart the iay iangil.[16] than the maunis[17] maid myrth, for to mok the merie.[18] the laucrok[19] maid melody vp in the skyie. the nychtingal al the nycht sang sueit notis. the tuebitis[20] cryit cheuis nok[21] quhen the plettis[22] clattrit.[23] tho garruling[24] of the stirlene[?][25] gart the sparrou cheip.[26] the lyntquhit[27] sang cuntirpoint quhen the ouzil[28] zulpit. the grene serone[29] sang sueit quhen the gukl spynk[30] chantit. the rede schank[31] cryit my fut my fut, and once[32] cry't tueit. the herrous gaif ane vyikl skrech as the kyl hed beue in fier, quhilk gart the quhaplis[33] for fleyitnes[34] fle far fra hame.

A still more ostentatious display of the wealth of the writer's native dialogue follows, in a description of a sea scene, ending in a fight. Into this he has poured a complete dictionary of naval terms, some of which set translation or explanation at defiance, but many of which are still in familiar use among the fishing population of the sea-coast of Fife, from whom either Lyndsay or Inglis would be likely enough to learn them. Leyden describes them generally as in part of Norman, in part of Flemish origin. We will pass on, and select for our next extract a portion of the author's natural philosophy; and here we shall strip his clear and expressive style of the cumbrous and capri-

---

[1] Imitative word for cry of ass. [2] Caused.
[3] Cackle. [4] Imitative word for cry of young birds.
[5] Glede, hawk. [6] Goslings. [7] Hoarse cry.
[8] Gull. [9] Cushat-dove.
[10] Rather gould, that is howled. [11] The hedge-sparrow.
[12] The cuckoo. [13] Dove. [14] Imitative word for cry of the dove.
[15] Jargoning. [16] Imitative word for cry of the jay. [17] Thrush.
[18] Blackbird. [19] Lark. [20] Lapwings.
[21] Imitative word for cry of lapwings. [22] Magpies.
[23] Chattered. [24] Garrulous noise. [25] Starling.
[26] Make a feeble noise. [27] Linnet.
[28] The ouzle, which means sometimes the thrush, sometimes the blackbird, sometimes, as here, apparently a different bird from either.
[29] Green Siren, or Green-finch. [30] Goldfinch.
[31] Fieldfare. [32] Small hedge-sparrow.
[33] Curlews. [34] Fear.

cious old spelling, which makes it look as if it were all over bespattered with mud to the eye of a modern reader :—

Now, to speak of the generation of the dew, it is ane humid vapour, generit in the second region of the air in ane fair calm night, and sine[1] descends in ane temperate caldness on the green erbs in small drops. The hair[7] rinne is ane cald dew, the whilk falls in misty vapours, and sine it freezes on the eird.[3] The mist, it is the excrement or the superfluity of the cluds, the whilk falls fra the air in ane sweet rain, whilk rain can nought be perceivit be the sight of men. Hail stones is ane congealit rain, whilk falls on the eird be grit vehemence, and it falls rather on the day light nor[4] on the night. The snaw is ane congealit rain, frozen and congealit in the second region of the air, and congeals in divers massive cluds, whilk stops and empeshes[5] the operation of the planets to exerce their natural course; than[6] the vehemence of the planets braks thay[7] cluds, fra the force of the whilk there comes fire, and ane grit sound, whilk is terrible to be hard, and that terrible sound is the thing that we call the thunder; but or[9] we bear the thunder, we see first the fire, howbeit[9] that they proceed at ane instant time. The cause that we see the fire or we hear the thunder is be reason that the sight and clearness of ony thing is mair swift towart us nor is the sound. The evil that the thunder does on the eird, it is done or we hear the crack of it. Oft times we will see fire-slaught,[10] how be it there be na thunder hard. The thunder slays mony beasts on the fields; and when it slays ane man that is sleepand, he sall be funden dead and his een[11] apen.[12] The thunder is maist dangerous for man and beast when there comes na rain with it. The fire-slaught will consume the wine within ane pipe in ane deep carr, and the pipe will resave na skaith. The fire-slaught slew ane man on the fields, and it meltit the gold that was in his bag, and it meltit nought the wax of ane seal that was in that samen bag. In Rome there was ane noble princess callit Martia grit with child; she was on the fields for her recreation, where that the fire-slaught straik her, and slew her nought, but yet it slew the child in her woime. There is three things that are never in danger of thunder nor fire-slaught; that is to say, the laury tree; the second is the selch,[13] whilk some men calls the sea wolf; the third thing is the eyrn,[14] that flies on high. The historiographers rehearses that Tiberius Caesar, emperor of Rome, had ever ane hat of laure tree on his head, and als he gart mak his pailyeons,[15] and tents on the fields of selch skins, to that effect that he might be furth of the danger of the thunder and fire-slaught. The best remede contrar thunder and fire-slaught is to men and women to pass in hen[16] caverns under the eird, or in deep caves, be cause the thunder does maist damage till high places.

[1] Then.	[2] Hoar.	[3] Earth.	[4] Than.
[5] Hinders.	[6] Then.	[7] Those.	[8] Ere.
[9] Although.	[10] Lightning.	[11] Eyes.	[12] Open.
[13] Seal.	[14] Eagle.	[15] Pavilions.	[16] Hollow

It is worthy of remark, that, although we have here unquestionably the Scottish dialect, distinctly marked by various peculiarities (indeed the author, in his prologue or preface expressly and repeatedly states that he has written in Scotch, " in our Scottis langage," as he calls it), yet one chief characteristic of the modern Scotch is still wanting—the suppression of the final *l* after a vowel or diphthong—just as it is in Barbour and Blind Harry. This change, as we before remarked, is probably very modern. It has taken place in all likelihood since Scotch ceased to be generally used in writing; the principle of growth, which, after a language passes under the government of the pen, is to a great extent suspended, having recovered its activity on the dialect being abandoned again to the comparatively lawless liberty, or at least looser guardianship, of the lips.

English Poets:—Hawes; Barklay.

The English poetical literature of the first half of the sixteenth century may be fairly described as the dawn of a new day. Two poetic names of some note belong to the reign of Henry VII.—Stephen Hawes and Alexander Barklay. Hawes is the author of many pieces, but is chiefly remembered for his Pastime of Pleasure, or History of Grand Amour and La Belle Pucelle, first printed by Wynkyn de Worde in 1517, but written about two years earlier. Warton holds this performance to be almost the only effort of imagination and invention which had appeared in our poetry since Chaucer, and eulogizes it as containing no common touches of romantic and allegoric fiction. Hawes was both a scholar and a traveller, and was perfectly familiar with the French and Italian poetry as well as with that of his own country. It speaks very little, however, for his taste, that, among the preceding English poets, he has evidently made Lydgate his model, even if it should be admitted that, as Warton affirms, he has added some new graces to the manner of that cold and wordy versifier. Lydgate and Hawes may stand together as perhaps the two writers who, in the century and a half that followed the death of Chaucer, contributed most to carry forward the regulation and modernisation of the language which he began. Barklay, who did not die till 1552,

when he had attained a great age, employed his pen principally
in translations, in which line his most celebrated performance
is his Ship of Fools, from the German of Sebastian Brandt,
which was printed in 1508.   Barklay, however, besides con-
sulting both a French and a Latin version of Brandt's poem,
has enlarged his original with the enumeration and description of a considerable variety of follies which he found
flourishing among his own countrymen.   This gives the work
some value as a record of the English manners of the time:
but both its poetical and its satirical pretensions are of the very
humblest order.   At this date most of our writers of what was
called poetry seem to have been occupied with the words in
which they were to clothe their ideas almost to the exclusion
of all the higher objects of the poetic art.   And that, perhaps,
is what of necessity happens at a particular stage in the progress of a nation's literature—at the stage corresponding to the
transition state in the growth of the human being between the
termination of free rejoicing boyhood and the full assurance of
manhood begun; which is peculiarly the season not of achieve-
ment but of preparation, not of accomplishing ends, but of
acquiring the use of means and instruments, and also, it may be
added, of the aptitude to mistake the one of those things for the
other.

SKELTON.

But the poetry with the truest life in it produced in the reign
of Henry the Seventh and the earlier part of that of his son
is undoubtedly that of Skelton.   John Skelton may have been
born about or soon after 1460; he studied at Cambridge, if not
at both universities; began to write and publish compositions in
verse between 1480 and 1490; was graduated as poet laureat
(a degree in grammar, including versification and rhetoric) at
Oxford before 1490; was admitted *ad eundem* at Cambridge in
1493; in 1498 took holy orders; was probably about the same
time appointed tutor to the young prince Henry, afterwards
Henry the Eighth; was eventually promoted to be rector of
Diss in Norfolk; and died in 1529 in the sanctuary at Westminster Abbey, where he had taken refuge to escape the vengeance of Cardinal Wolsey, originally his patron, but latterly the

chief butt at which he had been wont to shoot his satiric shafts.
As a scholar Skelton had a European reputation in his own day;
and the great Erasmus has styled him *Britannicarum literarum
decus et lumen* (the light and ornament of English letters). His
Latin verses are distinguished by their purity and classical
spirit. As for his English poetry, it is generally more of a
mingled yarn, and of a much coarser fabric. In many of his
effusions indeed, poured forth in sympathy with or in aid of some
popular cry of the day, he is little better than a rhyming buffoon;
much of his ribaldry is now nearly unintelligible; and it may
be doubted if a considerable portion of his grotesque and apparently incoherent jingle ever had much more than the sort of
half meaning with which a half-tipsy writer may satisfy readers
as far gone as himself. Even in the most reckless of these compositions, however, he rattles along, through sense and nonsense,
with a vivacity that had been a stranger to our poetry for many
a weary day; and his freedom and spirit, even where most
unrefined, must have been exhilarating after the long fit of
somnolency in which the English muse had dozed away the last
hundred years. But much even of Skelton's satiric verse is instinct with genuine poetical vigour, and a fancy alert, sparkling,
and various, to a wonderful degree. It is impossible, where the
style and manner are, if not so discursive, at least so rushing and
river-like, to give any complete idea of the effect by extracts;
but we will transcribe a small portion of the bitterest of his
attacks upon Wolsey, his satire, or "little book," as he designates
it, entitled Why come ye not to court? extending in all to nearly
1300 lines :—

> Our barons be so bold
> Into a mouse-hole they wold
> Run away and creep,
> Like a meiny of sheep;
> Dare not look out at dur
> For dread of the mastiff cur,
> For dread of the butcher's dog
> Wold wirry them like an hog. .
> For an this cur do gnar
> They must stand all afar,
> To hold up their hand at the bar.
> For all their noble blood,
> He plucks them by the hood,
> And shakes them by the ear,
> And brings them in such fear;

He baiteth them like a bear,
Like an ox or a bull:
Their wits he saith are dull;
He saith they have no brain
Their estate to maintain,
And maketh them to bow their knee
Before his majesty.

In the chancery where he sits,
But such as be admits
None so hardy as to speak:
He saith, Thou buddypeke,
Thy learning is too lewd,
Thy tongue is not well thewd,[1]
To seek[2] before our grace:
And openly in that place
He rages and he raves,
And calls them cankerred knaves.
Thus royalty doth he deal
Under the king's broad seal;
And in the Checker be them checks;
In the Star Chamber he nods and becks,
And beareth him there so stout
That no man dare rout.[3]
Duke, earl, baron, nor lord,[4]
But to his sentence must accord;
Whether he be knight or squire,
All men must follow his desire.

But this mad Amalek
Like to a Mamelek,[5]
He regardeth lords
No more than potshords;
He is in such elation
Of his exaltation,
And the supportation
Of our sovereign lord,
That, God to record,[6]
He ruleth all at will,
Without reason or skill;[7]
Howbeit the primordial
Of his wretched original,

---

[1] Well mannered.
[2] In original spelling seke. Qy. a typographical error for speke (or speak)?
[3] Snort.   [4] That is, no duke, &c.   [5] Mameluke.
[6] Witness.   [7] Regard to propriety.

And his base progeny,[1]
And his greasy genealogy,
He came of the sank royal[2]
That was cast out of a butcher's stall.

.   .   .   .   .

He would dry up the streams
Of nine kings' names,[3]
All rivers and wells,
All water that swells;
For with us he so mells[4]
That within England dwells,
I wold he were somewhere else;
For else by and by
He will drink us so dry,
And suck us so nigh,
That men shall scantly
Have penny or halfpenny.
God save his noble grace,
And grant him a place
Endless to dwell
With the devil of hell!
For, an he were there,
We need never fear
Of the feindes blake;
For I undertake
He wold so brag and crake,
That he wold than make
The devils to quake,
To shudder and to shake,
Like a fire-drake,[5]
And with a coal rake
Bruise them on a brake,[6]
And bind them to a stake,
And set hell on fire
At his own desire.
He is such a grim sire,
And such a potestolate,[7]
And such a potestate,
That he wold brake the brains
Of Lucifer in his chains,
And rule them each one
In Lucifer's trone.[8]

---

1 Progenitorship?   2 Sangue royal, blood royal.
3 Realms.   4 Meddles.
5 Fiery dragon.   6 Engine of torture.
7 "Equivalent, I suppose, to legato."—Dyce.   8 Throne.

I wold he were gone,
For among us is none
That raketh but he alone,
Without all good reason,
And all out of season, &c.

Another of Skelton's satirical invectives, his Bouge of Court
(that is, *Bouche à Court*, diet allowed at court), which is written
in the common stanza of seven decasyllabic lines, and altogether
with much more sobriety, has some strong allegorical painting,
but in a hard and heavy style; and the force is also more conspicuous than the invention. Another of his productions is a
drama, entitled Magnificence, a Goodly Interlude and a Merry,
in rhyme, and running to nearly 2600 long lines, the characters
being Felicity, Liberty, Measure, Counterfeit Countenance,
Crafty Conveyance, Cloaked Collusion, Courtly Abusion, and
other such shadowy personages. But Skelton's brightest and
in all respects happiest poetry is surely what of it is neither
allegorical nor satirical. The charm of his writing lies in its
natural ease and freedom, its inexhaustible and untiring vivacity;
and these qualities are found both in their greatest abundance
and their greatest purity where his subject is suggestive of the
simplest emotions and has most of a universal interest. His
Book of Philip Sparrow, for instance, an elegy on the sparrow of
fair Jane Soroop, slain by a cat in the nunnery of Carow, near
Norwich, extending (with the "commendation" of the "goodly
maid") to nearly 1400 lines, is unrivalled in the language for
elegant and elastic playfulness, and a spirit of whim that only
kindles into the higher blaze the longer it is kept up. The
second part, or "Commendation," in particular, is throughout
animated and hilarious to a wonderful degree :—the *refrain*,—

For this most goodly flower,
This blossom of fresh colour,
So Jupiter me succour,
She flourisheth new and new
In beauty and virtue;
Hac claritate gemina,
O Gloriosa femina, &c.—

recurring often so suddenly and unexpectedly, yet always so
naturally, has an effect like that of the harmonious evolutions of
some lively and graceful dance. Have we not in this poem, by-

the-by, the true origin of Skelton's peculiar dancing verse?   Is
it not Anacreontic, as the spirit also of the best of his poetry
undoubtedly is?*

·

·Roy; John Heywood.

Along with Skelton, viewed as he commonly has been only as a
satirist, is usually classed William Roy, a writer who assisted
Tyndal in his translation of the New Testament, and who is
asserted by Bale to be the author of a singular work entitled,
Read me and be not wroth, For I say nothing but troth, which
is supposed to have been first printed abroad about 1525.† This
is also a satire upon Wolsey and the clergy in general, and is as
bitter as might be expected from the supposed author, who,
having begun his life as a friar, spent the best-part of it in the
service of the Reformation, and finished it at the stake.   Among
the buffoon-poets of this age, is also to be reckoned John Heywood, styled the Epigrammatist, from the six centuries of Epigrams, or versified jokes, which form a remarkable portion of
his works.   Heywood's conversational jocularity has the equivo-
cal credit of having been exceedingly consoling both to the old
age of Henry VIII. and to his daughter Queen Mary: it must
have been strong jesting that could stir the sense of the ludicrous
in either of these terrible personages.   Besides a number of
plays, which are the most important of his productions, Heywood also wrote a long burlesque allegory, which fills a thick
quarto volume, on the dispute between the old and the new
religions, under the title of A Parable of the Spider and the
Fly; where it appears that by the spider is intended the Protestant party, by the fly the Catholic, but in which, according
to the judgment of old Harrison, " he dealeth so profoundly,
and beyond all measure of skill, that neither he himself that
made it, neither any one that readeth it, can reach unto the
meaning thereof."‡

* A most valuable and acceptable present has been made to the lovers of
our old poetry in a collected edition of Skelton's Poetical Works, 2 vols. 8vo.
Lond. Rodd, 1843, by the Rev. Alexander Dyce, who has performed his
difficult task in a manner to leave little or nothing further to be desired.
   † Ritson's Bibliog. Poet, p. 318.
   ‡ Description of England.

SCOTTISH POETS:—GAWIN DOUGLAS; DUNBAR; LYNDSAY.

But, while in England the new life to which poetry had awakened had thus as yet produced so little except ribaldry and buffoonery, it is remarkable that in Scotland, where general social civilization was much less advanced, the art had continued to be cultivated in its highest departments with great success, and the language had already been enriched with some compositions worthy of any age. Perhaps the Scottish poetry of the earlier part of the sixteenth century may be regarded as the same spring which had visited England in the latter part of the fourteenth,—the impulse originally given by the poetry of Chaucer only now come to its height in that northern clime. Gawin Douglas, Bishop of Dunkeld, who flourished in the first quarter of the sixteenth century, and who is famous for his translation of the Æneid, the first metrical version of any ancient classic that had yet appeared in the dialect of either kingdom, affects great anxiety to eschew "Southron," or English, and to write his native tongue in all its breadth and plainness; but it does not follow, from his avoidance of English words, that he may not have formed himself to a great extent on the study of English models. At the same time it may be admitted that neither in his translation nor in his original works of King Hart, and the Palace of Honour,—which are two long allegories, full, the latter especially, of passages of great descriptive beauty,—does Douglas convict himself of belonging to the school of Chaucer. He is rather, if not the founder, at least the chief representative, of a style of poetry which was attempted to be formed in Scotland by enriching and elevating the simplicity of Barbour and his immediate followers with an infusion of something of what was deemed a classic manner, drawn in part directly from the Latin writers, but more from those of the worst than those of the best age, in part from the French poetry, which now began in like manner to aspire towards a classic tone. This preference, by the Scottish poets, of Latin and French to "Southron," as a source from which to supply the deficiencies of their native dialect, had probably no more reasonable origin than the political circumstances and feelings of the nation: the spirit of the national genius was antagonistic to it, and it therefore never could become more than a temporary

fashion.* Yet it infooted more or less all the writers of this
age ; and amongst the rest, to a considerable extent, by far the
greatest of them all, William Dunbar. This admirable master,
alike of serious and of comic song, may justly be styled the Chaucer
of Scotland, whether we look to the wide range of his genius,
or to his eminence in every style over all the poets of his country
who preceded and all who for ages came after him. That of
Burns is certainly the only name among the Scottish poets that
can yet be placed on the same line with that of Dunbar ; and
even the inspired ploughman, though the equal of Dunbar in
comic power, and his superior in depth of passion, is not to be
compared with the elder poet either in strength or in general
fertility of imagination.† Finally, to close the list, comes another
eminent name, that of Sir David Lyndsay, whose productions
are not indeed characterised by any high imaginative power, but
yet display infinite wit, spirit, and variety in all the forms of
the more familiar poetry. Lyndsay was the favourite, throughout his brief reign and life, of the accomplished and unfortunate
James V., and survived to do perhaps as good service as any in
the war against the ancient church by the tales, plays, and other
products of his abounding satiric vein, with which he fed, and
excited, and lashed up the popular contempt for the now crazy
and tumbling fabric once so imposing and so venerated. Perhaps he also did no harm by thus taking off a little of the acrid
edge of mere resentment and indignation with the infusion of a
dash of merriment, and keeping alive a genial sense of the
ludicrous in the midst of such serious work. If Dunbar is to
be compared to Burns, Lyndsay may be said to have his best
representative among the more recent Scottish poets in Allan
Ramsay, who does not, however, come so near to Lyndsay by a
long way as Burns does to Dunbar.‡

* Douglas's Palace of Honour was reprinted for the Bannatyne Club, 4to.
Edin. 1827 ; and two vols. of a new edition of his translation of the Æneid
have also been produced by the same association, 4to. Edin. 1839.
† Portions of Dunbar's poetry had been previously published from the
MSS. by Ramsay, Hailes, and Pinkerton ; but the only complete edition is
that entitled The Poems of William Dunbar, now first collected, with Notes,
and a Memoir of his life, by David Laing : 2 vols. 8vo. Edin. 1834.
‡ The Poetical Works of Sir David Lindsay, with a Life, Glossary, and
Illustrative Dissertations and Notes, were published by the late George
Chalmers, in 3 vols. 8vo. London, 1806.

SURREY; WYATT.

Lyndsay is supposed to have survived till about the year 1567.[*] Before that date a revival of the higher poetry had come upon England like the rising of a new day. Two names are commonly placed together at the head of our new poetical literature, Lord Surrey and Sir Thomas Wyatt. Henry Howard, Earl of Surrey, memorable in our history as the last victim of the capricious and sanguinary tyranny of Henry VIII., had already, in his short life, which was terminated by the axe of the executioner in his twenty-seventh year, carried away from all his countrymen the laurels both of knighthood and of song. The superior polish alone of the best of Surrey's verses would place him at an immeasurable distance in advance of all his immediate predecessors. So remarkable, indeed, is the contrast in this respect which his poetry presents to theirs, that in modern times there has been claimed for Surrey, as we have seen, the honour of having been the first to introduce our existing system of rhythm into the language. The true merit of Surrey is, that, proceeding upon the same system of versification which had been introduced by Chaucer, and which, indeed, had in principle been followed by all the writers after Chaucer, however rudely or imperfectly some of them may have succeeded in the practice of it, he restored to our poetry a correctness, polish, and general spirit of refinement such as it had not known since Chaucer's time, and of which, therefore, in the language as now spoken, there was no previous example whatever. To this it may be added that he appears to have been the first, at least in this age, who sought to modulate his strains after that older poetry of Italy, which thenceforward became one of the chief fountain-heads of inspiration to that of England throughout the whole space of time over which is shed the golden light of the names of Spenser, of Shakespeare, and of Milton. Surrey's own imagination was neither rich nor soaring; and the highest qualities of his poetry, in addition to the facility and general mechanical perfection of the versification, are delicacy and tenderness. It is altogether a very light and bland Favonian breeze. The poetry of his friend Wyatt is of a different character, neither so

---

[*] Irving's Lives of the Scottish Poets. 2nd edit. 1810. II. 85.

flowing in form nor so uniformly gentle in spirit, but perhaps making up for its greater ruggedness by a force and a depth of sentiment occasionally which Surrey does not reach. The poems of Lord Surrey and Sir Thomas Wyatt were first published together in 1557.

We give one of Surrey's Sonnets in praise of his mistress, the Fair Geraldine, from Dr. Nott's edition of his Poems.* The spelling is modernised :—

Give place, ye lovers, here before
   That spent your boasts and brags in vain!
My lady's beauty passeth more
   The best of yours, I dare well sayn,
Than doth the sun the candle-light,
Or brightest day the darkest night.

And thereto hath a troth as just
   As had Penelope the fair ;
For what she saith ye may it trust,
   As it by writing sealed were :
And virtues hath she many mo
Than I with pen have skill to show.

I could rehearse, if that I would,
   The whole effect of Nature's plaint,
When she had lost the perfit mould,
   The like to whom she could not paint :
With wringing hands how she did cry,
And what she said, I know it, I.

I know she swore with raging mind,
   Her kingdom only set apart,
There was no loss by law of kind
   That could have gone so near her heart :
And this was chiefly all her pain ;
" She could not make the like again."

Sith Nature thus gave her the praise,
   To be the chiefest work she wrought,
In faith, methink, some better ways
   On your behalf might well be sought,
Than to compare, as ye have done,
To match the candle with the sun.

---

* Works of Henry Howard Earl of Surrey, and Sir Thomas Wyatt the Elder, 4to, Lond. 1815; vol. i. p. 4.

To Surrey we owe the introduction into the language of our present form of blank verse, the suggestion of which he probably took from the earliest Italian example of that form of poetry, a translation of the First and Fourth Books of the Æneid by the Cardinal Hippolito de' Medici (or, as some say, by Francesco Maria Molsa), which was published at Venice in 1541. A translation of the same two Books into English blank verse appeared in the collection of Surrey's Poems published by Tottel in 1557. Dr. Nott has shown that this translation was founded upon the metrical Scottish version of Gawin Douglas, which, although not published till 1553, had been finished, as the author himself informs us, in 1513. But it ought not to be forgotten that, as already remarked, we have one example at least of another form of blank verse in the Ormulum, centuries before Surrey's day.

The following earnestly passionate lines by Wyatt are supposed to have been addressed to Anne Boleyn :—

Forget not yet the tried intent
Of such a truth as I have meant;
My great travail so gladly spent
Forget not yet!

Forget not yet when first began
The weary life, ye know since whan;
The suit, the service, none tell can
Forget not yet!

Forget not yet the great assays;
The cruel wrong, the scornful ways,
The painful patience in delays,
Forget not yet!

Forget not! oh! forget not this!
How long ago hath been, and is,
The mind that never meant amiss,
Forget not yet!

Forget not then thine own approved,
The which so long hath thee so loved,
Whose steadfast faith yet never moved;
Forget not this!

THE ELIZABETHAN LITERATURE.

Of what is commonly called our Elizabethan literature, the greater portion appertains to the reign, not of Elizabeth, but of James—to the seventeenth, not to the sixteenth century. The common name, nevertheless, is the fair and proper one. It sprung up in the age of Elizabeth, and was mainly the product of influences which belonged to that age, although their effect extended into another. It was born of and ripened by that sunny morning of a new day,—"great Eliza's golden time,"— when a general sense of security had given men ease of mind and disposed them to freedom of thought, while the economical advancement of the country put life and spirit into everything, and its growing power and renown filled and elevated the national heart. But such periods of quiet and prosperity seem only to be intellectually productive when they have been preceded and ushered in by a time of uncertainty and struggle which has tried men's spirits: the contrast seems to be wanted to make the favourable influences be felt and tell; or the faculty required must come in part out of the strife and contention. The literature of our Elizabethan age, more emphatically, may be said to have had this double parentage: if that brilliant day was its mother, the previous night of storm was its father.

THE MIRROR FOR MAGISTRATES.

Our classical Elizabethan poetry and other literature dates only from about the middle of the reign; most of what was produced in the earlier half of it, constrained, harsh, and immature, still bears upon it the impress of the preceding barbarism. Nearly coincident with its commencement is the first appearance of a singular work, The Mirror for Magistrates. It is a collection of narratives of the lives of various remarkable English historical personages, taken, in general, with little more embellishment than their reduction to a metrical form, from the common popular chronicles; and the idea of it appears to have been borrowed

from a Latin work of Boccaccio's, which had been translated
and versified many years before by Lydgate, under the title of
The Fall of Princes. It was planned and begun (it is supposed
about the year 1557) by Thomas Sackville, afterwards distinguished as a statesman, and ennobled by the titles of Lord
Buckhurst and Earl of Dorset. But Sackville soon found himself
obliged to relinquish the execution of his extensive design,
which contemplated a survey of the whole range of English
history from William the Conqueror to the end of the wars of
the Roses, to other hands. The two writers to whom he recommended the carrying on of the work were Richard Baldwynne,
who was in orders, and had already published a metrical version
of the Song of Solomon, and George Ferrers, who was a person
of some rank, having sat in parliament in the time of Henry
VIII., but who had latterly been chiefly known as a composer of
occasional interludes for the diversion of the Court. It is a trait
of the times that, although a member of Lincoln's Inn, and
known both as a legal and an historical author, Ferrers was in
1552-3 appointed by Edward VI. to preside over the Christmas
revels at the royal palace of Greenwich in the office of Lord of
Misrule: Stow tells us that upon this occasion he "so pleasantly
and wisely behaved himself, that the king had great delight in
his pastimes."* Baldwynne and Ferrers called other writers
to their assistance, among whom were Thomas Churchyard,
Phaer, the translator of Virgil, &c.; and the book, in its first
form and extent, was published in a quarto volume in 1559.
"The work," says Baldwynne, in his Dedication "To the
Nobility" of a subsequent and enlarged edition of it in 1563,
"was begun and part of it printed in Queen Mary's time, but

* "On Monday the 4th of January," the Chronicler adds, "the said Lord of
Merry Disports came by water to London, and landed at the Tower-wharf,
entered the Tower, and then rode through Tower-street, where he was received
by Sergeant Vawce, Lord of Misrule to John Mainard, one of the sheriffs of
London, and so conducted through the city, with a great company of young
lords and gentlemen, to the house of Sir George Barne, Lord Mayor, where
he, with the chief of his company, dined, and after had a great banquet, and
at his departure the Lord Mayor gave him a standing cup with a cover of
silver and gilt, of the value of ten pound, for a reward, and also set a hogs-
head of wine and a barrel of beer at his gate for his train that followed him.
The residue of his gentlemen and servants dined at other aldermen's houses
and with the sheriffs, and so departed to the Tower-wharf again, and to the
Court by water, to the great commendation of the mayor and aldermen, and
highly accepted of the king and council."

hindered by the Lord Chancellor that then was;* nevertheless,
through the means of my Lord Stafford,† the first part was
licensed, and imprinted the first year of the reign of this our
most noble and virtuous Queen, and dedicated then to your
honours with this preface. Since which time, although I have
been called to another trade of life, yet my good Lord Stafford
hath not ceased to call upon me to publish so much as I had
gotten, at other men's hands; so that, through his lordship's
earnest means, I have now set forth another part, containing
as little of mine own as the first part doth of other men's." The
Mirror for Magistrates immediately acquired and for a considerable time retained great popularity; a third edition of it was
published in 1571; a fourth, with the addition of a series of new
lives from the fabulous history of the early Britons, by John
Higgins, in 1574; a fifth, in 1587; a sixth, with further additions, in 1610, by Richard Nichols, assisted by Thomas Blener-
hasset (whose contributions, however, had been separately
printed in 1578).‡ The copiousness of the plan, into which any
narrative might be inserted belonging to either the historical or
legendary part of the national annals, and that without any
trouble in the way of connexion or adaptation, had made the
work a receptacle for the contributions of all the ready versifiers
of the day—a common, or parish green, as it were, on which a
fair was held to which any one who chose might bring his wares
—or rather a sort of continually growing monument, or cairn,
to which every man added his stone, or little separate specimen
of brick and mortar, who conceived himself to have any skill in
building the lofty rhyme. There were scarcely any limits to the
size to which the book might have grown, except the mutability
of the public taste, which will permit no one thing, good or bad,
to go on for ever. The Mirror for Magistrates, however, for all
its many authors, is of note in the history of our poetry for
nothing else which it contains, except the portions contributed
by its contriver Sackville, consisting only of one legend, that of
Henry, Duke of Buckingham (Richard the Third's famous ac-

---

* He is supposed to mean Dr. Heath, Archbishop of York.

† Henry Lord Stafford, son and heir of Edward, last (Stafford) Duke of
Buckingham. He had been allowed, notwithstanding his father's forfeiture,
to sit in parliament as Lord Stafford; and lived till 1562.

‡ A reprint of the Mirror for Magistrates, in 2 (sometimes divided into 3)
vols. 4to., was brought out by the late Mr. Haslewood in 1815.

complice and victim, and grandfather of Lord Stafford, the great patron of the work), and the introduction, or Induction, as it is called, prefixed to that narrative, which however is said to have been originally intended to stand at the head of the whole work. The Induction begins with a picture of winter, which is drawn with vivid colours and a powerful pencil; then follow some brief reflections, suggested by the faded fields and scattered summer flowers, on the instability of all things here below; but suddenly the poet perceives that the night is drawing on faster, and thereupon redoubles his pace; when, he continues,

> In black all clad there fell before my face
> A piteous wight, whom woe had all forwast;
> Forth from her eyen the crystal tears outbrast,
> And, sighing sore, her hands she wrong and fold,
> Tearing her hair that ruth was to behold.
>
> Her body small, forwithered and forspent,
> As is the stalk with summer's drought opprest;
> Her wealked face with woful tears besprent,
> Her colour pale, and, as it seemd her best,
> In woe and plaint reposed was her rest;
> And, as the stone that drops of water wears,
> So dented were her cheeks with fall of tears.
>
> I stood aghast, beholding all her plight,
> 'Tween dread and dolour so distrained in heart,
> That, while my hairs upstarted with the sight,
> The tears outstreamed for sorrow of her smart.
> But, when I saw no end that could apart
> The deadly dole which she so sore did make,
> With doleful voice then thus to her I spake:
>
> Unwrap thy woes, whatever wight thou be!
> And stint betime to spill thyself with plaint:
> Tell what thou art, and whence; for well I see
> Thou can'st not dure, with sorrow thus attaint.
> And with that word, of sorrow, all forfaint,
> She looked up, and, prostrate as she lay,
> With piteous sound, lo! thus she gan to say:
>
> Alas, I wretch, whom thus thou see'st distrained,
> With wasting woes that never shall aslake,
> Sorrow I am; in endless torments pained
> Among the Furies in the infernal lake;
> Where Pluto, God of Hell, so grisly black,
> Doth hold his throne, and Lethe's deadly taste
> Doth rive remembrance of each thing forepast.

> Whence come I am, the dreary destiny
> And luckless lot for to bemoan of those
> Whom fortune in this maze of misery
> Of wretched chance most woeful mirrors chose;
> That when thou seest how lightly they did lose
> Their pomp, their power, and that they thought most sure,
> Thou may'st soon deem no earthly joy may dure.

Sorrow conducts the poet to the region of departed spirits; and then follows a long succession of allegoric pictures—including Remorse, Dread (or Fear), Revenge, Misery (that is, Avarice), Care, Sleep, Old Age, Malady, Famine, Death, War, Debate (or Strife), &c.; all drawn with extraordinary strength of imagination, and with a command of expressive, picturesque, and melodious language, nothing equal or approaching to which had till now been seen in our poetry, except only in Chaucer—and he can scarcely be said to have written in the same English the capabilities of which were thus brought out by Sackville. Both for his poetical genius, and in the history of the language, Sackville and his two poems in the Mirror for Magistrates—more especially this Induction—must be considered as forming the connecting link or bridge between Chaucer and Spenser, between the Canterbury Tales and the Fairy Queen.

For the sake of affording a means of comparison with the style and manner of the extracts we shall presently have to give from the latter work, we will add here another of Sackville's delineations :—

> And next in order sad OLD AGE we found,
> His beard all hoar, his eyes hollow and blind,
> With drooping cheer still poring on the ground,
> As on the place where nature him assigned
> To rest, when that the Sisters had untwined
> His vital thread, and ended with their knife
> The fleeting course of fast-declining life.
>
> There heard we him, with broke and hollow plaint,
> Rue with himself his end approaching fast,
> And all for nought his wretched mind torment
> With sweet remembrance of his pleasures past,
> And fresh delights of lusty youth forwast;[1]
> Recounting which how would he sob and shriek,
> And to be young again of Jove beseech !

---

[1] Utterly wasted and gone

But, as' the cruel fates so fixed be
That time forepast cannot return again,
This one request of Jove yet prayed he—
That, in such withered plight and wretched pain
As eld, accompanied with her loathsome train,
Had brought on him, all were it woe and grief,
He might awhile yet linger forth his lief,

And not so soon descend into the pit,
Where Death, when he the mortal corpse hath slain,
With reckless hand in grave doth cover it,
Thereafter never to enjoy again
The gladsome light, but, in the ground ylain,
In depth of darkness waste and wear to nought,
As he had ne'er into the world been brought.

But who had seen him sobbing how he stood
Unto himself, and how he would bemoan
His youth forepast,—as though it wrought him good
To talk of youth, all were his youth forgone—
He would have mused, and marvelled much, whereon
This wretched Age should life desire so fain,
And knows full well life doth but length his pain.

Crook-backed he was, tooth-shaken, and blear-eyed,
Went on three feet, and sometime crept on four ;
With old lame bones, that rattled by his side ;
His scalp all piled,[1] and he with eld forelore ;
His withered fist still knocking at death's door ;
Fumbling and drivelling as he draws his breath ;
For brief, the shape and messenger of Death.

Nothing is wanting to Sackville that belongs to force either of
conception or of expression. In his own world of the sombre
and sad, also, he is almost as great an inventor as he is a
colourist ; and Spenser has been indebted to him for many hints,
as well as for example and inspiration in a general sense : what
most marks the immaturity of his style is a certain operose and
constrained air, a stiffness and hardness of manner, like what
we find in the works of the earliest school of the Italian painters,
before Raphael and Michael Angelo arose to convert the art from
a painful repetition or mimicry of reality into a process of
creation—from the timid slave of nature into her glorified rival.
Of the flow and variety, the genuine spirit of light and life, that

[1] If.   [1] Peeled, bare, bald.

we have in Spenser and Shakespeare, there is little in Sackville; his poetry—ponderous, gloomy, and monotonous—is still oppressed by the shadows of night; and we see that, although the darkness is retiring, the sun has not yet risen.

ORIGIN OF THE REGULAR DRAMA.

From the first introduction of dramatic representations in England, probably as early, at least, as the beginning of the twelfth century, down to the beginning of the fifteenth, or perhaps somewhat later, the only species of drama known was that styled the Miracle, or Miracle-play. The subjects of the miracle-plays were all taken from the histories of the Old and New Testament, or from the legends of saints and martyrs; and, indeed, it is probable that their original design was chiefly to instruct the people in religious knowledge. They were often acted as well as written by clergymen, and were exhibited in abbeys, in churches, and in churchyards, on Sundays or other holidays. It appears to have been not till some time after their first introduction that miracle-plays came to be annually represented under the direction and at the expense of the guilds or trading companies of towns, as at Chester and elsewhere. The characters, or *dramatis personæ*, of the miracle-plays, though sometimes supernatural or legendary, were always actual personages, historical or imaginary; and in that respect these primitive plays approached nearer to the regular drama than those by which they were succeeded—the Morals, or Moral-plays, in which, not a history, but an apologue was represented, and in which the characters were all allegorical. The moral-plays are traced back to the early part of the reign of Henry VI., and they appear to have gradually arisen out of the miracle-plays, in which, of course, characters very nearly approaching in their nature to the impersonated vices and virtues of the new species of drama must have occasionally appeared. The Devil of the Miracles, for example, would very naturally suggest the Vice of the Morals; which latter, however, it is to be observed, also retained the Devil of their predecessors, who was too amusing and popular a character to be discarded. Nor did the moral-plays altogether put down the miracle-plays: in many of the provincial towns, at least, the latter continued to be represented almost to as late a date as the former. Finally, by a process of natural transition very similar to that by which the sacred and supernatural characters of the religious drama had been converted into the allegorical personifications of the moral-plays, these last, gradually becoming less and less vague and shadowy, at length, about the middle of the sixteenth century, boldly assumed life and reality, giving birth to the first examples of regular tragedy and comedy.

Both moral-plays, however, and even the more ancient miracle-plays, continued to be occasionally performed down to the very end of the sixteenth century. One of the last dramatic representations at which Elizabeth was present, was a moral-play, entitled The Contention between Liberality and Prodigality, which was performed before her majesty in 1600, or 1601. This production was printed in 1602, and was probably written not long before that time : it has been said to have been the joint production of Thomas Lodge and Robert Greene,* the last of whom died in 1592. The only three manuscripts of the Chester miracle-plays now extant were written in 1600, 1604, and 1607, most probably while the plays still continued to be acted. There is evidence that the ancient annual miracle-plays were acted at Tewkesbury at least till 1585, at Coventry till 1591, at Newcastle till 1598, and at Kendal down even to the year 1603.†

---

* By Edward Phillips, in his Theatrum Poetarum, 1675.

† The Towneley Mysteries (so called after the MS. containing them, formerly belonging to Mr. P. Towneley), which are supposed to have been acted at Widkirk Abbey in Yorkshire, have been printed for the Surtees Society, under the care of the Rev. Joseph Hunter and J. Stevenson, Esq., 8vo. Newcastle, 1831 ; the Coventry Mysteries, under the care of J. O. Halliwell, Esq., for the Shakespeare Society, 8vo. Lond. 1841 ; and the Chester Mysteries, for the same Society, under the care of Thomas Wright, Esq., vol. I. 8vo. Lond. 1843, and vol. II. 1847. See also Mr. Wright's Early Mysteries, and other Latin Poems of the twelfth and thirteenth centuries, 8vo. Lond. 1838. Mr. Collier, in a note to his Hist. of Eng. Dram. Poetry, ii. 123, 124, observes, that, although miracle-plays were at a very early date called Mysteries in France, and the term has been adopted by Warton, Percy, Hawkins, Malone, and other modern writers among ourselves, it was, he apprehends, unknown in England in that or any similar sense till comparatively a recent period. According to Mr. Wright Chester Plays, Introduction, pp. vii., viii.), while dramatic performances representing the legendary miracles attributed to the saints were properly called Miracula, Miracles, or Miracle-plays, those which were founded on Scripture subjects, and which were intended to set forth the mysteries of revelation, were distinguished by the title of Mysteria, or Mysteries. "In France," he adds, "the distinction between Miracles and Myste-

As has been observed, however, by Mr. Collier, the latest and best historian of the English drama, the moral-plays were enabled to keep possession of the stage so long as they did, partly by means of the approaches they had for some time been making to a more improved species of composition, "and partly because, under the form of allegorical fiction and abstract character, the writers introduced matter which covertly touched upon public events, popular prejudices, and temporary opinions."* He mentions, in particular, the moral entitled The Three Ladies of London, printed in 1584, and its continuation, The Three Lords and Three Ladies of London, which appeared in 1590 (both by R. W.), as belonging to this class.

Interludes of John Heywood.

Meanwhile, long before the earliest of these dates, the ancient drama had, in other hands, assumed wholly a new form. Mr. Collier appears to consider the Interludes of John Heywood, the earliest of which must have been written before 1521, as first exhibiting the moral-play in a state of transition to the regular tragedy and comedy. "John Heywood's dramatic productions," he says, "almost form a class by themselves: they are neither miracle-plays nor moral-plays, but what may be properly and strictly called interludes, a species of writing of which he has a claim to be considered the inventor, although the term interlude was applied generally to theatrical productions in the reign of Edward IV." A notion of the nature of these compositions may be collected from the plot of one of them, A Merry Play between the Pardoner and the Frere, the Curate and neighbour Pratte,

---

rice was carefully preserved to the latest times. In England, as early as the fourteenth century, there appears to have been some confusion in the application of these terms, and the name of Miracles was given frequently to all kinds of Scripture plays as well as to plays of saints' miracles." This account would seem to refute the conjecture which has been hazarded, that Mysteries meant properly dramatic representations by the *trades* of a town, and that the word was not *mysterium*, but *ministerium*, the original of the Italian *mestiere* and the French *métier*, anciently *mestier*.

* Hist. of Dramatic Poetry, II. 413.

printed in 1533, of which Mr. Collier gives the following account :—" A pardoner and a friar have each obtained leave of the curate to use his church,—the one for the exhibition of his relics, and the other for the delivery of a sermon—the object of both being the same, that of procuring money. The friar arrives first, and is about to commence his discourse, when the pardoner enters and disturbs him; each is desirous of being heard, and, after many vain attempts by force of lungs, they proceed to force of arms, kicking and cuffing each other unmercifully. The curate, called by the disturbance in his church, endeavours, without avail, to part the combatants; he therefore calls in neighbour Pratte to his assistance, and, while the curate seizes the friar, Pratte undertakes to deal with the pardoner, in order that they may set them in the stocks. It turns out that both the friar and the pardoner are too much for their assailants; and the latter, after a sound drubbing, are glad to come to a composition, by which the former are allowed quietly to depart."[*] Here, then, we have a dramatic fable, or incident at least, conducted not by allegorical personifications, but by characters of real life, which is the essential difference that distinguishes the true tragedy or comedy from the more moral. Heywood's interludes, however, of which there are two or three more of the same description with this (besides others partaking more of the allegorical character), are all only single acts, or, more properly, scenes, and exhibit, therefore, nothing more than the more rudiments or embryo of the regular comedy.

UDALL'S RALPH ROISTER DOISTER.

The earliest English comedy, properly so called, that has yet been discovered, is commonly considered to be that of Ralph Roister Doister, the production of Nicholas Udall, an eminent classical scholar in the earlier part of the sixteenth century, and one of the masters, first at Eton, and afterwards at Westminster. Its existence was unknown till a copy was discovered in 1818, which perhaps (for the title-page is gone) was not printed earlier than 1566, in which year Thomas Hackett is recorded in the register of the Stationers' Company to have had a licence for

* Hist. of Dramatic Poetry. ii. 386.

printing a play entitled Rauf Ruyster Duster; but the play is quoted in Thomas Wilson's Rule of Reason, first printed in 1551, so that it must have been written at least fifteen or sixteen years before.* This hypothesis would carry it back to about the same date with the earliest of Heywood's interludes; and it certainly was produced while that writer was still alive and in the height of his popularity. It may be observed that Wilson calls Udall's play an interlude, which would therefore seem to have been at this time the common name for any dramatic composition, as, indeed, it appears to have been for nearly a century preceding. The author himself, however, in his prologue, announces it as a Comedy, or Interlude, and as an imitation of the classical models of Plautus and Terence.

And, in truth, both in character and in plot, Ralph Roister Doister has every right to be regarded as a true comedy, showing indeed, in its execution, the rudeness of the age, but in its plan, and in reference to the principle upon which it is constructed, as regular and as complete as any comedy in the language. It is divided into acts and scenes, which very few of the moral-plays are; and, according to Mr. Collier's estimate, the performance could not have been concluded in less time than about two hours and a half, while few of the morals would require more than about an hour for their representation.† The dramatis personæ are thirteen in all, nine male and four female; and the two principal ones at least—Ralph himself, a vain, thoughtless, blustering fellow, whose ultimately baffled pursuit of the gay and rich widow Custance forms the action of the piece; and his servant, Matthew Merrygreek, a kind of flesh-and-blood representative of the Vice of the old moral-plays—are strongly discriminated, and drawn altogether with much force and spirit. The story is not very ingeniously involved, but it moves forward through its gradual development, and onwards to the catastrophe, in a sufficiently bustling, lively manner; and some of the situations, though the humour is rather farcical than comic, are very cleverly conceived and managed. The language also may be said to be on the whole, racy and characteristic, if not very polished. A few lines from a speech of one of the widow's handmaidens, Tibot Talkapace, in a conversation with her fellow-servants on the approaching marriage of their masters, may be quoted as a specimen :—

And I heard our Nource speake of an husbande to-day
Ready for our mistresse; a rich man and a gay :
And we shall go in our French hoodes every day ;
In our silke cassocks (I warrant you) freshe and gay ;
In our tricke ferdigews, and billiments of golde,
Brave in our suten of chaunge, seven double folde,
Then shall ye see Tibet, trende the mowse so trimme ;
Nay, why said I trende ? ye shall see hir glide and swimme,
Not lumperdee, clumperdee, like our spaniell Rig.[*]

GAMMER GURTON'S NEEDLE.

Ralph Roister Doister is in every way a very superior production to Gammer Gurton's Needle, which, before the discovery of

[*] Udall (the name is otherwise written Uvedale, Owdall, Dowdall, Woodall,
and Woddell) died in 1566. He was a zealous Lutheran, and one of the
most active writers for the press in his day. We have already had occasion
to notice the translation brought out in 1548 under his care of Erasmus's
Paraphrase of the New Testament. As an Eton master he appears to have
been noted for his severity : but the most remarkable fact belonging to this
part of his history is that in 1542 he was dismissed on the charge of having
been concerned in a robbery, and that in a letter in his own handwriting
still preserved among the Cotton MSS. he seems, to a considerable extent at
least, to admit his guilt. At this time, too, there is reason to believe that he
held a living in the church. The probability is that the robbery, described
as being of certain images of silver and other plate belonging to the college,
may have been prompted by some impulse of anti-Romanist zeal. On the
establishment, at any rate, of the reformed system under Edward, Udall was
made first a prebend of Windsor and soon after was presented to the rectory
of Calborne in the Isle of Wight ; and at last he was appointed to the head
mastership of Westminster School, from which, however, and probably also
from his ecclesiastical preferments, he was again ejected under Mary, soon
after the middle of whose reign he died. Upon the discovery of the printed
copy of Ralph Roister Doister in 1818 by the Rev. Mr. Briggs, that gentleman had a limited reprint made of it, and then presented the original copy to
the library of Eton College, where he had been educated. He did not then
know that the author had been one of the masters there, nor who the author
was ; nor did Dr. Bliss, when he soon after inserted in his new edition of
Wood's Athenæ Oxonienses the quotation from the play given by Wilson,
know that it was from Ralph Roister Doister. Another edition, with notes,
was produced in 1821 by Mr. F. Marshall ; and a third reprint by Mr.
Thomas White, in his Old English Drama, in 1830. But the standard copy
is now that edited for the Shakespeare Society in 1847 by Mr. William Dur-
rant Cooper, with an elaborate Life of Udall prefixed, and occasional notes,
in which Mr. Cooper states that he has largely availed himself of those
accompanying the reprint of 1821. According to Mr. Cooper, the authorship
of Ralph Roister Doister was first established by Mr. Collier, in his History of
English Dramatic Poetry (1831), vol. ii. p. 445.

Udall's piece, had the credit of being the first regular English comedy. At the same time, it must be admitted that the superior antiquity assigned to Ralph Roister Doister is not very conclusively made out. All that we know with certainty with regard to the date of the play is, that it was in existence in 1551. The oldest edition of Gammer Gurton's Needle is dated 1575: but how long the play may have been composed before that year is uncertain. The title-page of the 1575 edition describes it as "played on the stage not long ago in Christ's College, in Cambridge;" and Warton, on the authority of a manuscript memorandum by Oldys, the eminent antiquary of the early part of the last century, says that it was written and first printed in 1551.[*] Wright also, in his Historia Histrionica, first printed in 1669, states it as his opinion that it was written in the reign of Edward VI. In refutation of all this it is alleged that "it could not have been produced so early, because John Still (afterwards bishop of Bath and Wells), the author of it, was not born until 1543; and, consequently, in 1552, taking Warton's latest date, would only have been nine years old.[†] But the evidence that Bishop Still was the author of Gammer Gurton's Needle is exceedingly slight. The play is merely stated on the title-page to have been "made by Mr. S., Master of Arts;" and even if there was, as is asserted, no other Master of Arts of Christ's College whose name began with S. at the time when this title-page was printed, the author of the play is not stated to have been of that college, nor, if he were, is it necessary to assume that he was living in 1575. On the whole, therefore, while there is no proof that Ralph Roister Doister is older that the year 1551, it is by no means certain that Gammer Gurton's Needle was not written in that same year.

This "right pithy, pleasant, and merie comedie," as it is designated on the title-page, is, like Udall's play, regularly

[*] History of English Poetry, iv. 82. He adds, that it was "soon afterwards acted at Christ's College in Cambridge." And elsewhere (iii. 203) he says, that it was acted in that society about the year 1552. We do not understand how Mr. Collier (ii. 444) collects from a comparison of these two passages that "Warton states in one place that Gammer Gurton's Needle was printed in 1551, and in another that it was not written till 1552." Mr. Collier, it may be perceived, is also mistaken in adding, that Warton seems to have had no other evidence for these assertions than the opinion of Wright, the author of the Historia Histrionica.

[†] Collier, ii. 444.

divided into acts and scenes, and, like it too, is written in rhyme
—the language and versification being, on the whole, perhaps
rather more easy than flowing—a circumstance which, more than
any external evidence that has been produced, would incline us
to assign it to a somewhat later date. But it is in all respects
a very tame and poor performance—the plot, if so it can be
called, meagre to insipidity and silliness, the characters only a
few slightly distinguished varieties of the lowest life, and the
dialogue in general as feeble and undramatic as the merest
monotony can make it. Its merriment is of the coarsest and
most boisterous description, even where it is not otherwise offensive; but the principal ornament wherewith the author endeavours to enliven his style is a brutal filth and grossness of
expression, which is the more astounding when we consider that
the piece was the production, in all probability, of a clergyman
at least, if not of one who afterwards became a bishop, and that
it was certainly represented before a learned and grave university. There is nothing of the same high seasoning in Ralph
Roister Doister, though that play seems to have been intended
only for the amusement of a common London audience. The
Second Act of Gammer Gurton's Needle is introduced by a song,

> I cannot eat but little meat,
>   My stomach is not good, &c.

which is the best thing in the whole play, and which is well
known from having been quoted by Warton, who describes it as
the earliest *chanson à boire*, or drinking ballad, of any merit in the
language; and observes that " it has a vein of ease and humour
which we should not expect to have been inspired by the simple
beverage of those times." But this song is most probably not by
the author of the play: it appears to be merely a portion of a
popular song of the time, which is found elsewhere complete, and
has recently been so printed, from a MS. of the sixteenth century, by Dr. Dyce, in his edition of Skelton.* We will give, as
a specimen of the language of Gammer Gurton's Needle, the
introductory speech to the first Act, which is put into the
mouth of a character called Diccon the Bedlam,—that is, one

---

* See Account of Skelton and his Writings, vol. I. pp. 7—9. Mr. Dyce
states that the MS. from which he has printed the song is certainly of an
earlier date than the oldest-known edition of the play (1575).

of those mendicants who affected a sort of half-madness, and were known by the name of Bedlam Beggars :[*]—

> Many a myle have I walked, divers and sundry walks,
> And many a good man's house have I bin at in my daies :
> Many a gossip's cup in my tyme have I tasted,
> And many a broche and spyt have I both turned and basted :
> Many a prece of bacon have I had out of thir balkes,
> In ronnyng over the countrey with long and were walkes :
> Yet came my foute never within those doore cheekes,
> To seek flesh or fysh, garlyke, onyons, or leekes,
> That ever I saw a sorte in such a plyght,
> As here within this house appeareth to my syght.
> There is howlynge and schowlyng, all cast in a dumpe,
> With wheuling and pewling, as though they had lost a trumpe :
> Syghing and sobbing, they weepe and they waylo ;
> I marvel in my mynd what the devil they ayle.
> The olde trot syts groning, with alas and alas,
> And Tib wringes her hands, and takes on in worse case ;
> With poore Corke, thoyr boye, they be dryven in such fyts
> I fear mee the folkes be not well in theyr wyts.
> Aske them what they ayle, or who brought them in this stays ?
> They aunswer not at all, but alacke and welaway !
> When I saw it booted not, out at doores I hyed mee,
> And caught a slyp of bacon, when I saw none spyed mee,
> Which I intend not far hence, unles my purpose fayle,
> Shall servo for a shoing horne to draw on two pots of ale.

MISOGONUS.

Probably of earlier date than Gammer Gurton's Needle, is another example of the regular drama, which, like Ralph Roister Doister, has been but lately recovered, a play entitled Misogonus, the only copy of which is in manuscript, and is dated 1577. An allusion, however, in the course of the dialogue, would seem to

* Diccon is the ancient abbreviation of Richard. It may be noticed that there is an entry in the Stationers' Books of a play entitled Diccon of Bedlam, under the year 1563 (see Extracts from the Registers of the Stationers' Company, edited by Mr. Collier for the Shakespeare Society, 1848, vol. i. p. 69), which is in all probability the same piece we are now considering. If so, this fact affords an additional presumption that Gammer Gurton's Needle was printed, or at least written, some years before the date of the earliest edition of it now extant.

prove that the play must have been composed about the year
, 1560.   To the prologue is appended the name of Thomas
Ilychardes, who has therefore been assumed to be the author.
The play, as contained in the manuscript, consists only of the
unusual number of four acts, but the story, nevertheless, appears
to be completed. For a further account of Misogonus we must
refer the reader to Mr. Collier's very elaborate analysis ;* only
remarking that the piece is written throughout in rhyming
quatrains, not couplets, and that the language would indicate it
to be of about the same date with Gammer Gurton's Needle. It
contains a song, which for fluency and spirit may very well bear
to be compared with the drinking-song in that drama. Neither
in the contrivance and conduct of the plot, however, nor in the
force with which the characters are exhibited, does it evince the
same free and skilful hand with Ralph Roister Doister, although
it is interesting for some of the illustrations which it affords of
the manners of the time. One of the dramatis personæ, in particular, who is seldom absent from the stage, Cacurgus, the buffoon
or fool kept by the family whose fortunes form the subject of the
piece, must, as Mr. Collier remarks, " have been a very amusing
character in his double capacity of rustic simpleton and artful
mischief-maker." "There are few pieces," Mr. Collier adds, " in
the whole range of our ancient drama which display the important character of the domestic fool in anything like so full and
clear a light."

CHRONICLE HISTORIES :—BALE'S KYNGE JOHAN ; ETC.

If the regular drama thus made its first appearance among us
in the form of comedy, the tragic muse was at least not far
behind.   There is some ground for supposing, indeed, that one
species of the graver drama of real life may have begun to emerge
rather sooner than comedy out of the shadowy world of the old
allegorical representations ; that, namely, which was long distinguished from both comedy and tragedy by the name of History,
or Chronicle History, consisting, to adopt Mr. Collier's definition, "of certain passages or events detailed by annalists put
into a dramatic form, often without regard to the course in which

* Hist. Dram. Poet. II. 463—481.

they happened ; the author sacrificing chronology, situation, and circumstance, to the superior object of producing an attractive play."* Of what may be called at least the transition from the moral-play to the history, we have an example in Bale's lately recovered drama of Kynge Johan,† written in all probability some years before the middle of the sixteenth century, in which, while many of the characters are still allegorical abstractions, others are real personages ; King John himself, Pope Innocent, Cardinal Pandulphus, Stephan Langton, and other historical figures moving about in odd intermixture with such mere notional spectres as the Widowed Britannia, Imperial Majesty, Nobility, Clergy, Civil Order, Treason, Verity, and Sedition. The play is accordingly described by Mr. Collier, the editor, as occupying an intermediate place between moralities and historical plays ; and "it is," he adds, "the only known existing specimen of that species of composition of so early a date." The other productions that are extant of the same mixed character are all of the latter half of the century ; such as that entitled Tom Tiler and his Wife, supposed to have been first printed about 1578, although the oldest known edition is a reprint dated 1661 ; The Conflict of Conscience (called a comedy), by Nathaniel Woods, minister of Norwich, 1581 ; &c.‡

TRAGEDY OF GORBODUC.—BLANK VERSE.

But the era of genuine tragedies and historical plays had already commenced some years before these last-mentioned pieces saw the light. On the 18th of January, 1562, was "shown before the Queen's most excellent Majesty," as the old title-pages

* Hist. Dram. Poet. II. p. 414.

† Published by the Camden Society, 4to. 1838, under the care of Mr. Collier.

‡ See an account of these and other pieces of the same kind in Collier, Hist. Dram. Poet. II. 333, &c. In assigning the first publication of Tom Tiler and his Wife to the year 1578, Mr. Collier professes to follow Ritson (Ancient Songs, ii. 31, edit. 1829), who, he observes, was no doubt as correct as usual. But, whatever may have been Ritson's correctness in matters of mere transcription, it is proper to note that in the present case he merely offers a conjecture ; so that we are left to depend, not upon his correctness, but upon his sagacity. The dependence to be placed upon that is certainly not great.

of the printed play inform us, " in her Highness' Court of Whitehall, by the Gentlemen of the Inner Temple," the Tragedy of Gorboduc, otherwise entitled the Tragedy of Ferrex and Porrex, the production of the same Thomas Sackville who has already engaged our attention as by far the most remarkable writer in The Mirror for Magistrates, and of Thomas Norton, who is said to have been a puritan clergyman, and who had already acquired a poetic reputation, though in a different province of the land of song, as one of the coadjutors of Sternhold and Hopkins in their metrical version of the Psalms. On the title-page of the first edition, printed in 1565, which, however, was surreptitious, it is stated that the three first acts were written by Norton, and the two last by Sackville; and, although this announcement was afterwards withdrawn, it was never expressly contradicted, and it is not improbable that it may have a general foundation of truth. It must be confessed, however, that no change of style gives any indication which it is easy to detect of a succession of hands; and that, judging by this criterion, we should rather be led to infer that, in whatever way the two writers contrived to combine their labours, whether by the one retouching and improving what the other had rough-sketched, or by the one taking the quieter and humbler, the other the more impassioned, scenes or portions of the dialogue, they pursued the same method throughout the piece. Charles Lamb expresses himself " willing to believe that Lord Buckhurst supplied the more vital parts."* At the same time he observes that " the style of this old play is stiff and cumbersome, like the dresses of its times;" and that, though there may be flesh and blood underneath, we cannot get at it. In truth, Gorboduc is a drama only in form. In spirit and manner it is wholly undramatic. The story has no dramatic capabilities, no evolution either of action or of character, although it affords some opportunities for description and eloquent declamation; neither was there anything of specially dramatic aptitude in the genius of Sackville (to whom we may safely attribute whatever is most meritorious in the composition), any more than there would appear to have been in Spenser or in Milton, illustrious as they both stand in the front line of the poets of their country and of the world. Gorboduc, accordingly, is a most unaffecting and uninteresting

* Specimens of Eng. Dram. Poets, i. 6 (edit. of 1835)

tragedy; as would also be the noblest book of the Fairy Queen or of Paradise Lost—the portion of either poem that soars the highest—if it were to be attempted to be transformed into a drama by merely being divided into acts and scenes, and cut up into the outward semblance of dialogue. In whatever abundance all else of poetry might be outpoured, the spirit of dialogue and of dramatic action would not be there. Gorboduc, however, though a dull play, is in some other respects a remarkable production for the time. The language is not dramatic, but it is throughout singularly correct, easy, and perspicuous; in many parts it is even elevated and poetical; and there are some passages of strong painting not unworthy of the hand to which we owe the Induction to the Legend of the Duke of Buckingham in the Mirror for Magistrates. The piece has accordingly won much applause in quarters where there was little feeling of the true spirit of dramatic writing as the exposition of passion in action, and where the chief thing demanded in a tragedy was a certain orderly pomp of expression, and monotonous respectability of sentiment, to fill the ear, and tranquillize rather than excite and disturb the mind. Sir Philip Sydney, while he finds fault with Gorboduc for its violation of the unities of time and place, declares it to be "full of stately speeches and well-sounding phrases, climbing to the height of Seneca in his style, and as full of notable morality, which it doth most delightfully teach, and so obtain the very end of poesy." It grieves him, he adds, that it is so "very defectuous in the circumstances,"—that is, the unities,—because that must prevent it from remaining for ever "as an exact model of all tragedies."[*] Rymer terms it, "a fable better turned for tragedy than any on this side the Alps;" and affirms that "it might have been a better direction to Shakespeare and Ben Jonson than any guide they have had the luck to follow."[†] Pope has delivered his opinion to the like effect, telling us that "the writers of the succeeding age might have improved by copying from this drama a propriety in the sentiments and dignity in the sentences, and an unaffected perspicuity of style, which are essential to tragedy." One peculiarity of the more ancient national drama retained in Gorboduc is the introduction, before every act, of a piece of machinery called the Dumb Show, in which was

* Defence of Poesy, p. 81 (edit. of 1810).
† Short view of Tragedy, p. 84.

shadowed forth, by a sort of allegorical exhibition, the part of
the story that was immediately to follow. This custom survived
on the English stage down to a considerably later date: the
reader may remember that Shakespeare, though he rejected it in
his own dramas, has introduced the play acted before the King
and Queen in Hamlet by such a prefigurative dumb show.[*]

Another expedient, which Shakespeare has also on two occasions
made use of, namely, the assistance of a chorus, is also adopted
in Gorboduc: but rather by way of mere decoration, and to
keep the stage from being at any time empty, as in the old
Greek drama, than to carry forward or even to explain the
action, as in Henry the Fifth and Pericles. It consists, to
quote the description given by Warton, "of Four Ancient and
Sage Men of Britain, who regularly close every act, the last
excepted, with an ode in long-lined stanzas, drawing back the
attention of the audience to the substance of what has just passed,
and illustrating it by recapitulatory moral reflections and poetical
or historical allusions."[†] These effusions of the chorus are all in
rhyme, as being intended to be of the same lyrical character with
those in the Greek plays; but the dialogue in the rest of the
piece is in blank verse, of the employment of which in dramatic
composition it affords the earliest known instance in the language. The first modern experiment in this "strange metre,"
as it was then called, had, as has already been noticed, been
made only a few years before by Lord Surrey, in his translation of
the Second and Fourth Books of the Æneid, which was published
in 1557, but must have been written more than ten years before,
Surrey having been put to death in January, 1547. In the mean
time the new species of verse had been cultivated in several
original compositions by Nicholas Grimoald, from whom, in the
opinion of Warton, the rude model exhibited by Surrey received

---

* Revides the original 1565 edition of Gorboduc, there was another in 1569
or 1570, and a third in 1590. It was again reprinted in 1736; and it has also
appeared in all the editions of Dodsley's Old Plays, 1744, 1780, and 1825. It
has now been edited for the Shakespearian Society by Mr. W. D. Cooper, in
the same volume with Ralph Roister Doister. Mr. Cooper has shown that the
edition of 1590 was not, as had been supposed, an exact reprint of that of
1565. He has also given us elaborate biographies both of Norton and of
Sackville, in the latter of which he has shown that Sackville, who died suddenly at the Council-table in 1608, was born in 1536, and not in 1527, as commonly supposed.

† Hist. Eng. Poet. iv. 181.

"new strength, elegance, and modulation."* Grimoald's pieces
in blank verse were first printed in 1557, along with Surrey's
translation, in Tottel's collection entitled Songs and Sonnets of
Uncertain Authors; and we are not aware that there was any
more English blank verse written or given to the world till the
production of Gorboduc. In that case, Sackville would stand
as our third writer in this species of verse; in the use of which
also, he may be admitted to have surpassed Grimoald fully as
much as the latter improved upon Surrey. Indeed, it may be
said to have been Gorboduc that really established blank verse
in the language; for its employment from the time of the appearance of that tragedy became common in dramatic composition,
while in other kinds of poetry, notwithstanding two or three
early attempts, such as Gascoigne's Steel Glass, in 1570, Aske's
Elizabetha Triumphans, in 1588, and Vallans's Tale of Two
Swans, in 1590, it never made head against rhyme, nor acquired
any popularity, till it was brought into repute by the Paradise
Lost, published a full century after Sackville's play. It is
remarkable that blank verse is never mentioned or alluded to by
Sir Philip Sidney in His Defence of Poesy, which could not
have been written more than a few years before 1586, the date of
Sidney's death, at the age of thirty-two. Yet he was acquainted
with Gorboduc, as it appears; and in one part of his tract he
treats expressly on the subject of versification, of which, he says,
"there are two sorts—the one ancient, the other modern: the
ancient marked the quantity of each syllable, and, according to
that, framed his verse; the modern observing only number, with
some regard to the accent, the chief life of it standeth in that
like sounding of the words which we call rhyme."† Even in
dramatic composition the use of blank verse appears to have been
for some time confined to pieces not intended for popular representation. Gorboduc, as we have seen, was brought out
before the Queen at Whitehall; and, although, after that example,
Mr. Collier observes, "blank verse was not unfrequently employed
in performances written expressly for the court and for representation before select audiences, many years elapsed before this
heroic measure without rhyme was adopted on the public stages
of London."‡

* Hist. Eng. Poet. iii. 340.　　† Defence of Poesy, p. 68.
‡ Hist. Dram. Poet. ii. 483.

OTHER EARLY DRAMAS.

Within a fortnight after the first performance of Gorboduc, it
is recorded that another historical play, entitled Julius Cæsar,
was acted at court; but of this piece—affording "the earliest
instance on record," Mr. Collier apprehends, "in which events
from the Roman history were dramatised in English "*—nothing
is known beyond the name. To about the same time, or it may
be even a year or two earlier, is probably to be assigned another
early drama, founded on the story of Romeo and Juliet; as is
inferred from the assertion of Arthur Brooke, in an advertisement prefixed to his poem upon that subject printed in 1562,
that he had seen "the same argument lately set forth on
the stage." But whether this was a regular tragedy, or only a
moral-play, we have no data for conjecturing. "From about
this date," says Mr. Collier, "until shortly after the year 1570,
the field, as far as we have the means of judging, seems
to have been pretty equally divided between the later morals,
and the earlier attempts in tragedy, comedy, and history. In
some pieces of this date (as well as subsequently) we see endeavours made to reconcile or combine the two different modes
of writing; but morals afterwards generally gave way, and
yielded the victory to a more popular and more intelligible
species of performance. The licence to James Burbage and
others in 1574 mentions comedies, tragedies, interludes, and
stage plays; and in the act of common council against their performance in the city, in the following year, theatrical performances are designated as interludes, tragedies, comedies, and
shows; including much more than the old miracle-plays, or more
recent moral-plays, which would be embraced by the words
interludes, shows, and even stage-plays, but to which the terms
tragedies, and comedies, found in both instruments, could not be
so properly applicable."† We may add, in order to finish the
subject here, that in the licence granted by James I., in 1603, to

* Hist. Dram. Poet. II. 415.
† Hist. II. 417.   Mr. Collier adds in a note, as an instance of how the
names designating the different kinds of plays were still misapplied, or what
vague notions were as yet attached to them, that, so late as in 1578, Thomas
Lupton called his moral of All for Money both a tragedy and a comedy. He
calls it in the title "a moral and pitiful comedy;" and in the prologue, "a
pleasant tragedy;" but he seems, nevertheless, to use the words in their common acceptation—meaning by these quaint phrases that the piece is a mixture

Burbage, Shakespeare, and their associates, they are authorized to play "comedies, tragedies, histories, interludes, morals, pastorals, stage-plays, and such other-like;" and that exactly the same enumeration is found in the patent granted to the Prince Palatine's players in 1612; in a new patent granted to Burbage's Company in 1620;* and also in Charles I.'s patent to Hemings and Condell in 1625. Morals, properly so called, however, had disappeared from the stage long before this last date, though something of their peculiar character still survived in the pageant or masque. It may be observed that there is no mention of morals, any more than of miracle plays, in the catalogue of the several species of dramatic entertainments which Shakespeare has put into the mouth of Polonius in Hamlet, and in which he seems to glance slyly at the almost equally extended string of distinctions in the royal patents.

Of the greater number of the plays that are recorded to have been produced in the first twenty years after the appearance of Gorboduc, only the names have been preserved, from which it cannot in all cases be certainly determined to what class the piece belonged. From the lists, extracted from the accounts of the Master of the Revels, of those represented before the court between 1568 and 1580, and which no doubt were mostly the same that were exhibited in the common playhouses, it appears

---

of tragedy and comedy. The catastrophe is sufficiently tragical; Judas, in the last scene, coming in, says the stage direction, "like a damned soul in black, painted with flames of fire and with a fearful vizard," followed by Dives, "with such like apparel as Judas hath;" while Damnation (another of the *dramatis personæ*), pursuing them, drives them before him, and they pass away, "making a pitiful noise," into perdition. A few years before, in like manner, Thomas Preston had called his play of Cambyses, King of Persia, which is a mixture of moral and history, "a lamentable tragedy full of pleasant mirth" on the title-page, and in the running title A Comedie of King Cambises. Another play of about the same date, and of similar character, that of Appius and Virginia, by R. B., is styled "a tragical comedy." At a still earlier period, both in our own and in other languages, the terms tragedy and comedy were applied to other narrative compositions as well as to those in a dramatic form. The most illustrious instance of such a use of the term comedy is its employment by Dante for the title of his great poem, because—as he has himself expressly told us in his dedication of the Paradise to Cane della Scala, Prince of Verona—the story, although it began sadly, ended prosperously. Even the narratives in the Mirror for Magistrates, published, as we have seen, in the latter part of the sixteenth century, were still called tragedies.

* See it printed for the first time, in Collier, I. 416.

probable that, out of fifty-two, about eighteen were founded
upon subjects of ancient history or fable; twenty-one upon
modern history, romances, and stories of a more general kind;
and that, of the remainder, seven were comedies, and six
morals.* "Of these fifty-two dramatic productions," Mr. Collier
observes, "not one can be said to have survived, although
there may be reason to believe that some of them formed
the foundation of plays acted at a later period." Among the
very few original plays of this period that have come down to us
is one entitled Damon and Pythias, which was acted before the
queen at Christ Church, Oxford, in September, 1560, and was
the production of Richard Edwards, who, in the general estimation of his contemporaries, seems to have been accounted the
greatest dramatic genius of his day, at least in the comic style.
His Damon and Pythias does not justify their laudation to a
modern taste; it is a mixture of comedy and tragedy, between
which it would be hard to decide whether the grave writing or
the gay is the rudest and dullest. The play is in rhyme, but
some variety is produced by the measure or length of the line
being occasionally changed. Mr. Collier thinks that the notoriety
Edwards attained may probably have been in great part owing
to the novelty of his subjects; Damon and Pythias being one of
the earliest attempts to bring stories from profane history upon
the English stage. Edwards, however, besides his plays, wrote
many other things in verse, some of which have an ease, and
even an elegance, that neither Surrey himself nor any other
writer of that age has excelled. Most of these shorter compositions are contained in the miscellany called the Paradise of Dainty
Devices, which, indeed, is stated on the title-page to have been
"devised and written for the most part" by Edwards, who had,
however, been dead ten years when the first edition appeared in
1576. Among them are the very beautiful and tender lines,
which have been often reprinted, in illustration of Terence's
apophthegm,—

  " Amantium iræ amoris redintegratio est ;"

---

* See the lists in Collier, iii. 24, 25. But compare the list given by Mr. P.
Cunningham at the end of his Extracts from the Accounts of the Revels at
Court in the Reigns of Queen Elizabeth and King James I., printed for the
Shakespeare Society, 8vo. Lond. 1842. Some items in Mr. Collier's classifi-
cation may be questioned. For example, the story of Titus and Gisippus is
not a "classical subject drawn from ancient history or fable."

or, as it is here rendered in the burthen of each stanza,—

"The falling out of faithful friends renewing is of love."

Edwards, who, towards the end of his life, was appointed one of
the gentlemen of the Chapel Royal and master of the queen's
singing-boys, "united," says Warton, "all those arts and accomplishments which minister to popular pleasantry: he was the
first fiddle, the most fashionable sonnetteer, the readiest rhymer,
and the most facetious mimic, of the court."[*] Another surviving
play produced during this interval is the Tragedy of Tancred
and Gismund, founded upon Boccaccio's well-known story, which
was presented before Elizabeth at the Inner Temple in 1568, the
five acts of which it consists being severally written by five
gentlemen of the society, of whom one, the author of the third
act, was Christopher Hatton, afterwards the celebrated dancing
lord chancellor. The play, however, was not printed till 1592,
when Robert Wilmot, the writer of the fifth act, gave it to the
world, as the title-page declares, "newly revived, and polished
according to the decorum of these days." The meaning of this
announcement, Mr. Collier conceives to be, that the piece was in
the first instance composed in rhyme; but, rhymed plays having
by the year 1592 gone out of fashion even on the public stage,
Wilmot's reviving and polishing consisted chiefly in cutting off
many of the "tags to the lines," or turning them differently.
The tragedy of Tancred and Gismund, which, like Gorboduc, has
a dumb show at the commencement and a chorus at the close of
every act, is, he observes, "the earliest English play extant the
plot of which is known to be derived from an Italian novel."[†]
To this earliest stage in the history of the regular drama belong,
finally, some plays translated or adapted from the ancient and
from foreign languages, which doubtless also contributed to
excite and give an impulse to the national taste and genius in
this department. There is extant an old English printed version,
in rhyme, of the Andria of Terence, which, although without
date, is believed to have been published before 1530; and the
moral, or interlude, called Jack Juggler, which is founded upon
the Amphitruo of Plautus, appears from internal evidence to
have been written in the reign of Edward VI. or Mary, though

---

[*] Hist. of Eng. Poet. iv. 110.
[†] Hist. Dram. Poet. iii. 13.

not printed till after the accession of Elizabeth. These early
and very rude attempts were followed by a series of translations
of the tragedies of Seneca, all likewise in rhyme, the first of
which, the Troas, by Jasper Heywood, son of the celebrated
John Heywood, was published in 1559; the second, the Thyestes,
also by Heywood, in 1560; the third, the Hercules Furens, by
the same hand, in 1561; the fourth, the Œdipus, by Alexander
Nevyle, in 1563; the fifth and sixth, the Medea and the
Agamemnon, by John Studley, in 1566. The Octavia, by Thomas
Nuce, was entered on the Stationers' Books in the same year,
but no copy of that date is now known to exist. Versions of the
Hyppolytus and the Hercules Oetaeus by Studley, and of the
Thebais by Thomas Newton, were added when the whole were
republished together, in 1581, under the title of "Seneca his
Ten Tragedies translated into English." Of the authors of these
translations, Heywood and Studley in particular "have some
claim," as Mr. Collier remarks, " to be viewed in the light of
original dramatic poets; they added whole scenes and choruses
wherever they thought them necessary." But Heywood and his
coadjutors in this undertaking do not appear to have had any
view of bringing Seneca upon the English stage; nor is it probable that any of their translated dramas were ever acted. In
1566, however, The Supposes, a prose translation by George
Gascoigne from Gli Suppositi of Ariosto, and another play, in
blank verse, entitled Jocasta, taken from the Phœnissæ of
Euripides, by Gascoigne and Francis Kinwelmarsh, were both
represented at Gray's Inn. The Jocasta was, therefore, the
second English play written in blank verse. "It is," says
Warton, "partly a paraphrase and partly an abridgment of the
Greek tragedy. There are many omissions, retrenchments, and
transpositions. The chorus, the characters, and the substance of
the story are entirely retained, and the tenor of the dialogue is
often preserved through whole scenes. Some of the beautiful
odes of the Greek chorus are neglected, and others substituted in
their places, newly written by the translators."[*] These substitu-
tions, however, sometimes display considerable poetic talent;
and the versification throughout the piece, both in the old metre
(in which the choral passages are written) and in the new, flows
with a facility and smoothness which, as contrasted with any

* Hist. Eng. Poet. iv. 197.

English verse written twenty years before, indicates a rate of
progress during that space, in the subsidence of the language into
comparative regularity of grammatical and syntactical forms,
which is very surprising. Warton remarks, as a proof of the
rapidity with which the work of refinement or change went on
in the language at this time, that "in the second edition of this
play, printed again with Gascoigne's poems in 1587, it was
thought necessary to affix marginal explanations of many words,
not long before in common use, but now become obsolete and
unintelligible." In the present instance this was done, as the
author tells us, at the request of a lady, who did not understand
"poetical words or terms." But it was a practice occasionally
followed down to a much later date. To all the quarto editions,
for example, of Joshua Sylvester's metrical translation of Du
Bartas (1605, 1608, 1613) there is appended "A brief Index,
explaining most of the hardest words scattered through this
whole work, for ease of such as are least exercised in those kind
of readings." It consists of thirty double-columned pages, and
may contain about six hundred words.*

* Most of these are proper names; many others are scientific terms.
Among the explanations are the following :—*Annals*, Histories from year to
year.—*Acchiae' pheere*, Venus (pheere itself is not explained, and may therefore be supposed to have been still in common use).—*Bacchanalian frows*,
Women-priests of Bacchus, the God of Cups.—*Barn-geese* and *Barnacles*, a
kind of fowls that grow of rotten trees and broken ships.—*Demain*, possessions
of inheritance, time out of mind continued in the possession of the lord.—*Dual*,
single combat.—*Metaphysical*, supernatural.—*Poetasters*, base, counterfeit, unlearned, witless, and wanton poets, that pester the world either with idle
vanities or odious villanies.—*Patagons*, Indian cannibals, such as eat man's
flesh.—*Scaliger, Josephus*, now living, a Frenchman admirable in all languages
for all manner of learning (so in edition of 1613, though Jos. Scaliger died in
1609). These explanatory vocabularies are sometimes also, found appended
to prose works of the sixteenth and seventeenth centuries. Mr. Hallam, in a
note to his Introduction to the Literature of Europe, vol. iii. p. 370, has
observed that, in Pratt's edition of Bishop Hall's works, we have a glossary of
obsolete or unusual words, employed by him, which amount to more than 1100,
some of them Gallicisms, but the greater part of Latin or Greek origin.
This book was published after the Restoration. By that time we see the difficulty ordinary readers had was, to understand the old words that were going
out of fashion; whereas, that of their ancestors, in the days of Elizabeth and
James, was to understand the new words that were flowing so fast into their
mother-tongue. This little circumstance is very curiously significant, not
only of the opposite directions in which the language was moving at the two
periods, but of the difference, also, in other respects, between an age of
advancement and hope, and one of weariness, retrogression, and decrepitude.

SECOND STAGE OF THE REGULAR DRAMA: PEELE; GREENE.

It thus appears that numerous pieces entitled by their form to
be accounted as belonging to the regular drama had been produced before the year 1580; but nevertheless no dramatic work
had yet been written which can be said to have taken its place
in our literature, or to have almost any interest for succeeding
generations on account of its intrinsic merits and apart from its
mere antiquity. The next ten years disclose a new scene.
Within that space a crowd of dramatists arose whose writings
still form a portion of our living poetry, and present the regular
drama, no longer only painfully struggling into the outward
shape proper to that species of composition, but having the
breath of life breathed into it, and beginning to throb and stir
with the pulsations of genuine passion. We can only here
shortly notice some of the chief names in this numerous company
of our early dramatists, properly so called. One to whom much
attention has been recently directed is George Peele, the first of
whose dramatic productions, The Arraignment of Paris, a sort
of masque or pageant which had been represented before the
queen, was printed anonymously in 1584. But Peele's most
celebrated drama is his Love of King David and Fair Bethsabe,
first published in 1599, two or three years after the author's
death. This play Mr. Campbell has called " the earliest fountain
of pathos and harmony that can be traced in our dramatic poetry ;"
and he adds, "there is no such sweetness of versification and
imagery to be found in our blank verse anterior to Shakespeare."[*]
David and Bethsabe was, in all probability, written not anterior
to Shakespeare, but after he had been at least six or seven years
a writer for the stage, and had produced perhaps ten or twelve
of his plays, including some of those in which, to pass over all
other and higher things, the music of the verse has ever been
accounted the most perfect and delicious. We know at least
that The Midsummer Night's Dream, Romeo and Juliet, The
Merchant of Venice, Richard II., King John, and Richard III.,
were all written and acted, if not all printed, before Peele's play
was given to the world.[†]   But, independently of this considera-

* Spec. of Eng. Poet. i. 140.
† This is established by the often-quoted passage in Meres's Wit's Treasury,
published in 1598, in which these and others of Shakespeare's plays are
enumerated.

tion, it must be admitted that the best of Peele's blank verse, though smooth and flowing, and sometimes tastefully decorated with the embellishments of a learned and imitative fancy, is both deficient in richness or even variety of modulation, and without any pretensions to the force and fire of original poetic genius. It may be true, nevertheless, as is conceded by Mr. Collier, one of the modern critics with whom Peele has not found so much favour as with Mr. Campbell and with Mr. Dyce, to whom we are indebted for the first collected edition of his plays,* that " he had an elegance of fancy, a gracefulness of expression, and a melody of versification which, in the earlier part of his career, was scarcely approached."† Another of Peele's pieces, entitled The Old Wives' Tale, a Pleasant conceited Comedy, printed in 1595, has excited some curiosity from a resemblance it bears in the story, though in little or nothing else, to Milton's Masque of Comus.‡ Contemporary with Peele was Robert Greene, the author of five plays, besides one written in conjunction with a friend. Greene died in 1592, and he appears only to have begun to write for the stage about 1587. Mr. Collier thinks that, in facility of expression, and in the flow of his blank verse, he is not to be placed below Peele. But Greene's most characteristic attribute is his turn for merriment, of which Peele in his dramatic productions shows little or nothing. His comedy, or farce rather, is no doubt usually coarse enough, but the turbid stream flows at least freely and abundantly. Among his plays is a curious one on the subject of the History of Friar Bacon and Friar Bungay, which is supposed to have been written in 1588 or 1589,

* Dramatic Works of George Peele (with his Poems), by the Rev. Alexander Dyce, 2 vols. 8vo. London, 1829.

† Mr. Hallam's estimate is, perhaps, not quite so high : "Peele has some command of imagery, but in every other quality it seems to me that he has scarce any claim to honour ; and I doubt if there are three lines together in any of his plays that could be mistaken for Shakespeare's. . . . The versification of Peele is much inferior to that of Marlow ; and, though sometimes poetical, he seems rarely dramatic."—Lit. of Eur. ii. 273.

‡ This was first printed out by Isaac Reed in the appendix to his edition of Baker's Biographia Dramatica, 1782, vol. ii. p. 441. The subject has been examined at length by Warton in his Minor Poems of Milton, pp. 135, 136 ; and again, pp. 575—577 (2nd edit. Lond. 1791). He observes, " That Milton had an eye on this ancient drama, which might have been the favourite of his early youth, perhaps may be at least affirmed with as much credibility as that he conceived the Paradise Lost from seeing a mystery at Florence, written by Andreini, a Florentine, in 1617, entitled Adamo."

though first published in 1594. This, however, is not so much a story of diablerie as of mere legerdemain, mixed, like all the rest of Greene's pieces, with a good deal of farcical incident and dialogue; even the catastrophe, in which one of the characters is carried off to hell, being so managed as to impart no supernatural interest to the drama.*

MARLOW.

Of a different and far higher order of poetical and dramatic character is another play of this date upon a similar subject, the Tragical History of the Life and Death of Doctor Faustus, by Christopher Marlow. Marlow died at an early age in 1593, the year after Greene, and three or four years before Peele. He had been a writer for the stage at least since 1586, in which year, or before, was brought out the play of Tamburlaine the Great, his claim to the authorship of which has been conclusively established by Mr. Collier, who has further shown that this was the first play written in blank verse that was exhibited on the public stage.† "Marlow's mighty line" has been celebrated by Ben Jonson in his famous verses on Shakespeare; but Drayton, the author of the Polyolbion, has extolled him in the most glowing description,—in words the most worthy of the theme:—

> Next Marlow, bathed in the Thespian springs,
> Had in him those brave translunary things
> That the first poets had: his raptures were
> All air and fire, which made his verses clear:
> For that fine madness still he did retain,
> Which rightly should possess a poet's brain.‡

Marlow is, by nearly universal admission, our greatest dramatic writer before Shakspeare. He is frequently, indeed, turgid and bombastic, especially in his earliest play, Tamburlaine the Great, which has just been mentioned, where his fire, it must be con-

* Greene's plays are collected under the title of The Dramatic Works of Robert Greene, to which are added his Poems; with some Account of the Author, and Notes; by the Rev. Alexander Dyce; 2 vols. 8vo. 1831.

† Hist. Dram. Poet. iii. pp. 107—120.

‡ Elegy. "To my dearly beloved friend Henry Reynolds, Of Poets and Poesy."

fossed, sometimes blazes out of all bounds and becomes a mere
wasting conflagration— sometimes only raves in a furious storm
of sound, filling the ear without any other effect. But in his fits
of truer inspiration, all the magic of terror, pathos, and beauty
flashes from him in streams. The gradual accumulation of the
agonies of Faustus, in the concluding scene of that play, as the
moment of his awful fate comes nearer and nearer, powerfully
drawn as it is, is far from being one of those coarse pictures of
wretchedness that merely oppress us with horror: the most
admirable skill is applied throughout in balancing that emotion
by sympathy and even respect for the sufferer,—

> ———— for he was a scholar once admired
> For wondrous knowledge in our German schools,—

and yet without disturbing our acquiescence in the justice of his
doom; till we close the book, saddened, indeed, but not dissatisfied, with the pitying but still tributary and almost consoling
words of the Chorus on our hearts,—

> Cut is the branch that might have grown full straight,
> And burned is Apollo's laurel-bough
> That sometime grew within this learned man.

Still finer, perhaps, is the conclusion of another of Marlow's
dramas—his tragedy of Edward the Second. "The reluctant
pangs of abdicating royalty in Edward," says Charles Lamb,
"furnished hints which Shakespeare scarce improved in his
Richard the Second; and the death-scene of Marlow's king moves
pity and terror beyond any scene, ancient or modern, with which
I am acquainted."* Much splendour of poetry, also, is expended
upon the delineation of Barabas, in The Rich Jew of Malta; but
Marlow's Jew, as Lamb has observed, "does not approach so
near to Shakespeare's [in the Merchant of Venice] as his Edward
the Second." We are more reminded of some of Barabas's
speeches by the magnificent declamation of Mammon in Jonson's
Alchymist.†

---

* Spec. of Eng. Dram. Poets, i. 31.
† The works of Christopher Marlow, with Notes and a Life, have been
edited by Mr. Dyce, in 3 vols. 8vo. Lond. 1850.

LYLY; KYD; LODGE.

Marlow, Greene, and Peele are the most noted names among those of our dramatists who belong exclusively to the age of Elizabeth; but some others that have less modern celebrity may perhaps be placed at least on the same line with the two latter. John Lyly, the Euphuist, as he is called, from one of his prose works, which will be noticed presently, is, as a poet, in his happiest efforts, elegant and fanciful; but his genius was better suited for the lighter kinds of lyric poetry than for the drama. He is the author of nine dramatic pieces, but of these seven are in prose, and only one in rhyme and one in blank verse. All of them, according to Mr. Collier, "seem to have been written for court entertainments, although they were also performed at theatres, most usually by the children of St. Paul's and the Revels." They were fitter, it might be added, for beguiling the listlessness of courts than for the entertainment of a popular audience, athirst for action and passion, and very indifferent to mere ingenuities of style. All poetical readers, however, remember some songs and other short pieces of verse with which some of them are interspersed, particularly a delicate little anacreontic in that entitled Alexander and Campaspe, beginning—

> Cupid and my Campaspe played
> At cards for kisses, &c.

Mr. Collier observes that Malone must have spoken from a very superficial acquaintance with Lyly's works when he contends that his plays are comparatively free from those affected conceits and remote allusions that characterise most of his other productions. Thomas Kyd, the author of the two plays of Jeronimo and the Spanish Tragedy (which is a continuation of the former), besides a translation of another piece from the French, appears to be called Sporting Kyd by Jonson, in his verses on Shakespeare, in allusion merely to his name. There is, at least, nothing particularly sportive in the little that has come down to us from his pen. Kyd was a considerable master of language; but his rank as a dramatist is not very easily settled, seeing that there is much doubt as to his claims to the authorship of by far the most striking passages in the Spanish Tragedy, the best of

his two plays. Lamb, quoting the scenes in question, describes
them as "the very salt of the old play," which, without them,
he adds, "is but a *caput mortuum*." It has been generally assumed
that they were added by Ben Jonson, who certainly was employed
to make some additions to this play; and Mr. Collier attributes
them to him as if the point did not admit of a doubt—acknowledging, however, that they represent Jonson in a new light, and
that "certainly there is nothing in his own entire plays equalling
in pathetic beauty some of his contributions to the Spanish
Tragedy." Nevertheless, it does not seem to be perfectly clear
that the supposed contributions by another hand might not have
been the work of Kyd himself. Lamb says, "There is nothing
in the undoubted plays of Jonson which would authorise us to
suppose that he could have supplied the scenes in question. I
should suspect the agency of some 'more potent spirit.' Webster
might have furnished them. They are full of that wild, solemn,
preternatural cast of grief which bewilders us in the Duchess of
Malfy." The last of these early dramatists we shall notice,
Thomas Lodge, who was born about 1550, and began to write for
the stage about 1580, is placed by Mr. Collier "in a rank
superior to Greene, but in some respects inferior to Kyd." His
principal dramatic work is entitled The Wounds of Civil War,
lively set forth in the true Tragedies of Marius and Sylla; and
is written in blank verse with a mixture of rhyme. It shows
him, Mr. Collier thinks, to have unquestionably the advantage
over Kyd as a drawer of character, though not equalling that
writer in general vigour and boldness of poetic conception.
His blank verse is also much more monotonous than that of Kyd.
Another strange drama in rhyme, written by Lodge in conjunction with Greene, is entitled A Looking-glass for London and
England, and has for its object to put down the puritanical outcry against the immorality of the stage, which it attempts to
accomplish by a grotesque application to the city of London of
the Scriptural story of Nineveh. The whole performance, in
Mr. Collier's opinion, "is wearisomely dull, although the authors
have endeavoured to lighten the weight by the introduction of
scenes of drunken buffoonery between 'a clown and his crew of
ruffians,' and between the same clown and a person disguised as
the devil, in order to frighten him, but who is detected and well
beaten." Mr. Hallam, however, pronounces that there is great
talent shown in this play, "though upon a very strange

canvass."[*] Lodge, who was an eminent physician, has left a
considerable quantity of other poetry besides his plays, partly in
the form of novels or tales, partly in shorter pieces, many of
which may be found in the miscellany called England's Helicon,
from which a few of them have been extracted by Mr. Ellis, in
his Specimens. They are, perhaps, on the whole, more credit-
able to his poetical powers than his dramatic performances. He
is also the author of several short works in prose, sometimes
interspersed with verse. One of his prose tales, first printed in
1590, under the title of Rosalynde: Euphues' Golden Legacie,
found in his cell at Siloxtra (for Lodge was one of Lyly's
imitators), is famous as the source from which Shakespeare
appears to have taken the story of his As You Like It. "Of
this production it may be said," observes Mr. Collier, "that our
admiration of many portions of it will not be diminished by a
comparison with the work of our great dramatist."[†]

It is worthy of remark, that all these founders and first
builders-up of the regular drama in England were, nearly if not
absolutely without an exception, classical scholars and men who
had received a university education. Nicholas Udall was of
Corpus Christi College, Oxford; John Still (if he is to be considered the author of Gammer Gurton's Needle) was of Christ's
College, Cambridge; Sackville was educated at both universities;
so was Gascoigne; Richard Edwards was of Corpus Christi,
Oxford; Marlow was of Bonet College, Cambridge; Greene, of
St. John's, Cambridge; Peele, of Christ's Church, Oxford; Lyly,
of Magdalen College, and Lodge of Trinity College, in the same
university. Kyd was also probably a university man, though
we know nothing of his private history. To the training
received by these writers the drama that arose among us after
the middle of the sixteenth century may be considered to owe
not only its form, but in part also its spirit, which had a learned
and classical tinge from the first, that never entirely wore out.
The diction of the works of all these dramatists betrays their
scholarship; and they have left upon the language of our higher
drama, and indeed of our blank verse in general, of which they were
the main creators, an impress of Latinity, which, it can scarcely
be doubted, our vigorous but still homely and unsonorous Gothic

* Literature of Eur. li. 274.

† Hist. of Dram. Poet. lii. 213. See upon this subject the Introductory
Notice to As You Like It in Knight's Shakspere, vol. iii. 247—263.

speech needed to fit it for the requirements of that species of composition. Fortunately, however, the greatest and most influential of them were not mere men of books and readers of Greek and Latin. Greene and Peele and Marlow all spent the noon of their days (none of them saw any afternoon) in the busiest haunts of social life, sounding in their reckless course all the depths of human experience, and drinking the cup of passion, and also of suffering, to the dregs. And of their great successors, those who carried the drama to its height among us in the next age, while some were also accomplished scholars, all were men of the world—men who knew their brother-men by an actual and intimate intercourse with them in their most natural and open-hearted moods, and over a remarkably extended range of conditions. We know, from even the scanty fragments of their history that have come down to us, that Shakespeare and Jonson and Beaumont and Fletcher all lived much in the open air of society, and mingled with all ranks from the highest to the lowest: some of them, indeed, having known what it was actually to belong to classes very far removed from each other at different periods of their lives. But we should have gathered, though no other record or tradition had told us, that they must have been men of this genuine and manifold experience from the drama alone which they have bequeathed to us,—various, rich, and glowing as that is, even as life itself.

EARLIER ELIZABETHAN PROSE:—LYLY; SIDNEY; SPENSER; NASH; ETC.

Before leaving the earlier part of the reign of Elizabeth, a few of the more remarkable writers in prose who had risen into notice before the year 1500 may be mentioned. The singular affectation known by the name of *Euphuism* was, like some other celebrated absurdities, the invention of a man of true genius—John Lyly, noticed above as a dramatist and poet—the first part of whose prose romance of Euphues appeared in 1578 or 1579. "Our nation," says Sir Henry Blount, in the preface to a collection of some of Lyly's dramatic pieces which he published in 1632, "are in his debt for a new English which he taught them.

Euphues and his England* began first that language; all our
ladies were then his scholars; and that beauty in court which
could not parley Euphuism—that is to say, who was unable to
converse in that pure and reformed English, which he had
formed his work to be the standard of—was as little regarded as
she which now there speaks not French." Some notion of this
"pure and reformed English" has been made familiar to the
reader of our day by the great modern pen that has called back
to life so much of the long-vanished past, though the discourse
of Sir Piercie Shafton, in the Monastery, is rather a caricature
than a fair sample of Euphuism. Doubtless, it often became a
purely silly and pitiable affair in the mouths of the courtiers,
male and female; but in Lyly's own writings, and in those of
his lettered imitators, of whom he had several, and some of no
common talent, it was only fantastic and extravagant, and
opposed to truth, nature, good sense, and manliness. Pedantic
and far-fetched allusion, elaborate indirectness, a cloying smoothness and drowsy monotony of diction, alliteration, punning, and
other such puerilities,—those are the main ingredients of
Euphuism; which do not, however, exclude a good deal of wit,
fancy, and prettiness, occasionally, both in the expression and
the thought. Although Lyly, in his verse as well as in his
prose, is always artificial to excess, his ingenuity and finished
elegance are frequently very captivating. Perhaps, indeed, our
language is, after all, indebted to this writer and his Euphuism
for not a little of its present euphony. From the strictures
Shakespeare, in Love's Labours Lost, makes Holofernes pass on
the mode of speaking of his Euphuist, Don Adriano de Armado
—"a man of fire-new words, fashion's own knight—that hath a
mint of phrases in his brain—one whom the music of his own
vain tongue doth ravish like enchanting harmony"—it should
almost seem that the now universally adopted pronunciation of
many of our words was first introduced by such persons at this
refining "child of fancy:"—"I abhor such fanatical fantasms,
such insociable and point device companions; such rackers of
orthography as to speak *dout*, fine, when he should say *doubt*; *det*,
when he should pronounce *debt*, d, e, b, t; not d, e, t: he clepeth a
calf, *cauf*; *half*, *hauf*; *neighbour* vocatur *nebour*; *neigh*, abbreviated
ne; this is abhominable (which he would call *abominable*): it

insinuateth me of insanie." Here, however, the all-seeing poet laughs rather at the pedantic schoolmaster than at the fantastic knight; and the euphuistic pronunciation which he makes Holofernes so indignantly criticise was most probably his own and that of the generality of his educated contemporaries.

A renowned English prose classic of this age, who made Lyly's affectations the subject of his ridicule some years before Shakespeare, but who also perhaps was not blind to his better qualities, and did not disdain to adopt some of his reforms in the language, if not to imitate even some of the peculiarities of his style, was Sir Philip Sidney, the illustrious author of the Arcadia. Sidney, who was born in 1554, does not appear to have sent anything to the press during his short and brilliant life, which was terminated by the wound he received at the battle of Zutphen, in 1586; but he was probably well known, nevertheless, at least as a writer of poetry, some years before his lamented death. Puttenham, whose Art of English Poesy, at whatever time it may have been written, was published before any work of Sidney's had been printed, so far as can now be discovered, mentions him as one of the best and most famous writers of the age "for eclogue and pastoral poesy." The Countess of Pembroke's Arcadia, as Sidney's principal work had been affectionately designated by himself, in compliment to his sister, to whom it was inscribed—the "fair, and good, and learned" lady, afterwards celebrated by Ben Jonson as "the subject of all verse"—was not given to the world even in part till 1590, nor completely till 1593. His collection of sonnets and songs entitled Astrophel and Stella, first appeared in 1591, and his other most celebrated piece in prose, The Defence of Poesy, in 1595. The production in which he satirises the affectation and pedantry of the modern corrupters of the vernacular tongue is a sort of masque, supposed to pass before Queen Elizabeth in Wanstead garden, in which, among other characters, a village schoolmaster called Rombus appears, and declaims in a jargon not unlike that of Shakespeare's Holofernes. Sidney's own prose is the most flowing and poetical that had yet been written in English; but its graces are rather those of artful elaboration than of a vivid natural expressiveness. The thought, in fact, is generally more poetical than the language; it is a spirit of poetry encased in a rhetorical form. Yet, notwithstanding the conceits into which it frequently runs—and which, after all, are mostly rather the frolics of a nimble wit, somewhat too solicitous of display, than the sickly perversities of a coxcombical or effeminate taste—and, notwithstanding also some want of animation and variety, Sidney's is a wonderful style, always flexible, harmonious, and luminous, and on fit occasions rising to great stateliness and splendour; while a breath of beauty and noble feeling lives in and exhales from the whole of his great work, like the fragrance from a garden of flowers.

Among the most active occasional writers in prose, also, about this time were others of the poets and dramatists of the day, besides Lodge, who has been already mentioned as one of Lyly's imitators. Another of his productions, besides his tale of Rosalynd, which has lately attracted much attention, is a Defence of Stage Plays, which he published, probably in 1579, in answer to Stephen Gosson's School of Abuse, and of which only two copies are known to exist, both wanting the title-page.* Greene was an incessant pamphleteer upon all sorts of subjects; the list of his prose publications, so far as they are known, given by Mr. Dyce extends to between thirty and forty articles, the earliest being dated 1581, or eight years before his death. Morality, fiction, satire, blackguardism, are all mingled together in the stream that thus appears to have flowed without pause from his ready pen. "In a night and a day," says his friend Nash, "would he have yarked up a pamphlet as well as in seven years; and glad was that printer that might be so blest to pay him dear for the very dregs of his wit."† His wit, indeed, often enough appears to have run to the dregs, nor is it very sparkling at the best; but Greene's prose, though not in general very animated, is more concise and perspicuous than his habits of composition might lead us to expect. He has generally written from a well-informed or full mind, and the matter is interesting even when there is no particular attraction in the manner. Among his most curious pamphlets are his several tracts on the rogueries of

* See Mr. Collier's Introduction to the Shakespeare Society's editions of Gosson's School of Abuse, 1841; and of Northbrooke's Treatise against Dicing, Dancing, Plays, and Interludes, 1843. See also his History of Dramatic Poetry, ii. 277, &c. By far the amplest and most satisfactory account that has been given of Lodge and his productions (nearly twenty of which are enumerated and described), will be found prefixed to a reprint of his Answer to Gosson, and other two of his very rare publications, edited for the Shakespeare Society by Mr. David Laing, 8vo. Lond. 1853. His Rosalynd is included in Collier's Shakespeare's Library, 2 vols. 8vo. 1843.

† Strange News, in answer to Gabriel Harvey's Four Letters.

London, which he describes under the name of Coney-catching —a favourite subject also with other popular writers of that day. But the most remarkable of all Greene's contributions to our literature are his various publications which either directly relate or are understood to shadow forth the history of his own wild and unhappy life—his tale entitled Never too Late; or, A Powder of Experience, 1590; the second part entitled Francesco's Fortunes, the same year; his Groatsworth of Wit, bought with a Million of Repentance, and The Repentance of Robert Greene, Master of Arts, which both appeared, after his death, in 1592. Greene, as well as Lodge, we may remark, is to be reckoned among the Euphuists; a tale which he published in 1587, and which was no less than five times reprinted in the course of the next half-century, is entitled Menaphon; Camilla's Alarum to slumbering Euphues, in his melancholy cell at Silexedra, &c.; and the same year he produced Euphues his Censure to Philautus; wherein is presented a philosophical combat between Hector and Achilles, &c. But he does not appear to have persisted in this fashion of style. It may be noticed as curiously illustrating the spirit and manner of our fictitious literature at this time, that in his Pandosto, or, History of Dorastus and Fawnia, Greene, a scholar, and a Master of Arts of Cambridge, does not hesitate to make Bohemia an island, just as is done by Shakespeare in treating the same story in his Winter's Tale. The critics have been accustomed to instance this as one of the evidences of Shakespeare's ignorance, and Ben Jonson is recorded to have, in his conversation with Drummond of Hawthornden, quoted it as a proof that his great brother-dramatist " wanted art," and sometimes sense." The truth is, as has been observed,† such deviations from fact, and other incongruities of the same character, were not minded, or attempted to be avoided, either in the romantic drama, or in the legends out of which it was formed. They are not blunders, but part and parcel of the fiction. The making Bohemia an island is not nearly so great a violation of geographical truth as other things in the same play are of all the proprieties and possibilities of chronology and history—for instance, the co-existence of a

* Yet Jonson has elsewhere expressly commended Shakespeare for his art. See his well-known verses prefixed to the first folio edition of the Plays.
† See Notice on the Costume of the Winter's Tale in Knight's Shakspere, vol. iv.

kingdom of Bohemia at all, or of that modern barbaric name,
with anything so entirely belonging to the old classic world as
the Oracle of Delphi. The story (though no earlier record of it
has yet been discovered) is not improbably much older than
either Shakespeare or Greene : the latter no doubt expanded and
adorned it, and mainly gave it its present shape; but it is most
likely that he had for his groundwork some rude popular legend
or tradition, the characteristic middle age geography and chronology of which he most properly did not disturb.

But the most brilliant pamphleteer of this age was Thomas
Nash. Nash is the author of one slight dramatic piece, mostly
in blank verse, but partly in prose, and having also some lyrical
poetry interspersed, called Summer's Last Will and Testament,
which was exhibited before Queen Elizabeth at Nonsuch in
1592; and he also assisted Marlow in his Tragedy of Dido,
Queen of Carthage, which, although not printed till 1594, is
supposed to have been written before 1590. But his satiric was
of a much higher order than his dramatic talent. There never
perhaps was poured forth such a rushing and roaring torrent of
wit, ridicule, and invective, as in the rapid succession of pamphlets which he published in the course of the year 1589 against
the Puritans and their famous champion (or rather knot of champions) taking the name of Martin Mar-Prelate ; unless in those
in which he began two years after to assail poor Gabriel Harvey,
his persecution of and controversy with whom lasted a much
longer time—till indeed the Archbishop of Canterbury (Whitgift)
interfered in 1597 to restore the peace of the realm by an order
that all Harvey's and Nash's books should be taken wherever
they might be found, "and that none of the said books be ever
printed hereafter." Mr. D'Israeli has made both these contro-
versies familiar to modern readers by his lively accounts of the
one in his Quarrels, of the other in his Calamities, of Authors ;
and ample specimens of the criminations and recriminations
hurled at one another by Nash and Harvey have also been given
by Mr. Dyce in the Life of Greene prefixed to his edition of that
writer's dramatic and poetical works. Harvey too was a man of
eminent talent ; but it was of a kind very different from that of
Nash. Nash's style is remarkable for its airiness and facility ;
clear it of its old spelling, and, unless it be for a few words and
idioms which have now dropt out of the popular speech, it has
quite a modern air. This may show, by-the-by, that the lan-

guage has not altered so much since the latter part of the sixteenth century as the ordinary prose of that day would lead us to
suppose; the difference is rather that the generality of writers
were more pedantic then than now, and sought, in a way that
is no longer the fashion, to brocade their composition with what
were called ink-horn terms, and outlandish phrases never used
except in books. If they had been satisfied to write as they
spoke, the style of that day (as we may perceive from the example
of Nash) would have in its general character considerably more
resembled that of the present. Gabriel Harvey's mode of writing
exhibits all the peculiarities of his age in their most exaggerated
form. He was a great scholar—and his composition is inspired
by the very genius of pedantry; full of matter, full often of good
sense, not unfrequently rising to a tone of dignity, and even
eloquence, but always stiff, artificial, and elaborately unnatural
to a degree which was even then unusual. We may conceive
what sort of chance such a heavy-armed combatant, encumbered
and oppressed by the very weapons he carried, would have in a
war of wit with the quick, elastic, inexhaustible Nash, and the
showering jokes and sarcasms that flashed from his easy, natural
pen. Harvey, too, with all his merits, was both vain and
envious; and he had some absurdities which afforded tempting
game for satire. In particular he plumed himself on having
reformed the barbarism of English verse by setting the example
of modelling it after the Latin hexameter: "If I never deserve
any better remembrance," he exclaims in one of his pamphlets,
"let me be epitaphed the inventor of the English hexameter!"
Nash, again, profanely characterises the said hexameter as "that
drunken staggering kind of verse, which is all up hill and down
hill, like the way betwixt Stamford and Beechfield, and goes like
a horse plunging through the mire in the deep of winter—now
soused up to the saddle, and straight aloft on his tiptoes" (in
these last words, we suppose, exemplifying the thing he describes
and derides).

ENGLISH HEXAMETER VERSE.

Harvey, however, did not want imitators in his crotchet; and
among them were some of high name. He boasts, in the same
place where he claims the credit of the invention, of being able

to reckon among his disciples, not only "learned Mr. Stanyhurst,"—that is Richard Stanyhurst, who in 1583 produced a
most extraordinary performance, which he called a translation of
the First Four Books of the Æneid, in this reformed verse,* but
"excellent Sir Philip Sidney," who, he observes, had not disdained to follow him in his Arcadia and elsewhere. This is
stated in his Four Letters and certain Sonnets, especially touching Robert Greene, 1582.† But from a preceding publication,
entitled Three Proper and Witty Familiar Letters lately passed
between two University Men, touching the Earthquake in April
last, and our English Reformed Versifying, which were given to
the world in 1580,‡ we learn that Edmund Spenser too seemed,
or professed himself, for a short time half inclined to enlist himself among the practitioners of the new method. The two
University men between whom the Letters had passed are
Spenser (who is designated Immerito) and Harvey, with whom
he had become intimate at Cambridge (they were both of Pembroke Hall), and by whom he is supposed to have been introduced
to Sidney a short time before this correspondence began. The
Letters are in fact five in number; the original three, before the
pamphlet was published, having had two others added to them,
"of the same men's writing, both touching the foresaid artificial
versifying and certain other particulars, more lately delivered
unto the printer." The publication is introduced by a Preface
from "a Well-willer" to both writers, who professes to have
come by the letters at fourth or fifth hand, through a friend,
"who with much entreaty had procured the copying of them out
at Immerito's hands." He had not, he declares, made the
writers privy to the publication. The merits of Harvey's letters
in particular—which form indeed the principal part of the
pamphlet, and to which the only one by Spenser originally
designed to be given is merely introductory—are trumpeted
forth in this Preface in a very confident style:—"But show me
or Immerito," exclaims the Well-willer, "two English letters in
print in all points equal to the other two, both for the matter
itself and also for the manner of handling, and say we never saw

* This very scarce volume was reprinted, under the care of Mr. Maidment,
in 4to., at Edinburgh in 1836.
† Reprinted by Sir E. Brydges in the second volume of the Archaica, 1815.
‡ Reprinted in the second volume of Ancient Critical Essays upon English
Poets and Poesy, edited by Joseph Haslewood, 2 vols. 4to, Lond. 1811—15.

good English letters in our lives." "And yet," he adds, "I am credibly informed by the foresaid faithful and honest friend, that himself [the writer of the said two letters] hath written many of the same stamp both to courtiers and others, and some of them discoursing upon matters of great weight and importance, wherein he is said to be fully as sufficient and habile as in those scholarly points of learning." Nevertheless, this well-wisher, or his faithful and honest friend, was strongly suspected at the time to be no other than Harvey himself. Nash declares in one of his pamphlets that the compositor by whom the Well-willer's epistle, or Preface, was set up, swore to him that it came under Harvey's own hand to be printed. And in another place, addressing Harvey, he says, "You were young in years when you privately wrote the letters that afterward were publicly divulged by no other but yourself. Signior Immerito was counterfeitly brought in to play a part in that his interlude of epistles. I durst on my credit undertake Spenser was in no way privy to the committing of them to print. Committing I will call it, for in my opinion G. H. should not have reaped so much discredit by being committed to Newgate, as by committing that misbelieving prose to the press." Nash's authority, however, is none of the best; and it is fair to add that Harvey himself, in one of his Four Letters published in 1592, speaks of the present letters as having been sent to the press either by some malicious enemy or some indiscreet friend. It can hardly be supposed that he designed to conceal himself under the latter description.

But to return to what Spenser tells us of his studies and experiments in English hexameters and pentameters. In one letter, written from Leicester House, Westminster, in October, 1579, he says: "As for the two worthy gentlemen, Mr. Sidney and Mr. Dyer [afterwards Sir Edward Dyer, and greatly esteemed as a writer of verse in his day], they have me, I thank them, in some use and familiarity, of whom and to whom what speech passeth to your credit and estimation I leave yourself to conceive; having always so well conceived of my unfeigned affection and zeal towards you. And now they have proclaimed in their ἀρεοπάγῳ a general surceasing and silence of bald rhymers, and also of the very best too; instead whereof they have, by authority of their whole senate, proscribed certain rules and laws of quantities of English syllables for English verse; having had thereof already great practice, *and almost drawn me into their*

faction."   Afterwards he goes farther: "I am more in love," he
says, "with English versifying [that was the name by which
Harvey and his friends distinguished the now invention] than
with rhyming; which I should have done [with?] long since if
I would then have followed your counsel."   And he concludes,
"I received your letter sent me the last week, whereby I perceive you continue your old exercise of versifying in English;
which glory I had now thought should have been ours at London
and the court."   "Trust me," he adds, "your verses I like pass-
ingly well, and envy your hidden pains in this kind, or rather
malign and grudge at yourself that would not once impart so
much to me."   He remarks, however, that Harvey has once or
twice made a breach in the rules laid down for this new mode of
versifying by Master Drant, that is, Thomas Drant, chiefly
known as the author of two collections of Latin poetry, entitled
Sylva and Poemata Varia, but also the author of some verse
translations from the Latin and Greek.   "You shall see," says
Spenser in conclusion, "when we meet in London (and when it
shall be, certify us), how fast I have followed after you in that
course: beware lest in time I overtake you."   And, as a sample
of what he had been doing, he subjoins a few English Iambics.

Six months later we find him still occupied with the new
method.   Writing to Harvey again in the beginning of April
1580, he says: "I like your late English hexameters so exceedingly well that I also enure my pen sometimes in that kind;
which I find, indeed, as I have often heard you defend in word,
neither so hard nor so harsh [but] that it will easily and fairly
yield itself to our mother-tongue."   Yet from what follows it
almost looks as if he were all the while making sport of his
solemn friend and his preposterous invention.   "The only or
chiefest hardness which seemeth," he goes on, "is in the accent;
which sometime gapeth, and, as it were, yawneth, ill-favouredly,
coming short of that it should, and sometime exceeding the
measure of the number; as in *Carpenter*, the middle syllable
being used short in speech, when it shall be read long in verse
seemeth like a lame gosling, that draweth one leg after her; and
Heaven, being used short as one syllable, when it is in verse
stretched out with a diastole is like a lame dog that holds up one
leg."   Nash's ridicule is hardly so unmerciful as this.   Spenser,
however, adds, by way of consolation, "But it is to be won with
custom, and rough words must be subdued with use."   After-

wards he sets down four lines of English Elegiac verse—asking,
"Seem they comparable to those two which I translated you ex-
tempore in bed the last time we lay together in Westminster?—

> That which I eat did I joy, and that which I greedily gorged;
> As for those many goodly matters left I for others."

This can hardly have been written, or even, one would think,
have been intended to be taken, seriously. "I would heartily
wish," he concludes, "you would either send me the rules and
precepts of art which you observe in quantities, or else follow
mine, that M. Philip Sidney gave me, being the very same
which M. Drant devised, but enlarged with M. Sidney's own
judgment, and augmented with my observations; that we might
both agree and accord in one, lest we overthrow one another,
and be overthrown of the rest."

From this it would appear that, after all, Drant (whose era
was between 1560 and 1570) was, in this matter of English
hexameters, before Harvey. But, indeed, long before this Sir
Thomas More had amused himself with the same fancy. And
the attempt to mould English verse into the form of Latin (which
long afterwards exercised the ingenuity of Milton, and which
has been revived in our own day) continued to engage some
attention down to the close of the sixteenth century. In 1602
was published a small pamphlet entitled Observations on the
Art of English Poesy, by Thomas Campion: wherein it is
demonstratively proved, and by example confirmed, that the
English toong will receive eight several kinds of numbers,
proper to itself, which are all in this book set forth, and, were
never before this time by any man attempted. Thomas Campion, or Champion, was a poet of some celebrity in his day; his
name occurs, along with those of Spenser and Shakespeare (the
others are Sidney, John Owen, Daniel, Hugh Holland, Ben Jonson,
Drayton, Chapman, and Marston), in Camden's enumeration in his
Remains concerning Britain (first published in 1604) of the most
pregnant poetical wits then flourishing. His tract was answered
the next year by his brother-poet, Samuel Daniel, in A Defence of
Ryme against a pamphlet entitled Observations in the Art of English Poesy: wherein is demonstratively proved that Ryme is the
fittest harmony of words that comports with our language.* This

---

* Both Campion's Observations and Daniel's Defence are reprinted in the
second volume of the Ancient Critical Essays, edited by Haslewood.

reply appears to have terminated the controversy for the present; and, indeed, although Milton in a later day, in addition to imitating, or attempting to imitate, the metres of Horace, also, like Campion, denounced the Gothic barbarism and bondage of rhyme, it never was again seriously proposed, we believe, to reform our poetry by the entire abolition of the natural prosody of the language, and the substitution of the Greek or Latin.

EDMUND SPENSER.

If Harvey had seriously infected Spenser with the madness of his hexameters and pentameters, the reformed versifying might have been brought for a short time into more credit, although Spenser's actual performances in it, as has been remarked, are bad enough to countenance even those of his friend the inventor. But, besides that to change, as this system appears to have required, the entire pronunciation and musical character of a language is as much beyond the power of any writer, or host of writers, as to change the direction of the winds (the two cases being alike governed by laws of nature above human control), Spenser was of all writers the one least likely to be permanently enthralled by the pursuit of such an absurdity. Of all our great poets he is the one whose natural tastes were most opposed to such outlandish innovations upon and harsh perversions of his native tongue—whose genius was essentially the most musical, the most English, and the most reverential of antiquity.

Edmund Spenser has been supposed to have come before the world as a poet so early as the year 1569, when some sonnets translated from Petrarch, which long afterwards were reprinted with his name, appeared in Vander Noodt's Theatre of Worldlings: on the 20th of May in that year he was entered a sizer of Pembroke Hall, Cambridge; and in that same year, also, an entry in the Books of the Treasurer of the Queen's Chamber records that there was "paid upon a bill signed by Mr. Secretary, dated at Windsor 18° Octobris, to Edmund Spenser, that brought letters to the Queen's Majesty from Sir Henry Norris, Knight, her Majesty's ambassador in France, being at Thouars in the said realm, for his charges the sum of 6l. 13s. 4d., over and besides

96. presented to him by Sir Henry Norris."[*] It has been supposed that this entry refers to the poet. The date 1510, given
on that of the year of his birth upon his monument in Westminster Abbey, erected long after his death, is out of the question; but the above-mentioned facts make it probable that he was
born some years before 1553, the date commonly assigned.

He has himself commemorated the place of his birth: "At
length," he says in his Prothalamion, or poem on the marriages
of the two daughters of the Earl of Worcester,

> At length they all to merry London came,
> To merry London, my most kindly nurse,
> That to me gave this life's first native source,
> Though from another place I take my name,
> An house of ancient fame.

It is commonly said, on the authority of Oldys, that he was born
in East Smithfield by the Tower. It appears from the register
of the University that he took his degree of Bachelor of Arts in
1572, and that of Master of Arts in 1576. On leaving Cambridge
he retired for some time to the north of England. Here he appears to have written the greater part of his Shepherd's Calendar,
which, having previously come up to London, he published in
1579. And he had already, as we learn from his correspondence
with Harvey, finished two works entitled his Dreams and Dying
Pelican, of which nothing is now known, unless the former (as
has been conjectured) be the same afterwards published under
the titles of The Visions of Petrarch, The Visions of Bellay, and
Visions of the World's Vanity; and he had begun his Fairy
Queen, as well as at least designed, and perhaps made some progress in, a poem in Harvey's new mode of versifying, to be
entitled Epithalamion Thamesis; "which book," he says, "I
dare undertake will be profitable for the knowledge, and now for
the invention and manner of handling." The subject was to be
treated in the same manner as it is in the Fourth Book of the
Fairy Queen. He also speaks of another work which he calls
his Stemmata Dudleiana, probably a poem in honour of the family
of his patron, the Earl of Leicester, uncle of Sir Philip Sidney,
of which he says that it must not lightly be sent abroad without

---

* First published in Mr. Cunningham's Introduction (p. xxx.) to his Extracts from the Accounts of the Revels at Court, printed for the Shakspeare
Society, 8vo. Lond. 1842.

more advisement—adding, however, "But trust me, though I never do well, yet in my own fancy I never did better." And Harvey congratulates him on nine Comedies, which he had either written, or was engaged with :—" I am void of all judgment if your Nine Comedies, whereunto, in imitation of Herodotus, you give the names of the Nine Muses, come not as near Ariosto's Comedies, either for the fineness of plausible elocution or the rareness of poetical, as the Fairy Queen doth to his Orlando." But he published nothing more for some years.

In his Letter to Harvey written from Leicester House in October, 1579, and more especially in a long Latin valedictory poem included in it, he speaks of being immediately about to proceed across the seas in the service of Leicester, to France, as it would appear, if not farther. "I go thither," he writes, " as sent by him, and maintained (most-what) of him; and there am to employ my time, my body, my mind, in his honour's service." But whether he actually went upon this mission is unknown. In the beginning of August, 1580, on the appointment of Arthur Lord Grey of Wilton as Lord Deputy of Ireland, Spenser accompanied his lordship to that country as his secretary; in March, the year following, he was appointed to the office of Clerk in the Irish Court of Chancery; but on Lord Grey being recalled in 1582 Spenser probably returned with him to England. It has been conjectured that he may have been the person mentioned in a letter to Queen Elizabeth from James VI. of Scotland, dated at St. Andrews, the 2nd of July, 1583 (the original of which is preserved among the Cotton MSS.), where James says in the postscript, " Madam, I have stayed Maister Spenser upon the letter quilk is written with my awin hand, quilk sall be ready within twa days."*

Of how he was employed for the next three or four years nothing is known; but in 1586 he obtained from the crown a grant of above 3000 acres of forfeited lands in Ireland: the grant is dated the 27th of July, and, if it was procured, as is not improbable, through Sir Philip Sidney, it was the last kindness of that friend and patron, whose death took place in October of this year. Spenser proceeded to Ireland to take possession of his estate, which was a portion of the former domain of the Earl of

* See Note by Mr. David Laing on p. 12 of his edition of Ben Jonson's Conversations with William Drummond, printed for the Shakespeare Society. 8vo. Lond. 1842.

Desmond in the county of Cork; and here he remained, residing in what had been the earl's castle of Kilcolman, till he returned to England in 1590, and published at London, in 4to., the first three Books of his Fairy Queen. If he had published anything else since the Shepherd's Calendar appeared eleven years before, it could only have been a poem of between four and five hundred lines, entitled Muiopotmos, or the Fate of the Butterfly, which he dedicated to the Lady Carey. He has himself related, in his Colin Clout's Come Home Again, how he had been visited in his exile by the Shepherd of the Ocean, by which designation he means Sir Walter Raleigh, and persuaded by him to make this visit to England for the purpose of having his poem printed. Raleigh introduced him to Elizabeth, to whom the Fairy Queen was dedicated, and who in February, 1591, bestowed on the author a pension of 50l. This great work immediately raised Spenser to such celebrity, that the publisher hastened to collect whatever of his other poems he could find, and, under the general title of Complaints: Containing sundry small poems of the World's Vanity; printed together, in a 4to. volume, The Ruins of Time, The Tears of the Muses, Virgil's Gnat, Mother Hubberd's Tale, The Ruins of Rome (from the French of Bellay), Muiopotmos (which is stated to be the only one of the pieces that had previously appeared), and The Visions of Petrarch, &c., already mentioned. Many more, it is declared, which the author had written in former years were not to be found.

Spenser appears to have remained in England till the beginning of the year 1592: his Daphnaida, an elegy on the death of Douglas Howard, daughter of Lord Howard, and wife of Arthur Gorges, Esq., is dedicated to the Marchioness of Northampton in an address dated the 1st of January in that year, and it was published soon after. He then returned to Ireland, and, probably in the course of 1592 and 1593, there composed the series of eighty-eight sonnets in which he relates his courtship of the lady whom he at last married,* celebrating the event by a splendid Epithalamion. But it appears from the eightieth sonnet that he had already finished six Books of his Fairy Queen. His next publication was another 4to. volume which appeared in 1595,

* She was not, as has been commonly assumed, a peasant girl, but evidently a gentlewoman, a person of the same social position with Spenser himself. I have shown this, for the first time, in Spenser and his Poetry, vol. iii. pp. 253, &c.

containing his Colin Clout's Come Home Again, the dedication
of which to Raleigh is dated "From my house at Kilcolman,
December the 27th, 1591," no doubt a misprint for 1594; and also
his Astrophel, an elegy upon Sir Philip Sidney, dedicated to his
widow, now the Countess of Essex; together with The Mourning
Muse of Thestylis, another poem on the same subject.   The same
year appeared, in 8vo., his sonnets, under the title of Amoretti,
accompanied by the Epithalamion.   In 1596 he paid another visit
to England, bringing with him the Fourth, Fifth, and Sixth
Books of his Fairy Queen, which were published, along with a
new edition of the preceding three books, in 4to., at London in
that year.   In the latter part of the same year appeared, in a
volume of the same form, a reprint of his Daphnaida, together
with his Prothalamion, or spousal verse on the marriages of the
Ladies Elizabeth and Catharine Somerset, and his Four Hymns
in honour of Love, of Beauty, of Heavenly Love, and of Heavenly Beauty, dedicated to the Countesses of Cumberland and
Warwick, in an address dated Greenwich, the 1st of September,
1596.   The first two of these Hymns he states had been composed
in the greener times of his youth; and, although he had been
moved by one of the two ladies to call in the same, as "having
too much pleased those of like age and disposition, which, being
too vehemently carried with that kind of affection, do rather
suck out poison to their strong passion than honey to their
honest delight," he "had been unable so to do, by reason that
many copies thereof were formerly scattered abroad."   At this
time it was still common for literary compositions of all kinds to
be extensively circulated in manuscript, as used to be the mode
of publication before the invention of printing.   These Hymns
were the last of his productions that he sent to the press.   It
was during this visit to England that he presented to Elisabeth,
and probably wrote, his prose treatise entitled A View of the
State of Ireland, written dialogue-wise between Eudoxus and
Irenaeus; but that work remained unprinted, till it was published
at Dublin by Sir James Ware in 1633.

Spenser returned to Ireland probably early in 1597; and was
the next year recommended by the Queen to be sheriff of Cork;
but, soon after the breaking out of Tyrone's rebellion in October,
1598, his house of Kilcolman was attacked and burned by the
rebels, and, one child having perished in the flames, it was with
difficulty that he made his escape with his wife and two sons.

He arrived in England in a state of destitution; but it seems unlikely that, with his talents and great reputation, his powerful friends, his pension, and the rights he still retained, although deprived of the enjoyment of his Irish property for the moment, he could have been left to perish, as has been commonly said, of want: the breaking up of his constitution was a natural consequence of the sufferings he had lately gone through. All that we know, however, is that, after having been ill for some time, he died at an inn in King Street, Westminster, on the 16th of January, 1599. Two Cantos, undoubtedly genuine, of a subsequent Book of the Fairy Queen, and two stanzas of a third Canto, entitled Of Mutability, and forming part of the Legend of Constancy, were published in an edition of his collected works, in a folio volume, in 1609; and it may be doubted if much more of the poem was ever written. As for the poem called Britain's Ida, in six short Cantos, which also appeared in this volume, it is certainly not by Spenser. Besides the works that have been enumerated, however, the following compositions by Spenser, now all lost, are mentioned by himself or his friends:—His Pageants, The Canticles Paraphrased, a poetical version of Ecclesiastes, another of the Seven Penitential Psalms, The Hours of our Lord, The Sacrifice of a Sinner, Purgatory, A Se'ennight's Slumber, The Court of Cupid, and The Hell of Lovers. He is also said to have written a treatise in prose called The English Poet.

The most remarkable of Spenser's poems written before his great work, The Fairy Queen, are his Shepherd's Calendar and his Mother Hubberd's Tale. Both of these pieces are full of the spirit of poetry, and his genius displays itself in each in a variety of styles.

The Shepherd's Calendar, though consisting of twelve distinct poems denominated Æclogues, is less of a pastoral, in the ordinary acceptation, than it is of a piece of polemical or party divinity. Spenser's shepherds are, for the most part, pastors of the church, or clergymen, with only pious parishioners for sheep. One is a good shepherd, such as Algrind, that is, the puritanical archbishop of Canterbury, Grindall. Another, represented in a much less favourable light, is Morell, that is, his famous antagonist, Elmore, or Aylmer, bishop of London. Spenser's religious character and opinions make a curious subject, which has not received much attention from his biographers. His connexion with Sidney and Leicester, and afterwards with Essex, made

him, no doubt, be regarded throughout his life as belonging to
the puritanical party, but only to the more moderate section of it,
which, although not unwilling to encourage a little grumbling at
some things in the conduct of the dominant section of the hierarchy, and even professing to see much reason in the objections
made to certain outworks or appendages of the established system,
stood still or drew back as soon as the opposition to the church
became really a war of principles. Spenser's puritanism seems
almost as unnatural as his hexameters and pentameters. It was
probably, for the greater part, the product of circumstances,
rather than of conviction or any strong feeling, even while it
lasted; and it never appears afterwards in such prominence as in
his Shepherd's Calendar, the first work that he published. It
has even been asserted that his Blatant Beast, in the Sixth Book
of the Fairy Queen, is meant for a personification of Puritanism.
At any rate, it is evident that, in his later years, his Christianity
had taken the form rather of Platonism than of Puritanism. The
puritanical spirit of some parts of the Shepherd's Calendar, however, probably contributed to the popularity which the poem long
retained. It was reprinted four times during the author's life
time, in 1581, 1586, 1591, and 1597. Yet it is not only a very
unequal composition, but is, in its best executed or most striking
parts, far below the height to which Spenser afterwards learned
to rise. We may gather from it that one thing which had helped
to give him his church-reforming notions had been his study and
admiration of the old poetry of Chaucer and the Visions of Piers
Ploughman. One of his personages, who, in one of the Æclogues,
discourses much in the style of the principal figure in Langland's
poem, is called Piers; and Chaucer is not only in various passages affectionately commemorated under the name of Tityrus,
but several of the Æclogues are written in a peculiar versification
which appears to be intended as an imitation of that of Chaucer's
poetry. So far as Spenser, at this time of his life, can be accounted any authority in such a matter, it may be admitted that
he seems to have regarded the verse of his great predecessor as
only accentually, not syllabically, regular; but it is still more
evident, at the same time, that these intended imitations of
Chaucer in the Shepherd's Calendar do not really give a true
representation of his prosody, according to any theory of it that
may be adopted. The flow of the verse is rather that of the
Visions of Piers Ploughman, only without the regular alliteration

and with the addition of rhyme. As a specimen of the Shepherd's Calendar, we will give, from the second Ægloguo, which is one of those composed in this peculiar measure, the Tale of the Oak and the Briar, as told by the old shepherd Thenot, who says he conned it of Tityrus in his youth :—

There grew an aged tree on the green,
A goodly Oak sometime had it been,
With arms full strong and largely displayed,
But of their leaves they were disarrayed;
The body big and mightily pight,[1]
Throughly rooted, and of wondrous height :
Whilom he had been the king of the field,
And mochel[2] mast to the husband[3] did yield,
And with his nuts larded many swine ;
But now the grey moss marred his rine;[4]
His bared boughs were beaten with storms,
His top was bald and wasted with worms,
His honour decayed, his branches sere.

Hard by his side grew a bragging Brere,
Which proudly thrust into th' element,
And seemed to threat the firmament ;
It was embellished with blossoms fair,
And thereto aye wonted to repair
The shepherds' daughters to gather flowers,
To paint their garlands with his colours ;
And in his small bushes used to shrowd
The sweet nightingale, singing so loud ;
Which made this foolish Brere wex so bold,
That on a time he cast him to scold
And snob the good Oak, for he was old.

Why stand'st there, quoth he, thou brutish block ?
Nor for fruit nor for shadow serves thy stock.
Seest how fresh my flowers been spread,
Dyed in lilly white and crimson red,
With leaves engrained in lusty green,
Colours meet to clothe a maiden queen ?
Thy waste bigness but cumbers the ground,
And dirks[5] the beauty of my blossoms round ; .
The mouldy moss which thee accloyeth[6]
My cinnamon smell too much annoyeth :
Wherefore soon, I rede[7] thee, hence remove,
Lest thou the price of my displeasure prove.

---

[1] Strongly fixed.	[2] Much.	[3] Husbandman.	[4] Bind.
[5] Darkens	[6] Coils around.	[7] Advise.	

So spake this bold Brere with great disdain;
Little him answered the Oak again;
But yielded, with shame and grief adawed[1]
That of a weed he was over-crawed.

It chanced after upon a day
The husbandman's self to come that way,
Of custom to surview his ground,
And his trees of state in compass round:[2]
Him when the spiteful Brere had espied,
He causeless complained, and loudly cried
Unto his lord, stirring up stern strife;—

O my liege lord! the God of my life,
Please of you pond[3] your suppliant's plaint,
Caused of wrong and cruel constraint,
Which I your poor vassal daily endure:
And, but your goodness the same secure,
Am like for desperate dole to die,
Through felonous force of mine enemy.

Greatly aghast with this piteous plea,
Him rested the goodman on the lea,
And bade the Brere in his plaint proceed.
With painted words tho[4] gan this proud weed
(As most usen ambitious folk)
His coloured crime with craft to cloak:—

Ah, my Sovereign! lord of creatures all,
Thou placer of plants both humble and tall,
Was not I planted of thine own hand,
To be the primrose of all thy land,
With flowering blossoms to furnish the prime,[5]
And scarlet berries in summer time?
How falls it then that this faded Oak,
Whose body is sere, whose branches broke,
Whose naked arms stretch unto the fire,[6]
Unto such tyranny doth aspire,
Hindering with his shade my lovely light,
And robbing me of the sweet sun's sight?
So beat his old boughs my tender side,
That oft the blood springeth from woundes wide.
Untimely my flowers forced to fall,
That been the honour of your coronal;
And oft he lets his canker-worms light
Upon my branches, to work me more spite;

---

[1] Daunted.
[2] Perhaps the true reading is "encompass round," that is, circumambulate.
[3] Ponder, consider.   [4] Then.   [5] Spring.
[6] The meaning seems to be, are ready for firewood.

And oft his hoary locks down doth cast,
Wherewith my fresh flowrets been defast.
For this, and many more such outrage,
Crave I[1] your goodlyhead to assuage
The rancorous rigour of his might;
Nought ask I but only to hold my right,
Submitting me to your good sufferance,
And praying to be guarded from grievance.

To this the Oak cast him to reply
Well as he couth;[3] but his enemy
Had kindled such coals of displeasure,
That the goodman[2] nould[4] stay his leisure,
But home him hasted with furious bent,
Increasing his wrath with many a threat:
His harmful hatchet he hent[5] in hand
(Alas! that it so ready should stand!)
And to the field alone he speedeth
(Aye little help to harm there needeth),
Anger nould let him speak to the tree,
Enaunter[6] his rage mought cooled be,
But to the root bent his sturdy stroke,
And made many wounds in the wasted Oak:
The axe's edge did oft turn again,
As half unwilling to cut the grain;
Seemed the senseless iron did fear,
Or to wrong holy eld did forbear;
For it had been an ancient tree,
Sacred with many a mystery,
And often crossed with the priests' crew,
And often hallowed with holy water due;
But like fancies weren foolery,
And broughten this Oak to this misery;
For nought mought they quitten him from decay;
For fiercely the goodman at him did lay.
The block oft groaned under his blow,
And sighed to see his near overthrow.
In fine[7] the steel had pierced his pith;
Tho down to the ground he fell therewith.
His wondrous weight made the ground to quake;
The earth shrank under him, and seemed to shake:
There lieth the Oak, pitied of none.

Now stands the Briere like a lord alone,

---

[1] The common reading is "craving."
[2] Farmer.
[4] Lett that.
[5] Would not.
[6] At last.
[3] As well as he could.
[5] Took.

Puffed up with pride and vain pleasance :
But all this glee had no continuance ;
For eftsoons winter gan to approach,
The blustering Boreas did encroach
And beat upon the solitary Brere,
For now no succour was seen him near.
Now gan he repent his pride too late ;
For, naked left and disconsolate,
The biting frost nipt his stalk dead,
The watery wet weighed down his head,
And heaped snow burthened him so sore
That now upright he can stand no more ;
And, being down, is trod in the dirt
Of cattle, and bruized,[1] and sorely hurt.
Such was the end of this ambitious Brere,
For scorning eld.

The story is admirably told, certainly ; with wonderful facility
of expression, as well as with a fancy and invention at once the
most just and spirited, and the most easy and copious—altogether
so as to betoken a poet such as had not yet arisen in the language since it had settled down into its existing form. This
earliest work of Spencer's, however, betrays his study of our
elder poetry as much by its diction as by the other indications
already mentioned : he has thickly sprinkled it with words and
phrases which had generally ceased to be used at the time
when it was written. This he seems to have done, not so much
that the antiquated style might give the dialogue an air of
rusticity proper to the speech of shepherds, but rather in the
same spirit and design (though he has carried the practice much
farther) in which Virgil has done the same thing in his heroic
poetry, that his verse might thereby be the more distinguished
from common discourse, that it might fall upon the ears of men
with something of the impressiveness and authority of a voice
from other times, and that it might seem to echo, and, as it
were, continue and prolong, the strain of the old national minstrelsy ; thus at once expressing his love and admiration of the
preceding poets who had been his examples, and, in part, his
instructors and inspirers, and making their compositions reflect
additional light and beauty upon his own. This is almost the
only advantage which the later poets in any language have
over the earlier ; and Spenser has availed himself of it more or

[1] Bruised.

less in most of his writings, though not in any later work to the
same extent as in this first publication. Perhaps also there may
be discovered in the Shepherd's Calendar some other traces of
his studies in experimental versification at this time (to which
his attention may have been awakened by his friend Harvey's
lucubrations), besides his attempts to imitate the metre of
Chaucer or Piers Ploughman. The work is, at least, remarkable
for the variety of measures in which it is composed. The most
spirited of its lyric passages is a panegyric upon Elizabeth in the
Fourth Æclogue, of which, as the work is not much read, we
may transcribe a few verses.[1] It is recited by Hobbinol (Gabriel
Harvey), who, on the request of Thenot that he would repeat to
him one of his friend Colin's songs, framed before his love for
Rosalind had made him break his pipe, replies :—

> "Contented I ; then will I sing his lay
> Of fair Eliza, queen of shepherds all,
> Which once he made as by a spring he lay,
> And tuned it unto the water's fall :"—
>
> . . . .
>
> See where she sits upon the grassy green,
> (O seemly sight !)
> Yclad in scarlet, like a maiden queen,
> And ermines white ;
> Upon her head a crimson coronet,
> With damask roses and daffadillies set :
> Bay leaves between,
> And primroses green,
> Embellish the sweet violet.
>
> . . . .
>
> I see Calliope speed to the place
> Where my goddess shines,
> And after her the other Muses trace[1]
> With their violins.
> Been they not bay branches which they do bear,
> All for Eliza in her hand to wear ?
> So sweetly they play,
> And sing all the way,
> That it a heaven is to hear.
>
> Lo, how finely the Graces can it foot
> To the instrument !
> They dancen defly, and singen soot[2]
> In their merriment.

---

[1] Walk. [2] Sweet.

Wants not a fourth Grace to make the dance even?
Let that room to my Lady be yeven.[1]
She shall be a Grace
To fill the fourth place,
And reign with the rest in heaven.

And whither rens this bevy of ladies bright,
Ranged in a row?
They been all Ladies of the Lake behight[2]
That unto her go.
Chloris, that is the chiefest nymph of all,
Of olive branches bears a coronal:
Olives been for peace,
When wars do surcease;
Such for a princess been principal.

Ye shepherds' daughters that dwell on the green,
Hie you there apace:
Let none come there but that virgins been,
To adorn her grace;
And, when you come whereas[3] she is in place,
See that your rudeness do not you disgrace.
Bind your fillets fast,
And gird in your waste,
For more fineness, with a tawdry lace.

Bring hither the pink and purple cullumbine,
With gillyflowers;
Bring coronations, and sops in wine,
Worn of paramours:
Strow me the ground with daffadowndillies,
And cowslips, and kingcups, and loved lillies:
The pretty pance
And the chevisance
Shall match with the fair flower-delice.

Now rise up, Eliza, decked as thou art
In royal ray;[4]
And now ye dainty damsels may depart,
Each one her way.
I fear I have troubled your troops too long;
Let Dame Eliza thank you for her song;
And, if you come hither[5]
When damsons I gather,
I will part them all you among.

Executed in a firmer and more matured style, and, though
with more regularity of manner, yet also with more true bold-

---

[1] Given.   [2] Called, named.   [3] Where.   [4] Array.   [5] Hither.

ness and freedom, is the admirable Prosopopœia, as it is designated, of the adventures of the Fox and the Ape, or Mother
Hubberd's Tale, notwithstanding that this, too, is stated to have
been an early production—"long sithens composed," says the
author in his dedication of it to the Lady Compton and Mont-
eagle, "in the raw conceit of my youth." Perhaps, however,
this was partly said to avert the offence that might be taken at
the audacity of the satire. It has not much the appearance,
either in manner or in matter, of the production of a very young
writer, although it may have been written before any part of the
Fairy Queen, at least in the matured form of that poem; for we
can hardly believe that the work spoken of under that name as
in hand in 1579 was the same the first part of which was not
published till eleven years afterwards. We should say that
Mother Hubberd's Tale represents the middle age of Spenser's
genius, if not of his life—the stage in his mental and poetical
progress when his relish and power of the energetic had attained
perfection, but the higher sense of the beautiful had not yet
been fully developed. Such appears to be the natural progress
of every mind that is capable of the highest things in both these
directions: the feeling of force is first awakened, or at least is
first matured; the feeling of beauty is of later growth. With
even poetical minds of a subordinate class, indeed, it may sometimes happen that a perception of the beautiful, and a faculty of
embodying it in words, acquire a considerable development
without the love and capacity of the energetic having ever
shown themselves in any unusual degree: such may be said to
have been the case with Petrarch, to quote a remarkable example.
But the greatest poets have all been complete men, with the
sense of beauty, indeed, strong and exquisite, and crowning all
their other endowments, which is what makes them the greatest;
but also with all other passions and powers correspondingly
vigorous and active. Homer, Dante, Chaucer, Spenser, Shakespeare, Milton, Goethe, were all of them manifestly capable
of achieving any degree of success in any other field as
well as in poetry. They were not only poetically, but in all
other respects, the most gifted intelligences of their times; men
of the largest sense, of the most penetrating insight, of the most
general research and information; nay, even in the most worldly
arts and dexterities, able to cope with the ablest, whenever
they chose to throw themselves into that game. They may not

any of them have attained the highest degree of what is called
worldly success; some of them may have even been crushed by
the force of circumstances or evil days; Milton may have died
in obscurity, Dante in exile; "the vision and the faculty
divine" may have been all the light that cheered, all the estate
that sustained, the old age of Homer; but no one can suppose
that in any of these cases it was want of the requisite skill or
talent that denied a different fortune. As for Spenser, we shall
certainly much mistake his character if we suppose, from the
romantic and unworldly strain of much—and that, doubtless,
the best and highest—of his poetry, that he was anything
resembling a mere dreamer. In the first place, the vast extent
of his knowledge, comprehending all the learning of his age, and
his voluminous writings, sufficiently prove that his days were
not spent in idleness. Then, even in the matter of securing a
livelihood and a position in the world, want of activity or eagerness is a fault of which he can hardly be accused. Bred, for
whatever reason, to no profession, it may be doubted if he had
any other course to take, in that age, upon the whole so little
objectionable as the one he adopted. The scheme of life with
which he set out seems to have been to endeavour, first of all, to
procure for himself, by any honourable means, the leisure necessary to enable him to cultivate and employ his poetical powers.
With this view he addressed himself to Sidney, the chief professed patron of letters in that day (when, as yet, letters really
depended to a great extent for encouragement and support upon
the patronage of the great), hoping, through his interest, to
obtain such a provision as he required from the bounty of the
crown. In thus seeking to be supported at the public expense,
and to withdraw a small portion of a fund, pretty sure to be
otherwise wasted upon worse objects, for the modest maintenance
of one poet, can we say that Spenser, being what he was, was
much, or at all, to blame? Would it have been wiser, or more
highminded, or in any sense better, for him to have thrown
himself, like Greene and Nash, and the rest of that crew, upon
the town, and, like them, wasted his fine genius in pamphleteer-
ing and blackguardism? He knew that he would not eat that
public bread without returning to his country what she gave
him a hundred and a thousand fold; he who must have felt and
known well that no man had yet uttered himself in the English
tongue so endowed for conferring upon the land, the language,

and the people what all future generations would prize as their
lost inheritance, and what would contribute more than laws or
victories, or any other glory, to maintain the name of England in
honour and renown so long as it should be heard of among men.

But he did not immediately succeed in his object. It is
probably true, as has been commonly stated, that Burghley
looked with but small regard upon the poet and his claims.
However, he at last contrived to overcome this obstacle; and
eventually, as we have seen, he obtained from the crown both
lands, offices, and a considerable pension. It is not at all likely
that, circumstanced as he was at the commencement of his
career, Spenser could in any other way have attained so soon to
the same comparative affluence that he thus acquired. Probably
the only respect in which he felt much dissatisfied or disappointed was in being obliged to take up his residence in Ireland,
without which, it may have been, he would have derived little
or no benefit from his grant of land. Mother Hubberd's Tale
must be supposed to have been written before he obtained that
grant. It is a sharp and shrewd satire upon the common modes
of rising in the church and state; not at all passionate or declamatory,—on the contrary, pervaded by a spirit of quiet
humour, which only occasionally gives place to a tone of greater
elevation and solemnity, but assuredly, with all its high-minded
and even severe morality, evincing in the author anything rather
than either ignorance of the world or indifference to the ordinary
objects of human ambition. No one will rise from its perusal
with the notion that Spenser was a mere rhyming visionary, or
singing somnambulist. No; like every other greatest poet, he
was an eminently wise man, exercised in every field of thought,
and rich in all knowledge—above all, in knowledge of mankind,
the proper study of man. In this poem of Mother Hubberd's
Tale we still find also both his puritanism and his imitation of
Chaucer, two things which disappear altogether from his later
poetry. Indeed, he has written nothing else so much in
Chaucer's manner and spirit; nor have we nearly so true a
reflection, or rather revival, of the Chaucerian narrative style—
at once easy and natural, clear and direct, firm and economical,
various and always spirited—in any other modern verse. We
will pass over the description of the brave and honourable
courtier (intended for Sidney), which is probably known to most
of our readers, and the still more famous passage in which the

miserable state of a suitor for court favour (supposed to be the author's own case at the time) is depicted with such indignant force and bitterness of expression. What a fulness of matter and driving sleet of words there is in the following description of the moral anarchy wrought by the Ape and the Fox after the former had stolen the lion's hide and other royal emblems, and seated himself on the throne, with his companion and instigator for his chief counsellor and minister!—

First, to his gate he 'pointed a strong guard,
That none might enter but with issue hard ;
Then, for the safeguard of his personage,
He did appoint a warlike equipage
Of foreign beasts, not in the forest bred,
But part by land and part by water fed ;
For tyranny is with strange aid supported :
Then unto him all monstrous beasts resorted,
Bred of two kinds, as griffons, minotaurs,
Crocodiles, dragons, beavers, and centaurs ;
With these himself he strengthened mightily,
That fear he need no force of enemy.
Then gan he rule and tyrannize at will,
Like as the Fox did guide his graceless skill,
And all wild beasts made vassals of his pleasures,
And with their spoils enlarged his private treasures.
No care of justice, nor no rule of reason,
No temperance, nor no regard of season,
Did thenceforth ever enter in his mind :
But cruelty, the sign of currish kind,
And 'sdainful pride, and wilful arrogance ;
Such fellows those whom Fortune doth advance.
    But the false Fox most kindly[1] played his part ;
For whatsoever mother wit or art
Could work he put in proof ; no practice sly,
No counterpoint of cunning policy,
No reach, no breach, that might him profit bring,
But he the same did to his purpose wring.
Nought suffered he the Ape to give or grant,
But through his hand alone must pass the fiant.[2]
All offices, all leases by him lept,
And of them all whatso he liked he kept.
Justice he sold, injustice for to buy,
And for to purchase for his progeny.
Ill might it prosper that ill gotten was ;
But, so he got it, little did he pass.

----

[1] According to his nature.   [2] Warrant.

He fed his cubs with fat of all the soil,
And with the sweet of others' sweating toil;
He crammed them with crumbs of benefices,
And filled their mouths with meeds of malefices.
He clothed them with all colours save white,
And loaded them with lordships and with might,
So much as they were able well to bear,
That with the weight their backs nigh broken were.
He chaffered chairs in which churchmen were set,
And breach of laws to privy farm did let.
No statute so established might be,
Nor ordinance so needful, but that he
Would violate, though not with violence,
Yet under colour of the confidence
The which the Ape reposed in him alone,
And reckoned him the kingdom's corner-stone;
And ever, when he aught would bring to pass,
His long experience the platform was;
And, when he aught not pleasing would put by,
The cloak was care of thrift and husbandry,
For to increase the common treasure's store;
But his own treasure he increased more,
And lifted up his lofty towers thereby,
That they began to threat the neighbour sky;
The whiles the prince's palaces fell fast
To ruin; for what thing can, ever last?
And whilst the other peers for poverty
Were forced their ancient houses to let lie,
And their old castles to the ground to fall,
Which their forefathers, famous over all,
Had founded for the kingdom's ornament,
And for their memories' long moniment.
But he no count made of nobility,
Nor the wild beasts whom arms did glorify,
The realm's chief strength, and girland of the crown;
All those, through feigned crimes, he thrust adown,
Or made them dwell in darkness of disgrace;
For none but whom he list might come in place.
Of men of arms he had but small regard,
But kept them low, and straitened very hard.
For men of learning little he esteemed;
His wisdom he above their learning deemed.
As for the rascal commons, least he cared,
For not so common was his bounty shared;
Let God, said he, if please, care for the many;
I for myself must care before else any.
So did he good to none, to many ill;
So did he all the kingdom rob and pill;

Yet none durst speak, nor none durst of him plain,
So great he was in grace, and rich through gain ;
Ne would he any let to have access
Unto the prince but by his own address ;
For all that else did come were sure to fail ;
Yet would be further none but for avail.[1]
For on a time the Sheep, to whom of yore
The Fox had promised of friendship store,
What time the Ape the kingdom first did gain,
Came to the court her case there to complain,
How that the Wolf, her mortal enemy,
Had sithence[2] slain her lamb most cruelly,
And therefore craved to come unto the king
To let him know the order of the thing.
Soft, Goody Sheep, then said the Fox, not so ;
Unto the king so rash ye may not go ;
He is with greater matter busied
Than a lamb, or the lamb's own mother's head ;
Ne certes may I take it well in part
That ye my cousin Wolf so foully thwart,
And seek with slander his good name to blot ;
For there was cause, else do it he would not.
Therefore surcease, good dame, and hence depart :
So went the Sheep away with heavy heart :
So many mo,[3] so every one was used,
That to give largely to the box refused.

We must add the winding up of the story, as a sample of the
more descriptive portions of the poem. What is going on at last
attracts the notice of the powers above :—

Now, when high Jove, in whose almighty hand
The care of kings and power of empires stand,
Sitting one day within his turret high,
From whence he views with his black-lidded eye
Whatso the heaven in his wide vault contains,
And all that in the deepest earth remains,
The troubled kingdom of wild beasts beheld,
Whom not their kindly[4] sovereign did weld,[5]
But an usurping Ape, with guile suborned,
Had all subverned, he 'sdainfully it scorned
In his great heart, and hardly did refrain
But that with thunderbolts he had him slain.

---

[1] Bribe.   [2] Since.   [3] More.
[4] Natural.   [5] Wield.

Jove forthwith calls Mercury to him, and despatches him to the earth :—

> The son of Maia, soon as he received
> That word, straight with his azure wings he cleaved
> The liquid clouds and lucid firmament,
> Ne stayed till that he came with steep descent
> Unto the place where his prescript did show ;
> There stooping, like an arrow from a bow,
> He soft arrived on the grassy plain,
> And fairly paced forth with easy pain,
> Till that unto the palace nigh he came ;
> Then gan he to himself new shape to frame,
> And that fair face, and that ambrosial hue,
> Which wonts to deck the gods' immortal crew
> And beautify the shiny firmament,
> He doft, unfit for that rude rabblement.

Mercury puts on his hat of invisibility, and, taking his caduceus in his hand, makes a survey of the scene of extortion, oppression, and lawlessness. He sees on all sides more of ill of all kinds than can be told :—

> Which when he did with loathful eyes behold
> He would no more endure, but came his way,
> And cast to seek the Lion where he may,
> That he might work the avengement for his shame
> On those two caitives which had bred him blame ;
> And, seeking all the forest busily,
> At last he found where sleeping he did lie.
> The wicked weed, which there the Fox did lay,
> From underneath his head he took away,
> And then him waking forced up to rise.
> The Lion, looking up, gan him avize,
> As one late in a trance, what had of long
> Become of him, for fantasy is strong.
> Arise, said Mercury, thou sluggish beast,
> That here lies senseless, like the corpse deceast,
> The whilst thy kingdom from thy head is rent,
> And thy throne royal with dishonour blent.
> Arise, and do thyself redeem from shame,
> And be avenged on those that breed thy blame.
> Thereat enraged, soon he gan upstart,
> Grinding his teeth, and grating his great heart ;
> And, rousing up himself, for his rough hide
> He gan to reach, but nowhere it espied.
> Therewith he gan full terrible to roar,
> And chaufed at that indignity right sore ;

But, when his crown and sceptre both he wanted,
Lord, how he fumed, and swelled, and raged, and panted,
And threatened death, and thousand deadly dolours,
To them that had purloined his princely honours!
With that, in haste, disrobed as he was,
He towards his own palace forth did pass;
And all the way he rared as he went,
That all the forest with astonishment
Thereof did tremble, and the beasts therein
Fled fast away from that so dreadful din.
At last he came unto his mansion,
Where all the gates he found fast locked anon,
And many warders round about them stood:
With that he rared aloud as he were wood,
That all the palace quaked at the stound,
As if it quite were riven from the ground;
And all within were dead and heartless left,
And the Ape himself, as one whose wits were reft,
Fled here and there, and every corner sought,
To hide himself from his own feared thought.
But the false Fox, when he the Lion heard,
Fled closely forth, straightway of death afrard.
And to the Lion came full lowly creeping,
With feigned face, and watery eyne half weeping,
To excuse his former treason and abusion,
And turning all unto the Ape's confusion;
Nathless[1] the royal beast forbore believing,
But bade him stay at ease till further prieving.[2]
Then, when he saw no entrance to him granted,
Roaring yet louder, that all beasts it daunted,
Upon those gates with force he fiercely flew,
And, rending them in pieces, felly slew
Those warders strange, and all that else he met.
But the Ape, still flying, he nowhere might get:
From room to room, from beam to beam he fled,
All breathless, and for fear now almost dead.
Yet him at last the Lion spied and caught,
And forth with shame unto his judgment brought.
Then all the beasts he caused assembled be,
To hear their doom, and sad ensample see:
The Fox, first author of that treachery,
He did uncase, and then away let fly;
But the Ape's long tail (which then he had) he quite
Cut off, and both ears pared of their height;
Since which all apes but half their ears have left,
And of their tails are utterly bereft.

---

[1] Nevertheless. [2] Proving.

It would not have been possible to take the apologue of the Ape and the Fox for any covert representation of the state of the English court or government at the time when this poem appeared, or even perhaps to discover the veiled likeness of an existing minister or courtier in any of its delineations;—but the satire was certainly not without some strokes that were likely enough to be felt by powerful individuals, and the entire exposition was not calculated to be agreeable to those at the head of affairs. It was probably, therefore, just as fortunate for Spenser that, in whatever humour or with whatever view it was written, it did not see the light till after he had obtained both his grant of land and his pension.

The Fairy Queen was designed by its author to be taken as an allegory—" a continued allegory, or dark conceit," as he calls it in his preliminary Letter to Raleigh "expounding his whole intention in the course of this work." The allegory was even artificial and involved to an unusual degree; for not only was the Fairy Queen, by whom the knights are sent forth upon their adventures, to be understood as meaning Glory in the general intention, but in a more particular sense she was to stand for "the most excellent and glorious person" of Queen Elizabeth; and some other eminent individual of the day appears in like manner to have been shadowed forth in each of the other figures. The most interesting allegory that was ever written carries us along chiefly by making us forget that it is an allegory at all. The charm of Bunyan's Pilgrim's Progress is that all the persons and all the places in it seem real—that Christian, and Evangelist, and Mr. Worldly Wiseman, and Mr. Greatheart, and the Giant Despair, and all the rest, are to our apprehension not shadows, but beings of flesh and blood; and the Slough of Despond, Vanity Fair, Doubting Castle, the Valley of Humiliation, and the Enchanted Ground, all so many actual scenes or localities which we have as we read before us or around us. For the moral lessons that are to be got out of the parable, it must no doubt be considered in another manner; but we speak of the delight it yields as a work of imagination. That is not increased, but impaired, or destroyed, by regarding it as an allegory—just as would be the humour of Don Quixote, or the marvels of the Arabian Nights' Entertainments, by either work being so regarded. In the same manner, whoever would enjoy the Fairy Queen as a poem must forget that it is an

allegory, either single or double, either compound or simple.
Nor in truth is it even much of a story. Neither the personages
that move in it, nor the adventures they meet with, interest us
much. For that matter, the most ordinary novel, or a police
report in a newspaper, may often be much more entertaining.
One fortunate consequence of all this is, that the poem scarcely
loses anything by the design of the author never having been
completed, or its completion at least not having come down to
us. What we have of it is not injured in any material respect
by the want of the rest. This Spenser himself no doubt felt
when he originally gave it to the world in successive portions;—
and it would not have mattered much although of the six Books
he had published the three last before the three first.

These peculiarities—the absence of an interesting story or
concatenation of incidents, and the want of human character and
passion in the personages that carry on the story, such as it is—
are no defects in the Fairy Queen. On the contrary, the poetry
is only left thereby so much the purer. Without calling Spenser
the greatest of all poets, we may still say that his poetry is the
most poetical of all poetry. Other poets are all of them something else as well as poets, and deal in reflection, or reasoning,
or humour, or wit, almost as largely as in the proper product of
the imaginative faculty; his strains alone, in the Fairy Queen,
are poetry, all poetry, and nothing but poetry. It is vision
unrolled after vision, to the sound of endlessly varying music.
The "*shaping* spirit of imagination," considered apart from moral
sensibility—from intensity of passion on the one hand, and
grandeur of conception on the other—certainly never was possessed in the like degree by any other writer; nor has any other
evinced a deeper feeling of all forms of the beautiful; nor have
words ever been made by any other to embody thought with
more wonderful art. On the one hand invention and fancy in
the creation or conception of his thoughts; on the other the most
exquisite sense of beauty, united with a command over all the
resources of language, in their vivid and musical expression—
these are the great distinguishing characteristics of Spenser's
poetry. What of passion is in it lies mostly in the melody of
the verse; but that is often thrilling and subduing in the highest
degree. Its moral tone, also, is very captivating: a soul of
nobleness, gentle and tender as the spirit of its own chivalry,
modulates every cadence.

Spenser's extraordinary faculty of vision-seeing and picture-drawing can fail to strike none of his readers; but he will not be adequately appreciated or enjoyed by those who regard verse either as a non-essential or as a very subordinate element of poetry. Such minds, however, must miss half the charm of all poetry. Not only all that is purely sensuous in poetry must escape them, but likewise all the pleasurable excitement that lies in the harmonious accordance of the musical expression with the informing idea or feeling, and in the additional force or brilliancy that in such inter-union is communicated by the one to the other. All beauty is dependent upon form; other things may often enter into the beautiful, but this is the one thing that can never be dispensed with; all other ingredients, as they must be contained by, so must be controlled by this; and the only thing that standing alone may constitute the beautiful is form or outline. Accordingly, whatever addresses itself to or is suited to gratify the imagination takes this character: it falls into more or less of regularity and measure. Mere passion is of all things the most unmeasured and irregular, naturally the most opposed of all things to form. But in that state it is also wholly unfitted for the purposes of art; before it can become imaginative in any artistic sense it must have put off its original merely volcanic character, and worn itself into something of measure and music. Thus all impassioned composition is essentially melodious, in a higher or lower degree; measured language is the appropriate and natural expression of passion or deep feeling operating artistically in writing or speech. The highest and most perfect kind of measured language is verse; and passion expressing itself in verse is what is properly called poetry. Take away the verse, and in most cases you take away half the poetry, sometimes much more. The verse, in truth, is only one of several things by the aid of which the passion seeks to give itself effective expression, or by which the thought is endowed with additional animation or beauty; nay, it is only one ingredient of the musical expression of the thought or passion. If the verse may be dispensed with, so likewise upon the same principle may every decoration of the sentiment or statement, everything else that would do more than convey the bare fact. Let the experiment be tried, and see how it will answer. Take a single instance. "Immediately through the obscurity a great number of flags were seen to be raised, all richly coloured:" out of these words, no doubt, the reader or hearer might, after some meditation, extract the conception of a very imposing scene. But, although they intimate with sufficient exactness and distinctness the same literal fact, they are nevertheless the deadest prose compared with Milton's glorious words :—

> "All in a moment through the gloom were seen
> Ten thousand banners rise into the air,
> With orient colours waving."

And so it would happen in every other case in which true poetry was divested of its musical expression: a part, and it might be the greater part, of its life, beauty, and effect, would always be lost ; and it would, in truth, cease to be what is distinctively called poetry or song, of which verse is as much one of the necessary constituents as passion or imagination itself. Those who dispute this will never be able to prove more than that their own enjoyment of the sensuous part of poetry, which is really that in which its peculiar character resides, is limited or feeble ; which it may very well be in minds otherwise highly gifted, and even endowed with considerable imaginative power. The feeling of the merely beautiful, however, or of beauty unimpregnated by something of a moral spirit or meaning, is not likely in such minds to be very deep or strong. High art, therefore, is not their proper region, in any of its departments. In poetry they will probably not very greatly admire or enjoy either Spenser or Milton—and perhaps would prefer Paradise Lost in the prose version which Osborne the bookseller in the last century got a gentleman of Oxford to execute for the use of readers to whom the sense was rather obscured by the verse.

Passing over several of the great passages towards the commencement of the poem — such as the description of Queen Lucifera and her Six Counsellors in the Fourth Canto of the First Book, that of the visit of the Witch Duessa to Hell in the Fifth, and that of the Cave of Despair in the Ninth—which are probably more familiarly known to the generality of readers, we will give as our first specimen of the Fairy Queen the escape of the Enchanter Archimago from Braggadoccio and his man Trompart, and the introduction and description of Belphoebe, in the Third Canto of Book Second :—

He stayed not for more bidding, but away
Was sudden vanished out of his sight :
The northern wind his wings did broad display
At his command, and reared him up light,
From off the earth to take his airy flight.
They looked about, but nowhere could espy
Tract of his foot ; then dead through great affright
They both nigh were, and each bade other fly ;
Both fled at once, ne ever back returned eye ;

Till that they came unto a forest green,
In which they shrowd themselves from causeless fear ;
Yet fear them follows still, whereso they been ;
Each trembling leaf and whistling wind they hear
As ghastly bug[1] does greatly them afear ;
Yet both do strive their fearfulness to feign.[2]
At last they heard a horn, that shrilled clear
Throughout the wood, that echoed again,
And made the forest ring, as it would rive in twain.

Eft[3] through the thick they heard one rudely rush,
With noise whereof he from his lofty steed
Down fell to ground, and crept into a bush,
To hide his coward head from dying dreed ;
But Trompart stoutly stayed, to taken heed
Of what might hap.   Eftsoon there stepped fourth
A goodly lady clad in hunter's weed,
That seemed to be a woman of great worth,
And by her stately portance[4] born of heavenly birth.

Her face so fair as flesh it seemed not,
But heavenly pourtrait of bright angels' hue,
Clear as the sky, withouten blame or blot,
Through goodly mixture of complexions due ;
And in her cheeks the vermeil red did shew
Like roses in a bed of lillies shed,
The which ambrosial odours from them threw,
And gazers' sense with double pleasure fed,
Able to heal the sick, and to revive the dead.

In her fair eyes two living lamps did flame,
Kindled above at the heavenly Maker's light,
And darted fiery beams out of the same,
So passing persant and so wondrous bright
That quite bereaved the rash beholder's sight :
In them the blinded god his lustful fire
To kindle oft assayed, but had no might ;

---

[1] Bugbear.   [2] Conceal.   [3] Soon.   [4] Carriage.

For with dread majesty and awful ire
She broke his wanton darts, and quenched base desire.

Her ivory forehead, full of bounty brave,   •
Like a broad table did itself dispread
For Love his lofty triumphs to engrave,
And write the battles of his great godhead :
All good and honour might therein be read,
For there their dwelling was ; and, when she spake,
Sweet words like dropping honey she did shed,
And twixt the pearls and rubins[1] softly brake
A silver sound, that heavenly music seemed to make.

Upon her eyelids many graces sate,
Under the shadow of her even brows,
Working belgardes[2] and amorous retrate ;[3]
And every one her with a grace endows,
And every one with meekness to her bows :
So glorious mirror of celestial grace,
And sovereign monument of mortal vows,
How shall frail pen descrive[4] her heavenly face,
For fear through want of skill her beauty to disgrace ?

So fair, and thousand thousand times more fair,
She seemed, when she presented was to sight ;
And was yclad, for heat of scorching air,
All in a silken camus[5] lilly white,
Purfled[6] upon with many a folded plight,[7]
Which all above besprinkled was throughout
With golden aigulets, that glistened bright,
Like twinkling stars ; and all the skirt about
Was hemmed with golden fringe.

Below her ham her weed[8] did somewhat train ;[9]
And her straight legs most bravely were embailed[10]
In gilden[11] buskins of costly cordwain,[12]
All barred with golden bends, which were entailed[13]
With curious antickes,[14] and full fair aumailed ;[15]
Before they fastened were under her knee
In a rich jewel, and therein entrailed[16]
The ends of all the knots, that none might see
How they within their foldings close enwrapped be.

Like two fair marble pillars they were seen,
Which do the temple of the gods support,
Whom all the people deck with girlonds[1] green,
And honour in their festival resort;
Those same with stately grace and princely port
She taught to tread, when she herself would grace;
But with the woody nymphs when she did sport,
Or when the flying libbard[2] she did chase,
She could them nimbly move, and after fly apace.

And in her hand a sharp boar-spear she held,
And at her back a bow and quiver gay
Stuffed with steel-headed darts, wherewith she quelled
The salvage beasts in her victorious play,
Knit with a golden baldric, which forelay
Athwart her snowy breast, and did divide
Her dainty paps; which, like young fruit in May,
Now little, gan to swell, and, being tied,
Through her thin weed their places only signified.

Her yellow locks, crisped like golden wire,
About her shoulders weren loosely shed,
And, when the wind amongst them did inspire,
They waved like a penon wide dispread,
And low behind her back were scattered;
And, whether art it were or heedless hap,
As through the flowering forest rash she fled,
In her rude hairs sweet flowers themselves did lap,
And flourishing fresh leaves and blossoms did enwrap.

Such as Diana, by the sandy shore
Of swift Eurotas, or on Cynthus green,
Where all the nymphs have her unwares forlore,[3]
Wandereth alone, with bow and arrows keen,
To seek her game; or as that famous queen
Of Amazons, whom Pyrrhus did destroy,
The day that first of Priam she was seen,
Did show herself in great triumphant joy,
To succour the weak state of sad afflicted Troy.

Our next extract shall be part of the Masque of Cupid displayed to Britomart the Fair and Bold, the representative of
Chastity, in the house of the enchanter Busyrane, from the
Twelfth Canto of the Third Book; being the conclusion of the
first-published portion of the poem :—

_____

[1] Garlands.   [2] Leopard.   [3] Forsaken.

All suddenly a stormy whirlwind blew
Throughout the house, that clapped every door,
With which that iron wicket open flew
As it with mighty levers had been tore ;
And forth issued, as on the ready floor
Of some theatre, a grave personage
That in his hand a branch of laurel bore,
With comely haveour and countenance sage,
Yclad in costly garments, fit for tragic stage.

Proceeding to the midst he still did stand,
As if in mind he somewhat had to say,
And, to the vulgar beckoning with his hand,
In sign of silence, as to hear a play,
By lively actions he gan bewray
Some argument of matter passioned ;
Which done, he back retired soft away,
And, passing by, his name discovered,
Ease, on his robe in golden letters cyphered.

The noble maid still standing all this viewed,
And mervelled at his strange intendiment :
With that a joyous fellowship issued
Of minstrels making goodly merriment,
With wanton bards and rhymers impudent ;
All which together sung full cheerfully
A lay of love's delight with sweet consent ;
After whom marched a jolly company,
In manner of a masque, enranged orderly.

The whiles a most delicious harmony
In full strange notes was sweetly heard to sound,
That the rare sweetness of the melody
The feeble senses wholly did confound,
And the frail soul in deep delight nigh drowned ;
And, when it ceased, shrill trumpets loud did bray,
That their report did far away rebound ;
And, when they ceased, it gan again to play,
The whiles the masquers marched forth in trim array.

The first was Fancy, like a lovely boy,
Of rare aspect, and beauty without peer,
Matchable either to that imp of Troy
Whom Jove did love, and chose his cup to bear,
Or that same dainty lad which was so dear
To great Alcides, that whenas he died
He wailed womanlike with many a tear,
And every wood and every valley wide
He filled with Hylas' name ; the nymphs eke Hylas cried.

His garment neither was of silk nor say,
But painted plumes in goodly order dight,
Like as the sunburnt Indians do array
Their tawny bodies in their proudest plight:
As those same plumes so seemed he vain and light,
That by his gait might easily appear;
For still he fared¹ as dancing in delight,
And in his hand a windy fan did bear,
That in the idle air he moved still here and there.

And him beside marched amorous Desire,
Who seemed of riper years than the other swain,
Yet was that other swain this elder's sire,
And gave him being, common to them twain:
His garment was disguised very vain,
And his embroidered bonnet sat awry;
'Twixt both his hands few sparks he close did strain,
Which still he blew and kindled busily,
That soon they life conceived, and forth in flames did fly.

Next after him went Doubt, who was yclad
In a discoloured coat of strange disguise,
That at his back a broad capuccio had,
And sleeves dependent Albanese-wise;
He looked askew with his mistrustful eyes,
And nicely trod, as thorns lay in his way,
Or that the floor to shrink he did avize;²
And on a broken reed he still did stay
His feeble steps, which shrunk when hard thereon he lay.

With him went Danger, clothed in ragged weed
Made of bear's skin, that him more dreadful made;
Yet his own face was dreadful, ne did need
Strange horror to deform his grisly shade:
A net in the one hand, and a rusty blade
In the other was, this mischief, that mishap;
With the one his foes he threatened to invade,
With the other he his friends meant to enwrap;
For whom he could not kill he practised to entrap.

Next him was Fear, all armed from top to toe,
Yet thought himself not safe enough thereby,
But feared each shadow moving to or fro;
And his own arms when glittering he did spy,
Or clashing heard, he fast away did fly,
As ashes pale of hue, and winged-heeled;
And evermore on Danger fixed his eye,

---

¹ Moved forward.   ² Think.

Gainst whom he always bent a brazen shield,
Which his right hand unarmed fearfully did wield.

With him went Hope in rank, a handsome maid,
Of cheerful look, and lovely to behold ;
In silken samite[1] she was light arrayed,
And her fair locks were woven up in gold :
She always smiled, and in her hand did hold
An holy-water-sprinkle, dipped in dew,
With which she sprinkled favours manifold
On whom she list, and did great liking shew,
Great liking unto many, but true love to few.

And after them Dissemblance and Suspect
Marched in one rank, yet an unequal pair ;
For she was gentle and of mild aspect,
Courteous to all, and seeming debonair,
Goodly adorned, and exceeding fair ;
Yet was that all but painted and purloined,
And her bright brows were decked with borrowed hair ;
Her deeds were forged, and her words false-coined :
And always in her hand two clews of silk she twined :

But he was foul, ill-favoured, and grim,
Under his eyebrows looking still askance ;
And, ever as Dissemblance laughed on him,
He lowered on her with dangerous eye-glance,
Showing his nature in his countenance ;
His rolling eyes did never rest in place,
But walked each where for fear of hid mischance,
Holding a lattice still before his face,
Through which he still did peep as forward he did pace.

Next him went Grief and Fury, matched yfere ;[2]
Grief all in sable sorrowfully clad,
Down hanging his dull head with heavy cheer,
Yet inly being more than seeming sad ;
A pair of pincers in his hand he had,
With which he pinched many to the heart,
That from thenceforth a wretched life they lad[3]
In wilful languor and consuming smart,
Dying each day with inward wounds of Dolour's dart.

But Fury was full ill apparelled
In rags, that naked nigh she did appear,
With ghastly looks and dreadful drearihead ;
For from her back her garments she did tear,

---

[1] Satin. [2] Together. [3] Led.

And from her head oft rent her snarled[1] hair:
In her right hand a firebrand she did toss
About her head ; still running here and there,
As a dismayed deer in chace embost,[2]
Forgetful of his safety, hath his right way lost.

After them went Displeasure and Pleasance ;
He looking lumpish and full sullen sad,
And hanging down his heavy countenance ;
She cheerful, fresh, and full of joyance glad,
As if no sorrow she ne felt ne drad,[3]
That evil-matched pair they seemed to be :
An angry wasp the one in a vial had,
The other in her's an honey lady-bee.
Thus marched these six couples forth in fair degree.

After all these there marched a most fair dame,
Led of two grisly villains ; the one Despite,
The other cleped[4] Cruelty by name :
She, doleful lady, like a dreary sprite
Called by strong charms out of eternal night,
Had Death's own image figured in her face,
Full of sad signs, fearful to living sight ;
Yet in that horror she wed a seemly grace,
And with her feeble feet did move a comely pace.

Her breast all naked, as nett ivory
Without adorn of gold or silver bright,
Wherewith the craftsman wonts it beautify,
Of her due honour was despoiled quite,
And a wide wound therein (O rueful sight !)
Entrenched deep with knife accursed keen,
Yet freshly bleeding forth[5] her fainting sprite,
(The work of cruel hand) was to be seen,
That dyed in sanguine red her skin all snowy clean.

At that wide orifice her trembling heart
Was drawn forth, and in silver basin laid,
Quite through transfixed with a deadly dart,
And in her blood yet steaming fresh embayed ;[6]
And those two villains (which her steps upstayed,
When her weak feet could scarcely her sustain,
And fading vital powers gan to fade[7])
Her forward still with torture did constrain,
And ever more increased her consuming pain.

----

1 Entangled, knotted.   2 Hard run and wearied out.
3 Dreaded.   4 Called.   5 Out of, forth from.   6 Bathed.
7 It may be doubted if this be the right word. Perhaps it should be
" gan to vade "—that is, to pass away.

Next after her the winged God himself
Came riding on a lion ravenous,
Taught to obey the menage of that elf,
That man and beast with power imperious
Subdueth to his kingdom tyrannous:
His blindfold eyes he bade awhile unbind,
That his proud spoil, of that same dolorous
Fair dame, he might behold in perfect kind;
Which seen, he much rejoiced in his cruel mind.

Of which full proud, himself uprearing high,
He looked round about with stern disdain,
And did survey his goodly company,
And marshalled the evil-ordered train;
With that the darts which his right hand did strain
Full dreadfully he shook, that all did quake,
And clapped on high his coloured wings twain,
That all his meany[1] it afraid did make;
Tho,[2] blinding him again, his way he forth did take.

Behind him was Reproach, Repentance, Shame;
Reproach the first, Shame next, Repent behind:
Repentance feeble, sorrowful, and lame;
Reproach despiteful, careless, and unkind;
Shame most ill-favoured, bestial, and blind:
Shame loured, Repentance sighed, Reproach did scold;
Reproach sharp stings, Repentance whips entwined,
Shame burning brand-irons in her hand did hold:
All three to each unlike, yet all made in one mould.

And after them a rude confused route
Of persons flocked, whose names is hard to read:
Amongst them was stern Strife, and Anger stout,
Unquiet Care, and fond Unthriftihead,
Lewd Loss of Time, and Sorrow seeming-dead,
Inconstant Change, and false Disloyalty,
Consuming Riotise, and guilty Dread
Of heavenly vengeance, faint Infirmity,
Vile Poverty, and, lastly, Death with Infamy.

There were full many moe[3] like maladies,
Whose names and natures I note readen[4] well;
So many moe as there be fantasies
In wavering women's wit, that none can tell,
Or pains in love, or punishments in hell;
All which disguised marched in masquing wise
About the chamber by the damozell,

---

[1] Company, attendants.   [2] Then.   [3] More.
[4] Know not (wot not) to read.

> And then returned, having marched thrice,
> Into the inner room, from whence they first did rise.

A volume of poetry such as this, Spenser might fitly, and with some pride in the worth of the offering, as well as " in all humility, dedicate, present, and consecrate, to the Most High, Mighty, and Magnificent Empress, Elizabeth, to live with the eternity of her fame." The latter Books of the Fairy Queen have less continuity of splendour than the three first; but, besides innumerable single stanzas and short passages of exquisite beauty, they contain not a few pictures on a more extended canvas, which must be reckoned among the most remarkable in the work. Among others may be mentioned those of the Temple of Venus in the Tenth, and of the gathering of the rivers at the marriage of the Thames and the Medway, in the Eleventh Canto of the Fourth Book; those of the night spent by Sir Caledon among the shepherds in the Ninth, and of the Dance of the Graces in the Tenth Canto of Book Fifth; and that of the procession of the Seasons in the second of the Two Cantos of Mutability. But, passing over these more brilliant displays of an inventive and florid fancy, we will select, as our sample of this portion of the poem, one of its more soberly coloured passages, in which, nevertheless, there may perhaps be thought to be as much of "the vision and the faculty divine," though otherwise exercised, as in any of those we have yet quoted. The following, from the Second Canto of the Fifth Book, might seem to be a satire written in our own day on the folly and madness of seventy years ago, and it is difficult to believe that it was published two centuries before the events which it so strikingly prefigures :—

> There they beheld a mighty giant stand
> Upon a rock, and holding forth on high
> An huge great pair of balance in his hand,
> With which he boasted, in his surquedry,[1]
> That all the world he would weigh equally,
> If aught be had the same to counterpoise:
> For want whereof he weighed vanity,
> And filled his balance full of idle toys;
> Yet was admired much of fools, women, and boys.

---

[1] Pride, presumption.

He said that he would all the earth uptake,
And all the sea, divided each from either;
So would he of the fire one balance make,
And one of the air, without or wind or weather;
Then would he balance heaven and hell together,
And all that did within them all contain,
Of all whose weight he would not miss a feather;
And look, what surplus did of each remain,
He would to his own part restore the same again.

For why, he said, they all unequal were;
And had encroached upon other's share;
Like as the sea (which plain he showed there)
Had worn the earth; so did the fire the air;
So all the rest did other's parts impair;
And so were realms and nations run awry;
All which he undertook for to repair,
In sort as they were formed anciently,
And all things would reduce unto equality.

Therefore the vulgar did about him flock,
And cluster thick unto his leasings vain,
Like foolish flies about an honey-crock,
In hope by him great benefit to gain,
And uncontrolled freedom to obtain.
All which when Artegal did see, and hear
How he misled the simple people's train,
In 'sdainful wise he drew unto him near,
And thus unto him spake, without regard or fear:

" Thou that presum'st to weigh the world anew,
And all things to an equal to restore,
Instead of right, meseems, great wrong dost shew,
And far above thy force's pitch to soar:
For, ere thou limit what is less or more
In every thing, thou oughtest first to know
What was the poise of every part of yore,
And look then how much it doth overflow
Or fail thereof; so much is more than just, I trow.

" For at the first they all created were
In goodly measure by their Maker's might,
And weighed out in balances so near
That not a dram was missing of their right;
The earth was in the middle centre pight,[1]
In which it doth immovable abide,
Hemmed in with waters like a wall in sight,[2]

Pitched, fixed.   [2] Perhaps, site.

And they with air, that not a drop can slide ;
All which the heavens contain, and in their course guide.

" Such heavenly justice doth among them reign,
That every one do know their certain bound,
In which they do these many years remain,
And 'mongst them all no change hath yet been found ;
But, if thou now should'st weigh them new in pound,
We are not sure they would so long remain ;
All change is perilous, and all chance unsound ;
Therefore leave off to weigh them all again,
Till we may be assured they shall their course retain."

" Thou foolish elf," said then the Giant wroth,
" See'st not how badly all things present be,
And each estate quite out of order goth ?
The sea itself dost thou not plainly see
Encroach upon the land there under thee ?
And the earth itself, how daily it's increased
By all that dying to it turned be ?
Were it not good that wrong were then surceased,
And from the most that some were given to the least ?

" Therefore I will throw down these mountains high,
And make them level with the lowly plain ;
These towering rocks, which reach unto the sky,
I will thrust down into the deepest main,
And, as they were, them equalise again.
Tyrants, that make men subject to their law,
I will suppress, that they no more may reign,
And lordings curb that commons over-awe,
And all the wealth of rich men to the poor will draw."

" Of things unseen how canst thou deem aright,"
Then answered the righteous Artegal,
" Sith thou misdeem'st so much of things in sight ?
What though the sea with waves continual
Do eat the earth, it is no more at all,
Ne is the earth the less or loseth aught ;
For whatsoever from one place doth fall,
Is with the tide unto another brought ;
For there is nothing lost that may be found if sought.

" Likewise the earth is not augmented more
By all that dying unto it do fade ;
For of the earth they formed were of yore :
However gay their blossom or their blade
Do flourish now, they into dust shall vade ;[1]

---

[1] Pass away.

What wrong then is it if that when they die
They turn to that whereof they first were made?
All in the power of their great Maker lie;
All creatures must obey the voice of the Most High.

" They live, they die, like as he doth ordain,
Ne ever any asketh reason why.
The hills do not the lowly dales disdain;
The dales do not the lofty hills envy.
He maketh kings to sit in sovereignty;
He maketh subjects to their power obey;
He pulleth down, he setteth up on high;
He gives to this, from that he takes away;
For all we have is his; what he list do he may.

" Whatever thing is done by him is done,
Ne any may his mighty will withstand;
Ne any may his sovereign power shun,
Ne loose that he hath bound with stedfast band;
In vain, therefore, dost thou now take in hand
To call to count, or weigh his works anew,
Whose counsels' depth thou canst not understand,
Sith of things subject to thy daily view
Thou dost not know the causes nor their courses due.

" For take thy balance, if thou be so wise,
And weigh the wind that under heaven doth blow;
Or weigh the light that in the east doth rise;
Or weigh the thought that from man's mind doth flow:
But, if the weight of these thou canst not show,
Weigh but one word which from thy lips doth fall:
For how canst thou those greater secrets know,
That dost not know the least thing of them all?
Ill can he rule the great that cannot reach the small."

Therewith the Giant, much abashed, said,
That he of little things made reckoning light;
Yet the least word that ever could be laid
Within his balance he could weigh aright.
" Which is," said he, " more heavy, then, in weight,
The right or wrong, the false or else the true?"
He answered that he would try it straight;
So he the words into his balance threw,
But straight the winged words out of his balance flew.

Wroth waxed he then, and said that words were light,
Ne could within his balance well abide;
But he could justly weigh the wrong or right.
" Well, then," said Artegal, " let it be tried;
First in one balance set the true aside."

He did so first, and then the false he laid
In the other scale; but still it down did slide,
And by no mean could in the weight be stayed;
For by no means the false will with the truth be weighed.

" Now take the right likewise," said Artegale,
" And counterpoise the same with so much wrong."
So first the right he put into one scale,
And then the Giant strove, with puissance strong,
To fill the other scale with so much wrong;
But all the wrongs that he therein could lay
Might it not poise; yet did he labour long,
And swat, and chaufed, and proved every way;
Yet all the wrongs could not a little right downweigh.

Which when he saw he greatly grew in rage,
And almost would his balances have broken;
But Artegal him fairly gan assuage,
And said, " Be not upon thy balance wroken,[1]
For they do nought but right or wrong betoken;
But in the mind the doom of right must be;
And so likewise of words, the which be spoken,
The ear must be the balance to decree
And judge whether with truth or falsehood they agree.

" But set the truth and set the right aside,
For they with wrong or falsehood will not fare,
And put two wrongs together to be tried,
Or else two falses, of each equal share,
And then together do them both compare;
For truth is one, and right is ever one."
So did he, and then plain it did appear
Whether of them the greater were attone;[2]
But right sat in the middest of the beam alone.

But he the right from thence did thrust away,
For it was not the right which he did seek;
But rather strove extremities to weigh,
The one to diminish, the other for to eke,
For of the mean he greatly did mislike;[3]
Whom when so lewdly minded Talus found,
Approaching nigh unto him cheek by cheek,
He shouldered him from off the higher ground,
And, down the rock him throwing, in the sea him drowned.

Like as a ship, whom cruel tempest drives
Upon a rock with horrible dismay,

---

[1] Revenged.   [2] Taken all together.   [3] Mislike.

Her shattered ribs in thousand pieces rives,
And, spoiling all her gears and goodly ray,[1]
Does make herself misfortune's piteous prey;
So down the cliff the wretched Giant tumbled;
His battered balances in pieces lay,
His timbered bones all broken rudely rumbled:
So was the high-aspiring with huge ruin humbled.

That when the people, which had thereabout
Long waited, saw his sudden desolation,
They gan[2] together in tumultuous rout,
And mutining to stir up civil faction,[3]
For certain loss of so great expectation;
For well they hoped to have got great good
And wondrous riches by his innovation;
Therefore, resolving to revenge his blood,
They rose in arms, and all in battle order stood.

In old Greece and Rome the Poet was regarded as a species of
Prophet, and called by the same name; both were held to be
alike divinely inspired; but there are not many unveilings of
the distant future in poetry so remarkable as this anticipation
and refutation of the Liberty and Equality philosophism of the
end of the eighteenth century in the end of the sixteenth. Nor
has the kernel of that false philosophy ever perhaps been so
acutely detected as it is in those verses, by the exposure, first, of
the assumption involved in the original notion that equality is
anywhere a law or principle of nature; secondly, of the impossibility of either establishing true equality, or even of ascertain-
ing its existence, by such rude, superficial, almost mechanical
methods as human legislation has alone at its command. The
essence or reality of things will not be weighed in any scales
which its hand can hold.

OTHER ELIZABETHAN POETRY.

In the six or seven years from 1590 to 1596, what a world of
wealth had thus been added to our poetry by Spenser alone!
what a different thing from what it was before had the English
language been made by his writings to natives, to foreigners, to

---

[1] Array.   [2] Perhaps misprint for "ran."
[3] The reading of this line may be doubted.

all posterity! But England was now a land of song, and the busiest and most productive age of our poetical literature had fairly commenced. What are commonly called the minor poets of the Elizabethan age are to be counted by hundreds, and few of them are altogether without merit. If they have nothing else, the least gifted of them have at least something of the freshness and airiness of that balmy morn, some tones caught from their greater contemporaries, some echoes of the spirit of music that then filled the universal air. For the most part the minor Elizabethan poetry is remarkable for ingenuity and elaboration, often carried to the length of quaintness, both in the thought and the expression; but, if there be more in it of art than of nature, the art is still that of a high school, and always consists in something more than the mere disguising of prose in the dress of poetry. If it is sometimes unnatural, it is at least very seldom simply insipid, like much of the well-sounding verse of more recent eras. The writers are always in earnest, whether with their nature or their art; they never write from no impulse, and with no object except that of stringing commonplaces into rhyme or rhythm; even when it is most absurd, what they produce is still fanciful, or at the least fantastical. The breath of some sort of life or other is almost always in it. The poorest of it is distinguished from prose by something more than the mere sound.

WARNER.

The three authors of the poems of most pretension, with the exception of the Fairy Queen, that appeared during the period now under review, are Warner, Drayton, and Daniel. William Warner is supposed to have been born about the year 1558; he died in 1609. He has told us himself (in his Eleventh Book, chapter 62), that his birthplace was London, and that his father was one of those who sailed with Chancellor to Muscovy, in 1555: this, he says, was before he himself was born. Warner's own profession was the not particularly poetical one of an attorney of the Common Pleas. According to Anthony Wood, who makes him to have been a Warwickshire man, he had before 1586 written several pieces of verse, "whereby his name was cried up among the minor poets;" but this is probably a mistake; none of this early poetry imputed to Warner is now known to

exist; and in the Preface to his Albion's England, he seems to
intimate that that was his first performance in verse. "Written,"
he says, "have I already in prose, allowed [that is, with the
approbation] of some; and now offer I verse, attending indifferent
censures" [impartial judgments]. In his Dedication to Henry
Carey, the first Lord Hunsdon, he speaks of a former book, which
he had dedicated to the son of that Lord—"To him that from
your honour deriveth his birth." This, we suppose, must be his
prose work entitled Syrinx, or a Sevenfold History, pleasant
and profitable, comical and tragical, of which the only edition
known to exist is dated 1597, but which was licensed in 1584,
and was probably first printed about that time. In the Dedication to his poem he explains the meaning of the title, which is
not very obvious: "This our whole island," he observes, "anciently called Britain, but more anciently Albion, presently
containing two kingdoms, England and Scotland, is cause (right
honourable) that, to distinguish the former, whose only occur-
rents [occurrences] I abridge from our history, I entitle this my
book Albion's England." Albion's England first appeared, in
thirteen Books, in 1586; and was reprinted in 1589, in 1592,
in 1596, in 1597, and in 1602. In 1606 the author added a
Continuance, or continuation, in three Books; and the whole
work was republished (without, however, the last three Books
having been actually reprinted) in 1612. In this last edition
it is described on the title-page as "now revised, and newly
enlarged [by the author] a little before his death." It thus
appears that, so long as its popularity lasted, Albion's England
was one of the most popular long poems ever written. But that
was only for about twenty years: although the early portion of
it had in less than that time gone through half a dozen editions,
the Continuation, published in 1606, sold so indifferently that
enough of the impression still remained to complete the book
when the whole was republished in 1612, and after that no other
edition was ever called for, till the poem was reprinted in
Chalmers's collection in 1810. The entire neglect into which
it so soon fell, from the height of celebrity and popular favour,
was probably brought about by various causes. Warner, according to Anthony Wood, was ranked by his contemporaries
on a level with Spenser, and they were called the Homer and
Virgil of their age. If he and Spenser were ever equally
admired, it must have been by very different classes of readers.

Albion's England is undoubtedly a work of very remarkable
talent of its kind.   It is in form a history of England, or Southern
Britain, from the Deluge to the reign of James I., but may fairly
be said to be, as the title-page of the last edition describes it,
"not barren in variety of inventive intermixtures." Or, to use
the author's own words in his Preface, he certainly, as he hopes,
has no great occasion to fear that he has grossly failed "in verity,
brevity, invention, and variety, profitable, pathetical, pithy, and
pleasant." In fact, it is one of the liveliest and most amusing
poems ever written.   Every striking event or legend that the
old chronicles afford is seized hold of, and related always clearly,
often with very considerable spirit and animation.   But it is far
from being a mere compilation ; several of the narratives are not
to be found anywhere else, and a large proportion of the matter
is Warner's own, in every sense of the word.   In this, as well
as in other respects, it has greatly the advantage over the Mirror
for Magistrates, as a rival to which work it was perhaps originally produced, and with the popularity of which it could
scarcely fail considerably to interfere.   Though a long poem
(not much under 10,000 verses), it is still a much less ponderous
work than the Mirror, absolutely as well as specifically.   Its
variety, though not obtained by any very artificial method, is
infinite : not only are the stories it selects, unlike those in the
Mirror, generally of a merry cast, and much more briefly and
smartly told, but the reader is never kept long even on the same
track or ground : all subjects, all departments of human knowledge or speculation, from theology down to common arithmetic,
are intermixed, or rather interlaced, with the histories and
legends in the most extraordinary manner.   The verse is the
favourite fourteen-syllable line of that age, the same in reality
with that which has in modern times been commonly divided
into two lines, the first of eight, the second of six syllables, and
which in that form is still most generally used for short compositions in verse, more especially for those of a narrative or otherwise popular character.   What Warner was chiefly admired for
in his own day was his style.   Meres in his Wit's Treasury
mentions him as one of those by whom the English tongue in
that age had been "mightily enriched, and gorgeously invested
in rare ornaments and resplendent habiliments."   And for
fluency, combined with precision and economy of diction,
Warner is probably unrivalled among the writers of English

verse. We do not know whether his professional studies and habits may have contributed to give this character to his style; but, if the poetry of attorneys be apt to take this curt, direct, lucid, and at the same time flowing shape, it is a pity that we had not a little more of it. His command of the vulgar tongue, in particular, is wonderful. This indeed is perhaps his most remarkable poetical characteristic; and the tone which was thus given to his poem (being no doubt that of his own mind) may be conjectured to have been in great part the source both of its immense popularity for a time, and of the neglect and oblivion into which it was afterwards allowed to drop. That Warner's poetry and that of Spenser could have ever come in one another's way is impossible. Albion's England must from the first have been a book rather for the many than the few,—for the kitchen rather than the hall; its spirit is not, what it has been sometimes called, merely naive, but essentially coarse and vulgar. We do not allude so much to any particular abundance of warm description, or freedom of language, as to the low note on which the general strain of the composition is pitched. With all its force and vivacity, and even no want of fancy, at times, and graphic descriptive power, it is poetry with as little of high imagination in it as any that was ever written. Warner's is only at the most a capital poetical business style. Its positive offences, however, in the way of broadness and indecency of allusion are also very considerable—and are more pervading, run more through its whole texture, than the same thing will be found to do in the writing of any other eminent poet of that time. When the poem was first produced, the middle classes in general, for whom we must suppose it to have been principally intended, were still unrefined enough not to be scared or offended by this grossness, but rather to relish and enjoy it; this is proved by the eagerness with which so many editions were called for in so short a time. We do not believe that, as has been said, "Its publication was at one time interdicted by the Star-Chamber for no other reason, that can now be assigned, but that it contains some love-stories more simply than delicately related."* The prohibition by the Star-Chamber was of the first edition, and apparently before it had been published; and the ground seems to have been merely the invasion of the property of one printer by another (in whose house a seizure of the copies he had thrown

* Campbell, Specimens, p. 71 (edit. of 1844).

off was made by the wardens of the Stationers' Company, he, it is stated, having been forbidden to print the book both by the Archbishop of Canterbury and by the wardens, and his doing so being also contrary to the late decrees of the Honourable Court of Star-Chamber).* If the book had been attempted to be suppressed for the nakedness of some of the descriptions, it probably would not have appeared at all—whereas it was given to the world that same year from the press of another printer, and·was afterwards freely multiplied, as we have seen, in a rapid succession of new editions. But by the first years of the next century a new generation had grown up—and even among the most numerous class of readers a change of manners had taken place which made it impossible that such a work as Albion's England should retain the favour it had once enjoyed. It was probably now universally voted vulgar, and held to have been suitable only for a more barbarous age. Nevertheless, the poem, as we have said, has very remarkable merit in some respects, and many passages, or rather portions of passages, in it may still be read with pleasure. It is also in the highest degree curious both as a repository of our old language, and for many notices of the manners and customs of our ancestors which are scattered up and down in it. All that is commonly known of Warner is from the story of Argentile and Curan, which has been reprinted from his Fourth Book by Mrs. Cooper in The Muses' Library (1738), and by Percy in his Reliques, and that of The Patient Countess, which Percy has also given from his Eighth Book. We shall endeavour to select a few such short passages as may convey a fair notion of what the work contains and of the manner in which it is executed. It is difficult, for the reason that has been stated above, to find many pages, at least in the more interesting parts of the poem, that can be transcribed entire.

The following passage from the Third Book, being the conclusion of the 17th Chapter, is a specimen of Warner's very neatest style of narration.—He has related Cæsar's victory over the Britons, which he says was won with difficulty, the conquest of the country having been only accomplished through the submission of that "traitorous knight, the Earl of London," whose disloyal example in yielding his charge and city to the foe was followed by the other cities; and then he winds up thus :—

* See Ritson's Bibliographia Poetica, p. 383, note.

But he, that won in every war, at Rome in civil robe
Was stabbed to death : so certainly is underneath this globe ;
The good are envied of the bad, and glory finds disdain,
And people are in constancy as April is in rain ;
Whereof, amidst our serious pen, this fable entertain :—
    An Ass, an Old Man, and a Boy did through the city pass ;
And, whilst the wanton Boy did ride, the[1] Old Man led the Ass.
See yonder doting fool, said folk, that crawleth scarce for age,
Doth set the boy upon his ass, and makes himself his page.
Anon the blamed Boy alights, and lets the Old Man ride,
And, as the Old Man did before, the Boy the Ass did guide.
But, passing so, the people then did much the Old Man blame,
And told him, Churl, thy limbs be tough ; let ride the boy, for shame.
The fault thus found, both Man and Boy did back the ass and ride ;
Then that the ass was over-charged each man that met them cried.
Now both alight and go on foot, and lead the empty beast ;
But then the people laugh, and say that one might ride at least.
The Old Man, seeing by no ways he could the people please,
Not blameless then, did drive the ass and drown him in the seas.
Thus, whilst we be, it will not be that any pleaseth all ;
Else had been wanting, worthily, the noble Cæsar's fall.

The end of Richard the Third, in the Sixth Book (Chapter
26th), is given with much spirit :—

Now Richard heard that Richmond was assisted, and on shore,
And like unkenneled Cerberus the crooked tyrant swore,
And all complexions act at once confusedly in him ;
He studieth, striketh, threats, entreats, and looketh mildly grim ;
Mistrustfully he trusteth, and he dreadingly doth[2] dare,
And forty passions in a trice in him consort and square.
But when, by his convented force, his foes increased more,
He hastened battle, finding his corrival apt therefore.
    When Richmond orderly in all had battailed his aid,
Enringed by his compliers, their cheerful leader said :—
Now is the time and place, sweet friends, and we the persons lo
That must give England breath, or else unbreathe for her must we.
No tyranny is fabled, and no tyrant was indeed,
Worse than our foe, whose works will act my words if well he speed.
For ills[3] to ills superlative are easily entiteal,
But entertain amendment as the Gergesites did Christ.

---

[1] In the printed copy "a." The edition before us, that of 1612, abounds
with typographical errata.
[2] There can be no question that this is the true word, which is misprinted
"did" in the edition before me.
[3] Misprinted "ill."

Be valiant then ; he biddeth so that would not be outbid
For courage, yet shall honour him, though base, that better did.
I am right heir Lancastrian, he in York's destroyed right
Usurpeth ; but, through either source,[1] for neither claim I fight,
But for our country's long-lacked weal, for England's peace, I war ;
Wherein He speed us, unto whom I all events refer.

Meanwhile had furious Richard set his armies in array,
And then, with looks even like himself, this or the like did say :—
Why, lads ? shall yonder Welshman, with his stragglers, overmatch ?
Disdain ye not such rivals, and defer ye their dispatch ?
Shall Tudor from Plantagenet the crown by craking snatch ?
Know Richard's very thoughts (he touched the diadem he wore)
He metal of this metal : then believe I love it more
Than that for other law than life to supersede my claim ;
And lesser must not be his plea that counterpleads the same.

The weapons overtook his words, and blows they bravely change,
When like a lion, thirsting blood, did moody Richard range,
And made large slaughters where he went, till Richmond be espied,
Whom singling, after doubtful swords, the valorous tyrant died.

Others of Shakespeare's historical or legendary subjects are
also in Albion's England; particularly the story of Lear, and
that of Macbeth. In the former, which is in the Third Book
(Chapter 14), the following well-turned lines occur :—

His aged eyes pour out their tears, when, holding up his hands,
He said, O God ! whoso thou art that my good hap withstands,
Prolong not life, defer not death ; my self I overlive
When those that owe to me their lives to me my death would give.
Thou town, whose walls rose of my wealth, stand evermore to tell
Thy founder's fall, and warn that none do fall as Letr fell.
Did none affy in friends ; for say, His children wrought his wrack ;
Yea, those that were to him most dear did loath and let him lack.
Cordelia, well Cordelia said, she loved as a child ;
But sweeter words we seek than sooth, and so are men beguiled.
She only rests untried yet ; but what may I expect
From her, to whom I nothing gave, when these do me reject ?
Then die : nay, try ; the rule may fail, and nature may ascend ;
Nor are they ever surest friends on whom we most do spend.

The three last books, forming the continuation published in
1606, are occupied with the history of the Scots and Welsh; and
the story of Macbeth is told in the Fifteenth Book (Chapter 94).
Shakespeare's witches (as they are commonly called) are here
designated the " three fairies," and also " the weird-elves."

---

[1] This is the only reading like sense we can make out of " through either's
own," which is the nonsense of the edition before us.

There are occasionally touches of true pathos in Warner, and one great merit which he has is, that his love of brevity generally prevents him from spoiling any stroke of this kind by multiplying words and images with the view of heightening the effect, as many of his contemporaries are prone to do.   His picture of Fair Rosamond in the hands of Queen Eleanor is very touching:—

> Fair Rosamund, surprised thus ere thus she did expect,
> Fell on her humble knees, and did her fearful hands erect :
> She blushed out beauty, whilst the tears did wash her pleasing face,
> And begged pardon, meriting no less of common grace.
> So far, forsooth, as in me lay, I did, quoth she, withstand ;
> But what may not so great a king by means or force command ?
> And dar'st thou, minion, quoth the Queen, thus article to me ?
> . . . .
> With that she dashed her on the lips, so dyed double red :
> Hard was the heart that gave the blow ; soft were those lips that bled.
> Then forced she her to swallow down, prepared for that intent,
> A poisoned potion . . . . .

But we must also give an example or two of the eloquence of another kind with which the poem more abounds.   Much of it is in the style of the following curious passage (from Book IX. Chap. 47):—

> The younger of these widows (for they both had thrice been so)
> Trots to the elder's cottage, hers but little distance fro :
> There, cowering o'er two sticks across, burnt at a smokey stock,
> They chat how young men them in youth, and they did young men mock ;
> And how since threescore years ago (they aged fourscore now)
> Men, women, and the world were changed in all, they knew not how.
> When we were maids, quoth the one of them, was no such new-found
>   pride ;
> Yet served I gentles, seeing store of dainty girls beside.
> Then wore they shoes of ease ; now of an inch broad, corked high :
> Black karsey stockings ; worsted now, yea silk of youthful'st dye :
> Garters of lists ; but now of silk, some edged deep with gold :
> With costlier toys—for coarser turns than used, perhaps, of old.
> Fringed and embroidered petticoats now beg : but heard you named,
> Till now of late, busks, periwigs, masks, plumes of feathers framed,
> Supporters, pooters,[1] fardingales above the loins to wear ?
> . . . .
> Some wives, grey headed, shame not locks of youthful borrowed hair ;
> Some, tiring art, attire their heads with only tresses bare.

---

[1] Chalmers has "posters."

Some (grosser pride than which, think I, no passed age might shame)
By art abusing nature, beads of antick't hair do frame.
Once lacked each foresaid term,[1] because was lacking once the toy ;
And, lacked we all those toys and terms, it were no grief but joy :
But, lawful were it some to such, should all alike be coy ?
Now dwells each drossel in her glass : when I was young, I wot,
On holydays (for seldom else such idle times we got)
A tub or pail of water clear stood us instead of glass.

My parents they were wealthy, and myself in wanton youth
Was fair enough, but proud enough, so fool enough in truth.
I might have had good husbands, which my destiny withstood :
Of three now dead (all grief is dry, gossip, this ale is good)
In faith not one of them was so ; for by this drink I swear
(Requarrelling the cup) we—and her lips imparted were
When the other beldam, great with chat (for talkative be cups)
The former's prate, not worth the while, thus fondly interrupts :—
When I, quoth she, the country left to be a London lass,
I was not fairer than myself believed fair I was.
Good God! how formal, prankt, and pert became I in a trice,
As if unto the place it were a nature to be nice.

And so the dialogue proceeds, though with more spirit than
refinement, for a couple of pages farther. In another place
(Book XIV. Chap. 91) a Lar, or Elf, is introduced inveighing
against the decay of ancient manners, in the following strain :—

To farmers came I, that at least their loaf and cheese once freed
For all would eat, but found themselves the parings now to need ;
So do their landlords rack their rents : though in the manor place
Scarce smoked a chimney, yet did smoke perplex me in strange case.
I saw the chimneys cleared of fire, where ne'ertheless it smoked
So bitterly as one not used to like it might have choked.
But, when I saw it did proceed from nostrils and from throats
Of ladies, lords, and silly grooms, not burning skins nor coats,
Great Belzebub! thought I, can all spit fire as well as thine?
Or where am I ? It cannot be under the torrid line.
My fellow Incubus . . . . . .

Did put me by that fear, and said it was an Indian weed,
That fumed away more wealth than would a many thousands feed.
Freed of that fear, the novelty of coaches scathed me so,
As from their drifts and cluttering I knew not where to go.
These also work, quoth Incubus, to our avail, for why?
They tend to idle pride, and to inhospitality.
With that I, comforted, did then peep into every one,
And of my old acquaintances spied many a country Joan,

---

[1] Chalmers has " Once starching lacked the term."

Whose fathers drove the dung-cart, though the daughters now will none.
I know when prelates and the peers had fair attendance on
By gentlemen and yeomanry ; but that fair world is gone :
For most, like John, hurry with pedanties two or three,
Yet all go down the wind, save those that hospitalious be.
Greatest ladies, with their women, on their palfreys mounted fair,
Went through the streets, well waited on, their artless faces bare,
Which now in coaches scorn to be saluted of the air.
I knew when men judicial rode on sober mules, whereby
They might of suitors, those and they, ask, answer, and reply.
I know when more was thrived abroad by war than now by peace,
And English feared where they be frampt since hostile terms did cease :
But by occasion all things are produced, be, decrease.
Times were when practice also preached, and well said was well done ;
When courtiers cleared the old before they on the new world run ;
When no judicial place was bought, lest justice might be sold ;
When quirks nor quillets overthrew or long did causes hold ;
When lawyers more deserved their fees, and fatted less with gold ;
When to the fifteenth Psalm sometimes had citizens recourse ;
When Lords of farmers, farmers of the poor, had more remorse ;
When poverty had patience more ; when none, as some of late,
Illiterate, ridiculous, might on the altar wait ; &c.

Warner's most abusive invectives, however, in which he exhausts the vocabulary of the kitchen and the streets, are directed against the old religion. But we cannot afford room for any further specimens.

DANIEL.

The great work of Samuel Daniel, who was born at Taunton, in Somersetshire, in 1562, and died in 1619, is his Civil Wars between the Two Houses of Lancaster and York, in eight Books, the first four published in 1595, the fifth in 1599, the sixth in 1602, the two last in 1609 ; the preceding Books being always, we believe, republished along with the new edition. He is also the author of various minor poetical productions, of which the principal are a collection of fifty-seven Sonnets entitled Delia his Musophilus, containing a General Defence of Learning, some short epistles, and several tragedies and court masques. And he wrote, besides, in prose, a History of England, from the Conquest to the end of the reign of Edward III., as well as the Defence of Rhyme (in answer to Campion) which has been already men-

tioned. Very opposite judgments have been passed upon Daniel.
Ben Jonson, in his conversations with Drummond, declared him
to be no poet: Drummond, on the contrary, pronounces him
"for sweetness of rhyming second to none." His style, both in
prose and verse, has a remarkably modern air: if it were weeded
of a few obsolete expressions, it would scarcely seem more
antique than that of Waller, which is the most modern of the
seventeenth century. Bishop Kennet, who has republished
Daniel's History, after telling us that the author had a place at
Court in the reign of King James I., being groom of the privy
chambers to the Queen, observes, that he "seems to have taken
all the refinement a court could give him;" and probably the
absence of pedantry in his style, and its easy and natural flow,
are to be traced in great part to the circumstance of his having
been a man of the world. His verse, too, always careful and
exact, is in many passages more than smooth; even in his dramatic writings (which, having nothing dramatic about them
except the form, have been held in very small estimation) it is
frequently musical and sweet, though always artificial. The
highest quality of his poetry is a tone of quiet, pensive reflection
in which he is fond of indulging, and which often rises to dignity
and eloquence, and has at times even something of depth and
originality. Daniel's was the not uncommon fate of an attendant
upon courts and the great: he is believed to have experienced
some neglect from his royal patrons in his latter days, or at least
to have been made jealous by Ben Jonson being employed to
furnish part of the poetry for the court entertainments, the supply
of which he used to have all to himself; upon which he retired
to a life of quiet and contemplation in the country. It sounds
strange in the present day to be told that his favourite retreat
from the gaiety and bustle of London was a house which he
rented in Old Street, St. Luke's. In his gardens here, we are
informed by the writer of the Life prefixed to his collected poems,
he would often indulge in entire solitude for many months, or at
most receive the visits of only a few select friends. It is said to
have been here that he composed most of his dramatic pieces.
Towards the end of his life he retired to a farm which he had at
Beckington, near Philip's Norton, in Somersetshire, and his
death took place there. "He was married," says the editor of
his works, "but whether to the person he so often celebrates
under the name of Delia, is uncertain." Fuller, in his Worthies,

tells us that his wife's name was Justina. They had no children. Daniel is said to have been appointed to the honorary post of Poet Laureate after the death of Spenser.

In his narrative poetry, Daniel is in general wire-drawn, flat, and feeble. He has no passion, and very little descriptive power. His Civil Wars has certainly as little of martial animation in it as any poem in the language. There is abundance, indeed, of "the tranquil mind;" but of "the plumed troops," and the rest of "the pride, pomp, and circumstance of glorious war," Daniel seems, in composing this work (we had nearly written in this composing work) to have taken as complete a farewell as Othello himself. It is mostly a tissue of long-winded disquisition and cold and languid declamation, and has altogether more of the qualities of a good opiate than of a good poem. We will therefore take the few extracts for which we can make room from some of his other productions, where his vein of reflection is more in place, and also better in itself. His Musophilus is perhaps upon the whole his finest piece. The poem, which is in the form of a dialogue between Philocosmus (a lover of the world) and Musophilus (a lover of the Muse), commences thus:—

Philocosmus.

Fond man, Musophilus, that thus dost spend
In an ungainful art thy dearest days,
Tiring thy wits, and toiling to no end
But to attain that idle smoke of praise!
Now, when this busy world cannot attend
The untimely music of neglected lays,
Other delights than these, other desires,
This wiser profit-seeking age requires.

Musophilus.

Friend Philocosmus, I confess indeed
I love this sacred art thou set'st so light:
And, though it never stand my life in stead,
It is enough it gives myself delight,
The whilst my unafflicted mind doth feed
On no unholy thoughts for benefit.

Be it that my unseasonable song
Come out of time, that fault is in the time;
And I must not do virtue so much wrong
As love her aught the worse for others' crime;
And yet I find some blessed spirits among
That cherish me, and like and grace my rhyme.

A gain that [1] I do more in soul esteem
Than all the gain of dust the world doth crave;
And, if I may attain but to redeem
My name from dissolution and the grave,
I shall have done enough; and better deem
To have lived to be than to have died to have.

Short-breathed mortality would yet extend
That span of life so far forth as it may,
And rob her fate; seek to beguile her end
Of some few lingering days of after-stay;
That all this Little All might not descend
Into the dark an universal prey;
And give our labours yet this poor delight
That, when our days do end, they are not done,
And, though we die, we shall not perish quite,
But live two lives where others have but one.

Further on in the dialogue, Musophilus exclaims:—

So fares this humorous world, that ever-more,
Rapt with the current of a present course,
Runs into that which lay contemned before;
Then, glutted, leaves the same, and falls to a worse:
Now zeal holds all, no life but to adore;
Then cold in spirit, and life is of no force.

Strait all that holy was unhallowed lies,
The scattered carcases of ruined vows;
Then truth is false, and now hath blindness eyes;
Then zeal trusts all, now scarcely what it knows;
That evermore, to foolish or to wise,
It fatal is to be seduced with shows.

Sacred Religion! Mother of Form and Fear! [2]
How gorgeously sometimes dost thou sit decked!
What pompous vestures do we make thee wear!
What stately piles we prodigal erect!
How sweet perfumed thou art! how shining clear!
How solemnly observed! with what respect!

Another time, all plain, all quite thread-bare,
Thou must have all within, and nought without;
Sit poorly, without light, disrobed; no care
Of outward grace, to amuse the poor devout;
Powerless, unfollowed; scarcely men can spare
The necessary rites to set thee out.

----

[1] Erroneously printed in the edition before us (2 vols. 12mo. 1718) "Again that."

[2] This fine line has been adopted by Wordsworth, a reader and admirer of Daniel, in one of his sonnets on the Duddon.

> Either Truth, Goodness, Virtue are not still
> The selfsame which they are, and always one,
> But alter to the project of our will ;
> Or we our actions make them wait upon,
> Putting them in the livery of our skill,
> And cast them off again when we have done.

Afterwards he replies very finely to an objection of Philocosmus to the cultivation of poetry, from the small number of those who really cared for it :—

> And for the few that only lend their ear,
> That few is all the world ; which with a few
> Do ever live, and move, and work, and stir.
> This is the heart doth feel, and only know ;
> The rest, of all that only bodies bear,
> Roll up and down, and fill up but the row ;
>
> And serve as others' members, not their own,
> The instruments of those that do direct.
> Then, what disgrace is this, not to be known
> To those know not to give themselves respect ?
> And, though they swell, with pomp of folly blown,
> They live ungraced, and die but in neglect.
>
> And, for my part, if only one allow
> The care my labouring spirits take in this,
> He is to me a theatre large enow,
> And his applause only sufficient is ;
> All my respect is bent but to his brow ;
> That is my all, and all I am is his.
>
> And, if some worthy spirits be pleased too,
> It shall more comfort breed, but not more will.
> But what if none ?   It cannot yet undo
> The love I bear unto this holy skill :
> This is the thing that I was born to do ;
> This is my scene ; this part must I fulfil.

Our last extract shall be from his epistle to the Lady Margaret, Countess of Cumberland (the mother of Lady Anne Clifford, afterwards Countess of Pembroke, Dorset, and Montgomery, to whom Daniel had been tutor) :—

> He that of such a height hath set his mind,
> And reared the dwelling of the thoughts so strong,
> As neither fear nor hope can shake the frame
> Of his resolved powers ; nor all the wind
> Of vanity or malice pierce to wrong
> His settled peace, or to disturb the same ;

What a fair seat hath he from whence he may
The boundless wastes and weals of man survey!

And with how free an eye doth he look down
Upon those lower regions of turmoil!
Where all the storms of passions mainly beat
On flesh and blood ; where honour, power, renown
Are only gay afflictions, golden toil ;
Where greatness stands upon as feeble feet
As frailty doth, and only great doth seem
To little minds who do it so esteem.

. . . .

Thus, Madam, fares that man that hath prepared
A rest for his desires ; and sees all things
Beneath him ; and hath learned this Book of Man,
Full of the notes of frailty ; and compared
The best of glory with her sufferings :
By whom, I see, you labour all you can
To plant your heart, and set your thoughts as near
His glorious mansion as your powers can bear.

Which, Madam, are so soundly fashioned
By that clear judgment, that hath carried you
Beyond the feeble limits of your kind,
As they can stand against the strongest head
Passion can make ; inured to any hue
The world can cast ; that cannot cast that mind
Out of the form of goodness ; that doth see
Both what the best and worst of earth can be.

Which makes that, whatsoever here befals,
You in the region of your self remain,
Where no vain breath of the impudent molests ;
That lieth [1] secured within the brazen walls
Of a clear conscience ; that, without all stain,
Rises in peace, in innocency rests,
Whilst all what malice from without procures
Shows her own ugly heart, but hurts not yours.

And, whereas none rejoice more in revenge
Than women use to do, yet you well know
That wrong is better checked by being contemned
Than being pursued ; leaving to Him to avenge
To whom it appertains. Wherein you show
How worthily your clearness hath condemned
Base malediction, living in the dark,
That at the rays of goodness still doth bark.

---

[1] This apparently must be the true word. The edition before us has " hath."

Knowing the heart of man is set to be
The centre of this world, about the which
These revolutions of disturbances
Still roll; where all the aspects of misery
Predominate; whose strong effects are such
As he must bear, being powerless to redress;
And that, unless above himself he can
Erect himself, how poor a thing is man!

     .   .   .   .

And this note, Madam, of your worthiness
Remains recorded in so many hearts,
As time nor malice cannot wrong your right
In the inheritance of fame you must possess:
You that have built you by your great deserts,
Out of small means, a far more exquisite
And glorious dwelling for your honoured name
Than all the gold of[1] leaden minds can frame.

DRAYTON.

  Michael Drayton, who is computed to have been born in 1563, and who died in 1631, is one of the most voluminous of our old poets; being the author, besides many minor compositions, of three works of great length:—his Barons' Wars (on the subject of the civil wars of the reign of Edward II.), originally entitled Mortimeriados, under which name it was published in 1596; his England's Heroical Epistles, 1598; and his Polyolbion, the first eighteen Books of which appeared in 1612, and the whole, consisting of thirty Books, and extending to as many thousand lines, in 1622. This last is the work on which his fame principally rests. It is a most elaborate and minute topographical description of England, written in Alexandrine rhymes; and is a very remarkable work for the varied learning it displays, as well as for its poetic merits. The genius of Drayton is neither very imaginative nor very pathetic; but he is an agreeable and weighty writer, with an ardent, if not a highly creative, fancy. From the height to which he occasionally ascends, as well as from his power of keeping longer on the wing, he must be ranked, as he always has been, much before both Warner and Daniel. He has

[1] The text before us has "that," which is nonsense.

greatly more elevation than the former, and more true poetic life than the latter. His most graceful poetry, however, is perhaps to be found in some of his shorter pieces—in his Pastorals, his very elegant and lively little poem entitled, Nymphidia; or, the Court of Fairy, and his verses on Poets and Poesy, in which occur the lines on Marlow that have been quoted in a preceding page. From a mass of verse extending in all to not far from 100,000 lines, the few extracts that we can give must be far from affording a complete illustration of the author's genius. The following is from the commencement of the Thirteenth Book, or Song, of the Polyolbion, the subject of which is the County of Warwick, of which Drayton, as he here tells us, was a native:—

Upon the mid-lands now the industrious muse doth fall ;
That shire which we the heart of England well may call,
As she herself extends (the midst which is decreed)
Betwixt St. Michael's Mount and Berwick bordering Tweed,
Brave Warwick, that abroad so long advanced her Bear,
By her illustrious Earls renowned every where ;
Above her neighbouring shires which always bore her head.

  My native country, then, which so brave spirits hast bred,
If there be virtues yet remaining in thy earth,
Or any good of thine thou bred'st into my birth,
Accept it as thine own, whilst now I sing of thee,
Of all thy later brood the unworthiest though I be.

. . . .

When Phœbus lifts his head out of the water's [1] wave,
No sooner doth the earth her flowery bosom brave,
At such time as the year brings on the pleasant spring
But Hunt's up to the morn the feathered sylvans sing ;
And, in the lower grove as on the rising knowl,
Upon the highest spray of every mounting pole
These quiristers are perched, with many a speckled breast :
Then from her burnished gate the goodly glittering East
Gilds every mountain-top, which late the humorous night
Bespangled had with pearl, to please the morning's sight ;
On which the mirthful quires, with their clear open throats,
Unto the joyful morn so strain their warbling notes
That hills and valleys ring, and even the echoing air
Seems all composed of sounds about them every where.
The throstle with shrill sharps, as purposely he sung
To awake the lustless sun, or chiding that so long
He was in coming forth that should the thickets thrill ;
The woosel near at hand; that hath a golden bill,

---

[1] Or, perhaps, "watery." The common text gives "winter's."

As nature him had marked of purpose t' let us see
That from all other birds his tunes should different be;
For with their vocal sounds they sing to pleasant May;
Upon his dulcet pipe the merle doth only play.
When in the lower brake the nightingale hard by
In such lamenting strains the joyful hours doth ply
As though the other birds she to her tunes would draw
And, but that Nature, by her all-constraining law,
Each bird to her own kind this season doth invite,
They else, alone to hear that charmer of the night
(The more to use their ears) their voices sure would spare,
That moduleth her notes so admirably rare
As man to set in parts at first had learned of her.
To Philomel the next the linnet we prefer;
And by that warbling bird the woodlark place we then,
The red-sparrow, the nope, the redbreast, and the wren;
The yellow-pate, which, though she hurt the blooming tree,
Yet scarce hath any bird a finer pipe than she.
And, of these chanting fowls, the goldfinch not behind,
That hath so many sorts descending from her kind.
The tydy, for her notes as delicate as they;
The laughing hecco; then, the counterfeiting jay.
The softer with the shrill, some hid among the leaves,
Some in the taller trees, some in the lower greaves,
Thus sing away the morn, until the mounting sun
Through thick exhaled fogs his golden head hath run,
And through the twisted tops of our close covert creeps
To kiss the gentle shade, this while that sweetly sleeps.

   And, near to these our thicks, the wild and frightful herds,
Not hearing other noise but this of chattering birds,
Feed fairly on the lawns; both sorts of seasoned deer;
Here walk the stately red, the freckled fallow there;
The bucks and lusty stags amongst the rascals strewed,
As sometime gallant spirits amongst the multitude.
Of all the beasts which we for our venerial name
The hart among the rest, the hunter's noblest game.
Of which most princely chase sith none did e'er report,
Or by description touch to express that wondrous sport
(Yet might have well beseemed the ancients' noble songs)
To our old Arden here most fitly it belongs.
Yet shall she not invoke the Muses to her aid,
But thee, Diana bright, a goddess and a maid;
In many a huge-grown wood, and many a shady grove
Which oft hast borne thy bow, Great Huntress, used to rove,
At many a cruel beast, and with thy darts to pierce
The lion, panther, ounce, the bear, and tiger fierce;
And, following thy fleet game, chaste mighty forest's queen,
With thy dishevelled nymphs attired in youthful green,

About the lawns hast scoured, and wasted both far and near,
Brave huntress! But no beasts shall prove thy quarries here
Save those the best of chase, the tall and lusty red.
The stag, for goodly shape and stateliness of head,
Is fittest to hunt at force. For whom when, with his hounds,
The labouring hunter tufts the thick unbarbed grounds,
Where harboured is the hart, there often from his feed
The dogs of him do find; or, thorough skilful heed,
The huntsman by his slot, or breaking earth, perceives,
Or entering of the thick by pressing of the greaves,
Where he had gone to lodge. Now, when the hart doth hear
The often bellowing hounds to vent his secret leir,[1]
He rousing rusheth out, and through the brakes doth drive,
As though up by the roots the bushes he would rive;
And, through the cumbrous thicks as fearfully he makes,
He with his branched head the tender saplings shakes,
That, sprinkling their moist pearls, do seem for him to weep,
When after goes the cry, with yellings loud and deep,
That all the forest rings, and every neighbouring place.
And there is not a hound but falleth to the chace;
Rechasing with his horn, which then the hunter cheers,
Whilst still the lusty stag his high-palmed head upbears,
His body showing state, with unbent knees upright,
Expressing, from all beasts, his courage in his flight.
But when, the approaching foes still following, he perceives
That he his speed must trust, his usual walk he leaves,
And o'er the champain flies; which when the assembly find,
Each follows as his horse were footed with the wind.
But, being then embost, the noble stately deer
When he hath gotten ground (the kennel cast arrear)
Doth beat the brooks and ponds for sweet refreshing soil;
That serving not, then proves if he his scent can foil,
And makes amongst the herds, and flocks of shag-woolled sheep,
Them frighting from the guard of those who had their keep;
But, whenas all his shifts his safety still denies,
Put quite out of his walk, the ways and fallows tries.
Whom when the ploughman meets, his team he letteth stand,
To assail him with his goad; so, with his hook in hand,
The shepherd him pursues, and to his dog doth hollo,
When, with tempestuous speed, the hounds and huntsmen follow;
Until the noble deer, through toil bereaved of strength,
His long and sinewy legs then failing him at length,
The villagers attempts, enraged, not giving way
To any thing he meets now at his sad decay.
The cruel ravenous hounds and bloody hunters near,
This noblest beast of chace, that vainly doth not[2] fear,

----

[1] Lair.   [2] "But" is the common reading.

Some bank or quick-set finds; to which his haunch opposed,
He turns upon his foes, that soon have him inclosed,
The churlish-throated hounds then holding him at bay;
And, as their cruel fangs on his harsh skin they lay,
With his sharp-pointed head he dealeth deadly wounds.
The hunter, coming in to help his wearied hounds,
He desperately assails; until, oppressed by force,
He, who the mourner is to his own dying corse,
Upon the ruthless earth his precious tears lets fall.

This passage, though long, will scarcely be felt to be tedious.
It is one of the most animated descriptions in poetry. We add a
short specimen of Drayton's lighter style from his Nymphidia—
the account of the equipage of the Queen of the Fairies, when
she set out to visit her lover Pigwiggen. The reader may compare it with Mercutio's description in Romeo and Juliet:—

Her chariot ready straight is made;
Each thing therein is fitting laid,
That she by nothing might be stayed,
For nought must be her letting;
Four nimble gnats the horses were,
Their harnesses of gossamer,
Fly Cranion, her charioteer,
Upon the coach-box getting.

Her chariot of a snail's fine shell,
Which for the colours did excel,
The fair Queen Mab becoming well,
So lively was the limning;
The seat the soft wool of the bee,
The cover (gallantly to see)
The wing of a pied butterflee;
I trow 'twas simple trimming.

The wheels composed of cricket's bones,
And daintily made for the nonce;
For fear of rattling on the stones
With thistle down they shod it;
For all her maidens much did fear
If Oberon had chanced to hear
That Mab his queen should have been there,
He would not have abode it.

She mounts her chariot with a trice,
Nor would she stay for no advice
Until her maids, that were so nice,
To wait on her were fitted;

But ran herself away alone ;
Which when they heard, there was not one
But hasted after to be gone,
    As she had been dismitted.

Hop, and Mop, and Drab so clear,
Pip and Trip, and Skip, that were
To Mab their sovereign so dear,
    Her special maids of honour ;
Fib, and Tib, and Pink, and Pin,
Tick, and Quick, and Jill, and Jin,
Tit, and Nit, and Wap, and Win,
    The train that wait upon her.

Upon a grasshopper they got,
And, what with amble and with trot,
For hedge nor ditch they spared not,
    But after her they hie them :
A cobweb over them they throw,
To shield the wind if it should blow ;
Themselves they wisely could bestow
    Lest any should espy them.

JOSEPH HALL.

Here should not be omitted a name of great note, that of
Joseph Hall, who was born in 1574, and was successively bishop
of Exeter and Norwich, from the latter of which sees, having
been expelled by the Long Parliament, he died, after protracted
sufferings from imprisonment and poverty, in 1656. Hall began
his career of authorship by the publication of Three Books of
Satires, in 1597, while he was a student at Cambridge, and only
in his twenty-third year. A continuation followed the next
year under the title of Virgidemiarum the Three last Books ;
and the whole were afterwards republished together, as Virgidemiarum Six Books ; that is, six books of bundles of rods.
" These satires," says Warton, who has given an elaborate
analysis of them, " are marked with a classical precision to which
English poetry had yet early attained. They are replete with
animation of style and sentiment. . . . The characters are
delineated in strong and lively colouring, and their discrimina-
tions are touched with the masterly traces of genuine humour.

The versification is equally energetic and elegant, and the fabric of the couplets approaches to the modern standard."* Hall's Satires have been repeatedly reprinted in modern times.

SYLVESTER.

One of the most popular poets of this date was Joshua Sylvester, the translator of The Divine Weeks and Works, and other productions, of the French poet Du Bartas. Sylvester has the honour of being supposed to have been one of the early favourites of Milton.† In one of his publications he styles himself a Merchant-Adventurer, and he seems to have belonged to the Puritan party, which may have had some share in influencing Milton's regard. His translation of Du Bartas was first published in 1605; and the seventh edition (beyond which, we believe, its popularity did not carry it) appeared in 1641.‡ Nothing can be more uninspired than the general run of Joshua's verse, or more fantastic and absurd than the greater number of its more ambitious passages; for he had no taste or judgment, and, provided the stream of sound and the jingle of the rhyme were kept up, all was right in his notion. His poetry consists chiefly of translations from the French; but he is also the author of some original pieces, the title of one of which, a courtly offering from the poetical Puritan to the prejudices of King James, may be quoted as a lively specimen of his style and genius :—" Tobacco battered, and the pipes shattered, about their ears that idly idolize so base and barbarous a weed, or at leastwise overlove so loathsome a vanity, by a volley of holy shot thundered from Mount Helicon."§ But, with all his general flatness and frequent absurdity, Sylvester has an uncommon flow of harmonious words at times, and occasionally even some fine lines and felicitous expressions. His

* Hist. of Eng. Poet. iv. 328.

† Milton's obligations to Sylvester were first pointed out in Considerations on Milton's Early Reading, and the Prima Stamina of his Paradise Lost, together with Extracts from a Poet of the Sixteenth Century, by the Rev. Charles Dunster (who had a few years before produced his well-known edition of the Paradise Regained). 1800.

‡ Ritson, in his Bibliographia Poetica, makes the edition of 1613 to have been only the third; but it is called the fourth on the title-page.

§ 8vo. Lond. 1615.

contemporaries called him the "Silver-tongued Sylvester," for
what they considered the sweetness of his versification—and
some of his best passages justify the title. Indeed, even when
the substance of what he writes approaches nearest to nonsense,
the sound is often very graceful, soothing the ear with something
like the swing and ring of Dryden's heroics. But, after a few
lines, is always sure to come in some ludicrous image or expression which destroys the effect of the whole. The translation of
Du Bartas is inscribed to King James in a most adulatory and
elaborate Dedication, consisting of a string of sonnet-shaped
stanzas, ten in all, of which the two first are a very fair sample
of the mingled good and bad of Sylvester's poetry :—

To England's, Scotland's, France', and Ireland's king ;
  Great Emperor of Europe's greatest isles ;
Monarch of hearts, and arts, and everything
  Beneath Boötes, many thousand miles ;
  Upon whose head honour and fortune smiles ;
About whose brows clusters of crowns do spring;
  Whose faith him Champion of the Faith enstyles ;
Whose wisdom's fame o'er all the world doth ring :
Mnemosyne and her fair daughters bring
  The Daphnean crown to crown him laureate ;
Whole and sole sovereign of the Thespian spring,
  Prince of Parnassus and Pierian state ;
And with their crown their kingdom's arms they yield,
Thrice three pens sable in a Cynthian field ;
Signed by themselves and their High Treasurer
Bartas, the Great ; engrossed by Sylvester.

Our sun did set, and yet no night ensued ;
  Our woeful loss so joyful gain did bring.
In tears we smile, amid our sighs we sing ;
So suddenly our dying light renewed.
As when the Arabian only bird doth burn
  Her aged body in sweet flames to death,
  Out of her cinders a new bird hath breath,
In whom the beauties of the first return ;
From spicy ashes of the sacred urn
  Of our dead Phœnix, dear Elizabeth,
  A new true Phœnix lively flourisheth,
Whom greater glories than the first adorn.
So much, O King, thy sacred worth presume-I-on,
James, thou just heir of England's joyful un-i-on.

It is not to be denied that there is considerable skill in versifi-

cation here, and also some ingenious rhetoric ; but, not to notice
the pervading extravagance of the sentiment, some of the best
sounding of the lines and phrases have next to no meaning ; and
the close of each stanza, that of the last in particular, is in the
manner of a ludicrous travesty. Many of Sylvester's conceits,
however, belong to the original upon which he worked, and
which upon the whole may be considered as fairly represented,
perhaps occasionally improved, in his translation. Some passages are very melodiously given—the following, for instance,
the commencement of which may put the reader in mind of
Milton's "Hail, holy light ! offspring of heaven first-born ":—

> All hail, pure lamp, bright, sacred, and excelling ;
> Sorrow and care, darkness and dread repelling ;
> Thou world's great taper, wicked men's just terror,
> Mother of truth, true beauty's only mirror,
> God's eldest daughter ; O ! how thou art full
> Of grace and goodness ! O ! how beautiful !
>
> . . . . . .
>
> But yet, because all pleasures wax unpleasant
> If without pause we still possess them present,
> And none can right discern the sweets of peace
> That have not felt war's irksome bitterness,
> And swans seem whiter if swart crows be by
> (For contraries each other best descry),
> The All's architect alternately decreed
> That Night the Day, the Day should Night succeed.
> The Night, to temper Day's exceeding drought,
> Moistens our air, and makes our earth to sprout :
> The Night is she that all our travails eases,
> Buries our cares, and all our griefs appeases :
> The Night is she that, with her sable wing
> In gloomy darkness hushing every thing,
> Through all the world dumb silence doth distil,
> And wearied bones with quiet sleep doth fill.
> Sweet Night ! without thee, without thee, alas !
> Our life were loathsome, even a hell, to pass ;
> For outward pains and inward passions still,
> With thousand deaths, would soul and body thrill.
> O Night, thou pullest the proud masque away
> Wherewith vain actors, in this world's great play,
> By day disguise them. For no difference
> Night makes between the peasant and the prince,
> The poor and rich, the prisoner and the judge,
> The foul and fair, the master and the drudge,

The fool and wise, Barbarian and the Greek ;
For Night's black mantle covers all alike.
  He that, condemned for some notorious vice,
Seeks in the mines the baits of avarice,
Or, melting at the furnace, fineth bright
Our soul's dire sulphur, resteth yet at night.
He that, still stooping, tugs against the tide
His laden barge alongst a river's side,
And, filling shores with shouts, doth melt him quite,
Upon his pallet resteth yet at night.
He that in summer, in extremest heat
Scorched all day, in his own scalding sweat,
Shaves with keen scythe the glory and delight
Of motley meadows, resteth yet at night,
And in the arms of his dear phere forgoes
All former troubles and all former woes.
Only the learned Sisters' sacred minions,
While silent Night under her sable pinions
Folds all the world, with painless pain they tread
A sacred path that to the heavens doth lead ;
And higher than the heavens their readers raise
Upon the wings of their immortal lays.

CHAPMAN'S HOMER.

Of the translators from the ancients in this age, by far the
greatest is Chapman. George Chapman was born at Hitching
Hill, in the county of Hertford, in 1557, and lived till 1634.
Besides his plays, which will be afterwards noticed, he is the
author of several original poetical pieces ; but he is best and
most favourably known by his versions of the Iliad and the
Odyssey. "He would have made a great epic poet," Charles
Lamb has said, in his Specimens of the English Dramatic Poets,
turning to these works after having characterized his dramas,
"if, indeed, he has not abundantly shown himself to be one : for
his Homer is not so properly a translation as the stories of
Achilles and Ulysses re-written. The earnestness and passion
which he has put into every part of these poems would be incredible to a reader of mere modern translations. His almost Greek
zeal for the honour of his heroes is only paralleled by that fierce
spirit of Hebrew bigotry with which Milton, as if personating
one of the zealots of the old law, clothed himself when he sat

down to paint the acts of Samson against the uncircumcised.
The great obstacle to Chapman's translations being read is their
unconquerable quaintness. He pours out in the same breath the
most just and natural, and the most violent and forced expressions. He seems to grasp whatever words come first to hand
during the impetus of inspiration, as if all other must be inade-
quate to the divine meaning. But passion (the all in all in
poetry) is everywhere present, raising the low, dignifying the
mean, and putting sense into the absurd. He makes his readers
glow, weep, tremble, take any affection which he pleases, be
moved by words or in spite of them, be disgusted and overcome
that disgust." Chapman's Homer is, in some respects, not unworthy of this enthusiastic tribute.　Few writers have been
more copiously inspired with the genuine frenzy of poetry—with
that "fine madness," which, as Drayton has said in his lines on
Marlow, "rightly should possess a poet's brain." Indeed, in the
character of his genius, out of the province of the drama, Chapman bears a considerable resemblance to Marlow, whose unfinished translation of Musæus's Hero and Leander he completed.
With more judgment and more care he might have given to his
native language, in his version of the Iliad, one of the very
greatest of the poetical works it possesses.　But what, except the
most extreme irregularity and inequality,—a rough sketch rather
than a finished performance,—was to be expected from his boast
of having translated half the poem—namely, the last twelve
books—in fifteen weeks? Yet, rude and negligent upon the
whole as it is, Chapman's is by far the most Homeric Iliad we
yet possess.　The enthusiasm of the translator for his original is
uncompromising to a degree of the ludicrous.　"Of all books,"
he exclaims in his Preface, "extant in all kinds, Homer is the
first and best:" and in the same spirit, in quoting a passage from
Pliny's Natural History in another portion of his preliminary
matter, he proceeds first to turn it into verse, "that no prose
may come near Homer."　In spite, however, of all this eccen-
tricity, and of a hurry and impetuosity which betray him into
many mistranslations, and, on the whole, have the effect perhaps
of giving a somewhat too tumultuous and stormy representation of
the Homeric poetry, the English into which Chapman transfuses
the meaning of the mighty ancient is often singularly and delicately beautiful.　He is the author of nearly all the happiest of
the compound epithets which Pope has adopted, and of many

others equally musical and expressive. "Far-shooting Phœbus,"
—"the ever-living gods,"—"the many-headed hill,"—"the ivory-
wristed queen,"—are a few of the felicitous combinations with
which he has enriched his native tongue. Carelessly executed,
indeed, as the work for the most part is, there is scarcely a page
of it that is not irradiated by gleams of the truest, poetic genius.
Often in the midst of a long paragraph of the most chaotic versification, the fatigued and distressed ear is surprised by a few
lines,—or it may be sometimes only a single line,—"musical as
is Apollo's lute,"—and sweet and graceful enough to compensate
for ten times as much ruggedness. Such, for instance, is the
following version of part of the description of the visit paid by
Ulysses and his companions to the shrine of Apollo at Chrysa,
in the First Book :—

> —— The youths crowned cups of wine
> Drunk off, and filled again to all : that day was held divine,
> And spent in pæans to the Sun ; who heard with pleased ear :
> When whose bright chariot stooped to sea, and twilight hid the clear,
> All soundly on their cables slept, even till the night was worn ;
> And when the Lady of the Light, the rosy-fingered morn,
> Rose from the hills, all fresh arose, and to the camp retired,
> While Phœbus with a fore-right wind their swelling bark inspired.

And here are a few more verses steeped in the same liquid
beauty, from the Catalogue of the Ships, in the Second Book :—

> Who dwell in Pylos' sandy soil and Arene[1] the fair,
> In Thryon near Alpheus' flood, and Aepy full of air,

---

[1] This name is incorrectly accented, but Pope has copied the error.
Warton had a copy of Chapman's translation, which had belonged to Pope,
and in which the latter had noted many of the interpolations of his predecessor,
of whom, indeed, as Warton remarks, a diligent observer will easily discern
that he was no careless reader.— Hist. Eng. Poet. iv. 272. This copy,
described in the newspaper account as having been presented to Warton by
Bishop Warburton, is stated to have been knocked down for 12l. at the sale
by auction in April 1800 of the library of the late Rev. John Mitford.
In the preface to his own Iliad, Pope has allowed to Chapman, "a daring
fiery spirit that animates his translation, which is something like what
one might imagine Homer himself might have writ before he arrived to
years of discretion." Dryden has told us also that Waller used to say he
never could read it without incredible transport. In a note upon Warton's
History, by the late Mr. Park, it is stated that "Chapman's own copy of his
translation of Homer, corrected by him throughout for a future edition, was
purchased for five shillings from the shop of Edwards by Mr. Steevens, and,
at the sale of his books in 1800, was transferred to the invaluable library of
Mr. Heber." This important copy, it appears, cannot now be found. Chap-

In Cyparysseus, Amphigen, and little Pteleon,
The town where all the Eleots dwell, and famous Dorion ;
Where all the Muses, opposite, in strife of poesy,
To ancient Thamyris of Thrace, did use him cruelly :
He coming from Eurytus' ' court, the wise Oechalian king,
Because he proudly durst affirm he could more sweetly sing
Than that Pierian race of Jove, they, angry with his vaunt,
Bereft his eyesight and his song, that did the ear enchant,
And of his skill to touch his harp disfurnished his hand :
All these, in ninety hollow keels, grave Nestor did command.

Almost the whole of this Second Book, indeed, is admirably
translated: in the harangues, particularly, of Agamemnon and
the other generals, in the earlier part of it, all the fire of Homer
burns and blazes in English verse.*

HARINGTON ; FAIRFAX ; FANSHAWE.

Of the translators of foreign poetry which belong to this
period, three are very eminent. Sir John Harington's translation of the Orlando Furioso first appeared in 1591, when the
author was in his thirtieth year. It does not convey all the glow
and poetry of Ariosto; but it is, nevertheless, a performance of
great ingenuity and talent. The translation of Tasso's great epic
by Edward Fairfax was first published, under the title of Godfrey
of Bulloigne, or the Recoverie of Jerusalem, in 1600. This is a
work of true genius, full of passages of great beauty ; and,
although by no means a perfectly exact or servile version of the
Italian original, is throughout executed with as much care as
taste and spirit.† Sir Richard Fanshawe is the author of versions
of Camoens's Lusiad, of Guarini's Pastor Fido, of the Fourth

---

man's Iliad in a complete form was first printed without date, but certainly
after the accession of James I., to whose son, Prince Henry, it is dedicated.
The Odyssey, which is in the common heroic verse of ten syllables, was published in 1614.

¹ This name is also miscounted. Both works are probably very incorrectly printed.

* Chapman's Translation of the Iliad, formerly a scarce book, has now been
rendered generally accessible by two reprints of it ; the first edited by the late
Dr. W. Cooke Taylor, 2 vols. 8vo. 1843; the second along with the Odyssey
and others of Chapman's translations, by Mr. R. Hooper, 5 vols. 8vo. 1857.

† Reprinted in the Tenth and Fourteenth Volumes of KNIGHT'S WEEKLY
VOLUME.

Book of the Æneid, of the Odes of Horace, and of the Querer
por Solo Querer (To love for love's sake) of the Spanish dramatist Mendoza. Some passages from the last-mentioned work,
which was published in 1649, may be found in Lamb's Specimens,[*] the ease and flowing gaiety of which never have been
excelled even in original writing. The Pastor Fido is also
rendered with much spirit and elegance. Fanshawe is, besides,
the author of a Latin translation of Fletcher's Faithful Shepherdess, and of some original poetry. His genius, however, was
sprightly and elegant rather than lofty, and perhaps he does not
succeed so well in translating poetry of a more serious style: at
least, Mickle, the modern translator of Camoens, in the discourse
prefixed to his own version, speaks with great contempt of that
of his predecessor; affirming not only that it is exceedingly un-
faithful, but that Fanshawe had not "the least idea of the dignity
of the epic style, or of the true spirit of poetical translation."
He seems also to sneer at Fanshawe's Lusiad because it was "published during the usurpation of Cromwell,"—as if even the poets
and translators of that time must have been a sort of illegitimates
and usurpers in their way. But Fanshawe was all his life a
steady royalist, and served both Charles I. and his son in a succession of high employments. Mickle, in truth, was not the man
to appreciate either Fanshawe or Cromwell.

DRUMMOND.

One of the most graceful poetical writers of the reign of
James I. is William Drummond, of Hawthornden, near Edinburgh; and he is further deserving of notice as the first of his
countrymen, at least of any eminence, who aspired to write in
English. He has left us a quantity of prose as well as verse;
the former very much resembling the style of Sir Philip Sidney
in his Arcadia,—the latter, in manner and spirit, formed more
upon the model of Surrey, or rather upon that of Petrarch and
the other Italian poets whom Surrey and many of his English
successors imitated. No early English imitator of the Italian
poetry, however, has excelled Drummond, either in the sustained
melody of his verse, or its rich vein of thoughtful tenderness.

[*] Vol. ii. pp. 242—253.

We will transcribe one of his sonnets as a specimen of the fine moral painting, tinged with the colouring of scholarly recollections, in which he delights to indulge:—

> Trust not, sweet soul, those curled waves of gold
>   With gentle tides that on your temples flow,
>   Nor temples spread with flakes of virgin snow,
> Nor snow of cheeks with Tyrian grain enrolled.
> Trust not those shining lights which wrought my woe
>   When first I did their azure rays behold,
> Nor voice whose sounds more strange effects do show
>   Than of the Thracian harper have been told ;
> Look to this dying lily, fading rose,
>   Dark hyacinth, of late whose blushing beams
> Made all the neighbouring herbs and grass rejoice,
>   And think how little is 'twixt life's extremes :
> The cruel tyrant that did kill those flowers
> Shall once, ay me ! not spare that spring of yours.

DAVIES.

A remarkable poem of this age, first published in 1599, is the Nosce Teipsum * of Sir John Davies, who was successively solicitor- and attorney-general in the reign of James, and had been appointed to the place of Chief Justice of the King's Bench, when he died, before he could enter upon its duties, in 1626. Davies is also the author of a poem on dancing entitled Orchestra, and of some minor pieces, all distinguished by vivacity as well as precision of style; but he is only now remembered for his philosophical poem, the earliest of the kind in the language. It is written in rhyme, in the common heroic ten-syllable verse, but disposed in quatrains, like the early play of Misogonus already mentioned, and other poetry of the same era, or like Sir Thomas Overbury's poem of The Wife, the Gondibert of Sir William Davenant, and the Annus Mirabilis of Dryden, at a later period. No one of these writers has managed this difficult stanza so successfully as Davies: it has the disadvantage of requiring the sense to be in general closed at certain regularly and quickly recurring turns, which yet are very ill adapted for

---

* The full title is Nosce Teipsum. This oracle expounded in two elegies : —1. Of human knowledge.—2. Of the soul of man and the immortality thereof.

an effective pause; and even all the skill of Dryden has been unable to free it from a certain air of monotony and languor,—a circumstance of which that poet may be supposed to have been himself sensible, since he wholly abandoned it after one or two early attempts. Davies, however, has conquered its difficulties; and, as has been observed, "perhaps no language can produce a poem, extending to so great a length, of more condensation of thought, or in which fewer languid verses will be found."[*] In fact, it is by this condensation and sententious brevity, so carefully filed and elaborated, however, as to involve no sacrifice of perspicuity or fullness of expression, that he has attained his end. Every quatrain is a pointed expression of a separate thought, like one of Rochefoucault's Maxims; each thought being, by great skill and painstaking in the packing, made exactly to fit and to fill the same case. It may be doubted, however, whether Davies would not have produced a still better poem if he had chosen a measure which would have allowed him greater freedom and real variety; unless, indeed, his poetical talent was of a sort that required the suggestive aid and guidance of such artificial restraints as he had to cope with in this, and what would have been a bondage to a more fiery and teeming imagination was rather a support to his. He wrote, among other things, a number of acrostics upon the name of Queen Elizabeth; which, says Ellis, "are probably the best acrostics ever written, and all equally good; but they seem to prove that their author was too fond of struggling with useless difficulties."[†] Perhaps he found the limitations of the acrostic, too, a help rather than a hindrance.

DONNE.

The title of the Metaphysical School of poetry, which in one sense of the words might have been given to Davies and his imitators, has been conferred by Dryden upon another race of writers, whose founder was a contemporary of Davies, the famous Dr. John Donne, Dean of St. Paul's. Donne, who died at the age of fifty-eight, in 1631, is said to have written most of his poetry before the end of the sixteenth century, but none of it

[*] Hallam, Lit. of Europe, ii. 227.
[†] Spec. of Early Eng. Poets, ii. 570.

was published till late in the reign of James. It consists of
lyrical pieces (entitled Songs and Sonnets), epithalamions or
marriage songs, funeral and other elegies, satires, epistles, and
divine poems. On a superficial inspection, Donne's verses look
like so many riddles. They seem to be written upon the
principle of making the meaning as difficult to be found out as
possible—of using all the resources of language, not to express
thought, but to conceal it. Nothing is said in a direct, natural
manner; conceit follows conceit without intermission; the most
remote analogies, the most far-fetched images, the most un-
expected turns, one after another, surprise and often puzzle the
understanding; while things of the most opposite kinds—the
harsh and the harmonious, the graceful and the grotesque, the
grave and the gay, the pious and the profane—meet and mingle
in the strangest of dances. But, running through all this bewil-
derment, a deeper insight detects not only a vein of the most
exuberant wit, but often the sunniest and most delicate fancy,
and the truest tenderness and depth of feeling. Donne, though
in the latter part of his life he became a very serious and devout
poet as well as man, began by writing amatory lyrics, the strain
of which is anything rather than devout; and in this kind of
writing he seems to have formed his poetic style, which, for such
compositions, would, to a mind like his, be the most natural
and expressive of any. The species of lunacy which quickens
and exalts the imagination of a lover, would, in one of so soothing a brain as he was, strive to expend itself in all sorts of novel
and wayward combinations, just as Shakespeare has made it do in
his Romeo and Juliet, whose rich intoxication of spirit he has by
nothing else set so livingly before us, as by making them thus
exhaust all the eccentricities of language in their struggle to
give expression to that inexpressible passion which had taken
captive the whole heart and being of both. Donne's later poetry,
in addition to the same abundance and originality of thought,
often running into a wildness and extravagance not so excusable
here as in his erotic verses, is famous for the singular movement
of the versification, which has been usually described as the
extreme degree of the rugged and tuneless. Pope has given us a
translation of his four Satires into modern language, which he
calls The Satires of Dr. Donne Versified. Their harshness, as
contrasted with the music of his lyrics, has also been referred to
as proving that the English language, at the time when Donne

wrote, had not been brought to a sufficiently advanced state for
the writing of heroic verse in perfection.* That this last notion
is wholly unfounded, numerous examples sufficiently testify:
not to speak of the blank verse of the dramatists, the rhymed
heroics of Shakespeare, of Fletcher, of Jonson, of Spenser, and
of other writers contemporary with and of earlier date than
Donne, are, for the most part, as perfectly smooth and regular as
any that have since been written; at all events, whatever
irregularity may be detected in them, if they be tested by Pope's
narrow gamut, is clearly not to be imputed to any immaturity in
the language. Those writers evidently preferred and cultivated,
deliberately and on principle, a wider compass, and freer and
more varied flow, of melody than Pope had a taste or an ear for.
Nor can it be questioned, we think, that the peculiar construction
of Donne's verse in his satires and many of his other later poems
was also adopted by choice and on system. His lines, though
they will not suit the see-saw style of reading verse,—to which
he probably intended that they should be invincibly impracticable,—are not without a deep and subtle music of their own, in
which the cadences respond to the sentiment, when enunciated
with a true feeling of all that they convey. They are not smooth
or luscious verses, certainly; nor is it contended that the endeavour to raise them to as vigorous and impressive a tone as
possible, by depriving them of all over-sweetness or liquidity,
has not been carried too far; but we cannot doubt that whatever
harshness they have was designedly given to them, and was
conceived to infuse into them an essential part of their relish.

Here is one of Donne's Songs:—

Sweetest love, I do not go
For weariness of thee,
Nor in hope the world can show
A fitter love for me;
But, since that I
Must die at last, 'tis best
Thus to use myself in jest
By feigned death to die.

Yesternight the sun went hence,
And yet is here to-day;
He hath no desire nor sense,
Nor half so short a way:

---

* See article on Donne in Penny Cyclopædia, vol. ix. p. 85.

> Then fear not me,
> But believe that I shall make
> Hastier journeys, since I take
>   More wings and spurs than he.
>
> O how feeble is man's power!
>   That, if good fortune fall,
> Cannot add another hour,
>   Nor a lost hour recall;
>   But come bad chance,
> And we join to it our strength,
> And we teach it art and length
>   Itself o'er us to advance.
>
> When thou sigh'st thou sigh'st not wind,
>   But sigh'st my soul away;
> When thou weep'st, unkindly kind,
>   My life's blood doth decay.
>   It cannot be
> That thou lov'st me as thou say'st,
> If in thine my life thou waste,
>   Which art the life of me.
>
> Let not thy divining heart
> Forethink me any ill;
> Destiny may take thy part
> And may thy fears fulfil;
>   But think that we
> Are but laid aside to sleep:
> They who one another keep
>   Alive ne'er parted be.

Somewhat fantastic as this may be thought, it is surely, notwithstanding, full of feeling; and nothing can be more delicate than the execution. Nor is it possible that the writer of such verses can have wanted an ear for melody, however capriciously he may have sometimes experimented upon language, in the effort, as we conceive, to bring a deeper, more expressive music out of it than it would readily yield. We add one of his elegies as a specimen of his more elaborate style:—

> Language, thou art too narrow and too weak
> To ease us now; great sorrows cannot speak.
> If we could sigh our accents, and weep words,
> Grief wears, and lessens, that tears breath affords.
> Sad hearts, the less they seem, the more they are;
> So guiltiest men stand mutest at the bar;
> Not that they know not, feel not their estate,
> But extreme sense hath made them desperate.

Sorrow! to whom we owe all that we be,
Tyrant in the fifth and greatest monarchy,
Was 't that she did possess all hearts before
Thou hast killed her, to make thy empire more?
Knew'st thou some would, that knew her not, lament,
As in a deluge perish the innocent?
Was 't not enough to have that palace won,
But thou must raze it too, that was undone?
Had'st thou stay'd there, and looked out at her eyes,
All had adored thee, that now from thee flies;
For they let out more light than they took in;
They told not when, but did the day begin.
She was too sapphirine and clear for thee;
Clay, flint, and jet now thy fit dwellings be.
Alas, she was too pure, but not too weak;
Whoe'er saw crystal ordnance but would break?
And, if we be thy conquest, by her fall
Thou hast lost thy end; in her we perish all:
Or, if we live, we live but to rebel,
That know her better now, who knew her well.
If we should vapour out, and pine and die,
Since she first went, that were not misery;
She changed our world with hers; now she is gone,
Mirth and prosperity is oppression.
For of all moral virtues she was all
That ethics speak of virtues cardinal:
Her soul was Paradise; the cherubin
Set to keep it was grace, that kept out sin:
She had no more than let in death, for we
All reap consumption from one fruitful tree.
God took her hence lest some of us should love
Her, like that plant, him and his laws above;
And, when we tears, he mercy shed in this,
To raise our minds to heaven, where now she is;
Who, if her virtues would have let her stay,
We had had a saint, have now a holiday.
Her heart was that strange bush, where sacred fire,
Religion, did not consume, but inspire
Such piety, so chaste use of God's day,
That what we turn to feast she turned to pray,
And did prefigure here, in devout taste,
The rest of her high Sabbath, which shall last.
Angels did hand her up, who next God dwell,
For she was of that order whence most fell.
Her body 's left with us, lest some had said
She could not die, except they saw her dead;
For from less virtue, and less beauteousness,
The Gentiles framed them Gods and Goddesses.

The ravenous earth that now woos her to be
Earth too will be a Lemnis;[1] and the tree
That wraps that crystal in a wooden round[2]
Shall be took up spruce filled with diamond.
And we, her sad glad friends, all bear a part
Of grief, for all would break a Stoic's heart.

SHAKESPEARE'S MINOR POEMS.

In the long list of the minor names of the Elizabethan poetry appears the bright name of William Shakespeare. Shakespeare published his Venus and Adonis in 1593, and his Tarquin and Lucrece in 1594; his Passionate Pilgrim did not appear till 1599; the Sonnets not till 1609. It is probable, however, that the first mentioned of those pieces, which, in his dedication of it to the Earl of Southampton, he calls the first heir of his invention, was written some years before its publication; and, although the Tarquin and Lucrece may have been published immediately after it was composed, it, too, may be accounted an early production. We have no positive evidence that any wholly original drama, such as would be considered a work of invention, had yet been produced by Shakespeare; and, notwithstanding the force of some of the reasons which have been lately urged[3] for carrying back some of his original plays to a date preceding the year 1593, we are still inclined to think it probable that all the other poetry we have of Shakespeare's was composed at least before he had fairly given himself up to dramatic poetry, or had done anything in that line to which he could properly set his name, or by which he could hope that he would live and be remembered among the poets of his country. But, although this minor poetry of Shakespeare sounds throughout like the utterance of that spirit of highest invention and sweetest song before it had found its proper theme, much is here also, immature as it may be, that is still all Shakespearian—the vivid conception, the inexhaustible fertility and richness of thought and imagery, the

[1] The earth of the Isle of Lemnos was supposed by the ancients to be medicinal.
[2] We have ventured to introduce this word instead of "Tomb," which is the reading in the edition before us (Poems, &c., 8vo. Lond. 1640), and which cannot possibly be right.
[3] Both by Mr. Knight and by Mr. Collier. Mr. Knight conceives, also, that the Tarquin and Lucrece is a composition of seven or eight years' later date than the Venus and Adonis.

glowing passion, the gentleness withal that is ever of the poetry
as it was of the man, the enamoured sense of beauty, the living
words, the ear-delighting and heart-enthralling music; nay, even
the dramatic instinct itself, and the idea at least, if not always
the realization, of that sentiment of all subordinating and con-
summating art of which his dramas are the most wonderful
exemplification in literature.

Resuming now the history of that dramatic poetry which is the
chief glory of the Elizabethan age of our literature, we begin
with a notice of these productions, which constitute by much the
most valuable part of it.

SHAKESPEARE'S DRAMATIC WORKS.

William Shakespeare, born in 1564, is enumerated as one of
the proprietors of the Blackfriars Theatre in 1589; is sneered at
by Robert Greene in 1592, in terms which seem to imply that
he had already acquired a considerable reputation as a dramatist
and a writer in blank verse, though the satirist insinuates that
he was enabled to make the show he did chiefly by the plunder
of his predecessors;[*] and in 1598 is spoken of by a critic of the
day as indisputably the greatest of English dramatists, both for
tragedy and comedy, and as having already produced his Two
Gentlemen of Verona, Comedy of Errors, Love's Labours Lost,
Love's Labours Won (generally supposed to be All's Well that
Ends Well),[†] Midsummer Night's Dream, Merchant of Venice,
Richard II., Richard III., Henry IV., King John, Titus Andronicus, and Romeo and Juliet.[‡] There is no ground, however,
for feeling assured, and, indeed, it is rather improbable, that we

[*] "There is an upstart crow, beautified with our feathers, that, with his
tiger's heart wrapt in a player's hide, supposes he is as well able to bombast
out a blank verse as the best of you; and, being an absolute *Johannes Fac-
totum*, is, in his own conceit, the only *Shake-scene* in a country."—Greene's
Groatsworth of Wit, 1592.

[†] But the Rev. Joseph Hunter, in the Second Part of New Illustrations of
the Life, Studies, and Writings of Shakespeare, 8vo. Lond. 1844, and previously in a Disquisition on the Tempest, separately published, has contended
that it must be the Tempest; and I have more recently stated some reasons
for supposing that it may be the Taming of the Shrew (see The English of
Shakespeare, 1857; Prolegomena, pp. 8, 9).

[‡] Palladis Tamia; Wit's Treasury. Being the Second Part of Wit's Commonwealth. By Francis Meres. 1598, p. 282.

have here a complete catalogue of the plays written by Shakespeare up to this date; nor is the authority of so evidently loose a statement, embodying, it is to be supposed, the mere report of the town, sufficient even to establish absolutely the authenticity of every one of the plays enumerated. It is very possible, for example, that Meres may be mistaken in assigning Titus Andronicus to Shakespeare; and, on the other hand, he may be the author of Pericles, and may have already written that play and some others, although Meres does not mention them. The only other direct or positive information we possess on this subject is, that a History called Titus Andronicus, presumed to be the play afterwards published as Shakespeare's, was entered for publication at Stationers' Hall in 1593; that the Second Part of Henry VI. (if it is by Shakespeare), in its original form of The First Part of the Contention betwixt the Two Famous Houses of York and Lancaster, was published in 1594; the Third Part of Henry VI. (if by Shakespeare), in its original form of The True Tragedy of Richard Duke of York, in 1595; his Richard II., Richard III., and Romeo and Juliet, in 1597; Love's Labours Lost and the First Part of Henry IV. in 1598 (the latter, however, having been entered at Stationers' Hall the preceding year); "a corrected and augmented" edition of Romeo and Juliet in 1599; Titus Andronicus (supposing it to be Shakespeare's), the Second Part of Henry IV., Henry V., in its original form, the Midsummer Night's Dream, Much Ado about Nothing, and the Merchant of Venice, in 1600 (the last having been entered at Stationers' Hall in 1598); the Merry Wives of Windsor, in its original form, in 1602 (but entered at Stationers' Hall the year before*): Hamlet in 1603 (entered likewise the year before); a second edition of Hamlet, "enlarged to almost as much again as it was, according to the true and perfect copy," in 1604; Lear in 1608, and Troilus and Cressida, and Pericles, in 1609 (each being entered the preceding year); Othello not till 1622, six years after the author's death; and all the other plays, namely, the Two Gentlemen of Verona, the Winter's Tale, the Comedy of Errors, King John, All's Well that Ends Well, As You Like It, King Henry VIII., Measure for Measure, Cymbeline, Macbeth, the Taming of the Shrew, Julius Cæsar, Antony and Cleopatra, Coriolanus, Timon of Athens, the Tempest, Twelfth Night, the

* This first sketch of the Merry Wives of Windsor has been reprinted for the Shakespeare Society, under the care of Mr. Halliwell, 1842.

First Part of Henry VI. (if Shakespeare had anything to do with that play*), and also the perfect editions of Henry V., the Merry Wives of Windsor, and the Second and Third Parts of Henry VI., not, so far as is known, till they appear, along with those formerly printed, in the first folio, in 1623.

Such then is the sum of the treasure that Shakespeare has left us; but the revolution which his genius wrought upon our national drama is placed in the clearest light by comparing his earliest plays with the best which the language possessed before his time. He has made all his predecessors obsolete. While his Merchant of Venice, and his Midsummer Night's Dream, and his Romeo and Juliet, and his King John, and his Richard II., and his Henry IV., and his Richard III., all certainly produced, as we have seen, before the year 1598, are still the most universally familiar compositions in our literature, no other dramatic work that had then been written is now popularly read, or familiar to anybody except to a few professed investigators of the antiquities of our poetry. Where are now the best productions even of such writers as Greene, and Peele, and Marlow, and Decker, and Marston, and Webster, and Thomas Heywood, and Middleton? They are to be found among our Select Collections of Old Plays,—publications intended rather for the mere preservation of the pieces contained in them, than for their diffusion among a multitude of readers. Or, if the entire works of a few of these elder dramatists have recently been collected and republished, this has still been done only to meet the demand of a comparatively very small number of curious students, anxious to possess and examine for themselves whatever relics are still recoverable of the old world of our literature. Popularly known and read the works of these writers never again will be; there is no more prospect or probability of this than there is that the plays of Shakespeare will ever lose their popularity among his countrymen. In that sense, everlasting oblivion is their portion, as everlasting life is his. In one form only have they any chance of again attracting some measure of the general attention—namely, in the form of such partial and very limited exhibition as Lamb

* See upon this question Mr. Knight's Essay upon the Three Parts of King Henry VI., and King Richard III., in the Seventh Volume of his Library Edition of Shakspere, pp. 1—119. And see also Mr. Halliwell's Introduction to the reprint of The First Sketches of the Second and Third Parts of King Henry the Sixth (the First Part of the Contention and the True Tragedy), edited by him for the Shakespeare Society, 1843.

has given us an example of in his Specimens. And herein we
see the first great difference between the plays of Shakespeare
and those of his predecessors, and one of the most immediately
conspicuous of the improvements which he introduced into
dramatic writing. He did not create our regular drama, but he
regenerated and wholly transformed it, as if by breathing into it
a new soul. We possess no dramatic production anterior to his
appearance that is at once a work of high genius and of anything
like equably sustained power throughout. Very brilliant flights
of poetry there are in many of the pieces of our earlier dramatists;
but the higher they soar in one scene, the lower they generally
seem to think it expedient to sink in the next. Their great
efforts are made only by fits and starts: for the most part it
must be confessed that the best of them are either merely extravagant and absurd, or do nothing but trifle or dose away over
their task with the expenditure of hardly any kind of faculty at
all. This may have arisen in part from their own want of
judgment or want of painstaking, in part from the demands of a
very rude condition of the popular taste; but the effect is to
invest all that they have bequeathed to us with an air of barbarism, and to tempt us to take their finest displays of successful
daring for mere capricious inspirations, resembling the sudden
impulses of fury by which the listless and indolent man of the
woods will sometimes be roused for the instant from his habitual
laziness and passiveness to an exhibition of superhuman strength
and activity. From this savage or savage-looking state our
drama was first redeemed by Shakespeare. Even Milton has
spoken of his " wood-notes wild;" and Thomson, more unpere-
moniously, has baptized him " wild Shakespeare,"[*]—as if a sort
of half insane irregularity of genius were the quality that chiefly
distinguished him from other great writers. If he be a " wild "
writer, it is in comparison with some dramatists and poets of
succeeding times, who, it must be admitted, are sufficiently
tame: compared with the dramatists of his own age and of the
age immediately preceding,—with the general throng of the
writers from among whom he emerged, and the coruscations of
whose feebler and more desultory genius he has made pale,—he
is distinguished from them by nothing which is more visible at
the first glance than by the superior regularity and elaboration

* " Is not wild Shakespeare thine and Nature's boast ?"—Thomson's Summer.

that mark his productions. Marlow, and Greene, and Kyd may
be called wild, and wayward, and careless; but the epithets are
inapplicable to Shakespeare, by whom, in truth, it was that the
rudeness of our early drama was first refined, and a spirit of high
art put into it, which gave it order and symmetry as well as
elevation. It was the union of the most consummate judgment
with the highest creative power that made Shakespeare the
miracle that he was,—if, indeed, we ought not rather to say that
such an endowment as his of the poetical faculty necessarily
implied the clearest and truest discernment as well as the utmost
productive energy,—even as the most intense heat must illuminate
as well as warm.

But, undoubtedly, his dramas are distinguished from those of
his predecessors by much more than merely this superiority in
the general principles upon which they are constructed. Such
rare passages of exquisite poetry, and scenes of sublimity or true
passion, as sometimes brighten the dreary waste of their productions, are equalled or excelled in almost every page of his;—
" the highest heaven of invention," to which they ascend only
in far distant flights, and where their strength of pinion never
sustains them long, is the familiar home of his genius. Other
qualities, again, which charm us in his plays are nearly unknown
in theirs. He first informed our drama with true wit and
humour. Of boisterous, uproarious, blackguard merriment and
buffoonery there is no want in our earlier dramatists, nor of
mere gibing and jeering and vulgar personal satire; but of true
airy wit there is little or none. In the comedies of Shakespeare
the wit plays and dazzles like dancing light. This seems to have
been the excellence, indeed, for which he was most admired by
his contemporaries; for quickness and felicity of repartee they
placed him above all other play-writers. But his humour was
still more his own than his wit. In that rich but delicate and
subtile spirit of drollery, moistening and softening whatever it
touches like a gentle oil, and penetrating through all enfoldings
and rigorous encrustments into the kernel of the ludicrous that
is in everything, which mainly created Malvolio, and Shallow,
and Slender, and Dogberry, and Verges, and Bottom, and Lancelot, and Launce, and Costard, and Touchstone, and a score of
other clowns, fools, and simpletons, and which, gloriously over-
flowing in Falstaff, makes his wit exhilarate like wine, Shakespeare has had almost as few successors as he had predecessors.

And in these and all his other delineations he has, like every other great poet, or artist, not merely observed and described, but, as we have said, created, or invented. It is often laid down that the drama should be a faithful picture or representation of real life; or, if this doctrine be given up in regard to the tragic or more impassioned drama, because even kings and queens in the actual world never do declaim in the pomp of blank verse, as they do on the stage, still it is insisted that in comedy no character is admissible that is not a transcript,—a little embellished perhaps,—but still substantially a transcript from some genuine flesh and blood original. But Shakespeare has shown that it belongs to such an imagination as his to create in comedy, as well as in tragedy or in poetry of any other kind. Most of the characters that have just been mentioned are as truly the mere creations of the poet's brain as are Ariel, or Caliban, or the Witches in Macbeth. If any modern critic will have it that Shakespeare must have actually seen Malvolio, and Launce, and Touchstone, before he could or at least would have drawn them, we would ask the said critic if he himself has ever seen such characters in real life; and, if he acknowledge, as he needs must, that he never has, we would then put it to him to tell us why the contemporaries of the great dramatist might not have enjoyed them in his plays without ever having seen them elsewhere, just as we do,—or, in other words, why such delineations might not have perfectly fulfilled their dramatic purpose then as well as now, when they certainly do not represent anything that is to be seen upon earth, any more than do Don Quixote and Sancho Panza. There might have been professional clowns and fools in the age of Shakespeare such as are no longer extant; but at no time did there ever actually exist such fools and clowns as his. These and other similar personages of the Shakespearian drama are as much more poetical phantasmata as are the creations of the kindred humour of Cervantes. Are they the less amusing or interesting, however, on that account?—do we the less sympathize with them?—nay, do we feel that they are the less naturally drawn? that they have for us less of a truth and life than the most faithful copies from the men and women of the real world?

But in the region of reality, too, there is no other drama so rich as that of Shakespeare. He has exhausted the old world of our actual experience as well as imagined for us new worlds of his own.[*] What other anatomist of the human heart has searched its hidden core, and laid bare all the strength and weakness of our mysterious nature, as he has done in the gushing tenderness of Juliet, and the "fine frenzy" of the discrowned Lear, and the sublime melancholy of Hamlet, and the wrath of the perplexed and tempest-torn Othello, and the eloquent misanthropy of Timon, and the fixed hate of Shylock? What other poetry has given shape to anything half so terrific as Lady Macbeth, or so winning as Rosalind, or so full of gentlest womanhood as Desdemona? In what other drama do we behold so living a humanity as in his? Who has given us a scene either so crowded with diversities of character, or so stirred with the heat and hurry of actual existence? The men and the manners of all countries and of all ages are there: the lovers and warriors, the priests and prophetesses, of the old heroic and kingly times of Greece,—the Athenians of the days of Pericles and Alcibiades,—the proud patricians and turbulent commonalty of the earliest period of republican Rome,—Cæsar, and Brutus, and Casius, and Antony, and Cleopatra, and the other splendid figures of that later Roman scene,—the kings, and queens, and princes, and courtiers of barbaric Denmark, and Roman Britain, and Britain before the Romans,—those of Scotland in the time of the English Heptarchy,—those of England and France at the era of Magna Charta,—all ranks of the people of almost every reign of our subsequent history from the end of the fourteenth to the middle of the sixteenth century,—not to speak of Venice, and Verona, and Mantua, and Padua, and Illyria, and Navarre, and the Forest of Arden, and all the other towns and lands which he has peopled for us with their most real inhabitants.

Nor even in his plays is Shakespeare merely a dramatist. Apart altogether from his dramatic power he is the greatest poet that ever lived. His sympathy is the most universal, his imagination the most plastic, his diction the most expressive, ever given to any writer. His poetry has in itself the power and varied excellences of all other poetry. While in grandeur, and beauty, and passion, and sweetest music, and all the other higher gifts of song, he may be ranked with the greatest,—with Spenser, and Chaucer, and Milton, and Dante, and Homer,—he is at the

---

[*] " Each change of many-coloured life he drew,
Exhausted worlds, and then imagined new."—Johnson.

same time more nervous than Dryden, and more sententious than
Pope, and more sparkling and of more abounding conceit, when
he chooses, than Donne, or Cowley, or Butler.   In whose
handling was language ever such a flame of fire as it is in his?
His wonderful potency in the use of this instrument would alone
set him above all other writers.*   Language has been called the
costume of thought: it is such a costume as leaves are to the
tree or blossoms to the flower, and grows out of what it adorns.
Every great and original writer accordingly has distinguished,
and as it were individualised, himself as much by his diction as
by even the sentiment which it embodies; and the invention of
such a distinguishing style is one of the most unequivocal
evidences of genius.   But Shakespeare has invented twenty
styles.   He has a style for every one of his great characters, by
which that character is distinguished from every other as much
as Pope is distinguished by his style from Dryden, or Milton
from Spenser.   And yet all the while it is he himself with his
own peculiar accent that we hear in every one of them.   The
style, or manner of expression, that is to say,—and, if the manner
of expression, then also the manner of thinking, of which the
expression is always the product—is at once both that which
belongs to the particular character and that which is equally
natural to the poet, the conceiver and creator of the character.
This double individuality, or combination of two individuali-
ties, is inherent of necessity in all dramatic writing; it is what
distinguishes the imaginative here from the literal, the artistic
from the real, a scene of a play from a police report.   No more
in this than in any other kind of literature, properly so called,
can we dispense with that infusion of the mind from which the
work has proceeded, of something belonging to that mind and to

---

* Whatever may be the extent of the vocabulary of the English language,
it is certain that the most copious writer has not employed more than a frac-
tion of the entire number of words of which it consists.   It has been stated
that some inquiries set on foot by the telegraph companies have led to the
conclusion that the number of words in ordinary use does not exceed 3000.
A rough calculation, founded on Mrs. Clarke's Concordance, gives about
21,000 as the number to be found in the Plays of Shakespeare, without counting inflectional forms as distinct words.   Probably the vocabulary of no other
of our great writers is nearly so extensive.   Todd's Verbal Index would not
give us more than about 7000 for Milton: so that, if we were to add even fifty
per cent. to compensate for Milton's inferior voluminousness, the Miltonic
vocabulary would still be not more than half as copious as the Shakespearian.

no other, which is the very life or constituent principle of all art, the one thing that makes the difference between a creation and a copy, between the poetical and the mechanical.

CHAPMAN; WEBSTER; MIDDLETON; DECKER; CHETTLE; MARSTON; TAILOR; TOURNEUR; ROWLEY; THOMAS HEYWOOD.

Shakespeare died in 1010. The space of a quarter of a century, or more, over which his career as a writer for the stage extends, is illustrated also by the names of a crowd of other dramatists, many of them of very remarkable genius; but Shakespeare is distinguished from the greater number of his contemporaries nearly as much as he is from his immediate predecessors. With regard to the latter, it has been well observed by a critic of eminent justness and delicacy of taste, that, while they "possessed great power over the passions, had a deep insight into the darkest depths of human nature, and were, moreover, in the highest sense of the word, poets, of that higher power of creation with which Shakespeare was endowed, and by which he was enabled to call up into vivid existence all the various characters of men and all the events of human life, Marlow and his contemporaries had no great share,—so that their best dramas may be said to represent to us only gleams and shadowings of mind, confused and hurried actions, from which we are rather led to guess at the nature of the persons acting before us than instantaneously struck with a perfect knowledge of it; and, even amid their highest efforts, with them the fictions of the drama are felt to be but faint semblances of reality. If we seek for a poetical image, a burst of passion, a beautiful sentiment, a trait of nature, we seek not in vain in the works of our very oldest dramatists. But none of the predecessors of Shakespeare must be thought of along with him, when he appears before us, like Prometheus, moulding the figures of men, and breathing into them the animation and all the passions of life."* "The same," proceeds this writer, "may be said of almost all his illustrious contemporaries. Few of them ever have conceived a consistent character, and

---

* Analytical Essays on the Early English Dramatists (understood to be by the late Henry MacKenzie), in Blackwood's Magazine, vol. ii. p. 657.

given a perfect drawing and colouring of it; they have rarely, indeed, inspired us with such belief in the existence of their personages as we often feel towards those of Shakespeare, and which makes us actually unhappy unless we can fully understand everything about them, so like are they to living men. . . . The plans of their dramas are irregular and confused, their characters often wildly distorted, and an air of imperfection and incompleteness hangs in general over the whole composition; so that the attention is wearied out, the interest flags, and we rather hurry on, than are hurried, to the horrors of the final catastrophe."* In other words, the generality of the dramatic writers who were contemporary with Shakespeare still belong to the semi-barbarous school which subsisted before he began to write.

George Chapman, already mentioned as the translator of Homer, was born six or seven years before Shakespeare, but did not begin to write for the stage till about the year 1595, after which date he produced sixteen plays that have survived, besides one in the composition of which he was assisted by Ben Jonson and Marston, and two others in which he and Shirley joined. One anonymous play, The Second Maiden's Tragedy (printed for the first time in 1824), and five others that are lost, have also been attributed to him. All these pieces were probably produced before the year 1620, although he lived till 1634. Chapman's best known, and probably also his best, plays are his tragedy of Bussy d'Ambois, reprinted in the third volume of Dilke's Old Plays (1814); his comedy of Monsieur d'Olive, in the same collection; and his comedies of All Fools, The Widow's Tears, and Eastward Hoe (the last the piece in which he was assisted by Jonson and Marston), in Dodsley's collection.† "Of all the English play-writers," says Lamb, " Chapman perhaps approaches nearest to Shakespeare in the descriptive and didactic, in passages which are less purely dramatic. Dramatic imitation was not his talent. He could not go out of himself, as Shakespeare could shift at pleasure, to inform and animate other existences; but in himself he had an eye to perceive, and a soul to embrace, all forms."‡ He was a great poet; but his genius was essentially epic, not dramatic.

* Blackwood's Magazine, vol. II p. 657.
† The comedy of All Fools appeared for the first time in the second (Reed's) edition of Dodsley.   ‡ Specimens, I. 107.

Webster, Middleton, Decker, Chettle, Marston, Robert Tailor, Tournour, and Rowley, may also be reckoned among the dramatic writers of considerable note who were the contemporaries of Shakespeare, though most, or all, of them survived him, and none of them began to write so early as he did. John Webster was parish clerk of St. Andrews, Holborn, and a member of the Merchant Tailors' Company. Of four dramatic pieces of which he is the sole author, besides two comedies which he wrote in conjunction with Rowley, and other two in which he assisted Decker, his tragedies of The White Devil and the Duchess of Malfy are the most celebrated. The character of Vittoria Corombona, the White Devil, is drawn with great spirit; and the delineation of the Duchess of Malfy displays not only remarkable power and originality of imagination, but a dramatic skill and judgment which perhaps no one of the other writers we have named along with Webster has anywhere matched. None of them has either so little extravagance, or so much of the true terrific. "To move a horror skilfully," says Lamb,—"to touch a soul to the quick,—to lay upon fear as much as it can bear,— to wean and weary a life till it is ready to drop, and then stop in with mortal instruments to take its last forfeit,—this only a Webster can do. Writers of an inferior genius may 'upon horror's head horrors accumulate,' but they cannot do this."[*] Webster seems to have been a slow writer, which it may be presumed few of his contemporaries were. In an advertisement prefixed to his White Devil, he says, "To those who report I was a long time in finishing this tragedy, I confess I do not write with a goose-quill winged with two feathers; and, if they will needs make it my fault, I must answer them with that of Euripides to Alcestides, a tragic writer. Alcestides objecting that Euripides had only in three days composed three verses, whereas himself had written three hundred; Thou tell'st truth, quoth he; but here's the difference—thine shall only be read for three days, whereas mine shall continue three ages." It will be seen from this passage that Webster was not wanting in a due sense of his own merits; he seems also to have had a sufficient contempt for the public taste of his day, or at least for that of the ordinary audiences of the theatre where his piece had been brought out: "I have noted," he says, "most of the people that come to that playhouse resemble those ignorant asses who, visit-

[*] Specimens, i. 231.

ing stationers' shops, their use is not to inquire for good books, but new books;"_and he adds, "Should a man present to such an auditory the most sententious tragedy that ever was written, observing all the critical laws, as height of style and gravity of person; enrich it with the sententious Chorus, and, as it were, enliven death in the passionate and weighty Nuntius; yet, after all this divine rapture, ... the breath that comes from the uncapable multitude is able to poison it." It is difficult to discern in all this the modesty which Lamb so much praises.*
Neither does Webster greatly shine as a critic of the performances of others in a subsequent paragraph of his advertisement or preface, in which he gives us his opinion of some of his contemporaries:—"I have ever," he observes, "truly cherished my good opinion of other men's worthy labours, especially of that full and heightened style of Master Chapman; the laboured and understanding works of Master Jonson; the no less worthy composures of the most worthily excellent Master Beaumont and Master Fletcher; and lastly, without wrong last to be named, *the right happy and copious industry of Master Shakespeare, Master Decker, and Master Heywood.*" All this may be frank enough, as Lamb calls it, but it is certainly not very discriminating.

Thomas Middleton is the author, in whole or in part, of between twenty and thirty dramatic pieces; his associates in those which he did not write entirely himself being Decker, Rowley, Jonson, Fletcher, and Massinger. One of his plays, a comedy called The Old Law, which he wrote in conjunction with Rowley (and which was afterwards improved by Massinger), appears to have been acted so early as 1599; and another was published in 1602. The greater number of his pieces are comedies, and, compared with most of his contemporaries, he has a good deal of comic talent; but his most noted dramatic production is his tragi-comedy of The Witch, which remained in manuscript till a small impression of it was printed, in 1778, by Isaac Reed, after it had been suggested by Steevens that it had probably been written before Macbeth, and might have been the source from which Shakespeare borrowed his Witches in that play. The commentators would have everything, in Shakespeare and everybody else, to be borrowed or stolen: they have the genius and the zeal of thief-catchers in ferreting out and exposing all transferences among writers, real and imaginary, of thoughts, words,

* Specimens, I. 230.

and syllables; and in the present case, as in many others, their professional ardour seems to have made a great deal out of very little. Lamb, in an admirable criticism, has pointed out the essential differences between the witches of Shakespeare and those of Middleton,* from whose play, however, Shakespeare appears to have taken a few lines of his incantations; unless, indeed—which we think not improbable—the verses in question were common popular rhymes, preserved among the traditions of the nursery or the country fireside. Middleton's witches have little of the supernatural awfulness of Shakespeare's. "Their names, and some of the properties," as Lamb observes, "which Middleton has given to his hags, excite smiles. The Weird Sisters are serious things. Their presence cannot co-exist with mirth. But, in a lesser degree, the witches of Middleton are fine creations. Their power, too, is, in some measure, over the mind. They raise jars, jealousies, strifes, *like a thick scarf o'er life.*"

Still another and lower species of witch—"the plain, traditional, old woman witch, of our ancestors," as Lamb has called her, "poor, deformed, and ignorant, the terror of villages, herself amenable to a justice," is the heroine of the tragi-comedy of The Witch of Edmonton, the joint production of Rowley, Ford, and Decker. Thomas Decker was the author of, or a contributor to, more than thirty plays in all, nearly two-thirds of which, however, have perished. He has not much high imagination, but considerable liveliness of fancy, and also no little power of pathos. His best pieces are his comedies of Old Fortunatus and The Honest Whore; and his spirited Satiromastix, the principal character in which, Horace Junior, is a humorous caricature of Ben Jonson, who had previously ridiculed Decker upon the stage, in Crispinus, the hero of his satirical comedy of The Poetaster. Decker is also supposed to be the author of the best parts of the very touching play of Patient Grissil, which appeared in 1603, and which has been reprinted, from a unique copy of that edition, for the Shakespeare Society, under the care of Mr. Collier, 1841. It was written by him in conjunction with William Haughton, who is the author of several plays of little merit, and Henry Chettle, who was one of the most active and prolific dramatic writers of this time, although of eight-and-thirty plays in which he is stated to have been more or less concerned, only the present

* Specimens, i. 187.

and three others have been preserved. He has force as well as fertility, but it is apt to run into rant and absurdity. John Marston is the author of eight plays, and appears to have enjoyed in his own day a great reputation as a dramatist. He is to be classed, however, with Sackville and Chapman, as having more poetical than dramatic genius; although he has given no proof of a creative imagination equal to what is displayed in the early poetry of the former, and the best of Chapman's is instinct with a diviner fire. But he is, nevertheless, a very imposing declaimer in verse. Besides his plays, Marston published two volumes of poetry: the second, by which he is best known, a collection of satires, in three books, entitled The Scourge of Villainy, a set of very vigorous and animated Juvenalian chants. Of Robert Tailor nothing is known, except that he is the author of one play, a comedy, entitled The Hog hath Lost his Pearl, which was acted in 1613, and published the following year. It is reprinted in Dodsley's Collection, and Mr. Lamb has extracted from it the most interesting scenes, which, however, derive their interest rather from the force of the situation (one that has been turned to better account in other hands) than from anything very impressive in its treatment. The merit of a perspicuous style is nearly all that can be awarded to this writer. Cyril Tourneur is known as the author of two surviving dramas—The Revenger's Tragedy, and The Atheist's Tragedy, besides a tragi-comedy, called The Nobleman, which is lost.* The Revenger's Tragedy, in particular, which is reprinted in Dodsley's Collection, both in the development of character and the conduct of the action evinces a rare dramatic skill, and the dialogue in parts is wonderfully fine—natural and direct as that of real passion, yet ennobled by the breathing thoughts and burning words of a poetic imagination,—by images and lines that plough into the memory and the heart.

William Rowley, whose co-operation in the Witch of Edmonton with Dekker and Ford has been already noticed, owes the greater part of his reputation to his having been taken into part-

* Drake, in his work entitled Shakespeare and his Times (vol. ii. p. 570), speaks of The Nobleman as if he had read it—telling us that it, as well as Tourneur's two tragedies, contains "some very beautiful passages and some entire scenes of great merit." In fact, the play is believed never to have been printed; but a manuscript copy of it was in the collection of Mr. Warburton, the Somerset herald, which was destroyed by his cook.

nership, in the composition of some of their pieces, by Middleton,
Webster, Massinger, and other writers more eminent than himself; but he has also left us a tragedy and three comedies of his
own. He has his share of the cordial and straightforward manner
of our old dramatists; but not a great deal more that is of much
value. Of the style of his comedy a judgment may be formed
from the fact, recorded by Langbaine, that certain of the scenes
of one of his pieces, A Shoemaker's a Gentleman, used to be
commonly performed by the strolling actors at Bartholomew and
Southwark fairs. Though he appears to have begun to write, at
least in association with others, some ten years before the death
of Shakespeare, Rowley probably survived the middle of the
century. So, also, it is supposed, did Thomas Heywood, the
most rapid and voluminous of English writers, who appears to
have written for the stage as early as 1596, but whose last-
published piece, written in conjunction with Rowley, was not
printed till 1655.* Heywood, according to his own account, in
an Address to the Reader prefixed to his tragi-comedy of The
English Traveller, published in 1633, had then, as he phrases it,
"had either an entire hand, or, at the least, a main finger," in
the incredible number of two hundred and twenty dramatic productions! "True it is," he adds, "that my plays are not exposed
unto the world in volumes, to bear the title of Works, as others.
One reason is that many of them, by shifting and change of companies, have been negligently lost; others of them are still
retained in the hands of some actors who think it against their
peculiar profit to have them come in print; and a third, that it
never was any great ambition in me to be in this kind volumi-
nously read." Besides his plays, too, Heywood, who was an actor,
and engaged in the practice of his profession for a great part of
his life, wrote numerous other works, several of them large
volumes in quarto and folio. Among them are a translation of
Sallust; a folio volume entitled The Hierarchy of the Blessed
Angels; a General History of Women; and another work entitled Nine Books of Various History concerning Women, a folio
of between four and five hundred pages, which, in a Latin note
on the last page, he tells us was all excogitated, written, and
printed in seventeen weeks. Of his plays above twenty are still
extant,—about a tithe of the prodigious litter. Two of them, his
tragedy of A Woman Killed with Kindness, and his historical

* See Dodsley's Old Plays, edit. of 1826; vii. 218 and 222.

play of The Four 'Prentices of London, are in Dodsley; three more, his tragi-comedies of The English Traveller, The Royal King and Loyal Subject, and A Challenge for Beauty, are in Dilke's Collection; and about a dozen others have been reprinted for the Shakespeare Society. Lamb has very happily characterized Heywood in a few words: "Heywood is a sort of prose Shakespeare. His scenes are to the full as natural and affecting. But we miss *the part*, that which in Shakespeare always appears out and above the surface of *the nature.*" His plays, however, are for the greater part in verse, which at least has ease of flow enough; and he may be styled not only a prose Shakespeare, but a more poetical Richardson. If he has not quite the power of Lillo in what has been called the domestic tragedy, which is the species to which his best pieces belong, he excels that modern dramatist both in facility and variety.[*]

BEAUMONT AND FLETCHER.

But the names of the dramatic writers of the present period that hold rank the nearest to Shakespeare still remain to be mentioned. Those of Beaumont and Fletcher must be regarded as indicating one poet rather than two, for it is impossible to make anything of the contradictory accounts that have been handed down as to their respective shares in the plays published in their conjoint names, and the plays themselves furnish no evidence that is more decisive. The only ascertained facts relating to this point are the following:—that John Fletcher was about ten years older than his friend Francis Beaumont, the former having been born in 1576, the latter in 1585; that Beaumont, however, so far as is known, came first before the

---

[*] Mr. Hallam (Introd. to Lit. of Eur. iii. 345) states that between forty and fifty plays are ascribed to Heywood; in fact, only twenty-six existing plays have been ascribed to him, and only twenty-three can be decisively said to be his (see Dodsley, edit. of 1826, vii. 218, *et seq.*). Mr. Hallam is also not quite correct in elsewhere stating (ii. 275) that Heywood's play of A Woman Killed with Kindness bears the date of 1600, and in speaking of it as certainly his earliest production. The earliest known edition, which is called the third, is dated 1617; and the earliest notice of the play being acted is in 1603. Two other plays, the First and Second Parts of The Death of Robert Earl of Huntingdon, otherwise called Robin Hood, which have been ascribed to Heywood, were published in 1601. But there is some doubt as to his claim to these pieces.

world as a writer of poetry, his translation of the story of
Salmacis and Hermaphroditus, from the Fourth Book of Ovid's
Metamorphoses, having been published in 1602, when he was
only in his seventeenth year; that the Masque of the Inner
Temple and Gray's Inn (consisting of only a few pages), produced in 1612, was written by Beaumont alone; that the
pastoral drama of the Faithful Shepherdess is entirely Fletcher's;
that the first published of the pieces which have been ascribed
to the two associated together, the comedy of The Woman-Hater,
appeared in 1607; that Beaumont died in March, 1616; and
that, between that date and the death of Fletcher, in 1625, there
were brought out, as appears from the note-book of Sir Henry
Herbert, Deputy Master of the Revels, at least eleven of the
plays found in the collection of their works, besides two others
that were brought out in 1626, and two more that are lost.
Deducting the fourteen pieces which thus appear certainly to
belong to Fletcher exclusively (except that in one of them, The
Maid in the Mill, he is said to have been assisted by Rowley),
there still remain thirty-seven or thirty-eight which it is possible
they may have written together in the nine or ten years over
which their poetical partnership is supposed to have extended.[*]
Eighteen of Beaumont and Fletcher's plays, including the
Masque by the former and the Pastoral by the latter, were published separately before 1640; thirty-four more were first published together in a folio volume in 1647; and the whole were
reprinted, with the addition of a comedy, supposed to have been
lost (The Wild Goose Chase),[†] making a collection of fifty-three
pieces in all, in another folio, in 1679. Beaumont and Fletcher
want altogether that _white heat_ of passion by which Shakespeare
fuses all things into life and poetry at a touch, often making a
single brief utterance flash upon us a full though momentary
view of a character, which all that follows deepens and fixes,
and makes the more like to actual seeing with the eyes and
hearing with the ears. His was a deeper, higher, in every way
more extended and capacious nature than theirs. They want his
profound meditative philosophy as much as they do his burning
poetry. Neither have they avoided nearly to the same degree

[*] One, the comedy of The Coronation, is also attributed to Shirley.
[†] This play, one of the best of Fletcher's comedies, for it was not produced
till some years after Beaumont's death, had been previously recovered and
printed by itself in 1652.

that he has done the degradation of their fine gold by the intermixture of baser metal. They have given us all sorts of writing,
good, bad, and indifferent, in abundance. Without referring in
particular to what we now deem the indecency and licentious-
ness which pollutes all their plays, but which, strange to say,
seems not to have been looked upon in that light by anybody in
their own age, simply because it is usually wrapped in very
transparent *double entendre*, they might, if judged by nearly one-
half of all they have left us, be held to belong to almost the
lowest rank of our dramatists instead of to the highest. There
is scarcely one of their dramas that does not bear marks of haste
and carelessness, or of a blight in some part or other from the
playhouse tastes or compliances to which they were wont too
easily to give themselves up when the louder applause of the
day and the town made them thoughtless of their truer fame.
But fortunately, on the other hand, in scarcely any of their
pieces is the deformity thus occasioned more than partial : the
circumstances in which they wrote have somewhat debased the
produce of their fine genius, but their genius itself suffered
nothing from the unworthy uses it was often put to. It springs
up again from the dust and mud, as gay a creature of the
element as ever, soaring and singing at heaven's gate as if it
had never touched the ground. Nothing can go beyond the
flow and brilliancy of the dialogue of these writers in their
happier scenes ; it is the richest stream of real conversation,
edged with the fire of poetry. For the drama of Beaumont and
Fletcher is an essentially poetical and imaginative, though not in
so high a style, as that of Shakespeare ; and they, too, even if
they were not great dramatists, would still be great poets.
Much of their verse is among the sweetest in the language ;
and many of the lyrical passages, in particular, with which their
plays are interspersed, have a diviner soul of song in them than
almost any other compositions of the same class. As dramatists
they are far inferior to Shakespeare, not only, as we have said,
in striking development and consistent preservation of character,
—in other words, in truth and force of conception,—but also
both in the originality and the variety of their creations in that
department ; they have confined themselves to a comparatively
small number of broadly distinguished figures, which they
delineate in a dashing, scene-painting fashion, bringing out their
peculiarities rather by force of situation, and contrast with one

another, than by the form and aspect with which each individually
looks forth and emerges from the canvas. But all the resources
of this inferior style of art they avail themselves of with the
boldness of conscious power, and with wonderful skill and effect.
Their invention of plot and incident is fertile in the highest
degree; and in the conduct of a story for the mere purposes of
the stage,—for keeping the attention of an audience awake and
their expectation suspended throughout the whole course of the
action,—they excel Shakespeare, who, aiming at higher things,
and producing his more glowing pictures by fewer strokes, is
careless about the mere excitement of curiosity, whereas they
are tempted to linger as long as possible over every scene, both
for that end, and because their proper method of evolving character and passion is by such delay and repetition of touch upon
touch. By reason principally of this difference, the plays of
Beaumont and Fletcher, in the great days of the stage, and so
long as the state of public manners tolerated their licence and
grossness, were much greater favourites than those of Shakespeare in our theatres; two of theirs, Dryden tells us, were
acted in his time for one of Shakespeare's; their intrigues,—
their lively and florid but not subtle dialogue,—their strongly-
marked but somewhat exaggerated representations of character,
—their exhibitions of passion, apt to run a little into the melo-
dramatic,—were more level to the general apprehension, and
were found to be more entertaining, than his higher art and
grander poetry. Beaumont and Fletcher, as might be inferred
from what has already been said, are, upon the whole, greater in
comedy than in tragedy; and they seem themselves to have felt
that their genius led them more to the former,—for, of their
plays, only ten are tragedies, while their comedies amount to
twenty-four or twenty-five, the rest being what were then called
tragi-comedies—in many of which, however, it is true, the
interest is, in part at least, of a tragic character, although the
story ends happily.* But, on the other hand, all their tragedies

* The following definition of what was formerly understood by the term
tragi-comedy, or tragic-comedy, is given by Fletcher in the preface to his
Faithful Shepherdess :—" A tragic-comedy is not so called in respect of
mirth and killing, but in respect it wants deaths (which is enough to make it
no tragedy): yet brings some near to it (which is enough to make it no
comedy): which (viz. tragic-comedy] must be a representation of familiar
people, with such kind of trouble as no life can be without; so that a god is
as lawful in this as in a tragedy; and mean people as in a comedy."

have also some comic passages; and, in regard to this matter, indeed, their plays may be generally described as consisting, in the words of the prologue to one of them,* of

" Passionate scenes mixed with no vulgar mirth."

Undoubtedly, taking them all in all, they have left us the richest and most magnificent drama we possess after that of Shakespeare; the most instinct and alive both with the true dramatic spirit and with that of general poetic beauty and power; the most brilliantly lighted up with wit and humour; the freshest and most vivid, as well as various, picture of human manners and passions; the truest mirror, and at the same time the finest embellishment, of nature.

JONSON.

Ben Jonson was born in 1574, or two years before Fletcher, whom he survived twelve years, dying in 1637. He is supposed to have begun to write for the stage so early as 1593; but nothing that he produced attracted any attention till his Comedy of Every Man in his Humour was brought out at the Rose Theatre in 1596. This play, greatly altered and improved, was published in 1598; and between that date and his death Jonson produced above fifty more dramatic pieces in all, of which ten are comedies, three what he called comical satires, only two tragedies, and all the rest masques, pageants, or other court entertainments. His two tragedies of Sejanus and Catiline are admitted on all hands to be nearly worthless; and his fame rests almost entirely upon his first comedy, his three subsequent comedies of Volpone or The Fox, Epicoene or The Silent Woman, and The Alchemist, his court Masques, and a Pastoral entitled The Sad Shepherd, which was left unfinished at his death. Ben Jonson's comedies admit of no comparison with those of Shakespeare or of Beaumont and Fletcher: he belongs to another school. His plays are professed attempts to revive, in English, the old classic Roman drama, and aim in their construction at a rigorous adherence to the models afforded by those of Plautus, and Terence, and Seneca. They are admirable for their elaborate

* The Custom of the Country.

art, which is, moreover, informed by a power of strong conception of a decidedly original character; they abound both in wit
and eloquence, which in some passages rises to the glow of
poetry; the figures of the scene stand out in high relief, every
one of them, from the most important to the most insignificant,
being finished off at all points with the minutest care; the
dialogue carries on the action, and is animated in many parts
with the right dramatic reciprocation; and the plot is in general
contrived and evolved with the same learned skill, and the same
attention to details, that are shown in all other particulars.
But the execution, even where it is most brilliant, is hard and
angular; nothing seems to flow naturally and freely; the whole
has an air of constraint, and effort, and exaggeration; and the
effect that is produced by the most arresting passages is the most
undramatic that can be,—namely, a greater sympathy with the
performance as a work of art than as anything else. It may be
added that Jonson's characters, though vigorously delineated,
and though not perhaps absolutely false to nature, are most
of them rather of the class of her occasional excrescences or
eccentricities than samples of any general humanity; they are
the oddities and perversions of a particular age or state of
manners, and have no universal truth or interest. What is
called the humour of Jonson consists entirely in the exhibition
of the more ludicrous kinds of these morbid aberrations; like
everything about him, it has force and raciness enough, but
will be most relished by those who are most amused by dancing
bears and other shows of that class. It seldom or never makes
the heart laugh, like the humour of Shakespeare,—which is,
indeed, a quality of altogether another essence. As a poet,
Jonson is greatest in his masques and other court pageants.
The airy elegance of these compositions is a perfect contrast to
the stern and rugged strength of his other works; the lyrical
parts of them especially have often a grace and sportiveness, a
flow as well as a finish, the effect of which is very brilliant.
Still, even in these, we want the dewy light and rich coloured
irradiation of the poetry of Shakespeare and Fletcher: the
lustre is pure and bright, but at the same time cold and sharp,
like that of crystal. In Jonson's unfinished pastoral of The Sad
Shepherd there is some picturesque description and more very
harmonious verse, and the best parts of it (much of it is poor
enough) are perhaps in a higher style than anything else he has

written; but to compare it, as has sometimes been done, either as a poem or as a drama, with The Faithful Shepherdess of Fletcher seems to us to evince a deficiency of true feeling for the highest things, equal to what would be shown by preferring, as has also been done by some critics, the humour of Jonson to that of Shakespeare. Fletcher's pastoral, blasted as it is in some parts by fire hot from heaven, is still a green and leafy wilderness of poetical beauty; Jonson's, deformed also by some brutality more elaborate than anything of the same sort in Fletcher, is at the best but a trim garden, and, had it been ever so happily finished, would have been nothing more.

MASSINGER; FORD.

After Shakespeare, Beaumont and Fletcher, and Jonson, the next great name in our drama is that of Philip Massinger, who was born in 1584, and is supposed to have begun to write for the stage soon after 1606, although his first published play, his tragedy of The Virgin Martyr, in which he was assisted by Decker, did not appear till 1622. Of thirty-eight dramatic pieces which he is said to have written, only eighteen have been preserved; eight others were in the collection of Mr. Warburton, which his servant destroyed. Massinger, like Jonson, had received a learned education, and his classic reading has coloured his style and manner; but he had scarcely so much originality of genius as Jonson. He is a very eloquent writer, but has little power of high imagination or pathos, and still less wit or comic power. He could rise, however, to a vivid conception of a character moved by some single aim or passion; and he has drawn some of the darker shades of villany with great force. His Sir Giles Overreach, in A New Way to Pay Old Debts, and his Luke in the City Madam, are perhaps his most successful delineations in this style. In the conduct of his plots, also, he generally displays much skill. In short, all that can be reached by mere talent and warmth of susceptibility he has achieved; but his province was to appropriate and decorate rather than to create.

John Ford, the author of about a dozen plays that have survived, and one of whose pieces is known to have been acted so early as 1613, has one quality, that of a deep pathos, perhaps more nearly allied to high genius than any Massinger has shown; but the range of the latter in the delineation of action and passion is so much more extensive, that we can hardly refuse to regard him as the greater dramatist. Ford's blank verse is not so imposing as Massinger's; but it has often a delicate beauty, sometimes a warbling wildness and richness, beyond anything in Massinger's fuller swell.

LATER ELIZABETHAN PROSE WRITERS.

Even the prose literature of the present period is much of it of so imaginative a character, that it may be considered to be a kind of half poetry. We have already traced the change which English prose-writing underwent in the course of the second and third quarters of the sixteenth century, passing from the familiar but elegant simplicity of the style of Sir Thomas More to the more formal and elaborate but still succinct and unincumbered rhetoric of Ascham, from thence to the affectations of Lyly the Euphuist and his imitators, and finally out of what we may call that sickly and unnatural state of transition to the richly decorated eloquence of Sidney. Along with Sidney's famous work, though of somewhat later date, may be mentioned his friend Spenser's View of the State of Ireland, written, as has been already intimated, probably in the year 1596. It is a composition worthy of the many-visioned poet—full of matter, full of thought, full of life, with passages of description in it that make present the distant and the past, like the painter's colours. The style has not so much that is outwardly imposing as Sidney's, but more inward vigour and earnestness, as well as more compactness and sinew; in short, more of the true glow of eloquence, more of a heart leaping within it, and sending a pulse through every word and cadence.

On the whole, by the end of the sixteenth century, our prose, as exhibited in its highest examples, if it had lost something in ease and clearness, had gained considerably in copiousness, in sonorousness, and in splendour. In its inferior specimens, also, a corresponding change is to be traced, but of a modified character. In these the ancient simplicity and directness had given place

only to a long-winded wordiness, and an awkwardness and
intricacy, sometimes so excessive as to be nearly unintelligible,
produced by piling clause upon clause, and involution upon
involution, in the endeavour to crowd into every sentence as
much meaning or as many particulars as possible.   Here the
change was nearly altogether for the worse; the loss in one
direction was compensated by hardly anything that could be
called a gain in another.   It ought also to be noticed that
towards the close of the reign of Elizabeth a singularly artificial
mode of composition became fashionable, more especially in
sermons and other theological writings, consisting mainly in
the remotest or most recondite analogies of thought and the
most elaborate verbal ingenuities or conceits.   This may be
designated the opposite pole in popular preaching to what we
have in the plainness and simplicity, natural sometimes even
to buffoonery, of Latimer.

Translation of the Bible.

The authorized translation of the Bible, on the whole so
admirable both for correctness and beauty of style, is apt, on the
first thought, to be regarded as exhibiting the actual state of
the language in the time of James I., when it was first published.   It is to be remembered, however, that the new translation was formed, by the special directions of the king, upon the
basis of that of Parker's, or the Bishops' Bible, which had been
made nearly forty years before, and which had itself been
founded upon that of Cranmer, made in the reign of Henry VIII.
The consequence is, as Mr. Hallam has remarked, that, whether
the style of King James's translation be the perfection of the
English language or no, it is not the language of his reign.   "It
may, in the eyes of many," adds Mr. Hallam, "be a better
English, but it is not the English of Daniel, or Raleigh, or
Bacon, as any one may easily perceive.   It abounds, in fact,
especially in the Old Testament, with obsolete phraseology, and
with single words long since abandoned, or retained only in
provincial use."*   This is, perhaps, rather strongly put; for
although the preceding version served as a general guide to

* Lit. of Eur. II. 404.

the translators, and was not needlessly deviated from, they have evidently modernized its style, not perhaps quite up to that of their own day, but so far, we apprehend, as to exclude nearly all words and phrases that had then passed out even of common and familiar use. In that theological age, indeed, few forms of expression found in the Bible could well have fallen altogether into desuetude, although some may have come to be less apt and significant than they once were, or than others that might now be substituted for them. But we believe the new translators, in any changes they made, were very careful to avoid the employment of any more words of yesterday, the glare of whose recent coinage would have contrasted offensively with the general antique colour of diction which they desired to retain. If ever their version were to be revised, whether to improve the rendering of some passages by the lights of modern criticism, or to mend some hardness and intricacy of construction in others, it ought to be retouched in the same spirit of affectionate veneration for the genius and essential characteristics of its beautiful diction; and a good rule to be laid down might be, that no word should be admitted in the improved renderings which was not in use in the age when the translation was originally made. The language was then abundantly rich enough to furnish all the words that could be wanted for the purpose.

THEOLOGICAL WRITERS:—JAMES I.; BISHOP ANDREWS; DONNE; HALL; HOOKER.

Besides the translation of the Bible, the portion of the English literature of the present period that is theological is very great in point of quantity, and a part of it also possesses distinguished claims to notice in a literary point of view. Religion was the great subject of speculation and controversy in this country throughout the entire space of a century and a half between the Reformation and the Revolution; and nothing can more strikingly illustrate the universality of the interest that was now taken in theological controversy, than the fact that both the kings whose reigns fill the first half of the seventeenth century have left us a considerable quantity of literary manufacture of their own, and that it is almost all theological. The writings

of Charles I. will be noticed afterwards.   King James, whose
works were collected and published in a folio volume in 1616,
under the care of Dr. Mountagne, bishop of Winchester, had
given to the world what he called a Fruitful Meditation upon
part of the Apocalypse, "in form of ano sermon," so early as the
year 1588, when he was only a youth of two-and-twenty. Indeed,
according to Bishop Mountagne's account, this performance was
"written by his majesty before he was twenty years of age."
Soon after, on the destruction of the Spanish Armada, he produced another Meditation on certain verses of one of the chapters of the First Book of Chronicles. Among his subsequent
publications are Meditations on the Lord's Prayer and on some
verses of the 27th chapter of St. Matthew.   And nearly all his
other works,—his Dæmonologie, first published in 1597; his
True Law of Free Monarchies, 1598; his Basilicon Doron, or
advice to his son Prince Henry, 1599; his Apology for the Oath
of Allegiance, 1605,—are, in the main, theological treatises.   It
is scarcely necessary to add that they are of little or no value,
either theological or literary; though they are curious as illustrating the intellectual and moral character of James, who was
certainly a person of no depth either of learning or of judgment,
though of some reading in the single province of theology, and
also of considerable shrewdness and readiness, and an inexhaustible flow of words, which he mistook for eloquence and
genius.

One of the most eminent preachers, perhaps the most eminent,
of the age of Elizabeth and James, was Dr. Lancelot Andrews,
who, after having held the sees of Chichester and Ely, died
bishop of Winchester in 1626.   Bishop Andrews was one of the
translators of the Bible, and is the author, among other works, of
a folio volume of Sermons published, by direction of Charles I.,
soon after his death; of another folio volume of Tracts and
Speeches, which appeared in 1629 ; of a third volume of Lectures
on the Ten Commandments, published in 1642; and of a fourth,
containing Lectures delivered at St. Paul's and at St. Giles's,
Cripplegate, published in 1657. He was, perhaps, the most
learned of the English theologians of that learned time, and was
besides a person of great vigour and acuteness of understanding;
so that his death was regarded by scholars both at home and
abroad as the extinction of the chief light of the English church.
Milton, then a youth of seventeen, bewailed the event in a Latin

elogy, full of feeling and fancy; and even in a tract written
many years afterwards, when his opinions had undergone a
complete change, he admits that "Bishop Andrews of late years,
and in these times the Primate of Armagh (Usher), for their
learning are reputed the best able to say what may be said " in
defence of episcopacy.* Both the learning and ability of
Andrews, indeed, are conspicuous in everything he has written;
but his eloquence, nevertheless, is to a modern taste grotesque
enough. In his more ambitious passages he is the very prince of
verbal posture-masters,—if not the first in date, the first in
extravagance, of the artificial, quibbling, syllable-tormenting
school of our English pulpit rhetoricians; and he undoubtedly
contributed more to spread the disease of that manner of writing
than any other individual. Not only did his eminence in this
line endear him to the royal tastes of Elizabeth and James;
all men admired and strove to copy after him. Fuller declares
that he was "an inimitable preacher in his way;" and then he
tell us that "pious and pleasant Bishop Felton, his contemporary and colleague, endeavoured in vain in his sermons to
assimilate his style, and therefore said merrily of himself, I had
almost marred my own natural trot by endeavouring to imitate
his artificial amble." Many a "natural trot" Andrews no doubt
was the cause of spoiling in his day, and long after it. This
bishop is further very notable, in the history of the English
church, as the first great asserter of those semi-popish notions
touching doctrines, rites, and ecclesiastical government with
which Laud afterwards blew up the establishment. Andrews,
however, was a very different sort of person from Laud,—as
superior to him in sense and policy as in learning and general
strength and comprehensiveness of understanding. A well-
known story that is told of him proves his moderation as much
as his wit and readiness: when he and Dr. Neal, bishop of
Durham, were one day standing behind the king's chair as he
sat at dinner (it was the day on which James dissolved his third
parliament, and the anecdote is related on the authority of
Waller, the poet, who was present), his majesty, turning round,
addressed the two prelates—My lords, cannot I take my subjects'
money when I want it, without all this formality in parliament?
"The bishop of Durham readily answered, God forbid, sir, but

* The Reason of Church Government argued against Prelacy (published in
1641), Book I. chap. 3.

you should; you are the breath of our nostrils. Whereupon the king turned, and said to the bishop of Winchester, Well, my lord, what say you? Sir, replied the bishop, I have no skill to judge of parliamentary cases. The king answered, No put-offs, my lord, answer me presently. Then, sir, said he, I think it is lawful for you to take my brother Neal's money, for he offers it."[*] Clarendon has expressed his belief that if Archbishop Bancroft had been succeeded in the see of Canterbury by Andrews, instead of Abbot, the infection of the Geneva fire would have been kept out, which could not afterwards be so easily expelled.[†]

Donne, the poet, was also a voluminous writer in prose; having left a folio volume of Sermons, besides a treatise against Popery entitled The Pseudo-Martyr, another singular performance, entitled Biathanatos, in confutation of the common notion about the necessary sinfulness of suicide, and some other professional disquisitions. His biographer, Izaak Walton, says that he preached "as an angel, *from* a cloud, but not in a cloud;" but most modern readers will probably be of opinion that he has not quite made his escape from it. His manner is fully as quaint in his prose as in his verse, and his way of thinking as subtle and peculiar. His sermons are also, as well as those of Andrews, overlaid with learning, much of which seems to be only a useless and cumbersome show. Doubtless, however, there are deep and beautiful things in Donne, for those that will seek for them; as has, indeed, been testified by some who in modern times have made themselves the best acquainted with these long-neglected theological works of his.[‡]

Another of the most learned theologians and eloquent preachers of those times was as well as Donne an eminent poet, Bishop Joseph Hall. Hall's English prose works, which are very voluminous, consist of sermons, polemical tracts, paraphrases of Scripture, casuistical divinity, and some pieces on practical religion, of which his Contemplations, his Art of Divine Meditation, and his Enochismus, or Treatise on the Mode of Walking with God, are the most remarkable. The poetic temperament of Hall reveals itself in his prose as well as in his verse, by the fervour of his

* Life of Waller, prefixed to his Poems, 1712.

† Hist. L 88 (edit. of 1717).

‡ The first edition of the collected Works of Dr. Donne was published by the Rev. Henry Alford, M.A., in 6 vols. 8vo. in 1839. Three folio volumes of his Sermons, however, had been successively published in 1640, 1649, and 1661.

piety, and the forcible and often picturesque character of his style, in which it has been thought he made Seneca his model. "The writer of the Satires," observes Warton, "is perceptible in some of his gravest polemical or Scriptural treatises; which are perpetually interspersed with excursive illustrations, familiar allusions, and observations on life." [*] It will be perceived, from all this, that both in style and in mind Hall and Donne were altogether opposed; neither in his prose nor in his verse has the former the originality of the latter, or the fineness of thought that will often break out in a sudden streak of light from the midst of his dark sayings; but, on the other hand, he is perfectly free from the dominant vices of Donne's manner, his conceits, his quaintness, his remote and fantastic analogies, his obscurity, his harshness, his parade of a useless and cucumbering erudition.

Last of all may be mentioned, among the great theological writers of this great theological time, one who stands alone, Richard Hooker, the illustrious author of the Eight Books of the Laws of Ecclesiastical Polity; of which the first four were published in 1594, the fifth in 1597, the three last not till 1632, many years after the author's death. Hooker's style is almost without a rival for its sustained dignity of march; but that which makes it most remarkable is its union of all this learned gravity and correctness with a flow of genuine, racy English, almost as little tinctured with pedantry as the most familiar popular writing. The effect also of its evenness of movement is the very reverse of tameness or languor; the full river of the argument dashes over no precipices, but yet rolls along without pause, and with great force and buoyancy.

BACON.

Undoubtedly the principal figure in English prose literature, as well as in philosophy, during the first quarter of the seventeenth century, is Francis Bacon. Bacon, born in 1561, published the first edition of his Essays in 1597; his Two Books of the Advancement of Learning in 1605; his Wisdom of the

[*] Hist. Eng. Poet. iv. 336. A complete collection of the works of Bishop Hall, edited by the Rev. Peter Hall, was brought out at Oxford, in 12 vols. 8vo. in 1837–39.

Ancients (in Latin) in 1610; a third edition of his Essays, greatly
extended, in 1612; his Two Books of the Novum Organum, or
Second Part of the Instauratio Magna, designed to consist of Six
Parts (also in Latin), in 1620; his History of the Reign of
Henry VII., in 1622; his Nine Books De Augmentis Scientiarum,
a Latin translation and extension of his Advancement of Learning, in 1623. He died in 1626. The originality of the Baconian
or Inductive method of philosophy, the actual service it has
rendered to science, and even the end which it may be most correctly said to have in view, have all been subjects of dispute
almost ever since Bacon's own day; but, notwithstanding all
differences of opinion upon these points, the acknowledgment that
he was intellectually one of the most colossal of the sons of men
has been nearly unanimous. They who have not seen his greatness under one form have discovered it in another; there is a
discordance among men's ways of looking at him, or their theories
respecting him; but the mighty shadow which he projects
athwart the two bygone centuries lies there immovable, and
still extending as time extends. The very deductions which are
made from his merits in regard to particular points thus only
heighten the impression of his general eminence,—of that something about him not fully understood or discerned, which, spite
of all curtailment of his claims in regard to one special kind of
eminence or another, still leaves the sense of his eminence as
strong as ever. As for his Novum Organum, or so-called new
instrument of philosophy, it may be that it was not really new
when he announced it as such, either as a process followed in the
practice of scientific discovery, or as a theory of the right method
of discovery. Neither may Bacon have been the first writer, in
his own or the immediately preceding age, who recalled attention
to the inductive method, or who pointed out the barrenness of
what was then called philosophy in the schools. Nor can it be
affirmed that it was really he who brought the reign of that
philosophy to a close: it was falling fast into disrepute before he
assailed it, and would probably have passed away quite as soon
as it did although his writings had never appeared. Nor possibly
has he either looked at that old philosophy with a very penetrating or comprehensive eye, or even shown a perfect understanding of the inductive method in all its applications and
principles. As for his attempts in the actual practice of the inductive method, they were, it must be owned, either insignificant

or utter failures; and that, too, while some of his contemporaries, who in no respect acknowledged him as their teacher, were turning it to account in extorting from nature the most brilliant revelations. Nay, can it be doubted that, if Bacon had never lived, or never written, the discoveries and the writings of Galileo, and Kepler, and Pascal, and others who were now extending the empire of science by the very method which he has explained and recommended, but most assuredly without having been instructed in that method by him, would have established the universal recognition of it as the right method of philosophy just as early as such recognition actually took place? That Bacon's Novum Organum has, even down to the present day, affected in any material degree the actual progress of science, may be very reasonably questioned. What great discovery or improvement can be named among all those that have been made since his time, which, from the known facts of its history, we may not fairly presume would have been made at any rate, though the Novum Organum had never been written? What instance can be quoted of the study of that work having made, or even greatly contributed to make, any individual a discoverer in science who would not in all probability have been equally such if he had never seen or heard of it? In point of fact, there is no reason to believe that almost any of those by whom science has been most carried forward since it appeared had either much studied Bacon's Novum Organum, or had even acquired any intimate or comprehensive acquaintance with the rules and directions therein laid down from other sources. Nor is it likely that they would have been more successful experimenters or greater discoverers if they had. For there is surely nothing in any part of the method of procedure prescribed by Bacon for the investigation of truth, that would not occur of itself to the sagacity and common sense of any person of an inventive genius pursuing such investigation; indeed, every discovery that has been made, except by accident, since science had any being, must have been arrived at by the very processes which he has explained. There can be little doubt that it would be found, on a survey of the whole history of scientific discovery, that its progress has always depended partly upon the remarkable genius of individuals, partly upon the general state of the world and the condition of civilization at different times, and not in any sensible degree upon the mere speculative views as to the right method of

philosophy that have at particular eras been taught in schools or
books, or otherwise generally diffused.   In fact it is much more
reasonable to suppose that such speculative views should have
been usually influenced by the actual progress of discovery than
it by them; for the recognition of sound principles of procedure,
in as far as that is implied in their practical application, though
not perhaps the contemplation and exposition of them in a systo-
matic form, is necessarily involved, as has been just observed, in
the very act of scientific discovery.   All this being considered,
there cannot well be attributed to Bacon's Novum Organum any
considerable direct share, nor even much indirect influence in
promoting the progress which science has made in certain do-
partments since his time; it is most probable that that progress
is to be traced to other causes altogether, and that it would have
been pretty nearly what it is though the Novum Organum never
had been written.   Galileo, and not Bacon, is the true father of
modern natural philosophy.   That, in truth, was not Bacon's
province at all; neither his acquirements nor the peculiar character and constitution of his mind fitted him for achieving anything on that ground.   The common mistake regarding him is
the same as if it were to be said that not Homer, but Aristotle,
was the father of poetry, because he first investigated and explained the principles or philosophy of a part of the art of poetry.
Bacon belongs not to mathematical or natural science, but to
literature and to moral science in its most extensive acceptation,
—to the realm of imagination, of wit, of eloquence, of æsthetics,
of history, of jurisprudence, of political philosophy, of logic, of
metaphysics and the investigation of the powers and operations
of the human mind.   He is either not at all or in no degree
worth mentioning an investigator or expounder of mathematics,
or of mechanics, or of astronomy, or of chemistry, or of any other
branch of geometrical or physical science; but he is a most penetrating and comprehensive investigator, and a most magnificent
expounder, of that higher wisdom in comparison with which all
these things are but a more intellectual sort of legerdemain.   All
his works, his essays, his philosophical writings, commonly so
called, and what he has done in history, are of one and the same
character; reflective and, so to speak, poetical, not simply demonstrative, or elucidatory of mere matters of fact.   What, then,
is his glory?—in what did his greatness consist?   In this, we
should say;—that an intellect at once one of the most capacious

and one of the most profound ever granted to a mortal—in its powers of vision at the same time one of the most penetrating and one of the most far-reaching—was in him united and reconciled with an almost equal endowment of the imaginative faculty; and that he is, therefore, of all philosophical writers, the one in whom are found together, in the largest proportions, depth of thought and splendour of eloquence. His intellectual ambition, also,—a quality of the imagination,—was of the most towering character; and no other philosophic writer has taken up so grand a theme as that on which he has laid out his strength in his greatest works. But with the progress of scientific discovery that has taken place during the last two hundred years, it would be difficult to show that these works have had almost anything to do. His Advancement of Learning and his Novum Organum have more in them of the spirit of poetry than of science; and we should almost as soon think of fathering modern physical science upon Paradise Lost as upon them.

A late distinguished writer, Mr. Hallam in his History of European Literature, although his estimate of what Bacon has done for science is much higher than we are able to go along with, yet in the following passage seems to come very near to the admission of, or at least very strongly to corroborate, much of what has just been advanced:—"It is evident that he had turned his thoughts to physical philosophy rather for an exercise of his reasoning faculties, and out of his insatiable thirst for knowledge, than from any peculiar aptitude for their [these, or such ?] subjects, much less any advantage of opportunity for their cultivation. He was more eminently the philosopher of human than of general nature. Hence he is exact as well as profound in all his reflections on civil life and mankind; while his conjectures in natural philosophy, though often very acute, are apt to wander far from the truth in consequence of his defective acquaintance with the phenomena of nature. His Centuries of Natural History give abundant proof of this. He is, in all these inquiries, like one doubtfully, and by degrees, making out a distant prospect, but often deceived by the haze. But if we compare what may be found in the sixth, seventh, and eighth Books De Augmentis, in the Essays, the History of Henry VII., and the various short treatises contained in his works, on moral and political wisdom, and on human nature, from experience of which all such wisdom is drawn, with the Rhetoric, Ethics, and

Politics of Aristotle, or with the historians most celebrated for
their deep insight into civil society and human character,—with
Thucydides, Tacitus, Philip de Comines, Machiavel, Davila,
Hume,—we shall, I think, find that one man may almost be compared with all of these together. When Galileo is named as
equal to Bacon, it is to be remembered that Galileo was no moral
or political philosopher, and in this department Leibnitz certainly falls very short of Bacon. Burke, perhaps, comes, of all
modern writers, the nearest to him; but, though Bacon may not
be more profound than Burke, he is still more copious and comprehensive."*

Burton.

A remarkable prose work of this age, which ought not to be
passed over without notice, is Burton's Anatomy of Melancholy.
Robert Burton, who, on his title-page, takes the name of Democri-
tus Junior, died in 1640, and his book was first published in 1621.

* Lit. of Eur. iii. 61. Among many other admirable things thickly scattered over the whole of this section on Bacon (pp. 23—68), Mr. Hallam has
taken an opportunity of pointing out an almost universal misapprehension into
which the modern expositors of Bacon's Novum Organum have fallen on the
subject of his celebrated Idola, which, as is here shown, are not at all what we
now call idols, that is, false divinities, but merely, in the Greek sense of the
word, images or fallacious appearances of things as opposed to realities (pp.
44—46). The reader may also be referred to another disquisition on Bacon,
of great brilliancy, by Mr. Macaulay, which originally appeared in the Edinburgh Review (No. 132, for July, 1837, pp. 1—104). And in addition to the
illustrative expositions of the Novum Organum, of a more scientific character,
by the late Professor Playfair, in his Dissertation on the Progress of Mathematical and Physical Science, prefixed to the Encyclopædia Britannica (pp.
453—474); and by Sir John Herschel, in his Preliminary Discourse on the
Objects, Advantages, and Pleasures of the Study of Natural Philosophy, in
Dr. Lardner's Cabinet Cyclopædia, may be mentioned, as containing some
views of the greatest importance, the Second Section of Coleridge's Introduction to the Encyclopædia Metropolitana (pp. 24—32), partly founded on what
had been previously published in the Friend. Coleridge is one of the very few
modern writers who have not fallen into the misconception noticed above
about Bacon's Idola. See his treatise, p. 28. But the most learned, elaborate,
and complete examination that Bacon's philosophical system and claims have
received, is what is given from the papers of the late R. H. Ellis, Esq., in the
new edition of his works, superintended by Mr. Spedding, Lond. 1857, et seq.
The reader may also be referred to a remarkable volume, entitled Francis
Bacon of Verulam, by Kuno Fischer; translated from the German by John
Oxenford, Lond. 1857.

It is an extraordinary accumulation of out-of-the-way learning, interspersed, somewhat in the manner of Montaigne's Essays, with original matter, but with this among other differences,—that in Montaigne the quotations have the air of being introduced, as we know that in fact they were, to illustrate the original matter, which is the web of the discourse, they but the embroidery; whereas in Burton the learning is rather the web, upon which what he has got to say of his own is worked in by way of forming a sort of decorative figure. Burton is far from having the variety or abundance of Montaigne; but there is considerable point and penetration in his style, and he says many striking things in a sort of half-splenetic, half-jocular humour, which many readers have found wonderfully stimulating. Dr. Johnson declared that Burton's Anatomy of Melancholy was the only book that ever drew him out of bed an hour sooner than he would otherwise have got up.

HISTORICAL WRITERS.

Among the historical writers of the reign of James may be first mentioned the all-accomplished Sir Walter Raleigh. Raleigh is the author of a few short poems, and of some miscellaneous pieces in prose; but his great work is his History of the World, composed during his imprisonment in the Tower, and first published in a folio volume in 1614. It is an unfinished work, coming down only to the first Macedonian war; and there is no reason to suppose that any more of it was ever written, although it has been asserted that a second volume was burnt by the author. Raleigh's History, as a record of facts, has long been superseded; the interest it possesses at the present day is derived almost entirely from its literary merits, and from a few passages in which the author takes occasion to allude to circumstances that have fallen within his own experience. Much of it is written without any ambition of eloquence; but the style, even where it is most careless, is still lively and exciting, from a tone of the actual world which it preserves, and a certain frankness and heartiness coming from Raleigh's profession and his warm impetuous character. It is not disfigured by any of the petty pedantries to some one or other of which most of the writers of books in that day gave way more or less, and it has altogether comparatively little of the taint of age upon it; while in some passages the composition, without losing anything of its natural grace and heartiness, is wrought up to great rhetorical polish and elevation.

Another celebrated historical work of this time is Richard Knolles's History of the Turks, published in 1610. Johnson, in one of his Ramblers, has awarded to Knolles the first place among English historians; and Mr. Hallam concurs in thinking that his style and power of narration have not been too highly extolled by that critic. "His descriptions," continues Mr. Hallam, "are vivid and animated; circumstantial, but not to feebleness; his characters are drawn with a strong pencil. . . . . In the style of Knolles there is sometimes, as Johnson has hinted, a slight excess of desire to make every phrase effective; but he is exempt from the usual blemishes of his age; and his command of the language is so extensive, that we should not err in placing him among the first of our elder writers."* Much of this praise, however, is to be considered as given to the uniformity or regularity of Knolles's style; the chief fault of which perhaps is, that it is too continuously elaborated and sustained for a long work. We have already mentioned Samuel Daniel's History of England from the Conquest to the reign of Edward III., which was published in 1618. It is of little historical value, but is remarkable for the same simple ease and purity of language which distinguish Daniel's verse. The contribution to this department of literature of all those that the early part of the seventeenth century produced, which is at the same time the most valuable as an original authority and the most masterly in its execution, is undoubtedly Bacon's History of the reign of Henry VII.

The series of popular national chronicles was continued in this period, from the publication of Edward Hall's Union of the Two Noble and Illustrious Families of York and Lancaster, in 1548, by that of Richard Grafton's Chronicle at Large, down to the First Year of Queen Elizabeth, in 1569; of Raphael Holinshed's Chronicles of England, Scotland, and Ireland, in 1577; and by the various publications of the laborious antiquaries John Stow and John Speed; namely, Stow's Summary of the English Chronicles, of which he published many editions between 1565 and 1598; his Annals, also frequently reprinted

* Lit. of Eur. III. 572.

with corrections and enlargements between 1573 and 1600; his Survey of London, first published in 1598, and again with additions in 1603; and Speed's Theatre of the Empire of Great Britain, 1606, and his History of Great Britain, coming down to the accession of James I., 1614. These various works of Stow and Speed rank among the head sources or fountains of our knowledge in the department of national antiquities.

CLASSICAL LEARNING.

With the exception of a magnificent edition of Chrysostom, in eight volumes folio, by Sir Henry Savile, printed at Eton, where Savile was provost of the College, in 1612, scarcely any great work in the department of ancient scholarship appeared in England in the portion of the seventeenth century which preceded the breaking out of the Civil War. It, however, produced a number of works written in Latin by Englishmen, which still retain more or less celebrity: among others, the illustrious Camden's Britannia, first published in 1586, but not enlarged to the form in which its author ultimately left it till the appearance of the sixth edition, in 1607; the same writer's Annales Rerum Anglicarum regnante Elizabetha, the first part of which was printed in 1615, the sequel not till after Camden's death; John Barclay's two poetical romances of the Euphormio, the first part of which was published in 1603, and the more famous Argenis, 1621; Lord Herbert's treatise De Veritate, 1624; and the Mare Clausum, the Uxor Hebraica, and other works of the most learned John Selden.

END OF VOL. I.

THE

ANNOTATED EDITION

OF THE

ENGLISH POETS.

BY

ROBERT BELL,

AUTHOR OF

'THE HISTORY OF RUSSIA,' 'LIVES OF THE ENGLISH POETS,' ETC.

———————

In Volumes, 2s. 6d. each, in cloth.

THE necessity for a revised and carefully Annotated Edition of the English Poets may be found in the fact, that no such publication exists. The only Collections we possess consist of naked and frequently imperfect Texts, put forth without sufficient literary supervision. Independently of other defects, these voluminous Collections are incomplete as a whole, from their omission of many poets whose works are of the highest interest, while the total absence of critical and illustrative Notes renders them comparatively worthless to the Student of our National Literature.

A few of our Poets have been edited separately by men well qualified for the undertaking, and selected Specimens have appeared, accompanied by notices, which, as far as they go, answer the purpose for which they were intended. But these do not supply the want which is felt of a Complete Body of English Poetry, edited throughout with judgment and integrity, and combining those features of research, typographical elegance, and economy of price, which the present age demands.

The Edition now proposed will be distinguished from all preceding Editions in many important respects. It will include the works of several Poets entirely omitted from previous Collections, especially those stores of Lyrical and Ballad Poetry in which our Literature is richer than that of any other Country, and which, independently of their poetical claims, are peculiarly interesting as Illustrations of Historical Events and National Customs.

By the exercise of a strict principle of selection, this Edition will be rendered intrinsically more valuable than any of its predecessors. The Text will in all instances be scrupulously collated, and accompanied by Biographical, Critical, and Historical Notes.

An Introductory Volume will present a succinct account of English Poetry from the earliest times down to a period which will connect it with the Series of the Poets, through whose Lives the History of our Poetical Literature will be continued to the present time. Occasional volumes will be introduced, in which Specimens, with connecting Notices and Commentaries, will be given of those Poets whose works are not of sufficient interest to be reproduced entire. The important materials gathered from previously unexplored sources by the researches of the last quarter of a century will be embodied wherever they may be available in the general design ; and by these means it is hoped that the Collection will be more complete than any that has been hitherto attempted, and that it will be rendered additionally acceptable as comprising in its course a Continuous History of English Poetry.

By the arrangements that will be adopted, the Works of the principal Poets may be purchased separately and independently of the rest. The Occasional Volumes, containing, according to circumstances, Poetry of a particular Class or Period, Collections Illustrative of Customs, Manners, and Historical Events, or Specimens, with Critical Annotations, of the Minor Poets, will also be complete in themselves.

As the works of each Poet, when completed, will be independent of the rest, although ultimately falling into their places in the Series, they will be issued irrespective of chronological sequence. This arrangement will present a greater choice and variety in the selection from time to time of poets of different styles and periods, and at the same time enable the Editor to take advantage of all new sources of information that may be opened to him in the progress of publication. General Title-pages will be finally supplied for combining the whole Collection into a Chronological Series.

Already Published.

POETICAL WORKS OF JOHN DRYDEN, including the most complete collection of his Prologues and Epilogues hitherto published, with Memoir and Notes, Critical and Historical. Three vols. 7s. 6d.

POETICAL WORKS OF THE EARL OF SURREY, of Minor Contemporaneous Poets, and of Sackville, Lord Buckhurst. With Notes and Memoir. 2s. 6d.

POETICAL WORKS OF WILLIAM COWPER, together with Illustrative Selections from the Works of Lloyd, Cotton, Brooke, Darwin, and Hayley. Notes and Memoirs. Three vols. 7s. 6d.

SONGS FROM THE DRAMATISTS. From the first regular Comedy to the close of the Eighteenth Century. With Notes, Memoirs, and Index. 2s. 6d.

POETICAL WORKS OF SIR THOMAS WYATT. With Notes and Memoir. 2s. 6d.

POETICAL WORKS OF JOHN OLDHAM. With Memoir and Notes. 2s. 6d.

POETICAL WORKS OF EDMUND WALLER. With Memoir and Notes. 2s. 6d.

POETICAL WORKS OF GEOFFREY CHAUCER. With Memoir, Introduction, Notes, and Glossary. Eight vols. 20s.

POETICAL WORKS OF JAMES THOMSON. With Memoir and Notes. Two vols. 5s.

POEMS OF WILLIAM SHAKSPEARE. With Memoir and Notes. 2s. 6d.

POETICAL WORKS OF SAMUEL BUTLER. With Memoir and Notes. Three vols. 7s. 6d.

POETICAL WORKS OF ROBERT GREENE and CHRISTOPHER MARLOWE. With Memoir and Notes. 2s. 6d.

EARLY BALLADS. Illustrative of History, Traditions, and Customs. With Introduction and Notes. 2s. 6d.

ANCIENT POEMS, BALLADS, and SONGS OF THE PEASANTRY OF ENGLAND. With Introduction and Notes. 2s. 6d.

POETICAL WORKS OF BEN JONSON. With Memoir and Notes. 2s. 6d.

London: GRIFFIN, BOHN, & CO., 10 Stationers' Hall Court.